A HISTORY OF COMMUNICATION STUDY

A BIOGRAPHICAL APPROACH

Everett M. Rogers

THE FREE PRESS
A Division of Macmillan, Inc.
NEW YORK

Maxwell Macmillan Canada
TORONTO

Maxwell Macmillan International
NEW YORK   OXFORD   SINGAPORE   SYDNEY

The Free Press
A Division of Macmillan, Inc.
866 Third Avenue, New York, N.Y. 10022

Maxwell Macmillan Canada, Inc.
1200 Eglinton Avenue East
Suite 200
Don Mills, Ontario M3C 3N1

Macmillan, Inc. is part of the Maxwell Communication Group of Companies.

Printed in the United States of America

printing number
1   2   3   4   5   6   7   8   9   10

Library of Congress Cataloging–in–Publication Data

Rogers, Everett M.
    A history of communication study: a biographical approach /
Everett M. Rogers.
        p.   cm.
    Includes bibliographical references and index.
    ISBN 0–02–926735–8
    1. Communication—History—19th century.   2. Communication—History—20th century.   I. Title.
P90.R613   1994
302.2'09—dc20   93–43281
                                                                          CIP

The epigraph is taken from the song "Joe Hill," by Earl Robinson and Alfred Hayes, in *Industrial Workers of the World Songbook,* 4th ed. (San Francisco, 1938).

I dreamed I saw Joe Hill last night
Alive as you and me.
Said I, "But Joe, you're ten years dead."
"I never died," said he.
"I never died," said he.
                    From the song "Joe Hill"

CONTENTS

PART III: ESTABLISHMENT OF THE COMMUNICATION FIELD

ILLUSTRATIONS

TABLES

PREFACE

From the window of my studio office, across Lake Lagunita and the red tile roofs of Stanford University, I can see the locations of the late Wilbur Schramm's Institute for Communication Research, originally in the Press Building, then in Cypress Hall, and now in the Stanford Quadrangle, with each move symbolizing the gradual acceptance of the field of communication. Erect above the campus is the Hoover Tower, which houses the Hoover Institution on War, Revolution, and Peace, and which hosted Harold Lasswell's content analysis project of the world's most prestigious newspapers just after World War II. Down to the right, stretching from Palo Alto to San Jose, twenty miles to the south, is Silicon Valley and the computer and microelectronics industry inspired by Claude E. Shannon's information theory. The think tank in which I am writing this book was established by Bernard Berelson of the Ford Foundation on the basis of Paul F. Lazarsfeld's proposal, thus providing the intellectual crossroads at which Schramm met Lasswell, where Shannon spent a year on leave from MIT, and where systems theory got its start. I am in the right place to write a book about the history of communication study.

I have gathered publications, dug through archival materials, and conducted oral history interviews with the pioneers of communication study. This book also grows out of six years of teaching a course on the history and philosophy of communication research and a course on advanced communication theories for doctoral students at the Annenberg School for Communication at the University of Southern California. I am grateful for the many contributions that the Annenberg School has made to this book. Dean Peter Clarke helped me at every turn. My colleague Peter Monge co-taught the doctoral theory course with me on several occasions, and I learned a great deal from him. I thank the Center for Advanced Study in the Behavioral Sciences for the fellowship in 1991–1992 that allowed me to complete this book and the National Science Foundation for providing my fellowship (as part of grant number BNS-8700864). My work was also supported by a grant from the Rockefeller Archives Center, North Tarrytown, New York, whose historical materials helped me trace the crucial role of the Rockefeller Foundation in establishing communication research in America.

I also acknowledge the help of the following scholars:

- Dr. Michael Noll, University of Southern California, who helped me get started on the history of information theory, and Dr. Klaus Krippendorff, University of Pennsylvania, who helped me finish this history.
- Dr. Robert Price, Raytheon Company, Lexington, Massachusetts, who shares my interest in Claude Shannon's information theory and guided me to valuable materials, including his 1984 taped interviews with Shannon.
- Dr. Tom Valente, Johns Hopkins University, who coauthored an earlier partial version (Rogers and Valente 1992) of Chapter 11 in this book on information theory.
- Dr. Robert K. Merton, Russell Sage Foundation, for helping me with Chapter 8 on Paul F. Lazarsfeld and more generally for teaching me important lessons about the history of science.
- Dr. Steven H. Chaffee, Stanford University, for our many fruitful discussions about Wilbur Schramm and "Daddy" Bleyer, and their visions of communication study.
- Dr. Rolf Wigand, professor of information studies at Syracuse University, for his advice, particularly about European influences on communication study.

I also thank Stacy Braslau, Donna Ivarone, Judy Herrman, Gail Light, and Jean Campbell of the Annenberg School and Virginia Heaton of the Center for Advanced Study in the Behavioral Sciences for their successful wrestling with my runaway handwriting.

My own personal history in communication study began during my Ph.D. program at Iowa State University in the mid-1950s, some thirty-nine years ago. My academic career overlapped with some of the founders and forerunners whose stories I tell here. This history is undoubtedly enriched by my having personally experienced certain of the ideas, events, and individuals described in this book.

Much of this book is organized around approaches to communication study that are closely associated with one theorist or a small group of theorists. This biographical approach to analyzing the history of communication study by focusing on the individual scholars who moved it forward is only one way to organize this material. Alternatively, a historian of communication study might organize this chronology by historical eras, by dominant philosophies (for example, progressivism), by the communication technologies of study (film, radio, television), or by other contextual factors. I chose to make sense out of the history of communication study on the basis of people, by means of biographical historiography.

This book concentrates on the big names and big institutions of the history of communication study. I rely heavily on the general consensus of informed observers about who played dominant roles in the history of communication study. By relying on the published scholarly literature, archival materials, and oral history interviews, I may have overlooked less well-known individuals and institutions. They may have played important roles too, but I was unable to capture them in my work.

Wilbur Schramm (1981) identified four founders of communication study:

> Thus, it was that in the 1930s and '40s four genuine giants emerged from the social sciences as specialists in human communication, and made a lasting mark on journalism. Adolf Hitler—no thanks to him, for it was involuntary—gave us two of them: Paul Lazarsfeld and Kurt Lewin. Robert Maynard Hutchins—no thanks to him, because he intended no such contribution—gave us a third one, Harold Lasswell. And the United States military establishment—perhaps somewhat to its surprise—gave us a fourth, by taking the most promising young experimental psychologist in the country and giving him wartime assignments that caused him to spend the rest of his life studying communication. This was Carl Hovland.

I question this received history of communication study. The myth of the four founders began with Bernard Berelson's (1959) attack on the field and was emphasized by Wilbur Schramm (who is *the* founder, if ever there were one). Berelson (1959) claimed that these four outstanding individuals were losing interest in communication research and that the field was thus "withering away." Schramm (1959a) disputed this field-is-dying assertion but nevertheless popularized the four founders myth in his writings over the next several decades (Schramm 1980, 1981, 1985).

The four founders myth is not totally incorrect. Lasswell, Lewin, Lazarsfeld, and Hovland did indeed play key roles in launching the field of communication, but there were many other founders, several of equal or greater influence in shaping communication study: Wilbur

Schramm, Robert E. Park, Theodor Adorno, Claude E. Shannon, Norbert Wiener, and Robert K. Merton. Further, the four founders in turn had "founders," that is, individuals who influenced their thinking about communication. For example. Harold Lasswell was directly influenced by Freud, and Theodor Adorno built on the theories of Freud and Marx. So are Freud and Marx also founders of the field of communication?

Important advances in communication study have often been made by schools composed of a coherent network of key scholars who are located in one institution. This book includes the Frankfurt school of critical theory, the Chicago school of symbolic interactionism, and the Palo Alto school of interactional communication—theory groups that are ignored by the four founders myth.

Why did Bernard Berelson and Wilbur Schramm select their seemingly arbitrary four founders in 1959? Lasswell, Lewin, Lazarsfeld, and Hovland were recent and immediate influences upon their own thinking. The four founders did their most important research and writing in the 1930s, 1940s, and 1950s, about the time that communication study was emerging as a distinct body of scholarly work in America. Nevertheless the four founders myth is a serious oversimplification of the history of communication study. It is not a very useful classification in understanding what happened and will not receive much further attention in this book.

The myth, for instance does not distinguish between forerunners and founders.* Scholars like Gabriel Tarde, Georg Simmel, Robert E. Park, George Herbert Mead, Kurt Lewin, Harold D. Lasswell, Carl I. Hovland, Norbert Wiener, and Claude E. Shannon certainly engaged in what we consider communication study by today's standards. These forerunners made important intellectual contributions to communication study, but they did not identify themselves as communication scholars, nor did their students, nor did they institutionalize the field by establishing schools or department of communication in universities.

Next came founders, scholars who were not trained formally in communication but conducted communication research and educated the first generation of communication scholars in the new discipline. The chief founder was Wilbur Schramm, who not only institutionalized communication study at Iowa, Illinois, and Stanford in the form of in-

---

*The definitions of forerunners and founders are adapted from Ben-David and Collins (1966).

stitutes for communication research but also taught many of the first Ph.D. holders in communication. Was Paul F. Lazarsfeld a forerunner or a founder? He certainly conducted communication research during his first two decades in America, but he identified himself as a sociologist, and his disciples worked as sociologists. Lazarsfeld was more a forerunner than a founder. Lasswell, Lewin, and Hovland were definitely forerunners, not founders. They did not give up their primary identification with political science, social psychology, and psychology, respectively.

Our main focus here is on North America, and especially the United States, because that is where the communication field grew to strength, although I detail its European roots (in Part I), and touch on the current status of communication study in Europe, Latin America, and elsewhere today (in Chapter 12). This book emphasizes the century from 1860 to 1960, an era that begins with publication of *On the Origin of Species* by Charles Darwin and ends with U.S. schools of communication becoming widely institutionalized in U.S. universities. Communication study came of age intellectually mainly in the United States during the 1900s, but its roots go back several decades earlier in Europe. The history of communication study is the story of the social sciences, with important contributions also from biology, mathematics, and electrical engineering.

My emphasis is on mass communication and, somewhat less, on interpersonal communication, but Carl I. Hovland, Kurt Lewin, George Herbert Mead, and John Dewey are included here. The distinction between interpersonal and mass communication has been greatly overstressed. It is not a useful way to divide the field of communication today, and I recommend its dismissal as a false dichotomy (Reardon and Rogers 1988). I do not include much of the humanistic origins of communication study here, such as rhetoric.

Just as "statistics is often taught with little reference to the men who developed the basic ideas of the field" (Tankard 1984, p. xi), so is communication often taught without much discussion of its roots. One result of this ahistorical nature of many communication courses today is that most students of communication do not know where their field came from. Some say that the field is so new that it does not yet have much history. Yet although departments or schools of communication began at most U.S. universities only after 1950, the roots go back a century. And if one begins counting the history of communication study with Aristotle's *Rhetoric* and Quintillian's *Models,* this field predates the other social sciences. There is plenty of history of communication study.

I interviewed forty-seven individuals who knew the early figures in communication study, including their students and surviving colleagues. Particularly valuable were the following oral history interviews:

- Dr. Theodore Peterson, Dr. Charles Sandage, Dr. Ellen Wartella, and Dr. David K. Berlo (on Wilbur Schramm).
- Dr. John H. Weakland, Dr. Paul Watzlawick, Dr. Heinz von Foerester, and Dr. Carol Wilder (on Gregory Bateson and the Palo Alto school).
- Dr. Martin Jay (on the Frankfurt school).
- Dr. Tamotsu Shibutani and Dr. Robert E. L. Faris (about the Chicago school).
- Dr. Alexander L. George and Joseph M. Goldsen (on Harold D. Lasswell).
- Dr. James S. Coleman, Dr. Elihu Katz, and Dr. Robert K. Merton (on Paul F. Lazarsfeld).
- The late Dr. Nathan Maccoby, Dr. William J. McGuire, Dr. Leonard Doob, Dr. Ernest R. Hilgard, and Dr. M. Brewster Smith (on Carl I. Hovland).
- Dr. Darwin Cartwright, Dr. Joan Lasko, Dr. Ralph K. White, Dr. Harold H. Kelley, and Dr. Miriam Lewin (on Kurt Lewin).
- Dr. Walter A. Rosenblith (on Norbert Wiener).
- Dr. John Pierce, Dr. Robert Fano, Dr. Peter Elias and Dr. Robert A. Scholtz (on Claude E. Shannon).

I used the following archives in writing this book:

- Oral History Research Office and the Rare Books and Manuscript Library, Butler Library, Columbia University, New York.
- MIT Libraries, Institute Archives and Special Collections, Cambridge, Massachusetts.
- Library of the American Philosophical Society, Philadelphia.
- Department of Special Collections, Joseph Regenstein Library, University of Chicago.
- Archives of the History of American Psychology, Bierce Library, University of Akron, Akron, Ohio.
- Rockefeller Archives Center, North Tarrytown, New York.

- U.S. Library of Congress, Washington, D.C.
- University of Iowa Archives, University Libraries, Iowa City.
- University Archives, University of Illinois Library, Urbana.
- Sterling Library, Yale University, New Haven, Connecticut.
- Department of Special Collections and University Archives, Stanford Libraries, Stanford, California.

The key events related in this book occurred in a very small number of places. Chicago is important as the site of the Chicago school, as is Frankfurt, Germany, for a parallel reason. The Frankfurt school is more formerly called the Institute for Social Research, which affiliated with the University of Frankfurt in the first years of its existence but then migrated in 1933 to New York City and had a loose affiliation with Columbia University. This arrangement continued for the next seventeen years, a period in which much of the institute's important work in critical theory was accomplished. Columbia University was also the headquarters for Paul F. Lazarsfeld's Office of Radio Research and his Bureau of Applied Social Research, which pioneered the early studies of mass communication effects.

Washington, D.C., was a key locus during the early World War II years, when Carl I. Hovland, Wilbur Schramm, Harold D. Lasswell, Kurt Lewin, Paul F. Lazarsfeld, and others came together to provide a new unity to communication study. Later these scholars moved back to their universities: Lasswell and Hovland to Yale, where Hovland established the Yale Program in Communication and Attitude Change, and Schramm to the University of Iowa.

Our story begins with Wilbur Schramm and Iowa City in the 1930s. It will end with Schramm at Stanford in the 1960s.

Almost all of the pioneers of communication study whose contributions are traced in this book are now gone (Claude E. Shannon is the exception; he lives in retirement in a Boston suburb). Like the labor organizer Joe Hill, these communication pioneers live on in their influential writings and in our thinking. They never died.

CHAPTER 1

WILBUR SCHRAMM AND THE FOUNDING OF COMMUNICATION STUDY

> The difficulty in summing up a field like human communi-
> cation is that it has no land that is exclusively its own. Com-
> munication is the fundamental social process.
>
> —Wilbur Schramm

On April 14, 1981, Wilbur Schramm returned from Honolulu, where he was living in retirement, to Iowa City, to give the Les Moeller Lecture at the School of Journalism and Mass Communication at the University of Iowa. It was a nostalgic visit. Schramm had first come to Iowa in 1930 to pursue his Ph.D. degree. In 1943 he had organized the first Ph.D. program in mass communication in the world while he was direc-tor of the Iowa journalism school. When he moved to Illinois in 1947, Les Moeller took over Schramm's position at Iowa. Schramm (1981) began the 1981 Moeller lecture in this way:

> Miss Betty [his wife] and I want to thank you for letting us come back to spend a few days with you on this campus for which we have so much affection and have not seen for so long. . . . It was about 48 years ago that I became aware of a slender, pretty girl in the front row of one of the first classes that I taught at Iowa. . . . About 18 months later she and I were married. . . . Iowa was a remarkable place in the 1930s and '40s, and chiefly because of the spirit of creativity that pervaded it. . . . Remember this was Iowa in the middle of the Depression, with a budget about one-eighth what I found when I went to Illinois in 1947. . . . In a place where one might not expect to find him, the Iowa Child Welfare Research Sta-tion, was one of the most creative psychologists in the world, Kurt Lewin.

I thank Lyle M. Nelson, Mary Schramm Coberly, and Guido Stempel III for reviewing this chapter.

1

I want to talk about what has happened to academic journalism and communication since the decade of the '30s when Ted [George] Gallup was a brand-new Ph.D., Frank Mott was a brand-new Director [of the School of Journalism] at Iowa, and the country was in its worst depression.

Thirty-eight years before this speech, in 1943, Schramm had returned to the University of Iowa from his wartime duties in Washington, D.C., with a vision of communication study, to found the first Ph.D. program in mass communication and the first communication research institute. At that time Schramm was influenced by Paul F. Lazarsfeld, Carl I. Hovland, and other social scientists who were conducting communication research connected with World War II, which brought together scholars from psychology, sociology, and political science to form the new field of communication. Wilbur Schramm was the founder of communication study and is the central figure in its history.

Figure 1.1. Wilbur Schramm (1907–1987) in about 1947, when he moved from the University of Iowa to the University of Illinois.

Source: University of Illinois at Urbana-Champaign, Institute of Communications Research.

WILBUR SCHRAMM

Wilbur Schramm (1907–1987) was born in Marietta, Ohio, on August 5, 1907 (Figure 1.1). This pastoral setting, located on the southern boundary of Ohio, was named by French explorers after their queen, Marie Antoinette. Schramm's ancestors came from Schrammsburg, Germany, and their Teutonic name caused difficulties for the family during World War I, when Schramm was a boy. His father was a lawyer in Marietta, whose legal practice suffered (Cartier 1988, p. 58).

Schramm's Stutter

Wilbur Schramm developed a severe stutter at age five due to "an amateurishly performed tonsillectomy" (Cartier 1988, p. 59). His speech difficulty was embarrassing to him and his family. As the stutter persisted, Schramm's father withdrew his interest in his only son, for whom he had dreamed of a career in law and politics (Coberly 1992). The boy's stutter was traumatic for him, such as when he had to recite a section of Martin Luther's catechism before the Lutheran Church congregation (Cartier 1988, p. 59). He avoided speaking in public. Instead of giving the valedictory address at his high school graduation, Schramm played "The Londonderry Air" on his flute. But when he graduated summa cum laude from Marietta College in history and political science in 1928, he did give a valedictory speech. Gradually Schramm learned to live with his stutter, which eventually became less pronounced. Nevertheless, his speech difficulty had an effect later in his life, eventually leading him into the field of communication for a second career (Table 1.1).

Even as a boy, Schramm displayed the can-do spirit that was to characterize a career in which his zest, creativeness, and intellectual abilities allowed him to master new fields. His only sister, Helen, a few years younger, once was struggling with a difficult piano piece. He finally said, "I don't see how you can possibly have so much trouble with that," and sat down and played it perfectly. On recalling this incident years later, Schramm's sister cried indignantly: "And he hadn't even studied the piano!" (Coberly 1992).

Schramm's mentors at the University of Iowa in the early 1930s did not feel that the brilliant young scholar could teach due to his stutter. But eventually, with speech therapy and perhaps with growing confi-

TABLE 1.1
Major Events in the Career of Wilbur Schramm

Date	Event
1907	Born in Marietta, Ohio
1928	Bachelor's degree in history and political science from Marietta College
1930	Master's degree in American Civilization from Harvard University
1932	Ph.D. in English Literature from the University of Iowa
1932–1934	American Council of Learned Societies postdoctoral fellow at the University of Iowa where he conducted experimental research with Dr. Carl E. Seashore
1934–1941	Assistant professor, associate professor, and professor of English, and founder and director of the Iowa's Writers' Workshop, University of Iowa
1942–1943	On leave from the University of Iowa to serve as educational director of the Office of Facts and Figures and the Office of War Information in Washington, D.C., during World War II, where he formed his vision of communication study
1943–1947	Director, School of Journalism, University of Iowa, and founder of the first doctoral program in mass communication
1947–1955	Founder and director of the Institute of Communications Research, dean of the Division of Communication, and assistant to the president of the University of Illinois
1955–1973	Professor of communication and director (1957–1973) of the Institute for Communication Research, Stanford University
1962–1973	Appointed the Janet M. Peck Professor of International Communication at Stanford University, until his mandatory retirement from Stanford at age sixty five
1973–1975	Director, East-West Communication Institute, Hawaii
1975–1977	Distinguished Center Researcher, East-West Communication Institute, Honolulu, Hawaii
1977	Ah Boon Hau Professor of Communication, Chinese University of Hong Kong
1987	Dies in Honolulu

dence about his verbal ability, Schramm overcame his stuttering problem bit by bit (Cartier 1988, p. 111). He made teaching his lifetime career, and in later life his stammer was a problem only occasionally.

Schramm spoke with difficulty but wrote easily, and he earned his college expenses as a part-time sports reporter for the *Marietta Register* and as a stringer for the Associated Press. He continued his part-time newspaper work at the *Boston Herald* during graduate work at Harvard University, completing his M.A. degree in American Civilization in 1930. Later, looking back to his Harvard studies, Schramm said that he was most influenced by Alfred North Whitehead, the famous philosopher (and, like Schramm, a stutterer), from whom he took a graduate-level course, illustrating Schramm's desire to seek out great minds.

Why did Schramm leave Harvard, after earning his master's degree, for the tree-lined banks of the Iowa River? Tuition at Harvard was $500 per semester, and Schramm had to struggle financially. At one time during his Harvard sojourn, he worked at six part-time jobs simultaneously (Schramm 1942–1943, p. 3). Later he was awarded a graduate fellowship, and the financial pressure eased somewhat, but then the stock market crashed, bringing on the Great Depression. Another reason Schramm moved to the University of Iowa for his doctorate was connected to his stuttering. One of the top experts in stuttering in the United States, Professor Lee Edward Travis, conducted research on, and treatment of, stuttering at Iowa. He theorized that wrong-handedness might be a factor in stuttering, so he strapped Schramm's right hand to his side with a leather contraption. It did not help.

Travis's work on stuttering was carried forward at Iowa by Wendell Johnson, and it was he who helped Schramm by means of counseling and therapeutic exercises. Johnson had been five years old when he began stuttering (a common age among the approximately 1 percent of the U.S. population afflicted with stuttering). Stuttering is often diagnosed by perfectionist parents whose child may actually have only the hesitations and repetitions characteristic of the normal speech of most young children. In that sense, stuttering is a socially defined malady. Further, most individuals seldom stutter when alone but only when talking face-to-face with others (Schramm did not stutter when talking on the telephone), especially in a stressful situation (such as giving a speech). While he was the director of the Iowa Speech Clinic in the 1930s, Wendell Johnson investigated these social aspects of stuttering. He discovered a tribe of Indians that had no stuttering—not a single member of the tribe stuttered, and the tribe had no word for stuttering or other speech defects in their language. "The Indian children were not criticized or evaluated on the basis of their speech" (Johnson, quoted by McElwain 1991, p. 112). Johnson was much more than just a speech therapist. He related his treatment and study of stuttering to linguistic theory and to general semantics.* He saw stuttering as what would today be called a communication problem. Certainly Johnson passed this viewpoint along to Schramm. His stuttering problem was thus one reason for Schramm's early interest in communication.

A Post-Doc in Experimental Psychology

Schramm's treatment for his stuttering made him keenly aware of the emerging field of communication study and led him eventually into experimental research on speech behavior. But Schramm majored in the humanities at Iowa, earning a Ph.D. in English literature in 1932. His dissertation was an analysis of Henry Wadsworth Longfellow's epic poem *Hiawatha*. Schramm then received a postdoctoral fellowship from the American Council of Learned Societies (Schramm 1935, p. 5) and stayed on at Iowa for two years of postdoctoral study with Professor Carl E. Seashore in the Psychology Department. Schramm conducted laboratory experiments on audiology problems and learned quantitative research approaches. He was acquiring the tools of a social scientist. The depression meant that faculty positions in English departments were scarce, and Schramm's postdoctoral fellowship at Iowa was a means of survival.

Also, Schramm felt that his scientific training needed strengthening. Throughout his lifetime, Schramm was attracted to individuals of excellence, and Seashore was an important academic figure at Iowa: professor of psychology, a pioneer experimental researcher, and long-time dean of the graduate school. A respected historian of the University of Iowa considers Seashore to be one of the most important shapers of the university's directions—even more important than several of the university's presidents (Persons 1990).

Born Carl Emil Sjöstrand in Sweden in 1866, Seashore migrated with his family at age three to an Iowa farm. Shortly, Seashore's parents changed the family name. Carl Seashore earned his Ph.D. degree in ex-

---

*Today, the facility for treating stutterers in the University of Iowa's Department of Speech Pathology and Audiology is housed in the Wendell Johnson Speech and Hearing Center.

perimental psychology at Yale University, getting in "on the ground floor" of this new field, as he liked to say (Persons 1990, p. 107). While on a European trip, he visited the experimental laboratory of Wilhelm Wundt at the University of Leipzig, considered the birthplace of psychology. In 1897, Seashore joined the University of Iowa as an assistant professor of psychology and combined his personal interest in music with his scientific expertise, conducting experiments on a variety of acoustical and speech problems. Seashore thus represented a scientific approach to Schramm's personal problem of stuttering.* He learned experimental design, the use of laboratory equipment, and how to think like a psychologist.

The fact that Schramm would conduct postdoctoral research in a field that he had not previously studied was a statement of his can-do spirit. Such a seemingly risky move signaled Schramm's later mid-career shift from English literature to journalism education and then to the new field of communication study that he created. This spirit characterized Schramm's entire life and was one of his most important qualities. He excelled in widely different fields. For example, he was an athlete, good enough to be offered a tryout at third base with the Columbus Red Birds, a Triple-A professional baseball farm club. While he was a graduate student at Harvard University, he played the flute with the Boston Civic Symphony Orchestra. He was a licensed airplane pilot. He once surprised David Berlo, his doctoral advisee at Illinois in the 1950s, by breaking off from a morning office conference in Urbana for travel to a luncheon meeting with the Kellogg Foundation trustees in Battle Creek, Michigan, and then resuming his office discussion with Berlo in the afternoon.† In the 1960s, while a senior faculty member at Stanford, Schramm bought a self-instruction manual and taught himself FORTRAN computer programming. Schramm wrote so profusely during his eighteen years at Stanford that he wore out several electric typewriters (Nelson 1977, p. 17). As his daughter noted, "He could no more stop writing then breathing. . . . In fact, he did stop the two together"

---

*A dozen years after Schramm's postdoctoral fellowship research with Seashore, he wrote an appealing short story, "Old Professors Never Die," published in the *Saturday Evening Post* (August 3, 1946), which drew on incidents of Seashore's well-known absent-mindedness (Stoddard 1950).

†Berlo (1992) also tells how Schramm, frustrated in trying to reach his colleague Charles Osgood by telephone at Indiana University (where Osgood was involved in a summer workshop on psycholinguistics), flew from Urbana to Bloomington and left a note on Osgood's pillow: "Charlie. Please call me in Urbana when you get well. Will."

(Coberly 1992). Schramm's life is "a gold mine of human interest material" (Starck 1991). Wilbur Schramm was good at almost everything he put his mind to. Everyone who knew him well begins by describing Schramm as a Renaissance man. The self-confidence thus displayed is an important quality for the founder of a new academic field.

THE IOWA WRITERS' WORKSHOP

From 1935 to 1942, Schramm was an assistant professor in the English Department at the University of Iowa, where he attained early fame as director of the Iowa Writers' Workshop, an intimate group of graduate students working closely with Schramm and several other faculty members in order to gain skills in fiction writing through an apprenticeship experience. The workshop grew out of a graduate seminar in fiction writing that had been taught by Professor Edwin Ford Piper for several years at the University of Iowa. Piper gave his course a regional focus, stressing Iowa culture, in order to balance the eastern seaboard bias of much American literature. The University of Iowa pioneered in granting M.F.A. and Ph.D. degrees for theses and dissertations that represented exemplary fiction writing.

In 1939, when Piper died, Schramm was named director of the workshop. His appointment came as a surprise to him: "When he [Piper] died suddenly of a heart attack, I had to take over. They should probably have gotten someone else at that time, and I rather expected them to, but I had a little while when no one else was there, and so had a lot of fun doing what I thought needed doing" (Schramm to Paul Engel, August 10, 1976, University of Iowa Libraries, Department of Special Collections). Piper's graduate seminar on fiction writing, widely called the "writers' workshop," thus grew into a program officially identified in the university catalog as the Iowa Writers' Workshop. The workshop consisted of ten to fifteen graduate students who were admitted each fall and five professors, most of whom taught part-time in the workshop. Schramm placed less emphasis on Iowa culture than had Piper. Students came from all over the United States, and the program became nationwide in focus. It rapidly achieved fame for its excellence.

In its teaching/learning style, the workshop was participatory and intimate. Schramm held an individual conference with each student once each week in his office (Wilbers 1980, p. 64). When a student had written something that Schramm considered ready, it was presented in a weekly seminar, which often met at Schramm's home. In its methods, although not in its content, the Iowa Writers' Workshop was a pilot for the doctoral programs in communication that Schramm was to launch subsequently at Iowa, Illinois, and Stanford.

The workshop, which remains one of the best graduate programs in creative writing in the United States, was small in size, elite, and of excellent quality. It taught students how to write fiction by having them write, with Schramm and other faculty acting as coaches. Such literary luminaries as James Michener, Robert Penn Warren, and John Cheever came to the workshop to teach and to write. Philip Roth wrote *Letting Go* and John Irving wrote *The World According to Garp* at the workshop, and Kurt Vonnegut wrote *Slaughterhouse Five* while he was teaching there. During the five years that Schramm directed the Iowa Writer's Workshop, ten books written by workshop students were published commercially.

In order to supplement his professorial salary, Wilbur Schramm did fiction writing on the side.* He published fantasy short stories about such characters as a farmer with a flying tractor, a horse that played third base for the Brooklyn Dodgers, the boatlike prairie schooner of a frontiersman named Windwagon Smith, and other free-spirited fictional personalities; most were published in the *Saturday Evening Post,* then a large-circulation magazine. Schramm gained a considerable reputation as a fiction writer; his magazine articles were republished in anthologies, he won the third-place award of the O. Henry Prize for fiction writing in 1942, and he published a fiction book, *Windwagon Smith and Other Yarns* (Schramm 1947b). He might have continued his career as an author and a professor of fiction writing, but this future was to be interrupted by World War II.

It was somewhat by chance that Schramm was at the University of Iowa. It was another accident that Kurt Lewin, an émigré psychologist from the University of Berlin, was there too. Schramm was drawn to Lewin and participated in Lewin's "Hot Air Club," which met weekly in

---

*Gladner (1990, p. 270) stated that Schramm wrote these fictional short stories during the World War II years in Washington in order to create a public opinion favorable to the war effort. Indeed, several of the magazine stories reflect an image of America as brave, patriotic, and virtuous, as is suggested by the stories' titles: "The Flying Cofffin," "The Story of Wilbur the Jeep," and "Boone over the Pacific." Even Schramm's Grandpa Hopewell, who powered his flying tractor with homemade cider, became a Pentagon consultant on high-octane jet fuels at the end of the story. But it seems implausible that these magazine stories were written as part of Schramm's wartime duties in the Office of Facts and Figures (Coberly 1992). In fact, a search of Schramm's personnel folder in the National Records Center (OFF Records E-7, Box 17) shows that he was concerned with other wartime duties.

an Iowa City café, the Round-Window Restaurant,* to discuss Lewin's field theory. Schramm (1981) recalled: "I don't know why journalism at Iowa made no more use of Lewin than it did, for so far as I know, I was the only one from our field here to have much contact with him or to know his students like Leon Festinger and Alex Bavelas. But I remember him well: Pacing back and forth in front of a class, with his round pink cheeks shining, drawing diagrams on the board to illustrate field theory, and saying over and over again, 'Vat haf ve vergassen?' or 'Vas haf ve vergotten?'" Although trained as a humanist in English literature, Schramm was gaining expertise in social science theory and research. His postdoctoral fellowship in psychology with Seashore and his informal association with Lewin at Iowa provided the background for his later founding of the scientific field of communication.

THE WORLD WAR II YEARS IN WASHINGTON, D.C.

World War II had a tremendous impact on the field of communication; it brought to the United States such immigrant scholars from Europe as Kurt Lewin, Paul F. Lazarsfeld, and Theodor Adorno; it attracted U.S. scholars like Carl I. Hovland and Harold D. Lasswell to communication research; and it connected these scholars who were to launch the field of communication study into a dense network. Thus an invisible college[†] of communication scholars came together in Washington, D.C. They met in formal conferences and informally in carpools,[‡] on military bases, and in federal government offices. Communication was considered crucial in informing the American public about the nation's wartime goals, and the details of food and gas rationing and other consumer

---

*The Round-Window Restaurant, more properly called Smitty's Restaurant (after its owners, Esther and Roland Smitty), was located near the corner of North Dubuque and Iowa Avenue, just off the University of Iowa campus. The Round-Window was only a couple of blocks down Iowa Avenue from East Hall (now the Seashore Building), where both Lewin and Schramm had their offices.

[†]An invisible college is a set of scholars sharing a common research interest who maintain contact with each other by formal (for example, conferences) and informal (for example, telephone calls) channels.

[‡]Because of the gasoline and tire shortage, Schramm and several other individuals organized a carpool from their homes in Silver Spring, Maryland, to their government offices in downtown Washington, D.C. Members of Schramm's carpool were anthropologist Margaret Mead, Philip Wylie, Clyde Vandenberg, William B. Lewis (a CBS official), and Leo Rosten, who had been a Ph.D. student in political science at Chicago under Harold Lasswell (Cartier 1988, p. 170).

sacrifices and in motivating the public to purchase war bonds, to avoid buying silk stockings and other scarce products on the black market, to grow victory gardens, and to support the war effort in other ways. Accordingly, communication research initially focused on studying the effects of communication. This consensus about the role of communication happened during World War II, and it happened mainly in Washington, D.C.

A Network of Social Scientists

The war caused the federal civil service to balloon at the rate of 97,000 new employees per month in 1941–1942, including substantial numbers of social scientists. Washington was actually a very small world for social scientists, consisting of three main research agencies linked by a set of common consultants: (1) the Research Branch of the Division of Information and Education, U.S. Army, directed by Samuel A. Stouffer, (2) the Surveys Division of the Office of War Information (OWI), directed by Elmo C. ("Budd") Wilson, and (3) the Division of Program Surveys of the U.S. Department of Agriculture (USDA) directed by Rensis Likert.* Each research group consisted of fewer than a hundred social scientists, interconnected by consultants like Paul F. Lazarsfeld, for example, who advised both the Research Branch and the OWI (Converse 1987, p. 163).

During World War II, Washington was the place to be for a social scientist. America's enemies represented such an unmitigated evil that very few social scientists opposed the war, especially after the fall of France in June 1940, when it became apparent that Hitler would dominate Europe.† America's war aims united these scholars in a common cause and brought them together into a network of relationships that would last throughout their careers. The war effort demanded an interdisciplinary approach, often centered on communication problems. World War II thus created the conditions for the founding of communication study.

As a wartime employee of the Office of Facts and Figures (OFF) and

*The Division of Program Surveys was located in the USDA because it had begun in 1939 to conduct studies of farmers' reactions to New Deal programs. Then it began conducting surveys for the OWI, Office of Price Administration, and the U.S. Department of the Treasury (Hyman 1991, pp. 3–4).

†The U.S. public supported the war effort so strongly that many young men falsified their medical records so that they would not be rejected by the draft (Coberly 1992).

the OWI, Schramm participated in an informal group that met regularly in a Washington hotel for dinner and discussions about interdisciplinarity in the social sciences. The other participants included Margaret Mead; Lyman Bryson, on leave from Columbia University's Teachers College for wartime duties as Schramm's boss at the OWI; Rensis Likert, director of the USDA's Division of Program Surveys; Goodwin Watson, a Columbia University psychologist; Ernest R. ("Jack") Hilgard, a Stanford psychologist who was working for Likert's Program Surveys, carrying out opinion research for the OWI; and Lawrence Frank, on leave from the Laura Spelman Rockefeller Memorial to do wartime work in Washington. The group met monthly during 1942 (Hilgard 1992).

None of the social scientists who collaborated in conducting wartime communication research had been trained in communication study; no doctoral programs in communication existed at that time. As one of the wartime Washington people, Nathan Maccoby, who conducted experiments on the effects of military training films in Sam Stouffer's Army Research Branch, said, "I tell my students that all I learned about communication, I learned on-the-job while doing experimental studies of U.S. military servicemen" (Maccoby 1987).

Lasswell's (1948) communication model—*"Who says what, to whom via what channels, with what effect?"*—was first published in a report of the Rockefeller Foundation Communication Seminars (November 1, 1940), which had met monthly in New York City during 1939 and 1940.* The Rockefeller Foundation report argued that the federal government should utilize communication research in the emergency situation of approaching war and detailed various types of research needed on communication, such as content analysis, surveys, and panel studies. This memorandum became a founding document for the emerging field of communication study. Lasswell's communication model provided the framework for the Rockefeller report, and thus for the wartime research in Washington, focusing on communication effects.

The federal government was engaged in several types of communication research during World War II, each of which had important long-term consequences for the field of communication. In the U.S. Army, Carl I. Hovland and others were conducting evaluations of military

*Actually, two lengthy memoranda resulted from the Rockefeller Communication Seminars: the November 1, 1940, report, *Public Opinion and the Emergency,* which recommended that the government invest in communication research in the approaching wartime emergency, and an October 17, 1940, report, *Needed Research in Communication,* which represented a broad call for communication research as essential to understanding modern society.

training films, out of which the tradition of persuasion research was to develop (see Chapter 9). At the Library of Congress, Harold D. Lasswell was conducting content analyses of Allied and Axis propaganda messages (see Chapter 6). At MIT in Cambridge, Professor Norbert Wiener was writing his "yellow peril" report* on the mathematics of how to improve antiaircraft gunfire accuracy, sponsored by the Pentagon. This work led to cybernetic theory, dealing with systems that regulate themselves through feedback (see Chapter 10). And at Bell Labs in New York, Claude E. Shannon was carrying out cryptographic analysis, which would help form the basis of information theory (see Chapter 11). At the OFF, Wilbur Schramm helped draft speeches for President Roosevelt's radio broadcasts to the nation, including his famous fireside chats. OFF and the OWI, its successor agency, were responsible for domestic and foreign propaganda. They informed the public about the progress of the war and of the sacrifices that the public was being asked to make. Schramm met regularly in planning meetings with other OFF and OWI staff and their consultants to design public communication campaigns and to study their effects. Thus, during 1942, he developed his vision of communication study.

Office of Facts and Figures/Office of War Information

The OFF was created in October 1941 to boost public morale. Although the United States would not enter World War II until six weeks later, on December 7, 1941, it had been obvious for more than a year that America would join the Allies. However, there was considerable public opposition to U.S. participation in the war in Europe, and the mass media were suspicious of OFF. Further, OFF sounded like a propaganda agency to U.S. newspeople (actually, it was, despite its name), so many newspapers launched vicious attacks on it. Poet Archibald MacLeish, the U.S. Librarian of Congress, was also appointed the Director of OFF, which got underway on October 24, 1941 (Bishop and MacKay 1971, p. 10).

Schramm knew MacLeish from his having lectured at the University of Iowa. Eight days after the Japanese attack on Pearl Harbor, Schramm wrote to MacLeish, volunteering for wartime service. He observed: "Perhaps more than any previous war this is likely to be a war of communi-

---

*The widely used nickname for this report arose because it contained such formidable mathematics, and because of its yellow covers, indicating its secret classification.

cation."* Within two weeks, MacLeish had appointed Schramm as OFF's educational director. Schramm's fifteen months with OFF and OWI "would drastically change his life—change the direction of his intellectual pursuits, thrust him into a circle of national decision-making elites, and prompt him to refer to himself as a social scientist rather than a literary humanist" (Gladner 1990, p. 269).

Eight months later, on June 13, 1942, when OFF was reorganized as the OWI, it had 400 employees and a budget of $1.5 million. One of the largest divisions within OFF was the Bureau of Intelligence, in charge of gauging public opinion about the war, headed by Budd Wilson. The staff of 140, assisted by another 160 in the USDA's Program Surveys Division, designed surveys to measure the public's understanding of war-related issues and conducted data gathering about the effectiveness of OFF's public information activities. For instance, surveys were conducted of the extent of home canning, the amount of pleasure driving (which was banned officially), participation in a wartime rubber salvage drive, and how effectively Boy Scouts were distributing government posters about the war. Enemy propaganda was analyzed as a basis for carrying out counterpropaganda efforts. OFF and OWI claimed to be providing accurate information about the progress of the war, which largely amounted to acknowledging U.S. and Allied losses in 1941 and 1942. However, media critics of OFF and OWI claimed that U.S. losses were intentionally underreported.

The director of OWI was Elmer Davis, a distinguished radio commentator who had been a Rhodes scholar, a fiction writer, and a news analyst for CBS Radio. In 1941, Davis broadcast a criticism of the confused organizational setup of public information in the federal government and as a result was promptly nominated by President Roosevelt to head the newly created OWI. Rationalizing the government's wartime public information efforts was an impossible task; the Army, Navy, and other agencies continued their own public communication activities, independent of the OWI (Bishop and MacKay 1971, p. 18). During 1943 the OWI experienced extreme difficulties. Its annual budget was cut from $8.9 million to $2.7 million by a Congress distrustful of the notion of wartime propaganda, internal conflict raged, and its leadership changed (Converse 1987, p. 472). The OWI retained its responsibility for "white" propaganda—aimed at the domestic audience—while the

*This December 15, 1941, letter from Schramm to MacLeish is in the University of Iowa Archives, University Libraries, Wilbur Schramm Vertical File.

Office of Special Services (OSS, later to become the Central Intelligence Agency) was responsible for "black" propaganda—communication messages in which the true identity of the communicator is falsified and which include false information—employed overseas against the enemy.

Schramm's Vision of Communication Study

Schramm's vision was formed during 1942, while he was the director of the education division of OFF, and later at OWI. His ideas about communication study probably grew gradually out of his everyday contacts with other scholars interested in the emerging field of communication, but he was most directly influenced by the two dozen staff members and consultants at OFF/OWI who met every two or three days around a long conference table in the U.S. Library of Congress building. Schramm participated with the following members of this planning group (Cartier 1988, p. 170; Hilgard 1992b): Sam Stouffer from the Research Branch of the U.S. Army; Ralph O. Nafziger, head of OFF's Media Division, on leave from the University of Minnesota's School of Journalism; Rensis Likert and Jack Hilgard from the Division of Program Surveys in the USDA, who conducted audience surveys for OFF/OWI; and George Gallup, Elmo Roper, Paul F. Lazarsfeld, and Frank Stanton, all consultants to OFF (Stanton 1992).*

The group met to decide what information should be communicated to the American public to boost domestic morale and what communication channels OFF could use to reach their intended audience. They tried to assess, through surveys, the effects of their communication activities on the public. The central concern of this planning group was to carry out large-scale communication campaigns guided by the best expertise available, with feedback about effects provided by audience surveys. As David Manning White, then a recent Ph.D. from the University of Iowa who was invited to the planning group sessions by Schramm,

---

*Not included in this group was Harold Lasswell, whom Schramm was not to meet until 1955 at Stanford, although Schramm's colleague Nafziger had been trained in content analysis methods by Lasswell in his War-Time Communications Project in the U.S. Library of Congress. Schramm was presumably informed about Lasswell's five-question model and the 1939–1940 Rockefeller Foundation Communication Seminars that this model dominated by Lyman Bryson, who had participated in the seminars and was Schramm's boss at the OWI in 1942 (Rowland 1983, p. 82).

stated: "Mass communication research *began* in the Library of Congress in 1942" (Cartier 1988, p. 171).

Thus was Wilbur Schramm's vision of communication study born during his fifteen months at the OFF and OWI. He returned to Iowa City to begin implementing his vision in 1943. Ralph O. Nafziger went back to the University of Minnesota when his two-year leave without pay ended in 1943, where he founded the Research Division in the Minnesota School of Journalism in 1944.* But while Nafziger was introducing some communication study into his school of journalism, Schramm at Iowa was seeking to launch a whole new field of academic study. He was preoccupied with "Why aren't *we* in *communication* asking those kinds of questions [the questions discussed by the planning group in OFF/OWI]? I wanted to do that so bad it hurt" (Cartier 1988, p. 174).

Schramm was happy to leave OWI and Washington in 1943, and return to the University of Iowa. He found OWI "tangled, messy, busy" and much of the work routine and uninteresting (Cartier 1988, p. 174). When he returned to the University of Iowa, he was quite a different man than when he had left. Then he was a professor of English, in charge of teaching creative writing. Now he had a vision for founding the new field of communication study.

THE IOWA PROGRAM IN MASS COMMUNICATION RESEARCH

When Wilbur Schramm returned to Iowa City, it was a fortuitous and opportunistic happenstance that he wound up in the School of Journalism at the university. The university's top administrators wanted to keep him at Iowa, and the School of Journalism needed a director since Frank Luther Mott had resigned effective August 1, 1942. Schramm was somewhat of an odd choice to be director because he had never been a full-time journalist. At the time, such experience as a reporter or editor was considered an essential requirement for being appointed as a journalism professor. Schramm was not at heart a journalism professor, and he did not teach courses in writing and editing skills at any time during his career. He was pursuing a broader vision of communication study and considered himself just temporarily alight in a school of journalism for the next few years.

---

*Along with the Minnesota Poll that it conducted, with both activities funded initially by the *Minneapolis Star* and the *Minneapolis Tribune*. By the mid-1950s, the Minnesota Poll was operated by the *Minnesota Tribune* (Stempel 1992).

Schramm would have more logically fit back in the Iowa Writers' Workshop, but another scholar, the poet Paul Engel, was in charge of the workshop. In 1981, Schramm was asked in an interview why he did not return from Washington to his previous faculty position in the Department of English at the University of Iowa: "I went to Harvard and worked with Alfred North Whitehead, did graduate work at Iowa with Carl Seashore and George Stoddard in psychology, then learned about statistics and quantitative research. Having such broad interests, it would have been hard coming back to Iowa and teaching the history of Chaucer" (McElwain 1991, p. 18).

Schramm did not want to return to his prewar position as workshop director in part because Norman Foerster, his former mentor while a doctoral student, was dean of the School of Letters, which included the Department of English and hence the workshop. In 1943, Foerster and Schramm's relationship had ruptured, and this split was a major reason that Schramm did not wish to return to his old post (Cartier 1988, p. 109).

Appointing Schramm as director of the School of Journalism solved another problem for the University of Iowa's administration; they wanted to keep him at Iowa. In fact, Schramm was offered a choice of administrative positions, including director of the University of Iowa libraries (Wilbers 1980, p. 12). Had he accepted that position, communication study might have grown out of library and information science. Instead, he fit his vision of communication study into the School of Journalism, thus shaping and constraining in important ways what the field of communication would later become.

Inauguration of the first communication Ph.D. program in a school of journalism, a professional training unit oriented to the print channel of communication, directly led to the division of the communication field into two subdisciplines: mass communication and interpersonal communication. Other doctoral programs in communication study were later launched in existing departments of speech, stressing interpersonal interaction. The communication Ph.D. program at Iowa could have begun in the Department of Speech and Dramatic Arts (now the Department of Communication Studies), devoted to studying interpersonal communication. This department was the first in the United States to study speech scientifically and had been awarding Ph.D. degrees since 1930, so Schramm might have initiated his idea for a doctoral program in communication study as part of an already-existing operation. He did not, and so Iowa was to have two different doctoral programs in communication. The Department of Communication Studies has awarded more than four hundred doctorates since 1930, and the School of Journalism and Mass Communication has awarded about two hundred such degrees since 1947. The potentially divisive situation of having two different academic units on the same university campus awarding Ph.D. degrees in communication is replicated on many university campuses today. This unusual arrangement stems from Wilbur Schramm at the University of Iowa in the 1940s.

An alternative would have been for Schramm to launch the first university unit in communication study in one of its parental disciplines like sociology, psychology, or political science, but at Iowa those departments already had Ph.D. programs. Additionally, Schramm had a doctorate in the humanities and was not acceptable as a faculty member in the other departments. So he launched the new discipline of communication in a school of journalism, although the doctoral curriculum that he created was interdisciplinary, drawing on courses in psychology, sociology, and political science.

Daddy Bleyer and the Bleyer Children

The teaching of journalism in U.S. universities began around 1900, although in 1869 Robert E. Lee, the former commander of the southern armies in the Civil War, had proposed college fellowships in journalism at Washington College (now Washington and Lee), when he was president of that institution.* Several universities lay claim to founding the teaching of journalism. The first journalism course still extant was offered at the University of Kansas in 1903. The following year, Willard G. "Daddy" Bleyer at the University of Wisconsin taught a course on newspaper libel law to twenty-five students. The next year, he offered a year-long course in journalism, in which forty students enrolled. Journalism at Wisconsin was thus launched. It grew into a department of journalism in 1912 (with Bleyer as chair) and a school of journalism in 1927. Thereafter, Wisconsin's school of journalism, with Bleyer as its director, became the key institution in producing professors of journalism in the United States. Bleyer recruited talented individuals who had newspaper experience and had been teaching journalism at the university level to teach journalism part time at Wisconsin while they pursued a Ph.D.

---

*Lee thought that well-trained journalists could play an important role in rebuilding the war-torn South (Dennis 1992).

degree in political science, sociology, or history, minoring in journalism by enrolling in doctoral seminars on public opinion and propaganda that Bleyer taught. The journalism minor doctoral program at Wisconsin was approved by the university administration in 1927 as part of the creation of the school of journalism.

Bleyer's strategy was to help schools of journalism survive in U.S. research universities by training a cadre of directors for these schools ("the Bleyer children") who had Ph.D. degrees in a social science and shared his vision of journalism as a social science. His students became the deans and directors of schools of journalism at Minnesota, Northwestern, Stanford, Illinois, and Michigan State, among others (Nafzinger 1970). This strategy was quite radical for its time, but it eventually was widely accepted. Professor Fred S. Siebert (1970) who served as an early director of the School of Journalism at Illinois and later as dean of the College of Communication at Michigan State, considered Daddy Bleyer the outstanding pioneer in journalism education: "He established the first real operating school of journalism, with [a] . . . research orientation at Wisconsin." Thus Wisconsin in the 1930s was the seed institution for journalism training based in the social sciences, and Daddy Bleyer was the pioneering figure.

Bleyer (1873–1935) was born into a family of newspaper people in Milwaukee. While an undergraduate student at the University of Wisconsin, majoring in English, he helped found the student newspaper, the *Daily Cardinal,* and served as its editor. He earned his bachelor's degree and then his master's in 1889, subsequently teaching high school English while doing newspaper work part-time. He returned to teach at the University of Wisconsin, earning his Ph.D. degree in English in 1904, when he began teaching the university's first course in journalism. Bleyer's academic title was soon changed to assistant professor of journalism (Sloan 1990, p. 77). Henry Ladd Smith (1992), who taught with Bleyer at Wisconsin for two years, described him as a very poor teacher: "In all my years in academia, he was the worst I've known at the lectern. It was obviously torture for him to stand against the blackboard wall, facing the volley of a hundred pairs of drooping eyelids. He sponged his dripping face at regular intervals. But his seminars were well worth the experience. Dull, yes, but respected." Daddy Bleyer was "dry as dust" in the classrooms, one of his students said (Nelson 1987, p. 5).

Bleyer pioneered in promoting journalism as a legitimate university discipline, with emphasis on teaching journalism as a social science rather than as a vocational subject. He believed that U.S. democracy could be improved through a more responsible press, staffed by news-people trained so that they not only knew how to write the news but also could understand the society whose events they were reporting. Further, Bleyer thought that journalism could not survive in research universities like Wisconsin if it were just vocational training. Journalism education had to gain academic respectability. Bleyer was a missionary for his journalism-as-social-science point of view, working through professional journalism associations and training a cadre of journalism professors. He wrote journalism textbooks that defined the field of journalism: *The Profession of Journalism* (1910), *Newspaper Writing and Editing* (1913), *Types of Newswriting* (1916), *How to Write Special Feature Articles* (1920), and *Main Currents in the History of American Journalism* (1927). Along with Walter Williams, dean of the more vocationally oriented school of journalism at the University of Missouri, Bleyer is considered the founding father of journalism education (Emery and McKerns 1987). Bleyer's vision of journalism education has had a lasting influence on the field, even though he is now fifty-eight years gone.

Bleyer's vision of journalism consisted of three components. First was a four-year undergraduate curriculum comprised of one-fourth journalism courses and three-fourths classes in the social sciences and humanities. Daddy Bleyer's journalism curriculum at the University of Wisconsin became "the basic command of accreditation" (Nelson 1987, p. 5) and was eventually accepted by most U.S. schools of journalism. Second, Bleyer conducted social science research on problems that he felt could improve the quality of newspapers and also provide a more adequate knowledge base for journalism teaching. For example, he carried out a newspaper readership survey in Madison in 1928 in order to determine the effects of newspapers on their readers. Finally, in 1922, he initiated a graduate seminar in public opinion, taught in the Department (later School) of Journalism at the University of Wisconsin, which centered on Walter Lippmann's (1922) important book, *Public Opinion*. In 1927, Bleyer obtained the approval of the graduate school at Wisconsin to offer a Ph.D. degree in political science, sociology, or history, with a minor in journalism. Bleyer's philosophy was of "a well-organized four-year course of study in preparation for journalism in which required and elective courses in history, economics, government and politics, sociology, psychology, science, and literature are being pursued at the same time that students are taking courses in journalism, [which] gives purpose and direction to the student's work and shows him what these other studies mean in relation to the life and work of the world." Some decades later, in the 1940s, when the accreditation of journalism schools got underway, Bleyer's vision of the ideal journalism curriculum became the standard for accrediting schools of journalism.

The first Ph.D. degree granted in the Wisconsin program of study was in 1929 to Ralph D. Casey, who had come to Madison after several years of newspaper experience and after teaching journalism at several universities. After earning his Ph.D. degree in political science with a minor in journalism, Casey moved to the University of Minnesota, where he became director of the journalism school in 1930. With Ralph O. Nafziger, Casey established a research division at Minnesota in 1944, the first of its kind. Two other "Bleyer children" followed in Casey's footsteps: Chilton R. ("Chick") Bush and Nafziger. Like Casey, both had newspaper and journalism teaching experience and then came to Wisconsin, where they earned Ph.D. degrees in political science with a journalism minor (in 1935 and 1936, respectively), while teaching part-time in the School of Journalism. Nafziger then taught at Minnesota in the School of Journalism for fifteen years (except for the World War II years, which he spent in Washington, D.C.). Chick Bush followed a similar career path to that of Nafziger, except that he devoted a year of his doctoral study to enrolling in political science at the University of Chicago. After earning his Ph.D. degree, Bush went from Wisconsin to Stanford, where he served as head of the department of communication and journalism from 1934 until his retirement in 1961. Bleyer's purpose in establishing the doctoral program at Wisconsin was to train a cadre of journalism professors with competence in the social science aspects of communication.

Daddy Bleyer was a strong critic of certain newspaper policies, particularly sensationalism. He also badgered newspaper owners and publishers to pay higher salaries to journalists. Bleyer had progressive gender attitudes for his day, encouraging women to study journalism. He was the only male elected to membership in the women's national journalism honorary. Bleyer was a brave man who on one occasion stood up to the president of the University of Wisconsin, in defense of a student journalist who had written a critical but accurate article in the *Daily Cardinal*.

Daddy Bleyer was in an advantageous position to promote his notion of the social sciences in undergraduate journalism training. As the informal founder of journalism education in U.S. universities, he helped create the American Association of Teachers of Journalism (AATJ) in 1912 and served as its first president. He chaired for several years the curriculum committee of the Association of American Schools and Departments of Journalism (AASDJ), the organization of administrators of journalism schools, through which he influenced the journalism curricula of other universities.

Bleyer was a strong promoter of research on journalism problems. He chaired the research committee of the AATJ during the late 1920s and regularly presented papers at the annual conferences that reported his research findings or outlined needed research topics. Bleyer's overall strategy was to help journalism schools survive by remaking them in a more scholarly direction, including an increased emphasis on research.

The general idea of the social sciences foundation for a journalism major did not originate with Bleyer. Where did he get his vision? Bleyer wrote in 1934, "This seems to have been the first attempt to carry out Pulitzer's and President Eliot's proposals for combining instruction in social sciences with that in journalism for the purpose of giving students broad background and some technical training in journalism" (Ross 1957), Joseph Pulitzer (1847–1911), a Hungarian émigré, had launched his newspaper empire with the *St. Louis Post-Dispatch* and grew it into a major newspaper chain whose flagship was the *New York World*. The *World* was known for its sensationalistic, yellow journalism press wars with William Randolph Hearst's newspaper chain, and one would not then associate Pulitzer's name with serious journalism. But in 1892 Pulitzer approached President Low of Columbia University with an offer to endow a school of journalism. He was initially rebuffed at Columbia and took up the matter with President Charles W. Eliot of Harvard, who drew up a program for the teaching of journalism.* Out of their discussions, Eliot and Pulitzer proposed a curriculum for a school of journalism that stressed courses in the social sciences and humanities, complemented by courses in journalistic skills. Harvard did not get the Pulitzer School of Journalism (it went to Columbia after all, in 1912),† but the journalism curriculum that Pulitzer and Eliot proposed became Daddy Bleyer's model at Wisconsin (although not at Columbia, where the curriculum is heavily professional and vocational). Pulitzer gave Columbia $2 million for a new building for journalism,

*President Eliot was no admirer of American journalists. Around 1890 he called them "drunkards, deadbeats, and bummers" (Mott 1950, p. 488).

†President Nicholas Murray Butler of Columbia was more receptive to Pulitzer's offer than his predecessor had been.

student fellowships, and for the Pulitzer Prizes for meritorious journalistic and literary achievements (Bleyer 1934).

Most newspaper editors of the day ridiculed Pulitzer's proposal for a school of journalism. He responded with an article in the *North American Review* (Pulitzer 1904) in which he explained that the objective of the school of journalism was "to make better journalists, who will make better newspapers, which will better serve the public. . . . My hope is that this College of Journalism will raise the standard of the editorial profession. . . . I wish to begin a movement that will raise journalism to the rank of a learned profession" (Pulitzer 1904).

Iowa School of Journalism

The University of Iowa began teaching journalism in the early 1900s, and the School of Journalism was established in 1924. One of the early journalism instructors at Iowa was George H. ("Ted") Gallup (1902–1984). He grew up in the county seat town of Jefferson, in western Iowa. As a high school boy, Gallup got a share of the profits from the six cows that he milked on his father's farm. He was also captain of his school's football and basketball teams, until Jefferson High School decided to drop sports when the coach was drafted into military service in World War I. Gallup told the school administrators that he would outfit the athletic teams in uniforms and also serve as the coach. "The only stipulation was that I got to keep the gate receipts at the games. They agreed," remembered Gallup (McElwain 1991, p. 1). Even at an early age, Gallup was very enterprising.

Gallup earned his B.A. degree at Iowa in 1923, his M.A. in 1925, and his Ph.D. in psychology in 1928, with a dissertation entitled "An Objective Method for Determining Reader Interest in the Content of a Newspaper." From 1924 to 1929, Gallup taught journalism courses at Iowa in news editing, copyreading, advertising, and magazine writing. Meanwhile, he worked out the basic idea of drawing a sample of survey respondents from a large population and then generalizing the research results. His specialty was studying newspaper audiences. While teaching at Iowa, Gallup founded Quill and Scroll Society, the international honorary society for high school journalists. Years later, long after Gallup had moved to New York and established the American Institute of Public Opinion (commonly called the Gallup Poll), the Quill and Scroll Foundation established a chaired professorship at Iowa named in his honor, the George H. Gallup Professorship in Journalism (McElwain

1991, p. 4). Gallup was a key founder of the field of polling research, and in the eyes of the American public, the words *Gallup* and *poll* are essentially synonymous. (In fact, *gallup* is the Finnish word for a poll.)

From 1927 to 1942, the director of the School of Journalism at Iowa was Frank Luther Mott. He grew up in a small-town Iowa newspaper family, earned his Ph.D. at Columbia University, and then came back to Iowa City to teach journalism and earned a Pulitzer Prize in history for his 1939 book, *History of American Magazines.* Mott organized the Society for the Prevention of Cruelty to Speakers, a behind-closed-doors drinking club (illegal during prohibition) that provided postlecture relaxation for noted speakers whom Mott had persuaded to travel to Iowa City: Robert Frost, e. e. cummings, Carl Sandburg, Henry Wallace, Lincoln Steffens, and Stephen Vincent Benét. Wilbur Schramm was one of the sixteen regular members of the society, which gloried in its ability to bring outstanding public figures to Iowa City.

Directing the Journalism School

When Frank Luther Mott resigned as director of the journalism school at Iowa in May 1942 to become dean of journalism at Missouri, a search process was launched to find a replacement. Schramm was contacted about the position and was asked to describe his proposed journalism program. A month later, in September 1942, he sent President Virgil Hancher "A Blueprint for a School of Journalism, with Fourteen Recommendations for the Iowa School." It stated: "I should like to see the kind of School of Journalism that would be not as weak as itself, but as strong as the university. Not a group of teachers and students sitting on the periphery of the university, playing with their toys, putting together the picture of who, what, where, and when in the first paragraph—not that, but a School that would be in the very heart of the university, which would begin with the assumption that the students it wants to produce will be the students in the whole university best equipped to understand and talk about the world they live in" (Cartier 1988, p. 246). This visionary statement reflected in part the perspectives on human communication that Schramm had absorbed from his wartime associates on the banks of the Potomac. It was not a vocational-type vision of journalism training but rather called for a Bleyer-style curriculum that would include a minimum of courses in journalism and a maximum of courses in the social sciences and humanities.*

Schramm's blueprint was evidently helpful; the university administration offered the position to him in March 1943 (Oukrop 1965, p. 55). Although Schramm had only several years of part-time newspaper experience, he had considerable personal charm and proved administrative experience in helping establish the Iowa Writers' Workshop and heading the Education Division of the OFF/OWI. He was 35 years old.

Schramm's blueprint included a plan for the Ph.D. degree in mass communication and for a communication research center. His vision for communication study at Iowa called for the School of Journalism to conduct research and to award doctoral degrees. Schramm went one big step beyond Bleyer: he established a doctoral program in mass communication, not in journalism as at Wisconsin.† The doctoral curriculum at Iowa included courses taught in the journalism school in communication theory, research methods, public opinion, propaganda analysis, and other social scientific topics, plus courses outside the school in psychology, sociology, and political science to buttress the curriculum. The idea of a school of journalism's giving a Ph.D. degree was new at the time. The University of Missouri had awarded the first Ph.D. in journalism in 1934, but only a couple of these degrees had been earned by 1943 (Oukrop 1965, p. 140). The first two Ph.D.s in mass communication were awarded at Iowa a year after Schramm left for Illinois, in August 1948, to Charles E. Swanson and Donald D. Jackson. Swanson was recruited to the new doctoral program by Wilbur Schramm while they were playing baseball on the campus down by the Iowa River one afternoon (McElwain 1991, p. 219). Swanson was working on his master's in the Iowa Writers' Workshop at the time. Schramm convinced him to test the new waters of a mass communication doctorate.

Notice that the new mass communication schools in the 1940s and 1950s were not located in the Ivy League universities or in the other

---

*Although how much Schramm knew at this time about Bleyer's Wisconsin journalism curriculum, or about the Bleyer-children at Minnesota, Illinois, Northwestern, and Stanford, is unclear. By 1947, four or five years later, however, Schramm (1947a) quoted Daddy Bleyer's vision in a statement about education for journalism. Lyle Nelson, a Stanford communication professor who was Schramm's best friend for several decades, says, "I never heard him mention Bleyer, nor have I run across references to Bleyer in his principal books" (Nelson 1992).

†Another important difference between the Bleyer and Schramm visions was that Bleyer stressed undergraduate training in journalism, while Schramm focused on doctoral-level training and on research.

high-prestige universities like Chicago or MIT. These elite universities were the locations of the forerunners of the field of communication: the Chicago school and Harold D. Lasswell at the University of Chicago; Paul F. Lazarsfeld at Columbia University; Kurt Lewin, Norbert Wiener, and Claude E. Shannon at MIT; and Carl I. Hovland and Lasswell at Yale University. America's most prestigious universities conducted the first communication research, but they resisted founding organizational units to provide communication study. (They still do.) Instead, the first doctoral programs in mass communication were founded at the large land-grant universities in the Midwest: Iowa, Illinois, Wisconsin, and Minnesota and, a West Coast outlier, Stanford. These universities already had journalism schools, and doctoral programs in communication study were grafted on to these existing structures. (In later years, these schools of journalism typically added "and mass communication" to their names.) Not accidentally, the Illinois, Wisconsin, Minnesota, and Stanford schools were all headed by Bleyer children. The only school of journalism in the Ivy League was at Columbia, thanks to the gift from Joseph Pulitzer. Iowa had a journalism school, and it had Schramm and his vision of communication study. Of course there were many other university schools of journalism that did not adopt the innovation of communication study until years later, and then only partially or halfheartedly, if at all. The innovator universities by that time had gained a big advantage in academic prestige from being first in the field. Today, Wisconsin, Stanford, Illinois, Minnesota, and Iowa are still considered among the top university schools of mass communication in the United States.

Communication Research Institutes

The founding of the doctoral programs in mass communication—at Iowa in 1943, at Illinois in 1947, at Wisconsin in 1950, at Minnesota in 1951, and at Stanford in 1952—was usually followed in each case by the founding of a communication research institute, each patterned loosely after Paul F. Lazarsfeld's Bureau of Applied Social Research at Columbia University (which was still called the Radio Research Project in 1943):

- The Research Division in the University of Minnesota's School of Journalism, founded by Ralph Casey and Ralph O. Nafziger in 1944 on Nafziger's return from OFF/OWI work. This was the first communication research institute in a school of journalism in the United States.

- Schramm's Bureau of Audience Research at the University of Iowa, founded in 1946.
- Schramm's 1947 Institute of Communications Research at the University of Illinois.
- The Mass Communications Research Center at the University of Wisconsin, founded in 1949 by Ralph O. Nafziger when he moved to Madison from Minnesota.
- Chilton Bush's 1955 Institute for Communication Research at Stanford University, which was directed by Wilbur Schramm after 1957.
- The Communication Research Center at Michigan State University, founded by Paul J. Deutschmann (who had been a doctoral student of Schramm's at Stanford University) in 1956.

These research institutes provided apprentice-style training for communication doctoral students and made it easier to enlist other social science disciplines in communication research. Sociologists and psychologists would be less likely to participate in communication study if such research were headquartered in a school of journalism, which other social scientists were likely to perceive as irrelevant to their research interests. A communication research institute could serve as a source of prestige for a school of journalism that may have been looked down upon by professors in other fields because of the perceived trade school nature of journalism training.

In 1946, radio station WMT in Cedar Rapids provided the Iowa School of Journalism with a grant of $5,000 to establish the Bureau of Audience Research, whose mission was to conduct audience studies for newspapers and radio stations. Leslie G. Moeller was recruited by Schramm to head the new bureau . Moeller was an experienced newspaperman and president of the Iowa Press Association, the trade association of Iowa newspapers. The bureau was intended to provide survey results to media institutions about the size and composition of their audience. Later, the media organizations also wanted to know the effects of their messages on their audience. The first newspaper readership studies under Schramm's direction at the Iowa Bureau of Audience Research were funded by George Gallup and his employer, Young and Rubicam advertising agency in New York. Later newspaper readership surveys were funded by the Iowa Press Association.

A research institute can be more flexible than a university department. It is easier to launch than is a department, and it can facilitate interdisciplinary collaboration. Thus, the institutes were an ideal place in which to launch the new field of communication study. But their flexibility also made them vulnerable, and most of the institutes for communication research founded in Schramm's era are now gone or relatively unimportant (including the Institute for Communication Research at Stanford, undoubtedly the most famous of the institutes, which continues to exist but seems to serve little purpose).

SCHRAMM'S DEPARTURE TO ILLINOIS

In 1947, Wilbur Schramm left Iowa City for the University of Illinois, where he became director of the Institute of Communications Research, director of the University of Illinois Press, and assistant to the president of the university. These duties were greatly expanded in 1950 when the Division of Communication was created, with Schramm as dean. The division encompassed the School of Journalism and Communications, the Library School, the University Libraries, the university's radio and television broadcasting stations, the Alumni Office, University Publicity, University Extension, Athletic Department Publicity, Agricultural Information, Allerton House Conference Center, the University Press, and the Institute of Communications Research. Table talk at the faculty club commonly referred to Schramm as the "communication czar" of the university, or the "duke of Allerton" after the name of the conference center.

Why did Schramm move from Iowa to Illinois? Illinois president George Stoddard had known Schramm at Iowa, where Stoddard had been the director of the Iowa Child Welfare Research Station and, later, dean of the graduate school. He promised Schramm that he could establish a research institute and a doctoral degree–granting program in communication at Illinois. That was a strong pull. There was also some push for Schramm to leave Iowa. He had drawn up an enthusiastic plan for communication study at Iowa for the next ten years, asking for $130,000 a year in operating costs, a level of resources that the university administrators felt they could not afford (Oukrop 1965, p. 69). So in April 1947, Schramm resigned at Iowa, to take up his new duties at Illinois effective the following September. Schramm became assistant to President Stoddard, joining his "kitchen cabinet" at Illinois, and participating in a "let's-get-the-university-moving-again" thrust (Hudson 1977, p. 311).

Professor Leslie G. Moeller replaced Wilbur Schramm as director of the Iowa School of Journalism in 1947 and continued in this position for the next twenty years. Moeller was born in 1904, grew up on an Iowa farm, and majored in journalism at the University of Iowa (Moeller 1970). After two decades of newspaper work, while serving in the U.S. Navy, Moeller wrote to Schramm, at the Iowa journalism school, raising penetrating questions about the role of journalism in society. Their exchange of letters impressed Schramm, who offered Moeller a faculty job in 1946, along with the position as head of the Bureau of Newspaper Research in the Iowa School of Journalism.

Schramm played a key role in the history of communication study. He was *the* founder of the field, the first individual to identify himself as a communication scholar; he created the first academic degree–granting programs with *communication* in their name; and he trained the first generation of communication scholars. Schramm authorized the textbooks at Illinois that helped launch the new field. Schramm's mass communication program in the Iowa School of Journalism was a pilot project for the doctoral program and for the communication research institute that he founded in 1947 at Urbana. At Illinois, Wilbur Schramm set in motion the patterns of scholarly work in communication study that continue to this day.

PART I

EUROPEAN BEGINNINGS OF COMMUNICATION STUDY

DARWIN, FREUD, AND MARX

The big three intellectuals of the nineteenth century were Europeans, born in England, Austria, and Germany, respectively. Darwin, Freud, and Marx each changed the mind of the world with their revolutionary ideas about human behavior and society. All three were creative rebels in an intellectual sense, all violated the social norms of the European society in which they lived, and all paid dearly for their intellectual radicalism.

Charles Darwin was accused of claiming that humans descended from the apes. This radical idea set off a firestorm of controversy, with religious leaders particularly opposed to his evolutionary theory. The public dispute about evolution continues to this day in the United States in the debate over teaching students about creationism (the belief that the world began in the way literally described in the biblical chapter of Genesis) versus evolution.

Sigmund Freud shocked Victorian Europe by theorizing that boys regard their fathers as rivals for their mothers' sexual attention. Hysteria, Freud claimed, was caused by childhood sexual seduction, and men as well as women could have hysteria. In 1933, Hitler called psychoanalysis a "Jewish science," books by Freud were burned, and most German and Austrian psychoanalysts were forced to migrate to America.

Karl Marx was exiled from his native Germany for his revolutionary political views—first to Paris, then to Belgium, and finally to London, where he could barely eke out an existence. Several of his children died from starvation and lack of medicine. Marxists in certain nations today are persecuted for their intellectual and political views. During the McCarthy era in the 1950s, American college professors, movie actors, and others accused of Marxist leanings were fired, ridiculed, and persecuted in various ways. George Stoddard, the University of Illinois president who brought Wilbur Schramm to Urbana, was fired, in part, for the several leftist professors employed at his university. Books by Marx are still forbidden in several nations today.

Darwin, Freud, and Marx are the three most important social theorists of the past century. Their ideas crossed the Atlantic and had important impacts on the beginnings of social science in America. The European theoretical foundations of evolutionary theory, psychoanalytic theory, and Marxism indirectly affected the rise of communication study in America after 1900. At the Chicago school, sociologists were attracted by evolutionary theory; the Frankfurt school combined Marxism and psychoanalytic theory; the Palo Alto school of interactional communication reacted against Freudian intrapersonal theory by studying relational communication; Harold D. Lasswell was an enthusiast for psychoanalytic thinking; and Carl I. Hovland's persuasion research had an indirect foundation in Freudian theory.

In order to understand these European influences on American scholarship, we go back five and a half centuries to the rise of Western civilization.

THE RENAISSANCE, 1450–1600

The early stirrings of modern science occurred in northern Italy, in and around the city of Florence, more than five hundred years ago as part of the Renaissance. The Renaissance was indeed a rebirth of European civilization, which had earlier flourished under the Greeks and Romans but had then been lost for several centuries after the fall of Rome to the tribes sweeping down over Europe from the Russian steppes. During the Dark Ages, Europe was a land of poverty and ignorance, with the Catholic church seeking in vain to preserve the advances in knowledge that had been made by the Greek thinkers: Aristotle, Socrates, Plato, and others. The surviving Greek manuscripts had been collected by Islamic peoples in the Middle East and North Africa and translated into Arabic. Only in this way was the knowledge of Aristotle and the other Greek thinkers preserved for us today.

In about 1450, this gloomy situation began to shift in important ways, and over the next 150 years, tremendous social changes occurred. Johannes Gutenberg invented the movable-type printing press in 1457 in Mainz, Germany, a wine-growing area. In fact, the Gutenberg printing press looked a lot like a wine press, the device from which it was adapted.* The press made books more widely available in Europe. Previously, books were reproduced by hand, and a "copyist" (usually a monk) could complete only two books a year. Books were thus rare and very valuable and were often kept chained to a reading table. In comparison, a printer using a Gutenberg printing press could produce one book a day (Pool 1983a, p. 14). The Renaissance thus got underway with an invention that greatly expanded access to knowledge. During the first fifty years of the Renaissance, an estimated twenty million copies were printed of 40,000 different books. Printing was such an important social change that its invention in Europe sets the date for the beginning of the Renaissance. Nevertheless, the full impact of the printing press was not immediate because of the low level of literacy among Europeans. (In fact, the first real mass medium did not occur until 376 years later, in 1833, with the advent of Benjamin Day's penny press newspaper, the *New York Sun*.)

At about the same time as Gutenberg's invention, bold Por-

---

*Gutenberg actually reinvented the printing press. The first movable-type printing press had been created by Pi-Sheng in China around 1041 A.D., several hundred years before Gutenberg, using clay type. Somewhat later, in 1241, Koreans invented metal type (Pool 1983a, p. 12).

tuguese explorers began utilizing improved means of navigation to sail thousands of miles down the west coast of Africa, around the Cape of Good Hope, to India. Through such exploration, the size of the known world expanded tremendously. Trade with Asia, mainly for spices, helped spark the rise of capitalism in Europe. Among the new rich were the Medici family of Florence, Italy, and they were very rich indeed. Cosimo de' Medici (1389–1464) was one of the richest men in the world. The Medicis more or less invented the idea of banking and soon had branch banks in Rome (to loan money at interest to the pope), Genoa, Naples, and other important trading centers. They generously endowed intellectuals like Galileo Galilei and Leonardo da Vinci and institutions supporting learning— universities, monasteries, schools, and hospitals. In Florence today, one can see the Medici coat of arms (seven red balls in a circle, the sign of a barber, suggesting that our word *medicine* may have been derived from *Medici*) that was cut in the stone walls of these buildings 500 years ago. The florin, the gold coin of Florence, became the standard monetary unit throughout the Western World, and Florence came to stand for all that was cultured, intellectual, and scientific. This northern Italian city was a kind of headquarters for the Renaissance, and the Medicis represented the new business class that was giving rise to modern capitalism.

Two individuals who lived in Florence during the Renaissance represent the early stirrings of science. One was Galileo Galilei (1564–1642), a pioneer in astronomy, physics, and mathematics. Galileo tutored the Medici children, and when he discovered the four moons of Jupiter in 1508, he named them after the four Medici brothers. This discovery was made possible with a 30-power telescope, the first such instrument utilized for astronomy. Galileo's fame derives particularly from his support of Copernicus's theory that the earth revolves around the sun, rather than vice versa, as previously believed. Galileo found evidence in support of the Copernican theory of a sun-centered universe, but the Catholic church forced him to recant his position.*

The other person was Leonardo da Vinci, a man of many outstanding talents: art, physiology, engineering, medicine, and inventor of a wide range of technological innovations, including the helicopter, submarine, and bicycle. Today we would call Leonardo a technologist, while Galileo was a scientist. Unlike Galileo, Leonardo was relatively unschooled and did not write books, nor was he connected with a university. He did not know Latin, the scholarly language of his day. But his many important contributions remind us that the Renaissance had a basis in technological innovation. Leonardo was the origin of the term *Renaissance man,* an individual who can do many different things, each with excellence.

Until the Renaissance, the Roman Catholic church was the only organized religion in Europe. After 1457 it was threatened by the increased availability of Bibles, due to printing. Catholic priests were no longer the sole interpreters of the Holy Word; monasteries lost control of the process of reproducing books, and the Catholic church lost power due to printing (Eisenstein 1968; Pool 1983a). Also, with the rise of trading and the beginnings of capitalism, many individuals began to believe that salvation could be earned by hard work and moral behavior while on earth, rather than only in the hereafter. The Protestant revolt against the Catholic church was thus aided by the printing press and by the rise of capitalism (Weber 1930).

The stream of Western civilization that had begun in Greece and Rome, which then halted and almost disappeared during the Dark Ages in Europe, began to flow again during the Renaissance.

---

*On successive nights in January 1508, Galileo noticed that certain of the four moons of Jupiter appeared on its opposite side, indicating that they were revolving around the planet. Galileo deduced that the earth and other planets in the solar system were revolving around the sun.

THE EUROPEAN UNIVERSITIES

The university played a key role in society after 1450. The great medieval universities grew out of the Catholic church: Padua and Bologna in Italy; Göttingen, Berlin, Frankfurt, and Heidelberg in Germany; the University of Paris; and Oxford and Cambridge in England. These early universities emphasized what we would today call a liberal arts approach, as did the first American universities, such as the Ivy League schools, that were modeled after their European predecessors. For example, John Harvard followed the model of Cambridge University where he had studied, founding the first American university in 1636. Most of the early American universities, like their European predecessors, were launched by religious denominations, particularly the Protestant faiths. These universities provided moralistic training to undergraduate students.

The model German research university was the University of Göttingen, founded in 1737. Here began the idea that professors should conduct research in order to discover new knowledge rather than just convey the conventional wisdom of their field to their students. Students were expected to play an active role in their studies, not just listen and recite back what they had heard. Göttingen's library was considered the best in Europe. After enjoying some years of high academic respect, the university collapsed during the Napoleonic wars of the early 1800s, and the University of Berlin rose rapidly (after its founding in 1810) to replace Göttingen. Berlin was one of the main models for Johns Hopkins University and the other research universities that were founded in America around 1890. Thus, two different university models were transferred from Europe to America: the Ivy League model of undergraduate, liberal arts education, and the German model of a research university that stressed graduate study.*

---

*A third, indigenous model for the American university was the land-grant college, which was established by the Morrill Act of 1862 to provide a vocational-type education in agricul-

The great ideas of Darwin, Freud, and Marx were based on a scientific perspective, and these three great thinkers were all trained at the leading European universities of their day, institutions that arose during the Renaissance. We begin with Darwin's evolutionary theory.

ture and engineering. Illinois, Wisconsin, Minnesota, Michigan State, and other land-grant universities in the Midwest played a key role in the diffusion of communication study in the United States.

CHAPTER 2

CHARLES DARWIN AND EVOLUTIONARY THEORY

The theory of evolution by natural selection was certainly the most important single scientific innovation in the nineteenth century.

—Jacob Bronowski, *The Ascent of Man*

The Origin of Species appeared, and the impression which it produced was enormous. No book dealing with a scientific subject had ever, I suppose, been so largely read by people who were not scientific.

—James Bryce, "Personal Reminiscences of Charles Darwin and the Reception of the 'Origin of Species'"

On the Origin of Species is one of the great books of Western civilization, ranking with Marx's *Das Kapital*. "The Darwinian revolution was the major revolution in the sciences in the nineteenth century" (Cohen 1985, p. 281). Darwinian theory compares with the Copernican revolution in its scientific importance, but it was even more contentious. Charles Robert Darwin (1809–1882) was a biologist, but his evolutionary theory affected the social sciences even more than the biological sciences (Figure 2.1). Charles Darwin was the grandson of Erasmus Darwin (1731–1802), a famous English evolutionist and naturalist whose book *Zoonomia, or the Laws of Organic Life* (1794–1796) contained a chapter on evolution. Evolutionary theory was in Charles Darwin's bloodlines. "His ancestry placed him securely in the purple of the British intellectual establishment" (Miller and Van Loon 1982, p. 46). He was born in Schrewsbury, England, where his father was a medical doctor (Barlow 1958, p. 21).

Darwin studied medicine at the University of Edinburgh but

Figure 2.1. Charles Darwin (1809–1882) in 1849.
Copyright of the Trustees of the British Museum.

dropped out because he could not stand the sight of blood. Then he pursued training to be a clergyman at Christ's College, Cambridge University. His "formal education had been a series of humiliating disasters" and "he seemed little more than an affable amateur" (Miller and Van Loon 1982, p. 6). While at Cambridge, Darwin spent much of his time hunting game and collecting beetles instead of studying to be a clergyman. But John Henslow (1796–1861), a professor of botany at Cambridge University, helped convert Darwin from a playboy student into a serious naturalist. They took long walks together in the English countryside, observing plants and other life. When the British Admiralty asked Professor Henslow to suggest a naturalist to sail on the HMS *Beagle*, a British Navy ship assigned to map the coast of South America, the professor recommended his protégé. Henslow's going-away gift to Darwin, a copy of Charles Lyell's book, *Principles of Geology*, would provide Darwin with useful background for his forthcoming evolutionary theory.

The voyage was a turning point in Darwin's career and was crucial in formulating his theory of evolution. In spite of his dubious academic

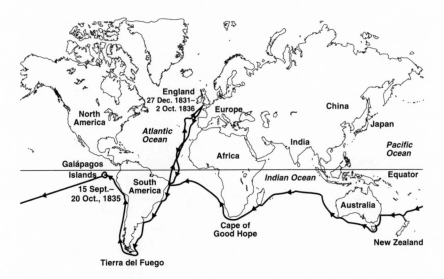

Figure 2.2. The Voyage of the *Beagle,* 1831–1836.

credentials, Darwin turned out to be a magnificent choice for investigation of the biological species found in the world's southern latitudes (figure 2.2). He was an acute observer of plant and animal life and gathered a significant set of valuable specimens on his voyage. During the trip, Darwin rapidly gained confidence in his ability to solve scientific puzzles. His inherited wealth allowed him to devote himself full-time to scholarly activities throughout his lifetime, as a kind of gentleman-scientist. Darwin was in daily correspondence with the best scientific minds in England while he was conceptualizing his evolutionary theory and, after its publication, while defending it.

In the century or two prior to Darwin's important contribution, the public had become extremely interested in evolution. One cause was the tremendous variety of new plants and animals that explorers were bringing back to Europe from Africa, Asia, and the Americas. The number of known plants and animals was approximately doubling every generation. The new sciences of botany and zoology were born. What could explain the tremendous diversity of living species? Their very existence began to challenge existing beliefs.

Until Darwin, many people thought that the number of species was unchanging over time, fixed at some point (such as the time of Noah's ark and the Great Flood). But Darwin established that new species originate over time—not by an act of divine creation but by natural selection, a process through which new species arise while certain other species become extinct through a process of differential survival. Individuals whose variations are best suited to their environment will have the greatest probability of reproducing their own kind (Cohen 1983, p. 292). Evolutionary theory was truly revolutionary (in Thomas Kuhn's sense of causing a scientific revolution), but Darwin was an odd kind of revolutionary: "A remarkably timid man who spend most of his life in seclusion; a semi-invalid riddled with doubts, fearing the controversy his theories might unleash; yet also the man who finally undermined belief in God's creation" (Miller and Van Loon 1982).

When Darwin's friend, Thomas H. Huxley, first read *On the Origin of Species* in 1859, he said: "How stupid not to have thought of it before" (Miller and Van Loon 1982, p. 3). Evolutionary thinking was an idea very much in the air at this time, and a variety of scientific explanations for how life changed had already been proposed before Darwin's book was published. In fact, most of the facts necessary for Darwin's evolutionary theory were available even before his around-the-world trip on the *Beagle* from 1831 to 1836 (twenty-eight years before publication of Darwin's book) to gather biological data and specimens. But no one had recognized their theoretical significance, until Darwin.

THE VOYAGE OF THE *BEAGLE*

A key event in the creation of evolutionary theory occurred when Darwin, only twenty-two years old, sailed on the *Beagle* in 1831 as a naturalist and gentleman-companion to the ship's captain. Darwin was a volunteer, not paid for his work, and fresh from his studies at Cambridge University. The *Beagle* stopped at numerous sites en route to South America, and at each Darwin was put ashore for several days or weeks or even months at a time. "At each landfall he went ashore and collected vast hoards of specimens. He dissected some, stuffed others, and threatened to overload the ship" (Miller and Van Loon 1982, p. 70). Although Darwin was gone from England for a total of five years, he actually was at sea for only eighteen months of this time. For three years and three months of his voyage, Darwin actually had a voyage on land. He detested sailing and was constantly seasick while on the *Beagle* (Browie and Neve 1989).

Darwin explored the coast of Brazil, the *pampas* of southern Argentina, Tierra del Fuego on the southern tip of the South American continent, the Falkland Islands off the coast of Argentina, and then up the west coast of Chile, Peru, and Ecuador (see Figure 2.2). The ship's crew plotted the coastline and took depth soundings while Darwin was ashore gathering specimens, making drawings of wildlife, and writing up his field observations. Then the ship would rendezvous with him and sail on to its next landing. Over a period of several years, the ship worked its way down the eastern coast of South America and back up the western coast, across the South Pacific to New Zealand and Australia, across the Indian Ocean to Cape Town, South Africa, and back to England (see Figure 2.2).

The *Beagle* was a Royal Navy sloop-brig, mounting ten guns. It was relatively small, only ninety feet long, and was powered by sails. It held 74 officers, men, and passengers. Darwin's beliefs conflicted with those of Robert FitzRoy, the ship's commander: "FitzRoy was difficult, imperious, and authoritarian; but he was also intelligent, fond of outdoor pursuits and natural philosophy, a good talker, thinker and companion" (Browie and Neve 1989, p. 25). Darwin and FitzRoy shared a mutual interest in geology, which drew them together during the long voyage, but on many other issues, they disagreed completely. FitzRoy was a zealous Christian, while Darwin had abandoned orthodox Christianity. The ship's captain completely opposed the idea of evolution. The two also disagreed about the subject of slavery (which they observed in Brazil) and about shipboard discipline. The young naturalist, however, curbed his tongue on the small ship: "Darwin had an almost pathological dislike for heated controversy" (Miller and Van Loon 1982, p. 69). This avoidance of trouble is one reason that Darwin later delayed publication of *On the Origin of Species* for twenty years. He knew that it would be a bombshell when it appeared.

When the *Beagle* sailed, Darwin "saw himself very much as a half-trained amateur sent out to collect specimens for the experts back home" (Bowler 1990, p. 52). He lacked self-confidence in his scientific ability. But gradually over the five years of the voyage, as he discovered new species and received encouraging letters from scientists in England, he became more confident. Darwin shipped boxes of the specimens that he collected, plus his written observations to John Henslow, his former botany professor at Cambridge. Henslow published abstracts of Darwin's letters to him and acted as a kind of scientific agent for Darwin in England. The most important result of the voyage was not "the evidence it supplied for the transmutation of species but Darwin's increased confidence in his own abilities as a scientific thinker, which encouraged him to tackle the deeper problems of the origin of species on his return" (Bowler 1990, p. 52).

One of Darwin's first scientific accomplishments was his discovery of a new species of South American ostrich (or rhea) on the *pampas* of Argentina. He was told about this new species by the *gauchos* (cowboys) with whom he was traveling. Darwin realized its significance rather belatedly: "The bird was cooked and eaten before my memory [of being told by the *gauchos* about the new species of ostrich] returned. Fortunately, the head, neck, legs, wings, many of the larger feathers, and a large part of the skin, had been preserved. From these a very nearly perfect specimen has been put together, and is now exhibited in the museum of the Zoological Society" (Darwin 1939, p. 107). Enough of the bird remained for it to be recognized as a new species. The ornithologist John Gould in London named it *Rhea darwinii* in his honor (Bowler 1990, p. 56). The existence of two species of ostrich in Argentina caused Darwin to ponder whether one species might have evolved from the other. The new, smaller species lived mainly to the south of the common ostrich, but both species flourished in an overlapping area, where they competed with each other for resources. This fact led Darwin to question the conventional wisdom that each species fit its home environment perfectly.

The *Beagle* stopped for more than a month in 1835 in the Galápagos Islands, which straddle the Equator about 600 miles off the coast of Ecuador in the Pacific Ocean. The Galápagos Islands are a natural laboratory for an evolutionist, due to the isolation of various species of bird and other life on the islands (there are no mammals). Among the assorted species are the famous giant turtles of the Galápagos; finches, whose shape of beak is adapted to their ecological niche; and mockingbirds, of which several distinct species had evolved due to the isolation of the islands. The main Galápagos Islands are thirty to fifty miles apart, and different species of turtles, finches, and mockingbirds have evolved due to this isolation. At the time, Darwin did not appreciate the evidence of evolutionary theory that he was encountering. He documented the island-to-island differences among the turtles and finches but was surprised when the governor of the Galápagos Islands told him that he could tell which island a turtle came from by its characteristics. Later, when he was writing up his observations of the Galápagos, he mulled over the governor's remarks.

Darwin returned to England on the *Beagle* in 1836 with a treasure of biological data, to find that his observations and specimens, which he had sent to England on other ships that the *Beagle* encountered during its voyage, had made him a scientific celebrity. He wrote the *Journal of the Voyage of the Beagle,* which became a popular travel book, but his evolutionary theory was not yet worked out.

We mainly think of Darwin as a biologist, but his initial fame immediately after returning from the voyage of the *Beagle* came from his work in geology. He explained the formation of coral reefs by the sinking of their underlying land surface. In February 1834, while Darwin was ashore near Valdivia, Chile, he experienced a severe earthquake. When the *Beagle* sailed into the harbor of Concepción a few weeks later, Darwin found that the land had been pushed up two or three feet, and nearby he observed mussels ten feet above the new high tide mark. In the Andes Mountains, he found older beds of shells at an altitude of 1,300 feet. Darwin began to speculate that South America had been elevated from the sea (Bowler 1990, p. 61). Two years later, in 1836, when the *Beagle* stopped in the Cocos islands, Darwin was able to observe coral reefs. He had recognized that South America was undergoing a gradual elevation, and he reasoned that the land underlying the South Seas might be sinking gradually. If so, the coral animals, which can live only in shallow water, would slowly build up a fringe around an island while the land gradually disappeared, finally leaving a coral atoll with a lagoon in its center (Bowler 1990, p. 65). Darwin published a volume on his theory of coral reefs, *The Structure and Distribution of Coral Reefs,* in 1842, six years after his return to England. It represented his growing confidence in his powers of scientific thinking (Bowler 1990, p. 65). He became an active member of the Geological Society, which brought him into contact with Charles Lyell and other good scientific minds.

He settled down in London and married, after making a careful list of the pros and cons of wedded life: "Like Freud and Marx, Darwin exploited the monotonous security of a happy marriage to work undisturbed at a revolutionary theory" (Miller and Van Loon 1982, p. 83). Darwin retired in 1842, at age thirty-three, to "a life of secluded individualism, working for a few hours a day before surrendering to an ordeal of nausea, weakness, headache, and palpitations" (Miller and Van Loon 1982, p. 87). In fact, Darwin was so weak from his various illnesses that he gave up shaving, which was too tiring. He usually could work only a few hours each day (Caudill 1989, p. 35).

Darwin moved to Down House in Kent, a pastoral setting, about twenty miles from London, where he resided in relative social isolation, raising six children, reading, writing, and carrying on a flourishing correspondence with other scientific thinkers. From Down House, Darwin gradually built up a network of scientific correspondents who supplied him with useful information and who later were to support him in the public battle over evolutionary theory (Bowler 1990, p. 7). Darwin wrote several lengthy letters each day, and this correspondence, available today in various archives, provides an understanding of his thinking processes as his evolutionary theory gradually developed. In the years following his return to England, Darwin gained confidence in his scientific abilities until he became a sophisticated detective in attacking the puzzle of evolution.

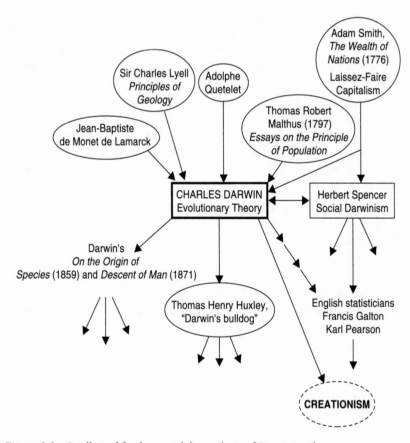

Figure 2.3.   Intellectual forebears and descendants of Darwinian theory.

INTELLECTUAL INFLUENCES ON DARWIN

Darwin's evolutionary theory was highly original, but he was influenced in his thinking by several other scholars (Figure 2.3). An invisible college of natural scientists were pushing evolutionary thinking forward, and a variety of evolutionary theories were available, each with proponents and critics. The members of this invisible college were divided about the nature of evolution. What were the major influences on Darwin's puzzle-solving process as he evolved his evolutionary theory?

Darwin read Thomas Malthus's *Essays on the Principle of Population* (1797) two years after his return on the *Beagle*. Malthus was a nonpracticing clergyman who had taught at the staff college of the British East Indies Company. Darwin picked up the book for amusement, not as part of his serious reading, but Malthus's basic idea of the selective role of competition turned out to be the key to Darwin's evolutionary theory. Malthus said that food increases arithmetically (in a progression of 1, 2, 3, 4, etc.) but that population increases geometrically (in a progression of 1, 2, 4, 16, etc.). An unchecked human population would double itself in twenty-five years. Malthus argued that his principle of population led to ghastly checks on population growth like famine, war, and natural disasters.* Darwin realized that population pressure creates a struggle for existence, as units in a population compete for available food. Thus, nature acts as a selective force, weeding out the weak and allowing the development of new species that are particularly fitted to their environment. If this process occurred for humans, it undoubtedly must also happen for other living things, Darwin reasoned.

Darwin had learned of Reverend Malthus's book from a citation to it in a publication by Adolphe Quetelet, a Belgian statistician-anthropologist-sociologist, from whom Darwin got the idea of a frequency curve for the distribution of a characteristic due to random variation. Quetelet had plotted such curves for variables like height and weight for thousands of individuals. In any given population, some individual units possess more of a certain characteristic and thus are enabled to fit better with their environment.

Darwin was also influenced in his evolutionary theory by the geologist Sir Charles Lyell (1795–1875) whose *Principles of Geology* (1830–1833) argued that the earth had undergone geological change. Darwin

---

*This statement by Malthus helped give economics a pessimistic tone, leading it to be called the dismal science.

began to think that biological changes had also occurred, although Lyell insisted on the contrary. After his return from the trip on the *Beagle,* Darwin became friends with the Scottish geologist (Barlow 1958, p. 100) and carried on an extensive correspondence with the older, established scholar, who served as a kind of mentor. Charles Lyell was a geologist, specializing in the fossil record, but his scientific interests were quite broad. He became a confidant of Darwin and later helped him through the difficulties of his priority claims to evolutionary theory with Alfred Russel Wallace.

Darwin reacted against the evolutionary theory of Jean-Baptiste de Monet de Lamarck (1744–1829), a French naturalist who introduced the word *biology,* to include both plants and animals. Lamarck claimed that needs determine the development of various body organs and the subsequent inheritance of these acquired characteristics. Lamarck's well-known example is giraffes, which feed on the leaves of trees. Over a long period of time, the giraffe acquired a long neck from constant stretching. Lamarck claimed that this longer neck was passed along to following generations, thus, a parent's modifications in anatomical structure could be inherited by its offspring. Later Lamarck's theory was proved wrong by advances in genetics research, but it was the most popular evolutionary theory before Darwin's. Between 3 million and 10 million species of plants and animals inhabit the earth today (Küppers 1990, p. 3). Is this number immutable over time? Lamarck was the first scholar to recognize biological evolution and to formulate a theory of descent, this in his book, *Zoological Philosophy* (Lamarck 1809). Darwin did not totally reject Lamarck's explanation of the evolution of new species, but he offered an alternate theory: due to random variation in sexual reproduction, some individuals are better suited to their environment, and over a lengthy period of time, these individuals have a slightly higher rate of reproduction and are more likely to survive in the struggle for existence. Thus, certain giraffes are born with longer necks, due to mutation and genetic variation. These giraffes can eat tree leaves that are higher and are more likely to survive, while shorter-necked animals succumb.

Another likely influence on Darwin's thinking was a contemporary who lived in London, the social philosopher Sir Herbert Spencer (1820–1903), who applied evolutionary theory to social life in what is known as social Darwinism. Spencer championed laissez-faire capitalism as the most efficient mechanism for making decisions in a system. The industrial revolution was underway in England and America, and the robber barons who led this revolution, like Andrew Carnegie, loved Spencer's theory. It fit perfectly with Carnegie's thinking that superior individuals should rise to the top of society. Darwin borrowed Spencer's term "survival of the fittest" for use in his evolutionary theory. In fact this term became, to the public, the most widely known component of Darwin's theory. "Survival of the fittest" means that living things that are best able to utilize the resources provided by their environment will produce the greatest number of offspring per period of time. Such over-production allows these living things to survive while their competitors will become extinct (Küppers 1990, p. 4). Units vary in their form because genetic material is copied from generation to generation with less than perfect accuracy, so a certain degree of mutation occurs. Darwin denied that his evolutionary theory was influenced by Spencer, whose work he did not regard with much respect. For example, on March 25, 1865, Darwin wrote to Charles Lyell: "I have read most of H[erbert] Spencer's Biology [the two-volume *The Principles of Biology*, 1864–1867] & agree with you. Some of his remarks are very clever & suggestive, but somehow I seldom feel any wiser after reading him, but often feel mortified [*sic*]" (Carroll 1976). Nevertheless, Herbert Spencer did most to popularize the term *evolution*, a word that Darwin hardly used (Bowler 1984, p. 9).

Adam Smith (1723–1790), the founding father of economics, is best known for arguing that individual self-interest through financial gain is a universal human motive in society. Smith's so-called invisible hand provided the mechanism through which free competition among individuals, each pursuing individual gain, leads to the maximum benefit for society. The role of government should be minimal, Smith argued, so as not to interfere with individual competition. This idea of free market forces provides an intellectual foundation for capitalism. Adam Smith's influential book, *The Wealth of Nations: An Inquiry into the Nature and Causes of the Wealth of Nations* (1776), provided a celebrated case of the division of labor and how it leads to the necessity of exchange. Smith observed that a single worker could produce one pin a day, working alone. But with a division of labor, ten specialized workers could produce 48,000 pins, 4,800 per worker per day. Obviously, the specialized workers would quickly force the single worker out of the pin-manufacturing business. Charles Darwin saw a biological parallel to economic competition in the struggle for food and territory by living creatures. This biological competition is most severe among individuals of the same species.

THE FINCHES OF GALÁPAGOS

The finches of the Galápagos Islands played a key role in the development of Darwin's theory of natural selection. The 600 miles from the mainland of South America to the Galápagos Islands were too great a distance for most continental species of birds to cross. The main islands of the Galápagos, desolate volcanic outcroppings, were distanced from each other in the Pacific Ocean as well. In this sparsely settled environment, the finches of Galápagos evolved into a variety of roles that would otherwise have been filled by other kinds of birds. Some finches adapted to seed crushing, others to eating various insects, and one set of finches even adapted to grasping and manipulating a cactus needle to dig insects out of plants (Gould 1980, p. 62). The names of the thirteen species of finches in the Galápagos label the niche occupied by each: tree finches, ground finches, cactus finches, warbler finches, vegetarian finches, woodpecker finches, and mangrove finches (Grant 1991). The Galápagos Islands thus provided Darwin with a natural laboratory in which to observe the process of isolation, independent adaptation, and the evolution of species. More than any other observation from his around-the-world voyage, the finches convinced Darwin of the reality of transmutation (Bowler 1990, p. 49). A line in his book *Journal of Researches* expressed Darwin's surprise at what he observed in the Galápagos archipelago: "I never dreamed that islands, about fifty or sixty miles apart, and most of them in sight of each other, formed of precisely the same rocks, placed under a similar climate, would have been differently tenanted" (Bowler 1990, p. 64).

Darwin did not recognize at first that the various species of finches had evolved from a common set of ancestors. That realization did not strike him until he had returned from his world voyage to London, when an ornithologist in the British Museum, John Gould, correctly identified all of the birds that Darwin had brought back from the Galápagos as finches (Gould 1980, p. 62). Even then, Darwin grasped his theory of evolution through natural selection only when he read widely outside biology. Darwin's personal notebooks and his extensive correspondence with other scholars explain the gradual process through which he developed evolutionary theory.

The voluminous notes that Darwin kept during the voyage of the *Beagle* show no awareness of evolutionary theory. But in November 1838 Darwin started a series of private notebooks on the transmutation of species. Publicly he pretended to hold conventional beliefs, while he gradually made sense out of his data. Four years later, Darwin had written a thirty-five-page outline of his evolutionary theory, and after two more years, he had in hand a 230-page book-length manuscript. He left instructions for its publication in case of his death (Miller and Van Loon 1982, p. 85).

Darwin gradually proposed, evaluated, and discarded hypotheses that would explain the biological data that he had gathered during his voyage on the *Beagle*. He had collected hundreds of specimens in the field, and his field notes were also available for him to ponder over and analyze. Darwin devoted himself to formulating a general theory of evolution. He read August Comte's book on positivist philosophy. Then he read Adam Smith on laissez-faire economics and was struck by the role of economic competition in bringing order to the economy as the result of the struggle for survival of businesses. He next turned to the volume by the Belgian statistician Adolphe Quetelet, who discussed Thomas Malthus's claim that a population grows geometrically while food supplies grow only arithmetically. In October 1838, Darwin read Malthus's *Essays on the Principle of Population,* going to the source that Quetelet discussed. The last pieces of the evolutionary puzzle were now falling in place for Darwin. It was two years after the *Beagle*'s return, and Darwin was thirty years old.

Notice that Darwin's theory of natural selection did not jump out at him from his data, nor did it come from the field of biology. Instead, "The immediate precipitators were a social scientist, an economist, and a statistician" (Gould 1980, p. 66). Key to the formulation of Darwin's evolutionary theory were his wide reading and his ability to identify the analogies to biology from other scientific fields. Creating his theory was a highly social process, involving its gradual construction through interaction with the ideas of others, both through reading and extensive correspondence with scientific colleagues.

ANTICIPATING THE STORM

Darwin had developed his theory of natural selection by 1838 and wrote it up in two unpublished sketches in 1842 and 1844. "Then, never doubting his theory for a moment, but afraid to explore its revolutionary implications, he proceeded to stew, dither, wait, ponder, and collect data for another fifteen years" (Gould 1980, p. 48). At the urging of his close friends, he began to write a tome that was intended to be four times the length of the voluminous *On the Origin of Species* that eventually resulted. He called his unpublished, unfinished book *Natural Selection*.

During the twenty-three-year period from the *Beagle*'s return to England in 1836, to publication of *On the Origin of Species* in 1859, Darwin read widely, corresponded with colleagues, and did further research. He talked to animal breeders in England in order to confirm that individual differences are inheritable. Shrewdly, Darwin saw the parallel between the choice exercised by domestic animal breeders and the selection made by nature (Miller and Van Loon 1982, p. 37). He spent eight years studying barnacles in England in order to gather more data about the evolutionary process. He identified an enormous variety of different species, but they were indistinguishable at the larval stage, suggesting to him that they had all descended from a common ancestor. Darwin established that an original single species could evolve into several distinct species that could no longer interbreed. One example of this kind of evolution came from the finches in the Galápagos Islands, but he also studied and documented many others. Darwin wanted to provide such an overwhelming mass of evidence that his evolutionary theory would be firmly supported, once it was published.

Darwin waited until 1859 to publish *On the Origin of Species*. One reason for the delay was to build up a community of evolutionary scientists in England. With an invisible college of backers finally in place, Darwin felt that he could better weather the controversy that he expected his theory to create. He had only one sentence in *On the Origin of Species* about humans. Nevertheless, he knew that a storm awaited publication of his evolutionary theory, especially from religious leaders and other individuals who would feel that evolutionary thinking threatened theological explanations of the origins of life. In 1844, a book entitled *The Vestiges of the Natural History of the Creation* was published anonymously, but it became known that the author was Robert Chambers, a Scottish naturalist. The tremendous uproar created by Chambers's book convinced Darwin to postpone publication of his book, whose detailed outline he had already drafted.

Darwin would have waited even longer to publish his theory, but his hand was forced by Alfred Russel Wallace (1823–1913), a young naturalist who independently formulated a theory of natural selection. "Wallace came from a poor background, lacking many advantages of the Darwin family" (Bowler 1990, p. 110). He was a professional collector of animal specimens for sale to zoos and others, traveling to the remote corners of the world, mainly Brazil, Indonesia, and Malaysia.* On June 18, 1858, Darwin received a letter from Wallace containing his draft paper, "On the Tendency of Varieties to Depart Indefinitely from the Original Type," which had been written in February 1858. Wallace had sent the paper to Darwin for his informal evaluation with a request to forward it to Sir Charles Lyell if the paper were of merit. Upon reading the essay, Darwin immediately realized that Wallace was an independent codiscoverer of natural selection as the key process in evolution. Wallace had once read Malthus's book on population and food supply. While Wallace was lying ill with malaria fever in Malaysia, Malthus's essay flashed through his mind, with the same result that had occurred to Darwin, who stated: "This [Wallace's] essay contained exactly the same theory as mine" [that is, Darwin's evolutionary theory in the yet-unpublished manuscript for *On the Origin of Species*] (Barlow 1958, p. 121).

What should Darwin do? He was troubled by the ethics of the situation. Wallace had sent him his paper in friendship, asking for suggestions. After discussing the problem via correspondence with his friend Lyell and the botanist J. D. Hooker, Darwin wrote a paper that abstracted the essence of evolutionary theory from his yet-unpublished *On the Origin of Species*. Darwin's paper (1858) and Wallace's (1858) were read to the Linnaean Society[†] in London on July 1, 1858, and then published in an issue of the *Journal of the Proceedings of the Linnaean Society of London (Zoology)*, with an explanatory note by Lyell and Hooker (1858), who stated: "These gentlemen having independently and unknown to one another, conceived the same very ingenious theory to account for the appearance and perpetuation of varieties and of specific form on our planet, may both fairly claim the merit of being original thinkers in this important line of inquiry; but neither of them having

---

*The Wallace Line, first identified by Alfred Russel Wallace, passes north-south through the fifty-mile strait between the Indonesian islands of Bali and Lombok, forming a divide between the zoological species of Australia and those of Europe, Asia, and the Americas. Wallace explained how this line had occurred as the result of the migration of species in an earlier period when the sea level was lower.

[†]The Linnaean Society in London had been founded in 1788 as a repository for the papers and other materials of Carolus Linnaeus (1707–1778), the great Swedish classifier of all forms of life (Boorstin 1983, p. 46). The society had evolved into one of the several important scientific associations in England, composed as a kind of fraternity of gentleman-scientists.

published his views, though Mr. Darwin has for many years past been repeatedly urged by us to do so, and both authors having now unreservedly placed their papers in our hand, we think it would best promote the interests of science that a selection from them should be laid before the Linnaean Society."

Darwin was not present at the Linnaean Society; he was grieving over the death of his young child from scarlet fever. Lyell and Hooker also presented the paper that Wallace had earlier mailed to Darwin (Gould 1980, p. 48). Charles Darwin acted in a proper way scientifically in his handling of the codiscovery of evolutionary theory. Wallace, for his part, insisted later that he did not deserve to be considered a codiscoverer of the theory. He argued that Darwin had worked for years on the theory that he had devoted only a few weeks to writing up.

Publication of the pair of articles in the *Journal of the Linnaean Society* met a quiet reception. So far, no storm of public controversy had occurred. But it was coming.

THE STORM

On November 24, 1859, all 1,250 copies of Charles Darwin's *On the Origin of Species, by Means of Natural Selection: Or the Preservation of Favored Races in the Struggle for Life* were sold the first day that they were available in London. A second printing of 3,000 copies sold out soon afterward. Within a few years of its publication, *On the Origin of Species* sold more than 25,000 copies (Cohen 1983, p. 289). The general idea of evolution was of great interest to the public in 1859. Darwin was already well known in England due to his prior publications from the journey of the *Beagle,* and *On the Origin of Species* created an immediate sensation.

According to the Book of Genesis, the earth was created in six days, and humans were created on the seventh day. Evolutionary theory suggested instead that humans had evolved gradually from some other life-forms. Thus, Darwin invited strong opposition from religious thinkers who believed in a literal meaning of the Bible. Darwin had been raised as a churchgoing Christian, and he had studied at Cambridge to be a clergyman, but after publication of his evolutionary theory, religious critics labeled him an anti-Christ. Darwin explained evolution by means of natural selection from accidental variation. While other theories of evolution had appeared prior to his, Darwin was the first to propose the mechanism of accidental variation. His theory denied that a purpose, such as from a deity like God, drove the process of evolution. In short, Darwin contradicted the Bible. *On the Origin of Species* posed "a battle in the ongoing war between science and religion for control of the human mind" (Bowler 1990, p. 2). Charles Darwin's wife, Emma, was deeply religious, and his reluctance to hurt her feelings was one reason for his delay in publishing *On the Origin of Species*. Shortly before they were married, she wrote to him about her fears for his salvation. Across the bottom of this letter he wrote: "When I am dead, know that many times I have kissed & cryed over this."

Darwin, in poor health, needed a "bulldog" to defend his evolutionary theory publicly. Thomas Henry Huxley became the second-in-command of Darwin's theory. Huxley was younger than Darwin, and in good health. Like Darwin, Huxley was an enthusiast for evolutionary theory. Huxley debated Dr. Samuel "Soapy Sam" Wilberforce, the bishop of Oxford, in a famous confrontation at the conference of the British Association for the Advancement of Science held at Oxford University in 1860. Bishop Wilberforce turned to Huxley on the speakers' platform and asked him sarcastically if it was through his grandfather or grandmother that he claimed descent from a monkey. Huxley responded that he would rather have an ape for a grandfather than "a man highly endowed by nature and possessed of great means and influence, and yet who employs these faculties for the mere purpose of introducing ridicule into grave scientific discussions" (Caudill 1989, p. 18). Most of Darwin's opponents accepted the basic idea of evolution, even while disagreeing about whether natural selection was the mechanism through which it occurred. They had no coherent alternative to natural selection. Darwin argued that the Creator's plans included natural selection. Darwin's opponents said that he claimed humans had descended from apes (he actually said that humans and apes had a common ancestor, probably in Africa). In 1859, the Neanderthal skull with the thick brow ridge of an ape was known. In 1891, Java Man was found in what is today Indonesia. The discovery of such artifacts lent credence to Darwin's claim of human-ape evolution from a common ancestor. In 1871, Darwin published *The Descent of Man and Selection in Relation to Sex*, dealing directly with human evolution. Charles Darwin did not like the term *evolution* because he felt that it implied biological progress, which was difficult to define, as there was no fixed direction of change. Herbert Spencer was not similarly troubled, equating social evolution with progress.

Louis Agassiz, professor of geology and zoology at Harvard University, led the opposition to Darwinian evolution in America (Lowenberg 1933), but there were many other detractors, and advocates, of evolutionary theory. The most famous debate was the "monkey trial" of John Thomas Scopes, a young high school teacher, held in Dayton, Tennessee, in 1925. Scopes was accused of teaching evolution to his students, an illegal act in Tennessee. The trial featured the spellbinding orator and fundamentalist preacher William Jennings Bryan versus the agnostic and liberal lawyer, Charles Darrow. Scopes was convicted of teaching evolution and fined $100 (Caudill 1989, p. 94). The main result of the highly publicized trial, as was intended by Scopes and the evolutionists, was to increase public awareness of evolutionary theory.

LATER RESEARCH ON EVOLUTION

Later findings of scientists helped further our understanding of evolution and led gradually to lessened interest in Darwin's theory per se among biologists. From 1890 to 1930, Darwinian theory was in eclipse as alternate theories of evolution abounded. But with new understandings of heredity, Darwinism made a comeback among biologists.

The field of genetics has advanced considerably since 1859 and in directions that shed light on the process of evolution. The research of an Augustine monk, Gregor Mendel, who had studied at the University of Vienna and then lived in what is now Slovakia, was conducted about the same time as publication of *On the Origin of Species*. His findings then lay dormant for twenty-four years, until they were rediscovered and popularized by William Bateson in 1890. Mendel's genetic research showed that acquired traits are not inherited and thus destroyed Lamarck's theory of evolution. For example, if a longhorn cow were dehorned by a farmer, its offspring would still be born with horns. Characteristics acquired by an adult's actions are not transmitted to its children. So Lamarck's giraffes, which stretched their necks to eat the leaves of tall trees, could not have passed their longer necks to their offspring. However, mutation and other genetic variation might lead to certain giraffes having longer necks, and such long-necked giraffes might be more likely to survive in the struggle for food, thus reproducing their type in greater numbers than short-necked giraffes.

Mendel created pure strains of garden peas by selectively inbreeding them for several generations. He could then identify seven dichotomous characteristics, such as tall or short, wrinkled seeds versus round seeds, mauve versus white flowers, yellow peas versus green peas, and so forth. He next cross-fertilized two true parents with opposite qualities, say, tall versus short, and found that all of the tall × short crosses were tall, because tall is a dominant, rather than a recessive, genetic trait. Then Mendel self-fertilized these offspring to obtain a second generation. In this second filial generation, three-fourths of the offspring were tall and one-fourth were short. The traditional viewpoint, prior to Mendel, was that of blending: the characteristics of hybrids would fall between the characteristics of the parents (so the height of all the offspring should be halfway between the tall and short heights). Mendel published his results in 1866 in a scientific journal, but no one paid much attention. Finally when Mendel's work on unlocking a basic puzzle of genetics was recognized, its significance for evolution began to sink in.

Darwin did not know of Mendel's work on genetics when *On the Origin of Species* was published. When Mendelian genetics became well known after 1890, it initially led to the questioning of evolutionary theory. Evolution now seemed to be explained by mutation, a change in genetic materials caused by physical damage, rather than by continuous variation, as Darwin had maintained. Eventually, after about 1930, as it was realized that both mutation and continuous variation are involved in evolution, Darwin's original theory was corrected and modified. "Only after the modern concept of genetic mutation confirmed that individual variation is essentially random were biologists forced to come to grips with the prospect that evolution might have the open-ended character predicted by Darwin" (Bowler 1990, p. 14).

Within two decades of the publication of Darwin's revolutionary book, most biologists were converted to the evolution of species. "The Darwinian revolution constituted a radical restructuring of natural science that has had major repercussions outside the narrow confines of evolutionary biology, especially in the social sciences" (Cohen 1983, p. 352).

IMPACTS OF EVOLUTIONARY THEORY

Karl Pearson (1857–1936) and Sir Francis Galton (1822–1911), key founders of the field of statistics, developed the techniques of the chi-square test and correlation, respectively, in order to test Darwin's theory of evolution (Tankard 1984, p. 62). Pearson's main career interest was statistical verification of Darwin's basis of evolution in natural selection (Greenwood 1949, p. 682). Galton was a first cousin of Charles Darwin

and was greatly influenced by him, becoming convinced to study heredity in human beings by reading *On the Origin of Species*. This volume also
led Galton to the controversial idea of eugenics, the improvement of the
human race by encouraging reproduction by the most capable individuals and discouraging reproduction by the least capable individuals.
Galton and Pearson embraced eugenics in an era long before Adolf Hitler tainted the concept by forcibly sterilizing individuals whom he considered inferior. But even in the day of Galton and Pearson, eugenics
was controversial.

Herbert Spencer and Social Darwinism

Sir Herbert Spencer (1820–1903) was a contemporary of Charles Darwin and Karl Marx, and they all lived in London at the same time. Spencer was the only child of stern parents. After only three months of formal education, he was tutored by his father, so that he had no peers. He
was a lifelong bachelor who led a difficult personal life as a semi-hermit
and a semi-invalid. Spencer suffered from insomnia and depression and
was neurotic. When he was thirty-three, a rich uncle died, leaving
Spencer a large inheritance, which supported him as a private scholar
for the rest of his life.

Spencer had no academic degrees, never held a university position,
and had no students. He read little and was not very scholarly. He developed his ideas by talking with leading scientists, often in the
London's men's clubs to which he belonged. Thomas Huxley (Darwin's
bulldog) was a frequent discussion partner. Spencer had broad interests
in psychology, philosophy, biology, and sociology. Politically, he was a
right-wing conservative thinker, perhaps one reason why sociologists,
mainly liberal, later viewed his writings with suspicion. He championed
Adam Smith's invisible hand and Thomas Malthus's apocalyptic population principle. Spencer defined social evolution as the change from a
state of incoherent, disorganized distribution of some phenomena to a
state of coherent, ordered variability. He traced the development of societies from simple to complex, using analogies from biology. Spencer
coined the term "survival of the fittest" about ten years prior to *On the
Origin of the Species*. He saw the Victorian England in which he lived as
the ultimate state of societal development. It has been said that "Herbert
Spencer and his philosophy were products of English industrialism."

Spencer had a "lifelong maniacal hatred of state power" and felt that the best government was the government that governed least. Like Darwin, Spencer responded to Thomas Malthus's theory of population growth (Hofstadter 1944, p. 39). Spencer claimed that all systems inevitably progress from a less organized to a more ordered state. In contrast, Darwin was chary of the idea of biological progress. Spencer and Darwin moved in the same social circles in London and met from time to time in their men's clubs, but Darwin said, "I am not conscious of having profited in my own work by Spencer's writings" (Barlow 1958, p. 109). Nevertheless, Darwin utilized Spencer's term "survival of the fittest," so it appears likely that at least some degree of intellectual exchange occurred between the two men. From his side, Spencer made no secret of his debt to Darwin: "I am simply carrying out the view of Mr. Darwin in their applications to the human race" (Spencer 1891, p. 438).

Spencer's social evolutionary theory served to attract the criticism of early U.S. scholars like Charles Horton Cooley and Robert E. Park but in the process got them interested in sociology. Cooley stated: "I imagine that nearly all of us who took up sociology between 1870, say, and 1890 did so at the instigation of Spencer. While he did not invent the word (though most of us had never heard it before), much less the idea, he gave new life to both [the word *sociology,* and what it meant]. . . . It is certain that nearly all of us fell away from him sooner or later and more or less completely" (Cooley 1920). Spencer is out of favor today among social scientists, who reject his notion that social evolution is progress.

In the three decades after the Civil War, it was impossible to be active in any field of intellectual work without mastering Spencer. Spencer's books sold very widely in the United States. In the first forty-three years of publication, about 370,000 copies were sold, "a figure unparalleled for works in such difficult spheres as philosophy and sociology" (Hofstadter 1944 pp. 33, 34). Spencer's supporters included John D. Rockefeller, president of the Standard Oil Company; James J. Hill, the railway magnate; and Andrew Carnegie, the steel tycoon, who became Spencer's personal friend and admirer.* Spencer told these business leaders what they wanted to hear: that laissez-faire capitalism was the

---

*Carnegie wrote a worshipful letter to Herbert Spencer in 1903 that began "Dear Master Teacher," and ended with these remarks: "The World jogs on unconscious of its greatest mind in Brighton lying silently brooding. But it will waken some day to its teachings and decree Spencer's place is with the greatest. I am ever gratefully, My Master, Your Devoted pupil, Andrew Carnegie" (Peel 1971, p. 2).

key to societal progress. The ruthless economic competition displayed by capitalism, Spencer argued, ought to be encouraged in order to achieve an efficiency in human society comparable to that exhibited in nature (Miller and Van Loon 1982, p. 171). In *Social Statics* (1851), Spencer claimed that free enterprise guaranteed the rapid adaptation of individuals and institutions to their changing environment. The suffering of those who failed to adapt provided a stimulus to do better the next time (Bowler 1990, p. 25). Thus capitalism was an ideal mechanism for social progress. Spencer's social Darwinism eventually fell into disrepute, but in the process, Spencer helped publicize evolutionary theory. In fact, his main role was to popularize Darwin's theory of evolution.

Nonverbal Communication

One of Darwin's books that is particularly important for communication scholars is *The Expression of the Emotions in Men and Animals,* which appeared thirteen years after *On the Origin of Species* and a year after *The Descent of Man,* in 1873. *The Expression of the Emotions* was also a bestseller. On its day of publication, a remarkable 5,267 copies were sold. This book established the field of nonverbal communication, although Darwin did not call it that. He argued that human emotional expression cannot be comprehended without understanding the emotional expressions of animals. "Our emotional expressions are in large part determined by our evolution" (Ekman 1973, p. ix). Charles Darwin supported his theory of the origins of nonverbal communication by describing emotional expressions in infants and children (obtained in part by observing his own baby son), in adults of various cultures, in the mentally ill, and in animals like apes and dogs.

On the centennial of the publication of *The Expression of the Emotions,* Paul Ekman (1973), a leading nonverbal communication scholar, pulled together the contemporary research evidence bearing on Darwin's nonverbal communication theory. Ekman's main conclusion was that "many of Darwin's observations, and a large part of his theoretical explanation and forecasts, are substantiated by current knowledge." Research evidence shows certain universal facial expressions like anger, fear, and happiness, are presumably due to some innate, genetic contribution to facial expression. The particular patterns of facial muscle movement associated with certain emotions stem from a genetic contribution rather than being learned (Ekman 1973, p. 5).

Population Ecology Theory

The organizational ecology perspective began in the 1970s as a shift in level of analysis from a single organization, to a number of organizations in relationship to each other. Population ecology theory, developed mainly by Professors Michael Hannan and John Freeman in the Department of Sociology at Cornell University, is based on evolutionary theory, although they do not acknowledge this basis (Hannan and Freeman 1977; Freeman and Hannan 1989; Young 1988, 1989).* Population ecology theory uses such evolutionary concepts as niche width,† environment, competition for scarce resources, and survival in order to predict the life or death of organizations over time. The theory is used to understand the survivability of a species of organizations. Hannan and Freeman tested their population ecology theory with such diverse populations as all of the restaurants in a city and the semiconductor companies in northern California's Silicon Valley. John Dimmick and Eric W. Rothenbuhler's (1987) research on the population ecology of mass media institutions explained why some media industries like radio broadcasting are partially displaced by the television industry.

The general purpose of population ecology theory is to explain reasons for the survival or extinction of units in a system. Population ecology researchers are reacting against much past investigation of organizational behavior, which looks inside a single organization and gathers data at only one point in time. Instead, population ecologists gather dynamic data and operate at a different level of analysis: that of a population of organizations (hence the name *population ecology*). The exact boundaries of a population of study—for example, all restaurants in a city—are not always as clear-cut as one might like. Just what is a species of organizations? The answer must usually be somewhat arbitrary.

CONTRIBUTIONS OF EVOLUTIONARY THEORY

In the 134 years since publication of *On the Origin of Species,* Charles Darwin's evolutionary theory has had important impacts on social science thinking and on communication study:

---

*However, population ecologists do acknowledge the human ecologists Robert Park and Amos Hawley as academic ancestors (Hannan and Freeman 1989).

†*Niche width* is a population's tolerance for changing levels of resources, ability to resist competitors, and response to other factors that inhibit growth (Freeman and Hannan 1983);

1. It directly influenced Karl Marx in formulating dialectical materialism (see Chapter 4).
2. The variant expressed by Herbert Spencer's social Darwinism attracted early American sociologists like Charles Horton Cooley and Robert E. Park to the field of sociology, although they later rejected social Darwinism. Cooley and especially Park were leaders of the Chicago school, and Park was the first theorist of mass communication (see Chapter 5). Park's work on urban ecology was directly influenced by Darwinian evolutionary theory.
3. Darwin helped launch the study of nonverbal communication, a specialty in communication study which continues to receive wide interest.
4. Many of the key concepts and the mechanism of evolutionary theory are currently utilized by scholars studying population ecology. This invisible college includes communication scholars.

Unlike Freudian psychoanalytic theory and Marxism, Darwin's evolutionary theory is not carried forward actively by a set of communication scholars today, except for students of nonverbal communication, and they do not generally recognize Darwin's role in launching their research tradition.

When Charles Darwin died of a heart attack on April 18, 1882, he was buried in the family cemetery in Kent. But a petition signed by scientists, clergymen, and members of Parliament pleaded that he should be buried in Westminster Abbey, and the change was made. Darwin's remains were laid to rest in the midst of England's great personages, close to another famous scientist, Sir Isaac Newton. Thus did his nation honor him.

---

a niche is thus a space in which a species can outcompete other species. With a wider niche width, a species can survive in a wider range of conditions. The advantage of a more specialized niche is that a species can exploit that space more completely (Hannan and Freeman 1977).

CHAPTER 3

SIGMUND FREUD AND PSYCHOANALYTIC THEORY

It has been remarked that it is almost impossible to overestimate the significance of sex in human affairs, but this impossibility Freud has achieved.
> —Robert S. Lynd, *Knowledge for What? The Place of
> Social Science in American Culture*

Sigmund Freud (1856–1939) was trained as a medical doctor, founded
the profession of psychoanalysis, and created psychoanalytic theory
(figure 3–1). Freud was not a social scientist, but certainly was a major
influence on the social sciences. His psychoanalytic theory had a strong
impact on psychology and has been an important influence on sociology, political science, and anthropology. It directly influenced the field
of communication through the critical school, the Palo Alto school,
Harold D. Lasswell, and, less directly, via Carl I. Hovland.

Freud's main contributions were his recognition of the unconscious,
the influence of psychological forces beyond our rational control, and
the role of sexuality in the psychological development of the individual
from infancy (Cohen 1983, p. 355). His discovery of infant sexuality
met tremendous antagonism, as children had been thought of as inno-
cent and free of sexual lust until puberty.

THE LIFE OF SIGMUND FREUD

Vienna was the birthplace of psychoanalytic theory at the turn of the
century. The capital of the Hapsburg Empire (Austro-Hungary), this
beautiful city of 1 million inhabitants was a great intellectual center.
Important ideas were in the air: the Bauhaus movement in architecture,
Arnold Schoenberg's radically innovative twelve-tone music, Otto
Neurath's Vienna Circle of logical positivists, and the philosophy of

Figure 3.1. Sigmund Freud (1856–1939) at age 70.
Used by permission of the Freud Museum, London.

Ludwig Wittgenstein. Turn-of-the-century Vienna was also characterized by puritanical norms, sexual repression, and a strict morality—a
hostile setting for Freud's ideas about the mind, particularly his emphasis on sexuality in explaining human behavior.

Freud's thought attacked many of the values of the Victorian age in
which he lived, especially the notion that sex was not a topic for scientific investigation (Fromm 1962, p. 135). Further, Freud's theory was a
marked departure from previous approaches to understanding human
behavior in that he focused on the individual's unconscious as a source
of explanation. Before Freud, psychologists and other scholars felt that
this dark, unexplored underside of the human personality could not be
probed scientifically. They were dubious about Freud's psychoanalytic
theory, which rested on the ability of psychoanalysts to understand the
unconscious. From its beginnings in Vienna, Freudian thought was
controversial.

Freud was born in Pribor, Moravia, in what is today Slovakia but was
then part of the Austro-Hungarian empire. His father was a fairly successful wool merchant. When Sigmund was four years old, he moved
with his family to Vienna, where he lived for the rest of his eighty-three
years, except for his final year in London. Freud identified himself as
Jewish. He had been given the Jewish name Schlomo after his grandfa-

ther, a rabbi. "Freud was, throughout his life, a *proud, chauvinistic*, even *vengeful* Jew" (Szasz, 1978, p. 139). One result was his lifelong interest in religion and religious history. The hostile anti-Semitism that he encountered early in his life left him feeling that "he belonged to a persecuted minority and attributed his creativeness partly to the fact that he had been compelled to think differently from the majority" (Ellenberger 1970, p. 464). Freud reacted to anti-Semitism by finding strength in his identification with Judaism.

Freud was a brilliant student, always at the head of his class wherever he studied. He trained at the University of Vienna, at the time one of the most distinguished universities in the world (Anzieu 1986, p. 27). Freud studied to be a medical doctor,* with the goal of becoming a medical scientist, but he could not acquire a university position because he was Jewish, so in 1886, when he was thirty years old, he began a private medical practice in Vienna (Table 3–1). He married Martha Bernays after a four-year-engagement, even though they had very little money; in fact, they had to pawn their watches (Schultz 1979, p. 303). Freud was a specialist in neurology, and, after several years of training to become a practicing physician, saw neurotic patients. They came to him for diagnosis and for treatment; Freud was expected to cure their neurotic tendencies. What curing techniques could he use? At first, he tried hypnosis. His patients were put into a state resembling sleep while they lay on a couch in his office. Freud, sitting beside them in a chair, pressed on their forehead with his hand to encourage them to concentrate on his questions. He continued to situate his patients on a couch even in later years when he no longer used hypnosis or forehead pressing. Thus, the psychoanalyst's couch, along with Freud's cigar, became symbols of psychoanalysis (Szasz 1978, p. 107).

Freud had learned hypnosis by studying for four months in 1885 and 1886 with Jean-Martin Charcot (1825–1893), a famous neurologist and director of the Salpêtrière Asylum for Women in Paris, who used hypnosis to treat hysteria (Sulloway 1979, p. 28). Freud hoped that hypnosis would be a means of learning about an individual's unconscious, and thus to find the causes of hysteria, an illness that had puzzled European physicians for centuries. Charcot, however, insisted that the causes of hysteria were strictly physical and prevented Freud from asking psychological questions of the patients. Nevertheless, Freud was convinced that the unconscious exists outside human awareness and that it is more

*Freud chose medicine because of reading Darwin (Schultz 1975, p. 301).

TABLE 3.1
Major Events in the Life of Sigmund Freud

Year	Event
1856	Born in Pribor, then located in Austro-Hungary, and soon moves with his family to Vienna, where he spends most of the rest of his life.
1881	Earns medical degree at the University of Vienna and hopes to become a medical researcher, but this career is blocked because he is Jewish.
1882	Begins developing psychoanalytic theory with his friend Josef Breuer, in discussions of the case of Anna O., a hysterical patient.
1885	Travels to Paris in order to study the use of hypnosis to treat hysteria, with Jean-Martin Charcot.
1886	Begins a private medical practice, specializing in neurotic patients.
1887	Breaks with his colleague Josef Breuer over the issue of childhood seduction as a cause of hysteria.
1895	With Breuer, publishes *Studies on Hysteria.*
1894–1899	Carries on an extensive correspondence with Wilhelm Fliess in Berlin.
1897	Self-analyzes his repressed feelings for his parents, which leads him to propose the oedipus complex.
1899	Publishes *The Interpretation of Dreams*, his most important book, based on his self-analysis.
1902	The Wednesday evening circle begins in Vienna, and six years later renames itself the Vienna Psychoanalytic Society.
1904	Argues in *The Psychotherapy of Everyday Life* that Freudian slips offer insight into the unconscious.
1905	Publishes *Three Essays on the Theory of Sexuality* and *Jokes and their Relation to the Unconscious.*
1908	The International Psychoanalytic Congress is held, and Carl Jung is elected president.
1938	The Nazis invade Austria, and Freud flees from Vienna to London.
1939	Freud dies from cancer.

powerful than the conscious mind in influencing certain individual behaviors (Freeman 1972, p. 189).

After returning from Paris, Freud was met with derisive laughter and
hostility when he announced at the Viennese Society of Physicians that
there were traumatic male hysterics in Paris (Lasswell 1930, p. 19). His
Viennese medical colleagues insisted that only women can become hysterical.* He was beginning to understand the resistance that his theories
were going to encounter. Freud found this hostile reception by Vienna's
leading medical scientists was disturbing and reacted with defiance. "He
felt he was leading a crusade against the accepted conventions of medicine, or at all events his seniors in Vienna, and he accepted his mission
wholeheartedly" (Jones 1953, p. 249). From this time on, Freud isolated himself from the Viennese medical world. He wanted to make a
great medical discovery and believed that his scientific peers would not
give him proper recognition.

During most of his life, Freud resided at Berggasse 19 with his wife
and six children and conducted his private medical practice there. His
apartment was centrally located in the old section of the city, near the
university, the opera house, and the Imperial Palace. "Freud was Viennese to his fingertips" (Ellenberger 1970, p. 465). He enjoyed all aspects
of Viennese culture: the coffeehouses, the theater, the music, and the
general intellectual milieu. Freud led a quiet, middle-class, rather traditional life-style. In 1936, he and his wife celebrated their fiftieth wed-
ding anniversary. Two years later in February 1938, the Nazis invaded
Austria, and Freud fled to London, taking with him most of his beloved
Greek statues and the other small antiquities that he kept on his desk
during psychoanalytic sessions with patients. He considered himself to
be an "archaeologist of the mind," digging for the past in each
individual's unconscious memory.† Following his eighty-third birthday
in 1939, after living for a year in London, Freud died after a sixteen-year
battle with cancer of the mouth, which kept him in constant pain and

---

*While classical male hysteria was no longer questioned by Viennese medical authorities,
Charcot's brand of traumatic male hysteria was doubted. Freud's medical colleagues at the
Viennese Society of Physicians felt that Freud was talking down to them in his overly enthu-
siastic presentation of Charcot's work.

†Freud was enamored of the Greek and Roman classics, and his trips to Athens and to
Rome were the great travel experiences of his life. He was fascinated by archeology and saw
his career as a quest into individuals' unacknowledged inheritance from the past (Boorstin
1983, p. 623).

required thirty-three operations to remove more and more of his palate and upper jaw. The cancer may have been brought on by Freud's liking for cigars (he smoked twenty a day). His former London home, at 20 Maresfield Gardens, is now the Freud Museum.

By 1920 or so, while in his sixties, Freud had attained world fame. Nevertheless, during his lifetime, Freud never received important scientific or medical awards for his psychoanalytic theory. But he did receive the Goethe Prize in 1930, near the end of his career, for his literary abilities.

PSYCHOANALYTIC THEORY: AN EXPLANATION

One of Freud's most important conceptualizations concerned the unconscious. Psychoanalytic theory seeks to explain human behavior by looking within the individual, and particularly into the individual's unconscious. Freud divided the human mind into three levels of self-awareness: (1) the conscious, which an individual can understand and describe to others with little difficulty; (2) the preconscious, which an individual can call up into consciousness; and (3) the unconscious, which is mainly inaccessible to an individual's conscious awareness, unless the individual is assisted by means of psychoanalysis. Repression is the process through which an individual prevents certain childhood events and other material from becoming accessible to conscious awareness. Projection is the process through which neurotic or moral anxiety at the unconscious level is converted into conscious fear. Thus, exchanges may occur between the conscious and unconscioius levels for an individual. Freud attempted various methods for understanding the unconscious of his patients by such means as hypnosis, free association, dream analysis, and the study of Freudian slips and jokes.

Perhaps Freud searched for the explanation of human behavior within the individual, rather than in the individual's social relationships with others, because he had gained an unfavorable view of society from the way that it had blocked him from his chosen profession of medical research due to religious prejudice. Freud perceived society as a negative influence on the lives of the sick patients whom he treated. He did not stress how society might be changed to solve the individual disorders that he treated but instead sought to cure his patients by helping them understand the causes of their mental dysfunctions, so that they could go on with their lives in a more effective manner. Psychoanalytic theory developed as an inward-looking, individualistic explanation of behavior through understanding the unconscious.

Freud's Methods

Freud utilized a variety of methods to probe the unconscious. At first, he tried hypnosis but eventually became dissatisfied with it when he found that it removed the symptoms but did not totally cure his patients. Later, he turned to lengthy, in-depth interviews with an individual. Freud urged his patients to relax on a couch while he encouraged them to say whatever came to mind. Because such free-association was often limited by inhibitions, Freud helped his patients overcome their resistance by accepting whatever they said in a completely nonjudgmental way. In 1892, Freud began using a couch, and in 1896 he coined the word *psychoanalysis*. He increasingly used the free-association technique, never censoring or judging what his patients said, hoping in this way to learn about traumatic events that were repressed in their unconscious.

Psychoanalytic theory was based on a relatively small number of detailed case studies. Freud typically saw each patient for an hour a day over a period of months or years, so each case study represented a very textured analysis. Freud's main knowledge base consisted of a dozen such case studies, although he also treated several hundred other patients. His dozen individuals of intensive study were a rather narrow sample. They were all very well-to-do (they had to be, in order to afford Freud's intensive therapy), and most of them were mentally disturbed women. They were neurotic, but not psychotic; that is, they were not so seriously disturbed that they had to be institutionalized. An example is Anna O., a young Viennese patient whose real name was Bertha Pappenheim (Schultz 1975, p. 303). Anna O. was an intelligent, attractive, and charming woman of twenty-one. She was troubled by a nervous cough, a squint, nausea, memory loss, and vision and speech problems, and her right arm and neck were paralyzed. Although German was her mother tongue, Anna O. could speak only English. Anna could not drink for a period of six weeks, even though she felt thirsty. Anna O. was a somewhat typical case of hysteria, and she was characteristic of Freud's patients in that she came from one of the wealthiest Jewish merchant families in Austria (Anzieu 1986, p. 57).

The data with which Freud worked consisted of his patients' verbal expressions about their past life events, particularly their childhood ex-

periences. The data—everything that came into his patients' consciousness—were thus qualitative. Freud did not use diagnostic tests or any
other quantitative measures of his patients' personality dimensions, and
he did not take notes while his patients talked to him, so his data consisted of what he remembered (Schultz 1975, p. 321). He did not test
hypotheses in a formal way but deduced the components of psychoanalytic theory in an interpretive fashion by identifying concepts, building
taxonomies, and suggesting possible relationships among his concepts,
perhaps illustrating them with an individual case study or two. Freud
included self-analysis as an important part of his research methodology.
He reserved the last half-hour of every workday for analyzing his own
thoughts, dreams, and memories. Many important components of psychoanalytic theory grew out of Freud's self-analysis, particularly of his
dreams. In fact, the key turning point in creating psychoanalytic theory
occurred between 1896 and 1901: "Freud invented psychoanalysis
when he was between 40 and 45, by personally embarking on a study
of his own dreams" (Anzieu 1986, p. 3).

Critics have pointed out that Freud sought to demonstrate the utility
of psychoanalysis through descriptions of largely unsuccessful cases,
that is, cases in which the patient did not fully recover as a result of
psychoanalytic treatment (Sulloway 1991). Freud published six detailed cases histories, but two of these six patients discontinued therapy
after only a few months, before any conclusive results were achieved.
Freud saw "Little Hans," who was obsessed with a horse phobia, once
and gathered most of his material about the case from the boy's father.
Freud never met his fourth case, Daniel Paul Schreber, but analyzed this
case through Schreber's published memoirs. The two remaining cases,
Rat Man and Wolf Man, are the most complete and are seemingly more
successful, but even in these cases the therapeutic results that Freud
claimed for them could not be reproduced by other psychoanalysts
(Sulloway 1991). In the light of this lack of firm scientific evidence
about the effectiveness of psychoanalysis, Freud's theory had to be accepted largely on the basis of its face validity.

Freud was a conscientious observer of the verbal and nonverbal behavior of his patients. He was a creative and courageous theory builder
and attracted other talented minds to the field of psychoanalysis, so that
his theory was carried forward as an intellectual movement that greatly
magnified the force of his ideas. Freud eventually quarreled with several
of his leading followers, however, splintering the psychoanalytic movement and destroying its unity.

The Talking Cure

Freud was a careful listener, and as he listened for hour after hour to his neurotic patients, he gradually began to create the theory of psychoanalysis. It helped Freud spin out his theory by discussing these cases with professional colleagues. The most important of these colleagues in

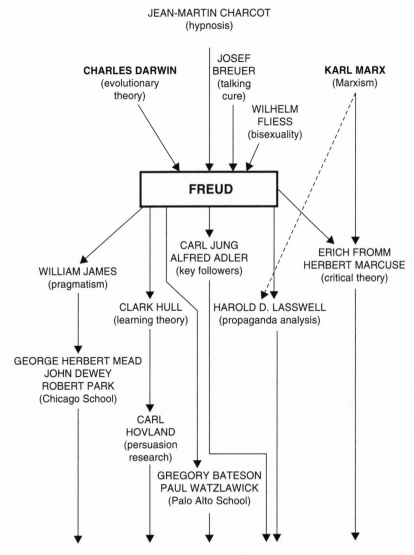

Figure 3.2. Intellectual forebears and descendants of Freudian theory.

Freud's early years of building psychoanalytic theory was Dr. Josef Breuer (1842–1925), an eminent Viennese medical doctor who cured patients by discussing their symptoms with them in the so-called talking cure. Psychoanalysis grew out of Freud's use of Breuer's talking cure and from discussions about their patients. Psychoanalytic theory was socially constructed, evolving out of Freud's talking with his patients and with his colleagues, especially Breuer, and, later, with his disciples (Figure 3–2).

Breuer was a senior colleague of Freud, fourteen years older and well established in Viennese medical circles. He had one of the wealthiest clienteles in Vienna and referred patients to Freud. Breuer was a warm and supportive friend of Freud and lent him substantial sums of money, funds that Freud could not repay for many years and that he eventually resented as an outgrown dependence. Breuer was also Freud's personal physician. Mainly, however, Breuer provided Freud with his own established scientific reputation, necessary for Freud to attract attention to his innovative ideas (Knight 1984).

Breuer's medical practice consisted mainly of young women who were called "hysterical": they complained of bodily symptoms but were not physically ill. Breuer told his friend Freud about the case of Anna O. in 1882. Her case played an important role in Freud's discussions with Breuer through which they advanced psychoanalytic theories. Anna O. became temporarily relieved of many of her symptoms when she told Dr. Breuer about the disagreeable events of her earlier life. For example, she told Breuer, under hypnosis, that she had once seen a dog drinking water from a glass, such a disgusting event that it prevented her from drinking. When Anna O. came out of the hypnotic trance, she asked for a glass of water and drank deeply. Her paralyzed arm was also cured by Breuer, when he forced her to recall a painful, traumatic event earlier in her life.

Eventually Anna O. recovered from her hysteria and became a leading social worker (the first in Germany and one of the first in the world) and feminist (Appignanesi and Zarate 1979, p. 33). The talking cure, which Anna O. also called "chimney sweeping," was renamed "catharsis" by Breuer and Freud.* **Catharsis** is the purging of an individual's strong emotions through vicarious means. The concept originally came from the Greek tragedies, which, as Aristotle noted, often cleansed or

---

*Her role in developing certain ideas in psychoanalysis was quite important. Anna O. "was the real discoverer of the cathartic method" (Jones 1953, p. 223).

purified an audience's emotions by depicting tragic events on the theater stage. Catharsis was seen as a useful release for individuals due to a kind of "hydraulic" theory of emotions: built-up emotions must be released or else they would "boil over" or "erupt." To Freud, catharsis was a therapeutic precursor of psychoanalysis. Symptoms were removed, as in the case of Anna O., by a patient's recalling forgotten, unpleasant events from the subconscious.

Freud convinced Breuer to join him as a coauthor of *Studien Über Hysteria* (*Studies on Hysteria*), published in 1895, which examined six cases of hysteria, one of which was that of Anna O. This was the world's first book on psychoanalysis (although the term *psychoanalysis* was not used by Freud until 1896), explicating such basic concepts as transference, resistance, and repression. Over the next five decades, Freud's psychoanalytic theory would unfold bit by bit, reported in his various books, each of which was a kind of summary of his work to that date. He continued to revise his theory and never supplied a complete statement of his theoretical system.

During his years of collaboration with Breuer, Freud became convinced that hysteria is sexually caused. He claimed that hysterical individuals had been seduced as children and that this child abuse caused hysteria in adult life. Freud accepted as true his patients' accounts that they had been molested by adults when they were children. This seduction theory shocked the public in turn-of-the-century Vienna, controversy erupted, and Breuer eventually broke with Freud, believing that he had been pressured to go along with Freud's seduction theory. After the spring of 1896, Breuer and Freud halted their intellectual collaboration; they never spoke to each other again. Such ruptured personal relationships were to become a repeated pattern throughout Freud's career.

In 1897, Freud himself dropped seduction theory, although he continued to insist that sexual problems were a primary cause of the mental problems of his patients. He proposed instead that their tales of sexual abuse were derived from sexual fantasy. It was a stunning blow to Freud when he realized that his patients' seduction accounts were fantasies. This severe disappointment turned him toward other methods of exploring the unconscious.

Freud's Creative Illness and Dream Analysis

In 1896, Freud's father died, bringing on a middle-age crisis and a neurotic illness that led Freud to self-analysis of his dreams. As he coped with his own neurosis, a kind of creative illness, Freud begin writing *The Interpretation of Dreams* (1899), his most important book. Freud felt that dreams contain valuable clues for understanding the causes of emotional disturbances. Dreams occur during sleep, when the conscious part of the mind is most relaxed and off-guard. To Freud, dreams represented the fulfillment of wishes, which were usually, but not always, sexual. Over a period of several years, from 1896 to 1899, Freud was able to recall the details of hundreds of his dreams, some going back to his childhood experiences. Then he analyzed this remembered material, just as he psychoanalyzed his patient's reports made during their sessions with him. Thus Freud used self-analysis to fight against his depressive tendencies. With the publication of *The Interpretation of Dreams*, Freud's neurosis ended. "The book could be called an autobiography in disguise" (Ellenberger 1970, p. 451).

Freud identified his major discovery to be that a dream is a fulfillment of a wish, the vicarious expression of a repressed, unacceptable sexual wish. The dream is a guardian of sleep in that feelings that would ordinarily awaken the dreamer are disguised so they are not disturbing (Ellenberger 1970, p. 492). Dreams provided Freud with a window into the unconscious mind—initially his own troubled mind and then others'. His focus on dream analysis was the key turning point in his career, helping him work out his own neurosis and to elaborate the basic principles of psychoanalysis. After 1900, Freud's "self-analysis had transformed the unsure young practitioner into a self-assured founder of a new doctrine and school, convinced that he had made a great discovery, which he saw as his mission to give to the world" (Ellenberger 1970, p. 459).

Transference and Identification

Transference is the shifting of emotional attitudes by a patient from parents or other individuals of the past to the therapist (Schultz 1979, p. 311). Such irrational feelings of love or hostility toward the therapist were considered by Freud to be a vital and necessary weaning of the patient from childish dependence. But sometimes transference could be troublesome to the therapist. For instance, when Breuer thought he had nearly cured Anna O. of her symptoms, she called him to her bedside one night and told him that she was pregnant with his child. He was so shocked that he left Vienna the next day, taking his wife on a second honeymoon. When Freud learned of these events from Breuer, he decided that the therapist would have to be aware of the process of transference and learn to manage it so as to help patients recover from their neurosis.

The concept of transference became an important part of Freud's theoretical apparatus. Transference was thought to be necessary before a patient could be cured, as it helped individuals work out their troubled personal relationships of the past. A concept related to transference is identification, the process through which an individual takes over the features of another person and incorporates them into his or her own personality. An individual might take on the manner, dress, style of speech, and other qualities of another person perceived as admirable and less vulnerable to the danger that gave rise to the individual's anxiety. Freud thought of identification as a long-lasting psychological attachment. He saw imitation, the mimicking of another person's behavior, as a kind of temporary identification.*

The Development of Psychoanalytic Theory

Many aspects of what we know today about Sigmund Freud come from his extensive correspondence with Wilhelm Fliess (1858–1928), a medical doctor who was a nose-and-throat specialist living in Berlin. Freud met Fliess when the latter enrolled in a postgraduate training course in Vienna. Fliess was one of very few people willing to listen to Freud at this stage. Freud carried on his famous correspondence with Fliess during a fifteen-year period from 1887 to 1902, and especially for the seven years between 1895 and 1902. They corresponded at length each week and had personal meetings during their vacations and at other times, which Freud glorified by calling them "conferences" (Szasz 1978, p. 109).†

Fliess had some strange theories, and the Freud-Fliess relationship

---

*Freud's concept of identification was utilized by Theodor Adorno and others in *The Authoritarian Personality* (1950), a study of prejudice in America. There is a vast literature on the concept of identification and on imitation, both important in communication study.

†The letters from Freud to Fliess were preserved, and are now available in the Freud Archives in the U.S. Library of Congress. Many of the letters have been published. However, Freud destroyed all of the letters *from* Fliess (Jones, 1953, p. 287). Fortunately for historical purposes, intellectuals like Freud and Darwin carried on an extensive daily correspondence, and their main ideas were thus preserved. Historians are concerned that contemporary intellectual figures may be communicating by telephone or by electronic systems, which may not leave a written record.

had "a tragic-comic flavor" (Jones 1953, p. 298). For instance, Fliess believed that sexual illness is caused by disturbances in the mucous membrane of the nose; he operated on Freud twice for nasal infections. From Fliess, Freud gained the notion of human bisexuality—that every individual has both male and female tendencies. Freud's passionate friendship with Fliess, someone intellectually his inferior, seems to have been motivated by Freud's need for collegial exchange during the period in which he was exploring his own unconscious mind and working out his theory of psychoanalysis (Jones 1953, p. 287), Fliess may have been particularly important to Freud during his neurotic illness from 1896 to 1899, but eventually the close relationship degenerated into feelings of competition and conflict. The friendship turned into hatred, after a final "conference" in September 1900, Freud and Fliess never spoke to each other again.

Freud's main contributions to psychoanalytic theory were made between 1896 and 1906, a decade that includes the six years of his close relationship with Fliess. He placed before the scientific world and the public the classic psychoanalytic ideas on hysteria, repression, dreams, infant sexuality, and the unconscious. He did not encounter any particular difficulties in disseminating these aspects of psychoanalytic theory—he was able to find publishers for his books—and most of his writings were favorably received, although "they evoked indignation and opposition as well" (Szasz 1978, p. 113). Freud's Oedipus complex—an incestuous attraction that exists between a mother and son attracted particular criticism. Some critics say that Freud did not get the Greek story of Oedipus quite straight. "Actually, Freud constructed the Oedipus complex by seizing upon some parts of the story, ignoring others, and reinterpreting quite arbitrarily the features he retained" (Szasz 1978, p. 130). Freud detected an Oedipus complex in his own childhood by writing out his dreams, then analyzing them, and publishing them in *The Interpretation of Dreams*. He found evidence of infantile sexuality in many of his own dreams, including jealousy of his father for his sexual relationship with Freud's mother. He distinguished two types of wish fulfillment:

1. The pleasure principle, which is made up of wishes and desires mainly of a sexual nature, which can be destructive to the individual in that they may call for behavior that is not very civilized. The pleasure principle dominates the unconscious.
2. The reality principle, which consists of more logical, organized

ideas, many of which assist the individual in reaching the goals of the pleasure principle. The reality principle mainly operates at the conscious level.

These two types of wish fulfillment are often in conflict, and an individual's behavior may represent a compromise.*

Personality Development

Freud's theory paid special attention to the stages of personality development in childhood and through the life cycle. Freud's sessions with his patients often probed their childhood because, as Freud liked to say, "The child is father of the man." He identified the following stages of personality development:

1. The three pregenital stages of early childhood. In the *oral stage*, from birth into the second year of age, the infant focuses on stimulation of the mouth, as in sucking and eating. This is generally a happy stage for a baby, in which cries of hunger lead to the response of being fed. But then teeth begin to erupt through the baby's gums, a painful process for the infant. In the *anal stage*, the young child focuses on the functions of bodily elimination. At first, such elimination is an uninhibited pleasure, but then toilet training begins. The external regulation of an instinctive impulse teaches the child to postpone the immediate pleasure of relieving anal tensions. Finally, in the *phallic stage* of development, beginning at the end of the third year or in the fourth year of age, the child focuses on the sexual organs. Here again, the uninhibited pleasure of aggressive sexual feelings are reined in by adult society, leading to the Oedipus complex, the Electra complex (in which the female child feels sexually attracted to her father and feels jealousy toward her mother), penis envy (by females), and castration anxiety (by male children).
2. A prolonged *latency period,* from about age six until puberty, during which sexual desires seem to disappear as the individual slowly matures.
3. The *adolescent period,* in which the pregenital sexual impulses are reactivated at puberty.

*Schramm (1949b) applied Freud's theory of the pleasure principle versus the reality principle to explain why individuals use the mass media for entertainment versus news.

4. The *genital stage* of maturity, at which heterosexual behavior typically begins.

Freud proposed that the individual personality is composed of three systems:

1. The id, consisting of everything of a psychological nature that is inherited at birth, such as instincts. The id, which consists of the biological component of the human personality, operates by means of the pleasure principle as a means of tension reduction. There is no good or evil for the id; it does not know morality.
2. The ego is the psychological component of the human personality. Here the reality principle suspends the pleasure principle temporarily. Thus, the individual learns to distinguish between ideas in the mind versus in the external world that surrounds the individual. The ego mediates between the self and its environment. Freud saw the ego as the executive of the personality.
3. The superego, the social component of the human personality that represents self-control, consists of the internalized representations of society's traditional ideals, as interpreted by the parents to their child. Here the individual is taught right from wrong and learns to strive for perfection rather than for pleasure. Thus, the superego is in conflict with the id.

These three components of personality tend to develop differently at the life-cycle stages described. Freud also coined the concept of libido (Latin for "desire") to describe the energy for such life instincts as hunger, thirst, and sex (these life instincts were called eros). The libido is contained in the id.

In 1904, Freud published *The Psychotherapy of Everyday Life*, in which he discussed various reasons for forgetting. This book also described parapraxis, the kind of mistakes of the tongue, pen, or memory that occur in daily life. These errors disclose unconscious wishes, which Freud felt offered insight into the individual's mind, as he argued in *Jokes and Their Relation to the Unconscious* (1905). Today we honor Freud's insight into this behavior by referring to our unconscious misstatements as Freudian slips. In 1905, Freud also published *Sexualtheorie* (*Three Essays on the Theory of Sexuality*), a book that outraged the public with its emphasis on sex as a primary human motivation. Sexuality was always at the center of Freud's psychoanalytic theory. Perhaps

Freud emphasized sex because of its physiological aspects and its connections to human biology. He was trained in medical science and only gradually during his career did he give more attention to social and cultural factors in psychoanalytic theory. Freud saw sexuality as one cause of individual dysfunction, perhaps reflecting his internalization of the Viennese sexual repression of his times.

THE RISE OF PSYCHIATRY IN EUROPE

Psychoanalytic theory grew to early strength in Vienna and then spread to Switzerland and Germany. Today Europe honors Freud as a past genius while largely ignoring psychoanalysis. America is now the world center of psychoanalysis. How did psychoanalytic theory spread out from Vienna to other European nations, and then migrate across the Atlantic?

Freud was not an isolated scientific genius. He developed his scientific theory in company with others; first Josef Breuer and then Wilhelm Fliess, and then a cult of followers that expanded rapidly. In 1902, he began a weekly discussion group in his home to teach psychoanalysis to a cadre of four protegés. This Wednesday evening circle grew to seventeen members by 1906, when Freud began corresponding with Carl G. Jung in Zurich, who had ben experimenting with the psychoanalytic approach for several years. In 1907, Jung traveled to Vienna to see Freud, and a strong bond was established between them. A year later, Jung organized the First International Congress of Psychoanalysis in Salzburg, Austria, attended by forty people from six nations (Sulloway 1991). Freud's Wednesday evening group renamed itself the Vienna Psychoanalytic Society. At the Second International Psychoanalytic Congress in 1910, an international association was organized, with Jung as its president.* Psychoanalytic theory was spreading rapidly.

With its success, the informal social movement was becoming bureaucratized into a formal organization. Freud and his followers decided that any individual wishing to become a psychoanalyst should first undergo a personal training analysis with an experienced psychoanalyst. This requirement restricted who could practice psychoanalysis and demanded a heavy financial sacrifice, as well as the surrender of the individual's privacy and indeed of the whole self (Ellenberger 1970,

---

*The annual congresses soon evolved into the International Psycho-Analytical Association, which continues to this day at the main professional body of psychoanalysts.

p. 552). "Instead of remaining within the already-established medical apparatus for training neurologists and psychiatrists, Freud created his own training institutes and sought to keep psychoanalysis independent from the medical schools" (Sulloway 1991). In the early days of Freud's psychoanalytic theory, a few individuals from other nations came to Vienna in order to be psychoanalyzed by Freud and thus to be trained as psychoanalysts. Soon more and more individuals, attracted by reading Freud's books and by his growing fame, traveled to Vienna for training in psychoanalysis. Next, psychoanalytic training centers were established in Berlin and in Vienna, though not in universities, perhaps indicating how far psychoanalysis was perceived as lying outside the conventional intellectual establishment. Psychoanalytic training was mainly limited to medical doctors as a postdoctoral specialization rather than becoming a specialty field of doctoral education in psychology.

Eventually the psychoanalytic movement became bureaucratized into a set of professional associations, training institutes, and other competing and overlapping organizations. The initial burst of scientific creativity by Freud and his immediate followers could not be sustained. Psychoanalysis became a professional specialization for medical doctors, who shared a theoretical viewpoint about individual dysfunctions and human behavior.

Freud felt that Jung's visibility as president of the International Congress of Psychoanalysis in 1910 would help establish psychoanalysis as something more than a Viennese and a Jewish science (Appignanesi and Zarate 1979, p. 115). On one hand, Freud was an extremely kind man, full of wit and humor and quite charming. But he was also a rather autocratic leader, who often put someone else in a figurehead position while retaining the real power to decide key issues—a strategy that was an invitation to conflict between Freud and his leading followers. The split with Jung was the most famous of all.

Carl G. Jung (1875–1961) was a psychiatrist at the Burghölzli Mental Hospital in Zurich. He was nineteen years younger than Freud. A Swiss medical doctor, Jung had taught at the University of Zurich but then resigned to start a private medical practice. Jung's interest in Freud began in 1900 when he read *The Interpretation of Dreams*. The two men began corresponding and finally met in 1907. Soon Freud called Jung the "crown-prince" of the psychoanalytic movement. Jung wrote to Freud that his veneration for him was something like a "religious crush" (Appignanesi and Zarate 1979, p. 115), but Jung did not accept all aspects of Freud's psychoanalytic theory and was critical of Freudian thought in his 1912 book, *The Psychology of the Unconscious*, which, when published, caused a break with Freud. The split became final in 1914, and they never saw each other again (Schultz 1975, p. 328). Their main difference dealt with the nature of the libido. To Jung, it was a generalized life energy. To Freud, it was sexual energy. Jung also rejected the Oedipus complex. He is most noted for his concept of archetypes, which are universal primordial images. Eventually Jung not only ended his relationship with Freud but left the psychoanalytic movement completely.

Freud's cult of followers helped him work out his psychoanalytic theory in the face of considerable opposition from the public and especially from the medical profession. Each of Freud's followers eventually broke with him. Jung argued that Freud overemphasized childhood sexuality. Karen Horney, another early follower of Freud, claimed that he misunderstood women, questioning his concept of penis envy. Horney (1885–1952) had earned her medical degree at the University of Berling, trained at the Berlin Psychoanalytic Institute from 1914 to 1918, and then became a faculty member there before migrating to Chicago in 1932. She rejected most of Freudian theory, claiming that Freud had overemphasized biology and underemphasized cultural factors in his formulations. She insisted that a child has a basic anxiety from feeling helpless in a potentially hostile world (Schultz 1975, p. 341).

Alfred Adler (1870–1937) was fourteen years younger than Freud and a dedicated Viennese follower of Freud. Adler was born in Vienna of wealthy parents and earned his medical degree at the University of Vienna. A charter member in Freud's Wednesday evening discussion group, Adler eventually differed with Freud by deemphasizing sex, arguing that individual psychology is determined by social factors and by personal relationships with others (Schultz 1975, p. 335). Adler did not feel that the libido was the main dynamic source of psychic life. In 1911, Adler split with Freud and founded a dissident society.

THE TRANSFER OF PSYCHOANALYTIC THEORY
TO THE UNITED STATES

Five lectures that Freud presented at Clark University in 1909 represented an important turning point in the introduction of psychoanalytic theory to America. He had been invited to America by G. Stanley Hall, an influential U.S. psychologist trained in Germany and the president of

Clark University, located in Worcester, Massachusetts. Freud's lectures were well received by many U.S. scholars. His books began to be read widely in the United States, and his psychoanalytic theory began to influence certain of the social sciences, especially anthropology and psychology.

World War I gave a boost to psychoanalysis as a means of treating shell shocked military serviceman, but the major infusion of Freudian thought in America occurred with the migration of hundreds of psychoanalysts from Germany and Austria to the United States following the rise of Hitler in the 1930s. These European-trained psychoanalysts did not need to search for jobs; they simply started a private practice as a psychoanalyst. The mass media began to popularize psychoanalysis to the public, and its use soon became widespread. Ernest Jones, an early disciple of Freud and later one of Freud's main biographers, founded the American Psychoanalytic Association. The United States was very receptive to psychoanalysis, where it was used to treat individuals diagnosed as psychotics, as well as neurotics. This extension of psychoanalytic theory had been pioneered by Carl Jung.

Psychoanalytic theory began to have an important intellectual impact in numerous fields: literature, religion, philosophy, the arts, and the social sciences. Harold D. Lasswell, a University of Chicago political scientist, studied psychoanalysis with Elton Mayo at Harvard and then underwent psychoanalytic training in Vienna and Berlin. Lasswell psychoanalyzed political leaders, practiced lay psychoanalysis at the University of Chicago, and drew on psychoanalytic theory in his prolific writings (see Chapter 6). Another key figure in bringing psychoanalysis to America was Harry Stack Sullivan (1892–1949) of Yale University, with whom Lasswell collaborated. Yale's Institute of Human Relations, funded generously by the Rockefeller Foundation during the 1930s, sought to construct a unified social science based on Freudian psychoanalytic theory (Sears 1985). Psychologist Clark Hull's behavior theory borrowed such concepts from Freud as frustration, aggression, regression, and repression and then tested hypotheses linking those concepts with experimental methods. Some parts of Freudian theory were generally supported by this psychological research; other aspects were not (Hornstein 1992).* Through Clark Hull's protégé, Carl I. Hovland, the

---

*A summary of the evidence supporting and not supporting hypotheses based on Freudian theory is provided by Fisher and Greenberg (1977).

Institute of Human Relations, and thus Freudian theory, influenced communication study.

Understandably, Freud is considered one of the important foundersof psychology.* However, the mainstream of American psychology developed in directions different from psychoanalytic theory. Modern psychology evolved from Wilhelm Wundt, the experimental psychologist who founded the first psychological laboratory at the University of Leipzig in Germany in 1879, about a decade before Freud began to create psychoanalytic theory. Although both psychology and psychoanalysis focused on intraindividual explanations of human behavior, they differed in several important ways:

1. Psychology was method centered (on the laboratory experiment), while psychoanalysis was problem centered (on neurosis). Psychoanalysis did not fit with psychology's attempt to be scientific through the use of experimental methods (Schultz 1975, p. 320).
2. Influenced by the natural sciences (especially physiology), psychology's data are quantitative, while psychoanalysis deals with the complexity of the individual's psychic life, using qualitative data from in-depth case studies.
3. The time frame of psychology is the here-and-now of the experiment, while psychoanalysis is concerned with the prior lifetime of the individual, drawing on remembrances of childhood events to explain adult neurosis.
4. The individuals of primary interest to psychologists are normal adults or children; psychoanalysts deal with neurotic patients.

There was a poor fit between psychology and psychoanalysis, and so they have mainly grown up as two separate, and often competing, academic and professional fields. Early sociologists in America, like their colleagues in psychology, took over such Freudian concepts as the inferiority complex, repression, rationalization, sublimation, transference, and, especially, wish fulfillment (Burgess 1939). But they rejected Freud's in-depth analytic methods, preferring their own research techniques, like the survey interview (which provides limited data from a large number of individuals). Psychoanalytic theory has had a consider-

---

*In fact, the key historian of psychology, Boring (1929, p. 753), designated Freud as the greatest figure in psychology.

able intellectual influence on anthropology, where the nature of the data and certain of the problems of study (such as the influence of culture on personality socialization) have a closer fit than in other social science fields. The intellectual influence of psychoanalytic theory on communication study occurred directly through Harold D. Lasswell and, less so, through Carl I. Hovland.

CONTRIBUTIONS OF PSYCHOANALYTIC THEORY TO COMMUNICATION STUDY

Sigmund Freud was one of the three major influences from nineteenth-century Europe on the social sciences as they developed in America. While Darwin's evolutionary theory and Marx's historical materialism were at the macro level of society, Freudian thought was individualistic, looking within the individual, especially the individual's childhood experiences, buried in the unconscious, for explanations of behavior. Freud maintained that childhood experiences shape adult behavior and that the unconscious explains human behavior.

Psychoanalytic theory assumes that explanations of human behavior lay within the individual, and especially in the unconscious. A number of important communication theories in use today look inside the individual for the forces impelling behavior change, although these are not psychoanalytic theories. Examples are Fritz Heider's (1946) balance theory, Leon Festinger's (1957) theory of cognitive dissonance, and Petty and Cacioppo's (1981, 1986) elaboration likelihood model of attitude change. These theories assume that an individual's unbalanced, inconsistent, or dissonant state, because it is uncomfortable to the individual, leads to the individual's behavior and change. The scholarly tradition of persuasion research begun by Carl I. Hovland grew out of Clark Hull's learning theory, which in turn was influenced by Freudian theory. Freudian theory also had an impact on Harold D. Lasswell's psychoanalytic studies of political leaders, although it did not as directly affect his communication research (see Chapter 6).

Freudian psychoanalytic theory combined with Marxism by the Frankfurt school of the 1930s and 1940s to give us today's critical theory of communication. The critical school's influential study of prejudice, reported in *The Authoritarian Personality* by Adorno and others (1950), represents a psychoanalytic theory of personality investigated with the methods of quantitative psychology. The long shadow of Sigmund Freud's thinking is clearly embedded in various lines of study of human communication today.

THE PALO ALTO GROUP AND INTERACTIONAL COMMUNICATION

The Palo Alto group focuses on the individual's communication relationships with others as a means of understanding the individual's behavior. The Palo Alto scholars have provided an alternative conceptualization of human behavior. A major paradigmatic shift occurred in the clinical field beginning in the 1950s and accelerating in the 1960s as the Freudian focus on the internal dynamics of the individual changed to a clinical emphasis on individuals' patterns of interaction or relationships (Rogers 1992). The Palo Alto group was one important part of this paradigmatic shift.

Formation of the Palo Alto Group

A unique, theoretically rich approach to relational communication has been espoused by the dedicated band of Palo Alto scholars for the past forty years. The Palo Alto group resulted from the gradual merger of two earlier theory groups in the Palo Alto area whose perspectives were highly compatible. One of these was led by Gregory Bateson, and was centered in the Veterans Administration hospital in Menlo Park, adjoining the city of Palo Alto. "They were investigating communication on a very wide range, but always on the principle that communication has a pragmatic, behavioral effect" (Wilder 1978). The VA hospital group investigated schizophrenic communication, the double bind, and, more broadly, paradox. Bateson's research program at the hospital was supported for nine years by a variety of funding sources, first by the Rockefeller Foundation (1952–1954) and then by the Macy Foundation.

The other group was headed by Dr. Don Jackson, who had participated in the VA hospital research and founded the Mental Research Institute (MRI) in Palo Alto in 1959. MRI staff originally conducted funded research projects, but later, when the grants ran out, the emphasis shifted to training in family therapy. The MRI group centered around Jackson, a medical doctor and psychiatrist who had trained with Harry

Stack Sullivan at the Washington-Baltimore Psychoanalytic Institute, John Weakland, an engineer trained in anthropology, and Jay Haley, a family therapist. Paul Watzlawick, who joined MRI in 1960, is a key figure in the Palo Alto group today. Watzlawick was born in Austria in 1921, earned his Ph.D. in psychology and modern languages from the University of Vienna in 1949, and then studied psychotherapy at the Carl Jung Institute for Analytical Psychology in Zurich. Today, in addition to his role as a main figure in the MRI, he has a private practice as a psychotherapist and holds an adjunct appointment in the Stanford Medical Center's Department of Psychiatry and Behavioral Sciences.

Participating in a network of talented intellectuals that are dedicated to understanding human communication in a new way was very attractive. MRI is the geographical and social center for the Palo Alto group today, but the group also involves other individuals than just the family therapists at MRI. They gather at morning and afternoon coffee sessions to discuss their cases, to participate in Thursday staff meetings and to view and critique videotapes of therapy sessions, and to provide joint family therapy to patients in the MRI Brief Therapy Center, a kind of R&D unit within MRI where cases are discussed and therapy is provided in order to develop and teach new therapy techniques. Today, and for the past several years, the MRI is a unique organization that operates without a director or even much of a hierarchical structure. The key individuals in the group have supported themselves by providing patient services and training programs through MRI. The group is vitally concerned with research and seeks to advance the interactional communication perspective.

Gregory Bateson was the theoretical mentor for both of the two interactionist communication groups in Palo Alto, and the two groups of scholars were completely compatible in their interactionist viewpoint. Eventually, Bateson's research grants at the VA hospital ran out, and the two sets of scholars gradually merged into what was by the late 1970s simply called the Palo Alto school or the Palo Alto group (Wilder 1979). It might have been more accurate to call these scholars the Interactional Communication School, which is its main theoretical focus. In the mid-1960s, Bateson moved to the Virgin Islands and to Hawaii to study dolphin communication, and then, in 1977, to Santa Cruz, 70 miles from Palo Alto, where he taught on the faculty of the University of California at Santa Cruz, until he died in 1980.

Don Jackson died in 1968. Several key figures moved away from the

Palo Alto area: For example, Janet Beavin Bavelas joined the psychology department at the University of Victoria (British Columbia), Canada; Jay Haley moved to Washington, D.C.; and Carlos Sluzki moved to Massachusetts. Today, the core members of the group who continue at MRI include Paul Watzlawick, John Weakland, and Richard Fisch.

Bateson was originally the key figure in the Palo Alto group, and with his departure some of the creative force went out of the group. Bateson had many of the stimulating ideas, and encouraged the Palo Alto scholars to think of themselves as "oddballs." The Palo Alto group is almost a social movement, centered around a theoretical perspective of human communication behavior as interactionist. As Carol Wilder (1979) stated in her review of the Palo Alto school: "I often felt in pursuing this piece [her review] that I was dealing with more of a social movement—even religion—than a communication theory; it may be that communication ideology is a more accurate term."

Gregory Bateson, Founder

Gregory Bateson was born in 1904, the son of William Bateson, England's famous geneticist who coined the word *genetics* in 1908 and rediscovered and popularized the important genetics experiments of Gregor Mendel. Gregory Bateson was named after the famous monk. "The Batesons were part of a circle of academic nobility that included the Darwins, Huxleys, and Whiteheads" (Goleman, 1978). Young Gregory resisted family pressures to become a biologist and instead earned his master's degree in anthropology at Cambridge University in 1930.* While doing field research in New Guinea in 1936, he met, and later married, anthropologist Margaret Mead. After they divorced in 1950, Mead and Bateson continued to work together as colleagues. Bateson's intellectual interests ranged widely across psychology, psychiatry, sociobiology, evolution, and communication among animals and humans.

During World War II, Bateson became a U.S. citizen so that he could serve with the OSS in the South Pacific. It was a demoralizing experience for him; he was unable to convince the U.S. military services to utilize anthropological understandings of South Pacific cultures. After

*Several good books have been written about Gregory Bateson, among them Lipset (1980), M. Bateson (1984), and M. Bateson and others (1977)

the war, he returned to the United States to participate in the Josiah Macy, Jr., Foundation Conferences on Cybernetics, where Norbert Wiener stimulated Bateson's interests in cybernetics theory (see Chapter 10). Bateson studied psychiatry and communication with Jurgen Ruesch at the Langely Porter Clinic of the University of San Francisco. Out of their collaboration, Bateson and Ruesch wrote *Communication: The Social Matrix of Psychiatry* (1951). Bateson underwent psychoanalysis with Elizabeth Hollensberg, a Jungian. His next step, in 1952, was to the Veterans Administration hospital project in Menlo Park, California, which launched the Palo Alto group.

Bateson was a truly interdisciplinary scholar, with no boundaries around his intellectual interests. "For most of his life, Gregory Bateson strove to develop a universal epistemology that would, in an essentially systems-theory frame of reference, give an integrated account of the capabilities of all living things to integrate information, organize and reorganize it, and communicate it outward from themselves" (Rieber 1989, p. 1). Bateson conducted ethnographic research in New Guinea, investigated communication among dolphins, and brought such concepts as metacommunication, paradox, and the double bind into communication study. He is the patron saint of the family therapy movement. His wide-ranging mind was not always easy to follow however, Bateson preferred complexity and ambiguity in his writings and was unable to explain his theoretical ideas so that readers could understand them easily. His most important book, *Steps to an Ecology of Mind* (1972), is complicated, difficult reading. Bateson argued that the human mind lies not within the brain or in some other part of the body, but outside the body, in an individual's relationships with other people—hence the title, "An Ecology of Mind." Such a conception stresses the importance of the individual's communication relationships with others, thus reflecting the central thesis of the Palo Alto group.

"Bateson's was a career of an intellectual nomad, traveling from place to place, and from one field to another, without ever settling into the safety of a secure niche. Too often, he was offered positions not entirely appropriate to his gifts or else he was offered posts that for reasons of intellectual conscience he could not accept" (Rieber 1989, p. 2). Bateson's academic marginality stemmed in part from his interdisciplinary interests; he did not fit the usual academic categories. Bateson spent his final ten years at the University of California at Santa Cruz, a unique academic institution that is organized primarily in residential colleges rather than in disciplinary departments. Here Bateson taught courses in "Bateson," unconstrained by disciplinary walls, until his death.

The Palo Alto Group and Communication Study

While relatively small in numbers, the Palo Alto group has not kept a low profile. Its members are widely published. At the time of Carol Wilder's (1979) stocktaking of the Palo Alto group, these relational scholars had published more than twenty books and several hundred articles. Since then, their intellectual output has increased considerably. In her study, Wilder (1979) concluded, "The work of this group . . . has been largely neglected in human communication research." The Palo Alto group is more widely recognized today, certainly, by scholars of communication. The interactional communication perspective has taken root and grown with less struggle in Europe than in the United States (Rogers 1992). Why has the Palo Alto School not received greater scholarly attention from U.S. communication scholars? The cause stems from two factors. First is a widespread misconception that members of the group study only communication pathologies, like schizophrenia. Several members of the group, including Bateson, worked at the Palo Alto Veterans Administration hospital in the 1950s and early 1960s, and their research was funded to study schizophrenic communication, but the central interest of the group has always been more general: to formulate a theory of interactionist communication. Schizophrenia is just one problem to which interactionist theory could be applied. This perspective also was applied to family therapy and to problems of organizational change by scholars at the Mental Research Institute.

Second, the conceptualization of communication by Gregory Bateson and his followers was of a nature that made it "difficult to create valid and workable research designs within the prevailing epistemologies of our [communication] discipline" (Wilder 1979). Translating concepts like paradox, the double bind, and metacommunication into researchable questions has proved to be very difficult, mainly because the individualistic research methodologies (centering on quantitative techniques) in which communication scholars are mostly trained are unsatisfactory tools for studying relational behavior. Again, we see a lack of fit between rich theoretical concepts and the available methodologies for testing them. Further, Bateson expressed his conceptual ideas in such complex language that it almost seemed that he did not want them to be understood.

The Palo Alto group was highly interdisciplinary in its academic makeup. Bateson was trained in anthropology and Don Jackson in psychiatry. Jay Haley has an M.A. degree in communication, as does Janet Beavin Bavelas; Watzlawick was trained in philosophy and linguistics, as well as psychiatry. John Weakland had been a chemical engineer and became interested in anthropology, with a special focus on China. This interdisciplinary nature of the group has resulted in a hybrid vigor.

Paul Watzlawick, Janet Beavin Bavelas, and Don Jackson wrote *Pragmatics of Human Communication: A Study of Interaction Patterns, Pathologies, and Paradoxes* (1967), in order to summarize the main viewpoint of the Palo Alto school. It is the core document expressing the interactional perspective and is the best-known work of the group. One of the authors, Janet Beavin Bavelas, has helped connect the work of the Palo Alto group with the field of communication study, primarily through her participation in the Interpersonal Communication Division of the International Communication Association (ICA).

Another important influence in the Palo Alto Group is Heinz von Foerster, who was born (in 1911) and grew up in Vienna. His uncle was Ludwig Wittgenstein, the philosopher. Von Foerster earned his Ph.D. degree in physics and worked on antiaircraft gunfire accuracy problems for the German army during World War II, the same scientific task that Norbert Viener and Claude Shannon were tackling for the Allied cause. When von Foerster came to America in 1949, he became an engineering professor at the University of Illinois at Urbana. Later, he founded the Biological Computation Center at Illinois. In 1975, he retired from Illinois and moved to Pescadero, a village on the Pacific coast south of San Francisco, about twenty miles from Palo Alto.

Paul Watzlawick knew of von Foerster through his important role in the post–World War II Macy Cybernetics Conferences, in which Bateson was a key participant. In 1976 von Foerster was invited to address an MRI conference, along with Bateson. Von Foerster pointed out that an observer of behavior, the observed phenomenon, and the process of observation form a cybernetic system. This viewpoint implied that what a scientist observes is a social construction and that attempts at absolute objectivity are futile. Thus, for example, a family therapist is also a participant in the family that is being helped, according to von Foerster's perspective. Von Foerster continues to be an intellectual influence on the contemporary Palo Alto group.

In addition to strong intellectual influences from Norbert Wiener's cybernetic theory and from general systems theory, the Palo Alto group drew from the work of Milton H. Erickson, a psychiatrist in Phoenix noted for his use of hypnosis (Haley 1976, p. 79).* MRI's contact with Erickson began in 1953, and the Palo Alto scholars continued to consult with him for several years. In addition, since the mid-1950s, Ray Birdwhistell, a specialist in nonverbal communication at the University of Pennsylvania, has influenced the Palo Alto school in analyzing the body movements of patients during family therapy (Haley 1976, p. 109).

Note that the Palo Alto group was not organized as a university department or school, centering on a single academic discipline, but rather as a loosely bundled coterie of scholars working on communication-related problems of mental health, family therapy, and schizophrenia. The group had a problem orientation (which can be limiting, if one lets it), to which human communication was explored as the main answer. The direct contact with patients at the VA hospital and at MRI was a source of intellectual inspiration for the members of the group. Bateson gained useful insight into the nature of paradoxical communication when he visited a training school for guide dogs for the blind. The dogs were taught to cope with contradictory commands such as when the trainer would order them "Go!" while holding back firmly on the dog's collar. Such training was intended to prepare the dogs for the paradoxical situations that they would encounter, such as when their blind owner might order them to walk across a street when the dog could see that it was dangerous (Weakland 1992).

The Palo Alto Group and Freudian Perspectives

The Palo Alto school is strongly opposed to Freudian approaches, instead reflecting a systems theory perspective in its view of communication. "It is difficult to overestimate the effect which cybernetics, information theory, and general systems theory had upon Bateson's thinking" (Wilder 1979). Gregory Bateson participated in most of the ten Macy Foundation Conferences on Cybernetics in New York in the 1940s and 1950s, where he was strongly influenced by Norbert Wiener and other cyberneticians.

Bateson and the Palo Alto group are definitely *not* Freudian: "The

---

*Bateson had become interested in trance states while he was doing fieldwork in Bali in 1936, which later led him to contact Erikson about the use of hypnosis (Watzlawick 1990, p. 88).

Palo Alto group express almost total disinterest in the Freudian individ-ualistic intrapsychic model, which stresses the importance of personal insight gained through exploring the past and the unconscious in a one-to-one relationship with the therapist" (Wilder 1979). The group takes as its unit of analysis the network of relationships between a focal indi-vidual and other individuals. Thus, the relational theory of the group is inherently of an interpersonal communication nature. "This shift of focus from the individual to the social network (from objects to pat-terns) has been likened to the shift from the earth to the sun as the center of a relational universe: The Copernican revolution in behavior science" (Wilder 1979). Watzlawick and others (1967, p. 28) stated that the psychoanalytic theory of Freud "postulates that behavior is pri-marily the outcome of a hypothesized interplay of intrapsychic forces considered to follow closely the laws of conservation and transforma-tion of energy in physics." Relational forces are in conflict with such an individualistic approach.

"Their [MRI and the Bateson VA project team] common denominator was precisely the rejection of the linear, monadic, intrapyschic model and its replacement by the interactional view" (Watzlawick 1981). What the original two components of the Palo Alto group shared was a common rejection of the medical model of therapy. According to the medical model, a person can "be changed if he were plucked out of his social situation and treated individually in a private office or inside a hospital. Once changed, he would return to his social milieu trans-formed because he had been 'cleared' of the intrapsychic problems caus-ing his difficulties. . . . The real world of the patient was considered sec-ondary since what was important was his perception of it" (Haley 1971, p. 2).

During the 1950s, the idea of trying to change a family occurred to various sets of therapists, as part of the general paradigmatic shift in the clinical field. Bateson was then on the staff of the VA hospital in Menlo Park, California, where his title, ethnologist, left him free to study al-most anything (Bateson 1972). Jay Haley (1971, p. 3), a member of Gregory Bateson's communication project at the VA hospital, describes what happened: "We had brought a schizophrenic patient together with his parents to try to find out why the patient could not be with them on visiting day for more than a few minutes without collapsing in an anxi-ety state. It was an information-gathering session, not a family treatment review. Yet what we observed so changed our views about treating schizophrenics that by the beginning of the next year we had started a systematic program of treating families of schizophrenics."

The hospitalized man was recovering from an acute schizophrenic episode. "When visited by his mother, he impulsively put his arm around her shoulder and she stiffened. When he withdrew his arms, she asked, 'Don't you love me anymore?' When he blushed, she said, 'Dear, you must not be so easily embarrassed and afraid of your feelings'" (Bateson and others, 1956; Wilder 1979). The patient was being given mixed messages by his mother, putting him in a double bind, which, as a schizophrenic, he did not have the ability to recognize or to escape.

The change in perspective from the medical model by the Palo Alto group required a different theoretic perspective, one that centered on the individual's interpersonal relationships with others. "The most consistently popular model was a system theory derived from cybernetics. This model could deal with interacting elements responding to one another in a self-corrective way, which is the way family members seemed to behave. Communication technology began to be part of the language of this field" (Haley 1971, p. 5). Intellectual connections with cybernetics and systems thinking continue to be made today by the Palo Alto group, particularly through Heinz von Foerster.

The Palo Alto group deviates most radically from the Freudian emphasis on insight as a therapeutic tool. Bateson did not believe that the unconscious should be made conscious. Instead, he (1972) asserted, "The unconscious is continually manifested in the exchange of messages, and one need go no further than behavioral data to comprehend the necessary dimensions of interaction" (Wilder 1979). An individual's problem can be alleviated, the Palo Alto group believes, regardless of its origins. The Palo Alto scholars refer to their approach as pragmatic because they focus on how communication affects human behavior (Watzlawick and others 1967, p. 22).

Metacommunication, Paradox, and the Double Bind

While Gregory Bateson was observing monkeys in the San Francisco Zoo one day, he noticed that when one monkey playfully nipped another, both monkeys understood that it was just play, even though it looked like real combat. Bateson (1972, pp. 177–193) concluded that the bite message must have been preceded by a metacommunication

(communication about communication) message that said: "This is play, not combat."

Bateson got the idea of communication and metacommunication at the first Macy Foundation Conference in March 1946, when Warren McCulloch, a neurophysiologist from the University of Illinois Medical School in Chicago, stated that the firing of every neuron has both a "report" and a "command" aspect. Bateson applied this metaphor to communication. The content of communication (Watzlawick and others 1967), which conveys the information contained in the message, is the report level. The relationship aspect of communication (equivalent to the command level) conveys the interpersonal relationships of the two or more participants in the communication process. The relationship dimension of a message classifies or frames the content of the message. Thus, it is one kind of metacommunication.

A means of operationalizing the relationship dimension of a communication dyad was developed by L. Edna Rogers and Richard V. Farace (1975), both then in the Department of Communication at Michigan State University. Each message so analyzed is a verbal intervention by one of the participants in a conversation. Each such message is classified as (1) "one-up," a movement toward gaining control of the exchange, (2) "one-down," or yielding control to the other person, or (3) "one-across," a movement toward neutralizing control. Such transactional analysis focuses on relationships as the units of analysis in communication research rather than on individuals. For example, consider the following exchange of messages between a husband and wife (Rogers and Farace 1975):

	Control Code
WIFE: We don't do anything together anymore.	One-up
HUSBAND: What do you mean?	One-down
WIFE: Well, as a family we don't do very much.	One-up
HUSBAND: Oh, I don't know.	One-across
WIFE: Don't you feel I do the major portion of the disciplining of the children?	One-down
HUSBAND: The time we're together you don't.	One-up
WIFE: Well, just for the record, I have to disagree.	One-up
HUSBAND: Well, just for the record, you're wrong.	One-up
WIFE: Well then, we completely disagree.	One-up

Rogers and Farace (1975), drawing on Bateson's (1936) *Naven*, his anthropological study of a tribe in New Guinea, use their codes to identify two basic types of relational control: (1) symmetry, or the exchange of equivalent control messages, so that one individual behaves toward the other as the other individual behaves toward him or her, and (2) complementarity, where the two participants in a communication dialogue exchange very unalike control messages. Here we see how the concepts of the Palo Alto group can be operationalized at the microlevel of conversational analysis.

A paradox, a contradiction that follows correct deduction from consistent premises (Watzlawick 1967, p. 188), occurs when a statement appears to include itself within its own scope, such as the injunction, "Ignore this statement." If one accepts the order, one cannot accept it— hence, the paradox. Another example is "I am lying." The solution to a paradox is to realize that the statement and the metastatement are of different logical types. One is a member; one is a class of members (Wilder 1979). The theory of types, proposed by Alfred North Whitehead and Bertrand Russell (1910), is based on the existence of hierarchies in levels of abstraction and states that in order to avoid paradox, a member of a class cannot be a class, nor can a class be a member of itself. In other words, each level of classification must be mutually exclusive without mixing the levels. Bateson utilized Whitehead and Russell's logic of types as a means of describing paradox in his double-bind theory of schizophrenia. The Whitehead-Russell type of logical paradox describes a computer that oscillates in a yes-no-yes fashion.*

The Palo Alto scholars specified these ingredients of a double bind:

1. Two or more individuals in an important relationship.
2. Repeted prior experience with the double-bind pattern.
3. A primary negative injunction (for example, "Don't do this or I'll punish you").
4. A secondary injunction that conflicts with the first at a more abstract level.
5. A third negative injunction prohibiting the individuals from escaping the situation.

In other words, a double bind occurs when one individual communi-

---

*Bateson was the first scholar to apply the theory of logical types of human communication (Haley 1976, p. 60).

cates two levels of messages to another: "When these two levels of messages both qualify and conflict each other, the other person is faced with an impossible situation. He cannot respond to either level without violating a prohibition at the other level, and so he is wrong whatever he does" (Haley 1976, p. 68). Double-bind situations occur in parent-child and in boss-employee relationships, for example.* Let us say that a child perceives that a parent is angry. The parent denies that she is angry and insists that the child deny it also. Should the child believe his own senses or believe the parent? If the former, the child maintains a sense of reality but loses the relationship with the parent. If the latter, the child maintains the relationship but distorts reality.

A schizophrenic individual, Bateson argued, loses the ability to metacommunicate, that is, to understand that a situation is binding and to rise to a higher level of abstraction in order to escape the bind, such as by saying, "You're giving me mixed messages" (Wilder 1979). Thus, an individual breaks out of the double bind by reframing the communication situation. Framing a communication exchange means to set it in context. Reframing is to change the context of the message exchange.

"One Cannot Not Communicate"

The Palo Alto school essentially equates communication with human behavior, as indicated by their famous dictum, "One cannot not communicate" (Watzlawick and others 1967, p. 48). This assertion makes us realize that not all communication is intentional. Communication happens through such nonverbal messages as shrugs, one's clothes, or via the perfume or aftershave that one wears, and whether one is late for an appointment, as well as through words (that is, verbal communication). Thus, the definition of communication must be very broad. To Watzlawick and others (1967), communication is practically synonymous with behavior (Motley 1990)—a very broad definition indeed. If communication must involve encoding (transforming an idea into the form of a message), then it must be possible *not* to communicate, that is, by producing nonencoded behavior (Motley 1990). The question is whether an unconscious behavior like an involuntary eye tic should be considered communication. Most scholars feel that it is.

Perhaps Watzlawick and others' assertion that "one cannot not

---

*Wishbow (1987) provides a useful summary of experimental evidence on double-bind communication.

communicate" is useful because it forces us to define the concept of communication in terms of the basic necessities in order for a behavior to qualify as communication. For instance, must communication be intentional? Must communication be interactive, with an active source and receiver playing back-and-forth roles? Must a message be encoded and decoded for communication to have occurred? These are important questions, and Watzlawick and others (1967) make us consider them when they assert, "We cannot not communicate" (Motley 1990).

One of the coauthors of the original statement that we cannot not communicate, Janet Beavin Bavelas (1990), wishes to modify her original view somewhat by identifying two substatements that she feels clarify the original intent: (1)"All behavior is *not* communication," but (2) "One probably cannot avoid communicating in a social setting." Think of the case of someone who does not want to communicate—for example, an airplane passenger who sits with his eyes closed in order to communicate that he does not want to speak with the person in the adjoining seat (Watzlawick and others 1967, p. 49). The simple presence of others in close proximity forces the individual to communicate the message of not wanting to communicate. But not all of the individual's behaviors are communicative; just some of these must be. "All behavior is not communicative, although it may be informative" (Bavelas 1990).

CONTRIBUTIONS OF THE PALO ALTO GROUP TO COMMUNICATION STUDY

One important lesson for communication study from the work of the Palo Alto group is to focus on problems of communication, as well as on the presumed positives. "The attention paid by Bateson, Watzlawick, and others to paradox, confusion, manipulation, noncontingency, and even 'disinformation'. . . . suggests a very different way of looking at human communication from that which has reigned in recent wisdom" (Wilder 1979). So, for example, communication study of such topics as self-disclosure and openness should be balanced by the study of ambiguity (Eisenberg 1984), deception, and deviousness. Certain situations like diplomacy, love, and business negotiation call for deliberate ambiguity rather than directness and clarity. The perspective of the Palo Alto group presses for an awareness of equivocal communication (Bavelas and others 1990), an understanding of communication pathologies, a search for the nature of self-referential contradiction like paradox, and to question whether more and clearer communication is always functional.

The group states that human communication is not just conscious, intentional, and successful as a step toward mutual understanding by two or more participants. The exchange of information between individuals can also be nonverbal, unintentional, paradox creating, and useful as a therapeutic technique. The perspective of the relational communication scholars is cybernetic, ecological, and based on systems theory. It does not fit with the dominant epistemology of communication study, which is one reason why the interactional theory of the Palo Alto group has not had more impact on communication study. The dominant focus of communication research is on investigating effects. In contrast, interactionist theory seeks to answer an entirely different kind of important question. This difference may explain why the Palo Alto group has not received more attention by mainstream communication scholars in the United States, who are chiefly concerned with studying effects.

The Palo Alto scholars oppose effects research, cast in terms of one-way models. "It could be argued that S-M-C-R (source-message-channel-receiver) was not extended as a 'model' of communication, that it met none of the tests of theoretical modeling, and that it was developed as an audiovisual aid to stimulate recall of the components of a communication relationship" (Berlo 1977, p. 12). One-way models may be quite appropriate for persuasion, propaganda, and studying mass communication effects, but the linear causality assumed by such directional models does not fit with a vision of human communication as interrelationships and as a process of mutual influence.

Bateson's VA hospital research project had an anthropological orientation in that the basic approach was to observe communication as it occurred in natural settings, without intrusion or intervention by the investigators. Bateson had an antiexperimental bias and thought that looking for cause-effect relationships between independent and dependent variables was foolish. Given his systems theory orientation and the anthropological perspective of the origins of the Palo Alto group, "it is not surprising to find a bad fit between the double-bind theory and conventional experimental method" (Wilder 1979). Many dozens of relational communication studies have used the Rogers-Farace coding system (one-up, one-down, and one-across) in order to quantify communication message exchanges. "The coding system has been used in a variety of settings, from TV interaction to labor negotiations, from learning-disabled children to job interviews, from classroom interaction to staff meetings to manager-subordinate dyads, etc., besides the more prevalent context of marital and family systems, both clinical and non-clinical" (Rogers 1992). The interactionist perspective will eventually become more widely understood and accepted among communication scholars. Then indeed the Palo Alto school will get the respect that it deserves.

CHAPTER 4

KARL MARX AND THE CRITICAL SCHOOL

Indisputably, Marx ranks as the most influential social theorist of all time. The validity of his theories has functioned, therefore, as *something like* the central problem of twentieth-century social science. But on all sides, the "great debate" on Marx has strongly tended to be more ideological than scientific.

—Lee Benson, "Marx's General and Middle-Range
Theories of Social Conflict"

No other theorist has so shaped the course of history as Karl Marx. One might think that his theory, Marxism, would be studied carefully by all students of social science; yet in many countries, Marx's books are banned. In the United States, only a few decades ago, many individuals were punished for reading Marx or for studying or teaching his ideas. The McCarthy era was a period of extreme anti-Marxism in America. So the intellectual power of Marxist theory, an imaginative attempt to explain social change in contemporary society, has often been limited by its political repercussions.

Here we describe Marx and Marxism and then focus on the critical school, a group of outstanding scholars who represent a merging of Marxist and Freudian theories and who have had a particularly important impact on communication study.

THE LIFE AND TIMES OF KARL MARX

Karl Marx (1818–1883) was born in Trier, Germany, in the Moselle River valley, a land of fine vineyards close to the Luxembourg and French borders (Figure 4.1). His sixty-five-year lifetime encompassed the fall of several European kingdoms through violent overthrow, in-

102

Figure 4.1. Karl Marx (1818–1883) While Living in London, at About 60 Years of Age.
Used by permission of Corinne L. Shefner.

cluding the French Revolution of 1848. Marx's theory is directly concerned with revolution. Marx grew up during a period of growing capitalism, expanding factories, and the building of colonial empires by European nations. His life was marked by personal frustration, flight, and tragedy (Boorstin 1983, p. 615). Although his father was a well-off lawyer, Marx sympathized with the poor, depressed, and exploited industrial workers of Europe. Marx's family included a long line of Jewish rabbis, but he became a Lutheran in his youth and an atheist while a university student. Later in life, Marx stated that "religion is the opiate of the masses" (Marx 1867).

Marx studied law at the University of Bonn, but he was not a serious student, spending much of his time drinking and dueling. He finished his law degree at the University of Berlin and became a young Hegelian. George Wilhelm Friedrich Hegel (1770–1831) theorized that society progresses because of wars, revolutions, and other struggles of the oppressed against their oppressors (Ruiz 1979, p. 21). Later, while Marx lived in Cologne and Paris, he was influenced by Ludwig Feuerbach and became anti-Hegelian. Hegel had written mainly about religious struggle, the conflict between spiritual ideas (Ruiz 1979, p. 22). Feuerbach wanted to put Hegel's theories into practice as applied to class struggle and to reject Hegel's idea of royal authority in religious matters. Marx absorbed the Freuerbach perspective on class conflict and made a contemporary application of its somewhat fuzzy ideas. He was clear-headed and precise in advocating an overthrow of the factory owners and government authorities. Out of his endless coffeehouse discussions as a student, Marx was becoming a radical subversive with class struggle as the driving force of his theory.

Karl Marx was "one of the most influential intellectuals of all time" (Westrum, 1991, p. 24). He earned his Ph.D. in philosophy from the University of Jena, specializing in a field then called political economy, which encompassed aspects of sociology, economics, and political science. He was blocked from entering an academic position in a German university due to his outspoken criticism of political leaders and he became active in exposing corrupt government officials and in documenting the conditions of the poor. His socialist politics and his radical writings led to his exile from Germany.

Marx was an excellent writer and became a competent newspaperman. In 1842 he became editor of the *Rheinische Zeitung (Rhenish Gazette)* and converted it into a tool of political journalism, exposing the dreadful living conditions of peasants in the Moselle district. The circulation of his newspaper grew rapidly until the German government shut it down because of its radical nature.

Marx was a strong critic of capitalism, "the finest critic capitalism has had" (Westrum 1991, p. 26). For example, he analyzed factory work life, especially in textile plants, which employed women and children. Marx felt that capitalism separates workers from ownership of the means of production, thus alienating them from themselves, and reducing them to less than full human beings (Westrum 1991, p. 25). Workers thus become powerless in influencing management decisions. Marx advocated a communist society in which every individual would share in ownership and control of the means of production.

In 1843, at twenty-five years of age, Marx converted himself to communism, mainly as a result of reading the history of the French Revolution (Benson 1979, p. 197). Marx was persecuted by the German government for his increasingly radical writings. He married the daughter of a wealthy family and then was exiled to Paris, where he edited a radical magazine. But the German government forced him to move again, pressuring the French government to expel him in 1845. Marx moved to Belgium, where he wrote *The Communist Manifesto* for the Communist League. Finally, in 1849, Marx was exiled again, this time to London, where he lived the last thirty-four years of his life in terrible poverty. Three of his six children died from lack of food and medicine. Marx eked out a bare living through his writing. For a time in 1863, he worked for the *New York Daily Tribune International* as a correspondent, but he refused to seek regular employment. He felt that to do so would allow bourgeois society to turn him into "a money-making machine" (Boorstin 1983, p. 617). Much of his reading, research, and writing was done in the Reading Room of the British Museum, in London, where he read the "blue books" of British factory inspectors, which documented the exploitation of workers of that day (Coser 1977, p. 64). Here too he wrote the three volumes of *Das Kapital*,* which focuses on the sordid conditions of the working class, such as women and children who worked as ragpickers, makers of clay tile, or in factories. They were overworked and underpaid, as was documented by the government inspectors' reports. Marx thrived on criticizing the establishment.

His friend, editor, and coauthor, Friedrich Engels (1820–1895), helped Marx financially. Marx had met Engels while living in Paris. Engels was the son of a rich textile manufacturer in Germany, and his personal contact with working-class misery radicalized him. Engels became an important collaborator and was Marx's coauthor of *The Communist Manifesto* (1848), which they wrote in Paris. The book begins: "A spectre is haunting Europe—the spectre of Communism." It also declares: "Workers of the World, unite!" This book and Marx's *Das Kapital* (1867) bracketed Charles Darwin's *On the Origin of Species* (1859). Marx wanted to dedicate *Das Kapital* to Darwin because he was so influenced by Darwinian evolutionary theory. In fact, Engels called Marx "the Darwin of sociology." Marx took a strictly revolutionary point of view. Conflict and struggle, he said, not peaceful growth and incremental change, were the main engines of social progress. His social conflict theory of change was based on class struggle, the irreconcilable conflicts between the exploitees and the exploiters that is based on individuals' differential access to the means of production (a scarce resource). An evolutionary mechanism drives Marxism.

Marx's theory had little immediate impact until well after his death in 1883. Lenin's Russian Revolution in 1917 marked a turning point in the attention give to Marxism. After that, Marx's writings became "the

---

*The first volume of *Das Kapital* was published in 1867; the other two volumes were prepared by Engels from Marx's notes and published after Marx's death.

working class bible" (Ruiz 1979, p. 34). "Few social theorists have so shaped the course of our world. His theories and concepts have stirred imaginations, started movements, fed revolutions, and spawned novel forms of government and economic systems" (Westrum 1991, p. 24). Karl Marx had a strong underdog complex; he empathized with the downtrodden and sought to bring about social change in a way that was humane. "Marx was able to institutionalize his ideas in powerful social movements that would later found governments and translate his ideas (with major adjustments) into practice" (Westrum 1991, p. 25). Often Marxist-type governments and political parties, however, have been rigidly and systematically brutal and inhumane, all in the name of Marxism. Why this distortion of Marx's ideas? Marx's works represent complex ideas at an abstract level, leaving much to their translation into actual policies, and many of his followers have been inept and inflexible. Further, Marx was a far better critic and analyst of capitalistic societies than he was a constructive planner for the communistic systems that he felt should replace them.

Karl Marx died in London on March 17, 1883, at sixty-five years of age. His body lies in Highgate Cemetery, not far from the grave of Sir Herbert Spencer, that great enthusiast for laissez-faire capitalism. For many decades, streams of visitors from the Soviet Union, Eastern bloc countries, the People's Republic of China, and Cuba paid their respect to Marx's remains. The number of visitors has fallen off sharply in recent years, however, as the European communist nations rejected Marxist philosophy.

WHAT IS MARXISM?

In this book we are talking about intellectual Marxism rather than about the political Marxism that was implemented in the form of socialist governments in various nations like the Soviet Union, the People's Republic of China, and Cuba. These countries' actual policies deviated widely from Karl Marx's intellectual theory. This distinction between intellectual and political Marxism has not always been kept clear, even by social scientists, a confusion that has limited the study of Marxist thought.

Central to Marx's theory of historical materialism are such concepts as the proletariat, socialism, communism, class struggle, the dictatorship of the proletariat, and *alienation,* the degree to which individuals are dominated by forces of their own creation that confront them as alien powers (Seaman 1959; Mutz 1987). Marx's lifetime coincided with the industrialization of Europe, characterized by increasing control of humanity over nature, by *efficacy* (the perceived ability of an individual to exert control over one's future), and by internal control. It is natural that Marx identified alienation as a key concept in his theoretical apparatus.

Marxism is the belief that material conditions like economic forces determine social change in society. Marxism is also called historical materialism, because it rests on a historical analysis of materialism (that is, of the economy) and is based on economic determinism. Historical materialism is the name given to Marx's doctrine of the evolution of human society, which is driven by the development of material goods (Ruiz 1979, p. 150). Increasing human control over nature, such as the growth of factory power and industrial production, leads to the development of productive forces and to the change from a slave society to a feudal system to a capitalistic society to socialism to communism.

According to Marx, the suppression of social classes and the transition to a classless and stateless system is brought about by the dictatorship of the proletariat, which is a temporary situation. Socialism is the doctrine that the struggle for the equal distribution of wealth can be achieved by eliminating private property and the exploitive ruling class and replacing it with public ownership (Ruiz 1979, p. 152). Communism is the stage of historical materialism following socialism when social classes cease to exist. The goal of socioeconomic equality was implied in Marx's famous sentence, written in 1875: "From each according to his ability, to each according to his needs." True communism, based on the doctrine of historical materialism of Marx and Engels, does not exist in the sense that class struggle has not ended in "communist" nations like China and Cuba. Despite their self-identification as communist, these nations are actually socialist in nature.

"Why study human behavior? According to Karl Marx, in order to change the world. Still more precisely, to develop theories useful to human beings struggling to create a better world" (Benson 1979, p. 189). Marx offered a macro-level theory of social change that he hoped would lead to a more egalitarian society. Marxism explains social change at the societal level, and not just through the aggregation of individual-level changes. Thus, Marxism is at the macro, rather than at the micro, level of analysis. In that sense, it is more sociological in nature rather than social-psychological. Marxists believe that society is in need of major social change. This pessimistic and radical viewpoint puts them on the left-hand side of the continuum of political beliefs.

Marx proposed a basic theoretical proposition: "In any society un-equal access to basic resources needed to sustain life invariably creates a culture that engenders significant social conflict of some type" (Benson 1979, p. 191). Note the normative ideology implied in this proposition: that inequality and social conflict are undesirable. Implied here also is the critical nature of Marxism—that society is imperfect and ought to be changed. Further, one can detect implications of Darwinian natural se-lection and the struggle for existence as important elements of Marxist theory.

Social class differences, which result from the mode of production, cause unequal access to resources in a system. Marx believed that the proletariat, the social class who survive by means of selling its labor, originated with the industrial revolution in England. He said that the proletariat, composed of industrial factory workers, which capitalistic society needs in large numbers, function as the universal social class. By uniting, the proletariat could gain the power needed to change society (Benson 1979, p. 199). Such unification depends on the proletariat's forming a class consciousness, that is, a self-identification as having a common role in society. Marx kept hoping for the coming revolution, but it never came. He argued that industrial workers were not develop-ing a proletarian class consciousness because the capitalistic bourgeoisie controlled the means of mental production (like the arts and the mass media) in society, thus creating a false consciousness among the prole-tariat. Marxists believe that the mass media belong to the superstructure of society, and that mass media content is dominated by social class relationships. The media reinforce the dominant values of society and are mainly antirevolutionary and antichange. Thus the mass media are often criticized by Marxists and by neo-Marxists, including the critical school of communication.

THE CRITICAL SCHOOL

The critical school, also known as the Frankfurt school and as the Insti-tute for Social Research, is an intellectual combining of Marxist and Freudian theories (Figure 4.2). The original, official name of this unique theory group was the Institute for Social Research, which was estab-lished in Frankfurt, Germany, in 1923. The Frankfurt school was the name given to them by others in the 1960s, after the school had passed its intellectual peak. They generally preferred to be called critical theorists, a name coined by their leader, Max Horkheimer, who became director

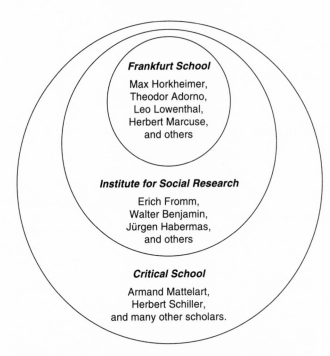

Frankfurt School

Max Horkheimer,
Theodor Adorno,
Leo Lowenthal,
Herbert Marcuse,
and others

Institute for Social Research

Erich Fromm,
Walter Benjamin,
Jürgen Habermas,
and others

Critical School

Armand Mattelart,
Herbert Schiller,
and many other scholars.

Figure 4.2. Key members of the Frankfurt School, the Institute for Social Research, and the Critical School.

of the Institute for Social Research in 1930, in his article, *"Traditionelle und Kritische Theorie"* (1937). Critical theory is Horkheimer's conception of Marxism; the phrase derives from the conventional description of Marxism as the critique of political economy and of capitalism.

"Critical school" is a name that applies not only to the dozen or so important intellectuals originally affiliated with the Frankfurt school but also to hundreds of other contemporary scholars who consider themselves intellectual descendants of the original Frankfurt scholars or at least fairly closely related to them in their thinking (Figure 4.2). A question might be raised as to whether critical scholars today are coherent enough to be considered a single school of thought, but we here follow the common convention of calling them the critical school, while acknowledging that neither the critical school today, nor the Frankfurt school of the 1930s and 1940s, represent a unified theoretical enterprise.

TABLE 4.1
Major Events in the History of the Critical School

Date	Event
1923	The *Institut für Sozialforschung* is established in Frankfurt, Germany, affiliates with the University of Frankfurt, and is directed by Carl Grünberg. The institute is financed by an endowment from Herman Weil, a wealthy German grain merchant who imported wheat from Argentina, through his Marxist son, Dr. Felix Weil.
1930	Max Horkheimer becomes director of the *Institut für Sozialforschung,* and its theoretical program is now called "materialism." The institute's affiliation with the University of Frankfurt is changed by Horkheimer from the Faculty of Economics to the Faculty of Philosophy. The institute begins to shift from an emphasis on history to a focus on social psychology with an increasing influence of Freudian psychoanalytic theory, introduced by Erich Fromm.
	Adolf Hitler comes to power in Germany, posing a threat to the institute whose scholars are Jews and socialists.
1932	The *Journal for Social Research* begins publication, and the institute shifts to publishing lengthy articles by its members instead of books.
1933	The institute is closed by the Nazi government of Germany, and the institute's scholars scatter to Geneva, Paris, London, and the United States.
1934	The Institute for Social Research affiliates with Columbia University, through the assistance of Paul F. Lazarsfeld and Robert Lynd, and locates at 429 West 117th Street in New York.
1937	Horkheimer provides a name for the critical school in his article "*Traditionelle und Kritische Theorie.*"
1938	Theodor Adorno escapes Hitler's Nazism by joining Lazarsfeld's Radio Research Project in Newark, New Jersey, but this attempted collaboration of empirical and critical scholars in radio music research ends unsuccessfully.
Early 1940s	Several scholars from the institute disperse to Washington, D.C., for wartime work with the Office of War Information, the Office of Secret Services, and other federal agencies. Horkheimer and Adorno move to Los Angeles in 1941, in part for health reasons, and the institute moves with them.
1950	Theodor Adorno and others publish *The Authoritarian Personality*, a large-scale survey of prejudice funded by the American Jewish Committee, and conducted in collaboration with psychologists at the University of California at Berkeley.

TABLE 4.1
Major Events in the History of the Critical School (*Cont.*)

Date	Event
	The Institute for Social Research is reestablished in Frankfurt, affiliated with the Johann-Wolfgang-Goethe University, and is directed by Max Horkheimer until his retirement in 1958 and then by Theodor Adorno until his death in 1969.
1960s	The critical perspective gradually becomes more widely popular among scholars in the United States and Europe, in part as the result of books like Herbert Marcuse's *One Dimensional Man* (1960) and *Dialectic of Enlightenment* (1949). The 1960 student movement develops a cultlike following of the critical school, to the latter's dismay.
Today	Jürgen Habermas is the leading critical scholar in Germany. In Latin America, Armand Mattelart (a Belgian who taught at a Chilean university for several years until 1973 and now is at the University of Paris) is the best-known critical scholar.

The major events in the history of the critical school are listed in Table 4.1. There are dozens of books and hundreds of articles about the school, but the most authoritative account is Martin Jay's *The Dialectical Imagination* (1973), written when "the main figures were alive and available for interviews, and correspondence and their private papers were not lost or dispersed, while they were old enough not to mind use being made of them" (Quinton 1974).

The Frankfurt School

The Frankfurt school concentrated on Marx, Freud, and avant-garde art and literature. The Frankfurt critical scholars were neo-Marxists, who were "driven from orthodox, Moscow-defined Marxism by the degradation of Stalinist tyranny, its ossification of thought, its enslavement of art and literature to propaganda, its maniacal vilification of everything in contemporary culture, Freud to surrealism, that was not an obvious instrument for the immediate purposes of Russian state powers" (Quinton 1974). Thus their ideology was left-Marxist, but it was also Freudian, philosophical, literary, humanistic, and intellectual.

These scholars were mainly trained in philosophy, and so they did not emphasize empirical data gathering, but it is an oversimplification to consider them as nonempirical or antiempirical. Rather, they observed the parts of society that they were critiquing and drew heavily on the history of their objects of study. On several occasions they conducted surveys, as in their investigation of working-class family and authority attitudes in Germany, Austria, and Switzerland in the early 1930s. On rare occasions, they utilized quantitative-type attitude scales, as in Adorno and others' *Authoritarian Personality* (1950).

The key figures in the Frankfurt school—Horkheimer, Adorno, Marcuse, and Leo Lowenthal—were truly outstanding intellectuals. In addition to their high level of academic quality, they were unique in the degree to which they collaborated with each other in their scholarly work. They wrote, critiqued each others' essays closely (although not harmoniously), and published them after extensive and repeated revisions in their journal. Dialogue among them was an important factor in the intellectual performance of the school. Their integration was aided by the institute's lack of affiliation with a single university department or discipline and its emphasis on scholarly research rather than university teaching (Jay 1988, p. 234).

The critical theorists enjoyed an unimpeded freedom of thought and expression, first in Germany's Weimar Republic, and then, after Hitler's takeover in 1933, in the United States (Quinton 1974).* Not only did the Frankfurt school have political freedom, but they also had economic independence, thanks to the generous endowment provided by the millionaire grain merchant Herman Weil. Thus, the critical theorists were free to act as a kind of conscience of society, to champion unpopular causes, and to oppose powerful establishment forces. Almost all of the Frankfurt scholars were able to escape Hitler's clutches (Adorno waited too long and barely made it, and Walter Benjamin committed suicide at the French-Spanish border, thinking that he could not escape).† The Frankfurt scholars were able to move their endowment from Frankfurt

---

*Hitler tightened his grip on Jews in Germany gradually. In spring 1933, he dismissed all Jews from university positions. On May 10, 1938, mass book burning occurred in which volumes by Jewish authors and by radical writers were destroyed. In 1938, after the *Kristallnacht* (Crystal Night) destruction of Jewish-owned stores, it became increasingly difficult for Jews to migrate from Germany.

†Benjamin committed suicide at the age of forty-eight, in September 1940. While fleeing German-occupied France, he was turned back at the border with Spain because of a technical hitch with his migration papers. That night he took his own life. The next morning the other refugees in Benjamin's party were allowed by the authorities to cross the frontier to freedom.

to the United States, although it eventually became insufficient to support them in New York.*

The fundamental doctrine of the Frankfurt school consisted of critiquing: (1) positivism (the belief that real, "positive" facts can be obtained from observation and experiments), claiming that social science is a form of false consciousness, which "endorses the status quo under a misleading veil of value-neutrality" (Quinton 1974), (2) Marxism for an insufficient emancipation from positivism and for thinking that "the proletariat will inevitably bring about a revolution that will eliminate alienation and dominance" (Quinton 1974), and (3) society for its irrationality in lulling individuals into a false acceptance of their conditions. The critical school seeks to bring the basic contradictions of capitalistic society to consciousness. Thus, the activities of critical theorists are intended to lead to an ideal society without human exploitation. In this, they reflect the normative position of Marxist theory.

Cynical observers referred to the Institute for Social Research as "Café Max" during its Manhattan sojourn—that is, Café Marx without the "r," in honor of its director, Max Horkheimer.† They claimed that the Frankfurt scholars were losing their Marxist orientation. It was indeed paradoxical that this gathering of Marxist scholars would relocate in New York City, an even greater world center of capitalism than Frankfurt. Perhaps this paradox explains, in part, why the Institute for Social Research strongly resisted integration with American culture during its sojourn. For example, the institute continued to publish its journal in German, though very few of its potential readers during World War II could read this language. The Frankfurt scholars regarded New York as only their temporary home, although they stayed for seventeen years in America.

---

*The Institute for Social Research had invested its endowment unwisely and was in a difficult financial situation after arriving in New York. Several members of the institute left Morningside Heights in 1942 to join the World War II effort in Washington. Max Horkheimer made contact with the American Jewish Committee in 1942 and directed a research program on studies in prejudice. One of the projects was the *Authoritarian Personality* study, carried out by Adorno and his Berkeley colleagues. Max Horkeimer should be credited with maintaining the institute during its sojourn in the United States. As Shils (1970, p. 776) remarked, the Frankfurt school is not just the story of a cat that landed on its feet in Germany, the United States, and again in Germany, but also of a shrewd administration.

†Critics of the institute also called it *"Grand Hotel Abgrund"* (Grand Hotel Abyss) in English (Heilbut 1983, p. 85). Another critic, Lubasz (1975), said, "Marxism is bourgeois theory about proletarian practice."

Who Were the Frankfurt Scholars?

The key figures in the Frankfurt school were the sons of Jewish upper-middle-class families. Their fathers were successful capitalists: Max Horkheimer's father was a prominent manufacturer, Adorno's was a wine merchant, and Leo Lowenthal's was a medical doctor. Their parents' affluence allowed the future Frankfurt scholars to enjoy an excellent formal education. The Frankfurter's parents typically pressured their sons to follow their fathers in the family business, an occupational commitment that the sons rejected. The sons also turned from their parents' capitalism to Marxism. Judaism in Nazi Germany was an alienating experience and made the Frankfurt scholars particularly conscious of prejudice and of anti-Semitism as a basis for authoritarianism (a topic that they investigated). Perhaps their Jewishness helped them identify with other objects of prejudice and more generally with the underdogs of society.

Of the key scholars in the Frankfurt school, only Max Horkheimer was a member when the Institute for Social Research officially began in 1923. Leo Lowenthal joined the institute in 1926, Theodor Adorno in 1928, and Herbert Marcuse in 1933. The school's central interests changed with the addition of new members. With Adorno came a focus on music, and with Lowenthal an analysis of literature. Later, Erich Fromm, who had a psychoanalytic practice (although he was not trained as a medical doctor), brought an interest in Freudian theory, as did Herbert Marcuse. The Frankfurt school was unique in bringing the theories of Marx and Freud together. No other group of academics had tried to do so. The two radically contrasting theories would not seem to mix, but they did at the hands of the Frankfurt scholars.

Several of the Frankfurter scholars were not trained as social scientists during their formal education, although they identified themselves as doing social research. Max Horkheimer (1895–1971) earned his doctorate in philosophy with a dissertation on Kant and taught philosophy at the University of Frankfurt as an assistant professor prior to joining the Institute for Social Research. Theodor Adorno (1903–1969) also earned his doctorate in philosophy and studied music in Vienna as a member of Arnold Schoenberg's circle of avant-garde musicians. Adorno was described as "the most pyrotechnically highbrow and, it must be said, unintelligible of the [Frankfurt school]" (Quinton 1974). Adorno displayed an abrasive personality and a tortuous writing style. During the years that he lived in America, he imperiously held to his European life-style. He wrote diatribes against jazz and held forth on the superiority of "serious music" (which to Adorno was not necessarily classical music; rather it was music that made an individual think seriously).

Leo Lowenthal (born in 1900) received a Ph.D. degree in philosophy, although he also studied literature, history, and sociology. Eric Fromm (1900–1980) received an intensive Jewish religious education, in keeping with his family name (*fromm* means "pious") (Burston, 1991). He studied philosophical anthropology, specializing in the study of religion, and earned his Ph.D. degree in sociology from the University of Heidelberg at age twenty-two. He then became interested in psychoanalysis. "Of the psychoanalysts who have contributed both to clinical and social psychology and the psychoanalytic movement, Erich Fromm was, for a time, among the most popular and prolific. His books, *Escape from Freedom* (1941), *The Sane Society* (1955), *The Art of Loving* (1956), and *Zen Buddhism and Psychoanalysis* (1960), were all best-sellers, commanding a wide and attentive audience. . . . His impact and relevance to the humanities and social sciences in the 1950's, 1960's, and 1970's is second to none" among psychoanalytic authors (Burston 1991). These popular books of Fromm's were written after he severed connections with the Institute for Social Research in 1938.

Combining Marxism with Freudian Theory

When the Frankfurt school began in the 1920s, the idea of combining Marxism with Freudianism seemed bizarre. The one country following a Marxist philosophy of government at that time, the Soviet Union, made Freudian thinking unwelcome. Moreover, Freud's pessimism about social change seemed irreconcilable with Marx's revolutionary thought (Jay 1973). While the Institute for Social Research was Marxist from the beginning, the Frankfurters' scholarly interest in psychoanalytic theory grew only slowly. The institute's first seven years, until Max Horkheimer became director in 1930, was mainly an era of orthodox Marxism. Leo Lowenthal, who joined the institute in 1926, underwent psychoanalysis and encouraged Horkheimer to do the same. He did, beginning in 1929, under Karl Landauer, a student of Freud (Held 1980). Horkheimer aided the establishment of an institute for Freudian psychoanalysis at the University of Frankfurt, directed by Landauer. The Institute for Social Research at Frankfurt had a loose relationship with this new Freudian institute, and soon, Erich Fromm, one of its key members, joined the Institute for Social Research.

World events contributed to the Frankfurt school's gradual shift away from its Marxist orientation. Hitler's takeover of the Weimar Republic in 1933, put an end to the Socialist party in Germany and to the hope for a socialist revolution. Then the Non-Aggression Pact of August 22, 1939, between Hitler and Stalin (leading to the invasion of Poland) marked the end of Marxist ideology in Russian communism (which had begun with the 1917 Russian revolution). Eventually the Frankfurt scholars became neo-Marxists, critical of classical Marxism.

As they became gradually disenchanted with orthodox Marxist analysis, they increasingly adopted Freudian theory, supplementing the macro level of Marxist explanations of social change with the micro level of Freudian social psychology of the individual. Erich Fromm was a dedicated Marxist, but he felt that Marx's framework was incomplete; he maintained that Freud's perspective also needed fleshing out. Freud accepted social structure as a given. Marx left psychological factors out of his explanation of economic factors as determinants of social structures. Fromm thought that family socialization of the individual was an important psychological agency in society and that even adult socialization was important as a means of social change.

Erich Fromm was particularly critical of certain aspects of Freudian theory. For example, he rejected Freud's interpretation of the Oedipus complex, claiming that the complex occurred only in patriarchal societies. This critique is a Marxist kind of viewpoint—that a social analysis should be limited to a specific historical and cultural context and that wider generalization is dangerous. Around 1938, Fromm dropped out of the Frankfurt band of scholars to migrate to America. When he struck off on his own, he was attacked by Horkheimer and Adorno in their writings. Although Freudian theory was somewhat deemphasized by the Frankfurt scholars during the 1940s, their research on authority and the family continued, eventually leading to Adorno and others' important book, *The Authoritarian Personality*, reporting a classic social science study.

Authoritarianism, Fascism, and Anti-Semitism

Given their treatment by German Nazism, it is understandable that the Frankfurt scholars became interested in the roots of Fascism. Their explanation of the causes of Fascism drew upon both Marxism and psychoanalytic theory. They argued that competitive capitalism was replaced with Fascist-style monopoly capitalism in order to deal with the crisis of capitalism, reflected by the worldwide economic depression of the early 1930s. The Frankfurt scholars adapted the Freudian criticism of civilization as a repression of human instincts, arguing that Fascist oppression was a function of the authoritarian personality, which arose because the bourgeois family–inculcated authoritarianism as a means of preserving the structure of the existing society in the face of the economic crisis.

A lengthy trail of intellectual influences led up to *The Authoritarian Personality* project in America in the 1940s. Around 1930, Wilhelm Reich, a Freudian psychoanalysts and Marxist, observed that sexual repression contributed to fascism. After moving to Berlin, where he personally experienced Hitler's rise to power, he traced the roots of fascism to the character structure of lower-middle class and working-class Germans (Samelson 1986).

Erich Fromm, also a psychoanalyst-turned-Marxist and an acquaintance of Reich, next took up the study of authoritarianism. Fromm and his colleagues in the Frankfurt Institute for Social Research carried out a survey of 1,150 blue-collar and white-collar workers in Germany, Austria, and Switzerland in 1929 and 1930, shortly before Hitler came to power. The personal interviews were transcribed and then psychoanalyzed (a unique use of psychoanalysis, which was to be used in a similar way in the United States study of the authoritarian personality). The theoretical framework for the European study, and certain of its results (such as that repressed individuals, trained by authoritarian parents, were later attracted to fascism), were reported in Horkheimer's *Studien Über Autorität und Familie* (*Studies on Authority and the Family*) (1936) and by Erich Fromm in his noted book *Escape from Freedom* (1941). This European research on authoritarianism led to *The Authoritarian Personality*, a large-scale empirical study of prejudice in the United States.

Anti-Semitism was not an important part of the 1929–1930 survey research in Europe—Hitler's persecution of the Jews had not yet begun—but it was central to *The Authoritarian Personality* study. Class consciousness dropped out of sight as a factor in the American study of authoritarianism. "Reich's original problem had been transformed to fit a liberal, empiricist, individual-psychology framework" (Samelson 1986). The American counterpart study to the European *Studies in Authority and the Family* was a hybrid product of Adorno's critical theory (combining Marxism and psychoanalytic theory) and American-style quantitative psychology (represented by Adorno's University of California at Berkeley coauthors Daniel Levinson, R. Nevitt Sanford, and Else Frenkel-Brunswik). All four coauthors were psychoanalytically inclined. Just how these four scholars came together to carry out the most widely known study of prejudice is a tale of accident and opportunity.

The Authoritarian Personality

Data gathering for *The Authoritarian Personality* research began in 1943, when Nevitt Sanford, a psychologist at the University of California at Berkeley, was asked by the university's provost if he could use $500 from an anonymous donor for a study of anti-Semitism. Sanford accepted the funding, hired Daniel Levinson, one of his doctoral students, and soon invited Else Frenkel-Brunswik, a psychologist in Berkeley's Institute of Child Welfare (today, known as the Institute for Human Development), to join the project. Later, Max Horkheimer became interested in the Berkeley research and obtained more adequate funding (about $40,000 per year for three years, 1945–1948) through the American Jewish Committee for a series of research projects on Studies in Prejudice.* Horkheimer suggested that Theodor Adorno join the research team in Berkeley, so Adorno commuted to the Berkeley project staff meetings once every few weeks from Los Angeles, where he was then living.

Few books with multiple authors are truly collaborative, but *The Authoritarian Personality* seems to have been. Three of the four authors were Jews, and the fourth, Nevitt Sanford, was a southern Protestant. Undoubtedly their backgrounds affected the nature of their research. Freudian influences come into *The Authoritarian Personality* study in several different ways. Sanford had studied with Henry Murray, a psychologist who had introduced psychoanalysis at Harvard University. Then Sanford took a psychoanalysis training course from Hans Sachs, one of Freud's colleagues (Sanford 1986). When Sanford began teaching in the psychology department at Berkeley in 1940, he maintained a part-time psychoanalytic practice, seeing his patients early in the morning and in the late afternoon (Sanford 1986).

Else Frenkel-Brunswik had been psychoanalyzed too but combined a

*Another important book in this series was Leo Lowenthal's *Prophets of Deceit* (1940), a study of German propaganda.

Freudian orientation with a quantitative psychological bent. Frenkel-Brunswik (1908–1958), a Central European, had studied for her doctorate in psychology with Karl Bühler at the University of Vienna. She continued at the university in a research position, while undergoing psychoanalysis, until the Nazi takeover of Austria in 1938 forced Frenkel-Brunswik and her husband, Egon Brunswik, to migrate to the United States (Levinson 1990). Under the neopotism rules of the day, his faculty appointment in psychology at Berkeley ruled out a tenure-track position for her, so Else Frenkel-Brunswik was employed in a research job at the Berkeley Institute of Child Welfare (Smith 1990, p. 89). In 1943, she joined Sanford, Levinson, and Adorno in the authoritarian personality study.

Theodor Adorno "was a most stimulating intellectual companion. He had what seemed to us a profound grasp of psychoanalytic theory, complete familiarity with the ins and outs of German Fascism, and, not least, a boundless supply of off-color jokes. He was very helpful when it came to thinking of items for the F [Fascism] scale" (Sanford 1986). Thomas Mann, the German refugee intellectual who lived near Adorno in Los Angeles in the early 1940s, described the critical theorist in these terms: "Adorno . . . is a person of similar [to his cousin Walter Benjamin] mental cast, uncompromising, tragically brilliant, operating on the highest level. Having grown up in an atmosphere entirely dominated by theory (political theory as well) and artistic, primarily musical, interests, he studied philosophy and music. . . . All his life this man of remarkable intellect has refused to choose between the professions of philosophy and music. He felt that he was actually pursuing the same thing in both divergent realms. His dialectic turn of mind and bent toward social history is interlinked with a passion for music" (Mann 1961, pp. 38–39).

Daniel Levinson was a doctoral student in psychology at Berkeley and had taken a course with a psychoanalytic perspective from Nevitt Sanford. Thus, all four coauthors of *The Authoritarian Personality* had a Freudian viewpoint, in addition to their individual skills in quantitative psychological methods, and to Adorno's critical-Marxist orientation.

The four scholars asked themselves whether individuals prejudiced against Jews were also prejudiced against other out-groups. They constructed the E (ethnocentrism) scale in order to find out. Then the scholars wondered whether the deep emotional needs causing prejudice were expressed in other ways—hence the F (fascism) scale (Sanford 1986). Typical scale items on the five-point Likert-type (strongly agree, agree, undecided, disagree, strongly disagree) E and F scales were:

1. One trouble with Jewish businessmen is that they stick to-gether and prevent other people from having a fair chance in competition (E).
2. The worst danger to real Americanism during the last 50 years has come from foreign ideas and agitators (E).
3. Obedience and respect for authority are the most important virtues children should learn (F).
4. An insult to our honor should always be punished (F).

They found that these scales were so highly interrelated that they concluded that anti-Semitism, ethnocentrism, and fascism together were parts of a general character structure that they called "authoritarian." In a review of the book, Brewster Smith (1950) stated: "The California investigators, to put it figuratively, set out to track a jackal and found themselves at grips with behemoth." The timing of their study added to its social significance: Hitler's persecution of the Jews in Europe had brought the issue of anti-Semitism to prominence. With the discovery of Hitler's concentration camps, the horror of the Holocaust became apparent to America. McCarthyism was waiting in the wings in the United States, a country that seemed to be turning toward a totalitarian state. Yet anti-Semitism had not been studied much by social psychologists.

The authoritarian personality that the Berkeley investigators identified is weak and dependent but seeks to maintain law and order by enforcing a punitive, conventional morality. The authoritarian individual thinks in stereotyped categories and feels strongly prejudiced against out-groups of all kinds. The individual's underlying self-attitudes of weakness and self-contempt lead to an "embittered struggle to prove to himself and others that he really belongs to the strong and good" (Smith 1950).

The data for the study came mainly from 2,099 respondents—Berkeley students, psychiatric patients in San Francisco, prison inmates at San Quentin, Lions and Rotary Club members, and a variety of other groups—who filled out the E and F scale questionnaires and provided other data about themselves. The sample, while large and diverse, was not representative of the U.S. population. Then the Berkeley scholars selected eighty respondents from their thousands of survey respondents who scored highest and lowest on the E scale and carried out open-ended personal interviews with them. Questions were asked about occupation, income, religion, politics, attitudes toward minorities, and race. The interview protocols were then scored for ethnocentrism, and a blind analysis was made to predict whether each respondent was in the high or low ethnocentrism category on the basis of the E scores. The two measures (the open-ended interview versus the attitude scale of ethnocentrism) agreed in 85 percent of the cases. The eighty high-low ethnocentrism individuals were also asked to respond to the TAT (Thematic Apperception Test) projective technique, and these data were then analyzed for indications of prejudice. Finally, in-depth case studies of two men, one high and one low in ethnocentrism, were conducted with psychoanalytic techniques.

In all, *The Authoritarian Personality* represented a triangulation of survey, clinical, and projective methods, as well as a hybrid of psychometric and psychoanalytic perspectives. The 1,000-page volume that resulted was "a physical landmark in the library shelves" (Smith 1950) and a formidable demonstration of Freudian-Marxism thinking applied to an important problem of the day, prejudice.

Prior to 1950, the study of prejudice was not fashionable among psychologists in America. *The Authoritarian Personality* set off a tremendous volume of research. In the three decades from 1950 to 1980, the F scale was utilized in published studies involving 30,000 American respondents plus 15,000 respondents in twenty-three other nations (Sanford 1986). By any indicator, *The Authoritarian Personality* was a very important study, and it is certainly the best-known work by any member of the Frankfurt school. Missing from this important study, unfortunately, was investigation of how individuals became prejudiced. Such inquiry would have focused the study more on a sociological, and communication, perspective. A number of communication studies in the 1960s, however, utilized Rokeach's dogmatism scale* as an intervening variable determining the degree to which individuals were affected by a communication message in a persuasion experiment.

A Return to Frankfurt and to Freud

The Frankfurt school returned to focusing on Freud after the reestablishment of the Institute for Social Research in Germany in 1950 by Horkheimer and Adorno. The institute's reinterest in psychoanalytic

---

*Milton Rokeach, who earned his Ph.D. in psychology at the University of California and worked as a research assistant on the *Authoritarian Personality* project, developed a dogmatism scale to measure closed-mindedness (Rokeach 1960). He argued that a possible leftist political bias might be represented by the Adorno scales in that a left-liberal individual can be just as prejudiced as a right-conservative.

theory was led by Herbert Marcuse, who had joined the institute in 1932 but whose major works appeared in the 1950s and 1960s. Like the other Frankfurt scholars, Marcuse (born in 1898) was the son of a prosperous Jewish family who earned his doctorate in philosophy. He became dissatisfied with Marxism in the late 1930s, due to the Spanish Civil War and to Stalin's purges in the Soviet Union, and became a neo-Freudian (Jay 1973). After a long incubation period, Marcuse's (1955) important book, *Eros and Civilization,* was published. This volume built on Freud's concepts of the life instinct (eros) and the death instinct (thanatos) to set them in a socioeconomic context. Marcuse argued that under certain material conditions, the individual could be freed from sexual repression and from the death instinct, so that an unrestrained life instinct would prevail. Marcuse's (1964) other important book, *One-Dimensional Man,* made him a cult figure in the 1960s student movement in the United States and Europe.

The post–World War II Frankfurt school mainly criticized late capitalism for its manipulation of people's minds by mass media advertising so that they would desire consumer products and so that they lost their critical and protesting line of thought (Quinton 1974). But when the 1960s student movement did protest against the establishment, the Frankfurt critical scholars were dismayed by the infantile destructiveness of student radicalism.

During recent decades, the Institute for Social Research at Goëthe University in Frankfurt has gradually faded in intellectual importance. As the original set of Frankfurt scholars retired or died, the intellectual force of critical theory spread out, attracting many scholars in different nations to adopt a critical perspective. Thus a widespread coterie of critical scholars rose.

The Critical School versus the Empirical School of Communication Research

Critical scholars and empirical scholars see the role of mass communication in society quite differently. Critical scholars think that the mass media are used by the establishment to control society, while empirical scholars see the media as able to help ameliorate social problems in society and as leading to incremental social change. Crucial issues to critical scholars are who owns and controls the mass media, a macro view. Empirical scholars are mainly concerned with the effects of the media on individual audience members, a micro view.

Critical scholars were strongly anti-Fascist prior to and during World War II; hence, their scholarly interests naturally turned to propaganda, prejudice, and other topics related to the rise of Hitler. Most contemporary critical scholars are not Marxists but may be somewhat leftist in their general orientation. Certainly they question society's status quo and often oppose the establishment.

For historical reasons tracing to their 1930s beginnings in Germany, critical scholars are generally anti-positivism, and many are oriented to philosophy. They are critical of empirical data, although such data were used in *The Authoritarian Personality* and also, after 1950, when the Institute for Social Research returned to Frankfurt. In fact, the post-1950 institute was influential in introducing American social research methods to European scholars.

Critical scholars focus on emancipation. They ask: Who gains and who loses from social research? Regarding mass communication and society (Heilbut 1983, p. 128), they look for the ways in which the media alienate individuals and commercialize popular culture. Some critical scholars engage in literary criticism, sometimes combining it with content analysis. One of the best-known examples is Leo Lowenthal's (1944) study of magazine articles about celebrities that appeared in *Collier's* in 1901 and in the *Saturday Evening Post* in 1941. Lowenthal showed that a change occurred from heroes of production to heroes of consumption during this forty-year period of American history (Heilbut 1983, pp. 128–130).

One critical scholar who believed in the consciousness-raising capability of the media was Walter Benjamin (1892–1940). Born into a family of wealthy German Jews, Benjamin received an excellent education and was a brilliant scholar. A friend of Theodor Adorno, he had a lengthy association with the Institute for Social Research, publishing in their journal and receiving a stipend from the institute's endowment. After an unfortunate association with German academia, Benjamin moved to Paris. His friendship with Bertolt Brecht led to a belief in the revolutionary potential of popular art, expressed in *Understanding Brecht* (Benjamin 1966). When Hitler's panzers invaded France in 1940, Benjamin delayed his escape despite desperate pleas from his Frankfurt school colleagues in New York. He almost reached freedom.

The opposing theoretical perspectives of critical and empirical scholars today often bring them into sharp conflict. In fact, the critical-empirical split is the strongest cleavage within the field of communication today.

CRITICAL THEORY TODAY

What is the status of the critical school today? The answer is different in Europe, in North America, and in Latin America. In the renewed Frankfurt school of recent decades, Jürgen Habermas and his student Albrecht Wellmer became the leading figures. Habermas received his doctorate in 1954 from the University of Bonn and then joined the Institute for Social Research at Frankfurt from 1956 to 1961. After various academic appointments, Habermas returned to the Institute for Social Research in 1983 as its director. He is also a professor of philosophy at the University of Frankfurt. Habermas is a grand theorist, operating at a high level of abstraction, who rejects positivism and emphasizes materialism. He wants communication to be emancipatory and free from exploitation in its effects. His books, available in English translation, are very difficult reading. In Europe, the former intellectual vigor of the Frankfurt school is gone. However, there are several hundred critical scholars of communication today, and several critical communication journals are published in Europe.

In North America, several centers of critical scholarship exist, for example, at the University of Illinois, the University of Iowa, and the University of California at San Diego. Several hundred critical communication scholars in the United States belong to a professional association, the Society for Democratic Communication. There are no U.S. journals specializing in critical theory, though one communication journal has "critical studies" in its name.

In Latin America, many communication scholars are interested in critical theory. The widely read book by Ariel Dorfman and Armand Mattelart, *How to Read Donald Duck: Imperialist Ideology in the Disney Comic* (1975), was originally published in Spanish in 1971. These critical scholars content-analyzed Walt Disney's Donald Duck comic strip as it appeared in Latin American newspapers, finding that these comics contain subtle themes of U.S. imperialism toward Third World nations. Dorfman and Mattelart concluded from their study that the staff of Disney Studios had imperialistic motivations. Dorfman and Mattelart assumed that the comics had effects on their readers in Latin America, an assumption that could have been tested by gathering data about effects from the comics' readers (Rogers 1985, p. 226).

The field of communication in Latin America is a hybrid, strongly flavored by both European critical scholarship and by North American empirical approaches (Chaffee, Gomaz-Palacio, and Rogers 1990). This hybrid flourishes particularly in Mexico and in Brazil, countries in which the university teaching of communication is particularly well established. For instance, Brazil in 1992 had 30,000 students enrolled in eighty university-level communication departments (see Chapter 12).

CONTRIBUTIONS OF MARX AND THE CRITICAL SCHOOL TO COMMUNICATION STUDY

Marxism and its latter-day theory group of critical scholars can serve as a source of ideas and concepts for empirical scholars (Rosengren, 1983). Critical scholars focus on issues of ownership and control of the mass media, topics that escaped the scholarly interests of empirical investigators like Paul F. Lazarsfeld, who instead took the communication field in the direction of investigating communication effects. The emphasis of critical scholars on the poor, disadvantaged, and weaker sectors of society could have a conscious-raising influence on noncritical scholars. The tension between critical and empirical communication scholars in America poses a fruitful intellectual challenge; however, the conflict prevents the interesting leads for communication study provided by the critical scholars from being investigated with the research methods and resources of the empirical school.

PART II

THE GROWTH OF COMMUNICATION STUDY IN AMERICA

The U.S. beginnings of communication study were a direct outgrowth of the field's European origins. The transfer of academic ideas across the Atlantic was greatly speeded up around 1930 by the rise of Hitler.

THE INTELLECTUAL MIGRATION
FROM EUROPE TO AMERICA

Americans today think of their universities as the best in the world, a nationalistic perception supported by such indicators as the number of American Nobel Prize winners* and the dominant number of American authors of scientific journal articles. Certainly Americans have been first in a number of spectacular scientific achievements, such as building the atomic bomb in the 1940s and putting a person on the moon in the 1960s.

It is easy for Americans today to forget that most American universities were not even founded until about a hundred years ago (although Harvard goes back to 1636), while several European universities—Cambridge, Oxford, and Paris, among others—have existed for over six hundred years. Further, until the 1930s, European universities were by any measure the tops in the world. German scientific universities were particularly outstanding. A generation of American social scientists attended German universities, studied for their doctorates there, and then formed an important intellectual bridge with European scholars by

---

*Prior to World War II, Americans won only 18 of 129 (14 percent) of the Nobel prizes awarded in physics, chemistry, and medicine. From 1945 to the mid-1970s, U.S. scientists won 56 percent of the awards in physics, 42 percent in chemistry, and 60 percent in medicine (Zuckerman 1977, pp. 282–288). Clearly World War II marked the phase-change in U.S. scientific excellence.

bringing European theories into American social science. Other early American scholars of communication study studied in Europe but did not earn their doctoral degrees there.

German universities rose to eminence worldwide for several reasons. First, education was highly valued by Germans, and the university professor commanded great public respect. The research university existed mainly to advance knowledge through scientific research rather than to impart training to undergraduate students who would become future professionals. The university in Germany of a century ago featured both freedom of teaching and freedom of learning. The university professor had freedom to choose lecture topics and to express his or her views without hindrance (Dobson and Bruce 1972). The professor should view the everyday world from a distance, it was thought, and feel free to comment on it. The German university student did not take tests in courses. Instead, a comprehensive examination was completed at the end of the student's curriculum. Thus, student knowledge of the details of lectures and attendance at lectures were deemphasized. Students could attend lectures on any topic that interested them, and they could move freely from university to university in German. Both faculty members and students had a very high degree of freedom in the German scientific university.

Until World War I, to study at the top university in any field and to learn from the really great minds meant to study in Europe, particularly in Germany. German universities attracted 9,000 Americans from 1815 to 1915, with the vast majority studying between 1870 and 1900 (Ross 1991, p. 55). The academic dependence of American scholars on their continental forbears was indicated by the longstanding U.S. university requirement that all doctoral students demonstrate a reading ability in French and German. Eventually, many of the classic writings in the sciences and in other fields were translated into English, and the foreign languages requirement was dropped by most U.S. universities in the late 1960s.*

The greatest European gift to American intellectual life was a result of Adolf Hitler, who came to power in Germany in 1933 and persecuted Jews and other individuals, such as gypsies and socialists. After the Crystal Night in 1938, when many Jewish stores were destroyed, Hitler made it increasingly difficult for Jews and others to avoid persecution by migrating to the United States, England, or to another haven. But much of the intellectual cream of the crop nevertheless managed to leave Germany, as well as Austria, France, and other European nations, as Hitler's German army invaded these neighboring states. The European intellectual migration to America included nineteen scientists who eventually won the Nobel Prize (Heilbut 1983, p. 350), several of whom, like Albert Einstein, Edward Teller, and Leo Czilard, played key roles in the invention of the atomic bomb in 1945. Meanwhile, Hitler's atom bomb project floundered (Coser 1984).

The intellectual exiles were physicists, chemists, mathematicians, and social scientists. The migrants to America were 43 percent of all the academics in German universities and 48 percent of all social scientists (Heilbut 1983, p. 75). The long list of famous social science scholars who came to America included Kurt Lewin, the well-known psychologist from the University of Berlin; Paul F. Lazarsfeld, the Viennese mathematician-sociologist; and the entire Frankfurt school. The Frankfurt school had its own endowment and settled near Columbia University, with which it formed a loose affiliation. Farther downtown in New York City, the New School for Social Research, led by the American Alvin Johnson, provided a home for exiled European scholars.

*Examples of particularly important translations in the social sciences are Hans Gerth and C. Wright Mills *From Max Weber: Essays in Sociology* (1946), Kurt H. Wolff, *The Sociology of Georg Simmel* (1950); Elsie Clews Parsons' translation of *The Laws of Imitation* by Gabriel Trade (1930); and Talcott Parsons's translation of *The Protestant Ethic and the Spirit of Capitalism* by Max Weber (1930).

Most of the social scientists settled in New York City, although eventually many U.S. universities, and almost every discipline and field, benefited immensely from the European intellectual migration.

The European escapees enriched almost every aspect of American cultural life. The émigré writers, musicians, actors, and directors mainly settled in Los Angeles. Among the well known were Bertolt Brecht, the German playwright, who became a Hollywood scriptwriter; Otto Preminger and Billy Wilder, who moved from Berlin to Hollywood as film writers and directors; Arnold Shoenberg, the Viennese avant-garde musician; Thomas Mann, the German intellectual and author of *Doctor Faustus;* and actors Marlene Dietrich, Greta Garbo, and Peter Lorre.

Between 1933 and 1941, 132,000 refugees left Nazi Germany for America. This intellectual migration was the key event in transferring the European roots of communication theory to America.

DIRECT SOURCES OF AMERICAN SOCIAL SCIENCE

Who were the main European theorists whose thinking was transferred to North America?*

Auguste Comte and Positivism. Auguste Comte (1798–1857), the father of sociology, argued in 1839 for recognition of sociology as the science of society. Comte also gave the world *positivism,* the belief that the scientific method can be applied to the study of human social behavior in order to help solve the social problems of society.

Emile Durkheim. Emile Durkheim (1858–1917) held the first chair of sociology (in 1913) at the University of Paris. He wrote *Suicide* (1897), an important early empirical

---

*In 1927, 258 American sociologists were asked to name the most influential foreign sociologists. The top choices, in order, were: Herbert Spencer, Georg Simmel, Gabriel Tarde, and Emile Durkheim (Levine, Carter, and Gorman 1976). In later decades, Karl Marx and Max Weber received important attention, while Simmel and Durkheim remained influential.

study of suicide rates. Durkheim also pioneered in sociological methodology with *The Rules of Sociological Methods*
(1895). He is considered the cofounder of *modern* sociology
(along with Georg Simmel).

George Simmel and the Chicago school. George Simmel
(1858–1918), the cofounder of modern sociology, was especially influential on the Chicago school. From Simmel,
we get the study of social networks and urban ecology and
the concepts of social distance and the marginal man. Robert Park of the Chicago school obtained his insights into the
role of the newspaper in public opinion while studying
with Simmel at the University of Berlin. Park then converted this theoretic perspective of Simmel into empirical
study of mass communication in America.

Gabriel Tarde. Gabriel Tarde (1843–1904) was a French
lawyer and judge, and later a sociologist, who based his initial observations about imitation on the behavior that he
saw in his courtroom. Tarde rose through the French judi-
cial system to become head of the Statistical Bureau in the
Ministry of Justice. Here he gathered statistical data about
crime and published several books about criminology.
Then he became professor of modern philosophy at the
College of France, in Paris. He wrote *Opinion and Masses*
(1901) and the *Underground Man* (1905), a futuristic utopia
about climatic change in a future society. His *The Laws of
Imitation* was published in 1900, four years before his
death, and influenced two contemporary research traditions, diffusion and social learning theory.

Diffusion is the process by which an innovation is communicated through certain channels over time among the
members of a social system (Rogers 1983). Tarde observed
that the rate of adoption of a new idea followed an s-
shaped curve over time and that higher-status individuals
adopted an innovation relatively earlier. An individual is
influenced to adopt an innovation by mimicking the behavior of another individual who has already adopted the new
idea. Social learning theory states that an individual's ob-

servation of the overt behavior of another individual often serves as a guide for the observer's behavior. Albert Bandura, a psychologist at Stanford University, pioneered the study of how individuals learn from interpersonal models and from models that they observe in the mass media. Bandura's theory has been particularly important in research on the effects of television violence on children's aggressive behavior.

Max Weber. Max Weber (1864–1920) was one of the most important sociologists of all time, although he was a professor of economics until relatively late in his life.* He pioneered various scholarly topics. In *The Protestant Ethic and the Spirit of Capitalism* (1930), he argued that Protestant religious values were associated with the rise of capitalism during the Renaissance. He gave us the concept of bureaucracy, the organization of large numbers of individuals in a hierarchy in order to carry out administrative tasks; *verstehen,* the empathic understanding of one's object of study by putting oneself in the other's role, and the methodological tool of ideal types (a contrasting set of extremes of some behavior or institution to which real-life cases can be compared); and charisma, the quality of an individual endowed with supernatural powers, was also explicated by Weber.

Wilhelm Wundt and Psychology. Wilhelm Wundt (1832–1920) launched the use of the scientific method of experimentation in psychology (Schultz 1975, p. 2). Trained as a physiologist, Wundt gradually became a psychologist during the years that he taught at the University of Leipzig, where he founded the world's first psychological laboratory and pioneered in conducting experiments. Wundt had considerable intellectual influence on several important American social scientists. For instance, John Dewey's and George Herbert Mead's idea of the reflex arc derived di-

*The pioneer generation of sociologists in Europe (and in America) had to have their degrees in some field other than sociology, though their work was essentially sociological. Often they did not think of themselves as sociologists, and only later were their writings defined as sociological. Max Weber was trained in law and economics, Gabriel Tarde and Emile Durkheim studied law, and Herbert Spencer and George Simmel were philosophers.

rectly from Wundt's notion of the gesture. Wundt had in turn been influenced by Darwin's (1872) *The Expression of the Emotions in Men and Animals.*

Each of the next seven chapters illustrates the transposition of these and other European theories to America, where they were studied empirically in communication study.

CHAPTER 5

THE CHICAGO SCHOOL

> The Harvard University pragmatist William James, in a letter written on October 29, 1903, said: "Chicago has during the past six months given birth to the fruit of its ten years of gestation under John Dewey. The result is wonderful—a *real school,* and *real thought.* Important thought, too! Did you even hear of such a city or such a University? Here [at Harvard] we have thought, but no school. At Yale a school, but no thought. Chicago has both.
>
> —*Letters to William James*

The Chicago School's influence on communication theory and research is so important for a number of reasons:

1. It represented the first important flowering of social science in America, serving as the intellectual beachhead for important European theories, particularly those of the German sociologist Georg Simmel.
2. It gave a strong empirical dimension to the social science study of social problems in the United States. The Chicago school was amelioristic, progressive, and pragmatic, seeking to improve the world by studying its social problems. At issue for the Chicago school was whether American democracy, born in a society of rural communities, could survive in the crowded immigrant slums of rapidly growing cities.
3. Chicago scholars formed a theoretical conception of personality socialization centering on human communication. To the Chicago sociologists, to be social and to be human was to communicate. They

I thank John Peters for critically reading the précis of this chapter that I presented at the Wichita Symposium, which is published as a chapter in the proceedings from that conference (Rogers, 1993).

attacked instinct explanations of human behavior and instead stressed a viewpoint later known as symbolic interactionism.
4. The Chicago school cast the mold for future mass communication research on media effects.

The experience of studying at Chicago had a deep and lasting impression on individuals who earned their Ph.D. degrees there. Tamotsu Shibutani, who received his doctorate in sociology at Chicago in the late 1940s, says, "Before I came to Chicago [from an undergraduate degree in sociology at Berkeley], I was like an individual in a dark room. I could make out objects, but I couldn't really see. Then the blinds were opened at Chicago. The sunlight streamed in, and I could understand human behavior. All the rest of my life, I have thought of myself as a Chicago sociologist" (Shibutani 1990). The Chicago school commanded great loyalty from the scholars trained there, and it "still represents a sort of mythical Eden to many contemporary sociologists who locate their personal pedigree and purpose in the profession by tracing back their lineage on the family tree planted in Chicago" (Van Maanen 1988, p. 20).

The important impact of the Chicago school on American social science is well documented; Kurtz's (1984) annotated bibliography lists more than 1,000 publications about the school. Here I synthesize the most important points about the development of the Chicago school, stressing its impacts on communication study. I give primary attention to Robert E. Park, the most influential member of the school and the scholar who pioneered research on mass communication. Other Chicago scholars like Charles Horton Cooley, John Dewey, and George Herbert Mead also placed communication at the center of their conception of human behavior.

WESTWARD EXPANSION AND THE ROBBER BARONS

After the Civil War, from 1865 to 1890, tremendous growth occurred in the United States. Natural resources were exploited by building railroads, making steel from iron and coal, raising capital, launching entrepreneurial ventures, and dividing the open prairie into farms and ranches. A set of robber barons led the major industries, amassing riches by dominating their business rivals and often engaging in questionable business practices. John D. Rockefeller was the biggest robber baron of all. In fact, the Sherman antitrust legislation was enacted originally to limit the near-monopoly power of Rockefeller's Standard Oil Company. Leland Stanford, Andrew Carnegie, and Cornelius Vanderbilt were born poor, worked hard, got ahead, and amassed huge fortunes. The robber barons ripped off their environment and exploited people, although their business activities were legal in their day. Few robber barons had a university education, and many were relatively unschooled. These men were entrepreneurs, took risks, made things happen, and created social changes. Late in his life, a robber baron might donate funds to private universities, libraries, or hospitals, often on a scale previously unknown. One lasting impact is the excellent private universities that they funded.

Johns Hopkins University opened its doors in 1876, founded by a large gift from Johns Hopkins, a prosperous Baltimore merchant who owned considerable stock in the Baltimore and Ohio Railroad. The twelve university trustees did not want to create just another undergraduate college like the 400 that already existed in the United States (Schmidt 1986, p. 5). As the university's first president, they chose Daniel Coit Gilman, who had studied in Berlin, because he was dedicated to emphasizing graduate education and research. Johns Hopkins was the first U.S. university to be a true university rather than just a college, and its founding marked an important turning point in the history of American higher education, serving as the model for other research universities in the United States, including, fifteen years later, the University of Chicago (Figure 5.1). The cynical newspaperman H. L. Mencken (1922) stated: "When [President Gilman] created the university, he achieved something colossal; he revolutionized the higher learning in America, and almost succeeded in making it intelligent." The revolution that Johns Hopkins created was the research university, an institution devoted to conducting research and to graduate education.

FOUNDING THE UNIVERSITY OF CHICAGO

A massive migration to the United States occurred from 1860 to 1912 as Europeans fled from war, revolution, and economic hardship and to the work opportunities and the promise of free farmland available in America. But large numbers of these immigrants were caught in slums, in rapidly urbanizing areas characterized by human exploitation and other social ills. Such problems were clearly evident on the South Side of Chicago, near Lake Michigan, where the University of Chicago was founded.

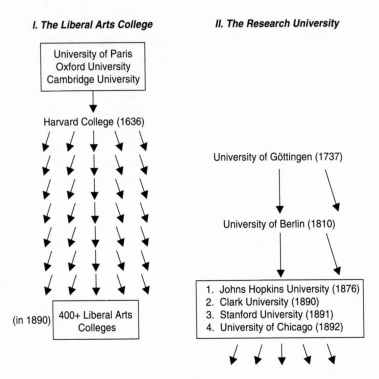

Figure 5.1. Development in the United States of the research university as an alternative model to the liberal arts college.

When the University was founded in 1892, thanks to a generous gift of $35 million from John D. Rockefeller, president of the Standard Oil Company, Chicago was America's second largest city, with almost 1.1 million people. The city's population had doubled in the decade from 1880 to 1890, and it doubled again by 1910. Chicago had an exceptional degree of cultural diversity. In 1900, half of its 1.7 million people were foreign born (Bulmer 1984, p. 13), and many others were the offspring of foreign-born parents. "Many of the immigrant men and women worked at the stockyards, the steel mills of South Chicago, garment factories, the McCormick agricultural [machinery] works, the railways, and the Pullman sleeping-car plant. Chicago's poverty and wealth, filth and luxury, agitation and crime, attracted international attention, as did its ill-managed and corrupt municipal government" (Diner 1975). When the great German sociologist Max Weber visited Chicago in 1904, he described the city as "like a man whose skin has been peeled off and whose intestines are seen at work" (1926, p. 286).

This huge and rapidly growing city did not have a major university. Baptist church leaders had decided to found a Baptist-related university in Chicago, partly because they already had a seminary there, and they turned to Rockefeller, a devout Baptist, for funding. They asked him for a large contribution to the new University of Chicago, and Rockefeller finally agreed to donate $600,000, if it were matched by $400,000 in contributions from other donors (Goodspeed 1916). The Baptist fundraising campaign reached its goal in a few months, with Marshall Field, the Chicago department store owner, agreeing to provide a sizable plot of land adjoining the mile-long Midway of the World's Columbian Exposition (hence, the campus is referred to as the Midway Campus). The agreement with Rockefeller specified that the new university would be located in the inner city rather than in a wealthy suburb, so the existing Baptist Union Theological Seminary was moved to the Midway campus.

Once the Baptist leaders had start-up funding plus a site for the campus, they hired a president, William Rainey Harper, then thirty-five years old and teaching Hebrew at Yale University. Harper had received his Ph.D. degree in classical languages from Yale at age eighteen and had taught at several universities, including the Baptist Union Theological Seminary, before moving to Yale. Harper had met many of the leading social scientists of his time, especially those involved in research designed to help solve social problems, through the Chautauqua movement for adult education.* That experience turned out to be important in heading Harper's new university toward social amelioration.

A shrewd bargainer, Harper agreed to come to Chicago if Rockefeller would donate an additional $1 million for divinity and graduate education. Rockefeller agreed, thus beginning the unique relationship between the go-getting young university president and his wealthy donor (Goodspeed 1916). For the next twenty years, the robber baron and Harper played a game that both understood and seemed to enjoy. Each year, President Harper grossly overspent the university budget. Then he appealed to Rockefeller for another million or so to save the new university in which Rockefeller had already invested so heavily. In this way, Harper gradually coaxed more and more millions out of Rockefeller. The strategy worked because Harper's new university was tremendously successful. Harper had a keen eye for academic talent, and he was a

---

*The Chautauqua movement was named for the town in New York State where the first Chautauqua was held. Each consisted of a two- or three-day public meeting at which noted speakers gave lectures. Chautauquas were an early from of adult education.

persuasive salesman when he went after the top scholars in each field. He typically doubled a professor's salary if he would join the Chicago faculty. By 1900, eight years after its founding, the University of Chicago was considered one of the top American universities in academic quality. It was the top-rated university in the Midwest and one of the five most prestigious in the United States. Rockefeller had responded generously to this success but finally told President Harper that he would make one final gift of $10 million; then the university was on its own. Rockefeller would continue to talk with Harper but not about the university's budget deficits. Harper agreed. Shortly after, Harper traveled to New York to see Rockefeller, who said that he would be happy to meet with him but not about deficits. Harper agreed and when he walked into Rockefeller's office said, "Let us pray" (that was the custom of the day). So they knelt and prayed, and President Harper told God all about the deficits. Rockefeller patiently underwrote Harper again.

Harper's vision for the University of Chicago was as a new kind of urban university. Speaking at the inauguration of Nicholas Murray Butler as president of Columbia University in 1902, Harper said, "A university which will adapt itself to urban influence, which will undertake to serve as an expression of urban civilization, and which is compelled to meet the demands of an urban environment, will in the end become something essentially different from a university located in a village or small city."

ROCKEFELLER FUNDING OF COMMUNICATION RESEARCH

Frederick T. Gates (1853–1929), a young Baptist minister and secretary of the American Baptist Education Society, was the key person in persuading John D. Rockefeller to make the initial gift of $600,000 to launch the University of Chicago. Rockefeller was impressed with Gates and a year or two later hired him to manage the Rockefeller philanthropy. In essence, Gates functioned as what was to become the Rockefeller Foundation, and when this institution was established several decades later (in 1913), Gates was one of the original trustees. He represented the idea of hiring professionals to give away money to deserving causes. Such professionals, and the private foundations in which they were employed, were needed by wealthy individuals like Rockefeller. Until he hired Gates, Rockefeller was continually hounded by individuals and groups seeking funding. And even with the help of Gates, Rockefeller could not increase his rate of giving to keep up with

TABLE 5.1
Contributions of the Rockefeller Foundation to the
Field of Communication Study

Date(s)	Source	Recipient	Amount
1891–1910	John D. Rockefeller	University of Chicago	$35 million to found and support the University of Chicago
1923–1932	Laura Spelman Rockefeller Memorial (merged with the Rockefeller Foundation in 1932)	The social sciences at the University of Chicago	$3.4 million
1933–1935	Rockefeller Foundation (Tracy Kitteridge)	Paul F. Lazarsfeld	Travel fellowship to the United States, about $8,000
1937–1944	Rockefeller Foundation (John Marshall)	Paul F. Lazarsfeld	Radio Research Project, $189,450
1929–1939	Rockefeller Foundation	Clark Hull, Carl I. Hovland, and other faculty at Yale University	$2 million, to found and support the Yale Institute of Human Relations
1948–1964	Rockefeller Foundation	Carl I. Hovland	$416,300, for the Yale Communication Research Project (on persuasion research)
1935–1945	Rockefeller Foundation (Lawrence K. Frank)	Kurt Lewin	$315,000, for his salary plus that of three research assistants at the University of Iowa
1939–1940	Rockefeller Foundation (John Marshall)	—	$1,500, for ten monthly meetings of the Rockefeller Communication Seminar

(Table continues on following page)

TABLE 5.1
Contributions of the Rockefeller Foundation to the Field of
Communication Study (*cont.*)

Date(s)	Source	Recipient	Amount
1940–1944	Rockefeller Foundation (John Marshall)	Harold D. Lasswell	$85,400, for the War-Time Communications Project (on propaganda analysis), U.S. Library of Congress
1948	Rockefeller Foundation	Wilbur Schramm	$2,000 for a communication research symposium at the University of Illinois
1951–1953	Rockefeller Foundation (John Marshall)	Wilbur Schramm	$9,150 for a conference at the University of Illinois on educational television
1946–1952	Rockefeller Foundation	Norbert Wiener	$28,000 for collaborative research at MIT on the cybernetics of brain physiology
1952–1955	Rockefeller Foundation	Gregory Bateson	$30,000 for cybernetic research and interactional communication

the growth of his wealth. Gates recommended to Rockefeller that he "wholesale" rather than "retail" his giving. In a sense, Gates invented the modern foundation, hiring subject-matter specialists in various scientific fields to manage Rockefeller's philanthropy. Rockefeller decided to fund research because, while he did not believe in giving money to street beggars, he felt it was appropriate to fund the study of the root causes of poverty (Prewitt 1991). The Rockefeller Foundation began in medical and public health research, branched out to agricultural research, and eventually encompassed other types of research.

Initially, the foundation was opposed to funding social science research; instead, the Laura Spelman Rockefeller Memorial (named after the wife of John D. Rockefeller), charged with improving public welfare through research, channeled Rockefeller monies into social research during the 1920s. The memorial was directed by Beardsley Ruml, a young Ph.D. in psychology from the University of Chicago. The memorial completely dominated social science funding in the 1920s. About $3.4 million of the approximately $21 million of total funding it provided from 1923 to 1932 (when it merged with the Rockefeller Foundation) went to the University of Chicago. This funding shaped the directions taken by American social science, for example, its stress on an empirical approach.

With the help of the Laura Spelman Rockefeller Memorial funding, the Chicago school was extremely productive. From 1923 to 1932, the Local Community Research Committee and the Social Science Research Committee (its successor) supported research that produced 84 books and monographs and 120 articles (Converse 1987, p. 492). By 1929, 79 local community research studies were completed but not published, although several of these were published later. A total of 162 research assistants were employed at that time by the Local Community Research Committee (Smith and White 1929, pp. 254–265). This was big-time research funding, the first for the social sciences. Until these massive grants, social science research had mainly been conducted by individual scholars. The Chicago school mounted a research program, consisting of a coordinated series of empirical studies, under the general direction of Robert E. Park.

The 1920s were a key decade for the development of the social sciences in America, and the die was cast mainly at the University of Chicago. In Chicago the new social problems associated with the industrial revolution in a twentieth-century democracy were particularly apparent. At the university, a highly competent set of social scientists, operated in an environment enriched by funding for their empirical research by the Laura Spelman Rockefeller Memorial (Prewitt 1991).

Not only were John D. Rockefeller and the Laura Spelman Rockefeller Memorial crucial ingredients at Chicago, but the Rockefeller Foundation funded each of the other forerunners of communication study. Without the Rockefeller Foundation, early communication study in America could not have flourished. The field is built on a foundation provided by oil (Table 5.1).

FOUNDING THE DEPARTMENT OF SOCIOLOGY

President Harper recruited Albion W. Small, then president of Colby College, a small Baptist institution in Waterville, Maine, to join the Chicago faculty. Small had studied history and political economy at the University of Berlin and at the University of Leipzig from 1879 to 1881 and then earned his Ph.D. degree from Johns Hopkins University in 1889. He also was an ordained Baptist minister, fitting the University of Chicago's twin demands for scholarly excellence and religious appropriateness. (Since its beginnings, the University of Chicago has not been very Baptist.) Small pioneered in teaching a sociology course at Colby College, and he had written an introductory textbook in sociology. He told President Harper that he wanted to be head of a sociology department at Chicago.

Small had a vision for the first American department of sociology, and he set out directly to put it into action. Small, who had translated and published the main writings of Georg Simmel, wanted his department to be the American outpost for German sociology.* But Small did not want Chicago sociologists just to popularize Simmel's theories. The Chicago School was to extend German sociological theories and apply them to investigating urban social problems. Chicago provided a natural laboratory for sociological investigation to test how U.S. democracy might be adjusted to function more effectively in the new urban milieu of turn-of-the-century America. Albion Small did not want his own ideas to dominate his colleagues and students.† Instead, Chicago sociology was to be pluralistic, a free marketplace of ideas. The resulting theoretical flexibility allowed the Chicago school to move away from its original close association with theology to the social problems orientation for which it became famous in the 1920s and 1930s. Small saw sociology as an amelioristic science. In the first issue of the *American Journal of Sociology* (which he founded and edited), he insisted that sociology should not be a "do-nothing" social science. Instead, he wanted it to "do-good."

Why did President Harper hire Albion Small in the then-unknown

---

*Simmel was the dominant European influence on the Chicago school, starting with Albion Small, who had been a fellow student with Simmel at the University of Berlin in 1880, and who maintained a friendship through correspondence and personal visits (Christakes 1978).

†As occurred at two other leading centers of American sociology: Yale University, led by William Graham Sumner, and Brown University under Lester Ward.

field of sociology as one of the original thirteen individuals selected as head professors at his new university? First, Small was one of very few Baptists with a Ph.D. degree and with German postgraduate training (Chistakes 1978, p. 20). As a bonus, Small was a college president and thus had administrative experience. So it seems that President Harper really wanted Small; he just happened to be a sociologist. "It is clear that the decision to establish a department of sociology at the University of Chicago and its subsequent intellectual development were largely products of Harper's policy of appointing particular persons because he thought them outstanding, rather than because he had definite ideas about what he wanted sociology to be" (Diner 1975). Had President Harper hired a different scholar (as indeed he tried to do) instead of Small, sociology at Chicago would have been subordinated in a department of political science.*

Thus, by a kind of hiring accident, Chicago had the first sociology department in the United States. It completely dominated early sociology in America. For example:

- By 1909, seventeen years after its founding, Chicago offered 100 of the 1,000 sociology courses then taught at 200 U.S. universities.
- From 1895 to 1915, Chicago awarded thirty-five of the ninety-eight United States doctorates in sociology (Hinkle 1980, p. 13).
- From 1915 to 1935, Chicago graduated sixty Ph.Ds, and eleven of them were among the first twenty-seven presidents of the American Sociological Society.
- By 1929, one-third of all graduate students in sociology in the United States were at the University of Chicago. They earned their Ph.D. degrees there, spread out to teach at other universities, and sent their star students back to Chicago to study for their doctorates. Many sociology departments in other U.S. universities thus became virtual "farm clubs" for Chicago.
- The leading textbooks in sociology were written at Chicago: *Introduction to the Science of Sociology,* edited by Robert E. Park and Ernest Burgess (1921), and W. I. Thomas and Florian Znaniecki, *The Polish Peasant in Europe and America* were sociological classics.

*The five core social science disciplines were formed around the turn of the century in America. Economics founded its professional association in 1885, psychology in 1892, anthropology in 1902, political science in 1903, and sociology in 1905. This division of social science into five disciplines were arbitrary and has been questioned from time to time but has retained its hold on American academic life (Prewitt 1991).

Albion Small launched the first scientific journal of sociology in the United States in 1905, the *American Journal of Sociology,* and he was its most prolific contributor, publishing thirty-eight articles in the first twenty years after its founding (Hinkle 1980, p. 13). Having command over this journal gave Chicago considerable influence over American sociology. Further, the Department of Sociology at Chicago also served as the executive offices for the American Sociological Society (now Association), the main professional organization for sociologists, for the first decades of its existence.

GEORG SIMMEL AND CHICAGO SOCIOLOGY

Georg Simmel and his French contemporary, Emile Durkheim, are often described as the cofounders of modern sociology (Caplow 1968, p. 12). Simmel (1858–1918) was born in Berlin of Jewish parents who converted to Catholicism. He studied at the University of Berlin and taught there for most of his academic life. Simmel was the consummate metropole, holding intimate salons in his home for the leading philosophers, artists, and intellectuals of his day. He had inherited a small fortune and lived as an independent scholar. Simmel wrote prodigiously, and much of his writings were about what would today be called modernity. Influenced by Charles Darwin and Herbert Spencer, Simmel taught and wrote about social evolution, urban social life, and the ecology of the city. His theoretical writings directly affected Chicago school, which served as a kind of empirical laboratory for his conceptualizations.

"Simmel was a cultivated man, thoughtful, detached, and worldly. He wrote on Italian architecture, lectured on German poetry, concerned himself with modern painting, women's fashions, and the history of pantheism. . . . The intellectual problems that interested him ranged beyond sociology: Freedom and free will, the metaphysics of death, and the psychological effects of metropolitan life. No subject was too large or too small for his consideration if it had a theoretical character" (Caplow 1968, p. 12). This extremely wide scope to his work was one reason for Simmel's difficulties with the academic establishment in Germany, which did not respect a dilettante.

Simmel would have been highly regarded had he not written on such a wide range of subjects: from the nature of exchange (in *The Philosophy of Money*), to the role of the stranger, to interpersonal networks as influences on human behavior. In fact, Simmel wrote essays on almost any theme. He could "Simmelize" a topic by bringing to bear his sociological perspective, whether it was fashion or capitalism or alienation. Simmel's work was speculative in nature; he did not engage in empirical investigation.

Simmel got little respect from his contemporary academics in Germany, and his faculty status did not advance (Levine 1989). He spent fifteen years, from 1885 to 1900, as only an assistant professor at the University of Berlin; in this academic rank, his university salary depended on student fees. Simmel was a popular lecturer, performing in the largest auditorium at the University of Berlin (Frisby 1984, p. 26–27). Perhaps his university colleagues were jealous of his popularity. His promotion had to be approved by the minister of education, who in Imperial Germany did not look favorably on Simmel's friendships with socialists and his articles in socialist publications. Sociology was a new and marginal academic field in turn-of-the-century Germany, and there were no university chairs in sociology until 1918. For all of these reasons, Simmel's academic career languished. Finally, in 1900, he was promoted to the rank of associate professor at the University of Berlin. He applied for a full professorship at various universities but was turned down each time. Simmel lamented that he would die without intellectual heirs. Only in 1914, at the age of fifty-six, did Simmel secure a professorship at the University of Strasbourg, which was not a very important university. Further, it was a chair in philosophy, not sociology (Frisby 1984, p. 22). Four years later, in 1918, Simmel died from liver cancer.

Among Simmel's important books are *The Stranger,* which inspired Robert Park at Chicago, and *The Web of Group-Affiliations* (1922), which led to network analysis. Simmel wrote about the triad,* a group composed of three individuals. He argued that a triad consists of unstable relationships in that two of the members of a triad usually form a dyadic coalition against the third member. In the 1950s and 1960s, considerable research on the triad was carried out by American sociologists, led by Theodore Caplow.

Simmel saw the progress of sociological analysis as one of gaining greater understanding by deeper thinking rather than by accumulating and analyzing facts. In contrast, Emile Durkheim's sociological style

---

*Simmel actually used the German word *dreierverbindung,* which does not imply the more integrated and harmonious relationship implied by the English word *triad* (Caplow 1968, p. 17). But Albion Small translated Simmel's term as *triad* in an early volume of the *American Journal of Sociology,* and thus it has remained since.

consisted of relying on statistical data obtained by empirical research, and Max Weber's approach framed sociological analysis around specialized concepts. Modern American sociology followed Durkheim and Weber and moved away from Simmel (Caplow 1968, p. 18). Simmel saw the central problem of sociology as the understanding of socialization (Spykman 1966, p. 40), a viewpoint carried forward and formulated into symbolic interactionism by Charles Horton Cooley, George Herbert Mead, and John Dewey of the Chicago school.

Simmel's theoretical perspective about communication, which Robert Park reflected in his research and writing, can be summarized (Levine, Carter, and Gorman 1976):

1. Society, the core concept of sociology, consists of communication among individuals.
2. All human communication represents some kind of exchange that has reciprocal effects on the individuals involved.
3. Communication occurs among individuals who stand at varying degrees of social distance from each other.
4. Human communication satisfies certain basic needs, such as for companionship or aggression, or to pursue income, education, or other desired goals.
5. Certain types of communication become stable or fixed with time and thus represent culture and social structure.

Simmel's focus on human communication influenced the Chicago school in a variety of ways. Fifteen of his articles were published in the *American Journal of Sociology,* the house organ of the sociology department at the University of Chicago and the leading American sociological journal of its day. Robert E. Park enrolled in courses from Simmel, including one in sociology at the University of Berlin, and later, when Park taught at Chicago, he was a conduit for Simmel's theoretical perspectives on human ecology, race relations, and the study of social problems. George Herbert Mead was influenced by Simmel and probably attended his lectures in Berlin.

COOLEY, DEWEY, MEAD, AND PARK

The flowering of social psychology and sociology at Chicago was the work of just a few scholars: Charles Horton Cooley, John Dewey,

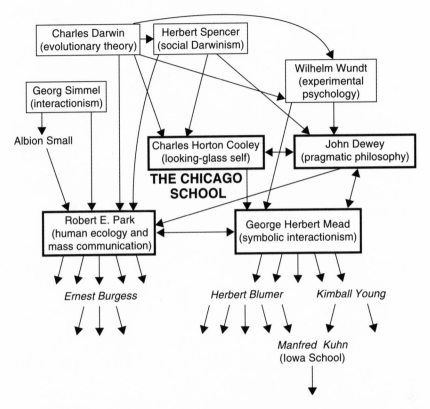

Figure 5.2. Intellectual forebears and descendants of the Chicago School.

George Herbert Mead, and Robert E. Park (Figure 5.2). These four important American scholars had a number of characteristics in common:

- They were born between 1859 and 1864, around the time of the American Civil War, and all shared a small-town upbringing. They were Protestant and moralistic in background, but through their scientific training they sought to become objective observers of social life. They were ameliorative—interested in attacking social problems by understanding them more accurately. They were optimists and felt that social progress was needed in order for American democracy to flourish in urban communities.
- They all had a University of Michigan–University of Chicago connection, high-prestige American universities at the time. John Dewey taught Cooley and Park at the University of Michigan. Cooley influenced Mead regarding his concept of the self. Dewey brought Mead

with him from the Michigan faculty to Chicago, where they were close friends. Although these four scholars were linked in an inter-personal network of intellectual influence and of intersecting ca-reers, each made separate intellectual contributions.

- Cooley and Mead founded interactionist social psychology (later and more popularly called symbolic interaction). They attacked instincts as forming the basis for human personality and saw interpersonal communication as central to the formation of personality.
- They stressed the subjectivism of human communication—that the receiver of a message interprets the content in a way that is idiosyn-cratic to that individual (rather than exactly as the message's source had intended). This subjectivism was later submerged by the Claude E. Shannon mathematical model of communication (see Chapter 11).
- The early Chicago school was empirical but not very quantitative. Park said that statistical methods were "parlor tricks," and it was not until the 1930s that Chicago sociology began to utilize statistical methods for the analysis of quantitative data.

Ann Arbor Beginnings: Charles Horton Cooley

The Chicago school actually got underway in Ann Arbor, Michigan, a university city about forty-five miles from Detroit. The University of Michigan is one of the highest-quality public universities in the United States, and it early grew to greatness, although it has not contributed very directly to communication study, except early on and indirectly through the Chicago school.

Charles Horton Cooley (1864–1929) was a go-blue Ann Arbor man. He was born there, spent almost his entire life in Ann Arbor, and died there. His father was the dean of the university's law school, and Cooley married the daughter of the university's medical school dean (Bierstedt 1981, p. 91). All of the other key figures in the Chicago school also grew up in small towns: Dewey in Burlington, Vermont; Park in Red Wing, Minnesota; and Mead in Hadley, Massachusetts. But they all cut their rural roots as soon as they could and lived urban lives. Cooley, on the other hand, stayed in Ann Arbor all of his life.

The young Cooley was a delicate boy who read a great deal, was pain-fully shy, suffered from a speech impediment, and was plagued by chronic constipation (Czitrom 1982, p. 94). He kept a journal all of his life, and many of his insights about human behavior came from intro-spection. Cooley contributed to our understanding of personality socialization by using observation as a research method. He was an arm-chair sociologist, observing his three children at play in his home and studying their use of personal pronouns like *I, me, my,* and *mine.* Cooley distrusted measurement and statistics. So he was empirical but not quantitative.

While he was a doctoral student at the University of Michigan in 1893, Cooley took a course in political philosophy from John Dewey. Cooley was deeply impressed by Dewey's lectures and incorporated their main theme into his own sociological theory: That the mass media of communication could restore a sense of community (Quandt 1970, p. 4).

Cooley was increasingly deaf after the age of forty but was still a very popular lecturer at the University of Michigan. In 1928 when he was sixty-four, 450 students were enrolled in his introductory sociology course. An intellectual recluse, Cooley found it a painful experience to attend academic conferences, especially when he was elected to the presidency of the American Sociological Society in 1918 (Bierstedt 1981, p. 89).

Cooley developed two main concepts:

1. The primary group (versus the secondary group)—face-to-face, in-timate, and important in forming a person's social nature. He called it "primary" because of its importance in personality socialization and also because such primary groups as parents, siblings, peers, and teachers come first in one's lifetime.
2. The looking-glass self—the idea that human interaction reflects the immediate environment to the individual, thus serving as a mirror for the mind.* "I am what I think you think I am." Cooley liked to quote: "Each to each a looking glass, reflects the other that doth pass." Cooley's (1902) colorful concept of the looking-glass self stressed the importance of interpersonal communication in person-ality socialization. It was a concept to be developed further by George Herbert Mead as the "self."

Cooley was a moralist but did not engage in reform. His writing is embarrassingly judgmental by today's standards, implying the superior-ity of Anglo-Saxons and Christian religion. He wanted to preserve the virtues of a rural society at a time of rapid urbanization. Cooley read

*Cooley got the concept of the looking-glass self from Adam Smith.

Spencer,* August Comte, and Gabriel Tarde, and he admired Darwin for his scientific imagination; he made no mention of Marx in his writings or of Freud. Cooley was influenced by William James's (1890) *Principles of Psychology,* an important early book that laid out the nature of psychology and also explained the perspective of pragmatism—that all ideas are hypotheses that can be tested by applying the scientific method to the social sciences of behavior.

Cooley wrote three main books: *Human Nature and the Social Order,* (1902), about childhood personality socialization, which included his conception of the looking-glass self; *Social Organization* (1909), which argued that society is tied together by the mass media and in which Cooley explained the concept of the primary group; and *Social Process* (1918), which dealt with the role of communication in society.

Key Figures in the Chicago School

The Department of Sociology at Chicago had a small faculty. Even if Dewey and Mead are included (sociology doctoral students often enrolled in their courses in the Department of Philosophy), we are talking about only a half-dozen key scholars (and a total faculty in sociology at any one time of from five to eight professors). Given the considerable accomplishments of the Chicago school and the hordes of doctoral students, these small numbers of faculty seem almost unbelievable. Briefly they are:

- Albion Small, founder of the Department of Sociology, who dominated the department in its early years, building the foundations for the greatness of the Chicago school.
- W. I. Thomas, who earned his Ph.D. in sociology at Chicago and also studied ethnology at Berlin and Göttingen and stated: "If men define situations as real, they are real in their consequences." Perceptions count, forming part of what Thomas called the individual's "definition of the situation." The five volumes of *The Polish Peasant in Europe and America,* a book of 2,250 pages about migration to America, written with Florian Znaniecki, a Polish sociologist, was published between 1918 and 1920. *The Polish Peasant* is "the first great classic in American empirical sociology" (Coser 1977). This study, the most

*John Dewey called Herbert Spencer's works to Cooley's attention while both Dewey and Cooley were at the University of Michigan.

important work establishing sociology as a discipline in America, stressed the concept of social disorganization and thus brought about a fundamental change in Chicago sociology, turning "scholars from the humanitarian interest in social problems toward an analysis of the sociological processes of disorganization which cause them" (Faris 1970 p. 17). Social disorganization freed the individual from the social control of the group. Two million Poles migrated to the Untied States from 1880 to 1910, and 80 percent of them worked in unskilled jobs in mass production industries: steel mills, packing-houses, textile factories, and coal mines. The shift from villages in Poland to urban Chicago represented a breakdown of primary group relationships and a loss of solidarity, which led to social disorganization. Thomas's strong intellectual influence on Chicago sociology ended in 1918, when he committed a sexual indiscretion.*

- Ernest Burgess, a family sociologist and human ecologist, who proposed the concentric circle theory of urban structure: that a city has a downtown business center with successive circles of lower-class, middle-class, and upper-class residential zones surrounding it. Burgess collaborated with Park (they were office-mates at the university) in ecological research on Chicago, launching the field of human ecology, which concerned individuals' relationship with their environment, and which borrowed directly from Darwin's evolutionary theory.

- John Dewey, who taught in the Department of Philosophy at Chicago from 1894 until 1904, when he left in anger for Columbia University. He was an exponent of pragmatism, the philosophy that interpretation of the meaning of beliefs should be made in terms of their practical effects or content, and of progressive education.

- George Herbert Mead, also in the Philosophy Department, who taught a course in advanced social psychology in which most sociology doctoral students enrolled. His important book *Mind, Self and Society* was compiled posthumously by one of his students, Charles W. Morris, from classroom notes taken during Mead's class in 1927. Mead argued that an individual's personality is formed through communication with other people, as self-images develop by means of interaction with others.

*Thomas was arrested by the FBI for an alleged violation of the Mann Act, which prohibited interstate transportation of women for immoral purposes and for false registration at a hotel. Although the charges against him were thrown out of court, Thomas was forced to resign from the University of Chicago (Kurtz 1984, p. 99).

- Robert E. Park, the scholar who best exemplified the Chicago school and can be considered the first academic student of mass communication.

In this chapter, we focus on Dewey, Mead, and, especially, Park.

CHARACTERISTICS OF CHICAGO SOCIOLOGY

The first externally funded social research in the United States, conducted at the University of Chicago, supported graduate students who worked with faculty on research projects. Mentor-apprentice relationships were important at Chicago in teaching how to conduct social research. Robert Park went into the field with his Ph.D. students, spending hours with each one, discussing their research. Park liked to say to his students, "Go get the seat of your pants dirty in *real* research" (Bulmer 1984, pp. 97–98).

Just as Bronislaw Malinowski and Franz Boas influenced anthropologists to engage in fieldwork, "the Chicago School of urban ethnography is usually regarded as the main force behind sociological fieldwork" (Van Maanen 1988, p. 17). Chicago research relied on close personal contacts between investigators and their respondents in order to capture their subjects' point of view empathically. The Chicago sociologists concentrated on the study of deviant subcultures, members of various down-and-out groups in Chicago: gangs (Thrasher, 1927), hobos (Anderson 1923), slum residents (Zorbaugh 1929), suicides (Shonle 1926), ghetto residents (Wirth 1926), and "taxi-dancers" (Cressey 1929).

An investigation typical of the Chicago approach to urban social problems was Cressey's (1929) study of a taxi-dance hall, which provided female dancing partners at ten cents a dance to men. The dancers "engaged in mildly erotic activities with paying customers under the guise of ballroom dancing." Cressey did not analyze taxi-dancing in a statistical or an objective manner. Instead this activity, viewed as unwholesome by reformers, was presented as a "legitimate topic for sympathetic understanding with moral horror." Pre-Park Chicago sociology, which had been colored by a Protestant reformist ideology, was thus converted to the scientific study of social problems. Recruits to Chicago sociology "went through a transformation away from 'do-goodism' to something akin to intellectual voyeurism" (Turner and Turner 1990, p. 48). The Chicago sociologists felt that appropriate policies for solving a social problem could be identified through sociological research. They wanted to study a social problem up close, mainly by such ethnographic methods as observation and in-depth interviews, although they also used quantitative data of an aggregate nature, like rates of prostitution or of juvenile delinquency in different sections of the city.*

A Chicago doctoral student typically chose a social problem for dissertation study, carried out the investigation, and then published a book about it with a lengthy introduction by Robert Park. "Park is reported to have said that he would rather encourage ten students to write ten books than write one book himself" (Burnet 1964). The Chicago school was a dense network of scholars carrying out research in one city about its social problems. Early Chicago scholars generally considered surveys to be unscientific, so the Chicago school had a greater concern with internal validity (the accurate understanding of behavior) than with external validity (the generalizability of the results). The typical Chicago doctoral dissertation was a case study of a social problem, and there were plenty of such problems to choose from in Chicago, with its huge slums and stockyards within walking distance of the university.† "Chicago sociologists . . . tried to construct a morally-relevant and socially-useful academic discipline" (Smith 1988, p. ix). *Progressivism* is the belief that social problems can be solved by scientific study. So progressivism, positivism, and reform marked the Chicago school, all in a context of attempted scientific objectivity.

The Chicago scholars moved U.S. sociology away from Herbert Spencer and macro-level evolution and toward a more finely grained micro-level social psychology. *Interactionism* is a perspective that says that human behavior is social, influenced by talking with others. *Symbolic interactionism* is the theoretical position that humans learn who they are through interacting with others. Humans construct meanings by means of interpersonal communication with others.

---

*The use of ethnographic methods by Chicago sociologists may have been facilitated by their organizational proximity to anthropologists at the University of Chicago. Anthropology did not split off into a separate department on the Midway campus until 1929 (Stocking 1979, p. 19).

†Typical of the muckraking literature of the turn-of-the century era is Upton Sinclair's *The Jungle* (1906), an exposé of the unsanitary conditions and labor exploitation of the Chicago meat-packing industry. This protest novel contributed to passage of the Pure Food and Drug Act of 1906. Sinclair was not connected with the Chicago school, although his book was read by the Chicago scholars.

Figure 5.3. John Dewey (1859–1952) in about 1904,
when he left the University of Chicago.
Used by permission of the University of Chicago Archives.

JOHN DEWEY AND PRAGMATIC PHILOSOPHY

John Dewey (1859–1952) was "the most widely known and influential philosopher this country has ever produced" (Haworth 1960). During his productive academic career, he published 36 books and 815 articles and papers—unfortunately, written in a dull style (Eastman 1941). Dewey believed that individuals can find self-realization only in the company of others; hence community is essential to democracy. Dewey was called "the philosopher of democracy" (Dearborn 1988, p. 6). Communication, to Dewey, was the means for getting people to be full, participating members of society (Peters 1989a). Dewey held that "society exists not only by transmission, by communication, but it may be fairly said to exist in transmission, in communication"; nevertheless, "Dewey

... is the path not taken by American mass communication research" (Peters 1989). In fact, most communication scholars do not recognize John Dewey as one of their forefathers; his work lies too far over the horizon for them to recognize his influence, and indeed many of his ideas are only indirect ancestors of contemporary communication study.

Dewey was born and grew up in Burlington, Vermont, where his father was a store owner and where students from the University of Vermont boarded at the Dewey home. During his junior year in college at the University of Vermont, Dewey read a textbook on evolution written by Thomas Henry Huxley ("Darwin's bulldog"). The young Dewey was "swept off his feet by the rapture of scientific knowledge" (Eastman 1941). He also read Herbert Spencer's book on social Darwinism. In his new excitement to understand the world, Dewey plunged ardently into his college studies, graduating first in his class and earning a bachelor's degree in philosophy. The practical problem for Dewey was what to do as a nineteen-year-old philosopher.

In 1879, American professors of philosophy were usually former clergy; their lectures contained a good deal of morality, and university administrators hoped that their philosophy professors would "see that science did not run away with the pupils' minds" (Eastman 1941). Dewey did not fit this mold of philosopher as moral educator, and in fact helped to change this image. He had a practical and progressive side and believed that scientific experimentation could provide one basis for knowing the world. After three unhappy years of teaching in public schools, Dewey went for his Ph.D. degree in philosophy at Johns Hopkins University, where his adviser, George Sylvester Morris, taught him a Hegelian perspective.* Hegel said that mind and nature have an essen-

---

*Although Dewey was attracted to Hegel during his doctoral student days at Johns Hopkins, he did not study the philosophy of Karl Marx. When asked by students or others about Marxism, he would reply, "I have never read Marx" (Eastman 1941). Eventually he did, and he was one of the first American liberals to visit the Soviet Union in the 1920s. One partial explanation for Dewey's changed perspective may have been his love affair with a beautiful, red-haired Polish émigré, Anzia Yezierska, with whom the sixty-year-old white-haired Dewey had an intense relationship in 1917–1918 (Dearborn 1988). Dewey wrote passionate poetry to Yezierska, who authored six books about immigrant life that were popular in the 1920s. A typical theme in her books was a "sweatshop Cinderella" who falls in love with an austere New Englander. Yezierska met Dewey when she lost her teaching position in New York, and she asked the dean of Columbia Teachers College, John Dewey, for help. He urged her to continue her writing career and gave her a typewriter. Later, they conducted a survey of Polish immigrants in Philadelphia's Jewish ghetto.

tial unity, so that in studying nature, one is studying the underlying reality of nature. Dewey also took classes in experimental psychology from G. Stanley Hall, who had trained with Wilhelm Wundt at Leipzig. After receiving his doctorate, Dewey accepted a faculty position at the University of Michigan, where his mentor, Morris, had moved. Shortly, Dewey moved to the University of Minnesota for one year but then returned to Michigan as professor and chair of the philosophy department (in 1888, at age thirty) upon the death of Morris.

In 1894, President William R. Harper of the University of Chicago offered Dewey the chairmanship of the combined Department of Philosophy, Psychology, and Pedagogy (education) at an annual salary of $5,000, considerably more than the $3,000 Dewey was earning at Michigan (Eastman 1941). The combined department was attractive to Dewey because of his growing interest in the psychology of the thought process and in progressive education.

He soon became involved in Jane Addams's Hull House at 800 South Halsted Street, north of the University of Chicago in a crowded slum of European immigrants near the Loop. Jane Addams was a reform-minded young woman who organized Chicago intellectuals to help the underclass, often through meetings at Hull House. The settlement house name came from an original owner, Charles J. Hull; its later owner, Helen Culver, was persuaded by Jane Addams in 1889 to donate Hull House to be the first settlement house in America. Hull House provided a facility for elites to come to the slums to live, observe the problems of the underdog, and discuss possible solutions.* It grew to cover an entire city block by the mid-1920s, when it had seventy residents who provided services to 9,000 women, men, and children per week. Jane Addams was awarded the Nobel Peace Prize in 1931 for her humanitarian contributions.† Dewey was involved in various types of social amelioration during his Chicago years, especially in education and particularly with Hull House. He greatly admired Jane Addams and named his daughter after her.

John Dewey has been described as "slender, quiet, introverted, con-

---

*Hull House was inspired by a house in which Oxford University graduates lived in a London slum. Jane Addams had visited this English settlement house and returned to Chicago to implement her modification of the original idea.

†Albion Small offered Addams a half-time faculty appointment in the Chicago Department of Sociology in 1913, but she declined the offer (Diner 1975). Nevertheless, there were close relationships between the department and Hull House.

templative" (McCaul 1961). Another account pictured him as "one of the greatest and most modest appearing man imaginable. . . . To see him on the platform in his gray sack coat, drooping mustache, hair parted in the middle and his 'excuse-me-for-intruding air'" (McCaul 1959). Dewey was not a neat dresser: "He used frequently to come into [his] class in Logical Theory with his necktie out of contact with his collar, a sock down around his ankle, or a pants leg caught up into his garter" (Eastman 1941). He was mild in nature but could be stubborn about a matter of principle. On one occasion he told the president of the University of Chicago that he would consider taking on the additional administrative duties of serving, in essence, as dean of education if his annual salary were increased from $5,000 to $7,000. President Harper said a salary of that size might embarrass Dewey with his colleagues, but Dewey thought he could cope with the pain. Later, Dewey recalled, "That demand for more pay did more to make a man of me than any other act of my life!" (Eastman 1941).

During his decade (1894–1904) at the University of Chicago, Dewey contributed mainly to psychology. After leaving the Midway, he applied psychology to educational and philosophical problems rather than contributing to psychology itself (Schultz 1975, pp. 155). Dewey's famous article, "Reflex Arc Concept in Psychology" (1896), drew on William Wundt's idea of the gesture and was later expanded by his Chicago colleague, George Herbert Mead. The main tradition of psychology when the Chicago school got underway was individualistic, without much attention to the individual's social relationships. Stimulus-response (S-R) theorizing predominated. An external stimulus was perceived by an individual; then it followed a nerve path to the proper muscles, whose action was the response, which ended the process. This type of S-R model might indeed describe certain behaviors—the knee-jerk reflex, for example—but it was an incomplete model of much human action, which is more social. The S-R model was inadequate in other ways too. A sharp noise might seem to be a stimulus to an individual's startled reaction (the response) but only if we ignore the quiet prior to the noise. Further, the stimulus and the response might be thought of as coordinated phases of a process through which an individual's response gives meaning to the stimulus (Faris 1970, pp. 90–91). Thus, Dewey, Mead, and other Chicago scholars questioned the oversimplification represented by the S-R model, the reflex arc, claiming that an individual's interpretation of the stimulus is also involved in determining the response in most cases. Thus, the S-R model was transformed to become a stimulus-interpretation-response model, with meanings (derived from interaction with others) as an important component.*

Dewey argued further that the reflex arc concept was fallacious because it distinguished between a stimulus that was regarded as external and a response that was considered wholly internal to the individual. This distinction was part of the mind-body dualism of early psychology and implied that the stimulus and response are not part of a coordinated whole. Exactly what an individual defines as a stimulus depends on what has gone on in the individual's preceding experience. For instance, once an individual has learned a new concept (like "trained incapacity," for example), illustrations of that concept are encountered with a surprising frequency. Interpretation is an important part of human action.

Dewey had five children, and they played a role in his increasing desire to reform education.† Dewey's philosophy of education grew out of the boredom and abstractness of his own early school experiences. His learning from life was much more exciting than his learning in school (Lagemann 1989) and he wanted formal education to capture the natural curiosity of children. Dewey founded an elementary school at the University of Chicago that served as a laboratory for the philosophy department. Commonly called the Dewey School, which could be written "Do-y School," after its slogan "To learn by doing" (Eastman 1941), "was the most important experimental venture in the whole history of American education" (Hook 1939, p. 15). Dewey was opposed to rote learning, to pumping children full of knowledge. Instead, he wanted schools to operate enough like society so that children became interested in learning spontaneously, through a natural curiosity that led to their active involvement in the teaching-learning process. The teacher's role is to provide the child with tools for learning. Dewey's motto was: "Teach the whole child." Math, for example, was taught through cooking and carpentry experience. The Dewey School was supported by the parents of its elite students and by gifts from wealthy Chicago families. Its enriched environment (23 teachers for only 140 students) provided ideal conditions for Dewey's reformist ideas and

---

*Dewey's conception of the reflex arc led directly to the idea of stages in the innovation-decision process through which an individual adopts a new idea (Rogers 1983).

†Dewey's style of working at home often entailed bouncing one child on his knee while another child had a finger in the inkwell of his writing desk (Dearborn 1988, p. 23).

launched the progressive movement in American education, which he led for several decades.

Dewey made the administrative error of appointing his wife Alice to be principal of the school without consulting President Harper. Such nepotism was unacceptable to the university president. She was a zealot for Dewey's ideas about educational reform. Eventually, in 1904, Mrs. Dewey was eased out as the school's principal by President Harper. She resigned from the school, and John Dewey left the University of Chicago.*

At that time, Dewey was so famous that "he could have had a chair in philosophy, psychology, or education in almost any university in the country" (Eastman 1941). Within a few weeks of his resignation from Chicago, Dewey, then forty-five years old, was appointed professor of philosophy at Columbia University. He spent the rest of his career there, eventually retiring in 1930 but continuing to write and publish his ideas about democracy, educational reform, and pragmatic philosophy until his death in 1952.[†]

Dewey stated, "The Great Society created by steam and electricity may be a society, but it is no community." The restoration of the sense of community was possible, however. "Till the Great Society is converted into a Great Community, the Public will remain in eclipse. Communication can alone create a great community" (Dewey 1927, pp. 98, 142). Dewey gave a series of lectures in 1926 at Kenyon College, Ohio, in which he expressed his concerns about American democracy. These lectures, later published as *The Public and Its Problems* (1927), argued that agricultural settlements in early America were the basis for community and for democracy. Dewey doubted that democracy could survive in an urbanized mass society unless certain of the essentials of the rural community could be restored. He hoped that modern media of communication, like newspapers, could again connect people with each other in the metropolitan society. Thus democracy might survive. Dewey's pondering about how American democracy could adapt to urban life

---

*The conflict between Dewey and Harper was complicated, involving more than just Mrs. Dewey (McCaul, 1961). For example, Dewey clashed with Harper over the merger of his school with another progressive school.

[†]Feminism was one of Dewey's strong beliefs, and in this matter he was far ahead of his time. He once marched down Fifth Avenue in New York carrying a sign that said, "Men can vote! Why can't I?" Dewey was bewildered at the amused smiles of the spectators (Dearborn 1988, p. 92).

was an issue carried forward by his Chicago school colleagues George Herbert Mead and Robert E. Park.

Today the Department of Psychology at the University of Vermont is housed in Dewey Hall. John Dewey and his wife are buried, at his wish, on the campus of the University of Vermont, with a view out over Lake Champlain. The house in which Dewey was born still stands, just a block from the university campus.

WILHELM WUNDT, FOUNDER OF EXPERIMENTAL PSYCHOLOGY

John Dewey's work on the reflex arc concept and George Herbert Mead's symbolic interaction had their foundation in Wilheim Wundt's experimental psychology. The degree to which the social sciences began in Europe, particularly in Germany, is illustrated by the case of experimental psychology (Dobson and Bruce 1972; Bringmann, Balance, and Evans 1975; Ben-David and Collins 1966; Hilgard 1987, pp. 38–47). The new discipline of experimental psychology got underway in Germany in the 1880s, mainly as a spin-off from physiology and philosophy. The discipline of physiology was already well developed in Germany; in fact, there was a surplus of well-qualified Ph.D.s in this field in comparison to the limited number of university professorships in physiology. Hence, pressure was created for a related field, psychology, in which physiologists could gain the professorships they felt they deserved. Philosophy was also an academic surplus field in Germany of the 1880s. Philosophy was mainly a speculative field, but certain philosophers were beginning to use empirical methods like experimentation.

Wilhelm Wundt (1832–1920) the founding father of experimental psychology, exemplifies this history of the field of psychology as it got underway as a recognized unit of university organization in Germany.* Before Wundt opened his Institute of Psychology, including a psychological laboratory, at Leipzig in 1879, psychology had been organized mainly as a specialty within philosophy. Wundt moved psychology away from the philosopher's armchair and into the experimental laboratory (Farr 1983). He was trained in physiology (as a medical doctor) and conducted physiological research for several years, before becoming a professor of philosophy at the University of Leipzig in 1875 and

---

*Tichener (1921), the respected historian of psychology, says that "Wundt is the founder, not of experimental psychology alone, but of psychology."

finally launching one of the world's first psychological laboratories, originally supported with his own funds until the university officially recognized his Psychological Institute a few years later (Bringmann, Balance, and Evans 1975). Wundt "is the first name who without reservation is properly called a psychologist" (Boring 1929). In fact, he trained almost every one of the first generation of psychologists in Germany and in America.* Many of those who were not his students were his "grandstudents." During his sixty-year university teaching career, he taught a remarkable 24,000 students (Bringmann, Balance, and Evans 1975).

Wundt had considerable intellectual influence on a number of early and important social scientists. G. Stanley Hall (1844–1924), who received the first American doctorate in psychology, visited Leipzig and returned to the United States to introduce psychological experimentation, first at Johns Hopkins (where he taught John Dewey) and then at Clark University. J. M. Cattell studied with Wundt and then established a psychological laboratory at Columbia University. Charles E. Spearman, the English statistician who devised rank-order correlation, earned his doctorate at Leipzig with Wundt and then taught at Cambridge University. Wundt was also influential outside psychology. Bronislaw Malinowski, who founded British social anthropology, studied at Leipzig. George Herbert Mead studied with Wundt, as did W. I. Thomas, both of the Chicago school. Dewey's and Mead's idea of the reflex arc derived directly from Wundt's notion of the gesture. Wundt had in turn been influenced by Darwin's *The Expression of the Emotions in Men and Animals* (1872), about what today is called nonverbal communication. Sigmund Freud wrote his book *Totem and Taboo* as a counterargument to Wundt's conception of the totemic age in human evolution (Farr 1983).

The idea of psychological experimentation actually started in two places in Europe in the 1880s: Leipzig and Paris. The Leipzig model for experimentation, pioneered by Wundt, called for both professors and students to participate in the research. In Wundt's institute, he and his students served as subjects and as experimenters, exchanging roles freely. The number of subjects per experiment was small, sometimes only one, and the names of the subjects were usually published." The role of data-source, or subject, was considered to be of higher or more

---

*At the time that Wundt began his Leipzig laboratory in 1879, "more American students were involved in graduate study in Europe than were similarly engaged at home" (Benjamin et al. 1992).

important status than was the experimenter" (Danziger 1985). Subject and experimenter were not strangers and saw themselves as engaged in a common enterprise. The Leipzig experiments investigated human thought processes, like remembering.

At the same time as Wundt's early psychological studies, a contrasting style of psychological experimentation was getting underway in Paris. Here the experimenters were male medical doctors and the subjects were generally female patients diagnosed as hysterical or with other illnesses. The experimenters were perceived as superior to the subjects, who were classified as abnormal. The Paris model of experimentation used the word *subject* for the individual respondents in an experiment, a term that came from medical practice.

Psychology in America mainly adapted the Paris model: the word *subject* was used, individual subjects became totally anonymous, and generally the number of subjects per experiment was quite large, perhaps several hundred (Danziger 1985). Collaborative, friendly relationships no longer characterized the subject-experimenter relationship.

For the first decade or so of psychology, until the 1880s, the discipline was almost completely German. Wundt authored the main textbook for experimental psychology and edited the first journal, *Psychological Studies*. German-language publications dominated until 1915, when the center of psychology as a discipline shifted to America with World War I. After 1933, due to Hitler's persecution of Jewish scholars, and then because of World War II, German psychology went into a steep decline and almost disappeared, with the number of American publications outnumbering German publications fifteen to one (Ben-David and Collins 1966).

GEORGE HERBERT MEAD AND SYMBOLIC INTERACTIONISM

George Herbert Mead (1863–1931) was born in Hadley, a small town in Massachusetts, where his father was a Congregational minister. Later, the senior Mead became a professor at Oberlin College in Ohio, where Mead studied for his bachelor's degree. About this time, he began to question religious dogma and to be troubled by self-doubts about his religiosity. Given that the field of philosophy and Christian beliefs were so closely tied, Mead's religious questioning posed difficulties for his intended future as a philosophy professor. Mead studied for one year at Harvard University with William James, the noted pragmatist, whose children he tutored, before enrolling at the University of Leipzig with

Figure 5.4. George Herbert Mead (1863–1931).
Used by permission of the University of Chicago Archives.

Wilhelm Wundt, specializing in the theory of the gesture. Mead said that the act is the basic unit of social science because of its symbolic significance. The act is social because it is interpreted by another individual. Mead also studied at the University of Berlin, perhaps with Georg Simmel, but he did not complete his Ph.D. degree. After teaching in Ann Arbor for several years, Mead moved from the University of Michigan to Chicago in 1894, at John Dewey's invitation. He taught at Chicago for thirty-seven years, until his death in 1931.

Mead and Dewey were very close. Although both were extremely shy in public, the two got along famously with each other. They worked together in the philosophy department at Michigan, and when Dewey was offered the position of department chair at Chicago, one of his conditions was to bring Mead with him from Ann Arbor. The Mead children, along with the Dewey children, attended Dewey's laboratory school on the Midway campus, and Mead participated actively in school affairs, including fund raising. "The personal connection that joined Dewey and Mead served as a conduit for the wholesale transfer of ideas" (Lagemann 1989).

George Herbert Mead had an original mind and made a notable contribution to social science by launching the theoretical perspective later known as symbolic interactionism. This social-psychological viewpoint was influenced by Charles Sanders Peirce, William James, Josiah Royce, James Mark Baldwin, John Dewey, and Charles Horton Cooley, plus Wilhelm Wundt and Chauncey Wright, but it was uniquely a Meadian conception (Lincourt and Hare 1973). Herbert Blumer, a latter-day Chicago sociologist, carried forward Mead's ideas into his own version of symbolic interactionism, which he vigorously defended from attack. There are other versions of Mead's theory, although Blumer's is best known. Mead's theoretical perspective was particularly attractive to sociologists, because it was social in nature. For many years, Mead was *the* social psychologist for sociologists (Bulmer 1984, p. 30).

Mead attacked mind-body dualism. He defined the "I" as the impulsive tendency of the individual's response to others. In contrast, the "me" is the incorporated others within the individual, consisting of all the attitudes of others with whom one has interacted and which one takes over into oneself. The "me" is thus an individual's view of how others see him or her—the attitudes of others that one assumes. An important concept for Mead was role taking, the ability of the self-individual to act socially toward himself or herself as toward others. Mead conceived of the mind as social, as developing through communication with others. Median theory states that individuals get to know themselves through interaction with others, who communicate to them who they are (Rogers 1986, p. 81).

Recall that Charles Horton Cooley coined the term "looking-glass self," an individual's self-conception constructed by imagining how others reflect one's image to oneself. Cooley, however, did not offer an explanation of how the self is formed. Mead did. He argued that no one is born with a self, and it does not develop instinctively. Instead, said Mead, the self is developed through a social process of interaction with others (Faris 1970, p. 96). The individual internalizes the interpretations and meanings of various others, obtained particularly early in life, to create a "generalized other," which is built up of the averaged expectations of many other individuals. "The human, physiologically among the most helpless and dependent creatures in the animal kingdom, thus obtains an emergent power which makes him the dominant species on earth" (Faris 1970, p. 98). The generalized other is those expectations of others with whom one interacts and who become a general guide to one's behavior. Gradually an individual learns to act not just in relation to the expectations of a few specific people but in terms of how other individuals in general would expect one to behave.* The essence of the self is reflexivity, the capacity to see oneself as an object of one's own reflection.

Mead taught a popular doctoral-level course, Advanced Social Psychology, which was an important part of the Chicago school of sociology and may have been the first course in social psychology in America. Most doctoral students in sociology enrolled in his course and thus were exposed to Mead's symbolic interactionist perspective. They adopted it enthusiastically in a theoretical sense, but it was not reflected directly or tested in their doctoral dissertation researches, and the many students who took Mead's famous course seldom cited their teacher in their scholarly publications. Nevertheless, the symbolic interactionism perspective oriented them toward the particular human behavior that they studied.

George Herbert Mead's work had been purely philosophical for forty years, but at Chicago he became reformist. He was active in helping establish Jane Addams's Hull House.† Mead was a close friend of Addams and served as treasurer for an association of Chicago settlement houses. Mead was also a member and officer of the City Club of Chicago, a private association devoted to the amelioration of social problems (Barry 1968). He was known as one of Chicago's leading reform figures (Bulmer 1984, p. 124) and between 1910 and 1912 directed a survey of Chicago's stockyard workers.

Mead might have been even more influential in Chicago school sociology but for the fact that he was a faculty member in another department, philosophy, where he taught social psychology. Mead provided a micro-level, individualistic perspective to sociology doctoral students, who then worked mainly in research on macro-level social problems. "Chicago was much more than just George Hebert Mead's social psychology. It was Park's approach. W. I. Thomas, Burgess, and many oth-

---

*Thus Mead's generalized other solved the problem created by Cooley's theory of the looking-glass self, which implied that an individual would have as many selves as there are people with whom the individual interacts. Mead said that we generalize the many others, making the expectations of the individual more manageable.

†Both Hull House and the Dewey School still stand today. Hull House is now surrounded by the campus of the University of Illinois at Chicago and serves as a museum. Dewey's laboratory school is located on the University of Chicago campus and serves as an elite school, mainly for faculty members' children.

ers. All were important parts of the whole of Chicago sociology" (Shibutani 1990).

The faculty and students who were at Chicago in its golden era, 1915–1935, did not refer to symbolic interactionism by that name. Instead, Herbert Blumer (1969) gave this name to the theoretic perspective only after he left Chicago and became the leading promoter and defender of symbolic interactionism. To the Chicagoans, symbolic interactionism was just the viewpoint espoused by George Herbert Mead in his advanced social psychology course. If Mead called his theory anything, it was "social behaviorism." The Chicagoans explicitly wanted to avoid getting labeled as any particular "ism" (Faris, 1990). (In fact, the Chicago school did not refer to itself as such during its heyday. Instead, that name was accorded to the sociology program at Chicago many years later, and mainly by non-Chicagoans.)*

Symbolic interactionism is a distinctly American theoretical perspective, grown by social psychologists at Chicago, with roots in pragmatic philosophy. It is a broad perspective rather than a specific theory and holds that human communication occurs through the exchange of symbols and their meanings. Human behavior can thus be understood by learning how individuals give meaning to the symbolic information that they exchange with others. Symbolic interactionism is based on the notions that individuals act toward objects on the basis of the meanings that these objects have for them, these meanings arise out of social interaction with one's fellows, and these meanings are modified through an interpretive process by the individual (Blumer 1986, p. 2).

Mead did not codify symbolic interactionism in a single book or article, and most of what we know of his theoretical perspective is based on publications edited from students' notes and published after his death in 1931.† Chief among these is *Mind, Self, and Society* (1934). Given this ambiguity in conveying Mead's thinking, it is not surprising that his intellectual descendants are not in complete agreement. Actually Mead left a legacy of confusion. Herbert Blumer was a foremost disciple, leading Mead's followers in stressing symbolic interactionism as a theoretical orientation and as a way of thinking about research problems. It

---

*To add to the confusion, there is also a Chicago school of economics, which has no connection to the Chicago school of sociology.

*Why didn't Mead publish his theory? "Mead shared Dewey's shyness to an extreme, so much so that he thought unduly little of his work and published sparsely throughout his career" (Diner 1980, pp. 35–36).

proved to be difficult to operationalize Mead's concepts like the self and the generalized other, particularly in survey research (Mullins 1973, p. 76).*

A splinter group of symbolic interactionists centered on Manfred Kuhn at the University of Iowa in the 1950s and 1960s, who had studied at the University of Wisconsin with Kimball Young, a Chicagoan. The fundamental divergence of the Iowa and Blumer schools of symbolic interactionism is methodological (Meltzer and Petras 1970). Kuhn and his followers operationalized symbolic interactionist concepts with a device called the Twenty Statements Test (TST), in which a respondent is asked to provide twenty answers to complete the sentence, "I am . . . " Individuals might respond, " . . . a young girl," " . . . a student," and so forth (Kuhn and McPartland 1954). Such self-identifications were used to categorize respondents.† Yet other Chicago sociologists also considered themselves symbolic interactionists but did not hew strictly to either the Blumer or the Kuhn line.‡ The significance of George Herbert Mead to contemporary communication scholars is that his symbolic interactionism put communication at the heart of sociological explanation.

A noted communication investigation that carried forward Herbert Blumer's version of Mead's symbolic interactionism was Erving Goffman's *The Presentation of Self in Everyday Life* (1959), which was based on his 1953 doctoral dissertation at Chicago, "Communication Conduct in an Island Community." Goffman (1922–1982) spent two years on the island of Unst (population 900), in the Shetland Islands off

---

*An exemplar of empirical research that embodies Meadian symbolic interactionism is Howard S. Becker's "On Becoming a Marihuana User" (1953), which takes the viewpoint of the respondent, follows a phenomenological approach, and portrays an individual's actions as rational from the perspective of the actor. Another exemplar is Erving Goffman's *The Presentation of Self in Everyday Life* (1959), which argues that human behavior is like a theater play on a stage.

†The TST has been utilized in over 100 investigations and achieved national attention when it was administered to the first batch of astronauts by NASA (Meltzer and Petras 1970, p. 9).

‡McSween's (1987) citation analysis of references to symbolic interactionism in the fifteen leading communication journals from 1972 to 1986 found that Herbert Blumer was most highly cited, followed by George Herbert Mead. Manfred Kuhn was hardly cited by communication scholars. The three symbolic interactionists were mainly cited in interpersonal communication-oriented journals like *Communication Monographs* and the *Quarterly Journal of Speech* and seldom cited in mass communication journals.

the coast of Scotland, "the most far-fetched island in Great Britain" (Winkin 1992).

Yves Winkin, a communication scholar at the University of Liège, in Belgium, retraced Goffman's steps to Unst and has reconstructed how and why this important study was carried out. Goffman's mentor in the Chicago Department of Sociology was Lloyd Warner, noted for his Yankee City series of ethnographic investigations of social class in a community. Goffman went to Unst in order to conduct a community study but instead pioneered a new type of research by studying conversational interaction in a community. He observed, recorded, and analyzed conversations in Unst, noting how people, with their words, positioned themselves to play out roles almost as if they were on a theatrical stage. They were on the stage of public life. Heavily influenced by reading the works of George Herbert Mead and by the teaching at Chicago of Herbert Blumer, Mead's disciple, Goffman took the symbolic interactionism perspective into a new type of empirical study. Although the Chicago sociologists were symbolic interactionists, they did not study interaction. Goffman's approach to analyzing human interaction was a radical departure from Chicago sociology. Later, while a faculty member at the University of Pennsylvania, Goffman studied the conversations of mental patients (*Asylums,* 1961), the handicapped (*Stigma,* 1963), and women (*Gender Advertisements,* 1979), pioneering the tradition of communication research called conversation analysis, which he called the interaction order.

ROBERT E. PARK AND CHICAGO'S GOLDEN ERA

Robert E. Park (1864–1944) was born near the end of the American Civil War. He shares his birth year with Charles Horton Cooley and Max Weber, who were six years older than Emile Durkheim and Georg Simmel, yet Park began his sociological career during World War I, when Cooley and the European sociologists were ending theirs. The reason is that Park began his academic career in 1913 at the University of Chicago at the venerable age of fifty. By any measure, he was a late bloomer, earning his Ph.D. degree at age thirty-nine, starting his teaching of sociology at fifty, and achieving his first professorial appointment at age fifty-nine. Within about a decade of taking up his first university teaching post in sociology, Park was elected president of the American Sociological Society, in 1925–1926.

Park has been described as "perhaps the single most influential per-

Figure 5.5. Robert E. Park (1864–1944) at the University of Chicago.
Used by permission of the University of Chicago Archives.

son in American sociology" (Boskoff 1969, p. 94), and it is said that "probably no other man has so deeply influenced the direction taken by American empirical sociology" (Turner 1967, p. ix). Park launched the scholarly study of four important topics: mass communication, race relations, human ecology, and collective behavior. "Thus the man who considered himself a failure at the age of 50 became the center of a great movement of social investigation" (Huges 1964).

Like his colleagues in the Chicago school, Park came from a rural, Protestant background. He was born on a farm in Pennsylvania and grew up in Red Wing, Minnesota, a small town on the Mississippi River. Red Wing had a number of foreign-born Scandinavian families, and the young Park was fascinated by them and in how they adjusted to American society. Park was an active boy and not bookish. He did not come out of an intellectual background.

The Education of Robert Park

Park attended the University of Michigan, where he was one of John Dewey's protégés; he took six philosophy courses from Dewey. He said in his memoirs (Park 1929a, p. 4): "It was there that I met John Dewey. He was an institution in philosophy, . . . an inspiring teacher, and his influence, while not perhaps designed or intended to do so, inspired and encouraged in me an intellectual curiosity in regard to the world for which there was no justification or explanation in the tradition in which I had been reared." Clearly Dewey was a strong intellectual influence on his student (Table 5.2). "Park took from Dewey a life-long interest in the role of communication as a force for integrating society and in devices for communication, especially the newspaper and the telephone" (Matthews 1977, p. 5). After Park's graduation in 1887, he worked as a newspaper reporter in Minneapolis, Detroit, Denver, and New York. Park was an investigative reporter and a reformer. For example, while employed by the *Minneapolis Journal* from 1887 to 1890, he exposed gambling houses and opium dens. When a diphtheria epidemic broke out, Park plotted the cases on a city map and identified the probable source of infection as an open sewer (Park 1929a, p. 5).

In 1892, Park decided to give up his newspaper career and join his father, now located in Watertown, South Dakota, in the grocery business. En route across the country, Park stopped in Detroit, where he learned that John Dewey, his former philosophy professor at Michigan, was starting a new kind of publication, *Thought News,* intended to link the expertise of university scholars with newspaper audiences by providing useful information about long-time social trends. Dewey's partner in this activity was a shadowy figure, Franklin Ford, who had edited a financial journal, *Bradstreet's,* in New York.* Professor Dewey who "had a lifelong weakness for quacks," was utterly fascinated by Ford, a kind of snake-oil salesman (Coughlan 1975, p. 96). Dewey introduced Park to Franklin Ford, and Park joined their visionary publishing venture. The copy for the first issue of *Thought News* was written in April 1892 but never published; the price of $1.50 for twelve issues per year was too high to attract subscribers. The venture failed, and Park went back to newspaper work, twenty-five dollars poorer, but his experience with *Thought News* changed the course of his life (Raushenbush 1979, p. 18). From then on, Park was interested in the relationship of the press to public opinion, a topic that he was to pursue in his doctoral dissertation a decade later. "It was . . . while I was a [newspaper] reporter and a

---

Bradstreet's and its competitor, *Dun's,* later combined to form Dun and Bradstreet, the credit and financial company that today publishes the *Wall Street Journal.*

TABLE 5.2
Major Events in the Career of Robert E. Park

Year	Events
1864	Born on a farm near Harveyville, Pennsylvania; moves with parents to Red Wing, Minnesota
1887	Earns a bachelor's degree at the University of Michigan in philosophy, where he is influenced by John Dewey
1887–1897	Works as a court reporter, police reporter, drama critic, general news reporter, and editor for the *Minneapolis Journal, Detroit Times, Denver Times, New York Morning Journal, New York World, Detroit Tribune, Detroit News*, and *Chicago Journal*
1892	Becomes involved in publishing *Thought News* with John Dewey and Franklin Ford
1897–1898	Earns a master's degree in philosophy at Harvard University
1899–1903	Does graduate study at Royal Friedrich-Wilhelms University, Berlin (taking his one course in sociology from Georg Simmel), the University of Strasbourg, and the University of Heidelberg, from which he earns his Ph.D. in philosophy with a dissertation, "The Crowd and the Public"
1903–1905	Assistant in the Department of Philosophy at Harvard University and secretary of the Congo Reform Association
1905–1912	Director of public relations at Booker T. Washington's Tuskegee Institute, Alabama
1913–1922	Professional lecturer, Department of Sociology, University of Chicago
1921	Coauthor (with Ernest W. Burgess) of a textbook, *Introduction to the Science of Sociology*, that defines the field of sociology
1922	Writes *The Immigrant Press and Its Control*
1923–1933	Appointed professor, Department of Sociology, University of Chicago
1925–1926	Elected president, American Sociological Society (now Association)
1929–1933	Travels in Japan, Indonesia, the Philippines, China, India, and South Africa and teaches at the University of Hawaii
1936–1944	Visiting professor of sociology, Fisk University, Nashville
1944	Dies on February 7, at age seventy-nine, in Nashville

city editor that I began my sociological studies. It was under the guidance of an extraordinary personality, Franklin Ford, himself a newspaper man, that I got my first understanding of the significance and the possibilities of the social survey as an instrument for social investigation" (Park 1929a).

While working for a Detroit newspaper in 1893, Park met George Herbert Mead, then a young professor of philosophy at the University of Michigan. Their paths would cross again two decades later in Chicago.

Park carried on a courtship by letter with Clara Cahill, daughter of a state judge in Lansing, 100 miles from Detroit. He wrote to her about himself and his newspaper work: "I love this crazy mixed-up world; if I didn't love it, I couldn't write about it" (Raushenbush 1979, p. 24). Park told Cahill, whom he later married, that eventually he would leave newspaper work to go into "the think business." He was indeed to become a philosopher and then a sociologist. In 1898, Park quit newspaper work to take up graduate study: "I went back to the university and spent altogether seven years at it—at Ann Arbor, Harvard, and in Germany. I did this because I was interested in communication and collective behavior and wanted to know what the universities had to say about it" (Raushenbush 1979, p. 28). At the turn of the century, the scholarly study of communication was not available in universities. So Park, the former newspaperman, studied philosophy, which at that time included what we today would call psychology and social psychology. In the fall of 1898, at age thirty-four, Park and his growing family moved to Cambridge, where he obtained an M.A. degree in philosophy from Harvard University a year later.

Park went to Harvard to understand communication, but Harvard did not give him what he was looking for. He studied with William James, Josiah Royce, and George Santayana, three brilliant philosophers, and also with Hugo Munsterberg, a former student of Wilhelm Wundt in experimental psychology. After earning his M.A., Park moved with his wife and children to Berlin, where he registered at the Royal Friedrich-Wilhelms University. In spring 1900, he took Georg Simmel's course in sociology, the only one on this topic in which Park would ever enroll. It gave him the fundamental point of view for the study of the newspaper and society for which he was searching (Park 1929a, p. 8).

Park next moved to the University of Strasbourg for two years to study with Wilhelm Windelband, whom Park felt had the requisite methodological expertise. Park enrolled in courses in philosophy and the social sciences and began his dissertation, *"Masse and Publikum: Eine Methodologische und Soziologische Untersuchung"* ("Crowd and Public: A Methodological and Sociological Inquiry").* In 1902, Windelband moved to the University of Heidelberg, and Park went with him, completing his dissertation in 1903. Then he returned to the United States and a position as assistant in philosophy at Harvard. Park did not want the role of the university professor for which he was now trained; he was tired of the academic world. Further, he was ashamed of his dissertation and the little book that was published from it, which represented the product of his seven years of graduate study. He felt that he was a failure. Later he stated: "I was disgusted with what I had done in the university, and had come to the conclusion that I couldn't do anything first rate on my own account. I decided the best thing I could do was to attach myself to someone who was doing something first rate" (Hughes 1964).

Park became the editorial secretary for the Congo Reform Association, an arm of the Baptist Missionary Society, which was protesting the harsh Belgian rule of the Congo and pressuring against European colonialization of Africa. Through his work in the Congo Reform Association, Park met Booker T. Washington, president of the Tuskegee Normal and Industrial Institute in Alabama, a vocational training school for young African-Americans in the South. Washington was an internationally known American leader (Huges 1964). Washington urged Park to see Tuskegee before visiting the Congo. Park came to Tuskegee, where he stayed for the next seven years as an editorial assistant to President Booker T. Washington, essentially in charge of public relations. The institute enrolled 1,600 students, and was a vital institution in the black community of the South. Park used his position at the Tuskegee Institute to gain insight into the problems of black people in America. He roamed widely over the South, observing the lives of the poor.

Washington and Park took a lengthy European trip together in 1910 to gather information about peasants, factory laborers, and government policies intended to help disadvantaged groups. As they traveled, mainly by railway, Park and Washington discussed what they had seen and been told. When they reached the next city, Washington would

*Park's dissertation was published as a book (in German) by Lack and Grunar in Bern, Switzerland, in 1904. An English translation by Charlotte Eisner, *Robert E. Park: The Crowd and the Public and Other Essays,* was published in 1972.

dictate his conclusions to a stenographer, and Park would then edit and rewrite the resulting manuscript into their important book, *The Man Farthest Down* (Washington and Park 1912). Park once said that his editing of Washington's and his wife Clara's writing could "make Clara sound more like Clara, and Washington sound more like Washington" than either could alone (Raushenbush 1979, p. 57). *The Man Farthest Down* argued that much more was being done in Europe to help the working class than was being done for blacks in America.* Washington took a stronger position on civil rights after the 1910 European trip, presumably as a result of what Park had helped him learn in Europe.

Park Moves to Chicago

During this period, Park met Albion Small at Roaring Brook, Michigan, where the Parks had a summer cabin. Small sounded Park out about teaching a summer school course at Chicago, but Park was not interested (Raushenbush 1979, p. 41). That attitude was to change a few years later, in 1912, during the International Conference on the Negro, held at Tuskegee and organized by Park, where W. I. Thomas of Chicago and Park each presented papers.

When Thomas and Park came together at the Tuskegee conference, they felt an instant rapport. "Thomas accepted the invitation to Tuskegee, expecting to remain for a couple of days. He stayed two weeks,[†] walking the red clay roads in company with the brooding, infinitely curious and well-read Park, of whom he had never heard" (Hughes 1964). It was more than just a meeting of two great sociological minds; it was a coming together of the top experts in two related forces that were changing American society. Park "knew the relations of Negroes with white Americans better than any social scientist in the country" (Hughes 1964). Thomas was the leading scholar in understanding what happened to rural European immigrants in American cit-

---

*The Booker T. Washington Papers in the U.S. Library of Congress show that Park also assisted Washington in writing two other books: *The Story of the Negro* (1909) and *My Larger Education* (1911). Washington's books were in part intended to attract donations to the Tuskegee Institute (Raushenbush 1979, p. 57).

†Actually, it could not have been two weeks; W. I. Thomas wrote a letter to Park from Chicago on April 24, 1912, four days after the conference ended. It began: "My dear brother in Christ: I am amazed to find how ignorant I was before I met you, and how wise I seem to be now" (Raushenbush 1979, p. 68).

ies. His monumental study, *The Polish Peasant in Europe and America,* was underway at the time of the Tuskegee conference. The masses of European immigrants in American cities aggravated social problems like poverty, slums, and crime. "So when Park and Thomas came together in 1912 in Tuskegee, and then became colleagues at Chicago, North American empirical sociology became the study of immigrants, ethnic groups, and what happens when several of them live in the same city, work in the same economy, and are citizens of the same body politic" (Hughes 1964).

After the 1912 Tuskegee conference, Thomas pushed Albion Small, chair of the Chicago Department of Sociology, to hire Park, but Small had agreed with the university administration that the sociology faculty was not to expand. Park began his teaching at Chicago as a very marginal man. He came in summer 1913 to offer a course on race relations, probably the first such course on this topic to be taught anywhere (Raushenbush 1979, p. 77). His original faculty appointment was in the university's Divinity School. Then he was appointed a professional lecturer in the Department of Sociology, a title that he held for nine years, until he was finally named full professor in 1923. Park's salary in 1914 was $500 to teach a single course, hardly enough to support his family.

Park had also been paid a nominal salary by the Tuskegee Institute, and this pattern continued during his first nine years at the University of Chicago. Park loved his work and did not feel concerned about his inadequate pay. Park's father had died about the time that Park moved to Chicago, and his inheritance allowed him to live comfortably. "Park was not exactly a rich man but he inherited a competence and there were no financial worries. He could go where he pleased and travel as much as he liked" (Faris 1944). By 1916, Park was teaching four courses at Chicago: The Newspaper, The Crowd and the Public, The Survey, and The Negro in America (Raushenbush 1979, p. 77).

When Robert Park arrived in the Department of Sociology, the Chicago school was a going concern, with Albion Small the founding figure and W. I. Thomas the intellectual driving force. The University of Chicago had already awarded thirty Ph.D. degrees in sociology before Park came in 1913. Another seventy-seven doctorates were awarded by 1934, when Park retired to emeritus status (Faris 1970, pp. 135–140). Park elevated the Chicago department into international prominence, forging a new type of empirically based social science.

Human Ecology and Social Disorganization

The local setting in which Park and Thomas were colleagues had a unique terrain: "So flat and uncomplicated that the forces that build cities could play themselves out in such a fashion that a map was also a systematic chart" (Hughes 1964). Park, his colleagues (especially Ernest Burgess), and his students plotted the location of juvenile crime, prostitution, mental illness, and other social problems on a map of Chicago (they called it a "spot-map"). The picture that typically emerged was of a concentric circle (a half-circle in the case of Chicago, due to Lake Michigan), with the greatest concentration of social problems lying just outside the downtown Loop. This type of sociological analysis came to be called human ecology, a term Park used in 1926, when he taught the first course on this topic (Huges 1968, p. 418).* Park and his students explored plant and animal ecology, mainly conducted in the light of Darwinian evolutionary theory, from which they borrowed such concepts as invasion, dominance, succession, and gradients of growth.

The research on urban social problems at Chicago was conducted by historians, political scientists, economists, anthropologists, and geographers, as well as sociologists, with Park "the natural, if never the official, leader of this very energetic movement" (Huges 1964). The Chicago school was more than just a school of sociology; it was, to a certain extent, a school of social sciences. Certainly the pragmatic and progressive nature of empirical research at Chicago infected anthropology, social psychology, philosophy, and political science, as well as sociology. The research focus on the urban problems of the city of Chicago was encouraged by the Local Community Research Committee and its successor, the Social Science Research Committee, funded mainly by the Laura Spelman Rockefeller Memorial between 1923 and 1932 (Park 1929b).

Park's interest in urban life, sparked by Georg Simmel, concentrated on the disruptions and social disorganization of the city, especially among new immigrants. Such an "anti-urban bias" is understandable, given Park's early lifetime experiences in a rural setting and in the light of the extreme difficulties of immigrants in adjusting to the rapidly growing city of Chicago in the 1913–1935 period. The research approach of Park and his doctoral students is illustrated by Nels

---

*The concept of ecology—the interrelationships among living organisms and between those organisms and their environment—had been coined in the 1890s by Ernst Haeckel, a German biologist and popularizer of Charles Darwin's evolutionary theory (Goist 1971).

Anderson's study of hobos, or what today are called homeless men. Chicago was estimated to have 30,000 hobos in the 1920s (Gillette 1928), many concentrated in the Madison-Halsted Street area, in what was called "Hobohemia." Nels Anderson, a Chicago doctoral student who was personally acquainted with the hobo life-style (from having previously lived as a hobo), in 1921 began to conduct informal interviews with individuals in Hobohemia in order to collect their life histories. He played the role of a hobo, acting as a participant observer (he was, perhaps, the first participant observer) in Hobohemia, emerging daily to attend his classes on the Midway campus. Park told Anderson: "Write down only what you see, hear, and know, like a newspaper reporter." This research was funded by a grant of $300. Anderson began to draft chapters, describing the Chicago urban world of the hobo, who were viewed as outcasts by society. Park and Burgess approved Anderson's dissertation, Park edited it into book form (without initially asking for Anderson's permission), added a preface, and six days later sent the manuscript off to the University of Chicago Press. *The Hobo* (Anderson 1923 was the first volume in the Sociological Series of the university press. It described the loathing with which hobos were held by the public, and how hobos reacted to being treated as pariahs in society.

Drawing on evolutionary theory, especially the Darwinian notion of the struggle for existence, Park distinguished four major social processes:

1. *Competition,* the struggle among units in a system for scarce resources.
2. Conflict, competition among units that are in contact or communication with each other. *Communication* was defined as occurring when minds meet so that two or more individuals mutually influence each other. Communication was thus defined as effective communication.
3. *Accommodation,* which occurs when conflict ceases, because of the allocation of status and power so that superordinate-subordinate relationships are fixed and controlled by the social structure.
4. *Assimilation,* the exchanging and sharing of cultural elements so that a common culture results. For example, Park studied the assimilation of European immigrants into American culture (which itself is an amalgamation of various immigrant cultures).

The Chicago sociologists found that each succeeding wave of European immigrants that had poured into the city's slums experienced the same severe social disorganization. As these populations prospered and migrated outward into higher-status residential areas over time, the rate of social disorganization declined (Faris 1970, p. 57). Park and his students found that this process occurred because most of the immigrants came from rural areas in Europe and had to learn how to live in a city. In a sense, slums were a kind of informal school for urban living. European Jews, who had lived in urban ghettos for 500 years, did not experience an equivalent degree of social disorganization when they migrated to America (Wirth 1926).

The Chicago slums were socially disorganized but not unorganized. Such institutions as the family, school, and church might break down in a crowded slum, but other forms of organization, like teenage gangs, flourished. The gangs attracted the children of foreign-born immigrants and often channeled these young people into serious types of crime (Faris 1970, p. 77). The Chicago sociologists found that juvenile delinquents seldom committed their first criminal act alone. The gang provided them information, motivation, and group support.

Paul G. Cressey's study of the taxi-dance hall is somewhat typical of the Chicago school's investigations of social disorganization. Cressey and four student research assistants gathered data in taxi-dance halls as covert observers. They pretended to be taxi-dance hall habitués, mixing with the patrons and not revealing their true identities. Cressey believed that through such informal contact with his respondents, he gained information that would otherwise not be revealed (Bulmer 1984, p. 105). Cressey also gathered life histories from the taxi-dance girls and their patrons in order to understand the full context of their respondents' situation, by asking respondents to describe their entire life. The life-history method has not been used much since the days of the Chicago school, as researchers depend more and more on the survey interview as a more structured tool for gathering quantitative data. The Chicago multimethod approach, however, continues to be valuable. The human ecology research on social disorganization is probably best known for its spot-maps of the city, on which the frequency of divorces, suicides, crimes, and other indicators of social disorganization were plotted (with each case indicated by a circular spot that was glued on to the map). The Chicago scholars combined quantitative data with insights and understandings that they mainly obtained by ethnographic methods that allowed them to get up close to their respondents.

The Stranger and Social Distance

Park elaborated Simmel's concept of social distance, the perceived lack of intimacy between two or more individuals or other categories.* He derived this concept from Simmel's idea of the stranger, and one of Park's students, Emory Bogardus, developed a social distance scale.[†] Park also adopted the role of marginal man from Simmel's concept of the stranger. A marginal person is one who lives between two worlds but belongs to neither—for example, children of immigrants to America who typically rejected their parents' language and culture but did not consider themselves to be full-fledged members of American society either. Park's student, Everett V. Stonequist, authored *The Marginal Man* (1937), building on Park's concept.

Certain of Simmel's basic concepts, like the related ideas of the stranger and social distance, stimulated considerable research in America (Levine, Carter, and Gorman 1976). Simmel's stranger, an outsider to the group, possessed certain advantages, such as objectivity and creativity in perceiving the group and its actions. Similarly, the social scientist, by remaining somewhat distant from his or her objects of study, maximizes objectivity. Studies of innovators, the first individuals in a system to adopt new ideas, show them to be cosmopolite and relatively unintegrated with their system. Thus, they enjoy a freedom from conformity to the system's norms (Rogers 1983). Robert Park and his Chicago students not only studied social distance and marginality, but Park insisted that his students become objective and detached observers of what they studied.[‡]

Park at Work

Park's role in Chicago sociology is illustrated by the experience of Norman Hayner, who kept a diary of his day-to-day activities in earning his

---

*Park utilized the concept of social distance in his analyses of race relations. He argued that the greater the social distance is between two individuals, the less they influence each other reciprocally (Coser 1977, p. 360).

[†]The Bogardus scale indexed, for instance, whether a white Caucasian perceived himself as closer to an individual of Chinese descent than to a black American (Bogardus 1929, 1933).

[‡]Although Park emphasized that a scholar should gain the subjective point of view of a respondent by empathically and imaginatively participating in the life of the respondent, in

Ph.D. degree. In 1921, Hayner enrolled in Park's course The Social Survey and became interested in Park's lectures about mobility and the stranger (Faris 1970, p. 80). Soon after, Park approved Hayner's proposal to study Chicago residential hotels and the individuals who lived in them. Hayner began to gather data through observation and personal interviews in downtown hotels and also in hotels near the University of Chicago. Park accompanied Hayner on an all-day walking visit to several Chicago hotels and to sources of information about them. Hayner noted, "Over lunch Park told his life story" (Faris 1970, p. 81). A few days later, Hayner presented his research proposal in Park's doctoral seminar, where it was well received. He continued gathering data through personal interviews with hotel residents, and he met regularly with Park to discuss his dissertation plans. By May 1922, Hayner began writing the first chapter of his dissertation, which Park approved, with some suggested revisions. Hayner completed his dissertation in 1923 and defended it in a meeting with his doctoral committee. Park was pleased with Hayner's study and encouraged him to publish it in book form. *Hotel Life,* which deals with Simmel's and Park's ideas about mobility and detachment behavior, applied to the empirical study of hotel residents, finally appeared in 1936.

Park thus introduced the guided dissertation into the Chicago Department of Sociology. Until then, a doctoral candidate followed the German pattern of choosing a topic, writing the dissertation in solitary confinement, and then presenting the final product to the professor, who judged its intellectual merit (Lazarsfeld 1962a). Park instead, treated his doctoral students as younger colleagues in a community of scholars. He served as their coach, telling them how to do social research in an apprenticeship relationship. Park had a special rapport with his students, representing one model for effective doctoral student-professor relationships. William Oscar Brown, whose 1930 Ph.D. dissertation dealt with racial prejudice, called Park "the greatest intellectual influence in my life. . . . He was never familiar with his students, but he respected them, he understood them, above all he was interested in them. He always respected you as a person." Everett V. Stonequist, another doctoral student of Park, noted, "In our early discussions he did

---

order to gain a real understanding of social actions. Park often quoted William James's "On a Certain Blindness in Human Beings," which argues that each of us is likely to misunderstand the meaning of other people's lives (Park 1950, p. 21). Park had heard a lecture by James on this topic while he was studying for his master's degree at Harvard University (White and White 1962, p. 157).

not offer advice on procedure, scope, or specific references but preferred discussing ideas. . . . Usually he would wait for a question, then turn it over in his mind and give his comments. He had a gift of making me feel like a collaborator rather than a student." Herbert Blumer, who earned his doctorate at Chicago and then stayed on to teach said, "In the course of my more than 30 years of observations in the field of graduate work, I have never seen any teacher who could be as successful as Park in awakening, mobilizing, and directing the talents of students and bringing them to their highest potentiality" (Raushenbush 1979, pp. 103, 105).

Edward Shils (1981), who took the last course that Park taught at Chicago, described him as "built like a bear, hunched over like a bear, putting his nose into everything like a bear, and growling and grunting like a bear." According to Robert Faris (1990), who studied for his Ph.D. degree at Chicago under Park between 1928 and 1931, this leader of the Chicago school was a gruff, frank "he-man," who on one occasion drove a female doctoral student in his classroom to tears when he exclaimed, "What a damn silly question!" This same Professor Park, however, frequently asked his doctoral students to dinner at his home near the Midway campus and invited them to accompany him and his family for weekends and vacations at their vacation cottage. Park treated his doctoral students like family members. He gave them advice (they did not always take it), rubbed off on them his tremendous enthusiasm for scholarly research, took pride in their accomplishments, and helped them secure faculty positions when they earned their Ph.D. degrees. Once they left Chicago, he corresponded with them, collaborated with them, and visited them on their university campuses whenever he could (Faris 1990).

Robert Faris remembers Park's courses as "very meaty, and very rich with suggestions of new things to think about. He was unique in the respect that you felt right up on the frontier every day. . . . Park had a way of establishing a real personal relationship with his graduate students, and giving his time by the hours in long talks, virtually by talking a book into them or talking a project into them and then letting the student do it and get the credit for it. . . . Park was a thinker, an absent-minded man, who forgot to get his hair cut, who forgot to wear a tie some days, and things like that. [He] came to class with soap in his ears" (Faris 1972).

Some of the Chicago doctoral students were brilliant, and others were mediocre. Park worked with all of them, bringing out the best in each, challenging them to perform in scholarly research at a level they did not themselves think was possible. Many, in fact, were not able to reach a comparable level of scholarly excellence in their careers after they left Chicago. Park felt that sociology had to make the most of the people it attracted rather than waiting for more capable individuals (Raushenbush 1979, p. 105). "If students faltered, Park kept after them with kindness and sometimes with brutality" (Shils, 1981).

Defining the Meaning of Sociology

The Chicago school, especially under Park's leadership, defined the meaning of sociology in two important ways. European sociology, prior to Chicago, had been theoretical and abstract in nature. Georg Simmel was prototypical in this sense. He lectured brilliantly and wrote analytically, but empirical (in the sense of gathering or analyzing data) he was not. Chicago sociology was grounded firmly in data, and after Chicago, American sociology based in the empirical world. Park believed in empirical research but not in statistical analysis. "Professor Park would sometimes hurl Jovian thunderbolts at the folly of the statisticians or the misguided Freudians" (Goldman 1973). He felt that searching for statistical relationships among variables would lead a sociologist away from understanding the nature of individuals' relationships.

The other, equally important redefinition of sociology at Chicago was to free it from a primarily normative concern, replacing this orientation with an emphasis on objectivity and a corresponding disdain for the applied field of social work. As Park (1929a) himself stated "Up to this time sociology had been popularly conceived and frequently described as 'a science of social reform' or 'the science of human welfare.'" Many of the early figures in American sociology were Protestant ministers or their sons, motivated to solve social problems through direct intervention; in short, sociology had been defined as "do-goodism." Park (1922) described the Chicago brand of sociology in these terms: "This approach became a logical scheme for a disinterested investigation of the origin and function of social institutions as they everywhere existed, and was in substance an application to society and social life of the pragmatic point of view which Dewey and Mead had already popularized in the [Chicago] department of philosophy."

Park (1922) credited W. I. Thomas with establishing the Chicago tradition of empirical and objective sociology, but after Thomas was forced out of the University of Chicago in 1919 (because of his arrest and morals charge), Park led in carrying forward the Chicago conception of sociology. He told the doctoral students in his classes, often in profane terms, that they should feel welcome to study a social problem, but they should do so independently of their own moral values. For example, a Chicago sociologist might conduct an investigation of prostitution, but the scholar's abhorrence of this profession should not affect how the research was conducted, the findings, or how they were interpreted. Park's conception of the role of the sociologist in social amelioration was that an individual's reformist ideas should be kept out of the research. From time to time, Park would growl his standard reproof at a Chicago doctoral student: "You're another one of those damn do-gooders" (Raushenbush 1979, p. 96). When Park returned from a year of teaching in China, he described the situation there of widespread poverty, hunger, and begging to the Chicago graduate students' Sociology Club. To the student who asked, "Dr. Park, what you described, these horrible conditions in China. Tell us, what would you do about it?" Park replied," Young man, I wouldn't do a thing. I wouldn't do a goddamn thing" (Lindstrom and Hardert 1988). Park was a progressive and wanted to work toward solving social problems through investigating them, but he did not engage directly in ameliorative activities himself. To do so, he felt, would detract sociologists from their main task of social research.

Park separated sociologists from social workers. In 1920, the School of Social Service Administration was created at the University of Chicago to train social workers. The new unit incorporated the university's previous program in home economics and was headed by Edith Abbott, who transferred from the Department of Sociology. Thus was the general pattern set at Chicago for the field: social work was defined as a woman's field, whereas sociology was mainly for male scholars. Social amelioration was the province of social work, leaving sociology free from concern with direct solutions to social problems. Intellectual hostility marred the relationship between sociology and social work at Chicago, and elsewhere (Diner 1975). "Academic training in social work, once generally allied with sociology in one department, has almost universally withdrawn into separate departments and schools, leaving behind the chill that is characteristic of the feelings between divorced couples" (Faris 1970, p. 13). "The field of sociology became more academic and isolated from social problems and the making of social change.

Those with an interest in reform (the 'applied') were channeled into social work, a 'woman's field' [sic] which sociologists regarded with a certain amount of disdain. Thus the 'pure vs. applied' division assumed
gender connotations, and the presence of early woman sociologists was
obscured from view" (Thorne 1990). The applied nature of sociology
during Chicago's golden era ended in 1920, with American sociologists
becoming increasingly uncomfortable with the social reform of social
problems.

The founding fathers of American sociology at the Chicago school
were indeed fathers, not mothers, and men continued to dominate the
new discipline. No woman sociologist was elected president of the
American Sociological Society from its founding in 1906 until 1931. At
Chicago, only 13 (12 percent) of the 112 Ph.D. degrees in sociology
granted through 1935 were awarded to women (Faris 1970, pp. 135–
140). Female sociologists tended to teach in women's colleges or in
schools of social work. As Deegan (1988) noted, the early female sociologists were practicing what was then considered mainstream sociology
but after 1920 was reinterpreted as social work.

The Park and Burgess book *Introduction to the Science of Sociology*
(1924) began in 1916 when Ernest W. Burgess returned to Chicago,
where he had previously earned his Ph.D., to teach an introductory
course in sociology. He and Park collaborated in planning the course
and selected 196 readings to illustrate fourteen sociological themes. The
1,000-page textbook that resulted cited the following scholars (in
order) most frequently: Simmel, Darwin, Spencer, Durkheim, Tarde,
Frederic Le Bon, Cooley, W. I. Thomas, Park, and William Graham
Sumner, with "the outstanding influence in the book . . . that of Park's
mentor, Georg Simmel" (Raushenbush 1979, p. 83). Simmel was cited
forty-three times, more than any other scholar (Coser 1977, p. 374).
The many citations to Darwin and Spencer indicate that evolutionary
theory was also an important influence on the Park-Burgess book, popularly known as the "green bible," which shaped the field of sociology in
its formative years and was "one of the most influential works ever written in sociology" (Faris 1970, p. 37). After its publication, most later
sociology textbooks have followed a generally standardized format. As
Faris (1970, p. 37) concluded: "The direction and content of American
sociology after 1921 was mainly set by the Park and Burgess text."

The Chicago school under Robert Park defined the new field of sociology as empirical, value free and detached from social applications, a

male province, and oriented toward the European theories of Darwinian evolution and Georg Simmel's interactionism.

Park's Communication Research

Park felt that his prior work as an investigative newspaper reporter was good preparation for his career in sociology: "Sociology, after all, is concerned with problems in regard to which newspaper men inevitably get a good deal of firsthand knowledge. . . . One might say that a sociologist is merely a more accurate, responsible, and scientific reporter" (Park 1939). Park's newspaper experience greatly aided his later sociological investigations of the city: "I expect that I have actually covered more ground, tramping about in cities in different parts of the world, than any other living man. Out of all this I gained, among other things, a conception of the city, the community, and the region, not as a geographical phenomena merely but as a kind of social organism" (Faris 1970, p. 29).

Robert Park's *The Immigrant Press and Its Control* (1922) (the only book he ever wrote) came about as the result of national concern with the possible disloyalty of European immigrants in the United States, generated by America's 1917 entry into World War I. Would the millions of German-Americans be loyal to the United States or to Kaiser Wilhelm? Would they spread propaganda and engage in sabotage? On the other hand, how could the civil rights of immigrants loyal to the United States be preserved? The Carnegie Corporation sponsored ten studies of immigrants. Park, who directed the study of the foreign-language press, found that newspapers in Yiddish, Polish, German, and so forth mainly helped recent immigrants learn how to survive in North America. Very little newspaper content encouraged loyalty to the original homeland. The foreign-language newspapers in America were gradually working themselves out of their role by aiding the assimilation of their immigrant audience into American culture. In fact, the number of foreign-language newspapers and the size of their audience dropped dramatically in the decades following World War I.*

Park has been called the "first theorist of mass communication" (Frazier and Gaziano 1979). He defined communication as "a social-psychological process by which one individual is enabled to assume, in

---

*More recently, in the 1980s and 1990s, foreign-language media in the United States have again become important, especially Spanish-language television, because of the large numbers of immigrants from Latin America.

some sense and to some degree, the attitudes and the point of view of another; it is a process by which a rational and moral order among men is substituted for one that is merely physiological and instinctual." Communication involves an empathic feeling into one's communication partner and thus makes possible the social nature of society. Park and his Chicago colleagues used communication as a synonym for human connectedness (Winkin July 27, 1992), viewing it as a potential solution to urban social problems. Communication, however, was not their main variable or focus of study.

THE PAYNE FUND STUDIES OF THE EFFECTS OF FILM

When a new mass media technology diffuses widely in America, it often is accepted first by children and teenagers. This pattern occurred for film in the 1920s, for television in the 1950s, and for microcomputers and video games in the 1980s. The heavy use of a new communication technology by youth typically sets off adult concern, which leads to scholarly research on the effects of the new technology and, occasionally, to actions by policymakers. Usually the main interest of parents and policymakers is in the effects, particularly the potential negative effects, of the new communication technology (Wartella and Reeves 1985). A prototype for this children-as-litmus-paper-for-a-medium's-effects is provided by the Payne Fund studies.

Film began to attract large audiences, especially of children, in the United States during the 1920s. Weekly movie attendance leaped from 40 million people in 1922 to 90 million in 1930. A coordinated program of thirteen investigations of the effects of movies on American children, conducted from 1929 to 1932, was financed by a foundation, the Payne Fund. The research project, Motion Pictures and Youth, was instigated by William Marston Seabury, a former lawyer in the movie industry who became concerned about the effects of movies on youth. Seabury worked out the proposal for the Payne Fund studies with Reverend W. H. Short, who obtained the funding of $65,800, donated by Frances Payne Bolton from monies that she had inherited from her father, a Cleveland industrialist (Jowett 1992), and established a New York headquarters office for the studies.

The purpose of the Payne Fund studies was to determine the possibly harmful effects of film viewing on children and youth. Most of the scholars conducting the research were at the University of Chicago, but several were at Ohio State University, and some were at other universities (for example, the child psychologist George Stoddard was at the University of Iowa). The studies were directed by W. W. Charters, head of the Bureau of Educational Research at Ohio State University. He asked Robert Park to participate, but Park was about to leave on a trip to China, so Park, got his Chicago colleague Herbert Blumer involved (Park later carried out a similar study of film effects on Chinese children in Hong Kong.) In all, the Payne Fund research represents one of the largest scientific programs ever conducted on media effects and "still constitutes the most extensive evaluation ever undertaken of the role of movies in American society and its effect on children" (Jowett 1992). Tens of thousands of children and youth served as respondents during the 1929–1932 study period.

The Payne Fund research showed that American children went to the movies about once a week and that 72 percent of feature films dealt with the themes of crime, sex, and love. The movies frequently showed the use of tobacco and liquor (and this during Prohibition). Understandably, parents were concerned about the effects of this new technology on their children, and with cause. In one study, a sample of children, asked questions about whether they had bad dreams after viewing a violent film, responded that they did.

The Payne Fund studies were conducted in an objective manner, but the findings were interpreted in a manner that was hostile to the film industry. The ten books emanating from the various Payne Fund projects, published in 1933, were generally written in careful social scientific prose, including the summary volume by Charters, but a popular treatment commissioned by the Payne Fund, *Our Movie-Made Children* (Forman 1933), was alarmist in tone (although Charters too concluded "The commercial movies are an unsavory mess"). The studies showed that movies had effects on children and youth; many of these effects did not meet with approval by parents, religious leaders, and others.*

The Payne Fund studies were of a different methodological nature than the typical Chicago school investigations. Statistical methods had

---

*These ten books are: Herbert Blumer, *The Movies and Conduct;* Herbert Blumer and Philip M. Hauser, *Movies, Delinquency, and Crime;* W. W. Charters, *Motion Pictures and Youth: A Summary;* Edgar Dale, *Children's Attendance at Motion Pictures* and *The Content of Motion Pictures,* W. S. Dysinger and Christian A. Ruckmick, *The Emotional Responses of Children to the Motion Picture Situation;* P. W. Holaday and George D. Stoddard, *Getting Ideas from the Movies;* Charles C. Peters, *Motion Pictures and Standards of Morality;* Ruth C. Peterson and L. L. Thurstone, *Motion Pictures and the Social Attitudes of Children;* and Frank K. Shuttleworth and Mark A. May, *The Social Conduct and Attitudes of Movie Fans.*

come into social science research during the 1920s, and the Payne Fund studies were mainly quantitative in nature. Lowery and DeFleur (1988, p. 34) concluded that "it was the coming together of two major social changes in American society—the development of a more precise research capability in the social sciences and the deepening public concern over the mushrooming growth of the movies—that gave birth to the scientific study of mass communication." The focus on media effects by communication scholars really began with the Payne Fund studies of movies and children.

WHY DID CHICAGO DECLINE?

The influence of the Chicago school fell off rapidly after 1935, about the time that Robert E. Park retired, for several reasons. First, it had created its own competition when its Ph.D. graduates left to teach at other universities. Many other good schools of sociology caught up with Chicago. For example, Columbia University after 1941 had two outstanding sociologists: Robert K. Merton, a social theorist, and Paul F. Lazarsfeld, a quantitative methodologist who studied the effects of mass communication. Another rival to Chicago was Harvard University, where sociological theorist Talcott Parsons was rising to prominence, to be joined in 1945 by the methodologist Samuel Stouffer, a Chicago Ph.D. As Chicago slipped back from its lead, the position of other universities, especially that of Columbia, but also Michigan, Wisconsin, North Carolina, and UCLA, rose (Faris 1970, p. 123). Chicago hired its own Ph.D. graduates as its new faculty members. Although collegial cohesion and intellectual homogeneity were resulting advantages, they were offset by such disadvantages as a lack of diversity and the loss of hybrid vigor among the faculty. The end of the Chicago school's preeminence was hastened by a kind of organizational exhaustion brought on by problems of personnel succession (Shibutani 1990).

Another problem was dissension among the faculty in the Chicago Department of Sociology, which detracted from their scholarly work and prevented them from making important decisions, such as about new faculty. For a six- or seven-year period after World War II, Chicago did not hire a single tenure-tracked faculty member, and at the same time important faculty members left: Herbert Blumer to Berkeley, Lloyd Warner to Michigan State, and Everett Hughes to Brandeis. Recent Chicago Ph.D.s were hired as temporary instructors to fill in for those who left. The department around 1950 had no assistant professors and one associate professor; all the rest of the faculty were full professors (Shibutani 1990), a top-heavy faculty structure that did not provide appropriate role models for the doctoral students.

The field itself had changed. American sociology moved from a social-problems focus on crime, prostitution, poverty, and other aspects of social disorganization to a focus on social status and work. Chicago eventually changed from its stress on qualitative ethnological methods to a quantitative and statistical approach but only after several years of conflict. At the Chicago sociology department's softball games, the graduate students and faculty divided into two teams: the Statisticians versus the Qualitatives. Chicago began to look somewhat old-fashioned to the rest of American sociology. Thus, while Chicago sociology was interpretive and broadly humanistic, after the 1930s American sociology became highly quantitative and statistical as it turned away from the Chicago school's approach. The main model for the social sciences was the natural sciences, which were already well established and highly respected, and this mimicking of the natural sciences took the social sciences toward empiricism and quantification. American sociology in the 1930s became increasingly concerned with the scientific status of the discipline, especially matters of methodology. Sociological methodology became centered on statistics, as exemplified by William F. Ogburn, who joined the faculty at Chicago in 1929 and influenced methodology to become "more self-conscious, precise, statistical, and determined to exclude the random insight and the unassimilated if revealing anecdote" (Matthews 1977, p. 179).*

Also important in Chicago's decline was the arrival in America of other European sociological theories like Max Weber's. Chicago sociology was based on the theoretical foundation provided by Georg Simmel,

---

*When U.S. president Herbert Hoover took office in 1928, he appointed the Research Committee on Recent Social Trends, headed by Wesley Mitchell, an economist, and Charles Merriam, a political scientist, both at the University of Chicago. William F. Ogburn, a recently arrived Chicago sociologist, was director of research for the committee, whose purpose was to identify the social and economic factors that brought on the depression. Hoover asked the Rockefeller Foundation to provide funds for the committee, which were granted. Four years later, a 1,600-page report was produced centering on Ogburn's theory of cultural lag: that technological change causes social problems like divorce, unemployment, and crime. The report recommended a greater emphasis on social planning, based on an increased role for social science research, but the committee's report led to little direct action when Hoover lost his reelection bid to Franklin D. Roosevelt (Prewitt 1991). Both the Research Committee on Recent Social Trends and the Payne Fund studies, which were underway at the same time, formed important networks among social scientists (centered on the University of Chicago) for the exchange of expertise (Robinson 1988).

who declined in influence in America by the 1930s (although attention to his theories would rise again later). The phase change in American sociology's choice of its European ancestry dated from Harvard sociologist Talcott Parson's book, *The Structure of Social Action* (1949), which drew on Weber, Durkheim, Freud, and Vilfredo Pareto but not on Simmel.

Finally, a revolt of professional sociologists in 1935 ended Chicago's monopoly control of the leading sociology journal and the headquarters of the professional association. This uprising did not end Chicago's important role in the sociology discipline, although it diminished it.* The 1935 disestablishment of the Chicago School's *American Journal of Sociology (AJS)* as the main professional journal for U.S. sociologists was led by L. L. Bernard, who, while president of the American Sociological Society in 1932, appointed hand-picked committees to review the *AJS* and propose a constitutional reform of the American Sociological Society. Bernard "took these steps [appointing the two committees] because the department of sociology at the University of Chicago under its leader at that time had become arrogant and was suspected of making the interests of the American Sociological Society subsidiary to those of the Chicago department" (Odum 1951, p. 410). A historical analysis shows that the successful revolt against Chicago in 1935 was spearheaded by a set of sociologists opposed to Chicago's dominance who had career anxieties caused by the great depression and were aware of the Chicago school's declining intellectual influence (Lengermann 1979). It was a political revolt against Chicago, not an intellectual revolt based on differences in sociological perspective.

The decline of Chicago's dominance of American sociology is indicated by the membership of the American Sociological Association in 1959. Twenty percent of ASA members who earned their doctorates in sociology before 1930 received their Ph.D. degree at Chicago. This figure dropped to only 8 percent from 1950 to 1959 (Riley 1960). Chicago's decline is also suggested by the relative falling off of sociologists' interest in social psychology as their main speciality.†

---

*The continuing importance of Chicago is shown by the fact that more than half of the presidents of the American Sociological Association had been faculty or students at Chicago, a dominance that continued after 1935 at about the same rate as before (Kurtz 1984, pp. 94–95).

†The members of the American Sociological Association chose social psychology as their most popular special interest in both 1930 and in 1959. Some 37 percent of the 1,832 ASA members in 1930 chose social psychology. By 1959, social psychology was still the most

James S. Coleman (1980a), who earned his doctorate in sociology at Columbia University and then spent most of his career at the University of Chicago, argues that the decline of the Chicago school was in part due to broader changes in American society: "The decline of the Chicago School was not merely a decline in the powerful personalities who shaped it. It was a decline in the kinds of problems the Chicago School had focused on. Immigration had declined, urban life had become somewhat more ordered, the marginality of men decreased." The Columbia school, built around Paul F. Lazarsfeld, gained dominance, "for New York was the center of the emerging communications industry, the emerging advertising industry, and the newly national marketing decisions" (Coleman 1980a). Instead of studying local community problems like the adaptation of European immigrants in Chicago and the marginal or deviant subcultures that ensued, Lazarsfeld and the Columbia scholars who replaced Park and the Chicagoans on center stage of American sociology emphasized national-level research problems like the effects of mass media communication.

THE CHICAGO SCHOOL AND COMMUNICATION STUDY

The conventional viewpoint of the history of communication study is that it emerged in the 1920s, 1930s, and 1940s as social scientists from several disciplines began to conduct empirical research on propaganda* (Lasswell 1927) and on radio's effects on its audiences (Lazarsfeld and Stanton 1942). I previously criticized the four founders myth: that Lasswell, Lazarsfeld, Lewin, and Hovland launched the field of communication study. Peters (1989) also questioned this conventional viewpoint, claiming instead that mass communication study deals with the larger issue of the role of the mass media in a healthy democracy. This broader view means that the roots of mass communication go back to scholars of the Chicago school and to Walter Lippmann (1922), for whom communication was the essence of human relationships. Park set the tone for the Chicago viewpoint by quoting Dewey *The Introduction to*

---

popular sociological specialty, but it was chosen by only 25 percent of the 6,345 ASA members (Riley 1960). Sociological social psychology was particularly a self-identification of the Chicago sociologists. By 1990, social psychology was chosen by 19 percent of the 13,265 members of the American Sociological Association as their specialty (Ennis 1992).

*Propaganda analysis helped get research on mass communication off the ground in the 1920s and 1930s but then was largely forgotten (Sproule 1987) or else lost its identity in the plethora of media effects studies that came to dominate the field of mass communication.

the Science of Sociology, the bible for early generations of American sociologists: "Society not only continues to exist *by* transmission, *by* communication, but it may fairly be said to exist *in* transmission, *in* communication. There is more than a verbal tie between the word common,
community, and communication" (Park and Burgess 1924, p. 36). To
the Chicago school, communication was much more than just the im-
parting or exchanging of information: communication created and
maintained society (Belman 1975, 170–175).

The Chicago school provided a more unified theory of
communication's place in society than did the so-called four founders of
the field of communication, who were prominent in the years after Chicago declined. Strangely, however, the Chicago School's theoretical perspective is rarely cited by communication scholars today. Peters (1986)
suggests that Lasswell, Lewin, Lazarsfeld, and Hovland were elevated to
founder status because they succeeded in the new form of methodologically sophisticated, quantitative, funded research: "This legacy [of the
"four founders"] has no body of ideas or canons of text but consists of
more an attitude or style of social research."

The so-called four founders of communication narrowed the focus of
communication study to an individualistic, short-term-effects paradigm. They thus shut out many areas of inquiry that scholars have only
recently reopened. Robert Park conducted the first mass communication research on newspaper content, audiences, and ownership structure—an example was his 1922 book, *The Immigrant Press and Its Control*—and in it raised research questions that are highly relevant today
(Rogers 1986, p. 79):

1. How does media content influence public opinion? (Today this is
   called the agenda-setting process.)
2. How are the mass media influenced by public opinion?
3. Can the mass media bring about social change?
4. How are interpersonal networks linked to the mass media?

In addition to anticipating later communication research on the agenda-
setting process, Park (1922, p. 328) identified another role of the mass
media: "Out of all the events that happen and are recorded every day by
correspondents, reporters, and the news agencies, the editor chooses
certain items for publication which he regards as more important or
more interesting than others. The remainder he condemns to oblivion
and the waste basket. There is an enormous amount of news 'killed'

every day." Kurt Lewin gave the name *gatekeeping* to this filtering process, and later communication scholars have studied the gatekeeping process in news media organizations.

Park defined communication as "a social-psychological process by which one individual is able to assume, in some sense and to some degree, the attitudes and the point of view of another." This definition centers on the Meadian-type empathy of the participants in the communication process with each other. Two or more individuals can give different meanings to identical information in a message that they receive. Contrast this two-way perspective with Claude Shannon's (1949d) linear model of communication: communication is how one mind influences another, as a one-way and intentional process.

"Communication was a fundamental human process to the Chicago sociologists, although other than Robert Park they did not point the specific directions that future communication research was to take. Perhaps this is one reason why the relationship of the Chicago School of Sociology to the modern discipline of communication science has been so little appreciated, and most often ignored by other observers tracing the history of communication research" (Rogers 1986, p. 79). We should recognize the important role played by the Chicago school in our past.

WAS CHICAGO A SCHOOL?

Finally, perhaps we should question whether the Chicago sociologists actually were a school. The notion of a school is a loose abstraction, used for convenience to describe a set of scholars whose viewpoints represent a certain degree of coherence. Some scholars (for example, Harvey 1987, p. 3) insist that a school must also have (1) a central figure who provides intellectual leadership, (2) an academic and geographical location, (3) financial support, and (4) a means of disseminating its work. By all of these indicators, Chicago was a school: it had (1) an intellectual leader in Robert Park, (2) a location at the University of Chicago, (3) funding from Rockefeller sources, and (4) disseminated its research work through its numerous books, published by the University of Chicago Press.

The main doubt about Chicago-as-a-school concerns the degree of consensus among its members. Certainly the Chicago scholars did not have a completely monolithic perspective. In fact, the Chicago school encouraged diversity of viewpoint and was quite interdisciplinary in orientation; an essential element in its credo was that all aspects of sociology should be represented. Albion Small, who served as department chair from its founding in 1892 until 1924, was oriented toward German sociological theory, especially that of Georg Simmel. Small also stressed a social problems perspective and a focus on the city of Chicago as a research laboratory. Thomas, Burgess, and Park were empirical researchers. Burgess and Park studied human ecology, investigating the nature of urban social disorganization. Dewey and Mead represented symbolic interactionism, a social type of social psychology. Later, in 1927, Chicago hired William Ogburn from Columbia University in order to bring in the statistical approach to analyzing sociological data. Clearly the Chicago school was eclectic, taking theoretical ideas from a variety of sources. Its intellectual center shifted considerably, even during its heyday.

The Chicago school of sociologists collaborated with scholars in anthropology, philosophy, and social psychology, along with political science and economics. The Social Sciences Research Building, constructed in 1929, was the first interdisciplinary center in the social sciences. A free exchange occurred between the Chicago school of sociology and other social sciences at the university.

How centered was the Chicago school on George Herbert Mead's symbolic interaction? Lewis and Smith (1980, p. xix) were "able to show—through counts of Mead's citations in articles, dissertations, and books, through course enrollments, responses by early Chicago sociologists to a survey questionnaire, and other relevant data—that Mead was not a central figure in the Chicago sociology program." They based this conclusion on the fact that only about three-fourths of all Chicago doctoral students enrolled in Mead's courses (mainly in his Advanced Social Psychology course), and of those who did, many did not use his theory in their dissertations (or even cite his publications in their footnotes). The early Chicago scholars took Mead's doctoral course in what we today call symbolic interaction, and although his theory affected their view of human behavior, the Chicago scholars then went off and did their dissertation research without paying much explicit attention to Meadian theory. Certainly their dissertations did not test it.

The general point here is that the Chicago school from 1915 to 1935 did not have a single coherent perspective that was rigidly followed. Its thought consisted of a strong dose of Robert Park's ecological approach to social disorganization, with social psychological and philosophical inputs from John Dewey and George Herbert Mead. The Chicago school did not have a unified theoretical viewpoint, but the Chicago scholars agreed about much of what they did and thought. Their lack of complete consensus should not prevent us from using the Chicago school as a convenient category.

The Chicago school was at the center of the rise of the social sciences in North America. It gained this high reputation not only through its intellectual accomplishments but also because of its well-publicized image. A thousand or so publications are now available about it. If an equivalent amount of attention were given to sociology at Columbia or Wisconsin or Yale around the turn of the century, would one of these places be considered the mecca for sociology? I do not think so. These other early strong spots for sociology were mostly one-man shows. When the one man declined, so did sociology at that university. Their view of sociology was unitary and limited, unlike the pluralistic diversity of the Chicago school. Further, such objective indicators as citation counts in the scholarly literature, the number of publications produced, and the patterns of where the early generation of U.S. sociologists earned their Ph.D. degrees all illustrate the central role of Chicago.

CONTRIBUTIONS OF THE CHICAGO SCHOOL

The main intellectual contribution of Chicago sociology to American social science was to ground it empirically in the study of social problems. The Chicago school gave an applied and amelioristic influence to American-style social science, with its scholars assuming that illuminating a social problem could lead to its solution.* It had other effects as well:

1. It conceptualized symbolic interactionism, a theoretical viewpoint that put communication at the center of how human personality is formed and changed.
2. It thought of mass communication as a possible means for American democratic society to survive in the face of urban social problems.
3. It conducted the Payne Fund studies of film effects on children in

---

*A spectacular example of this strategy is provided by Florence Nightingale during the Crimean War. She used statistical graphics to display the relationship between mortality rates and the lack of sanitary conditions in British army hospitals. She went public, anonymously, with her analysis of the large number of preventable deaths, and public opinion forced the British government to take action (Prewitt 1991).

the late 1920s, which provided an early prototype for the many later studies of communication effects.

4. It shunted female scholars like Jane Addams and her sociological colleagues connected with Hull House into social work as a separate and applied field.
5. Its methodological approach led to a contemporary set of communication scholars called the interpretive school.

THE INTERPRETIVE SCHOOL

"The most dramatic change in general communication theory during the last forty years has been the gradual abandonment of the idea of a passive audience, and its replacement by the concept of a highly active, highly selective audience, manipulating rather than being manipulated by a message—a full partner in the communication process" (Schramm 1971, p. 8). Once the notion of an active receiver (or, more properly, a participant in the communication process) is accepted, the search for standard effects of communication messages on audience individuals seems problematic. Instead, a scholar looks for the unique meaning that each audience individual gives to a message that is received.

The search for how people construct meanings is the main interest of interpretive communication scholars. The interpretive approach to communication study emphasizes the subjective meanings of a communication message to an individual. "The interpretive paradigm is informed by a concern to understand the world as it is, to understand the fundamental nature of the world at the level of subjective experience. It seeks explanation within the realm of individual consciousness and subjectivity, within the frame of reference of the participant, as opposed to the observer of the action" (Burrell and Morgan 1979, p. 28).

The interpretation of messages is usually studied by relatively less-structured, more qualitative research methods, but an interpretive perspective and qualitative methods are not identical. Interpretive research tends to be inductive, moving from the empirical level to the theoretical level. Theory defines the directions of research but is usually not used to derive specific hypotheses for testing. "Starting with data (usually qualitative data) does not mean that theory is absent, but that theory plays a different role than in the positivism approach, where theoretical implications are tested by hypotheses about relationships among concepts that have been operationalized at the empirical level. Instead, theory defines the objectives of interpretive research interest, and guides the formation of propositions from data about the subjective meanings of the actors in a social context" (Williams, Rice, and Rogers 1988). The central issue to interpretive scholars is meaning (Eisenberg 1984). These scholars borrow particularly from sociology, anthropology, linguistics, and literature. The Chicago school mainly conducted its field research in an interpretive style, and so it might provide a useful model for contemporary scholars of the interpretive school.

Ethnomethodology consists of data-gathering methods that allow respondents to provide data in ways that are structured by the respondent rather than by the scholar. Such ethnographic data reflect the respondents' point of view and capture the respondents' meanings—their constructions of reality. Thus, interpretive scholars generally gather qualitative data by observation and relatively unstructured interviewing. They search for "thick description," people's constructions of reality that are provided in depth. Interpretive scholars usually study a relatively small communication system, which they report in considerable detail. They are less concerned with a basis for generalizability of the results than in gaining an understanding in depth.

The interpretive approach has certain weaknesses. One important difficulty is managing and summarizing the large amounts of qualitative data in the form of field notes and transcripts. Such voluminous data pose difficulties for the interpretive scholar who is writing a twenty-page journal article out of materials from a year or two of data gathering. The richness of interpretive data causes data-reduction problems for interpretive scholars, as Matthew Miles (1979) implied in the title of his article, "Qualitative Data as an Attractive Nuisance."

Qualitative research approaches may face ethical problems (Punch 1986). An example is covert participant observation, in which the researcher masks his or her identity as an investigator when gathering data from respondents (Hilbert 1980), as Cressey did in his study of the taxi-dancers in Chicago.

Scholars of organizational communication use the interpretive approach to capture individuals' perceptions of an organization's culture (Putnam and Paconowsky 1983). The concept of culture is borrowed from anthropology (Geertz 1973), as are methods for studying organizational culture. An example is Paconowsky's (1988) study of W. L. Gore Associates, an innovative textile manufacturer in Delaware, which he found to be a self-sustaining system. Another well-known work by the interpretive school is a study of scientific communication among researchers in the Salk Institute in La Jolla, California, by Bruno Latour and Steven Woolgar (1979). Other interpretive scholars conduct conversation analysis of "cop talk" (Trujillo and Dionisopoulos 1987) or of macho remarks in an urban slum (Philipsen 1975, 1976).

An important new twist has been given to media communication research recently by focusing on how individuals "read" media messages. These studies of television viewers, for example, show that the individual is an active interpreter of the message content, not just a passive recipient. Often both quantitative and qualitative data-gathering methods are utilized by the investigator in order to understand how individuals interpret the media messages. These contemporary television viewing studies go a step beyond the simpler Lazarsfeld-type media effects research by asking how television characters are interpreted by the viewer and thus how effects are mediated. For example, consider older female views of the U.S. television series "Dynasty." If they perceive the heroine, Alexis Carrington Colby, as a successful, powerful older woman, they main gain an increase in self-esteem. But if they perceive her as an unattainable ideal, they may feel more depressed and helpless (Livingstone 1992, p. 61). Here we see how an audience member's perceptions of media messages mediate their effects. Obviously how individuals make sense out of media messages is an example of interpretive research.

Interpretive research is a reaction against the dominant style of communication research, which today is quantitative and, interpretive scholars claim, overly mechanistic. The relatively small but growing band of interpretive communication scholars find that their research is now being published by respected communication journals. Qualitative methods for communication study can fruitfully be combined with quantitative methods, as Paul F. Lazarsfeld argued in the 1950s. Communication study does not have to be either quantitative or qualitative.

In a way that contemporary interpretive scholars themselves do not recognize, they have returned to the research methodologies used by the Chicago school seventy years ago.

CHAPTER 6

HAROLD LASSWELL AND PROPAGANDA ANALYSIS

The Leonardo de Vinci of the behavioral sciences.
—Bruce Lannes Smith, "The Mystifying Intellectual
History of Harold D. Lasswell"

Master of the social sciences and pioneer in each; rambunctiously devoted to breaking down the man-made barriers between the social studies, and so acquainting each with the rest; filler-in of the interdisciplinary spaces between political science, psychology, and sociology; . . . sojourner in Vienna and selective transmitter of the Freudian vision to his American colleagues.
—American Council of Learned Societies, 1960

Harold D. Lasswell was trained as a political scientist, but his mind was so eclectic and wide ranging that he did not fit into any disciplinary box. "Such an interdisciplinary mind could not ignore such a fundamental human process as communication" (Rogers 1976, p. 99). Lasswell led the study of propaganda and virtually created the communication research method of content analysis. He published over 6 million scholarly words in his lifelong career, and the huge, three-volume *Propaganda and Communication in World History*, which he edited, was in press at the time of his death. Yet most communication scholars know him for only one sentence, which describes the field: "*Who* says *what* in *which channel* to *whom* with *what effects*?" (Lasswell 1948).

I thank Steven R. Brown for his review of this chapter.

203

Figure 6.1.   Harold D. Lasswell (1902–1978) at age 69.
Harold Dwight Lasswell Papers, Manuscripts and Archives, Yale University library;
used by permission.

THE LIFE AND TIMES OF HAROLD D. LASSWELL

Harold Dwight Lasswell (1902–1978) was born in Donnellson, Illinois,
with a population of 292, where his father was a Presbyterian minister
and his mother a high school teacher.* Both had active, inquiring
minds, and they took their son with them each summer to a Chautauqua to hear spellbinding political speakers like William Jennings Bryan,
noted for his Cross of Gold speech, and Robert La Follette, the Wisconsin liberal (Muth 1990, p. 3).

Harold Lasswell was a precocious boy who read widely. Young
Lasswell's uncle, a medical doctor, provided him with a copy of Freud's
1909 lectures at Clark University, thus launching Lasswell's lifelong intellectual interest in psychoanalytic theory and, more generally, in the

*Lasswell wrote lengthy letters home to his parents for the first several decades of his
career. These letters analyzed the history and politics of the places in which he traveled and
provided a report of Lasswell's daily activities. His voluminous correspondence is available to
scholars in archives at Yale University and at the University of Chicago. Many of Lasswell's
letters to his parents are presented, and discussed, in Muth (1990).

TABLE 6.1
Major Events in the Career of Harold D. Lasswell

Date	Events
1902	Born in Donnellson, Illinois
1918	Enrolls at the University of Chicago, at age sixteen, on a fellowship
1926	Earns a Ph.D. degree in political science at the University of Chicago, after study and data gathering in Switzerland, England, Germany, and France. His doctoral dissertation is a content analysis of propaganda messages during World War I
1927	Appointed assistant professor of political science at the University of Chicago; publishes his doctoral dissertation as *Propaganda Techniques in the World War*
1930	Publishes *Psychopathology and Politics*, marking his first major use of psychoanalytic theory to analyze political leaders
1936	Publishes *Politics: Who Gets What, When, How*, his book titled with the famous mapping sentence for the study of politics, arguing that the purpose of political science is to study power; promoted to associate professor with tenure at Chicago
1938	Resigns from the University of Chicago; the two trucks containing all of his data and personal effects crash and burn en route to New York
1939	Publishes (with Dorothy Blumentack) *World Revolutionary Propaganda: A Chicago Study*
1939–1940	Is the most influential member of the Rockefeller Foundation Seminar on Mass Communication, where he describes communication as "*Who* says *what* to *whom* via *what channels* with *what effect?*"
1940–1945	Serves as chief of the Experimental Division for the Study of War-Time Communications, U.S. Library of Congress
1946–1970	Appointed professor in the Law School at Yale University (and professor of political science, after 1952)
1970–1972	Serves as Distinguished Professor, City University of New York
1972–1976	Becomes Distinguished Professor, Temple University School of Law, and Albert Schweitzer Professor of International Affairs, Columbia University
1976–1978	Elected president, Policy Sciences Center, New York
1978	Dies on December 18 in New York City

role of personality in politics. At age sixteen, while Lasswell was an undergraduate student at the University of Chicago, he was surprised to discover that Freud was controversial (Reston 1969, p. 6).

Lasswell was editor of his high school newspaper and valedictorian of his class. His academic potential earned him a scholarship to the University of Chicago,* where he majored in economics and was a star debater (Muth 1990, p. 3). Lasswell entered the doctoral program in political science at Chicago in 1922; he felt that political science was properly challenging for him because the field was not so well developed. Actually, Lasswell never allowed the discipline of political science to confine his intellectual interests, which ranged over sociology, psychoanalysis, history, social psychology, and communication. "By the time he was well into graduate school, Lasswell was publishing across the board in the social sciences" (Smith 1969, p. 51). This multidisciplinarity caused problems for him during his career. For instance, some of his books received scathing reviews from disciplinary loyalists, and he did not fit easily into the Department of Political Science at Chicago or, later, in the Law School at Yale. Lasswell was an intellectual iconoclast (Marvick 1980), a radical innovator of theoretical perspectives and of research approaches.

Lasswell was an enthusiastic learner with a scholarly interest in diverse topics. One of his colleagues at the University of Chicago, Harold Gosnell, said, "[Charles Merriam, the department head] sent him [Lasswell] to England and he came back with an English accent, he sent him to Vienna and he came back with a full-grown psychoanalytic vocabulary, and he sent him to the Soviet Union and when he came back he showed that Marx could be reconciled with Freud" (Bulmer 1984, p. 194). Although he did not consider himself a communication scholar, "what we would today call a communication point of view pervaded much of Lasswell's thinking and writing, whatever the exact topic of scholarly concern" (Rogers 1986, p. 99). His academic interests included the study of propaganda, the formation of public opinion, the roles of political leaders, and content analysis of the mass media.

PSYCHOANALYTIC THEORY AND POLITICS

Lasswell's interest in psychoanalysis, begun when he was a teenager through his uncle's mentoring, became very strong while he was on the

---

*Lasswell won a competitive examination on modern history held at the University of Chicago for which the prize was a fellowship to attend the university (Smith 1969, p. 48).

political science faculty at Chicago. He associated with the maverick psychoanalyst Harry Stack Sullivan, who played a key role in introducing Freudian theory in America (Perry 1982), and with Edward Sapir, an anthropologist at the University of Chicago and later at Yale University, who was an enthusiast for psychoanalytic theory and pioneered the culture-and-personality approach in anthropology. In 1927, Lasswell spent six months studying with Elton Mayo, the Harvard University professor of industrial relations famous for the Hawthorne studies conducted in the Western Electric manufacturing plant in Chicago. Mayo was an English-Australian physician-psychiatrist who taught Lasswell how to utilize psychoanalytic interviewing and recording methods, which Lasswell later used to investigate the psychological aspects of political personalities. Mayo also taught Lasswell how to conduct psychoanalytic interviews and then allowed his student to conduct such analyses himself, mainly with students in the Harvard Business School, where Mayo taught, conducted research on management-worker relationships in factories, and served as a kind of a staff psychoanalyst (Trahair 1981–1982).

In 1928, Lasswell was awarded a travel fellowship by the Social Science Research Council for study of the psychiatric interview. He spent part of it in Boston in further work with Mayo and the rest in Vienna and Berlin, where he was psychoanalyzed by Theodor Reik, a follower of Freud. Upon his return to Chicago, Lasswell scandalized orthodox psychiatrists by analyzing volunteers, some of whom were students at the University of Chicago, in a model laboratory that he set up in his office in the Social Sciences Building. He wired up his "patients" to measure their galvanic skin response, pulse rate, and respiration and then related these indicators of emotional state to their spoken words (Almond n.d.). To critical observers, Lasswell's instrumentation looked like a lie detector. His attempts to relate psychoanalytic theory and behaviorism were resisted by scholars in both camps. Lasswell was learning that the academic world could be very antagonistic to psychoanalytic theory. Nor were psychoanalysts happy with Lasswell's innovative applications of psychoanalytic theory. Freudians were horrified.

There was considerable resistance to Lasswell's ideas on the part of political scientists. "On publication, [Lasswell's] *World Politics and Personal Insecurity* [his book about psychoanalytic theory and political leadership] was met with a kind of pop-eyed disbelief and dismay in many quarters. It received one of the most hostile reviews ever printed, in the *American Political Science Review*"(Smith 1969, p. 71). For a dozen years, from 1937 to 1950, none of Lasswell's articles was published in a political science journal. Instead, he published his work on psychoanalytic theory and politics in psychiatry journals. Eventually, younger political scientists accepted his perspective, and in 1955 he was elected president of the American Political Science Association, a high honor indeed for a scholar who attempted to introduce radical theoretical perspectives like Freudian psychoanalytic theory to political science. Lasswell had high impact on his original discipline: "There are few ideas in contemporary political science that cannot be found in Lasswell's early work" (Eulau 1962).

Heinz Eulau, a political scientist generally sympathetic toward Lasswell stated, "I am not sure whether it was what Lasswell said or how he said it that offended the sensibilities of political scientists. In conversations about him I sensed a good deal of respect for an intellectual effort that was not understood, but there was always some comment that he was slightly mad, and that what he wrote should not be taken too seriously." Eulau feels this resistance was due not only to Lasswell's psychoanalytic vocabulary and to his baffling style of expression but also to "the dim realization that Lasswell was a more consistent and threatening advocate than others of the 'behavioral revolution' in political science that smoldered at the University of Chicago in the late twenties and thirties" (Eulau 1962).

Lasswell founded the field of political psychology. His 1930 book, *Psychopathology and Politics*, was the key publication in launching this intersection of psychology and political science. He used psychoanalytic theory to explain why some political leaders became agitators while others became administrators. He advocated gathering and analyzing psychoanalytic biographies of political leaders, and several such researches were later carried out by Lasswell and by other political scientists (Smith 1969, p. 62). Lasswell was concerned with comprehensiveness and felt that the psychoanalytic methods of free association and prolonged interviewing could help political scientists understand the political motivations of their respondents, thus broadening the evidential base from which policy initiatives could be launched (Brown 1992).

While Lasswell was making the first applications of psychoanalytic theory in political science in the late 1920s, scholarly interest in Freudian theory was also being manifested elsewhere, Anthropology and psychiatry were coming together in studies of personality and culture, for example, in the research and writings by Edward Sapir. Margaret

Mead's *Coming of Age in Samoa* (1928) and Ruth Benedict's *Patterns of Culture* (1934) were markers for the emerging research tradition on culture and personality. Lasswell's *Psychopathology and Politics* appeared shortly before the Frankfurt school's *Studien Über Autorität und Familie* (Horkheimer 1936), the European study of authoritarianism that led eventually to Adorno and others' *The Authoritarian Personality* (1950). So Lasswell's work, while considered dangerously radical in political science, was part of the general infection of the social sciences by Sigmund Freud's psychoanalytic theory.

Lasswell was also heretical in advocating the political theory of Karl Marx, who was scarcely alluded to by U.S. political scientists in the 1920s (Smith 1969, p. 64). Lasswell first encountered Marxist theory from an unusual teacher in his Illinois high school, and he expanded his understanding of Marxism while traveling in Europe in the 1920s. His principal criticism of Marx and Engels was they they assumed that a world proletarian revolution was the only possible outcome after the age of capitalism had reached its zenith (Smith 1969, p. 76). Instead, Lasswell (1941) argued that the prolonged struggle between capitalist and communist nations might be so bitter that only police and the military could maintain order, creating a garrison state in which surveillance and repression would grip society.

Why was Lasswell such a radical innovator in pioneering new perspectives in the study of politics? One reason for Lasswell's eclecticism was that by "not being chained to an entourage of disciples, though often aided by able elaborators, Lasswell was able to continue as the spearhead of the movement" (Eulau 1962). Further, he was encouraged to search widely for useful ideas from other fields by his mentor at Chicago, Charles Merriam, who himself was pioneering a behavioral science approach in political science. Merriam was well connected with the Social Science Research Council and helped Lasswell obtain the grants for his travel to Europe that enabled him to study Freudian theory and Marxism.

Lasswell's interests were not limited by place, any more than they were by discipline. He utilized what today would be called a comparative cross-national analysis. He traveled widely in order to understand the politics of other nations and thus better understand the American political system. For an individual from tiny Donnellson, Illinois, Lasswell lived a very cosmopolite life. He spent 1923 and 1924 studying and traveling Europe and journeyed widely throughout the rest of his life. Lasswell resided in an apartment at 1 University Place in New York City for the last half of his life, to which he commuted from his work at the U.S. Library of Congress, at Yale University, and elsewhere. Clearly, Lasswell overcame space and distance as barriers to the spread of ideas.

CONTENT ANALYSIS OF PROPAGANDA MESSAGES

Lasswell's mentor at Chicago, Charles E. Merriam (1874–1955), chair of the Department of Political Science for many years, was an important figure in political science in the 1920s and 1930s, advocating a behavioral science approach to studying politics. Political science had been dominated by historical, legal, and philosophical methods (Almond n.d.). Merriam and Lasswell took the field toward the analysis of empirical data about individuals' political behavior.

The new approach to political science began at the University of Chicago, with a study of 6,000 nonvoters in the 1923 Chicago mayoral election by Merriam and Harold Godnell, and was carried forward by Lasswell, who promoted the idea that political scientists should study political behavior, not political ideas, and that power is the key concept in understanding politics. Merriam encouraged Lasswell to explore the psychoanalytical aspects of politics, and to pursue his interests in psychoanalysis, and helped him obtain a Social Science Research Council fellowship for travel and study at Harvard and in Europe. Merriam also introduced quantification into the study of political behavior, so he smiled on Lasswell's work on content analysis. Given these scholarly interests of his doctoral adviser, Lasswell's dissertation topic, a content analysis of World War I propaganda, seemed a logical choice of problem to study.* However, the topic was daring; little previous research had been conducted on it.

The Rise of Propaganda Research

Originally, *propaganda* was a rather neutral word, meaning "to disseminate or propagate an idea," coming from the Latin word "to sow." But over time, and especially since World War I, common usage has given it a very negative connotation, at least in English. Propaganda messages are perceived as dishonest, manipulative, and as brainwashing (Jowett

---

*Merriam (1919) had worked for the Creel Committee (the U.S. propaganda agency) during World War I in Italy.

and O'Donnell 1986, p. 15). The presumed effectiveness of Allied propaganda in hastening the collapse of German morale at the end of World War I guaranteed that propaganda would be a part of every major military conflict from then on (Qualter 1962, p. xi). During World War I, the U.S. government set up the Committee on Public Information, headed by George Creel and commonly called the Creel Committee, to conduct a massive domestic and international propaganda effort. An estimated 75 million copies of thirty different booklets about American ideals and wartime purposes were distributed in the United States, and millions of copies were distributed abroad. The Creel Committee also organized a corps of 75,000 speakers—called "four-minute men" for the length of their talks—who gave 755,000 patriotic speeches (Creel 1920, p. 7).

Creel's Committee on Public Information was so effective in seeking to stir up public support for the war that Americans learned to hate Germans. "Creel had oversold his product. Propaganda became a scapegoat in the postwar period of disillusion" (Winkler 1978, p. 3). Creel's own bombastic book about his committee's accomplishments, *How We Advertised America: The First Telling of the Amazing Story of the Committee on Public Information that Carried the Gospel of Americanism to Every Corner of the Globe* (1920), was a best-seller and helped convince the U.S. public that propaganda was an insidious force if left unchecked (Jowett 1987). Scholarly attention was attracted to the study of propaganda, particularly to investigations of the effects of such persuasive messages.

The research program on propaganda analysis in the 1920s and 1930s grew out of public disillusionment with the uses of propaganda by the United States, its allies France and Britain, and its enemies, especially Germany. Here was a perceived social problem, propaganda, that attracted the attention of scholars. While social scientific research on propaganda was one of the most important types of early communication research, propaganda analysis after the 1940s almost disappeared, routed by a competing paradigm of highly statistical communication research that used survey and experimental methods, rather than content analysis, to study communication effects (Sproule 1987, 1991). Why did experiments on persuasion, like those of Carl Hovland and his followers, and surveys of media effects, like those by Paul F. Lazarsfeld and his colleagues, push propaganda off center stage of communication research? One reason is that private foundations and the federal government were more eager to support research that was useful to policymakers but did not raise troubling questions about the interests and motives of the persuaders (Sproule 1987). The establishment was not eager to fund studies that might expose the questionable propaganda techniques it used.

Another reason for the decline of academic interest in propaganda analysis was its lack of a coherent theory, which in part derived from the diversity of social science disciplines that studied propaganda. In the late 1920s and early 1930s, the Social Science Research Council sponsored a standing committee, chaired by Lasswell and including scholars from various disciplines,* who sought to provide greater coherence to research on propaganda. After Lasswell had pioneered the study of propaganda with his doctoral dissertation and the resulting book, further study of this topic was promoted by the Institute for Propaganda Analysis, established in New York in 1937 with funding from Edward A. Filene (of Filene's Department Store in Boston) through the E. A. Filene Good Will Fund. The full name of the unit explains its orientation: Institute for Propaganda Analysis: A Non-Profit Corporation to Help the Intelligent Citizen Detext and Analyze Propaganda. Hadley Cantril, a psychologist at Princeton University, served as its first president, and Clyde R. Miller, a professor at Columbia University, directed the institute which was headquartered near the Columbia campus. The institute involved a loose network of scholars at various universities. In addition to encouraging scholarly research on propaganda, it identified seven propaganda strategies, such as name calling, the use of glittering generalities, card stacking, and the bandwagon effect. The institute was particularly concerned with the rise of Nazi power in Germany and the possible effects that Nazi propaganda might have in the United States or with the possibility of a Hitler figure's rising in the United States.

The issue of propaganda studies had become highly policized by 1941, and a few years later the institute was closed. Support of work on propaganda by the Social Science Research Council and by other funding sources dried up after World War II. Terms like *mass communication* and *communication research* began to be used in the mid-1940s, replacing such words as *propaganda* and *public opinion* to describe the work of scholars doing communication research (Delia 1987, p. 57).†

---

*One of whom was Ralph Casey, a journalism school professor at the University of Minnesota and one of the Bleyer children.

†Although several books such as Combs and Nimmo's *The New Propaganda* (1993) have been published in recent years, suggesting that scholarly work on propaganda may be experiencing a renaissance.

The rise of quantitative communication methods had an impact on Harold Lasswell's research on propaganda. His first study (of World War I propaganda) was qualitative and critical in tone (Lasswell 1927). He mainly exposed the nature of propaganda techniques that had been used by both sides in the conflict. His propaganda research during World War II, conducted fifteen years later, was mainly quantitative and statistical (Lasswell and Leites 1949).

Lasswell's study of propaganda in World War I was empirical in the sense that he cited specific examples of various propaganda techniques used by the Germans, British, French, and Americans. His dissertation was an example of rigorous scholarship: definitions of main concepts, classifications of propaganda strategies, and elaboration of factors that limited or facilitated the effects of such propaganda strategies (Almond n.d.). His propaganda analysis was based on interviews with officials in European nations and on the use of archival materials, as well as his qualitative content analysis of the propaganda messages.* Lasswell focused his doctoral research on the symbols used in the World War I propaganda messages. In this concern with symbols, Lasswell (1971, pp. xiii) said that he was mainly influenced by George Herbert Mead, although he did not take courses from Mead (or from Robert Park) at Chicago.

Lasswell's account of World War I propaganda was disquieting reading because he showed that modern warfare is total war—one in which the entire civilian population takes an active role. Warfare was no longer just for generals and military troops; it was a complete conflict in which public opinion mattered a great deal (Merelman 1981). Propaganda warfare posed an especially serious threat to democratic governments. Lasswell concluded that propaganda had strong effects: "When all allowances have been made, and all extravagant estimates pared to the bone, the fact remains that propaganda is one of the most powerful instrumentalities in the modern world."

What Is Propaganda?

Lasswell (1927) defined propaganda as "the management of collective attitudes by the manipulation of the significant symbols." It was, to him,

---

*Lasswell's first quantitative content analysis was his study of German schoolbooks, in which he tabulated the references to national superiority, foreign inferiority, military heroes, and so forth. (Lasswell 1925). Lasswell's first quantitative content analysis of propaganda came years later in his War-Time Communications Project during World War II.

not inherently bad or good; that determination depended on one's point of view and on whether the propaganda messages were truthful or dishonest. Propaganda is an attempt "to change other people's views in order to further one's own cause or damage an opposing one" (Petty and Cacioppo 1981, p. 3)—that is, a method for managing public opinion. It thus bears a close relationship to persuasion.* Both persuasion and propaganda are intentional communication, carried out by a source to change the attitudes of audience members. In the case of propaganda, the purpose of the persuasive effort is advantageous to the persuader but not to the individual being persuaded. Thus, advertising, public relations, and political campaigns are propaganda. Persuasion is often thought of as face-to-face, interpersonal communication, while propaganda is persuasion through the mass media (and hence aimed at a mass audience). This distinction on the basis of channel is not very important, however, because persuasion strategies can be utilized to construct mass media messages and propaganda strategies can be used interpersonally. Nevertheless, propaganda is usually one-way, while persuasion is often thought of as an interpersonal process and thus has a more interactive nature, even though it is one way in intention (that is, a source that seeks to persuade a receiver). In short, propaganda is mass persuasion.

Content Analysis

Content analysis is the investigation of communication messages by categorizing message content into classifications in order to measure certain variables. It "learned its methods from cryptography, from the subject-classification of library books, and from biblical concordances, as well as from standard guides to legal precedents" (Marvick 1977, p. 52). Lasswell content-analyzed World War I propaganda messages,

---

*Another definition of propaganda is provided by Jowett and O'Donnell (1986): "Propaganda is the deliberate and systematic attempt to shape perceptions, manipulate cognitions, and direct behavior to achieve a response that furthers the desired intent of the propagandist." Yet another well-known definition of propaganda is "the deliberate attempt by some individual or group to form, control, or alter the attitudes of other groups by the use of the instruments of communication, with the intention that in any given situation the reaction of those so influenced will be that desired by the propagandist" (Qualter 1962, p. 27). Later, Qualter (1985, p. 124) modified his definition: propaganda is "the deliberate attempt by the few to influence the attitudes and behavior of the many by the manipulation of symbolic communication."

such as leaflets dropped from balloons or airplanes or delivered by artillery shells over enemy lines and military recruiting posters, in order to identify the propaganda strategies used. The Allied forces made extensive use of propaganda balloons to distribute leaflets as far as 150 miles behind German lines. In the summer and autumn of 1918, with the wind generally at their backs, the Allies sent over five million leaflets per month (Lasswell 1927, p. 184).* In response, German propagandists published a well-read newspaper in French that featured lists of the names of captured French soldiers. Lasswell analyzed the persuasive strategies utilized in these propaganda leaflets, among them, attempts to divide the enemy (such as the Allied efforts to alienate Austria-Hungary from Germany), demoralizing the enemy (such as by stressing how many millions of American troops were arriving in France), and accusing the enemy of barbaric atrocities (such as the mistreatment of Belgian children by German soldiers).

Content analysts usually seek to infer the effects of the messages that they have analyzed, although actual data about such communication effects are seldom available to the content analyst. The picture that Lasswell drew of World War I propaganda was rather frightening, and his 1927 book heightened public concern about the inhumanity of warfare. Twenty years after World War I, propaganda was utilized even more thoroughly as a tool of warfare in World War II. And Lasswell content-analyzed those messages too.

Thus from his first research, Lasswell developed an important communication research tool, content analysis, and utilized it to study a socially significant problem of his day, propaganda. World War I was the first occasion in which propaganda was so widely used by combatants on both sides of the conflict. Understandably, U.S. policymakers and the public worried about the use of such Machiavellian techniques. Lasswell's research helped launch the teaching of university courses in propaganda and public opinion. He taught such courses himself at the University of Chicago for the dozen years after his initial appointment as an assistant professor of political science in 1926. His course Public Opinion and Propaganda at the University of Chicago, possibly the first one on the topic, and several of the other courses that he offered in the Department of Political Science, dealt with what we would today con-

---

*Captain Walter Lippman in the U.S. Army Expeditionary Force in France created many of these Allied propaganda leaflets that Lasswell analyzed.

sider communication (a term that was not used for university courses in the 1920s and 1930s). More specifically, what was called propaganda in courses like Lasswell's would be called mass communication today. Gradually, after World War II, the word propaganda dropped out of use in communication study (Sproule 1987, 1989, and 1991).*

LASSWELL'S MIDLIFE CRISIS

Lasswell taught at the University of Chicago for fourteen years, from 1924 to 1938, where he trained an outstanding set of Ph.D.s, including Nobel Laureate Herbert Simon and Ithiel de Sola Pool of MIT, and others. After two years as an instructor and six years as an assistant professor of political science at Chicago, Lasswell was promoted to associate professor with tenure in 1932. Six years later, he resigned. This decision was an important turning point in Lasswell's career, representing a kind of midlife crisis. It marked his move away from loyalty to political science and toward yet more interdisciplinary interests and encouraged him to play an important role in launching the new field of communication study in the 1940s.

Schramm (1980, 1985) argued that Lasswell left Chicago because he was denied promotion by University of Chicago president Robert Maynard Hutchins, and this conventional explanation is widely accepted. The actual case is different, and more complicated. Analysis of archival materials at the University of Chicago and at Yale University indicates that both a "push" and a "pull" were involved in Lasswell's departure from Chicago in 1938. Certainly President Hutchins was no fan of empirical social science, which Lasswell represented. The Department of Political Science was criticized for its quantitative and psychological emphases, as well as for recruiting its new faculty members internally (Torgerson 1991). President Hutchins, a legal scholar, had a nonquantitative, humanistic orientation toward political science and also disapproved of Lasswell's psychoanalytic interests. Charles Merriam, chair of the department and Lasswell's supporter, was nearing retirement and may not have provided a strong case to the university administration for keeping Lasswell. Lasswell nevertheless maintained good relationships over future years with both Merriam (whom Lasswell addressed as "Dear Chief" in his frequent letters; Merriam saluted Lasswell

*The early popularity of propaganda as a research topic is shown by the 4,500 publications included in an annotated bibliography on this topic (Lasswell, Casey, and Smith 1935).

as "Dear Judge"), and with President Hutchins, who appointed Lasswell to the Commission on Freedom of the Press (commonly called the Hutchins Commission) in 1946.*

Contrary to Schramm's explanation, Lasswell resigned from Chicago in 1938, where he had tenure and was already an associate professor, in order to establish an institute on psychiatry, culture, and politics with Harry Stack Sullivan and Edward Sapir in Washington, D.C. (Almond n.d.) Lasswell's June 29, 1938, letter of resignation to Dean Robert Redfield stated that he was "not requesting a leave of absence but is transferring to Washington."† The foundation that was to fund the new institute withdrew its promised financial support at the last moment, however, after Lasswell had resigned at Chicago, so he was left hanging.

Dwaine Marvick (1977, p. 32), in an analysis of Lasswell's career, says that Lasswell despaired of his career prospects at Chicago and resigned without any plans of certain employment. But my review of Lasswell's annual pay increases at Chicago (obtained from his university appointment papers in the President's Papers on file in the University of Chicago Library) shows that he was being treated well.‡ Nevertheless, Lasswell might have felt that he was not being moved ahead at the rate that he deserved, given his brilliant and productive career. After all, he had been an associate professor for six years.

Lasswell himself described his departure from the University of Chicago in 1938:

> Decided to act on a long-cherished plan to leave the University of Chicago for the purpose of developing an institute in Washington, D.C. devoted to the psychological and anthropological study of politics and society. The plan was to cooperate with Henry Stack Sullivan, M.D., of New York and Washington, D.C., and Professor Edward Sapir, anthro-

---

*In 1944, Henry Luce, owner of Time-Life Corporation, provided funding for a three-year study of the mass media in America by the Commission on Freedom of the Press. The commission of thirteen members, chaired by Hutchins, president of the University of Chicago, included Lasswell. The Hutchins Commission was concerned about the growing concentration of U.S. media ownership, a trend that was diminishing the level of newspaper competition. The commission's recommendations, such as the creation of an independent agency to appraise press performance, did not lead to action in most cases. However, its focus on press freedom, represented by the First Amendment, is a central value of American media people.

† This letter is in Folder 6, Box 36, President's Papers, Department of Special Collections, Regenstein Library, University of Chicago.

‡ One year before he left Chicago, Lasswell was given an annual salary increase from $4,000 to $4,500 for the 1937–1938 school year (Hutchins 1937).

pologist, of Yale University, in developing the new institution. The intention in 1938 was for HDL [Harold D. Lasswell] to become a member of the Washington School of Psychiatry (the William Alanson White Psychiatric Foundation)* and to develop a varied consultative practice until such time as the full financial program of the school could be realized. (Lasswell 1951, p. 9)

Harry Stack Sullivan (1892–1949) was an influential American psychoanalyst. A farm boy from New York State, he went on to earn his medical degree at the Chicago College of Medicine and Surgery. Sullivan specialized in treating schizophrenic patients and in analyzing the communication aspects of the therapy situation (Sullivan 1953). He argued for the social as well as the biological aspects of mental illness and called for a fusion of psychiatry and social science. Sullivan met Edward Sapir in 1926 at the University of Chicago, thus influencing Sapir's academic interest in culture and personality.

Sapir (1884–1939) was born in Germany and migrated with his family to New York as a young boy. He earned his Ph.D. degree in 1909 in anthropology at Columbia University with Franz Boas and rose to become an eminent linguist and anthropologist of American Indian cultures. Sapir taught at Chicago from 1925 until his move to Yale in 1931. His name is familiar to many for the Whorf-Sapir hypothesis, formulated with his student, Benjamin Lee Whorf, which argues that human thought is structured by language; for example, an Eskimo tribe that has twelve words for different types of snow can distinguish more forms of the substance than can English speakers, who have just the single word snow. Although he had not been psychoanalyzed, Sapir brought psychoanalytic theory into anthropology. Sullivan and Sapir were very close intellectually and in the 1930s added Lasswell to their plans for an interdisciplinary school of psychiatry in Washington, D.C. But Sapir became ill and died the following year, and the financial support for the new school of psychiatry in Washington was not forthcoming.[†] Then Lasswell had a fundamental disagreement with Sullivan, which ended their relationship.

The two moving vans containing all of Lasswells possessions, papers, and data skidded on an icy highway in northern Indiana, crashed, and

---

*This foundation was an umbrella for the newly founded Washington School of Psychiatry and for the interdisciplinary journal Psychiatry.

†The wealthy donor who had promised to fund the William Alanson White Psychiatric Foundation died just before the gift was finalized (Perry 1982, p. 360).

burned (Muth 1990, p. 14). His intellectual slate was thus wiped clean, ending his career in political science and encouraging the refocusing of his scholarly interests on the emerging field of communication study.*

These unexpected events left Lasswell at age thirty-six in Washington, D.C., with uncertain prospects. He improvised for a year or two, filling the time by make NBC radio broadcasts about great political figures of the past. Next, he became a part-time lecturer at the Yale Law School and served as a consultant to various federal government agencies and to the Rockefeller Foundation. The part-time visiting lectureship with the Law School at Yale University was arranged by Myres S. McDougal, a professor of law at Yale (Muth 1990, p. 14) and a longtime friend and admirer of Lasswell.

World War II soon began, and Lasswell became chief of the Experimental Division for the Study of War-Time Communications in the U.S. Library of Congress. This propaganda research was supported by a grant from the Rockefeller Foundation to the Library of Congress. Actually, Lasswell helped create the Library of Congress project throughout his influential role in the 1939–1940 Rockefeller Foundation Seminar on Mass Communication, organized by John Marshall of the foundation. The Rockefeller Communication Seminar also authored a persuasive plan for the federal government's use of mass communication in the approaching wartime emergency, a policy that Lasswell strongly encouraged and helped sell to high officials in Washington.

After a six-year marginal existence that included involvement in the World War II-related research at the Library of Congress, Lasswell settled down for most of the rest of his career (1946–1970) in a two-thirds' time appointment at the Yale Law School (McDougal 1991a). There were no Ph.D. students at the Yale Law School, and so Lasswell did not train a cadre of protégés to carry on his work, but he produced a record volume of scholarly publications. The Yale years involved "producing many books but adding little to wisdom or knowledge" (Shils 1981).

THE ROCKEFELLER COMMUNICATION SEMINAR

The Rockefeller Communication Seminar met monthly for ten months from September 1939 to June 1940 in the seminar room on the sixty-

*Some unburned fragments of Lasswell's personal library were left alongside the Indiana highway, including a book by Karl Marx. This fact was reported in the *Chicago Tribune*; later, during the McCarthy era in the 1950s, it caused Lasswell considerable difficulty with federal investigators.

fourth floor of Rockefeller Plaza, the building in which the Rockefeller Foundation had its offices. It had a dozen regular members:*

- Lyman L. Bryson, Columbia University's Teachers College, who edited the proceedings book from the seminar.
- Hadley Cantril, Department of Psychology, Princeton University.
- Lloyd A. Free, managing editor, *Public Opinion Quarterly*, at Princeton University, and a staff member of the Rockefeller Foundation–funded Radio Research Project, who served as secretary of the seminar.
- Geoffrey Gorer, Yale University, Institute for Human Relations.
- Harold D. Lasswell, William Alanson White Psychiatric Foundation, New York, and visiting professor at Yale Law School.
- Paul F. Lazarsfeld, director of the Radio Research Project, Columbia University.
- Robert S. Lynd, Columbia University, Department of Sociology.
- John Marshall, the Radio Research Project's research manager at the Rockefeller Foundation.
- Ivor A. Richards, a Cambridge University expert on semantics who was at Harvard University.
- Charles A. Siepmann, a British radio expert who had worked for the BBC.
- Donald Slesinger, American Film Center, a Rockefeller Foundation–supported program in New York.
- Douglas Waples, Graduate Library School, University of Chicago, who was conducting readership surveys.

In his letter of invitation to participants in the seminar, John Marshall stated that the objective was to provide general theoretical guidance to him about communication research, so that the Rockefeller Foundation would know what types of future projects to fund. But the signing of the German-Russian Nonaggression Pact in August 1939 and Hitler's invasion of Poland the next month marked the beginning of World War II in Europe. Almost from the first of the monthly seminars, in September 1939, their purposes change dramatically, to focus on how communication could be utilized by the federal government to cope with the approaching war. The final report of the Rockefeller Communication Sem-

---

*Three other Rockefeller Foundation officials, David Stevens, Stacy May, and R. J. Havighurst, also regularly participated in the seminar.

inar, *Needed Research in Communication*, dated October 17, 1940, declared that the U.S. government was obliged to take on wider responsibility for the welfare of its people and "that, if the exercise of that responsibility is to be democratic, more effective ways of keeping the government and the people in communication with each other will have to be created" (p. 3).

The minutes of the ten monthly seminars (which today are part of the Lyman L. Bryson Papers in the U.S. Library of Congress) show that Harold D. Lasswell was particularly influential in shaping the seminar discussions toward communication effects. His five-questions model of communication, in fact, was developed in the seminar: "*Who* says *what* to *whom* in *what channel* with *what effects?*" Lasswell's model became the basic framework for the entire seminar, pervading many of its discussions. Most of the papers presented and much of the spontaneous exchange at the sessions dealt with the effects of mass communication.

"The [five] question scheme—who says what to whom in what channel with what effect—became the dominant paradigm defining the scope and problems of American communications research. The behavioral science of communication became restricted to a rather narrow model that explained communication as essentially a process of persuasion" (Czitrom 1982, p. 132). Lasswell's five-questions model did not include "why?" that is, Why do those in control of communication choose to use it for the functions that they do? The Lasswell five-questions model was interpreted to focus communication research on media effects, which gave a coherence to such investigation, but it also steered communication scholars away from other important topics.

In Bernard Berelson's opinion, the Rockefeller Communication Seminar was seminal in the development of mass communication research (Morrison 1988). It established network links among the leading scholars interested in communication. The proceedings volume (Bryson 1948) was one of the first books to argue for communication as a field of study. The invisible college of communication scholars who participated in the Rockefeller Communication Seminar moved almost en masse to Washington, D.C., the following year to play an important role in World War II–related communication activities.

After the last seminar session in June 1940, Harold Lasswell suggested that the report be circulated to federal officials and that a meeting then be held with them to explore its implications in the light of the approaching World War II. In November 1940, a special report from the Rockefeller Communication Seminar, *Public Opinion and the Emer-*

gency, was prepared. It began: "This memorandum has grown out of the discussions of an informal group which originally intended to formulate a disciplined approach to the study of mass communications in present-day society. With the outbreak of war in Europe, however, this group agreed—for the time being at least—to turn its attention to the particular role of mass communications in the emergency so created" (Rockefeller Communication Seminar 1940b). The report described various types of communication underway or recommended.

A small conference was held on January 18, 1941, in the Princeton Club in New York City, at which the seminar's memorandum, which had been circulated previously, was discussed in reference to the approaching U.S. involvement in World War II (Rockefeller Foundation 1941). Present, in addition to the Rockefeller Communication Seminar's participants, were representatives of such U.S. government units as the Department of Justice, Library of Congress, Navy Department, Federal Communications Commission, Department of Agriculture, and Department of Interior.

Lasswell began the conference by summarizing the conclusions of the Rockefeller Communication Seminar and suggesting its implications for a government soon to be at war. His War-Time Communications Project was already underway at the U.S. Library of Congress, and its role as a coordinating unit for federal policymakers was discussed. A second conference was held in Washington, D.C., that month to sell the memorandum about communication research. Influential federal officials, such as the secretary to Harold Ickes, secretary of the interior, attended this conference (Marshall 1973, p. 123).

John Marshall and the Rockefeller Foundation played a crucial role in launching the field of communication, acting as a powerful catalyst to the birth of communication research. Prior to the Rockefeller Communication Seminar in 1939–1940, the words *communication research* were not even in common use. John Marshall, in his August 1939 letters inviting the dozen scholars to participate in the year-long seminar, coined the term *mass communication.**

---

*In his August 16, 1939, letter to Professor Ivor A. Richards of Cambridge University, John Marshall stated: "In the last couple of years, it has been increasingly clear that most of my work has been in a field which for lack of a better name I have come to call mass communications." This may have been the first use of the term *mass communication*. This letter is in the Rockefeller Archives Center, Collection RG, Record Group 1.1, Series 200, Box 223, Folder 2672. the words *communication* and *mass communication* began to be used in the early 1940s, and then rapidly spread into common use by scholars in journalism and related fields of mass communication, with Wilbur Schramm leading the way (Arcenas 1991).

Lasswell dominated the Rockefeller Communication Seminar. The Lasswell mapping of communication was expressed in the form of the five-questions model, which rapidly became very widely known.* Obviously, much of the complexity of actual communication behavior is not conveyed by Lasswell's five-questions statement, so it is not a communication model in any complete sense. For instance, Lasswell's five questions seem to assume that a communicator is present, that communication is intentional, and that messages flow unidirectionally from source to receiver, without feedback (Westley and MacLean 1955). What Lasswell's five questions do not say actually tells us a great deal about the way in which he, and other scholars of his time, saw communication: as an act, as Lasswell himself recognized, not a process. As one-way and intentional, oriented toward achieving a desired effect. The five questions focused communication research on effects.

Lasswell's contribution to the Rockefeller Communication Seminar also included his explication of the three functions of communication in society (Lasswell 1948):

1. Surveillance of the environment, the role of the media that allows an individual to look over the horizon in order to know about events in the broader world.
2. Correlation of society's response to events in the environment, such as when mass media communication tells an individual how to interpret some news events. Here the media help the individual to make sense out of what is going on in the world.
3. Transmission of the cultural heritage, as children are taught the history of their people, what is right and wrong, and how they differ from other peoples.

Later communication scholars added a fourth function of communication: entertainment. These four functions are still taught to students enrolled in most introductory courses in communication.

---

* Lasswell may have been stimulated to create his five-questions model by the journalist's ditty of Rudyard Kipling:

I kept six honest serving men
They taught me all I knew:
Their names are What and Why and When
And How and Where and Who.

LASSWELL'S WAR-TIME COMMUNICATIONS PROJECT

Harold Lasswell helped sell communication to the federal government at the start of World War II, along with such other communication pioneers as Paul F. Lazarsfeld, Kurt Lewin, and Wilbur Schramm. The U.S. government faced the Axis forces in a battle for people's minds, and communication would be essential to this effort. Even if communication were not an academic discipline that was taught in American universities, communication was becoming a kind of magic wand to the federal government. Harold Lasswell helped make it so.

The banks of the Potomac were an exciting place for social scientists during World War II: "What academic compartmentalization had made difficult in the university was a matter of ease in wartime Washington. Individual scholarship yielded to team research, and disciplinary isolation to interdisciplinary collaboration. These were years of liberation from the straitjacket that was called 'discipline.' We stopped defining ourselves and worked on problems" (Eulau 1968). The evil nature of Hitler's fascism in Europe served to unite American scholars in a community of effort.

One of Lasswell's main World War II tasks in Washington, D.C., was to conduct a content analysis of propaganda messages. He carried out a massive content analysis of Allied and Axis propaganda (summarized in Lasswell and Leites 1949). The purpose of the Rockefeller Foundation–sponsored project, funded by an $85,400 grant from 1940 to 1943, was to study wartime communication by developing improved methodologies for propaganda analysis. As Lasswell (1951) explained: "It was also desired to provide a training ground for technical personnel in case, as was anticipated, the U.S. would become more actively involved in propaganda and intelligence activities. Another purpose was to make it possible for HDL [Harold D. Lasswell], as a specialized student of propaganda, to be available in Washington where he could engage in consultation with public officials in developing the propaganda and intelligence programs of the government." Lasswell was not just analyzing propaganda; he was also helping to create it.

In his proposal to the Rockefeller Foundation, Lasswell justified his proposed research on this basis: "Should the United States become more intimately involved in the War, it would be important for us to formulate war aims in terms that would strengthen rather than weaken the morale of our allies. We need, therefore, to keep a watchful eye on the role of political symbols in the lives of our potential allies."*

One of the most frequent requesters of Lasswell's assistance was the U.S. Department of Justice. He trained sixty staff members in the department in how to carry out content analysis of thirty-nine foreign newspapers beyond those studied by the War-Time Communications Project, so that foreign propaganda in the United States could be detected. The results, it was hoped, could be utilized as courtroom evidence. Lasswell served as an expert witness in U.S. government trials of propagandists who were accused of fostering domestic propaganda in the United States, an activity forbidden by the McCormick Act of 1938.† Lasswell also served as an expert witness for the government in cases involving communists, German national socialists, and American fascists. He served as an expert witness until the admissibility of content analysis as evidence was established by a ruling of the U.S. Supreme Court. Lasswell and his staff continued to supply personnel consultative advice to the various federal agencies connected with propaganda administration: the Office of Facts and Figures, the Office of War Information, the Foreign Broadcast Intelligence Service of the Federal Communications Commission, Office of Censorship, Office of Strategic Services, the Psychological Warfare Branch of the U.S. Department of the Army, and the U.S. Department of State (Lasswell 1951). The War-Time Communications Project was much more than just a research project; it was in substantial part an intelligence effort. . . . as an intelligence operation, it was not particularly successful. It was operating beyond the state of the art, and as a result it contributed far more to content analysis methodology than to substantive understanding of the enemy at that time" (Pool 1969, p. 207).

The papers of Lasswell's War-Time Communications Project that are held today by the U.S. Library of Congress show that the contents of various newspapers—*Der Bund*, *Frankfurter Zeitung*, *Pravda*, *Le Matin*, *La Prensa*, *Egypt Gazette*, the *Omaha World-Herald*, and others—were analyzed. Lasswell and his corps of propaganda analysts, officed in the

---

*Lasswell's proposal is held in the Rockefeller Archive Center, Record Group RF RG1.1, Series 200R, Box 239, Folder 2852.

†For example, Lasswell testified against Transocean, which the federal government claimed was a Nazi news agency operating in the United States, by showing that Transocean presented a distorted treatment of the news, as compared with the *New York Times*.

Library of Congress Annex, now called the Adams Building, located near the U.S. Capitol building in Washington, D.C., tabulated the incidence of words like *war*, *nation*, *peace*, and *imperialism*. The main focus of the propaganda analysis was on media content during the period beginning with the outbreak of World War II in Europe in 1939. Lasswell's project found that German propaganda blamed other nations for starting World War II, exposed the claimed untruthfulness of French and British propaganda, and emphasized the weakness and decadence of Germany's enemies. The German propaganda also depicted a menacing characterization of Jews, a portent of the coming Holocaust.

Political scientist Heinz Eulau (1968) describes working on Lasswell's War-Time Communications Project: "The seemingly endless coding, all the pluses for strength and the minuses for weakness in the flow of symbols, and the poring over Lasswellian prose were richly rewarded by the company that Lasswell was keeping at the Library of Congress. He had assembled a research team of young men, including anthropologists, psychologists, sociologists, and political scientists, almost all of whom were to influence the course of behavioral science after the war." Ithiel de Sola Pool, Edward Shils, Morris Janowitz, Abraham Kaplan, and Sebastian de Grazia, among others, worked on the content analysis project.

Joseph M. Goldsen, who was Lasswell's second in command on the project, describes its staff as consisting of about twenty coders, who analyzed the contents of selected Allied and Axis newspapers, plus domestic and foreign radio broadcasts (Goldsen 1991). The coders were recruited through Lasswell's various network relationships. Several were his former students at the University of Chicago, and others were recommended by friends and colleagues.* Goldsen supervised the day-to-day coding activities, while Lasswell helped set up the coding categories, interpreted the findings of the content analysis, and fed the results to various government agencies in an attempt to influence policy decisions.

Lasswell's project was located in the U.S. Library of Congress because of the library's good collection of the various newspapers to analyze and because Archibald MacLeish, the U.S. Librarian of Congress, was a

---

*One of the individuals trained in content analysis methods by Lasswell was Ralph O. Nafziger, the University of Minnesota journalism professor then on leave to serve in the Office of Facts and Figures and the Office of War Information.

superpatriot and welcomed the project as one important step toward U.S. preparation for the approaching war. MacLeish, like most other American intellectuals, was convinced that U.S. intervention in World War II was inevitable when France fell in June 1940, leaving the British alone to oppose Hitler's military domination of Europe. The Library of Congress provided space for Lasswell's project at no charge.

When the propaganda project began in 1940, the United States had not entered World War II. President Roosevelt was campaigning for re-election, telling the American people that he would keep the United States out of involvement in the European war, while quietly aiding England and beginning preparations for mobilization. Thus, the project dealt with too sensitive a subject for it to be funded by the federal government, and John Marshall of the Rockefeller Foundation was willing to support it as one means of preparing the nation for the forthcoming war.

Ralph Casey, who earned his Ph.D. degree in political science with a journalism minor at Wisconsin in 1929 under Daddy Bleyer, was a key figure in extending Lasswell's propaganda analysis into the emerging field of communication study. Casey's doctoral dissertation, "Propaganda Technique in the 1928 Presidential Campaign," drew directly on Lasswell's dissertation and book, *Propaganda Technique in the World War* (1927), as is evident from its title. Casey became the director of the School of Journalism at Minnesota in 1930 and continued for the next twenty-eight years in that post. Lasswell and Casey collaborated in several ways. They both served on the Social Science Research Council's Committee on Pressure Groups and Propaganda form 1930 to 1934. Out of this work, they published an annotated bibliography, *Propaganda and Promotional Activities* (Lasswell, Casey, and Smith 1935), which was revised and updated in 1946 (Smith, Lasswell, and Casey 1946). During World War II, both Lasswell and Casey were consultants to the Office of Facts and Figures/Office of War Information. Through this connection, propaganda analysis became an important input into Wilbur Schramm's emerging vision of communication study.

Prior to World War II, most propaganda studies were reformist in nature, seeking to document the power of propaganda messages and to identify policies that could help curb such power. But after Harold Lasswell's War-Time Communications Project, which pioneered in quantitative methods of content analysis of Allied and Axis propaganda, the researcher became a neutral observer. World War II, the quantification of propaganda analysis, and Lasswell's project in the U.S.Library of

Congress together represent a turning point. Eventually the value-laden term *propaganda analysis* gave way to *communication research* (Sproule 1989, p. 16).

THE POLICY SCIENCES

In 1947, Lasswell became involved as a consultant to a large research project, the World Revolution of Our Time (also known as Revolution and the Development of International Relations, RADIR), underway at Stanford University's Hoover Institution on War, Revolution, and Peace, a conservative think-tank founded by U.S. President Herbert Hoover after World War I and depository of a rich collection of the world's newspapers and other media materials. This project, carried out from 1949 to 1953, was funded by the Carnegie Corporation in order to study the major political and social changes over the sixty-year period 1890–1950. It was a logical next step after Lasswell's propaganda project.

In collaboration with Ithiel de Sola Pool and Daniel Lerner, Lasswell content-analyzed 20,000 editorials in the most prestigious newspapers of five nations in order to identify changes in national elites and their political discourse. The rise and fall of political forces like democracy, authoritarianism, violence, and peace were traced over the six decades of study. *The Prestige Papers* (1952) by Ithiel de Sola Pool and others, was the most noted book reporting the study's results. The Hoover studies, as the project came to be called, consisted of three components: (1) the elite studies, which focused on government and political leaders, like the Nazi leaders of Germany, (2) the institutional studies, such as an investigation of Soviet economic organizations, and (3) the symbol studies, such as the analysis of the prestigious newspapers. These later investigations centered on mass communication. While Lasswell was officially just a consultant to the project, his theoretical framework for world revolution (Lasswell 1951) guided the entire research program, and many of the studies were carried out by his former students and by scholars who had worked with him in the War-Time Communications Project.

The Hoover studies represented "the first large-scale, quantitatively-based empirical research enterprise in contemporary political science" (Eulau 1977). The means of analyzing large data sets was advancing, which gave a boost to quantitative-type content analysis. Lasswell (1972) noted that the variety and uses of content analysis exploded about 1970: "Developments [in content analysis] were held back by the magnitude and repetitiousness of the material to be covered. Hence, the great, and in this instance, permanent leap forward with the emergence of the computer."

One important by-product of the Hoover studies was Lasswell's argument for development of the policy sciences, consisting of an integration of political science, law, sociology, and psychology and focusing on public choice and decision making. This hybrid field has not grown to vigorous maturity, but it has been one important thrust toward academic interdisciplinarity. Lasswell said that John Dewey was his inspiration for the policy science (Marvick 1980). Lasswell met Dewey when he was a high school student and then read many of his books (Torgerson 1990). By the time that Lasswell was a student at the University of Chicago, Dewey had been gone from the Midway campus for a dozen years, but some of Dewey's thinking may have been passed on to Lasswell through Robert E. Park, for whom Lasswell had "a genuine reverence" (Shils 1981).

Lasswell advocated the policy sciences as a means by which certain of the political and social problems facing modern societies could be resolved. He did not just advocate such direct approaches; he also participated directly in such ameliorative actions. One example is the Vicos Project in Peru. Lasswell became involved in this unusual field experiment in social power when he met Allen Holmberg, a Cornell University anthropologist specializing in Peruvian Indians, during their year together at the Center for Advanced Study in the Behavioral Sciences, at Stanford, in 1954–1955. Lasswell learned from Holmberg about the Vicos hacienda in the Andes Mountains. Some 1,700 Indians lived on about seventy square miles of rocky mountaintops, existing in a semi-feudal state of dismal poverty. Holmberg rented the hacienda from its absentee owners for $500 per year and instituted a self-development approach in which the Vicos peasant families were given power to operate their own system, with some advice from the North American scholars (Kunkel 1986; Dobyns, Doughty, and Lasswell 1964). This change in political power set off waves of economic and social development in Vicos. New potato seed and cultivation methods were introduced, leading to a doubling of potato yields and then a doubling again. Small businesses were formed, such as by Vicosiños who cut and sold the glacial ice found on the hacienda. They invested profits from such enterprises in building a school; in five years, the peasants were able to purchase the hacienda, ending their virtual serfdom. In a similar approach in the

United States, Lasswell was involved in placing the control of the Yale Psychiatric Institute in the hands of its inmates (Rubenstein and Lasswell 1966).

In 1946, Lasswell accepted a professorship at the Yale Law School, where he sought to broaden the nature of legal training by internationalizing it and introducing social science thinking. Lasswell felt that lawyers are to the policy sciences what engineers are to physics and medical doctors to biology. In 1952, he was also appointed on a courtesy basis in the Department of Political Science at Yale. Lasswell's main colleague in the Yale Law School was Professor Myres S. McDougal, a Mississippi-born lawyer who was educated at the University of Mississippi, Oxford University (where he was a Rhodes Scholar), and then at Yale University, where he earned his doctorate in international law. MacDougal was appointed to the faculty of the Yale Law School in 1934, and McDougal and Lasswell became acquainted in 1935 when McDougal was a visiting professor at the University of Chicago. They worked together as a highly productive team for over twenty-five years, writing about international legal problems. Their collaboration continued until Lasswell's death.

Lasswell retired from Yale in 1970 but continued his scholarly productivity until his death from pneumonia on December 18, 1978, in New York City. Lasswell had suffered a massive stroke a year earlier from which he never recovered.

LASSWELL'S STYLE

Lasswell's personal style was unusual. Arnold Rogow, a political scientist, practicing psychoanalyst, and a friend of Lasswell, described him thus: "He is, to begin with, a connoisseur of the good life, an epicure and a gourmet. He knows much about architecture, oriental culture, poetry, Renaissance furniture and painting (of which he owns several superb examples), science fiction, and the history of the cinema. His comments on modern art are apt to be pithy and to the point. He is also fully possessed of a creative imagination or inventive flair that is productive of ideas no matter what the subject. . . . He is without question America's most distinguished political scientist as well as one of our best known and most respected behavioral scientists" (Rogow 1969, pp. ix–x). McDougal (1991), Lasswell's long-time colleague in the Yale Law School, described him as "deeply humanitarian, a scholar whose intellect knew no boundaries. He was a shy, reserved man in person, but he was friends with politicians at the highest levels, and enjoyed talking with them at great length."

Despite their mutual interests in communication study, their being in Washington at the same time during World War II, and their many mutual friends, Lasswell and Wilbur Schramm did not meet until 1954–1955. When Lasswell was a fellow at the Center for Advanced Study in the Behavioral Sciences at Stanford, Schramm, who had just joined the Stanford faculty, went to Lasswell's studio at 2:00 P.M. in order to discuss a data-analysis problem in which he was engaged. Lasswell showed Schramm some sophisticated analysis that could be conducted with his data, and they became very involved in a discussion of what the data meant. Finally, Schramm says, they realized that it had grown dark and that they must have missed dinner. It was 8:00 P.M. Such was the nature of Lasswell's mind when challenged with an intellectual problem.

Peter Clarke, of the University of Southern California's Annenberg School for Communication, also attests to Lasswell's intensity. In the early 1960s, Clarke signed up for an informal luncheon session with Lasswell at the annual conference of the American Association for Public Opinion Research (AAPOR). The session included about thirty participants, who asked Lasswell questions about public opinion, mass communication, content analysis, and propaganda. Lasswell gave lengthy, highly involved answers using his usual abstract verbiage. At the end of the hour-long session with Lasswell, Clarke says that his mind felt so overloaded that he had to go to his hotel room to sleep for several hours. Such was the effect of direct exposure to Harold Lasswell.

Lasswell was a prolific scholar. Over his lengthy academic career, starting with a 1923 article in the *National Municipal Review,* "Chicago's Old First Ward," which dealt with machine politics, and ending with the several books that were published after his death in 1978, Lasswell authored or coauthored 325 articles and chapters and authored or edited 52 books (Muth, Finley, and Muth 1990). He was one of those extremely rare individuals who enjoy writing. Joseph Goldsen, Lasswell's assistant on the War-Time Communications Project, describes visiting him in his apartment at 10:00 A.M. to deliver some material. When Goldsen returned later that day at 5:00 P.M., Lasswell was still sitting at his typewriter. He had written an incredible fifty typed, double-spaced pages of scholarly prose. "He did not think of writing as work. It was pure pleasure for him" (Goldsen 1991). Lasswell's writing style, however, was "the combination of terseness and prolixity that makes his message sporadically unclear" (Marvick 1980).

Leo Rosten (1969, p. 1), a former student of Lasswell at the University of Chicago,* described him as "a bit of a freak: Pedantic, verbose, and quite ill at ease. He wore his hair in a short, stiff, Prussian cut, and his knowledge in a high, stiff, abrasive manner. He was only twenty-five, and he lectured us desperately, with a glazed stare into space, conspicuously unaware of whether we understood him and visibly unconcerned with what we might be thinking." Certainly Lasswell's verbal style was highly distinctive: "To him, talking is a form of testing, of dropping plumb lines into the gigantic reservoir of his knowledge. He talks the way other men daydream. His monologues are symposiums with invisible peers" (Rogow 1969, p. 3). Lasswell talked with his hands. "I was struck by the ballet of his hands. They are library hands, very pale, soft, unsullied by physical exertion. When Harold talks, over food or drinks, his hands make small gyrations, in the same ritual of gestures. The left hand is motionless, its thumb and forefinger forming an 'O'; the right hand hovers over and dances around the 'O'. . . . the right hand pulls the invisible thread through an invisible needle on a path horizontal to, and away from, the inert circle of the left hand 'O'" (Rosten 1969, p. 4).

CONTRIBUTIONS OF HAROLD LASSWELL
TO COMMUNICATION STUDY

Lasswell made these lasting contributions to the field of communication study:

1. His five-questions model of communication led to the emphasis in communication study on determining effects.[†] Lasswell's contemporary, Paul F. Lazarsfeld, did even more to crystallize this focus on communication effects.
2. He pioneered in content analysis methods, virtually inventing the

*Rosten studied Washington news correspondents (Rosten 1937) and Hollywood movie makers (Rosten 1941), and later wrote a book about Yiddish humor.

[†]Steven Brown (1992) points out that Lasswell was an integrator of diverse strands of knowledge and that he did not intend to restrict communication research to focus on effects. The effects orientation came about at the hands of later communication scholars who used Lasswell's model to guide their research.

methodology of qualitative and quantitative measurement of communication messages (propaganda messages and newspaper editorials, for example).

3. His study of political and wartime propaganda represented an important early type of communication study. The word *propaganda* later gained a negative connotation and is not used much today, although there is even more political propaganda. Propaganda analysis has been absorbed into the general body of communication research.

4. He introduced Freudian psychoanalytic theory to the social sciences in America. Lasswell integrated Freudian theory with political analysis, as in his psychoanalytic study of political leaders. He applied Freud's id-ego-superego via content analysis to political science problems. In essence, he utilized intraindividual Freudian theory at the societal level.

5. He helped create the policy sciences, an interdisciplinary movement to integrate social science knowledge with public action. The social sciences, however, generally resisted this attempt at integration and application to public policy problems.

WALTER LIPPMANN AND AGENDA SETTING

Walter Lippmann (1889–1974) was a fellow scholar with Harold Lasswell in work on propaganda analysis and public opinion, and he pioneered early thinking about what is now called the agenda-setting process. This influential newspaper columnist is best known for his 1922 book, *Public Opinion,* in which he spoke of "the pictures in our heads, and the world outside." He described agenda setting, the process by which a news topic is given a priority concern by the mass media, the public, and policy elites (Rogers and Dearing 1988). Unlike the other important early figures in communication study, Lippmann did not earn a graduate degree in a university, he never taught a university class, and he never adopted the research methods or the theoretical perspectives of social science, yet he was the most influential single writer about the role of the mass media in shaping public opinion, setting off the research tradition on the agenda-setting process that flourishes today. Walter Lippmann is undoubtedly the most influential nonacademic intellectual influence on communication study. *Public Opinion* is considered by James W. Carey (1982, p. 23) as the founding book for the field of communication study.

Lippmann's Life and Times

Lippmann was the only child of wealthy Jewish parents of German descent who were eager to be assimilated into New York society (Steel 1981). The young Lippmann was sent to Dr. Julius Sach's School for Boys, a private school favored by the richest Jewish families in New York. He summered with his parents in Europe, learning the charm and life-style that would be valuable to him later in life in his contacts with the rich and famous. As an undergraduate at Harvard University, he studied with William James, George Santayana, and Graham Wallas, a leftish British political scientist. He then continued for a master's degree in philosophy at Harvard, but he dropped out a few weeks before graduation to work for a socialist newspaper in Boston.

Journalism appealed to Lippmann because it allowed him to combine scholarly reading and writing with direct involvement with powerful policymakers. Early in his career, Lippmann felt that socialism offered solutions to America's social problems, and he assisted the famous muckraking journalist Lincoln Steffens in writing a series of magazine articles about Wall Street. But Lippmann grew disillusioned with socialism and with Steffens. Lippmann became an editor of the *New Republic,* an important intellectual magazine, for nine years. During World War I, he served as a U.S. Army captain in France, where he was a chief writer of front-line propaganda leaflets.

One of the several connections between Walter Lippmann and Harold Lasswell, in addition to their shared interests in propaganda and public opinion, was that U.S. Army Captain Walter Lippmann, as a leaflet writer for the propaganda unit of the Army Expeditionary Force in France, created much of the U.S. propaganda that Lasswell analyzed.[*] Like Lasswell, Lippmann was influenced by Freud, particularly by *The Interpretation of Dreams,* which Lippmann (1922) drew upon for his concept of a "pseudo-environment" that, he said, an individual creates as pictures in his or her head. Like Lasswell, Lippmann was influenced by Marxist theory early in his career, organizing the Harvard Socialist Club while he was an undergraduate student.

Adviser to Presidents

In 1921, Lippmann was hired by the *New York World,* New York's most influential liberal newspaper, where he wrote editorials. The *World*

---

[*]As Lasswell recognized (Lasswell 1971, p. xxxii).

folded in 1931, and Lippmann moved the the *New York Herald Tribune,* a conservative paper, where he began writing a four-times-a-week column, "Today and Tomorrow," for which he became famous; his column was syndicated and carried by hundreds of U.S. daily newspapers. In 1963, Lippmann shifted to the *Washington Post,* until he retired from writing his column in 1967.

Over his long life of eighty-six years (1889–1974), Lippmann acted as an influential shaper of political events, in addition to reporting and interpreting them as a newsperson. He helped draft President Woodrow Wilson's Fourteen Points in 1918, a proposed plan for world peace after World War I. Lippmann wrote editorials and "Today and Tomorrow" four days a week for thirty-six years. He wrote twenty books, of which *Public Opinion* is the most widely known. Incredibly, he was an adviser to twelve U.S. presidents from Teddy Roosevelt to Lyndon Johnson, until he broke with LBJ over the Vietnam War. Lippmann traveled frequently to other nations, where he conferred with heads of state, who often sought him out. His name opened every door (Steel 1981, p. xiv). During a trip to Greece in the mid-1950s, Lippmann made this casual entry in his diary: "Saw the king, the prime minister, etc.—the usual people." He was influential because his syndicated newspaper column, a dispassionate analysis of political matters, was read by millions of readers. Lippmann wrote clearly and had a special ability to simplify complexity. "He had an intellect of a sort that is rarely attracted to journalism" (Steel 1981, p. xiv). Without doubt, "Walter Lippmann was the most gifted and influential American political journalist of the twentieth century" (Curtis 1991). He was also a key analyst of the process of propaganda, public opinion, and agenda setting, in which he was an important participant during his career.*

The Pictures in Our Heads

Public Opinion was a tremendously influential book, both when it was published and over the years since. It drew on Lippmann's World War I propaganda experiences in France. For example, the French government felt that the war eventually would be decided on the basis of losses of military manpower. In late 1917, the French officer in charge of in-

---

*The inherent conflicts involved in Lippmann's contradictory roles as opinion shaper versus news reporter were acknowledged by him. In retrospect, he advocated "a large air space" between a journalist and a head of state.

telligence at Verdun, an important battlefield, invented a method of calculating troop losses that produced marvelous results. Every two weeks, the estimated number of German losses increased a hundred thousand or so: from 300,000, to 400,000, to 500,000 casualties. The French intelligence communiqués spoke of bloody sacrifices, heaps of corpses and other grisly details. This misinformation, Lippmann said, is propaganda. When a set of individuals can prevent an audience from having their own access to a news event and arrange the news about the event to suit their purposes, a potential for propaganda exists. "In order to conduct a propaganda, there must be some barrier between the public and the event" (Lippmann 1922, p. 28). Such restricted communication flows often occur during wartime, when government propagandists are the sole gatekeepers of news about important events. Lippmann thus defined propaganda as a situation in which communication flows are restricted and a set of individuals wish to distort the news.

Public Opinion was a key intellectual influence in creating public apprehension about the role of propaganda in a democratic society. People are irrational and react to symbols conveyed to them by the mass media. He showed how a government could censor the news and distort information flows by propaganda techniques. What solution did Lippmann offer to such problems? He felt that experts could serve as the saviors of American democracy by conveying their expert knowledge widely, so as to inform public opinion.

Lippmann (1922) identified stereotypes as a key factor in the public opinion process. A *stereotype* is a code that simplifies reality so that a source can convey it more easily to other individuals—for example, spoiled college students, gifted black athletes, and successful Asian businessmen.

Lippmann began *Public Opinion* with a chapter entitled "The World Outside and the Pictures in Our Heads." He described an island in the North Sea inhabited by English, French, and Germans in 1914. A mail boat that arrived once every two months was the sole contact with the wider world. In September 1914, the islanders "learned that for over six weeks now those of them who were English and those of them who were French had been fighting in behalf of the sanctity of treaties against those of them who were Germans. For six strange weeks they had acted as if they were friends, when in fact they were enemies." The "pictures in their heads," which had guided their behavior for the six weeks, had not corresponded with the "world outside." Once the islanders read the newspapers that were delivered by the mail boat, the world outside affected the picture in their heads. Here we see a spectacular example of the effects of the mass media.

The pictures in our heads often do not correspond to factual reality for several reasons, Lippmann (1922) said: we need simplified codes (like stereotypes) in order to give meaning to the buzzing, blooming confusion of the world, and the pseudo-environment that is conveyed to us by the media is the result of a high degree of gatekeeping in the news process. He pointed out that every newspaper is the result of a series of gatekeeping decisions. Lippmann and Charles Merz (1920) carried out a content analysis of the *New York Time*'s coverage of the Russian Revolution of 1917 and, concluded that the reporters wrote what they wanted to see or expected to see, rather than what actually happened.* The average newspaper reader spent only fifteen minutes per day with a newspaper at the time that Lippmann was writing. As a result of such limitations, Lippmann argued that the average person could not be expected to form intelligent opinions about important issues of the day. The democratic ideal of an informed public was as unlikely as that a fat man could be a ballet dancer. This skepticism about public opinion was expressed by the title of Lippmann's next book, *The Phantom Public* (1925).

AGENDA-SETTING RESEARCH

How did the early work by Harold Lasswell and, especially, by Walter Lippmann eventually result in an important type of communication research on agenda setting?[†]

Conceptualization of Agenda Setting

Agenda-setting research began with Lippmann's first chapter of *Public Opinion,* "The World Outside and the Pictures in Our Heads," in which he argued that the mass media are the principal connections between an event in the real world and the images in our minds of this event. Without using the term, Lippmann was talking about what we today call agenda setting. Forty years later, conceptualization of the agenda-setting process was advanced by the political scientist Bernard Cohen

---

*This difference between an actual event and its media coverage was later to be called a "pseudo-event" (Boorstin 1961).

[†]This section draws on Rogers, Dearing, and Bregman (1993).

(1963, p. 13), who observed that the press "may not be successful much of the time in telling people *what to think,* but it is stunningly successful in telling its readers *what to think about.* . . .The world will look different to different people, depending. . . .on the map that is drawn for them by writers, editors, and publishers of the paper they read" (emphasis added). Building on Lippmann's original idea, Cohen expressed the metaphor that led to agenda-setting research. He suggested that the mass media, in addition to whatever direct effects they may have ("telling people what to think"), have important indirect effects ("telling people what to think about").

But agenda setting was still just a theoretical idea, yet unnamed, until a classic study by Maxwell McCombs and Donald Shaw (1972) of the media's role in the 1968 presidential election campaign in Chapel Hill, North Carolina. They calculated the media agenda in Chapel Hill from a content analysis of the main mass media reporting the presidential campaign: newspapers, news magazines, and television news. They determined the relative frequency with which each issue (for example, foreign policy, inflation) was mentioned by the media in their reports of the presidential campaign, and then measured the public agenda by surveying 100 undecided voters who resided in Chapel Hill. Each respondent was asked, "What are the most important issues in the presidential campaign?" The media agenda correlated almost perfectly with the public agenda; that is, issues like foreign policy, law and order, and fiscal policy ranked similarly on both the media agenda and the public agenda. Perhaps the public's agenda was set by the media. How else could the public know (and agree on) what the issues were?

This study set off a research tradition by mass communication scholars, political scientists, sociologists, and other scholars who tried to answer this key question: How does an issue get on the policy agenda? The agenda-setting research tradition consisted of 233 scholarly publications by mid-1992 (Rogers, Dearing, and Bregman 1993), making it one of the most popular topics in mass communication research, with about a dozen publications appearing each year recently.

The agenda-setting process encompasses media agenda setting, public agenda setting, and policy agenda setting (Rogers and Dearing 1988). Media agenda setting is the process through which the relative amount of coverage of a particular news issue is determined by mass media gatekeepers, by the impact of major news events, and by audience interests. The media agenda is usually measured by content analysis (the research method developed by Harold Lasswell). Public agenda setting is the process by which the public decides which issues are of relatively greatest importance. Polls and surveys of the public are utilized by scholars to measure the public agenda. For instance, a national sample of the U.S. public are asked, "What are the most important problems facing America?" Policy agenda setting is the process by which the issue agenda of governmental bodies or elected officials is determined. The policy agenda may be indexed by the passage of laws or by the appropriation of funds (for example, the millions of dollars budgeted by the federal government for AIDS research, prevention, and treatment). It is usually assumed that the agenda-setting process consists of the media agenda's influencing the public agenda, which in turn influences the policy agenda:

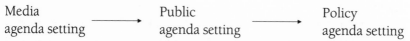

| Media | Public | Policy |
| agenda setting | agenda setting | agenda setting |

The agenda setting process describes how public opinion functions in a democracy. Ultimately, research on it seeks to offer one explanation of how social change occurs in modern society, particularly as a result of mass media communication. Notice that the media agenda presumably initiates the agenda-setting process, suggesting that at the macro level of society, the mass media may have strong effects in determining what we think about. The key role of the media agenda in the agenda-setting process also leads us to wonder how the media agenda gets set.

Communication Research on Agenda Setting

Communication scholars are attracted to agenda-setting research because it appears to offer a promising alternative to the scholarly search for direct media effects on overt behavior change. Earlier mass communication research had found only limited effects, which seemed counterintuitive to many mass communication researchers, especially to those who had previous mass media experience (like Maxwell McCombs and Donald Shaw). Further, the early mass communication Ph.D.s felt that the main purpose of the media was to inform rather than to persuade, so they looked for cognitive effects, like the agenda-setting process in which people are told what to think about rather than such affective effects as attitude change. Many of the agenda-setting publications by mass communication researchers state their main justification as an attempt to overcome the limited-effects findings of past communication research. For example, Maxwell McCombs stated in a 1981 overview: "It's [agenda setting] initial empirical exploration was fortuitously timed. It came at that time in the history of mass communication research when disenchantment both with attitudes and opinions as dependent variables, and with the limited-effects model as an adequate intellectual summary, was leading scholars to look elsewhere" (p. 121). The agenda-setting paradigm came along just when mass communication scholars were dismayed with their previous model of direct media effects, just as Thomas Kuhn (1962) predicts should happen in his notion of a scientific revolution.

How can the mass media have relatively few direct effects, but at the same time have strong indirect effects in setting the public agenda? McQuail and Windhal (1981, p. 62) stated: "The hypothesis [agenda setting] would seem to have escaped the doubts which early empirical research cast on almost any notion of powerful mass media effects, mainly because it deals primarily with learning and not with attitude change or directly with opinion change." Individuals learn information from the mass media about which issues are more important than others. The mass media are much less capable of changing directly attitudes and opinions, but they can tell us what to think about. This agenda-setting effect is not the result of receiving one or a few messages but rather is due to the aggregate impact of a very large number of messages, each of which has a different content but all of which deal with the same general issue. For example, for four years after the first AIDS cases were reported in the United States (in 1981), the mass media carried only a few stories about the epidemic. It was not yet on the media agenda, nor was the U.S. public fully aware of the AIDS issue (poll results indicated). Then, in mid-1985 two news events—movie actor Rock Hudson's death from AIDS and the refusal by the schools of Kokomo, Indiana, to allow a young boy with AIDS, Ryan White, to attend—led to a massive increase in media coverage of the AIDS issue. Almost immediately, public awareness of the epidemic increased; in a few months, 95 percent of U.S. adults knew about AIDS and understood how it was transmitted (Rogers, Dearing, and Chang 1991).

In 1966, almost fifty years after publication of Lippmann's *Public Opinion,* Max McCombs walked into the UCLA bookstore and bought a copy of Bernard Cohen's *The Press and Foreign Policy* (1963).*

---

*McCombs knew about Cohen's book from Wilbur Schramm's doctoral seminar at Stanford University, in which the volume by Cohen had been an assigned reading.

McCombs had just been sitting with faculty colleagues in a bar in Los Angeles, where they had discussed that day's front page of the *Los Angeles Times*. The headlines dealt with three different news events. McCombs and his colleagues speculated about the consequences of these front-page headlines for individuals who read one or the other of the headlines. McCombs' next step was to the UCLA bookstore, en route to Chapel Hill and his classic study of agenda setting with Donald Shaw.

McCombs was born in 1938 in Alabama and attended Tulane University, where he earned his bachelor's degree in journalism in 1960. Then he went to Stanford University for his master's degree under Chick Bush, who insisted that he gain media experience before continuing for his doctorate. McCombs then worked as a reporter for the *New Orleans Times-Picayune* for two years before returning to Stanford for his Ph.D. After a year's teaching at UCLA, McCombs moved to the School of Journalism at the University of North Carolina, where he taught for the next six years (later, McCombs' career would take him to Syracuse University and then to the University of Texas at Austin).

At North Carolina, McCombs met Donald L. Shaw (born in North Carolina in 1936), who had returned to Chapel Hill from the University of Wisconsin with a Ph.D. degree in mass communication. Shaw had earned his bachelor's and master's degrees in journalism at Chapel Hill. He worked as a reporter on the *Asheville Citizen* and the *Asheville Times* for a couple of years before enrolling in the doctoral program at Madison. His dissertation was a content analysis of newspapers to determine the effects of the telegraph on objectivity in news reports.

Shaw's and McCombs' faculty offices were next to each other at UNC, and in fall 1967, they submitted a small grant proposal to the National Association of Broadcasters (NAB) for a study of media effects on voting behavior in the forthcoming presidential election. The two communication scholars decided to interview 100 undecided voters in their small city of Chapel Hill, because they expected such undecided individuals to be most affected by the media's agenda of campaign issues (Tankard 1990, p. 281). Indeed they were. McCombs and Shaw found an almost perfect correspondence between the issues that the media said were relatively most important versus the issues that the undecided voters thought were most important. The results of this first study of agenda setting were published in 1972 in the journal *Public Opinion Quarterly*, in the process setting the agenda for agenda-setting research. The McCombs and Shaw paper has been cited by more than half (57 percent) of the 233 publications on agenda setting and is by far the most widely cited study in this research tradition. It achieved this prominence because it:

- Provided a name for the new research specialty and an empirical methodology for studying the agenda-setting process by juxtaposing a content analysis of the media agenda with a survey of the public agenda.
- Reported a spectacularly high relationship (a rank-order correlation of +.98) between the media agenda and the public agenda, suggesting that mass communication has indirect effects through the agenda-setting process, a finding that fulfilled the expectations of mass communication scholars at the time.
- Was originally presented as a paper at the 1971 American Association for Public Opinion Research and then published in 1972 in *Public Opinion Quarterly,* thus exposing it to both mass communication scholars who mainly study public agenda-setting, and to political scientists and sociologists who mainly investigate policy agenda setting.

What we today call agenda-setting research began with Walter Lippmann's *Public Opinion,* in which he expressed the basic notion that the media create symbolic images in our minds that may be quite different from the world that we experience "outside."* This vague notion of how the media set the public's agenda, however, did not lead directly toward forming the paradigm for agenda-setting research until Bernard Cohen's (1963) influential metaphor for agenda setting—that the media tell us "what to think about." However, the paradigmatic research study was not published for nine more years, until McCombs and Shaw's (1972) study of the 1968 presidential election campaign in Chapel Hill. These scholars provided one means of empirically testing the media agenda–public agenda relationship. Their seminal article led to a proliferation of investigations of the agenda-setting process, including, in recent years, a variety of methodological approaches that differ from the McCombs-Shaw content analysis—audience survey. For the first fifteen

---

*Several agenda-setting studies have found that real-world indicators (for example, the number of AIDS cases over time or the number of drug-related deaths per year) have little relationship to an issue's priority on the media agenda. See Rogers, Dearing, and Chang (1991) and Danielian and Reese (1989), respectively.

years or so, the invisible college of agenda-setting scholars went through a phase called "normal science" by Thomas Kuhn (1962) in which each empirical study builds incrementally on previous work. These investigations confirmed the McCombs-Shaw finding of the media agenda influencing public opinion. In other words, the media play an important role in forming public opinion.

In the late 1980s agenda-setting scholars began to break out of their rather stereotyped mold of content analyses and audience surveys of the media agenda–public agenda relationship. A creative variety of research designs and conceptualization began to be used. For example, some scholars traced a single issue (drugs, AIDS, or the environment) over time through the agenda-setting process. Others (Iyengar and Kinder 1987) conducted experiments of the public agenda-setting process at the micro level. Respondents viewed doctored videos of evening television news broadcasts in which extra material was spliced in about some issue. As might be expected, such individuals subsequently ranked that issue higher on their agenda.

Thus, the stream of communication research begun by Harold D. Lasswell and Walter Lippmann six or seven decades ago with their writings about public opinion and propaganda is now being carried forward by today's agenda-setting scholars. Although the words *propaganda* and *public opinion* have been replaced by terms like *mass communication* and *agenda setting,* the earlier conceptualizations continue to influence communication study.

CHAPTER 7

PAUL F. LAZARSFELD AND MASS COMMUNICATION EFFECTS

He was a wonderful talker, intense, clever, endlessly anec-
dotal. But it was his sheer energy that mainly transformed
our household when he visited.
　　　　　　—Bernard Bailyn [Lazarsfeld's son-in-law],
　　　　　　　　　　　　　　　"Recollections of PFL"

Paul F. Lazarsfeld . . . virtually created the fields of mathematical sociology, multivariate survey analysis, and the empirical study of both voting behavior and mass communications.
　　　—David L. Sills, "Paul Lazarsfeld . . . He Taught Us What
　　　　　　　　　　　　　Sociology Is—or Should Be"

On Saturday evening, November 23, 1941, Professor Robert K. Merton and his wife arrived for dinner at Paul F. Lazarsfeld's apartment in Manhattan.* A few months earlier, both Merton and Lazarsfeld had been appointed as new faculty members in the Department of Sociology at Columbia University. They represented a compromise on the part of the department, which was split down theory versus methodology lines: Merton was a promising young theorist and Lazarsfeld a methodologist who was directing the Office of Radio Research, already loosely attached to Columbia. "Paul and I had never heard of one another before coming to Columbia. We had not only not read one another; we had literally never heard of one another" (Merton 1987). Everyone in the Columbia

I thank Robert K. Merton, David L. Sills, Allen H. Barton, Rolf Wigand, and Ann Pasanella for critically reviewing this chapter, which also draws on Rogers (1992).

*Accounts of this memorable evening can be found in Merton (1979, 1987, and in press), Lazarsfeld (1975e), and Hunt (1961).

Department of Sociology expected Lazarsfeld and Merton to continue the theory versus methodology dispute, but for their first few months on the Morningside campus, they had little contact.

In November, Lazarsfeld decided to make a friendly move and invite the Mertons to dinner. After all, Merton was ten years his junior and an assistant professor (due to his greater experience, Lazarsfeld was appointed as an associate professor at Columbia). But when Professor and Mrs. Merton arrived that Saturday evening, Lazarsfeld met them at his apartment door to explain that he had to rush off to the NBC radio studios in New York in order to evaluate a radio program. "This Is War . . . ," for the U.S. Office of Facts and Figures (OFF), a new government agency set up to inform the public about preparations for America's expected entrance into World War II. OFF was in a hurry. They had telephoned Lazarsfeld just that afternoon, asking that he and his Office of Radio Research evaluate the radio message so as to make it more effective.

Merton accompanied Lazarsfeld to the radio studio, leaving their wives in the Lazarsfeld apartment with the uneaten dinner. Merton (1987) says, "Thus it was that Paul dragged me into the strange world of radio research." Test individuals in the studio were asked to record their responses to the radio broadcast on the Stanton-Lazarsfeld Program-Analyzer, a kind of polygraph to measure the radio message's effects. Then they were group interviewed about their likes and dislikes by one of Lazarsfeld's research assistants. In the radio studio, Merton whispered to Lazarsfeld that the interviewer was leading the respondents in the way that he asked questions. Lazarsfeld invited Merton to explain the problem to the interviewer. Merton then demonstrated how to ask the questions correctly with the next listener group to enter the studio. Lazarsfeld (January 8, 1962a) felt that Merton was a very effective interviewer. Meanwhile, Mrs. Merton and Mrs. Lazarsfeld were waiting impatiently, back at the Lazarsfelds' apartment. Late that Saturday evening, the husbands telephoned the wives to meet them at the Russian Tea Room at West 57th Street for champagne and caviar. The foursome talked until after midnight, about radio research, the forthcoming war, and Lazarsfeld's research institute at Columbia.

Robert Merton (in press) says, "And that's how it happened that I came to dinner and remained for 35 years." The Lazarsfeld-Merton team became one of the most effective and important collaborations in the history of their field, raising Columbia sociology to a dominant status in the nation. They spent the equivalent of a continuous three and a half years together, talking one-on-one, over the next thirty-five years, an estimated 18,000 hours.* This intense interaction is all the more amazing, considering that Lazarsfeld and Merton are "something like the original odd couple" (Merton 1992), with one the tool-maker and the other the theoretician.

Out of that remarkable evening came, in addition to the Lazarsfeld-Merton collaboration, the notion of focused group interviewing, in which a small group of respondents are questioned about a communication message to which they had just been exposed. Merton was induced to make an analysis of the data from the focused interview research during the following days. "The report was in the Office of Facts and Figures within a week" (Merton 1987). After the United States entered World War II, Merton found himself conducting focused interviews with U.S. soldiers in army camps about the effects of military training films, measured by the Program-Analyzer. In 1943, Merton, Fiske, and Curtis (1946) carried out individual (not group) focused interviews with 100 New Yorkers who had listened to the Kate Smith radio marathon that sold U.S. war bonds, in order to find out why Smith was so persuasive.

A few months later, in March 1942, Robert Merton complained in a letter to a friend that he had "gotten trapped" in radio research, but that it was so interesting that he was getting home at 1:00 or 2:00 every night (Lazarsfeld 1975, p. 36). The Lazarsfeld-Merton collaboration was well underway.

In this chapter we look backward to the World War II era when Paul F. Lazarsfeld was launching the study of mass communication and directing it toward investigating mass media effects. Our themes here also deal with the tension between critical and empirical scholarship and between theoretical and applied research.

THE LIFE AND TIMES OF PAUL F. LAZARSFELD

Paul F. Lazarsfeld was undoubtedly the most important intellectual influence in shaping modern communication research. But he did not consider himself mainly a communication scholar, and, indeed, it is dif-

*Merton estimates that he and Lazarsfeld talked an average of three hours per workday for forty weeks per academic year for thirty of the thirty-five years (they were not together at Columbia for five of the years).

Figure 7.1. Paul F. Lazarsfeld (1901–1976) and Frank Stanton (right), with their Lazarsfeld-Stanton Program-Analyzer, in about 1937.
Used by permission of Frank Stanton.

ficult to identify him with any single discipline. At times he called himself a mathematician, the field in which he had earned a Ph.D. degree at the University of Vienna, at other times a social psychologist, and, after mid-career, he identified himself as a sociologist (Sills 1987, p. 251).* Lazarsfeld was especially pleased in 1962 when he was appointed the Quetelet Professor of Social Science at Columbia University. He liked both the "Quetelet"—after a Belgian statistician Adolphe Quetlet, whom Lazarsfeld considered the founder of empirical social research—and the

---

*During the thirty-five years that Lazarsfeld and Robert K. Merton were colleagues at Columbia University, Lazarsfeld continually asked Merton, "What is sociology?" (Merton 1991). While their endless discussions of this topic were illuminating to both of them. Merton (in press) says that "Paul never believed there was such a subject as sociology."

"Social Science"—which was wide enough to include most of the disciplines to which Lazarsfeld contributed (Merton 1979, p. 21). Certainly Lazarsfeld was multidisciplinary. One of his former colleagues, David L. Sills (1987, p. 275) called him "a modern-day Leonardo da Vinci [who] largely ignored the traditional specialization of knowledge and sought to find new truths by bringing people and ideas together." Lazarsfeld did not pay much attention to disciplinary boundaries, preferring instead to focus on scholarly problems. He was a consummate methodologist, a toolmaker, and he applied these tools to a wide range of both academic and nonscholarly problems. As Robert Merton (in press) noted, Lazarsfeld's "fundamental interests were not substantive."

Lazarsfeld was more than just multidisciplinary, though. He was almost a disciplinary agnostic, as this statement in a 1973 interview indicates: "Look, [at Columbia, University] . . . I was defined as a sociologist, which really didn't mean anything. I mean, I always did the same work. In Vienna, it was called psychology and here it was called sociology" (Morrison 1976a, p. 106). Indeed, all through his life, Lazarsfeld investigated individual action (voting, buying consumer products, etc) in a social context. He was consistent, but the disciplinary labels changed during his career.

Lazarsfeld (1982, p. 18) said of himself that he "always would be an immigrant." He viewed himself as a stranger, as someone who did not really belong. The distinguished sociologist, James S. Coleman (1980b), a former doctoral student of Lazarsfeld at Columbia, described Lazarsfeld's strong energy and drive and also his insecurity: "Lazarsfeld was insecure, but for no good reason. He [was] America's most influential sociological methodologist." Nevertheless, "Lazarsfeld felt that he was somehow an outsider in America, a marginal person, never at the center of things. . . . He thought that it was the result of his Jewishness, his foreignness, his heavy accent, and his interest in such low-status activities as market research" (Sills 1987, p. 273). Lazarsfeld considered himself a permanent outsider: "I don't belong to the club" (Lazarsfeld 1975c). The club, to Lazarsfeld, was the establishment, from which he felt excluded by being Jewish and a foreigner. Perhaps by thinking of himself as number two, Lazarsfeld tried harder.

The Education of Paul Lazarsfeld

Paul F. Lazarsfeld (1901–1976) was born and spent the first three decades of his life in Vienna. His father was "a very poor and unsuccessful lawyer" (Lazarsfeld 1961a), so young Lazarsfeld decided that he would not become a lawyer or any other kind of professional person. He wanted to avoid having to chase after clients, administer an office, have his employees depend on him to bring in funding, and to have to dun his clients to pay their fees. This predisposition is particularly ironic considering that Lazarsfeld was to spend much of his career chasing after clients in order to keep a research institute solvent (Neurath 1983). His professional life consisted of tightroping between business and academe, with each of his university-connected research institutes threatened by financial collapse. Lazarsfeld created the idea of the university research institute but set a poor example of how to manage such an organization financially.

Lazarsfeld's mother, Sofie, was without formal training, but she became widely known for her 1931 book, *Wie die Frau den Mann erlebt* ("How the Woman Experiences the Male").* She wrote a newspaper column featuring marriage advice and maintained a weekend salon for political and academic figures in Vienna. The Lazarsfeld home was a haven for turn-of-the-century intellectuals, a hotbed of socialist politics, and a center of Freudian thought. Vienna was an exciting place in which to grow up, and it shaped the lifetime interests of Paul Lazarsfeld: "What you had in the Vienna of this time was a fabulous intellectual peak, you see, a mixture of politics, psychoanalysis, Marxism" (Lazarsfeld 1961, p. 40). Vienna's location astride several key European highways and the Danube gave it a cosmopolite air.

In his youth Lazarsfeld was politically active as a socialist. He was a leader of the Socialist High School Students in Vienna, led a *Horde* (a group of ten to twelve members) of Rote Falken (Red Falcons), the organization of young socialists in Austria, and taught socialist principles in the Rote Falken summer camps. Lazarsfeld was briefly jailed for courtroom disruption and for rowdy demonstrations in the streets outside the courtroom, when a guilty sentence was passed on Friedrich (Fritz) Adler, the 1916 assassin of the Austrian prime minister, Count Karl Stürghk. With his mother, Lazarsfeld frequently visited Adler in prison at the fortress of Stein, forty miles from Vienna.† Adler was an

---

*This book was translated and published in English in 1934 as *Rhythm of Life: A Guide to Sexual Harmony for Women* (London: Routledge and Son).

†The murderer, Friedrich Adler, was close to the young Paul Lazarsfeld. Adler had met Sofie Lazarsfeld when she was ill and living in a sanitarium. "There Friedrich Adler became very interested in my mother. . . . That lasted for 50 years. . . . Friedrich Adler and my mother

eminent physicist and mathematician. When Lazarsfeld was fifteen years old, he typed the manuscript for Adler's monograph criticizing Einstein's relativity theory, which Adler wrote while imprisoned at Stein (Lazarsfeld 1961a). From his prison cell, Adler wrote to the young Lazarsfeld: "Dear Paul: I'm glad to hear that you are doing well in mathematics. Whatever you do later, mathematics will always be useful to you" (Morrison 1988). Lazarsfeld was impressed that "a glorious murderer" wrote to him from jail to tell him to stick to doing mathematics. He did, all his life. His early training in mathematics provided the basic skills for his methodological expertise, which in turn provided the means of moving from one social science discipline to another and to founding the field of mass communication research.

In a 1973 interview (Morrison 1976, p. 116), Lazarsfeld recalled how he fell in love with quantitative methodology: "I stood in front of a bookstall in Vienna. I would be 19, and by coincidence there is a book which on the outside has one of the scatter diagrams—it was something like one would use describing a correlation [between two variables]. I didn't quite know what it was, but I found it so exciting. God knows . . . like seeing at that age the photograph of a nude girl or something." Lazarsfeld loved to work with data. "For some reason that I cannot understand at all, I tabulated questionnaires. I could do them for hours. I found endless pleasure in them. So it wasn't just a convergence of intellectual interest in social science and mathematics. It was a straight delight in the interpretation of tables which I found from the beginning to be terribly interesting" (Lazarsfeld, 1961a, p. 36).

Lazarsfeld received the excellent kind of formal education that was typical for the children of middle-class Viennese families. In 1925, at age twenty-four, he earned his Ph.D. degree in applied mathematics from the University of Vienna. In his doctoral dissertation, he applied Einstein's theory of gravitation to the movement of the planet Mercury, deriving a mathematical solution to the function that described the planet's orbit. He wrote his dissertation in three nights (Lazarsfeld

---

began to see each other a great deal" (Lazarsfeld 1962a, p. 183). Adler gave Sofie Lazarsfeld books to read and became a regular participant in her weekend salons. Her husband was drafted into the Austro-Hungarian Army and sent to the Italian front during World War I. "By then [1916], it was just a matter of course that the family consisted of my mother, Friedrich Adler, my sister, and myself" (Lazarsfeld 1962a, p. 189). In fact, Friedrich Adler was living in the Lazarsfeld home at the time that he assassinated Count Stürghk, a crime motivated by Adler's intention to create an anarchistic situation in which the Socialist party might gain control of the government. Adler's sentencing was delayed, and due to the events of World War I, he was never punished for the murder that he had committed.

1961a, p. 48).* University faculty positions were scarce, and so Lazarsfeld supported himself by teaching mathematics and physics in a *Gymnasium* (high school) in Vienna. With a doctorate in hand, Lazarsfeld was overqualified for teaching high school classes.

Lazarsfeld the Young Socialist

Austria, and especially Vienna, were in grave economic shape at the time that Lazarsfeld reached young adulthood. The Treaty of St. Germain, which Austria-Hungary signed in 1919 after losing World War I, had reduced the Hapsburg Empire of 50 million people to an Austria of only 6½ million, of whom 2½ million lived in Vienna. The city was of a size to command a large empire, but that empire no longer existed. Vienna was dominated politically by the Socialist party, mainly composed of working men and intellectuals. Jews, who made up about 10 percent of Vienna's population, were especially likely to support the Socialist party. To grow up in Vienna in the 1920s as Jewish and intellectual meant that one would likely be a socialist. How Lazarsfeld changed from being a young socialist in Austria to become the leader of administrative research (a name that he himself created) in America is a fascinating process.

Lazarsfeld came in contact with Professors Karl and Charlotte Bühler, who had founded the Department of Psychology[†] at the University of Vienna in 1923. The Bühlers represented one of the two main centers for psychology in Germany and Austria at that time (the other was the Gestalt psychology of Wolfgang Köhler at the University of Berlin). Lazarsfeld was invited by Charlotte Bühler to collaborate with her at the University of Vienna, following his presentation in her seminar of the results of questionnaire study by Otto Felix Kanitz, a socialist leader (Capecchi 1978). Kanitz had distributed 2,000 questionnaires at young socialists' meetings, and Lazarsfeld had analyzed the data. "At the age of about twenty-four, I listened to a leader of the Young Socialist Worker's Movement [Kanitz], who read from [a couple of the] questionnaires. . . . He used individual quotations to describe the misery of factory life. Immediately I asked myself why he did not make counts; he was surprised

---

*Which may not be such an unbelievable task as it sounds, given that doctoral dissertations in mathematics are often quite short.

[†]This unit, called an "institute" in German, is translated to English as "department." The Psychological Institute was "a benign but absolute monarchy presided [over] by Karl and Charlotte Bühler" (Smith 1990, p. 89).

at the idea, and turned the questionnaires over to me. I did the statistical analysis, which later formed the basis of one of my first papers" (Lazarsfeld 1982, p. 23). Lazarsfeld had to hand-tabulate the 2,000 questionnaires. "Helping with the tabulation was Mitzi Jahoda, who later became Lazarsfeld's first wife. (He eventually married three times.)

Lazarsfeld's presentation of the survey results at Charlotte Bühler's seminar impressed her and Lazarsfeld subsequently became an instructor in the Bühlers' department, offering courses in statistical methods (Lerg 1977) and, later, in social psychology and applied psychology, and guiding doctoral dissertations (Lazarsfeld 1969a, p. 274). However, his salary from the University of Vienna was so modest that he had to continue teaching at the *Gymnasium*. The Bühlers' Department of Psychology at the University of Vienna conducted studies of such contemporary social problems as the morale of unemployed men, how young people become work-minded, and how retired people attach meaning to their lives. The Bühlers and their students gathered diaries from young people, conducted personal interviews with elders, and observed family life. Lazarsfeld's later academic career was partly shaped by this social research experience.

In the Bühlers' department, "psychoanalysis was officially taboo, which did not prevent several members of the Institute from being psychoanalyzed, secretly as far as their professors were concerned. Although the Bühlers and Freud lived for many years in the same city and were attached to the same university, they never met in person" (Jahoda 1983). Lazarsfeld as a young scholar was close to Alfred Adler, the well-known Viennese psychoanalyst and follower of Freud. But when Lazarsfeld made a presentation about psychological testing at Adler's informal seminar, Adler responded by cutting him out of the seminar (Lazarsfeld, 1961b, p. 59). Young Lazarsfeld was learning about the conflict between qualitative and quantitative methodologies, a dichotomy that he later sought to break down but that continues to this day.

Lazarsfeld (1947, p. xvi) explains in his introduction to Hans Zeisel's book. *Say It with Figures:* "As an assistant to the Bühlers, I was in charge of training students to handle such materials. . . . The categories were more complex than usually treated by quantitative methods. . . . The goal was not to find isolated relationships. The results had to hang together, each as part of a consistent whole. This situation led to a kind of empirical work in which qualitative analysis is guided by conceptual schemes in which each empirical procedure is scrutinized as to its logical implications." This general approach to research that Lazarsfeld was formulating at the University of Vienna would characterize his later scholarly career.

LAZARSFELD'S VIENNA RESEARCH INSTITUTE

In 1925 Lazarsfeld sought relief from his personal financial problems by launching the Research Center for Economic Psychology (Wirtschafts-psychologische Forschungsstelle). This organization was important to the later development of sociology and communication in America. Following his migration to the United States, Lazarsfeld founded the Research Center of the University of Newark in 1936. A year later, in 1937, he directed the Office of Radio Research at Princeton University, which in 1939 moved to Columbia University, eventually to become the Bureau of Applied Social Research.* The bureau continued operation for forty years, until 1977, one year after Lazarsfeld's death (it was followed by the Center for the Social Sciences). Many other U.S. university research institutes were patterned after Lazarsfeld's model, including Wilbur Schramm's Institute of Communications Research at the University of Illinois in 1947 and his Institute for Communication Research at Stanford University in 1955. Today there are dozens of communication research centers at U.S. universities and abroad. All owe an intellectual debt for their organizational form to Paul F. Lazarsfeld.

One of Lazarsfeld's University of Vienna students, Lotte Danziger, was hired to do market research for an American company (Morrison 1976a, p. 138), and this helped Lazarsfeld realize there could be "a perfect conjunction" between market research and academic studies of why individuals act the way they do. Market research provided a source of funds that could finance scholarly research on human behavior (Lazarsfeld 1975a). (Alternative sources of research funding that are available today, such as private foundations and government, did not exist in Vienna in 1925, nor were they widely available in the United States until after 1941.)

*Lazarsfeld stated in a 1976 interview that "the only way I could stay in the United States (as I wanted to) was by emphasizing my skills as a research person and as a research organizer" (Stehr 1982). Another reason why Lazarsfeld started research institutes was his desire for status; in Europe, a professor should be director of his institute (that is, professor and department chair). Lazarsfeld thought that his becoming a professor in Vienna was blocked by his Jewishness; in America such an aspiration was made difficult by his being an immigrant.

The Vienna Research Center for Economic Psychology was the first university-connected research institute of its kind in Europe (Zeisel 1976–1977). It was such a chancy operation that Lazarsfeld only took a leave of absence from his *Gymnasium* teaching position rather than resign. He hoped that he could pay himself a modest salary out of the contracts for market research that his institute conducted for various companies. Lazarsfeld's institute carried out consumer market research studies of beer, butter, chocolate, coffee, milk, vinegar, shoes, perfume, and other products. It also conducted an audience study for Radio Vienna, one of the first media audience investigations in the world (Hyman 1991, p. 183). Obtaining market research contracts was not easy; Austria was undergoing very hard times, inflation was skyrocketing, and unemployment was widespread. In a shrewd move, Lazarsfeld enlisted Karl Bühler as chairman of a twenty-member advisory committee to his research institute, thus ensuring a connection with the Department of Psychology at the University of Vienna. The advisory committee included the leading businessmen, city officials, and professors of Vienna (Morrison 1976a, p. 92).

The employees of the research institute were mostly Lazarsfeld's leftish friends, many of whom he had trained in socialist principle in the Rote Falken. He transformed these young socialist intellectuals, many of them unemployed, and four or five years younger than Lazarsfeld, into social researchers (Morrison 1976b). The institute was a "flexible, adaptive, and non-hierarchical organization" (Jahoda 1983). The employees were highly motivated although not by financial rewards. They were paid very low wages, if at all. In fact, the institute barely survived economically. Lazarsfeld "created a penniless research center in a near-bankrupt society, and found his friends jobs studying unemployment" (Barton 1982). Hans Zeisel, one of Lazarsfeld's colleagues in the Forschungsstelle, described being confronted with an employee who had not been paid for a month: "Ah yes, four weeks isn't such a long time after all. I fear that the only thing we paid regularly was the coffee of our collaborators who worked on their labors in the depths of a Viennese coffee cellar. I'm sure that we never gave them any more than this because at the end of the month those among us that had a second job (for example, I was under instruction as a lawyer in my father's firm) had to put in part of their salary" (Morrison 1976a, p. 99). In a 1973 interview, Marie Jahoda noted that "the *Forschungsstelle* was every day in danger of bankruptcy and Paul was not a good administrator. He was absolutely shocking. You know he paid for an old study with the money from a new study, and of course the books didn't add up. He was a very messy administrator" (Morrison 1976a, p. 97).

One of Lazarsfeld's employees in the Vienna research center, Gertrud Wagner, described the organization: "Well, the *Forschungsstelle* was set up in 1925 in some rooms, and Paul started to get orders from firms and we started the market research. We started with nothing. Just the two rooms in the flat of a friend, and people made the questionnaires and we tried them out—actually quite good they were. Paul got a few co-workers to help—actually, we were friends of his" (Morrison, 1976a, p. 98).

Among the institute's several clients was the Frankfurt Institute for Social Research. Its director, Max Horkheimer, had planned a series of studies that were eventually published in a volume that he edited, *Studien über Autorität und Familie* (1936), that later influenced the important study of prejudice by Adorno and co-workers, *The Authoritarian Personality*. Lazarsfeld's Vienna Institute organized the Austrian part of the data gathering, which was carried out under the general direction of Erich Fromm of the Frankfurt school.*

One of the early studies by Lazarsfeld's institute was an attempt to understand the life and outlook of Viennese beggars. "To our surprise, we discovered that they regarded begging as work, that they had established an informal, powerful organization that regulated hours and places of work as well as fees for the hiring of children of various ages" (Jahoda 1983). The study of beggars may have helped in the design of the well-known Marienthal study of the unemployed, carried out a few years later.

The Vienna institute pioneered in several important methodologies: "The first real progress in question-and-interviewing design was made there. . . . The idea of cross-tabulation, how different methods and eventually integrating these methods in order to get a better view of the problem as a whole" (Zeisel 1986). This emphasis on advancing methodological techniques for social research would continue during Lazarsfeld's career in America.

In November 1936, the Austrian state police raided the Forschungsstelle. Marie Jahoda, its acting director while Lazarsfeld was in the United States, had been active in the underground since February

---

*However, Lazarsfeld did not meet Fromm, Horkheimer, or other members of the Frankfurt school until 1934, during Lazarsfeld's U.S. tour on a Rockefeller Foundation fellowship, when he worked with Fromm (then a refugee from the Hitler regime and living in New York) in analyzing the data that had been gathered a few years previously in Austria (Lazarsfeld 1961b).

TABLE 7.1
Major Events in the Career of Paul F. Lazarsfeld

Date	Event
1925	Founds the Research Center for Economic Psychology (Wirtschaftspsychologische Forschungsstelle), attached loosely to the University of Vienna
1931–1932	Carries out the Marienthal study of unemployment
1933–1935	Travels in the United States on a Rockefeller Foundation fellowship; migrates from Austria in 1935
1935–1936	Employed as a supervisor of student relief work in Newark, New Jersey
1936	Appointed acting director of the Research Center of the University of Newark, which he created
1937	Radio Research Project established at Princeton University, funded by the Rockefeller Foundation, and directed by Hadley Cantril, Frank Stanton (CBS), and Lazarsfeld, who conducts the study at the Research Center of the University of Newark
1939	Office of Radio Research project grant renewed by the Rockefeller Foundation, and moves with Lazarsfeld to New York City, where it is affiliated with Columbia University, and where Lazarsfeld is appointed a part-time lecturer without faculty status
1941	Appointed associate professor in the Department of Sociology at Columbia University; Robert K. Merton is appointed assistant professor
1944	Office of Radio Research at Columbia University is renamed the Bureau of Applied Social Research
1948	Appointed chair of the Department of Sociology, Columbia University
1950	Loses interest in communication research and he steps down as director of the bureau
1962	Named Quetelet Professor of Social Science at Columbia University
1969	Retires from Columbia and begins traveling weekly to the University of Pittsburgh, where he teaches sociology
1976	Dies of cancer

1934, when the Socialist party called a general strike. The police jailed her for ten months and then released her on the condition that she leave Austria immediately. The Forschungsstelle struggled on with Hans Zeisel as director until it was closed by the National Socialists in 1938. Lazarsfeld left his research institute deeply in debt when he migrated to America. The Bühlers, who were financially responsible for this debt, were very concerned until Lazarsfeld found a wealthy Swiss business-man, a Mr. Gold, who covered the debt in exchange for the dubious honor of becoming the director of the now-defunct Forschungsstelle (Morrison 1976a, pp. 82, 96, 100–101).

The entire idea of Lazarsfeld's Vienna institute seems somewhat sur-realistic: "A center organized by Socialists to advance social psychology and then conducting market research to increase businessmen's profits seems incongruous" (Hyman 1991, p. 182). But it must be remembered that other sources of funding for research were not available in Vienna in the early 1930s. Market research paid the bills.

THE MARIENTHAL STUDY OF UNEMPLOYMENT

Eventually Lazarsfeld's Vienna institute got a little money ahead, so that it could carry out a study for strictly scholarly purposes. Lazarsfeld pro-posed to investigate how people spent their leisure time. When he dis-cussed this proposal with Otto Bauer, leader of the Socialist party in Austria, the politician told him that it was silly to study leisure at a time of severe unemployment (Lazarsfeld 1969a, p. 275), so Lazarsfeld switched the research to focus on the unemployed. The Marienthal study was one of the first investigations of unemployment, an important social problem in the worldwide depression of the early 1930s (Lazarsfeld 1976). The project was supported by a small grant from the Rockefeller Foundation plus some minor funding from a central trades council in Vienna. The Rockefeller Foundation support later turned out to be important because it brought Lazarsfeld to the attention of the foundation's officials and led to his travel fellowship to the United States (Morrison 1976a, p. 99).

Lazarsfeld chose Marienthal, a village located sixteen miles southeast of Vienna, as the site for his study. Marie Jahoda directed the project, with help from Hans Zeisel and Lazarsfeld. Marienthal was a good place in which to study unemployment; 77 percent of the 478 families in Marienthal were out of work at the time of the study in 1931–1932 (Hyman 1979, p. 285). In addition to a survey of the households, the

Viennese researchers made personal observations, conducted in-depth case studies, and gathered historical materials. Further, such unobtrusive measures as library book use were obtained in order to determine if individuals' reading declined with unemployment (Freund 1978). It did, to about half of what it had been (Sills 1987, p. 257). Six months were required to carry out the field data gathering and eighteen months to analyze the data and to write up the results (Lazarsfeld 1962a, p. 229). The total cost of the Marienthal study was $1,000, plus lots of old clothes that Lazarsfeld and his colleagues collected in Vienna and then distributed in Marienthal in order to pay for local help with the data gathering. The researchers also arranged for free medical consultation once a week for needy cases in Marienthal.

Marienthal was a company town that had been dominated by Austria's largest spinning and weaving factory for nearly one hundred years. This textile company, Marienthal-Trumauer A.G., went bankrupt in 1929, throwing the town's citizens out of work (Freund 1978). Lazarsfeld and his colleagues executed a neat research design for studying the effects of unemployment. Unlike Robert and Helen Lynd's "Middletown" and W. Lloyd Warner's "Yankee City," which were selected as representative or average towns in America, Marienthal was chosen for study because it exemplified an acute social problem (Freund 1978).

The Marienthal findings showed "a portrait of a community living under great stress, in which the majority were losing a sense of involvement, of perspective, even of time. Resistance to unemployment as a 'state of mind' was slowly breaking down" (Freund 1978). One of the main research questions guiding the study was whether unemployed individuals were reacting by becoming revolutionary or apathetic. The answer was the latter, and it had implications for the Socialist party in Austria, foreshadowing the lack of resistance to Hitler's takeover of the country a few years later (Sills 1987, p. 257).

The desperation of the unemployed of Marienthal grew deeper by degrees. An employed worker was initially eligible for seven and one half months of unemployment relief, followed by a year of emergency help. Both paid from ten to twenty cents (U.S.) a day. Thereafter, no financial assistance was provided. Lazarsfeld and his colleagues found that although only 15 percent of the children of Marienthal had normal health, none of the children of workers who no longer received relief payments were healthy. These families made do with almost nothing: "There must be less food, of a poorer grade. Sugar must be eliminated entirely. The rent, although it amounts to only sixty cents a month, must be carefully hoarded. There can be no light at night. In the winter the family must remain a great part of the day in bed to conserve fuel. The only source of meat is an occasional cat or dog." The utter desperation of the unemployed is illustrated by the Austrian father who said, "Yesterday we ate our dog. I hated to do it because it had been our pet, but this is the third year that I have been without work and we had had no meat in more than a month. I told my wife and children that it was horseflesh and they liked it very much" (McMurray 1933).

The Marienthal residents, especially the men, were literally drowning in time. "Freed from the necessity of being punctual, or even hurrying, time has lost it meaning" (McMurray 1933). They stood for hours alone or in groups, holding long aimless conversations. Many no longer carried watches and could not even judge the time of day. The people realized that there was no work for them in Marienthal or in all of Austria. They gave up hope.

Many people in Marienthal reached what Lazarsfeld called the breaking point: "Some take to drink. Others run away. If the husband and not the wife breaks, she will usually maintain the home. When she breaks, the home collapses. The children are no longer cared for or sent to school; meals become irregular; housekeeping is neglected; every action is marked by a reckless irresponsibility" (McMurray 1933). These individuals classified as broken made up about one-third of the Marienthal families (Lazarsfeld 1932). As more and more families ran out of unemployment and emergency assistance, the Viennese scholars estimated that most of the rest of the Marienthal families would be broken. If these broken people were promised food, shelter, and work by a demagogue, Lazarsfeld believed that they would follow him, no matter how extreme his political program might seem (McMurray 1933). Hitler easily took over Austria a few years later.

The Marienthal project was the best-known study by the Forschungsstelle.* The book reporting the study was published in January 1933 by a German publisher in Leipzig, but "soon the bulk of the first edition fell victim to the [Nazi] book-burning because of its Jewish authors" (Jahoda 1983). The study gave Paul Lazarsfeld an academic reputation, one that would help him obtain a travel fellowship to the United States. How he first came to the attention of important American scholars happened in an unusual way. Lazarsfeld's mentor, Professor

---

*Marienthal was restudied fifty years after the original investigation by Dr. Michael Freund, a Viennese sociologist with a Ph.D. degree from Columbia University.

Charlotte Bühler, put his name on the program of the 1932 International Congress of Psychology, held in Hamburg, Germany. He told her that he wanted to talk about the art of asking *why,* his greatest intellectual passion at that time. Lazarsfeld recalled that she said, "You are an absolute idiot. Who at an international congress even listens to a methodological paper? It would just go down the drain. But you are in the middle of your study of Marienthal. . . . Anything you say about the effects of unemployment in 1931 will be terribly modern" (Lazarsfeld 1975d). His presentation was a big hit. Several American scholars, among them Gordon Allport of Harvard, Goodwin Watson at Columbia's Teachers College, and Edward C. Tolman at Berkeley, remembered his research on unemployment when he later came to the United States.

MIGRATION TO AMERICA

A Rockefeller Foundation official based in Paris, Tracy B. Kitteridge, was searching for young European researchers who wanted research experience in the United States (Capecchi 1978). Paul Lazarsfeld got a Rockefeller fellowship through very unusual circumstances. He was nominated for the fellowship as a kind of "second prize" because he was blocked from university advancement due to his being Jewish. In 1932, Professor Karl Bühler, whose wife, along with his two main assistants, were Jewish, felt that he could not promote Lazarsfeld to *Dozent,* a kind of adjunct assistant professor, even though he felt that Lazarsfeld had earned the promotion (Morrison 1976a, p. 126). Instead, Bühler appointed a gentile, Dr. Egon Brunswik, who taught theory and experimental methods. "By way of consolation, [Karl Bühler] put Lazarsfeld forward for the Rockefeller scholarship. Thus, the anti-semitism which had always hung over Lazarsfeld, blocking both his academic and political careers, was in a way instrumental in obtaining the fellowship" (Morrison 1988). Lazarsfeld (1975a) later remarked: "I would now be dead in a gas chamber, of course, if I could have become a *Dozent* at the University of Vienna."

Kitteridge was thus alerted to Lazarsfeld's academic abilities by Karl Bühler* and interviewed him for a Rockefeller Foundation fellowship in

---

*He also knew of Lazarsfeld from the Rockefeller Foundation's token funding of the Marienthal study in 1931 (Morrison 1976b, p. 99).

summer 1932 (Morrison 1976a, p. 139). He gave Lazarsfeld a copy of the application form and urged him to submit it, but Lazarsfeld did not think he had a chance so did not apply. In December he received a cable from Kitteridge in Paris: "Your application in this office misfiled. Urgently need new copy because decision has to be made before end of the year" (Lazarsfeld 1961a). Lazarsfeld promptly "reapplied" and was duly granted the study fellowship to America.

During his 1933–1935 fellowship tour of the United States, Lazarsfeld met a number of leading American scholars, including Samuel A. Stouffer at the University of Chicago and Robert S. Lynd at Columbia University, plus various market researchers (such as Rensis Likert at the Psychological Corporation in New York). These personal acquaintances were to prove very helpful to Lazarsfeld in later years, especially his relationship with Lynd. Robert Lynd was the son of a midwestern banker, who, after an undergraduate degree at Princeton, enrolled at Union Theological Seminary in New York. His observations of the wretched living conditions of Standard Oil workers in Elk Basin, Wyoming, led him to write critical articles in *Harper's* and other intellectual magazines (Smith 1991, p. 95). As a result, Lynd was funded by the Rockefeller Foundation–supported Institute for Social and Religious Research to conduct a study in Muncie, Indiana ("Middletown"). The Middletown research by Robert and Helen Lynd was a turning point in the history of American sociology in that social class and power became variables that were investigated in hypotheses. "The *Middletown* studies were the first empirical researches on a large scale which employed the new functional approach" (Lipset and Smelser 1961). The Middletown study originally focused on the role of the church in Muncie, Indiana, but the Lynds decided that they could understand the church only by analyzing the larger system of which the religious institution was a part (Lynd and Lynd 1929, p. 6). The husband and wife team first went to Muncie in 1924 and returned for a restudy in 1935, which they reported in their second book, *Middletown in Transition* (Lynd and Lynd 1937).*

The Middletown study did a great deal for the career of Robert Lynd. It was a classic sociological study, perhaps one of the most important empirical investigations in sociology since the Thomas and Znaniecki

---

*Muncie was restudied in 1977–1979 by Theodore Caplow of the University of Virginia.

(1927) study of the Polish peasant, the Chicago school classic carried out a decade earlier. Their first Middletown book achieved widespread acclaim for the Lynds. It went through six printings in 1929 alone, its first year of publication. Robert Lynd was offered a full professorship and a Ph.D. degree in sociology at Columbia University on the strength of *Middletown*.* Robert MacIver, then chair of the sociology department, who made the offer in 1931, later regretted this decision. Lynd was an empirical scholar who wanted sociology to deal with the applied problems of society; in contrast, MacIver was theoretical and felt that sociology should be the study of social organization (Lipset 1955, p. 293). The resulting division in the Columbia sociology department continued until Lazarsfeld and Merton came together in 1941.

Lazarsfeld (1962b, pp. 319–320) described his first meeting with Robert Lynd at Columbia University: "Here I come to the great Lynd and it is snowing, and the man is endlessly worried that I have no rubbers, and he begins to run from one office to another [to see] whether he can find a pair of rubbers so I don't get wet. Well, first, I don't care whether I get wet or not. And secondly, the idea that a complete stranger . . . " During Lazarsfeld's visit with Lynd at Columbia in 1933, he learned that Lynd had completed a survey of the effects of the depression on upper-middle-class families in Montclair, New Jersey, but he was stumped by data analysis problems. Lazarsfeld offered his services for free, but Lynd declined, so as not to exploit Lazarsfeld (Lazarsfeld 1961a, p. 20). Nevertheless, Lazarsfeld joined Lynd's doctoral seminar at Columbia, in which the students were writing papers out of the Montclair project. (The project's research results were never published.) Lazarsfeld later in life spoke about his relationship with Lynd:

> During the first few years of my life in this country, pretty much everything that I had I owed in some way to Lynd. . . . The first speeches I gave, which made me somewhat more known; my first job in Newark; and, of course, my appointment to Columbia. There's hardly anything I don't owe to him. . . . As long as I was just an underdog, just a poor immigrant, he had, so to say, unequivocal approval. Then, when I began to learn things on my own. . . . The existence of this Bureau even is due

---

*Minus the sections of their book written by Helen Lynd (Fox 1983).

to Lynd. The University would never really have accepted it if it hadn't been for Lynd (Lazarsfeld 1962b, p. 323).

While Lazarsfeld was in the United States on the Rockefeller Foundation fellowship between 1933 and 1935, his wife, Marie Jahoda, directed the Research Center for Economic Psychology. In 1936, the research center was raided by the police for its political underground activities, and two years later it was closed down. Jahoda was arrested and jailed for her socialist activities. Lazarsfeld's parents were also arrested. In February 1934, midway through Lazarsfeld's first fellowship year, a right-wing politician, Dollfuss, ousted the mayor of "Red Vienna," a Social Democrat. The Dollfuss government, propped up by Mussolini-type fascism, took over Austria. As a result of these political changes, Lazarsfeld lost his teaching position in the *Gymnasium* in Vienna, from which he had been on leave. He had no job in Austria to which he could return.

In the light of these ominous events in Vienna, Lazarsfeld decided to migrate to the United States in 1935. The Rockefeller Foundation extended his fellowship for a second year, and he desperately searched for a job offer from an American university (Pasanella 1990, p. 12). A position at the University of Pittsburgh's Research Bureau of Retail Training looked promising, but it fell through at the last minute.* By mid-1935, Lazarsfeld's Rockefeller Foundation fellowship completed, he was back in Vienna. Robert Lynd, however, helped in the job search, and wrote to Lazarsfeld in mid-1935: "Now here's something *not* to be Viennese about, but to write at once: In Newark on Friday afternoon, I unearthed a job that's crazy for you: The social agencies want someone to locate and appraise all available social data on Newark." Lazarsfeld applied, got the job, and booked passage to New York with the last $150 left from his Rockefeller Foundation fellowship (Neurath 1983, p. 373). When he arrived in Newark, he became director of a National Youth Administration research project on unemployment. Lazarsfeld rented a little room on West 113th Street west of Broadway, in Manhattan, and commuted to Newark.

---

*Fortunately, however, Lazarsfeld had the Pittsburgh job offer in hand in Vienna when he applied for an American visa. The day after the visa was granted by the U.S. embassy, Lazarsfeld received a cable from David Craig, director of the University of Pittsburgh Bureau, informing Lazarsfeld that Craig was moving to Washington, D.C., and that the position at Pittsburgh had thus evaporated (Morrison 1976a, p. 151).

THE RADIO RESEARCH PROJECT*

In a period of only a few years, Paul Lazarsfeld moved from directing his penniless research institute in Vienna to becoming director of the Bureau of Applied Social Research at Columbia University, soon to become "the most influential communication research organization in the world!" (Schramm 1981).

Lazarsfeld's Newark Research Center

Lazarsfeld's job in Newark was to oversee the research work of a small staff of students on relief who were tabulating data from some 10,000 questionnaires completed by unemployed young people (Sills 1987, p. 258). Within a year, Lazarsfeld got himself appointed as acting director of the Research Center at the University of Newark, an institute that he created out of thin air. It was not much of a job. The research staff consisted of one experienced scholar, Lazarsfeld, and his small cadre of student relief workers.[†] His contract stipulated that half of his $4,800 annual salary had to be earned from research contracts (Lazarsfeld 1969a, p. 288). The other half came from teaching courses at the University of Newark. In other words, the university president, Frank Kingdon, was not betting very heavily on the success of Lazarsfeld's research center.[‡] Symbolically, the Newark Research Center was housed in an old brewery.

An important step toward Lazarsfeld's financial survival occurred the following year through his affiliation with the Office of Radio Research,

---

*The important role of the Radio Research Project in shaping the directions of contemporary mass communication research is traced by Rogers (1992).

[†]In order to give the impression that the Newark center was a more substantial operation, Lazarsfeld published some of his work under another name, thus creating a nonexistent colleague, "Elias Smith." Lazarsfeld's pseudonym is "the perfect illustration of his wild inventiveness and its comic-ironic implications," says Hyman (1991, p. 186). Lazarsfeld originally created his alter-ego name as a means to foster the image that his Newark research center was more than just a one-man show, and also so that he would not seem to be such an overproducer of journal articles. Later, during the McCarthy period, Lazarsfeld was suspected by federal government authorities for having masqueraded as Elias Smith in the 1930s.

[‡]Nevertheless, Lazarsfeld's modest salary was enough to guarantee French visas for his father, mother, sister, brother-in-law, and nephew so that they could escape from Germany (Lazarsfeld 1975a).

which was established by a grant from the Rockefeller Foundation in September 1937 to the School of Public and International Affairs at Princeton University (Lazarsfeld, Cantril, and Stanton 1939). The full name of the Radio Research Project was The Essential Value of Radio to All Types of Listeners.

Background of the Radio Research Project

Lazarsfeld became involved in mass communication research in an accidental way; he was the right man, in the right place, at the right time. The radio industry had been developing for about fifteen years by the time Lazarsfeld began studying this new form of mass communication in the mid-1930s. Historians of radio date the beginning of the industry to KDKA in Pittsburgh, the first commercial radio station, founded by the Westinghouse Corporation in 1920 to sell the radio receiving sets it manufactured. A couple of years later, in 1922, AT&T launched WEAF in New York, the first radio station to sell advertising. There was a strong commercial interest in radio from the very beginning of the new industry.

The rate of adoption for radio among U.S. households was rapid (although two decades later, black-and-white television was adopted even more rapidly). By 1925, as shown in Figure 7.2, 10 percent of all U.S. households owned a radio; by 1930, radio ownership reached 46 per-

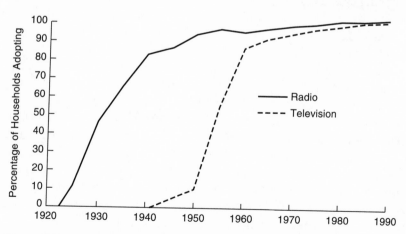

Figure 7.2. Adoption of radio and television by U.S. households.
Source: U.S. Census Bureau reports.

cent; and by 1940, 82 percent. At that time, the average radio was in use four and a half hours per day. In 1937, when the Radio Research Project began, a greater proportion of U.S. households had radios than had telephones, automobiles, plumbing, electricity, or newspapers.

In the late 1930s, the rising specter of Hitler's fascist Germany led to interest on the part of the federal government in propaganda and public opinion formation and thus in communication research. The rapid diffusion of the radio and the ways in which this new medium was used by Hitler's minister of propaganda, Josef Goebbels, focused particular interest on electronic means of communication. In the United States, the rise of advertising agencies led to the commoditization of culture and to the need for market research as a means of designing and marketing products to match consumers' needs. Finally, as part of President Franklin D. Roosevelt's New Deal program, designed to bring the nation out of its worst economic depression, increasing government regulation threatened the absolute freedom of the radio broadcasting industry. Paul F. Lazarsfeld's career intersected in various ways with each of these important trends in the mass communication industry (Robinson 1988). Migrating from middle Europe to the New York City area put Lazarsfeld at the geographical intersection of these important events that triggered the emergence of mass communication research.

In the several decades following the beginning of radio broadcasting in the United States, radio station officials forged a partnership with the emerging specialty of market research in order to obtain empirical data about radio's effects on its audiences. Such data were needed in order to persuade advertisers to buy radio advertising (Hurwitz 1988). The growth of commercial radio broadcasting paralleled the increasing importance of market research. The audiences for newspapers and magazines were measured by circulation figures, so that advertisers knew how many potential people a print ad could reach. But radio broadcasts reached an invisible audience of unknown size (Czitrom 1982, p. 126). Market research techniques were thus created to measure the size of the radio audience for various broadcasts and the demographic characteristics of listeners. Advertisers understandably wanted to know who listened to their ads and whether the advertisements led people to purchase the advertised products. A. C. Nielsen and other market researchers gathered audience ratings data that determined advertising rates and influenced radio program content.

The Radio Research Project was not the first empirical study of radio and its audience impacts in the United States, but previous investigations had been small and scattered and applied to the interests of the broadcasters (Hurwitz 1988). Lazarsfeld's Radio Research Project, and especially the three annual reviews of radio research coedited by Lazarsfeld and Frank Stanton of CBS, gave radio research a coherence and a visibility that it had not previously possessed (Lazarsfeld and Stanton 1942, 1944).

Designing the Radio Research Project

The roots of the Radio Research Project trace to John D. Rockefeller, Jr., son of the robber baron of the oil industry, who was responsible for the Rockefeller family's philanthropy. "In 1929, he had an idea that something might be done generally to improve the quality of radio programs."* When a member of the Rockefeller family expressed even mild interest in a topic, Rockefeller Foundation officials scurried to obtain relevant information, to write memoranda about alternative scenarios, and to consider various research approaches. The Radio Research Project grew out of this review and planning exercise at the Rockefeller Foundation.

John Marshall (1977), a Rockefeller Foundation official, explained how the Radio Research Project began: "The Trustees appointed a committee of review in 1933 . . . and suggested that one of the fields in which the Foundation might move was radio. I began to read and talk with people in the networks. The historic moment was when I read [Hadley] Cantril's [and Gordon Allport's] *The Psychology of Radio* [1935], which said that research on listeners was needed." Marshall (1903–1980) had long had an interest in radio, which began as a boy when he had owned a radio transmitter. He grew up in a middle-class Boston family and went on to study medieval history at Harvard University but discontinued his doctoral work there in order to go to work for the Rockefeller Foundation in 1933. He spent the rest of his career (thirty-seven years) with the foundation, mainly in the Humanities Division (which included the social sciences). John Marshall played a very important but low profile role in the rise of mass communication research. He created the expression *mass communication* in 1939 and funded many of the early investigations.

In 1936, Marshall believed that radio could be much more than just

---

*Quoted from a letter dated July 27, 1931, by A. W. Armour, a Rockefeller Foundation official, to Lawrence K. Frank, an official of the Laura Spelman Rockefeller Memorial. (Rockefeller Archive Center, Collection GEB, Series 918, Box 358, Folder 3696).

the mass/commercial/entertainment medium that it then was. He wanted to demonstrate to the radio networks that an audience existed for higher cultural fare (Morrison 1976a, p. 198), a view he shared with Professor Hadley Cantril at Princeton.* Marshall felt an intellectual distaste for the radio programs produced by the broadcasting networks and saw the Radio Research Project as part of a broader plan for cultural improvement of the public: "Basically, I felt that our interest in the Foundation in radio research was for the possibilities we believe it had of demonstrating that we didn't have to have the kind of radio programs we had. That is, there was an educational cultural value, and that by demonstrating this through research to the broadcasting companies, leverage could be asserted to adopt a more cultural and educationally valuable type of program" (Morrison 1976a). His hope proved to be naive; the broadcasting networks were fixed on achieving higher audience ratings through radio programming that appealed to the mass market.

Research on radio was needed, but the radio networks did not want to fund it themselves. A committee of the radio broadcasting industry had reviewed the Rockefeller Foundation research proposal and refused to fund it out of fear that the results might harm their relationships with advertising agencies and their advertising sponsors (Morrison 1976a, p. 200).† Nevertheless, they did not object to the Rockefeller Foundation–funded research, as long as Frank Stanton of CBS was involved. Stanton later said that his role in the

> Radio Research Project was 50/50 with Cantril until we brought PFL [Lazarsfeld] into the picture. Along with Had [Cantril], I wrote the proposal to the RF [Rockefeller Foundation], even typed it for Had's signature, since the grant had to be made to a non-profit organization. Originally . . . we planned to run the project jointly. Then Had went to Princeton [from Columbia University] and my work at CBS expanded, so that by the time RF made the grant, we were both so deeply involved in our own problems that neither could take on the full-time job of running the project. With RF's full knowledge and support, we proposed the or-

---

*Cantril enjoyed a close relationship with Rockefeller Foundation officials and with members of the Rockefeller family. Cantril and Nelson Rockefeller, a grandson of John D. Rockefeller, Sr., had been undergraduate roommates at Dartmouth.

†The networks' general lack of interest in research at this time is illustrated by an experience of Frank Stanton, director of research at CBS, in 1936. The conventional wisdom in the radio industry was that radio listening by audience members was mainly determined by radio

ganization of the project at Princeton with the two of us as associate directors and a director to be appointed. (Stanton 1991).

Marshall steered the proposal through the Rockefeller Foundation board of trustees for their approval. The project was funded for $67,000 for two years, with the provision that it could be extended.* Stanton had just been given additional responsibilities at CBS and declined the opportunity to direct the project. Cantril had helped found the journal *Public Opinion Quarterly* at Princeton and was also establishing the Office of Public Opinion Research at Princeton in order to become involved with George Gallup in polling research. Both men served as associate directors of the Radio Research Project but began searching for a full-time director. Robert Lynd recommended Paul Lazarsfeld, who was then, in August 1937, vacationing in Austria. Cantril cabled him an offer of an annual salary of $7,000 for two years and a research position on the Radio Research Project for Herta Herzog, Lazarsfeld's second wife (Hyman 1991, p. 190). After some difficult negotiations, Lazarsfeld convinced Cantril to allow him to work on the radio project at his Newark Research Center, with the funding channeled through the Office of Radio Research at Princeton. Lazarsfeld wrote to Lynd: "The entire arrangement is so favorable that somehow I cannot yet believe that it is true" (Hyman 1991, p. 191). The budget for the Radio Research Project was more than three times that of the entire Newark Research Center.

The seven-page proposal to the Rockefeller Foundation, "The Essential Value of Radio to All Type of Listeners," provided little detail about

---

signal strength, independent of the radio program content. However, Stanton found in a pilot survey that most listeners turned to the third or fourth radio station in order of reception quality. Stanton urged CBS to study the basis of radio listeners' likings. His proposed study was turned down by CBS officials on the basis that it had no commercial value (Morrison 1976a, p. 193). Later, however, Stanton began to apply research to other practical problems at CBS: "When I first came into the [radio] industry, daytime serials were interspersed with music and poetry and things of that kind, and you'd get high [ratings] points on the serials and low points on the poetry. I came up to management one day and said, 'Why don't we put these things back to back?'" (Bartos 1977). When CBS put blocks of serials together and grouped the evening news into another time block, they got higher ratings overall. The practice of grouping similar programs into formats continues to this day.

*Some months later, the General Education Board (a parallel unit to the Rockefeller Foundation) funded a $247,000 study of school radio broadcasting from 1937 to 1941 by W. W. Charters, Director of the Bureau of Educational Research, Ohio State University. A similar project was funded by the General Education Board at the University of Wisconsin. John Marshall was an official of the General Education Board, as well as the Rockefeller Foundation, and was involved with the school radio broadcasting projects. Marshall also funded research on film and books through the Rockefeller Foundation at about this time.

the exact research to be undertaken. In fact, the first two years of the project's duration called mainly for developing the research methodologies to be utilized in radio research. Perhaps this lack of specificity was appropriate, given the absence of much previous research on radio and the relative newness of the medium in American society. The loose structure gave free rein to Lazarsfeld to take it in directions that he would choose, an advantage that he immediately recognized. In an August 8, 1937, letter to Hadley Cantril (Morrison 1976a, p. 166), when Lazarsfeld was negotiating the offer to direct the Radio Research Project, he stated, "Radio is a topic around which actually any kind of research method can be tried out and can be applied satisfactorily." In fact, "Lazarsfeld's main priorities were methodological, and . . . he picked out substantive fields of study that were available and fundable to try out new methods" (Barton 1991). Lazarsfeld stated, "Look, you have to understand that I had no interest whatsoever in mass communication. I mean, everything in a way is interesting to a methodologist" (Morrison 1968). Clearly, Lazarsfeld was a rather diffident pioneer in studying the effects of mass media communication. He saw himself as a methodologist, and communication was just a convenient bathtub in which to float his research boats.

The Radio Research Project that Stanton and Cantril had proposed (the so-called Old Testament) was quite different from the actual project carried out by Lazarsfeld, which he dubbed the "New Testament." The Stanton-Cantril proposal called mainly for laboratory experiments, similar to those reported in the Cantril and Allport's The Psychology of Radio (1935). Lazarsfeld cut a much wider swath. He utilized survey research, content analyses of radio programs, ratings, and other types of secondary data. Comparisons of radio and print media audiences took Lazarsfeld and the Radio Research Project toward a science of mass communication (Czitrom 1982, p. 129). He drove the Radio Project widely over the landscape of communication study research, inventing and improvising as he went.

Why was the project funded at Princeton, given that its director was at the University of Newark? Lazarsfeld (1961a, p. 11) says this awkward arrangement arose because the Rockefeller Foundation officials thought that the University of Newark was "not distinguished." When the University of Newark went under in 1936 and the project moved with Lazarsfeld to offices in Union Square in New York City, it was still officially called the Princeton Radio Research Project. An alternative would have been for Lazarsfeld to be appointed as a faculty member at

Princeton, but Lazarsfeld, an immigrant Viennese Jew, was not accept-able there (Morrison 1976a, p. 225).

Frank Stanton

Lazarsfeld became director of the Radio Research Project by default be-cause Cantril was otherwise occupied with his teaching and other schol-arly duties and Frank Stanton was directing audience research for the CBS radio network. These two associate directors of the Radio Research Project nevertheless made important contributions to its success. Can-tril had a close relationship with George Gallup and helped Lazarsfeld obtain poll data about radio audiences and their reactions to different types of radio programs. A secondary reanalysis of these poll data by Lazarsfeld and his project staff helped them accomplish much more re-search than even the generous Rockefeller Foundation funding would have allowed. Cantril suggested that the project conduct a small num-ber of open-ended, in-depth personal interviews with individuals espe-cially affected by a radio program, such as fans of radio soap operas, in order to supplement the more quantitative surveys or ratings data from a large sample. This combination of qualitative and quantitative data about radio's effects became a stock-in-trade of the Radio Research Project.

"In addition to his intellectual abilities, Cantril was especially gifted in getting the rich and powerful to sponsor research" (Hyman 1991, p. 193). An illustration of the synergy made possible by the Lazarsfeld-Stanton-Cantril leadership of the radio project is exemplified by their study of Orson Welles's 1938 broadcast, "The War of the Worlds" (Can-tril with Gaudet and Herzog 1940), the Halloween Eve broadcast that panicked an estimated 1 million of the 6 million Americans who had tuned in. The Radio Research Project seized on this unique event to find out why the program had such dramatic effects in creating mass hyste-ria. Lazarsfeld telephoned Stanton the morning after the broadcast and asked for funding out of Stanton's CBS research budget to launch a "fire-house research project" (Hyman 1991, p. 193). Cantril and Lazarsfeld convinced the Rockefeller's General Education Board to contribute an extra $3,000 to the Radio Research Project for data gathering from a sample of radio listeners.* Herta Herzog conducted in-depth interviews

---

*The grant documents for this funding, dated November 29, 1938, are found in the Rockefeller Archive Center, Collection GEB, Box 361, Folder 3723.

with a small sample of panicked listeners, Stanton designed two quantitative surveys of the broadcast's effects, and George Gallup also carried out a survey. All four data sets were then analyzed by Cantril with Gaudet and Herzog, and reported in their book, *The Invasion from Mars* (1940), a classic in communication research.

Frank Stanton also made important contributions to the Radio Research Project. He guaranteed the collaboration of the powerful radio industry, essential to the project's effective operation; provided funding for the research on the effects of the "Invasion from Mars" broadcast, plus $5,000 for Merton's study of the 1943 Kate Smith radio marathon to sell U.S. war bonds; brought a variety of important research methodologies to the project's studies of radio's effects, not the least of which was the Lazarsfeld-Stanton Program-Analyzer; and coedited with Lazarsfeld the series of three books summarizing the fundings of the Radio Research Project and other related research on media effects (Lazarsfeld and Stanton, 1942, 1944, 1949).

Stanton had joined the two-person research department of the CBS radio network in New York after completing his Ph.D. dissertation, "A Critique of Present Methods and a New Plan for Studying Radio Listening Behavior," at Ohio State University in 1935. At that time, CBS was trying to catch up with NBC, the dominant radio broadcasting network. The CBS network had fewer radio station affiliates and a smaller national audience than did NBC. It was particularly interested in market research as a tool to persuade advertisers to buy ads on CBS. In fact, the CBS research division was part of the network's sales and promotion department. A first task for Stanton, the new Ph.D. in industrial psychology from Ohio State, upon his arrival in Manhattan, was to carry out research on audience exposure to CBS radio. Radio research began with the question of how many people were in the audience and who they were.

Stanton was uniquely prepared to study the audience behavior of radio listeners. He was born in 1908 in Muskegon, Michigan, and grew up in Dayton, Ohio. His father was a high school manual arts teacher and his mother was a potter, so Stanton learned how to work with tools and how to create gadgets. This ability came in handy in his doctoral studies in industrial psychology at Ohio State. With the help of a small grant of $100 from the CBS Radio Network, Stanton made a small device to record the station that a radio set was tuned to at given time intervals. Promptly after completing his degree, he was hired by CBS in New York. Stanton was twenty-seven years old and the first Ph.D. in the infant radio industry. He was to enjoy a long and important career in broadcasting.

Shortly after joining CBS, Stanton surveyed a sample of households around Scranton, Pennsylvania. He noted the station to which each radio set was tuned and whether it was on or off at the time, and he questioned household members about their radio listening preferences. Stanton presented the results of his audience listening survey at a hearing of the Federal Communications Commission (FCC) in Washington, D.C. (Smith 1990). By showing that its local station had a larger audience than had been assumed, the consequences were beneficial for CBS in its David-and-Goliath struggle with NBC, and this impressed William Paley, president of CBS, with the value of research. Stanton's stock in the corporation began to rise. He was hard-working, he had original and creative ideas, and he was competent; he also had a wonderful way in handling people and was a hard-working perfectionist. He even designed the official CBS letterhead stationery, back in the 1940s, with a small, almost invisible dot on the upper-left-hand margin, where CBS secretaries were instructed to start typing the letter's salutation (Metz 1975). A 1992 letter that I received from Frank Stanton was typed on CBS letterhead; the tiny dot is still there.* His "enduring concern with style in every aspect of the domain that he inhabited" was legendary (Merton 1992). Stanton's attention to detail at CBS was famed. Such attention takes time, lots of time; Stanton worked on nights and weekends, Christmas Day, and the Fourth of July, and other holidays.

Whenever a question arose at CBS—from advertising salespeople, from a CBS network affiliate station, or from government regulators at the FCC—and Stanton did not have the answer at hand, he would say, "Let's study it!" (Smith 1990, p. 152). Three years after his arrival at CBS, in 1938, Stanton was named director of research at the radio network, with a staff of 100. Four years later, in 1942, he became a vice-president, responsible for research, advertising, public relations, sales promotion, and such other duties as managing the CBS network's owned-and-operated radio stations. In 1946, eleven years after he had joined CBS, he was named president by William Paley, the founder and chairman of CBS. Frank Stanton continued as president until 1971, a twenty-five-year period during which CBS rose to become the number

*Stanton also created the original CBS logo of the "seeing eye," a well-known example of art design, and designed the elegantly simple stationery for the Center for Advanced Study in the Behavioral Sciences in 1955, when he was chair of the center's board of trustees. These Stanton-designed writing materials are also still in use today.

one broadcasting network, dominating television ratings in the United States. The greatest credit to Stanton's human relations skills is that he could continue as president of CBS for so many years under the tyrannical William Paley (Smith 1990).

Lazarsfeld the Toolmaker

Lazarsfeld was generally more interested in the methods of research than in the substantive content that was being studied, an orientation he shared with Samuel A. Stouffer, the sociologist who directed the American Soldier studies of the behavior of military personnel during World War II. In fact, it was Stouffer in 1935–1936 who introduced Lazarsfeld to fourfold contingency tables "by drawing one on a luncheon table-cloth one day in Newark" (Sills 1987, pp. 268–269). Stouffer showed Lazarsfeld how to classify individuals by education and then by occupational status. Lazarsfeld was to make a great deal of use of 2×2 tables, as well as three-variable (that is, $2 \times 2 \times 2$) contingency tables in order to tease out the relationships among the variables of study. "I was absolutely fascinated by this device [the three-variable table]. I'd never heard of it before. Immediately, I began to think what the implications of such could be" (Lazarsfeld January 8, 1962a).

This interest in toolmaking fit with Lazarsfeld's role in establishing and directing research institutes like the Office of Radio Research and, later, the Bureau of Applied Social Research at Columbia University. In order to maintain financial solvency for his scholarly research purposes, Lazarsfeld conducted market research on toothpaste, shampoo, and other consumer products. These studies had little substantive interest to scholars, but they could provide opportunities to advance research methodology. In order to achieve academic credibility, Lazarsfeld the toolmaker needed a career partner who was mainly a theorist. He found this counterpart in Robert K. Merton, and the two of them became the stars of American sociology in the 1950s, making Columbia University the premier department of sociology in the country. Engaging in such applied work as market research was strictly déclassé among American sociologists. Lazarsfeld's generally high academic prestige is thus all the more amazing, given the flagrant way in which he flouted the norms of academic sociology.

The Radio Research Project came along at the right time, for a number of reasons. Survey research methods were becoming more sophisticated in the 1930s with advances in sampling and in attitude measurement. Lazarsfeld utilized these methods and advanced them. He converted the poll into a scientific tool by combining the survey interview with multivariate data analysis methods in order to advance understanding of how individuals make decisions.

Two of Lazarsfeld's important methodological contributions were the Lazarsfeld-Stanton Program-Analyzer and focus group interviewing. Both were collaborative creations, and both grew out of the Radio Research Project.

Little Annie: The Lazarsfeld-Stanton Program-Analyzer

One by-product of the Radio Research Project was the development of a data-gathering apparatus called the *Lazarsfeld*-Stanton Program-Analyzer at the Radio Research Project (and the *Stanton*-Lazarsfeld Program-Analyzer at CBS). Nicknamed "Little Annie," the device allowed researchers to relate radio program or advertising content to its emotional effects on audience individuals. Instant likes and dislikes of experimental audiences were measured and recorded. As an individual listened to a radio broadcast, he or she was asked to indicate "likes" by pushing a green button and "dislikes" by pushing a red button. These responses were recorded by a stylus on a roll of continuously moving paper. After a group of respondents finished reacting to a program, they were asked to fill out a questionnaire about it. Then the radio broadcast was replayed to them by an investigator, who led them in a focus group discussion of the reasons for their likes and dislikes. Up to ten audience members' responses could be recorded simultaneously by the Program-Analyzer. It was a useful device for conducting formative evaluation of radio broadcasts, so that the effectiveness of the radio message could be improved by revising it. More generally, the Program-Analyzer could be used to learn more about radio audience behavior, especially the effects of radio broadcasts.

The Program-Analyzer grew out of both Lazarsfeld's and Stanton's previous devices for measuring communication effects. In Vienna, Lazarsfeld had investigated the emotional effects of music with a non-electronic type of program-analyzer. He set a metronome ticking while a half-dozen or so respondents listened to a piece of music. They were told to flip one page of a desktop calendar pad with each tick, after writing on the page whether they liked or disliked the music at that instant. When the musical piece was ended, Lazarsfeld interviewed the group of respondents about why they liked or disliked the music at each interval. The advantage of Lazarsfeld's device was that he could obtain more finely-grained data than if he had interviewed the same respondents weeks or months after hearing a certain piece of music, as would be the case in the usual audience survey of music listeners. The immediate postlistening interviews could measure listeners' reasons for their linking or disliking while they could still remember them (Levy 1982). The main disadvantage of the calendar-flipping device was that the respondents' music-listening experience was disturbed by having to make the written entries.

One Saturday afternoon in 1937, in the laboratory of the Princeton University Psychology Department, Lazarsfeld and Stanton were discussing how best to measure the effects of radio on its listeners. Lazarsfeld described the device he had used in his Vienna music study, and Stanton told Lazarsfeld about his little device, which recorded a radio listener's station choice on smoked paper. While he was teaching at Ohio State University, Stanton had used a cymograph (a device that records data on a time line) to measure his psychology students' understanding of films that Stanton had made of various laboratory experiments (Stanton 1981). Out of their shared experiences with such devices, Lazarsfeld and Stanton got the idea for their Program-Analyzer, and Stanton arranged to have it built by a laboratory shop technician. The Program-Analyzer was a wooden box, two feet long, one foot wide, and one foot high, that contained a constant-speed electric meter driving a six-inch wide roll of white recording paper, which moved at the rate of one-fifth of an inch per second (Levy 1982). Mounted just above the roll of paper were ten ink pens, each connected to an electromagnet attached to a six-foot-long electrical cord with an off-on switch at the other end. The Program-Analyzer was placed on a table, with up to ten respondents sitting around the table, each with an off-on switch, marked green for "like" and red for "dislike." When the dislike (on) switch was pressed, it lifted the corresponding pen slightly off the recording paper. It thus fixed a point in time when a respondent changed his or her reaction to the radio message. The group interview that followed allowed the investigator to probe the reasons for such changes. The data from all ten respondents could be accumulated into a composite distribution as a basis for the group interview.

Lazarsfeld's investigators claimed that the Program-Analyzer "focuses attention on the listener as the final judge of radio productions" in a kind "of jury trial with the listeners as jurors" (Hollonquist and Suchman 1944, pp. 265, 271). It allowed the broadcaster to determine "audience reactions to a particularly crucial statement, the effectiveness of a complex production technique, the recognition of a subtle pun, the qualities of the announcer, and listener acceptance of the authenticity of the material presented on the program. If the introduction is too long, if the sound effects do not contribute to listener orientation and enjoyment, if a punchline is delivered too fast, if the program structure is generally weak . . . " (Hollonquist and Suchman 1944, p. 272). In other words, the Program- Analyzer provided feedback to radio broadcasters about specific audience effects.

The Program-Analyzer had broad use. Lazarsfeld and Merton and their staff used it in the Radio Research Project. "Little Annie" went to war as a tool to measure U.S. soldiers' likes and dislikes of training and morale films. At CBS in New York, Stanton set up a laboratory in a special room in which the device was placed in a soundproof control booth (Wiebe 1981). Later, CBS constructed "Big Annie," to accommodate more than fifty respondents. Several Madison Avenue advertising agencies began using the Program-Analyzer, first with radio and film and later with television. The Program-Analyzer "had a considerable vogue among the entrepreneurs of Hollywood, Broadway, and Madison Avenue" (Abrams 1977). Eventually it fell out of use, although in the late 1970s the Children's Television Workshop created a microcomputer version of the Program-Analyzer to pretest segments of "3-2-1 Contact" with eight- to twelve-year-olds (Mielke and Chen 1983, pp. 31–55).

The Lazarsfeld-Stanton Program-Analyzer is still used today to evaluate pilots for new television programs—for example, CBS told Norman Lear, creator of "All in the Family," on the basis of its Program-Analyzer results from testing a pilot, to recast the roles of the daughter and the son-in-law (Mayer 1972, p. 94)—to test audience reactions to ads, and to understand better what audiences like and dislike about established shows. Essentially, the Lazarsfeld-Stanton Program-Analyzer was a media effects measurement machine.

Focus Group Interviewing

The November 23, 1941, coming together of Merton and Lazarsfeld in the Radio Research Project was also important because that is the night that focus group interviewing was created.* The Program-Analyzer and focused interviewing were originally linked, in that the time-interval likes-dislikes data were of little value unless followed by interviewing about the "why" of such individual likes and dislikes.

A focused interview consists of gathering data from respondents in a particular situation (such as hearing a radio program, observing a play, etc.) about their definition of the situation. It thus focuses on a particular experience of the respondent. The questions are usually asked in an open-ended way so as to elicit highly spontaneous data about the media message of study. The interview assumes that the investigator does not know enough in advance about the respondent's definition of the situation to be able to formulate all of the exact questions to be asked. It often follows a general list of topics or issues but without specifying in advance the exact questions to be asked. The resulting data are usually mainly qualitative in nature and can be helpful in the later design of a structured data-gathering device like a questionnaire (Merton, Fiske, and Kendall 1956, p. 3).

The focus group interview has an added dynamic in that each group member's responses often tend to stimulate statements made by other individuals in the group. It is the group interaction that produces the data, with the direction of the discussion spontaneous rather than predetermined by the investigator. One of the payoffs of focus group interviewing is the unanticipated responses that are elicited. From six to a dozen individuals are customarily included in a focus group, often seated in a circle, usually around a table, with the interviewer (or moderator). The focus group discussion may be observed by a researcher or research sponsors through one-way mirrors, and it may be videotaped. Today focus groups are one of the main tools of commercial market research. They play a key role in political campaigns and are also used by academic scholars of communication.† An example is Liebes and Katz's (1990) investigation of the meaning of the American television show "Dallas" to viewers in various cultures. These scholars led focus group interviews in people's homes immediately following their viewing an episode of "Dallas."

*Merton (1987) originally used the words *focussed group interview* and *focussed interview*. Editors insisted that *focussed* become *focused*. Then, through everyday usage by market researchers, *focused group interview* became *focus group*, the contemporary usage I use here.

†Included in the considerable literature about how to conduct focus groups are Calder (1977), Fern (1982), Morgan and Spanish (1984), and Morgan (1988). Morgan (1988, pp. 81–83) cites twenty-four how-to-do-it publications about focus groups.

The focused interview centers on an individual's perceptions of a media message, which are evoked by intensive, free-form interviewing in order to aid retrospection. The interview can center on hypotheses that are set up beforehand and then used as the focus of the interview, but focus groups are usually utilized to generate hypotheses, which are then tested with more quantitative data obtained by a survey or an experiment. In the case of the media effects studies conducted at Lazarsfeld's Office of Radio Research, the hypotheses generated by focus group interviews were that a particular message (such as a radio program or an advertising spot) would have certain effects, such as changing attitudes toward buying U.S. war bonds or changing the attitudes of highly educated people more than those with less education. Focus groups generated certain of the hypotheses about persuasion that were then tested by Carl Hovland in his World War II experiments with military personnel on the effects of training films.

Renewal of the Radio Research Project

"The Lazarsfeld Radio Research Project virtually created the field of mass communication research" (Sills 1987, p. 258). Among the outstanding products of the project were Herta Herzog's study of daytime radio soap opera audiences, Hadley Cantril's investigation of panic reactions to the famous 1938 Orson Welles broadcast "Invasion from Mars," Theodor Adorno's study of popular versus serious music, and Lazarsfeld's own studies of the comparative effects of radio listening versus reading. The Radio Research Project was very successful in terms of productivity: it resulted in four books and over forty articles (Pasanella 1990, p. 24). In fact, Lazarsfeld himself was so productive in publishing out of the Radio Project that he used an alias so as to appear to be less of an overproducer.

By 1939, however, bad feelings had developed between Lazarsfeld and Hadley Cantril, the Princeton professor who was an associate director of the Radio Research Project. When Lazarsfeld criticized Cantril for a student newspaper article about the "Invasion from Mars" study, which credited Cantril with leading the investigation, the Princeton scholar wrote Lazarsfeld (in a January 27, 1939, letter now held in Columbia University's Butler Library): "I am glad you expressed yourself on the release [to the Princeton student newspaper], but I must say that the reaction seems a bit infantile." Then Lazarsfeld and Cantril disagreed about who should be listed as authors of the study's publications. In the end, Cantril dropped out of directing the Radio Research Project, and it moved to Columbia University.

John Marshall, the Rockefeller Foundation official overseeing the project, became concerned in 1939 that Lazarsfeld was taking the research in a too-scattered direction by pursuing his personal interests rather than closely following a detailed project plan, which indeed did not exist. The Radio Research Project seemed to be whatever Lazarsfeld's whim of the moment happened to be. As the initial two-year support from the Rockefeller Foundation came to an end, Lazarsfeld pressed Marshall for further funding, but Marshall felt that Lazarsfeld should pull together the research results that were already in hand from the wide variety of radio studies that had been completed. He gave Lazarsfeld five months to finish a book-length monograph out of the Radio Research Project. Lazarsfeld met this deadline, and the 354-page report was published in 1940 as *Radio and the Printed Page: An Introduction to the Study of Radio and Its Role in the Communication of Ideas*. For his part, Marshall recommended to the foundation board that the project be funded for two more years at $20,000 per year. Nevertheless, he still felt that the project lacked coherence, so he established a communication seminar, composed of eminent scholars, that met monthly for a year to review the project and to plot the future directions of mass communication research. The Rockefeller Communication Seminar played a very important role in the history of communication research. The initial purpose of the seminar, focusing Lazarsfeld's shotgun approach in the Radio Research Project, was broadened to coordinate and stimulate the field of mass communication research, a change in direction that was in response to America's approaching involvement in World War II.

ADORNO AND THE RADIO PROJECT

During the Radio Research Project's brief stay at the University of Newark Research Center, Lazarsfeld invited Theodor Adorno of the Frankfurt school to join the project. Lazarsfeld's motive was in part to help Adorno escape from Germany. Adorno had overstayed in Europe, despite desperate pleas from Max Horkheimer and his other Frankfurt school colleagues who were then in exile in New York. Lazarsfeld's cable offering the Newark job allowed Adorno to obtain a U.S. visa in order to migrate to America. But Lazarsfeld had other motives as well. He needed Adorno's specialized help. Adorno was noted for his expertise on music, and one subproject of the Radio Research Project dealt with the role of radio music. In a 1973 interview, Lazarsfeld explained: "My motivation in inviting Adorno was first in wanting a music division [in the Radio Research Project], and secondly I wanted someone . . . with a theoretical background, and I think a very important part was that the Horkheimer Institute had been very helpful to me when I had this little place at Newark—this Research Center. Horkheimer subsidized us—paid our secretary or something,* so I felt very indebted to Horkheimer, and I knew he wanted to get Adorno here, and it was really almost repayment of the help he had given me" (Morrison 1976a, p. 264).

In a broad sense, perhaps Lazarsfeld offered the Radio Research Project position to Adorno because he wanted to see if the critical school and the empirical school could collaborate in a common research endeavor. Lazarsfeld found out that they could not, at least in this case. Part of the problem was Adorno: he was abrasive, imperious, intolerant, and insulting, and his writing style was tortuous, although displaying brilliance and imaginative creativity (Morrison 1978). Lazarsfeld begged Adorno not to litter his text with so many Latin words and not to write about the radio industry with such insulting remarks (Morrison 1978). Adorno ignored these suggestions.

For his part, Adorno was shocked by "the factory-like atmosphere" of the Radio Research Project: "My first impression of the researches already in progress there was not exactly marked by any great understanding. At Lazarsfeld's suggestion I went from room to room and spoke with colleagues, heard words like 'Likes and dislikes study,' 'Success or failure of a program,' of which I at first could make very little. . . . For the first time, I saw 'Administrative Research' before me. I don't recall whether Lazarsfeld coined this phrase, or I myself in my astonishment at a practically-oriented kind of science, so entirely unknown to me." To an elitist European scholar like Adorno, the Radio Research Project looked like a highly applied kind of research and rather shabby. He viewed it with complete disdain. Lazarsfeld described Adorno "as impossible" (Morrison 1976a, p. 117). The disagreement

---

*Morrison (1976a, p. 170) states that Lazarsfeld offered the position on the Radio Research Project to Adorno in return for a loan of $1,000 made to Lazarsfeld's Newark Research Center in 1936 by Horkheimer's Institute for Social Research, which kept the new center alive for its first four months until funding was provided by the University of Newark. The Frankfurt scholars also provided another $1,000 to fund Mirra Komarovsky's (1940) study of the effects of unemployment on families.

between Lazarsfeld and Adorno was not a scholarly squabble but a fundamental theoretical dispute about the nature of communication research (Towers 1977, p. 133).

Nevertheless, in spite of persistent complaints about Adorno by Rockefeller Foundation officials and by leaders in the radio industry, Lazarsfeld stuck by his critical school collaborator, defending Adorno to Stanton and Cantril. It was "a great relief to me to have someone around whose problem is that he has too many ideas and not too few" (Lazarsfeld to Stanton and Cantril, March 7, 1938, Lazarsfeld Papers, Butler Library, Columbia University). Lazarsfeld attempted to pair the explosive Adorno with Gerhard Wiebe, a German-speaking Mennonite with a Ph.D. in psychology from Ohio State University, who was also a professional jazz player (Morrison 1976a, p. 265). Their personal chemistry did not work: Adorno rejected Wiebe, who then was employed by Frank Stanton at CBS Research.

Adorno saw himself as an erudite European with a much superior culture to the American musical material that he was assigned to study. He detested jazz, for example.* Adorno sincerely doubted that radio listeners' likes and dislikes for different kinds of music could be measured, and even if they could, the idea that radio programming should be guided by such listener preferences was repugnant to him. Radio listeners, Adorno felt, should learn to like "good music." The close association of the Radio Research Project with the radio broadcasting networks was abhorrent to Adorno. He felt that scholarly research should be conducted to advance the frontiers of knowledge, not so that wealthy media moguls could become wealthier. To regard an art form like music as a commodity was ridiculous. Finally, Adorno thought it was problematic to impute causal relationships to the effects of radio music on listeners. "It would be naive to take for granted an identity between the social implications to be discerned in the stimuli and those embodied in the 'responses'" (Adorno 1969, p. 353). However, Adorno also stated that it would be "no less naive to consider the two things as totally uncorrelated."

Lazarsfeld's "Adorno Project" ended in failure. Rockefeller Foundation executives rejected Adorno's reports and terminated funding for the radio music research subproject. Lazarsfeld asked John Marshall to

---

*Lazarsfeld first knew of Adorno, in fact, from reading his article, "Über Jazz," published in 1936 in the *Zeitschrift für Sozialforschung* (the house organ of the Frankfurt school). Adorno published the article under a pseudonym, Hektor Rottweiler (Morrison 1976a, p. 264).

continue Adorno's funding of $3,000 in 1941, but Marshall refused (Morrison 1976a, p. 305), so Adorno left the project and moved to Los Angeles. The failure of the Lazarsfeld-Adorno collaboration set the tone for future difficult relations between the empirical school and the critical school (Towers 1977). Perhaps their incompatibility was more perceived than inevitable, however. The two camps could work together, at least under different conditions. The prickly Theodor Adorno successfully collaborated with empirical scholars a few years later in *The Authoritarian Personality*. That study was certainly empirical research, and it was mainly quantitative, but it was not administrative research (at least to the degree that Adorno considered that the Radio Project was).

CRITICAL VERSUS ADMINISTRATIVE RESEARCH

In a response to an article by Max Horkheimer *"Traditionelle und Kritische Theorie"* (1937), Lazarsfeld (1941a) wrote "Remarks on Administrative and Critical Communications Research." He recommended that critical theory be included in American communication studies along with Lazarsfeld's own style of research, which he termed "administrative communication research." This choice of name ("administrative" research) tells a great deal about how Lazarsfeld saw his empirical research as being in the service of government and mass media institutions. Through his personal contacts with Max Horkheimer, Erich Fromm, Theodor Adorno, and other critical scholars in the Institute for Social Research, Lazarsfeld was well acquainted with the Frankfurt school's critical theory* and felt this work deserved greater attention by American scholars. He sought to build a pluralistic bridge to critical scholarship, hoping that its convergence with American-style empirical research would serve as a source of "challenging problems and new concepts useful in the interpretation of known, and in the search for new, data" (Lazarsfeld 1941). His attempts at such bridge building failed.

Lazarsfeld saw critical scholarship as useful for posing challenging problems and new concepts that empirical researchers could use. "If it were possible in terms of critical research to formulate an actual research operation which could be integrated with empirical work, the people involved, the problems treated, and, in the end, the actual utility of the work would greatly profit." However, he also typified critical the-

*In fact, Lazarsfeld and Robert K. Merton had helped arrange the affiliation of the Institute of Social Research with Columbia University.

ory as "speculative" (Lazarsfeld 1969a, p. 325) and as contributing little to "fact-finding on constructive suggestions" (Lazarsfeld 1941). "Critical theory scorns the use of definitions," Lazarsfeld (1969, p. 324) asserted, so it is dangerously imprecise. Lazarsfeld viewed the utility of critical scholarship as preliminary and auxiliary to empirical communication research (McLuskie 1975, p. 37). In a 1973 interview, David Morrison (1988) questioned Lazarsfeld as to whether he was really sincere in relating to the Frankfurt School. Lazarsfeld insisted that he was indeed serious, because the Frankfurt scholars had "a core of intellectual integrity, and at the same time seemed to be foolish and irresponsible. It was always [on Lazarsfeld's part] a mixture of curiosity, interest, respect, and irritation."

Many critical scholars did not agree with the contributory role in which Lazarsfeld sought to place them. Most are opposed to administrative communication research, and the idea of their being co-opted into this enterprise is unacceptable to them. Lazarsfeld's attempts at bridge building were doomed to failure.

QUANTITATIVE AND QUALITATIVE RESEARCH

The Lazarsfeld tradition of social research sought to combine qualitative and quantitative methods, participant observation and depth interviewing, content analysis and biographies, panel studies and focused interviews (Merton and Kendall 1946). A variety of methodological innovations were pioneered by Lazarsfeld and his colleagues at the Bureau of Applied Social Research. For example, Lazarsfeld introduced deviant case analysis, in which individual cases are examined that do not fit a general statistical pattern. This research method is used to look in greater depth at the individuals whose behavior does not conform to a relationship characterizing most of the other people in a study. Let us say that Erie County, Ohio, voters are classified into a 2 × 2 table of high/low formal education versus voting for the Republican/Democratic presidential candidate. Most individuals are on the diagonal of the table, in two of the four cells—high education/Republican or low education/Democratic—but a few individuals are in the other two cells. An investigator should scrutinize these deviant cases closely by rereading their survey questionnaires, for example, and perhaps by reinterviewing them. Perhaps a third variable explains an individual's deviance from the generally positive relationship between the independent variable and the dependent variable. For instance, maybe a high education/Democratic voter is a housewife married to a low education/Democratic husband who influenced her to vote for the Democratic candidate.

Lazarsfeld combined his mathematical background with his life-long involvement in conducting social research in order to achieve a fruitful scholarly production of books and articles about mass communication, unemployment, higher education, political behavior, and so forth, and a series of important methodological advances. Fundamentally, Paul F. Lazarsfeld was a toolmaker, and only secondarily was he a communication scholar, although he was the most important single individual in launching mass communication research.

Lazarsfeld was an early proponent of triangulation—using multiple methods of measurement, data gathering, and data analysis in order to obtain a many-sided view of the object of study—long before the idea of triangulation became popular among social scientists. He stated his creed for social research in the form of four rules, all calling for triangulation, that he derived from his Vienna research experience (Glock 1979, p. 25; Lazarsfeld, 1969a, p. 232):

1. Any phenomenon should be measured with objective observations as well as with introspective reports.
2. Case studies should be combined with statistical information.
3. Data gathering should be combined with information about the history of what is being studied.
4. Data from unobtrusive measures should be combined with questionnaire and other self-reported data.*

THE 1940 ERIE COUNTY STUDY

The Erie County study led to Lazarsfeld's first famous book in America, *The People's Choice* (1944). This classic study of media effects was originally designed as an investigation of the impact of U.S. Department of Agriculture radio broadcasts promoting federal farm policies. Although Lazarsfeld (1969a p. 330) could not remember exactly how, this USDA proposal was somehow converted into a panel study of the November

---

*Glock (1979, p. 34) clarified that Lazarsfeld meant unobtrusive measures by "natural data," and data mainly from questionnaires by "experimental data," two terms that he used in his original statement.

1940 U.S. presidential election. Mainly it was because "Lazarsfeld simply wanted to do a panel study" (Sills 1987, p. 261).* The political research in Erie County, Ohio, was conducted in Lazarsfeld's tradition of marketing research (Chaffee and Hochheimer 1985) in the sense that a sample of individuals were asked why they made their voting choices. As in his market research studies in Vienna and in the United States, Lazarsfeld investigated mass media and interpersonal communication influences on individual's decisions. In the Erie County study, Lazarsfeld expected the media to be very important in changing individuals' voting choices.

The size of a radio audience is not reflected in public records, unlike the print media of books, magazines, and newspapers, so as the radio audience grew rapidly in the United States, the use of polling grew with it in order to measure the size of the listenership, its sociodemographic composition, and the effects of the broadcasts. Lazarsfeld took the opinion poll, which had been used mainly for descriptive purposes, and applied it to measure the effects of radio on its audiences. "This transformation of the opinion poll into multifaceted survey research constitutes one of Lazarsfeld's major accomplishments" (Sills 1976, p. 262). A panel consists of repeated measurements of the same respondents over time. The panel design for the Erie County study consisted of seven personal interviews, conducted at monthly intervals from May to November, with a sample of 600 respondents. This panel design fit well with the problem of studying radio's effects. Because individuals tune in and tune out of a radio program, the panel design allowed Lazarsfeld to determine the time-order of various independent variables on the dependent variable of changes in voting intention, the indicator of media effects.

Lazarsfeld had to find about $100,000 for the Erie County project. He had $15,000 left from the Rockefeller Foundation grant to the Office of Radio Research at Columbia. He sold the first reprint rights of the study's results to *Life Magazine* for $10,000 or $15,000. He obtained another $10,000 from radio set manufacturers in exchange for putting a question in the survey about which make of radio his respondents preferred. But he still did not have enough funding for the Erie County project, so he put in a survey question about what make of refrigerators his survey respondents preferred (Converse 1987, p. 271). Through

---

*Lazarsfeld's first panel study had been conducted of the New Jersey gubernatorial election of 1938 (Lazarsfeld and Rosenberg 1955; Lazarsfeld 1961b, p. 83).

such nickel-and-diming, an illustration of his entrepreneurial skills par excellence, Lazarsfeld was able to put together the needed funding. (Keep in mind that in 1940 there was a virtual absence of funding for empirical and methodological research from private foundations or from federal government sources like the National Science Foundation, which only reluctantly included some support for social research when it was created in 1950 [Merton 1991].)

Early propaganda theorists championed the powerful mass media, but later communication scholars did not find evidence of such strong effects when they investigated the impacts of the media in voting behavior, consumer decisions, and other types of behavior change. The main scholar to begin questioning the notion of powerful mass media was Paul F. Lazarsfeld, and it was his Erie County study that started him questioning. The voting study launched the era of limited effects in mass communication research. Lazarsfeld expected the Erie County project to find that the mass media had direct, powerful effects in making up people's minds about how to vote in a presidential election. He found the opposite: the media informed and persuaded only a few key individuals, called opinion leaders by the Bureau researchers, who in turn magnified this effect through interpersonal communication links with their followers, in a kind of two-step flow of communication. Opinion leadership was a very important idea in mass communication research for several decades after publication of *The People's Choice* in 1944, although Lazarsfeld's measure of opinion leadership left much to be desired, and the empirical evidence for a two-step flow of communication was actually scanty. In other words, the conceptual contribution of the Erie County study far outweighed its research findings about opinion leadership and the two-step flow of communication.

Lazarsfeld acknowledged his intellectual debt for the concept of opinion leadership to Edward L. Bernays, the father of public relations in the United States. Soon after his arrival in New York in 1933, Lazarsfeld had visited Bernays at his office in Manhattan in order to learn more about the field of public relations. Bernays had already written several books (1923, 1928) about public relations and public opinion and was an early and influential practitioner of public relations. Bernays and Lazarsfeld became friends in New York, and Bernays says that out of their discussions, Lazarsfeld drew the concept of opinion leaders (Bernays 1991). Bernays, in turn, got the general idea of opinion leadership from Walter Lippmann's influential book *Public Opinion,* although Lippman did not use the term.

When he designed the Erie County study, Lazarsfeld assumed that voting decisions in a presidential election would be made during the course of the campaign and would be influenced by news and feature stories about the election issues and the candidates appearing in the mass media. However, many of the Erie County voters had made up their minds before the electoral campaign began. Only 54 of the 600 respondents ever shifted from one candidate to the other, and only a few of these switchers were directly influenced to do so by the mass media (Converse 1987, p. 299). The voter who keeps an open mind to the issues and the candidates and then decides on the basis of what is best for the nation is a fiction. In sum, Lazarsfeld concluded, the media had minimal effects in the 1940 presidential election campaign. The soundness of this conclusion has since been disputed by some critics, who argue that other evidence indicates the media did have effects. For example, Chaffee and Hochheimer (1985) pointed out that "more than one-half [of the Erie County respondents] said either radio or newspapers had been the single most important source [of information about the campaign], but less than one-fourth cited a personal source as important. Despite this seemingly preponderant evidence of media impact, the authors concluded that 'more than anything else people can move other people.'" Just how important the media's effects were in the 1940 election is thus partly a matter of interpretation and of what types of data are considered. Lazarsfeld concluded that media effects were relatively weak and thus launched the era of limited media effects, which was to dominate the thinking of U.S. communication scholars for the next several decades. The media effects were indeed weaker than he had expected them to be, but there were such effects.

The People's Choice study "marked the beginning of the new discipline of voting research" (Zeisel 1976–1977). Soon Lazarsfeld's approach to political survey studies was taken up by scholars at the University of Michigan's Institute for Social Research, who have carried out national sample surveys in each U.S. presidential election ever since, asking certain of the same questions in each survey.* These every-four-year, one-shot national surveys are quite different from the Erie County panel design, in which the 600 citizens were interviewed about their

*Lazarsfeld (1975d) felt that Michigan's Institute for Social Research completely overshadowed his Bureau of Applied Social Research in voting research, after closely copying the bureau's research approach that was demonstrated in the Erie County study. The shift from Columbia to Michigan as the center of voting research is traced by Sheingold (1973), showing how the study of network influences on voting behavior got shortchanged in the process.

voting intentions each month for six months prior to the 1940 Willkie-Roosevelt contest.

One of the most biting critics of Paul Lazarsfeld is sociologist Todd Gitlin (1978), who stated: "The dominant paradigm in the field [of media sociology] since World War II has been, clearly, the cluster of ideas, methods, and findings associated with Paul F. Lazarsfeld and his school: The search for specific, measurable, short-term, individual, attitudinal and behavioral 'effects' of media content, and the conclusion that media are not very important in the formation of public opinion." Survey methodology influenced the way in which scholars conceptualized media effects. Perhaps effects became defined as what audience surveys could measure: short-term, individual-level attitude change (Gitlin 1978). Surveys, of course, can measure other indicators of effects than just attitude change, such as how much information about a topic is learned from the media and the relative salience of various issues (as in agenda-setting research).

A strong, and much-quoted, statement about the minimal effects of mass media communication by Klapper (1960) represents the extreme position of Lazarsfeld's Bureau in the 1950s: "Mass communication does not ordinarily serve as a necessary and sufficient cause of audience effects, but rather functions through a nexus of mediating factors. These mediating factors are such that they typically render mass communications a contributory agent, but not the sole cause, in a process of reinforcing the existing conditions."

The Bureau's emphasis on the social psychology of short-term effects of the mass media, and the limited effects research conclusions, turned many scholars away from what had been a hot research topic (Katz 1987). Chaffee and Hochheimer (1985, p. 270) stated: "The marketing orientation to research has been so intimately intertwined with much of communication research that it would seem inseparable to many scholars. The search for 'effects' of the media stems from the procurers of goods to sell their products through the use of advertising, product and packaging design, pricing decisions, and so forth." Why is market research close to mass communication research? Because one scholar founded both: Paul F. Lazarsfeld.

THE BUREAU OF APPLIED SOCIAL RESEARCH

The Bureau of Applied Social Research was not the first social science research center at a U.S. university, but it was by far the most influential in shaping quantitative research methods (Converse 1987, p. 267), and it was the birthplace of mass communication research.*

Institutionalizing the Bureau at Columbia University

Lazarsfeld's research institute settled into Columbia University by degrees, and Robert Lynd helped it at every step.† In 1939, Lazarsfeld was appointed a lecturer without faculty status in the Department of Sociology. The following year, his Office of Radio Research moved somewhat nearer to the Columbia campus, when the university provided it with office space in the old building of the College of Physicians and Surgeons, sixty blocks from the main university campus. This location, now part of the Lincoln Center area but then a high-crime area, was appropriately called Hell's Kitchen. The old medical school building was huge— three or four stories high and covering a half-block (Merton 1991). The office space was rent free; in fact, the building had been condemned and was eventually destroyed.

Lynd continued to act as Lazarsfeld's angel. He was chair of the Department of Sociology and thus facilitated Lazarsfeld's appointment as a lecturer. He was also chair of the university committee that oversaw social science research at Columbia and thus provided the rent-free office space for the Radio Research Project (Converse 1987, p. 268). The Office of Radio Research was funded by Lazarsfeld's Rockefeller Foundation grant, plus market research studies for *Life* and *Time* magazines, Green River Whiskey, wine, Sloan's Liniment, refrigerators, greeting cards, toothpaste (Kolynos Tooth Powder), vitamins, and Bisodol (a stomach powder). An anonymous poem, written by a Bureau researcher in 1949 (Sheridan 1979, p. 65), began:

The Bureau does investigations
On everything but sex relations—

Toothpaste, soap, and breakfast cereals,
Whiskey, clothes, and such materials.

*More would be known about the golden era of the Bureau of Applied Social Research but for a flood in the Bureau's basement that destroyed most of the historical materials for the period from the late 1940s to the 1960s.

†Two research centers had been founded previously: the social science research program at the University of Chicago in the 1920s and the Institute for Research in Social Science at

Commercially sponsored research made up about half of the budget for the office in its early years (Converse 1987, p. 269). Columbia University did not fund the office except for providing free space. Amazingly, during these several years, the Bureau and the university did not have a written agreement. Their relationship just evolved, bit by bit. In 1945, an investigatory committee discovered there was "nothing in writing to authorize the existence of the Bureau" (Converse 1987, p. 274).

By 1944, the Rockefeller Foundation funding for the Office of Radio Research was coming to an end, and the office's radio studies were only one part of its total research program. Because its name no longer fit what it did, Lazarsfeld renamed it the Bureau of Applied Social Research, at the suggestion of Robert Merton (although the word *Applied* was at Lazarsfeld's strong insistence).* The Office of Radio Research continued but now as one of the several departments in the Bureau. In the mid-1940s, Columbia University began to contribute $5,000 annually (later increased to $10,000) to support the Bureau, in recognition of its important role in training graduate students. In 1949, the Bureau moved adjacent to the Columbia campus.

Not only was the Bureau gradually becoming integrated into Columbia University, but Lazarsfeld was moving up the ladder of faculty status. He was appointed associate professor of sociology in 1941 (thanks to Robert Lynd) and later to full professor, department chair of sociology, and, finally, Quetelet Professor of Social Science. Robert K. Merton became associate director of the Bureau in 1943, formalizing his lifetime friendship and close professional collaboration with Lazarsfeld.† Their personal association represented the close integration of theory and research methodology, it boosted sociology at Columbia into nationwide intellectual dominance during the 1950s and early 1960s, and it brought the talented mind of Robert Merton into communication research for several decades. The Lazarsfeld-Merton collaboration was reflected in Merton's important conception of theories of the middle range

---

the University of North Carolina, founded in 1924 by Howard Odum to study racial and economic problems of the South. Both were quite different from Lazarsfeld's Bureau.

*Merton proposed "Columbia Bureau of Social Research," but "Paul, in effect, said he'd rather die" (Merton, in press). Lazarsfeld badly wanted *Applied* in the title because he thought it accurately described the Bureau's work, even if most sociologists thought that applied research was of low prestige. Merton, who thought of the Bureau as mainly Lazarsfeld's organization, gave way on its name (Merton 1991).

†Lazarsfeld admired Merton for his intellectual panache and his academic respectability.

(Merton 1957), by which he meant theories at a level of generality that facilitated the empirical testing of theoretically derived hypotheses.* His much-cited essay on theories of the middle range grew out of the intensive discussions between Lazarsfeld the toolmaker and Merton the sociological theorist (Morrison 1976a, p. 229).†

That the Bureau could flourish as it did (it employed about 100 individuals and had an annual budget of about $500,000 in the early 1960s) was somewhat of a miracle. Certainly its success was not due to strong support from the Columbia University administration. They did not understand completely what the Bureau did, and such a "soft money" research institute did not fit the pattern of most other academic units at Columbia. "The Bureau achieved eminence in spite of Columbia administrators and other scholars by the force and diffusion of its publications and graduates" (Converse 1987, p. 279). The dependence of Bureau researchers on money from outside funding sources necessarily meant a hand-to-mouth orientation. The completion of academic books and other scientific publications out of Bureau research projects was delayed, sometimes for up to a decade. The Bureau was forced to conduct market research and to study other topics on "the margins of academic respectability" (Converse 1987, p. 272). Lazarsfeld had to devote considerable time to raising research funds, which detracted from his academic research and from his work with doctoral students at Columbia. Only his tremendous energy made it possible for him to fill these multiple and conflicting roles.

The Bureau's Golden Era

The Bureau's golden era occurred in the late 1940s through the mid-1960s, while Lazarsfeld was the director, associate director, and an active researcher in the Bureau.‡ A number of praiseworthy research pro-

---

*Merton followed his own guidelines for conducting research at the middle range. In the 1950s he carried out a study of the social structure of several planned housing communities but refused to publish a book out of this excellent investigation because it did not have an adequate theoretical foundation.

†Merton is a heavily cited social science scholar, with his influential book *Social Theory and Social Structure* (1949) receiving some 5,000 citations for the period from 1954 (when the *Science Citation Index* was established) and 1972 (when the *Social Science Citation Index* was founded) to 1992, an estimated 60 percent of all of Merton's citations (Garfield 1980).

‡After Lazarsfeld resigned as director of the bureau, his successors, in order, were Kingsley Davis, Charles Y. Glock, Bernard Berelson, David Sills, and Allen H. Barton.

jects were carried out during this period: the Coleman-Katz-Menzel (1966) study of the diffusion of a medical drug, an investigation of the role of the mass media in modernization of the Middle East (Lerner 1958), and Lazarsfeld and Thielens's (1953) research on the effects of McCarthyism on American professors.

During its peak years, the Bureau of Applied Social Research had from twelve to twenty faculty, mostly part-time, plus a staff of about a hundred, mainly composed of doctoral students in sociology at Columbia (Converse 1987). At its high point, the annual budget was almost $1 million (Hyman 1991, p. 206). World War II marked the rise of government funding of Bureau research, beginning with the War Department's sponsorship of evaluation research on military training films. Within a few years, government funding made up more than half of the Bureau's annual budget.*

In 1941, as the United States was entering World War II, Lazarsfeld told all of the Bureau staff they had to learn Spanish, which he thought would be important for future research after the war, when the United States would aid Latin American development (Morrison 1976a, p. 160). Lazarsfeld guessed wrong. The postwar U.S. government aided Europe and Japan through the Marshall Plan.

The Bureau was incredibly productive. From 1937 to 1960, it published 52 books plus 350 articles, book chapters, and other publications (Converse 1987, p. 287). This volume of scholarly publications compared favorably with the Institute for Social Research at the University of Michigan from 1946 to 1960, perhaps the university-based social research institute most similar to the Bureau (Converse 1987, p. 377). Lazarsfeld's Bureau outproduced Michigan's institute in books, 52 to 22, but the Institute for Social Research published more journal articles (103 to 62) and book chapters (94 to 45).

An important influence of the Bureau of Applied Social Research was through the doctorates that it helped produce, many of whom rose to academic note in the field of sociology: James S. Coleman, Peter Blau, Peter H. Rossi, Seymour Martin Lipset, Alice S. Rossi, David Sills, Charles Y. Glock, Elihu Katz, and Morris Rosenberg. Seven of the last twenty presidents of the American Sociological Association (through

*Sheridan (1979, p. 126), the Bureau's administrator for its last decade, reported that in 1949–1950, 50 percent of the Bureau's income came from government sources, including the National Science Foundation and the Department of Labor. This figure jumped to 83 percent in 1951–1952 and to 91 percent in 1973–1974.

1992) received their doctorates at Columbia, and most had worked at the Bureau.

Robin Hooding at the Bureau

Paul Lazarsfeld managed the Bureau of Applied Social Research as "a kind of academic Robin Hooding" (Morrison 1988). Bernard Berelson (Morrison 1983) stated: "You know the joke around the Bureau was that you paid the deficit of the last study with the grant for the next study; that's how people lived around here." And Allen H. Barton (1982), a long-time Bureau employee and its director for several years, recalled that Lazarsfeld "brought new meaning to the term 'nonprofit,' scrambling from one debt-ridden project to another."

The Bureau's projects, especially during its prime in the 1940s, 1950s, and early 1960s, were distinctive in that Lazarsfeld was able to get many of them funded by private corporations at such a high level that he was able to carry out an academic research project at the same time that he conducted the applied research for the corporate sponsors (Turner and Turner 1990, p. 101). Typically, a descriptive report was provided immediately after the study for the sponsor, and then, after a delay of several years, an academic book, usually coauthored by Lazarsfeld or Merton and one or more of the Bureau staff would appear, aimed at a scholarly audience. Such a unique serving of two masters could work effectively only under special conditions. An essential ingredient was an entrepreneurial and charismatic professor like Lazarsfeld, who could sell overpriced research projects to corporation executives. Both he and the sponsors were conveniently located in Manhattan, then the center of corporate power. "Lazarsfeld's practice was to give luncheon talks to corporate leaders, an activity for which there were endless opportunities. When one of the members of the audience remarked to him on some similar issue that had arisen in his own company, Lazarsfeld would arrange to have lunch with him and try to persuade him to fund a research project to study it" (Turner and Turner 1980, p. 102).

Lazarsfeld's close relationship with Frank Stanton at CBS was a useful resource for the Bureau. Two largely qualitative studies were carried out by the Office of Radio Research on the effects of unscheduled events. One was *The Invasion from Mars*, the 1939 study of the audience effects of Orson Welles's radio broadcast of a fictional invasion by aliens. The other firehouse research on an unscheduled event was the Merton-Fiske-Curtis (1946) study of the Kate Smith war bond marathon. In both cases, Lazarsfeld (1982, p. 49) "had phoned [Frank] Stanton the morning after the event, and he provided money from his CBS research budget for immediate preliminary work. Today the bureaucratization of research applications make such improvisations difficult."

David Sills (1976), a student and colleague of Lazarsfeld for twelve years at Columbia University, said that "the decade of the 1950's in Columbia Sociology is recalled by some as a Golden Age, but it was hardly that. . . . There was, nonetheless, something magical about a place where Paul Lazarsfeld was our teacher, boss, colleague, critic, and—so we hoped—our friend. We joked endlessly about his impossible work habits, his outrageous demands upon our time, his nearly impenetrable Viennese accent, his ever-present cigar, his comments during hurried conferences in taxi rides downtown, his making three appointments for lunch at the Faculty Club and keeping them all by skillful table-hopping, and his ability to juggle a dozen projects and research assistants simultaneously."

Lazarsfeld was phenomenal at identifying promising research problems of study. In fact, he generated research questions at such a rate that they outran his time, money, and other resources. He was insistent in recruiting other people to study his problems. Most of the faculty and doctoral students in Columbia sociology were working, at least to some degree, on Lazarsfeld's research problems. Some of them resented Lazarsfeld's attempts at influence, perceiving him as a scheming conniver. James S. Coleman (1992), who was at Columbia with Lazarsfeld from 1951 to 1955, likened him to someone who threw bones to people: "Here, you take this bone. You take this one. Lazarsfeld could take a bone away from someone, and give it to someone else." When he turned an intellectual task over to one of his researchers, he expected the same level of expertise that he himself exhibited. Such high standards were difficult to fulfill.

Sills (1987, p. 251) speaks of Lazarsfeld's "personal magnetism" in attracting people to his Bureau projects. Lazarsfeld "worked with and through other people to an extraordinary degree; until late at night, he was seldom alone" (Sills 1981b). Most of Lazarsfeld's important publications are coauthored (Sills 1987, p. 251).

Lazarsfeld did not rule the Bureau absolutely. For instance, the Bureau staff had moral objections to a cigarette smoking study sponsored by the Philip Morris Corporation. Accordingly, Lazarsfeld conducted the research under a personal contract with the company rather than through the Bureau, and he reframed the project so that it was more balanced in its approach, to studying reasons for nonsmoking as well as for smoking.* "At the Bureau, research under Lazarsfeld was a collective (but not egalitarian) enterprise. . . . All participants were encouraged to bring in new ideas or raise questions or criticisms or suggest new directions. But it was Lazarsfeld as Bureau director who took the major responsibility for meeting with clients and overseeing the reports and publications emerging from the projects" (Pasanella 1990).

The Decatur Study of *Personal Influence*

The Bureau of Applied Social Research existed in part by doing what its name implied—conducting applied research for government, labor, business, and community organizations—but the practical problems that these sponsors brought to the Bureau usually got transformed "into sociological studies of some significance" (Glock 1979, p. 27). One of the Bureau's best-known investigations, resulting in the famous book *Personal Influence* (Katz and Lazarsfeld 1955), began with a "rather trivial question" (Glock 1979, p. 27) that was posed to Bureau researchers by the publishers of a popular family magazine. MacFadden Publications wanted to upgrade their audience to higher-status households. The *Personal Influence* study of 800 women respondents in Decatur, Illinois, in 1945 determined how individuals obtained information and others' opinions in decisions about what movies to see, how to vote, and what fashions to buy. This investigation advanced scholarly understanding of the interplay between mass media and interpersonal communication in the process of opinion leadership (Glock 1979, p. 27). After only *The People's Choice, Personal Influence* was the best-known book to come out of the Bureau of Applied Social Research.

The Decatur project, funded by a $30,000 grant from MacFadden Publications, grew out of an earlier project by the Bureau, directed by Robert K. Merton, in Dover, New Jersey (called "Rovere"), that had been sponsored by *Time* magazine. *Time* knew that it reached bankers, medical doctors, and other upper-middle class, well-educated opinion leaders. Did other types of opinion leaders exist in American communities?

---

*The research findings from the smoking study are reported in Meyer, Friedman, and Lazarsfeld (1973, pp. 243–254).

The Bureau's Rovere study of about one hundred respondents in a snowball sample sought to find out.* Unfortunately for the project's sponsor, the Bureau scholars found that many of the Rovere "influentials" (the term used instead of *opinion leaders*) did not read *Time,* and some could not even read.[†] MacFadden Publications, whose *True Story* was read by the lower-class influentials in Rovere, then agreed to sponsor the Decatur study (Lazarsfeld 1962b, p. 374).

Lazarsfeld had the funding. Now he needed the right scholar to lead the research project. C. Wright Mills, a promising young sociologist then teaching at the University of Maryland, was appointed to the faculty at Columbia at the suggestion of Robert K. Merton. At the time that he joined the Bureau, Mills was becoming well known for his somewhat radical sociology. The dispute between Mills and Lazarsfeld tells something about both of them. Mills, born in Waco, Texas, earned his bachelor's degree at the University of Texas at Austin, where he set a brilliant academic record, and then pursued his Ph.D. in sociology at the University of Wisconsin. He had contentious relationships with the department chair and with several of the faculty, based on an anti-authority attitude that was to characterize his later career. Mills then taught at the University of Maryland but made frequent trips to Greenwich Village in New York, where he came in frequent contact with critical intellectuals, including Horkheimer, Adorno, and Herbert Marcuse of the Frankfurt school, then living in exile in New York (Horowitz 1983, p. 72). Robert Merton knew of Mills's desire to move to New York and recommended him to the Columbia faculty and to Lazarsfeld, who appointed him to the Bureau in 1945.

Conflict with Lazarsfeld quickly ensued. Lazarsfeld claimed that Mills ignored the technical supervision of the survey sampling (which was Lazarsfeld's main interest), while gathering data from community leaders like newspaper editors and city officials about community power in Decatur (Mills's main interest). So Lazarsfeld fired Mills as director of the Decatur project and later from the Bureau (Lazarsfeld 1962b, p. 356; Horowitz 1983). Mills took the project over its budget and was assigned to make up for this deficit by directing, for free, a research project on Puerto Rican migrants to New York. During the

---

*Snowball sampling consists of gathering data from an initial sample of respondents, who are asked with whom they interact; a similar procedure is followed with this second sample, and so on.

[†]A detailed report of the Rovere study is provided by Merton (1949, pp. 441–474).

1950s, Mills wrote a series of much-talked-about books: *White Collar: The American Middle Classes* (1951), *The Power Elite* (1956), about those at the top of society, and *The Sociological Imagination* (1959), Mills's statement about what was right and wrong with sociology as a field. This last book also served to even old scores with Lazarsfeld. Mills had attained "an aura of heroic proportions" by 1959, and so his criticism of the Decatur study and the research tradition that Lazarsfeld represented caused considerable discussion among social scientists (Horowitz 1983, p. 173). The basic dispute was one of academic perspective: Mills was dedicated to the problems of radical social change, and he claimed that Lazarsfeld's perspective centered on system maintenance (Horowitz 1983, p. 173).

Finally, fourteen years after the Decatur study was conceived in 1942 and a decade after the survey data were gathered in 1945, the book reporting the results, *Personal Influence* (Katz and Lazarsfeld 1955), was published. Part I is a synthesis of Kurt Lewin–style group dynamics research, showing the importance of group influences on individuals' decisions and arguing that generalizations from small-group research could be extended to the mass communication process. (In essence, Katz and Lazarsfeld thus argued that interpersonal communication and mass media communication belonged together in one field.) Part II reports the empirical results from the Decatur study about the role of mass and interpersonal communication in the decision-making behavior of the housewife-respondents. *Personal Influence* centered on the rediscovery of Charles Horton Cooley's primary group in the mass audience of individuals, which was expressed through social relationships among people: neighbors, friends, and relatives. Messages in the mass media provided information to many individuals, but it was when this information was transmitted from one individual to another as personal influence that individuals were motivated to make decisions and to take action.

The Medical Diffusion Study

A similar silk-purses-from-sows'-ears story occurred in the mid-1950s when Joseph Precker, director of market research at Pfizer Drug Company, approached the Bureau about determining whether Pfizer should continue to advertise a new drug in the *Journal of the American Medical Association* (Glock 1979, p. 27). Elihu Katz, a Bureau staff member already had drafted a research proposal to study a sample of individuals, each of whom would be asked to designate sociometrically the several network partners with whom they discussed some topic. Then the network partners would also be interviewed about the same topic (Katz 1990). The snowball design was a logical next step, after the Rovera and Decatur studies of personal influence, in determining more precisely the process of interpersonal communication in the spread of ideas in a mass population. Pfizer's rather prosaic advertising question was merged with the basic idea of the Katz snowball proposal to create an investigation that represented a major advance in understanding the diffusion of innovations. In fact, this study is one of the most valuable diffusion studies of all time.

The Bureau researchers gathered data through personal interviews with medical doctors in selected specialties in four Illinois cities, asking them when they had adopted tetracycline. Pfizer's new antibiotic. These adoption data were checked against pharmacists' prescription records for the doctors of study. The respondents were also asked to report their interpersonal network links with other physicians (Coleman, Katz, and Menzel 1966). The Bureau's drug study established that the diffusion of innovations was a fundamentally social process of people talking to people about a new idea (Rogers 1983). The first individuals to adopt an innovation, the innovators, are not respected by other individuals in the system, and so the rate of adoption increases slowly at first. Then person-to-person discussions about the innovation cause the S-shaped diffusion curve to spurt upward after the opinion leaders in the system adopt.* Thus, over time, the rate of adoption displays a characteristic S-shape (as illustrated by Figure 7.1 for the rate of adoption of radios and television was in the United States).

The Bureau's Research Style

The Bureau of Applied Social Research was unique in several important ways. It did not conduct national sample surveys, and it did not maintain a permanent interviewing staff. Lazarsfeld believed that the infrastructure of such national surveys would lead his Bureau to pursue research contracts for studies that lacked immediate or potential scholarly value (Glock 1979, p. 27). The general style of Bureau projects was to

---

*Burt (1987) conducted a network analysis of the patterns of relationships among the medical doctors by reanalyzing the drug diffusion data some thirty-two years after the original data gathering. Valente (1991) then reanalyzed these data to understand better the nature of the critical mass in the S-shaped diffusion curves in the four Illinois communities.

gather data from a sample (or a census) of respondents in a community that was selected as representative. Such localized designs, in contrast to random samples of the U.S. population, permitted researchers to investigate interpersonal communication and social relationships, such as the diffusion of a new drug from doctor to doctor, the passing of political information from voter to voter, and the spread of consumer information from housewife to housewife. The Bureau researchers were sociologists with a central interest in communication processes. Their localized survey sociometry style fit with their disciplinary and intellectual interests in focusing on the social influences on individuals' decisions. That was the research tradition that Lazarsfeld had started years earlier in Vienna and that he continued throughout his career. Lazarsfeld's focus on individual social action led him to study how individuals make decisions. The mass media, group, and other influences on individual decisions could be investigated conveniently with survey methods, one of Lazarsfeld's areas of expertise. Using the individual as the unit of analysis also headed Lazarsfeld in the direction of studying media effects.

Another unique quality of Bureau research, shockingly unbelievable to most graduate students today, is that statistical tests of significance were never used. This absence of chi-square, F, and t values to test hypotheses in Bureau publications is indeed surprising, given that American social science research, and especially sociological research, in the 1940s, 1950s, and 1960s was deeply enamoured of statistical tests of significance. Lazarsfeld was even a mathematician, but he did not believe in using statistical tests of significance with survey data. The Bureau position against statistical tests, explained in methodological appendixes to several of their books and in other publications,* was that the Columbia researches were mainly exploratory in nature, designed to formulate hypotheses about human behavior rather than to provide a definitive test of such hypotheses (a task left to other, later researchers). In other words, the Bureau of Applied Social Research was in the business of identifying tentative understandings rather than in replicating and rigorously testing hypotheses about human behavior. The research design of the typical Bureau project was an intensive study of one system, often a local community or an organization. Such designs argued

---

*For example, Lipset, Trow, and Coleman (1956), Kendall (1970, pp. 301–305), and Selvin (1957). These arguments against using statistical tests of significance, and counterarguments by critics of the Bureau's position, are found in Morrison and Henkel (1970).

against the need for generalizing the findings from a random sample to a larger population. Tests of significance, and the statistical inference that they provide, were unnecessary and inappropriate for most Bureau researches, the argument went. Nevertheless, some critics argued, without statistical tests of significance, the Columbia investigators were left with only their intuitive judgment as a basis for accepting or rejecting hypotheses (Converse 1987, p. 285; Davis 1970, pp. 91–93).

I remember visiting the Bureau of Applied Social Research in 1959 as a guest of Herbert Menzel, who had directed the medical drug diffusion study. The Bureau was in a venerable hulk called the Vanderbilt Building near the Columbia campus. Tiny offices were crammed with doctoral research assistants and piles of questionnaires and other data. The Bureau researchers struck me as serious and dedicated, with little wasted motion. At noontime a new research proposal was presented and discussed over brown bag lunches. The Bureau scholars did not stop to greet each other or to have idle bull-sessions as they passed in the narrow halls. The work that I discussed with Menzel and his colleagues was at the cutting edge of social research. When I left the Bureau at the end of the day, I felt that I had seen social research at its best, albeit conducted in a somewhat factory-like fashion characterized by high efficiency.

Many of the Bureau studies were published as books. For a period in the 1950s, the Free Press practically became the publishing arm of the Bureau of Applied Social Research. Among these many books are the following:

- Paul F. Lazarsfeld's *Mathematical Thinking in the Social Sciences* (1954).
- Elihu Katz and Paul F. Lazarsfeld's *Personal Influence: The Part Played by People in the Flow of Mass Communication* (1955).
- Seymour Martin Lipset, Martin A. Trow, and James S. Coleman's *Union Democracy: The Internal Politics of the International Typographical Union* (1956), an important labor union in the New York newspaper industry. This book pioneered the use of survey data to illuminate how organizational structures affect individual behavior.
- Robert K. Merton, Marjorie Fiske, and Patricia L. Kendall's *The Focused Interview: A Manual of Problems and Procedures* (1956).
- David L. Sills's *The Volunteers* (1957), a study of the National Foundation for Infantile Paralysis, which raised money for research through the annual March of Dimes campaign and was the largest

voluntary health organization in the United States at the time of the study.

- James S. Coleman's *Community Conflict* (1957).
- Paul F. Lazarsfeld and Wagner Thielens's *The Academic Mind: Social Scientists in a Time of Crisis* (1958), a study of social science professors in the McCarthy era.
- Daniel Lerner's *The Passing of Traditional Society: Modernizing the Middle East* (1958), a report of survey research on the mass media and modernization in six Middle Eastern nations.
- Joseph T. Klapper's *The Effects of Mass Communication* (1960), the summary statement from Bureau studies about the minimal effects of the mass media.

These important volumes reported a wide diversity of methodological and substantive intellectual directions. They reflect the outpouring of excellent research being conducted at the Bureau during its golden era. These books also helped put the Free Press on the map. In fact, the Free Press became the major publisher in sociology for a time.*

Lazarsfeld stepped down as director of the Bureau of Applied Social Research in order to become chair of the Department of Sociology at Columbia University. He had begun to lose interest in communication research, bit by bit, during the 1950s, and after he relinquished directorship of the Bureau, he no longer needed to secure funding to support the other Bureau staff. Accordingly, he stopped going after small research projects of an applied nature, which often had a communication aspect (for example, the effects of an advertising campaign for a new brand of coffee). Instead, he was applying to private foundations and to federal government agencies for large grants to study substantive and methodological problems directly that would gain for him the academic respect of his sociological peers. For example, in about 1952, Lazarsfeld received a large grant from the Office of Naval Research for research on mathematical models of human behavior (Coleman 1992). The Columbia Department of Sociology was considered number one in the United

---

*This rapid rise of the new publishing house was not just due to Lazarsfeld and the Bureau, however. Jeremiah Kaplan, editor of the Free Press, was put in touch with Talcott Parsons of Harvard by Edward Shils of Chicago. The Free Press published Parsons's *The Structure of Social Action* (1949), and his other important books. Kaplan also published another major sociological classic in 1949, Robert K. Merton's *Social Theory and Social Structure*. Another factor in the success of the Free Press in the 1950s was the growing market for sociology books (Kaplan November 27, 1991).

States, and Lazarsfeld's personal work style was becoming somewhat less frenetic. Lazarsfeld was going through an academic change of life, one that took him out of communication research, although he did not completely lose his interest in communication research. In 1974, he, along with the social psychologist William J. McGuire, made a research proposal to the Markle Foundation to restudy daytime serials forty years after the Bureau's original work on this topic. It was Lazarsfeld's final proposal, and it was unsuccessful. On August 30, 1976, he died in New York, from cancer.

Wilbur Schramm (1981) related a story that Lazarsfeld once told him about the early days of his radio research. Lazarsfeld had conducted an audience survey of Radio Station WOI, an educational broadcasting station at Iowa State University, and traveled to Ames to deliver the completed research report in person. Dr. Charles Friley, the university president, met Lazarsfeld at the Ames train station with a black limousine. Unaccustomed to such attention and ill at ease at a "cow college" like Iowa State, Lazarsfeld tried to make casual conversation as they drove through the pastoral campus. As they passed the university's radio tower, Lazarsfeld, to his absolute horror, heard himself saying to the university president, "Oh, so you have a broadcasting station." Lazarsfeld wanted to melt through the floor of the car, but fortunately, President Friley took it as a joke.

Lazarsfeld realized from that moment what mass communication meant to him: messages and their effects on people. "He knew nothing of what went on in making [radio] programs or producing newspapers or any of the operations behind the communication product itself" (Schramm 1981). Such an orientation led Lazarsfeld away from investigating the source organizations for mass media communication.* He told Schramm the story just related in the context of giving advice to a new research institute director. Lazarsfeld told Schramm (in press): "This is what we most envy you and your colleagues. Most of you have worked in the media. Most of you know what happens inside a newspaper office or inside a broadcasting station."

---

*Lazarsfeld, in a February 21, 1975, oral history interview, stated: "I never understood the importance of studying the inside of the communications industry." Such problems of ownership, control, and functioning of media institutions did not fit well with Lazarsfeld's predominant methodological style of survey research on individual action. On the other hand, Allen H. Barton (1992) called my attention to several studies of mass media institutions that were carried out by Bureau scholars, so media institutions were not ignored completely at the Bureau.

Eventually Lazarsfeld's scholarly interests took him out of communication research. But the seventeen years that he had invested in communication study gave it a tremendous intellectual boost and a prestige-by-association with America's most famous sociological methodologist. Lazarsfeld took communication in the direction of studying individual action in a social context. Lazarsfeld directed the field of communication to the study of effects.

WORKING WITH MERTON

The considerable importance of Robert K. Merton as a theoretical influence on Lazarsfeld's intellectual contributions has not been fully realized (Coleman 1980b, p. 171). In fact, Merton was so important to the Bureau of Applied Social Research's program in communication research that perhaps we ought to refer to "Lazarsfeld-Merton" as the most important creators of the field of mass communication research in the United States.

Merton was born of immigrant parents in a South Philadelphia slum area in 1910. He received his B.A. degree in sociology from Temple University in 1931 and his Ph.D. from Harvard in 1936 as a member of the first cohort of doctoral students in sociology. He stayed on to teach for three years; he became an associate professor and, then in his second year, professor and chairman of the Department of Sociology at Tulane University, until he was called to Columbia in 1941. Merton's 1938 paper, "Social Structure and Anomie," had established him as a leading young theorist. "It brought him immediately to the attention of the sociological fraternity in the United States" (Bierstedt 1981, p. 455). Merton argued that both conformity and deviance are products of social structure. Thus, social structure not only constrains an individual's actions, as Freud believed, but helps to activate actions.

Robert MacIver, chair of the Department of Sociology at Columbia, wanted to hire Merton. His opponent in the department, Robert Lynd, wanted Lazarsfeld, a methodologist. The conflict was finally settled by Nicholas Murray Butler, president of the university, who made a Solomonic intervention: hire both.* The Lazarsfeld-Merton duo was to prove a winning combination, raising the Columbia University Department of Sociology to a high level of excellence.

*The details of this important hiring decision are related by MacIver (1968) and Lipset (1955, pp. 297–299).

When Lazarsfeld was being considered for the faculty position at Columbia University, Sam Stouffer (1941) wrote in a letter to the Columbia selection committee: "He [Lazarsfeld] is not a conventionally trained sociologist, but with respect to the three traits I mentioned (originality, versatility, and ingenuity), he ranks so high above the general run of sociologists that I can think of no one else with whom to compare him. He is not an orderly worker, and if he gets a bright idea, he is likely to pursue it to the detriment of orderly routines. I rather admire that kind of guy myself. . . . From the standpoint of statistical competence, I would rate Paul very highly, with emphasis on his ingenuity and inventiveness rather than upon his systematic knowledge of the literature."

Bernard Berelson in a 1973 interview (Morrison 1976a, p. 322) said that Lazarsfeld got theoretical respectability "by having some of Merton rub off on him." The noted sociologist Peter Blau, a doctoral student at Columbia in the late 1940s said: "The atmosphere at Columbia in those days, when Merton was becoming increasingly involved in empirical research and had already started his fruitful collaboration with Paul F. Lazarsfeld, tended to destroy the preconception, which most of us students initially shared, that a social theorist is not concerned with systematic empirical investigations. My new interest in the integration of theory and research motivated me to take all the courses and seminars on research methods Lazarsfeld offered, and to decide to do an empirical investigation" (Blau 1964, p. 20). Columbia sociology now had two influential scholars who worked together so closely that the department's doctoral program combined rigorous theoretical training and on-the-job research work.

James Coleman (1992) remembers a doctoral seminar on bureaucracy taught by Lazarsfeld and Merton. Lazarsfeld played the role of the uninformed novice, continually asking the wise Merton a series of somewhat elementary questions. These were questions that the typical doctoral student in the class wanted to know but might have been afraid to ask. The contrasting roles of the two professors gave a very effective dynamic to the seminar, as Coleman remembers it, despite the fact that Lazarsfeld was not ordinarily an effective teacher.

Merton is an urbane intellectual, widely admired for his remarkable choice of words in writing and speaking. Certainly Lazarsfeld had high respect for him, whom he called "Mr. Sociology in this country, and unbelievably brilliant" (Morrison 1976a, p. 177). Merton had tremendous influence in the field of sociology in the United States during the 1950s, 1960s, and 1970s, as Lazarsfeld (1962a, p. 148) noted: "You could almost define what sociology means for the younger generation [of sociologists]—it is whatever Merton picks [to study]." Indeed, during his long career Merton launched the sociology of science,* analyzed status relationships in a bureaucracy, proposed theories of the middle range to guide empirical inquiry, and became one of the leading exponents of structural and functional analysis in sociology.[†] A content analysis of some 2,500 articles in which Merton was cited from 1970 to 1977 shows that two-thirds are for his concepts rather than for his research findings (Garfield 1980). The formulation and elaboration of concepts is one of Merton's main theoretical contributions (Sztompka 1986, p. 15).

Merton (1949, p. 39) defined theory as a logically connected set of propositions from which empirical uniformities can be derived. Each proposition consists of a postulated relationship between two or more conceptual variables. Obviously, each concept must be defined in a precise way because concepts are the building blocks of theory. The basis for postulating the relationships in a set of theoretical propositions (or hypotheses) is provided by the underlying mechanism, or driving force of the theory.

Lazarsfeld and Merton were colleagues for thirty-five years. "There are few examples in the history of science of two such brilliant and accomplished colleagues developing and maintaining such a strong personal and scientific relationship for such an extended period. . . . Merton was the anonymous collaborator on almost everything that Lazarsfeld published. On the title pages of the copy he gave Merton of a long chapter on latent structure analysis, Lazarsfeld wrote: 'Bob, this is the first item in 20 years you did not have to work on. P.'" (Sills 1987, p. 270). Further, Merton's diplomatic skills were called on to extricate Lazarsfeld from various problems with Columbia University, his colleagues, and his research sponsors. In a festschrift for Lazarsfeld, Merton referred to him as "brother" (Sills 1987, p. 271).

Robert K. Merton was an important scholar of mass communication, independent of his influence on Lazarsfeld's work. His study with Fiske

---

*With his doctoral dissertation at Harvard, a revision of which was later published in book form in 1938 and later in 1970 and 1993 as *Science, Technology and Society in Seventeenth Century England,* a study of the relationship of religion, the economy, and science.

[†]Merton's intellectual contributions are described by Sztompka (1986), Crothers (1987), Clark, Modgil, and Modgil (1990), Coser (1975), and Bierstedt (1981). A sampling of Merton's contributions are represented by his much-admired *Social Theory and Social Structure* (1949).

and Curtis (1946) of the Kate Smith War Bond drive on the CBS radio network centered on a highly unusual event that took place on September 21, 1943. Kate Smith, a popular singer and radio personality, stayed on the air for eighteen hours, from 8:00 A.M. to 2:00 P.M. the next day. The radio marathon, featuring sixty-five one- to two-minute emotional appeals from Kate Smith, mixed in with musical numbers brought in an incredible $39 million of purchases and pledges for U.S. war bonds. Two previous drives had gathered only $1 million and $2 million, respectively. Merton, Fiske, and Curtis's book, *Mass Persuasion,* was based on 100 focused interviews with respondents in New York City, of whom 75 had called in pledges to buy war bonds. They were interviewed soon after the broadcast. Another sample of 978 people in New York City were interviewed with a survey questionnaire. Merton's investigation concluded that the media can have direct effects on a massive scale when the persuasive messages are highly emotional and come from a source made credible by "technicians of sentiment."

The Kate Smith broadcast, so obviously staged, led to the concept of pseudo-Gemeinschaft, the feigning of personal concern for another individual in order to manipulate the individual more effectively (Merton, Fiske, and Curtis 1946, p. 142).* The Bureau scholars found that Smith was able to persuade the U.S. mass audience to buy war bonds because she conveyed the impression of a genuine, highly personalized concern with the war effort and American soldiers. The respondents often contrasted Kate Smith's sincerity with the pretense and exception they observed in their everyday experiences. She was a symbol of caring and credibility. She pleaded with her radio audience to buy war bonds in order "to bring home the American fighting boys." The concept of pseudo-Gemeinschaft has since been explicated and utilized by various scholars (Beniger 1987).

"With few exceptions, research has been almost wholly concerned with the content rather than the effects of propaganda. Inquiry in this field has been focused on the appeals and rhetorical devices, the stereotypes and emotive language which make up the propaganda materials. But the actual processes of persuasion have gone largely unexamined" (Merton, Fiske, and Curtis 1946, p. xii). The Kate Smith war bond

---

*Related to Merton's concept of pseudo-Gemeinschaft is that of para-social interaction, the degree to which an individual perceives a mass medium as being like an interpersonal relationship (Horton and Wohl 1956). For example, I found that some viewers of a popular television soap opera in India actually carry on conversations with their favorite television character during the broadcasts (Singhal and Rogers 1989a, 1989b).

study used both the focused interview and the more common survey interview. The 1943 investigation dealt mainly with studying media effects, as was the general pattern in most other Bureau researches of that era.

Given Robert K. Merton's important role as a communication scholar in his own right, as well as in tandem with Lazarsfeld, it is perplexing that his contribution has not been more fully recognized by contemporary communication scholars.

CONTRIBUTIONS OF PAUL LAZARSFELD TO COMMUNICATION STUDY

Paul F. Lazarsfeld is best known for three contributions to communication study:*

1. He initiated the media effects research tradition, which was to become the dominant paradigm in U.S. mass communication research. He helped launch mass communication research with the first radio audience survey in 1930–1931 in Vienna (Heilbut 1983, p. 95), followed in America after 1937 with the Radio Research Project. He lent the prestige of his reputation to the emerging field of mass communication research in America. Lazarsfeld developed several important theoretical concepts, such as opinion leadership and the two-step flow of communication. He pioneered studying the role of interpersonal versus mass media channels in communication campaigns.

2. He advanced survey methodology through methods of gathering data like unobtrusive measurement and the focused interview, triangulation strategies, and various data analysis methods. He transformed public opinion polling methods into survey analysis, using sample surveys analytically "to draw inferences about causal relations that affect the actions of individuals" (Coleman 1980b, p. 155). Such a methodological style fit with

---

*Lazarsfeld, looking back over his career near its end, felt that his three most important contributions (in order) were the invention of university research institutes, the emphasis that he gave to research methodology, and his studies of how individuals make decisions, as in voting, in making an occupational choice, or in buying coffee (Lazarsfeld 1976). I generally agree. In a 1973 personal interview (Morrison 1976a, p. 428), Lazarsfeld said that his goal was also "to produce Paul Lazarsfelds." He counted among his blessings a half-dozen former Ph.D. students who had become very prominent.

Lazarsfeld's lifelong focus on the empirical analysis of individual action. He did not analyze the community in which his field surveys were conducted but instead studied individual decision making in the community. Unfortunately, this approach failed to capture much about social structure (Coleman 1980b, p. 165).

3. He created the prototype of the university-based research institute.* After he founded the Research Institute for Economic Psychology in Vienna in 1927, he launched two university research institutes in America. More famous was the Bureau of Applied Social Research at Columbia University, which served as the model for many other university research institutes, including many communication research institutes today. Lazarsfeld saw himself as a "managerial scholar"—a university professor who directs a research bureau (Lazarsfeld 1976). Compared to university departments, institutes are more flexible and focused and less subject to criticism for taking innovative directions. That is why the academic field of communication started in research institutes, at Illinois, Stanford, and elsewhere. Lazarsfeld created the organizational form through which communication study was first introduced in several universities. Lazarsfeld created the research institute as one important component of the U.S. research university. In the process, he helped put the stamp of administrative research on communication theory, and, more broadly, on much social science research.

Finally, Lazarsfeld brought Robert K. Merton into his Bureau of Applied Social Research and thus into communication study.

Center for Advanced Study in the Behavioral Sciences

In 1950, Lazarsfeld sought to change the Bureau into a professional school for training in social research (Lazarsfeld 1972). In collaboration with Merton, he wrote a memo to the Columbia University administration, but the plan did not have interdepartmental support at Columbia; the cost of the proposed professional school to the university was

---

*A considerable literature about U.S. university research institutes exists, much of if about the marginality of such institutes: Sieber (1972), Ikenberry and Friedman (1972), and Sheridan (1979). Many university-based research institutes remain on the periphery of the university, as was Lazarsfeld's Bureau, which depended on outside funding for about 95 percent of its budget during the years of its existence (Sheridan 1979, p 2).

another obstacle (Glock 1979, p. 31). In the early 1950s, Lazarsfeld was among those who advised the Ford Foundation on planning for the Center for Advanced Study in the Behavioral Sciences, located adjacent to the Stanford University campus. This think tank was established with Ford Foundation funding arranged by Bernard Berelson, a former colleague of Lazarsfeld in the bureau.* In 1951, Berelson became director of the Ford Foundation's Program in the Behavioral Sciences. McCarthyism was prevalent, and social science was confused with socialism by right-wing extremists. "Behavioral sciences" had a noncontroversial ring and was a broader concept, including history, philosophy, and psychiatry, for instance. Berelson "virtually created the term 'behavioral sciences'" (Sills 1981).[†]

Lazarsfeld's plan for the think tank in Palo Alto urged that it be organized to allow promising doctoral students and new Ph.D.s to collaborate with senior faculty members in joint research activities (Glock 1979, p. 31). Instead, the Center for Advanced Study in the Behavioral Sciences invited mainly established scholars in the behavioral sciences (along with younger scholars of distinct promise). "I wanted the Ford Center [the Center for Advanced Study in the Behavioral Sciences] to be a center for applied social research," Lazarsfeld said ruefully. Instead it became "absolutely opposite of what I had in mind" (Lazarsfeld 1975c). So Lazarsfeld was not able to launch his dream of a professional school for social research, either at Columbia or in Palo Alto.

---

*Berelson (1912–1979) was born in Spokane, Washington, and earned a Ph.D. degree in library science from the University of Chicago in 1941. His dissertation reported findings from the Erie County voting study, in which he collaborated with Lazarsfeld. Berelson then continued at Chicago as a professor and became dean of the Library School, which he took in the direction of communication research. His early investigations were studies of book readers. During World War II, Berelson worked for the Office of War Information as an analyst of German public opinion and morale. Near the end of the war, he moved to Columbia University's Bureau for Applied Social Research, where he helped Lazarsfeld analyze the data from the Erie County voting study and became a coauthor with Lazarsfeld of *The People's Choice*. He also took advantage of a newspaper strike in New York in order to determine what missing the newspaper means to readers (Berelson 1949).

†Berelson was an enthusiast for empirical social research, which he conducted himself and funded for others. For instance, he funded Leon Festinger's research leading to his book, *Theory of Cognitive Dissonance*. Berelson believed in making propositional inventories as a way of pulling together research-based knowledge into a form more useful for policymakers. His most noted example is the book with Gary Steiner, *Human Behavior: An Inventory of Scientific Findings* (1964). Berelson ended his career as president of the Population Council, a Rockefeller-funded organization that promotes family planning in Third World nations.

As a consultant to the Ford Foundation, Lazarsfeld in 1963 helped found the Institut für Höhere Studien (Vienna Institute of Advanced Studies in the Social Sciences) (Zeisel 1976–1977). Thus, his idea of the research institute had come full circle from his Vienna Forschungsstelle of the 1920s. The present-day institute was "a social-democratic maneuver to break the dominance of the conservatives in Austrian academia" (Freund 1991).

Criticisms of Lazarsfeld's Work

Paul Lazarsfeld was deeply devoted to empirical social science research. Robert S. Lynd (1939, p. 120) commented on the seductive quality of empirical research: "To carry it on, one usually places oneself inside the going system, accepts temporarily its values and goals, and sets to work at gathering data. . . . [One] tends to be drawn deeper within the net of assumptions by which the institution he is studying professes to operate." Empirical research can keep one from asking troublesome questions about the adequacy of the system of study (Rogers 1986, p. 107). For example, Lazarsfeld looked at audience effects of the mass media but not at the media institutions that produced the messages.

C. Wright Mills, Lazarsfeld's younger colleague in sociology at Columbia University, had harsh words for what he called "abstracted empiricism": "As a style of social science, abstracted empiricism is not characterized by any substantive propositions or theories." There is little doubt about the particular scholar that Mills was targeting with his remarks. He stated: "It must be interesting to political scientists to examine a full-scale study of voting which contains no reference to the party machinery for 'getting out the vote'; or indeed to any political institutions. Yet that is what happens in *The Peoples Choice,* a duly accredited and celebrated study of the 1940 election in Erie County, Ohio. From the book we learn that rich, rural, and Protestant persons tend to vote Republican; people of opposite type incline toward the Democrats; and so on. But we learn little about the dynamics of American politics." Finally, C. Wright Mills criticized Lazarsfeld for the bureaucratization of social research: "One reason for the thin formality or even emptiness of these fact-cluttered studies is that they contain very little or no direct observation by those in charge of them. The 'empirical facts' are facts collected by a bureaucratically guided set of usually semi-skilled individuals. It has been forgotten that social observation requires high skill and acute sensibility; that discovery often occurs precisely when an imaginative mind sets itself down in the middle of social realities" (Mills 1959, pp. 52–53, 55, 70).*

Paul F. Lazarsfeld was an academic entrepreneur spanning the boundary between the university's scholarly focus on theory and research versus the applied interests of government and private industry. This entrepreneurial role was worrisome to many U.S. sociologists, who placed a high value on keeping academic sociology well removed from applications to help solve practical problems. Lazarsfeld violated these norms by involving sociology in direct applications. Perhaps the dubious attitude of the sociological establishment toward him is indicated by the fact that he was not elected president of the American Sociological Association until his third try.† Once in office, he had the audacity to select "Applied Sociology" as the theme for the ASA's 1962 convention. In the face of strong objections from the other officers of the association, Lazarsfeld changed the conference theme to "The Uses of Sociology." The session chairs of the conference generally ignored the official theme in any event and scheduled theoretical papers as usual. But Lazarsfeld persevered with the applied theme and eventually published a book based on the conference's proceedings, *The Uses of Sociology* (Lazarsfeld, Sewell, and Wilensky 1967).

One of Lazarsfeld's academic colleagues, Bernard Berelson (Morrison 1988), discussed the keep-sociology-pure criticism of Lazarsfeld: "Well, the academics didn't really trust him. He was . . . too pushy, he was foreign, he was too bright, he was too self-confident, arrogant—sometimes to them—and too tied-in with the business and commercial world." The causes of the hostility toward Lazarsfeld are explained by James S. Coleman (1982, p. 1): "Paul Lazarsfeld was one of those rare sociologists who shaped the direction of the discipline for the succeeding generation. . . . Had it not been for Lazarsfeld, they [many sociologists] might have been pursuing quite different directions in sociology, and pursuing them in a different manner. Here, too, is the key to the hostility that some sociologists felt toward him (in particular, those sociologists engaged in scholarly, nonempirical, social philosophy in the

---

*Indeed, when Mills was directing the Decatur study in 1945, Lazarsfeld came only as far as Chicago for their meetings about the fieldwork, rather than traveling the last 150 miles to Decatur (Lazarsfeld 1962b, p. 354).

†Lazarsfeld ran for president of the American Sociological Association for three successive years. In 1958, he lost to Howard Becker; in 1959, he lost to Robert E. L. Faris; in 1960, he defeated Thorsten Sellin.

European tradition). They saw a discipline being captured, taken away from them, moved in directions they neither liked nor had the skills to pursue." Coleman (1980b, p. 164) criticized Lazarsfeld's influence on sociology for focusing on the analysis of individual action without considering sociological factors at a more macro (and social) level of analysis that indicated social structure.

Perhaps one of Lazarsfeld's most important roles was that of serving as a bridge between Europe and America. In his memoir, Lazarsfeld (1969a, pp. 270–271) stated: "When my academic career began, the social sciences in Europe were dominated by philosophical and speculative minds. . . . At the same time in the United States behaviorism and operationalism dominated the intellectual climate. . . . In this situation I became a connecting cog. A European 'positivist' was a curiosity welcomed by men aware of the subtler trends in the American social sciences."

James S. Coleman (1980a) has identified the decline of the Chicago school and the rise of Columbia at the center of American sociology due in part to changes in U.S. society, from studying local social problems resulting from European immigration to an interest in such national problems as the effects of mass media communication. Just as Chicago was situated at the intersection of urban social problems, so were Lazarsfeld and his Bureau located perfectly, just a few blocks uptown from Madison Avenue, for investigating the problems and issues raised by national media, the advertising industry, and the market research agencies that served both radio and advertising.

This phase change in the center of American sociology was paralleled by another shift: "From research which was unfunded or funded by socially concerned philanthropists, to research which was funded by interested parties" (Coleman 1980a). The interested parties in the case of Lazarsfeld's research were the mass communication industry, the corporations concerned with advertising and with marketing consumer products to the public, labor unions, and the U.S. government. "This change from unfunded research, or 'disinterested' funding, to financing of research parties is one which has never since been reversed, although there has been a change in the interested parties" (Coleman 1980a). Over the past several decades, government funding of social science research has been of growing importance.

Columbia's academic dominance eventually came to an end also, "with 1960 as perhaps the beginning of the end" (Coleman 1980a). Like the Chicago school, Columbia had its brief era of a few decades at center stage of American sociology. Then the field moved on, leaving Columbia sociology as just another of the several outstanding departments in the United States.

The Effects Orientation of Communication Research

More than any other individual, Paul F. Lazarsfeld directed communication research toward the study of effects. The effects orientation has a cost in paths not taken. Other important research issues were not studied or received scant attention; for example, questions of ownership and control of the mass media generally were ignored, as critical scholars point out. The macro-level issues involving the context of communication were shortchanged by the heavy emphasis on studying micro-level effects. The telephone's two-way, interactive effects could not be studied adequately with a one-way effects paradigm, so communication scholars ignored investigating them, concentrating instead on the one-way media: television, radio, and newspapers. The reason for this focus is that the field of communication got underway when the main media of study were one-way (film, radio, and television) and with effects, especially on children, that were a matter of widespread public concern. A theoretical paradigm, Claude E. Shannon's information theory (Shannon and Weaver 1949), and a set of methodological tools for examining cross-sectional data, developed particularly by Paul F. Lazarsfeld, became available at about this time, leading to the heavy focus on communication effects in communication research, especially in America.

The telephone and other two-way media, such as the telegraph and personal letters, represent research paths not taken by communication scholars. The telephone's effects were neglected as this medium expanded worldwide from 41 million telephones in 1945 to 494 million in 1982, an increase of 1,200 percent. The effects paradigm of communication scholars did not fit with the investigation of such an interactive medium. Further, study of the telephone was shortchanged because it was already widely diffused among U.S. households before communication study began. Moreover, examination of the telephone's diffusion and social impacts was made more difficult by the fact that such studies could begin only after the time at which almost all U.S. households had telephones. Finally, the telephone is a demassified channel, and any particular kind of content can be communicated through it. This fact poses serious problems for the usual approach to studying media effects, which depend on a standard content such as a film or a television program viewed by everyone in the exposed audience.

The early mass communication research by Lazarsfeld led to a minimal effects conclusion (that the media seldom had strong effects), which set off a search for alternative research approaches, like agenda-setting research. Essentially, this shift in perspective meant that communication researchers began to look for indirect effects (such as the effects of effects) rather than for direct effects only.

Lazarsfeld and Merton first came together on November 23, 1941, with important consequences for communication research. Fifty years later, on November 23, 1991, with some friends, I returned to the Russian Tea Room in New York. It is still decorated in red silk, with an old-style European air. One could easily imagine Lazarsfeld, Merton, and their wives sitting at the next table, talking about focused group interviewing, the Program-Analyzer, and Lazarsfeld's radio research institute. Maybe that was the night that communication effects research was born.

CHAPTER 8

KURT LEWIN AND GROUP DYNAMICS

The group dynamics movement that became the cutting
edge of the discipline [social psychology] in the decade following World War II was an apt response to the external
needs [caused by the war]. Most of the excitement emanated
from researchers associated with Kurt Lewin.
—William J. McGuire, "The Vicissitudes of Attitudes
and Similar Representational Constructs
in Twentieth Century Psychology"

Kurt Lewin (1890–1947) was a famous experimental psychologist at the
University of Berlin who fled as a refugee from Hitler's regime, became
a social psychologist in America, and pioneered classic experiments in
group communication. Like several other key figures in the history of
communication theory, he encountered a midlife disruption that led
him toward communication study. As in the case of Paul F. Lazarsfeld,
Lewin's crisis was caused by Hitler's fascism, which led to his exile in
America, shifting him from a more individualistic psychology to the social psychology of small-group communication. "If I were required to
name the one person who has had the greatest impact upon the field [of
social psychology], it would have to be Adolf Hitler" (Cartwright 1979).
Psychology was largely an American enterprise in its early decades of
development, but émigré European scholars in the 1930s gave social
psychology in the United States a strong German accent.

I thank Dorwin Cartwright, Miriam Lewin, and Sheila T. Murphy for their helpful comments on drafts of this chapter.

316

Figure 8.1. Kurt Lewin (1890–1947) at the University of Iowa.
Used with permission of Miriam Lewin.

Lewin is noted for founding research and training in group dynamics and for establishing the participative management style in organizations. He did not see himself as studying communication processes, although his research contributed directly to the emerging field of communication study, helping to put the group into communication theory and research.

THE LIFE AND TIMES OF KURT LEWIN

Lewin was born in Mogilno, East Prussia (in today's Poland), on September 9, 1890. His parents were poor Jewish farmers who also operated a small dry goods store. Prejudice was very strong in Germany at that time, and, in Mogilno, anti-Semitism was especially strong. In order to obtain a better education for their children, Lewin's family moved to Berlin, but the family continued to experience anti-Semitism. This prejudice was to have an influence on Lewin's scholarly interests later in his career.

Lewin earned a Ph.D. degree in psychology in 1914 at the Royal Friedrich-Wilhelms University of Berlin, at the time one of the top German universities. He was influenced in his psychological theorizing by his prior study of medicine, mathematics, and, especially, physics. Lewin was also directly influenced by his professor of philosophy, Ernst Cassirer, who inspired Lewin's lasting interest in the philosophy of science. The Psychological Institute at the University of Berlin was led by Wilhelm Stumpf, a proponent of the experimental approach, and the institute was noted at the time as the center for Gestalt psychology. Gestaltism had been founded and then flourished there between 1894 and 1921. Gestalt psychology investigates the subjective processes of an individual's immediate experience; it deals in wholes, in how an individual's perceived environment influences the individual's behavior.* The Gestaltists concentrated on "qualities in the whole that are absent in the individual parts of which the whole is composed" (Sahakian 1974, p. 295). Gestalt psychology centers on how the way in which an object is perceived is influenced by the total context in which the object is embedded (Hall and Lindzey 1957, p. 206). For example, individuals prefer the symmetry of geometric shapes, which often leads them to complete broken circles. Similarly, we tend to fill in a partial lack of information about an individual so as to form an overall impression.

Wolfgang Köhler (1887–1967), who followed Stumpf as director of the Institute of Psychology, was the founder of Gestalt psychology, along with Max Wertheimer (1880–1943) and Kurt Koffka (1886–1941). Gestalt psychology was experimental in its methodology but represented a turning away from the Wilhelm Wundt tradition of psychological research that had been underway for twenty-five years at Leipzig. The Berlin Gestaltists focused on studying problems of individual perception and learning. Although Lewin earned his doctorate at the University of Berlin and taught there after World War I, where he was a colleague with Köhler and Wertheimer, he was not a strict Gestaltist. His work was "Gestalt-like in orientation, but it centers on needs, personality, and social factors, whereas the Gestaltists emphasized perception and learning" (Schultz 1975, p. 285). Lewin was mainly interested

---

*Gestalt psychology directly influenced the balance theory of Fritz Heider (1946), Leon Festinger's (1957) cognitive dissonance, and Charles E. Osgood and Percy H. Tannenbaum's (1955) congruity principle.

in forces leading to individual action. The rise of Hitler in 1933 eventually broke up the Gestalt school at Berlin, and its key figures migrated to America.*

Although Lewin had taken fourteen courses from Professor Stumpf, the custom precluded him from speaking directly to Stumpf about his Ph.D. research. Instead, an assistant took Lewin's dissertation proposal to Stumpf and later relayed Stumpf's acceptance of the proposal to Lewin, who was waiting anxiously outside his professor's office. For the next four years, Lewin carried out his experiments without further contact with Stumpf, until the occasion of his doctoral examination. Such were the norms of German university culture concerning student-professor contact—norms that Lewin later rejected totally during his career as a professor. Lewin was a natural democrat, completely free of status consciousness, quite unlike the stereotype of the German professor. He told his students in both Berlin and America, to call him "Kurt." He often invited his doctoral students to his home for dinner and thought nothing of dropping in at their homes unannounced. He was extremely humble and refused to be drawn into acrimonious debates about his field theory with Clark Hull and his followers. Instead, Lewin encouraged friendly discussions of his differences with other viewpoints in psychology.

Following his doctorate at the University of Berlin, Lewin enlisted in 1914 as a private in the German Army and, after four years of fighting in World War I, left as a lieutenant decorated with the Iron Cross. During the war, Lewin was wounded and hospitalized. He used this period to write an article, "The War Landscape," published in 1917. He noted that "peace things" were perceived differently from "war things." For example, Lewin had noticed that a farmer's barn located in no man's land has quite a different meaning from a similar barn in a peaceful landscape. While in the military hospital, Lewin also began writing his *Habilitation* thesis, for the advanced degree in Germany that is past the Ph.D. and is required to qualify as a professor.

Lewin began teaching in 1921 at the Psychological Institute at the University of Berlin as an untenured faculty member. He began establishing his scholarly reputation through a series of important experiments carried out by his doctoral students. The first seven were female and came from Russia. He was wonderfully capable in attracting young

*Köhler migrated to the United States in 1935 and taught at Swarthmore College until 1958. Max Wertheimer migrated to the New School for Social Research in New York, and Kurt Koffka moved to Smith College in Northampton, Massachusetts.

scholars to psychological research. During the 1920s, Lewin began to formalize his field theory (also called group dynamics and topological psychology by Lewin) which later made him famous on both sides of the Atlantic. "By 1930 Lewin was a world figure in psychology" (Wolf 1973). He published forty articles in German before he came to the United States and about sixty publications after migrating (Stivers and Wheelan 1986).

FIELD THEORY

The general point of field theory is to study the individual in his or her "field," since events are determined by forces in an individual's immediate surroundings. This field, also called a lifespace, is the personal environment of the individual's activities, or the social situation around the individual. Field theory is very general; it is a kind of metatheory about theory-building. Yet it is more than an approach to theory; it is also an integrated set of concepts and the theoretical relationships among them. Lewin borrowed the methods of representing his field theory from physics (where one speaks of a "field of magnetic force," for example), although he did not lift concepts and their theoretical relationships wholesale from physics and apply them directly to psychology (Hall and Lindzey 1957, p. 206). Instead, he took concepts from physics and gave them a special meaning for psychology. For example, he defined a valence as the tension—a motivation or need—in an individual at a point in time (something like Freudian wishes). A vector was a force pushing or pulling an individual toward a negative or positive perception of an object. A barrier prevented an individual from fulfilling a wish (that is, from releasing a tension). These concepts—valence, vector, and barrier—illustrate how Lewin was influenced by physics in general and by topology in particular. Topological analysis fit with his "blackboard psychology" (Schultz 1975, p. 285).

One impact of Lewin and field theory on American psychology in the 1930s was to put subjectivism back into it (White 1992). Both Edward C. Tolman and Lewin offered a cognitive-type alternative to Clark Hull's behaviorism, which centered on S-R learning and was based on Freudian theory (White 1943). Tolman, "the cognitivist for experimental psychology," and Lewin, "the cognitivist for social psychology," pioneered the cognitive approach to psychology, which holds a central position in the field of psychology today (Zajonc 1992). In this sense, Lewin was closely related in his theoretical position to communication, for "cognation is both a product and an origin of communication. What is in your mind is the product of received communication, and what you tell others is taken from the contents of that same mind—contents that have undergone transformations and interacted with each other" (Zajonc 1992). It was this close correspondence between the cognitive emphasis of field theory and human communication processes that led to Lewin's elevation as a forefather of communication study.

Lewin followed a phenomenological approach in his field theory research, combining the humanistic with the scientific. For example, he personally debriefed each of his respondents after an experiment in order to understand their perceptions of their behavior. He had little use for statistical tests of significance because he worried that the individual case would get lost in the aggregation inherent in statistical analysis. However, he did not discourage his doctoral students from taking courses in statistical methods. At both Iowa and MIT, these courses were taught by Leon Festinger, Lewin's star protégé.

As part of his Americanization, Lewin shifted from philosophical and fundamental concerns in psychology toward more applied problems (Heims 1991, p. 223). "Nothing," he said, "is as practical as a good theory." The main biography of Kurt Lewin is titled *The Practical Theorist* (Marrow 1969). Lewin was interested in application, an activity that eventually required much of his time. Many other psychologists of his day resisted this orientation, but Lewin believed that applying a theory is one way to test its validity. Nevertheless, his research was clearly driven by theory, not data. His work was both practical and theoretical.

LEWIN'S BERLIN RESEARCH

Lewin was close to his doctoral students in Berlin, a teaching style uncommon in German universities at that time. Every Sunday morning at ten, he gathered his institute graduate students at the Schwedisches Café across the Schlossplatz from the Psychological Institute in Berlin for what he jokingly called their weekly *Quasselstrippe* (roughly translated as "chatter line"). He used these group discussions to advance his theory and research.

Lewin's most noted experiment during his Berlin era began during one of the regular *Quasselstrippe* meetings:

> As is the custom in European cafes, you have a cup of coffee and talk and chat, then you order a piece of cake, more time goes by, some more cake,

another cup of coffee, a process that may go on for two or three hours. On one such occasion, somebody called for the bill and the waiter knew just what everyone had ordered. Although he hadn't kept a written reckoning, he presented an exact tally to every person when the bill was called for. About a half hour later Lewin called the waiter over and asked him to write the check again. The waiter was indignant. "I don't know any longer what you people ordered," he said, "You paid your bill" (Morrow 1969, p. 27).

Lewin used field theory to explain this event in the Schwedische Café. He reasoned that the intention to carry out a specific task builds a psychological tension, which is released when the intended task is completed. If the task is interrupted, the tension is not discharged, and the uncompleted activity will be remembered longer than a completed task. The point is similar to Freud's statement that wishes persist until they are satisfied. Slips of the tongue, dreams, and similar behavior are outcroppings of an individual system seeking to discharge tension (Morrow 1969, p. 42).

Bluma Zeigarnik, a Russian doctoral student at Lewin's institute, designed a laboratory experiment to test the theory of interrupted tasks and tension reduction. She hypothesized a stronger recall of interrupted tasks. Her respondents, 164 children and adults, were each assigned twenty-two tasks to complete—among them, making a list of cities, drawing one's monogram, stringing beads, solving riddles, and counting backward from 55. Each individual was allowed to complete half of the tasks; the other half of the tasks, randomly determined, were interrupted before completion. Immediately afterward, each individual was asked to recall as many of the tasks as possible. The uncompleted tasks were recalled about twice as often as were the completed tasks: 90 percent of the interrupted tasks were remembered but only 45 percent of the completed tasks. Zeigarnik's research (Zeigarnik 1927) gained prominent attention from experimental psychologists worldwide (it should be remembered that Germany was then the international center for the discipline of psychology), and the stronger recall of interrupted tasks is called the Zeigarnik effect. This study helped to make Lewin well known among psychologists because the findings demonstrated the existence of psychic tensions, fundamental to Lewin's field theory. This experiment was also one of the first attempts to measure an intention or will. This experiment illustrates how Lewin was a master at transposing an everyday problem into a psychological experiment. The

Zeigarnik effect, which began with Lewin's acute observation in the Schwedisches Café, took him a long way.

COMING TO AMERICA

In 1929, Lewin* was invited to travel from Berlin to the International Congress of Psychology, held at Yale University. Today the black-and-white group photograph of the conference participants, shows surprisingly few attendants—only sixty or seventy individuals. Contrast this modest group with the tens of thousands of psychologists who attend an American Psychological Association conference today. But many of the famed psychologists of the day—Pavlov, Piaget, Clark Hull—were at the New Haven meeting. Lewin's talk, "The Effect of Environmental Forces," was difficult for the audience to follow. It was presented in German and based on field theory, with which they were then unfamiliar, but they were tremendously impressed by the short film that Lewin narrated of a small, blond German child, Hanna, who was trying to sit on a large rock while keeping eye contact with it.[†] While backing up to the rock, she missed it several times, falling to the ground. Finally she circled the rock several times. Then she looked backward between her legs, backed carefully against the rock, and sat down. Success. Lewin's narration of the film illustrated his field theory. The film "made an enormous impression" (Patnoe 1988, p. 3). One psychologist who was particularly impressed was Lewis Terman, chair of the Department of Psychology at Stanford University. In 1932, Terman invited Lewin to lecture for six months at Stanford.[‡]

Hitler came to power in 1933 as Lewin was returning from Stanford to Germany.[**] Lewin resigned from the Psychological Institute in Ber-

---

[*]In America his name is pronounced both "Luh-veén'" (the German pronunciation), and "Léw'-in," (the American pronunciation).

[†]Little Hanna was the eighteen-month-old niece of Kurt Lewin's wife. A copy of the film can be viewed at the Archives for the History of Psychology, University of Akron. Lewin was innovative among psychologists of his day in making films of his experiments as a means of recording one type of datum and as a means of illustrating his findings.

[‡]At Stanford, Lewin taught a psychology doctoral student named Angus Campbell, who was later to play a key role in finding in academic home at the University of Michigan for Lewin's Research Center for Group Dynamics after his death in 1947.

[**]Lewin decided to leave Germany while in Moscow—a stopover on his way home to Berlin from Stanford University. On April 30, 1933, upon hearing of Hitler's rise to power in

lin and migrated to the United States. He was relatively early to emigrate compared to other Jewish scholars in Germany, because he had extensive contacts with U.S. professors and other individuals outside of Germany. His move to America had a strong impact on his scholarly work, converting him from his earlier specialty of perception and learning psychology to become a social psychologist interested in prejudice, authoritarian leadership, and group influence.* Lewin's experiences with anti-Semitism in Berlin had a lasting effect on his scholarly interests. Ringing in his memories were the shouts of *"Juden heraus! Juden heraus!"* ("Jews out! Jews out!") that he heard on the streets of Berlin in the early 1930s (Marrow 1969).

After Lewin came to America, he became centrally interested in group influences on individual behavior. "Membership in a group," he stated, "is part of the 'ground' upon which a person stands" (M. Lewin 1976, p. 128). Lewin believed that identification with a group provides an individual with a point of view, a perspective, and a self-meaning. When an individual receives information through a communication process, the meaning of the message is determined, in part, by the group to which the person belongs.

Lewin was especially interested in the phenomena of self-hatred among Jews, and he wrote an important article on this topic in 1941, arguing that members of minority groups are often subject to self-hatred (Lewin 1948, p. 186). One of his examples concerned a summer camp for Jewish children that employed only non-Jewish counselors, held Christian services, and had no Jewish activities. What was the source of such evident self-hatred? Lewin (1941) explained that ordinarily a person will leave a group whose negative aspects outweigh the positive attractions, but no member of a minority group is allowed to leave it because of the greater power of the majority group. Thus, a Jew who converts is still considered a Jew by others. For instance, individuals living in Germany who had Jewish ancestry but were not practicing Judaism and did not consider themselves Jewish were still so classified by the Nazis and sent to concentration camps. The individual no longer

---

Germany, Lewin cabled Fritz Heider in the Boston area: "Gertilaz [a code name for Germany] impossible. Stop. Are possibilities there? Wire question to Boring, Lashley, Tolman, Ogdea, MacDougall. Staying till May 6th with Vygotski, Serpuchouska 17/1. Lewin."

*Lewin's mother died in a Nazi concentration camp while he was in the United States. She moved from Germany to the Netherlands, and Lewin tried to arrange a visa for her to migrate to Cuba. But his efforts were stalled, the Germans invaded the Netherlands, and his mother was shipped to a concentration camp in Poland.

practicing Judaism will move as far as possible from conventional Jewish behavior but will nevertheless feel frustrated by still being classified by others as Jewish, a situation that leads to aggression. The majority group is too powerful to attack, so the individual turns against his or her own minority group and himself or herself. The result, Lewin argued, is self-hatred among Jews and other minority groups.

The crisis represented by Lewin's migration to America led him to become more and more of a social psychologist and less and less of an individual learning-and-perception psychologist, a midlife change that led him to investigate human communication problems, although communication did not then exist as an academic field. During his nine years at Iowa, Lewin became interested in group psychology, especially through the influence of one of his doctoral students, Ronald Lippitt, who came to Iowa with a bachelor's degree in group work (Patnoe 1988, p. 31) and with a background as a Boy Scout executive. As the results of the group leadership experiment on autocratic, democratic, and laissez-faire leaders that Lewin conducted with Lippitt attracted tremendous public and scholarly attention, Lewin became increasingly a social psychologist in his own mind and was so defined by others (White 1992).

Although Kurt Lewin was one of the main fathers of social psychology, the field had been developing for many years before he became involved in it. Gordon Allport, Muzafer Sherif, Theodore Newcomb, and Daniel Katz, among others, had done, and were doing, important research. But Lewin brought new ingredients to social psychology and chose socially significant problems to investigate, many of them related to real-world events and processes. He tried "to create in the laboratory, powerful social situations that made big differences" (Festinger 1980, p. 239). One sign of Lewin's lasting influence on social psychology in the United States is the field's continuing interest in prejudice.

Lewin's Marginal University Status

Despite his eminence as a leading German psychologist in Berlin and his important role in fathering the field of social psychology in America, "Kurt Lewin never held a tenured academic appointment in any university" (Patnoe 1988, p. 4). At the Psychological Institute in Berlin, he was an untenured faculty member from 1921 to 1933. In order for a scholar to be eligible to be promoted to a professorial position in the German university system, the individual must conduct a major research past

the Ph.D. dissertation and defend it. Lewin passed his *Habilitation* examination in 1921 and in 1927 was promoted to the academic rank of
Ausserordentlicher nicht beamteter Professor (associate professor without
civil service rank and tenure). This honorary rank was as high as most
Jews could go in the German system of that time (Marrow 1969, p. 54).

On his arrival in America in 1933, the only position that Lewin could
obtain immediately was a temporary two-year appointment in the
School of Home Economics at Cornell University, supported by a grant
from the Laura Spelman Rockefeller Memorial and from the Emergency
Committee in Aid of Displaced Foreign Scholars. At Cornell, he conducted research in the university's nursery school on the influence of
social pressures on the eating habits of young children, exploring the
practical problem of why many "terrible twos" refuse to eat.

Teaching home economics at Cornell was a long way down for the
famous German psychologist from the University of Berlin, but the
Great Depression was underway and academic jobs were extremely
scarce. Lewin secured the position at Cornell through some lucky
breaks. Dr. Ethel B. Waring, a child development professor at Cornell,
had once visited Lewin in Berlin for two weeks and returned with copies
of films that he had taken of his experiments. Robert M. Ogden, dean of
the College of Arts and Sciences at Cornell, had also met Lewin in Berlin. Cornell University president Livingston Farrand was the chairperson of the executive committee of the Emergency Committee in Aid of
Displaced Foreign Scholars. Half of Lewin's $2,000 per year salary was
guaranteed by the Emergency Committee,* and the other half came
from the Laura Spelman Rockefeller Memorial, which had previously
been funding child development research at Cornell. This research
grants program of the memorial was managed by Dr. Lawrence K.
Frank, who also was impressed by Lewin when he met him on a 1928
trip to Berlin (Ash, 1992).

Lewin held his position at Cornell for just two years. During the
second year, in January 1935, Frank invited both Lewin and George
Stoddard, director of the Iowa Child Welfare Research Station of the
University of Iowa, to a small conference on Gestalt psychology at
Princeton University, where "Lewin clearly made a strong impression
on Stoddard" (Ash 1992). Within a month, Stoddard began the process

---

*When Farrand circulated a memo to the Cornell faculty, asking for expressions of inter-
est in various European refugee scholars, Waring was the only professor to speak out for
Lewin (Waring 1964).

of recruiting Lewin to Iowa, with the assistance of Frank. For several years, the Laura Spelman Rockefeller Memorial had been funding Stoddard's Iowa Child Welfare Research Station at $90,000 per year, two or three times the budgetary contribution of the University of Iowa, so it was a relatively easy matter for Frank to designate part of this funding for Lewin's salary and that of his three research assistants (Ash 1992). The grant from Frank for Lewin's work at Iowa was for a three-year period and was renewable.*

In 1935, Lewin, now forty-five years old, accepted the faculty position at the Iowa Child Welfare Research Station. The Iowa Child Welfare Research Station consisted of seven or eight faculty-level individuals (several of whom were part-time), plus research assistants, secretaries, and other staff, with offices located in the basement of the education building on the university campus. Despite its seemingly humble nature, the Iowa Child Welfare Research Station was the model for other institutes of child development research around the United States, also funded by the Laura Spelman Rockefeller Memorial. The atmosphere "at Iowa was in some ways tense for Lewin" (Patnoe 1988, p. 33). He was appointed to the Child Welfare Research Station, not the Psychology Department, and was sponsored by the director of the Child Welfare Research Station, George Stoddard, who was also the dean of the graduate school at Iowa. The Psychology Department was soon to be chaired by Kenneth Spence, a behaviorist co-worker of Clark Hull at Yale University and a strong opponent of Lewin's field theory approach. Academic controversy was soon to erupt between Spence and Lewin.

After leaving Iowa in 1945, for three years until his death in 1947, Lewin was a faculty member at MIT, where he headed the Research Center for Group Dynamics, within the Department of Economics and Social Sciences. By this time, he was very famous in America but still did not have tenure. Did his marginal academic positions affect the direction of his scholarly work? His dependence on soft money meant that he had to spend part of his time seeking research funds from outside the university, and during his final years at MIT, he was gone from campus most of the time (Patnoe 1988). The research funds usually came with strings attached, such as the expectation that solutions to a practical problem would be found in the research. This soft money dependence may be one reason why Lewin was oriented to solving social problems,

---

*Frank provided the funding for Lewin at Iowa in part to discourage him from joining the faculty at Hebrew University, in Jerusalem (Heims 1991, p. 196).

particularly at Iowa and MIT. Applied research paid its own way, as Paul F. Lazarsfeld found out at the Columbia University Bureau of Applied Social Research. But most psychologists feared that applied research would distract them from basic research on scholarly problems. Lewin, however, claimed that applied research could be conducted with rigor and that one could test theoretical propositions in applied studies. In essence, Lewin held that the dichotomy between basic research and applied research that might be valid in physics and chemistry need not exist in the social sciences.

Lewin attracted the very best young social psychologists to his doctoral training program, at both Iowa and MIT. Clearly the applied nature of his research did not drive away talented graduate students. However, his focus on action research did not earn him the respect that he felt he deserved from the field of U.S. psychology. "Lewin was outside the main stream of psychology, and seemed to be kept in the periphery by the psychology 'establishment'" (Wolf 1973). This lack of respect from academics traced to Lewin's interest in practical applications, which, along with the complexity of his field theory, put off some psychologists. Lewin's theoretical perspective was puzzling to some scholars because of the vectors, arrows, and other visualizations that he utilized (White 1992).

Authoritarian, Democratic, and Laissez-Faire Leadership

Lewin was not particularly concerned about the ownership of academic ideas, and indeed it was difficult to identify exactly who came up with certain conceptualizations since much of the research planning took place in group discussions. An example is Lewin's famous experiment on leadership styles. This project began when Ron Lippitt, a new doctoral student, arrived at the Iowa Child Welfare Research Station in 1936 and was assigned to Professor Lewin. Lippitt had majored in group work as an undergraduate, and Lewin began a discussion with him about German and American differences in leadership styles, with the German style being more autocratic and the American more democratic. With Lewin's encouragement, Lippitt did his master's thesis research comparing the effects of leadership style on the performance of two groups of boys. Their task was to construct theatrical masks out of papier-mâché and other materials. The boys in the group with a democratic leader outperformed the boys in the group with an autocratic leader, a research finding that fit with American values on democracy.

The results of this first experiment were promising, and Lewin encouraged Lippitt to redesign and expand the experiment for his doctoral dissertation. The study of experimentally created group climates was conducted by Lippitt and a newly arrived postdoctoral fellow, Ralph K. White, recruited by Roger Barker as his replacement in the postdoctoral fellowship at Iowa.* Barker and White had known each other at Stanford University, when both were studying for their Ph.D. degrees. White then taught for three years at Wesleyan University near Boston before coming to Iowa City. He had read Lewin's book, *The Dynamics of Personality,* and had heard Lewin lecture at Yale in 1935, but he did not know about the leadership experiment that was underway until he arrived at Iowa in 1937 (White 1992).

Two experiments were conducted, both with groups of five eleven-year-old boys in Iowa City. In the first study, Experiment I, carried out in 1938, four boys' clubs each met eleven times over three weeks in order to make theatrical masks. They were supplied with all of the materials (like papier-mâché, glue, paint, and tools) they would need and had a group leader (Lippitt and White played the roles of group leader). Two of the boys' clubs worked in a democratic way: the adult leader consulted with the boys and frequently asked their opinions. The adult leader in the other two clubs acted in an autocratic way, giving orders and demanding that they be followed.

The experiment was carried out in the spacious, otherwise empty attic of the education building at the University of Iowa. A special room about fifteen feet by twenty feet was created with partitions made of chicken wire, covered with burlap cloth. In a darkened area, but in sight of the two groups of boys, were a movie camera, six observers, and four stenographers[†] who kept a complete record of the interaction. Three observers for each group recorded various dimensions of the boys' behavior. (Two groups of boys met at the same time in the room but were separated by a bench on which the tools and construction materials were placed.)

---

*The resulting study was reported by Lewin and Lippitt (1938); Lewin, Lippitt, and White (1939); and White and Lippitt (1980).

[†]One of the stenographers was Joan Kalhorn Lasko, an undergraduate psychology major who got the job because she knew shorthand. When the experiment was completed, Lewin asked her to help analyze the data. Next she became Lewin's part-time secretary and eventually earned a master's degree at Iowa and then a Ph.D. in psychology at Ohio State. Lasko was another one of the many individuals whose career was affected by the magic touch of Kurt Lewin (Lasko 1991).

The boys in the authoritarian group were found to be unhappy and less productive than the boys in the democratic groups, who were friendlier with each other and showed more group spirit. The boys in the autocratic groups became restless and aggressive and fought among themselves. Their level of hostility and scapegoating was about thirty times higher than in the groups with the democratic leader. The boys functioned as individuals, without much concern for the group's goals or for the interests of other group members.

Experiment I was flawed in a number of important ways—the sample size was very small, with only two groups in each experimental condition, and the boys were not randomly assigned to one or the other of the two leadership conditions—the article reporting the research results would not be accepted for publication in a social psychology journal today. Yet the study received much fame, becoming a social science classic. Undoubtedly the main reason is that it dealt with such a socially significant topic. By 1938–1939, Adolf Hitler was overrunning Austria, Czechoslovakia, and Poland. Investigating the impacts of democratic and authoritarian leadership was an ideological coup.

The following year, 1939, Experiment II was designed to avoid certain of the methodological problems of the previous research. Again, four boys' clubs were studied.* each with a leader. Each club had one of three types of leadership: authoritarian, democratic, or laissez-faire. This third condition was created inadvertently when Ralph White played a democratic leader role in a do-nothing, hands-off style, and Lewin decided to incorporate this third type of leadership into the experiment. Lippitt recalls: "Ralph [White], who had drawn the role of democratic leader in the first time period, behaved in a way that was quite different from the other democratic-leader roles as we had defined them. He was obviously getting quite a different effect in terms of responses of the children. Kurt's observation of this, as he stood behind the burlap barrier and operated the movie camera, led to an excited gleam in his eye as he perceived a basic genotypic difference between the democratic pattern and what we labeled the laissez-faire pattern of leadership. So instead of correcting Ralph's style, we moved it more to-

*The twenty boys taking part in Experiment II were selected from the fifth grade of two public schools in Iowa City. The boys were asked to complete such sociometric questions, as, "What other boys would you like to have in the same club with you?" "Who would you rather not have in the same club with you?" The least-chosen boys in the two schools were not invited to participate in the experiment (White and Lippitt 1980, pp. 16–17).

ward a pure case of laissez-faire pattern" (Marrow 1969, p. 124). In fact, adding the third (laissez-faire) leadership style as an experimental condition helped clarify the meaning of democratic leadership and became the most important aspect of the study (White 1992).

Autocratic leadership was defined as "a high degree of control by the leader without much freedom by the members or participation by them in group decisions." The democratic and the laissez-faire leaders had a low degree of control but differed in that the democratic leader was "very active in stimulating group discussion and group decisions," while the laissez-faire leader played "a passive, hands-off role." A manipulation check by the experimenters showed that the three types of group leaders indeed carried out with the boys the type of leadership they were assigned to perform. The autocratic leaders, as scored by the group observers, gave orders in 45 percent of their remarks: "Get your work aprons on," "Vinnie, help Ben," and "All right, put your brush away," for example. In contrast, the democratic leaders gave orders only 3 percent of the time and the laissez-faire leaders 4 percent (White and Lippitt 1980, pp. 12, 31–33).

Experiment II had several ingenious manipulations, in addition to the main treatment of type of leadership. For instance, while the experiment was in progress, the adult leader of each group was called outside the room, and a graduate student unknown to the boys entered their meeting dressed as a janitor in order to replace a light bulb or to sweep the floor. He would then criticize the theatrical masks being made by some of the boys or by the whole group. This disguised procedure measured whether the group members would form a united resistance to the stranger, take the criticism docilely, or make a scapegoat of one of their members (White and Lippitt 1980, p. 24).

Each of the four groups had one of three leadership styles for six weeks, followed by six weeks of a different style, so each boy had the experience of working in a group with two leadership styles. The results again showed that the democratic leadership groups were happiest and most productive, with the authoritarian leadership groups least so, and the laissez-faire leadership groups midway. Members of the laissez-faire groups who had previously experienced autocratic leadership were frightened and disturbed. All but one of the twenty boys in the total experiment said afterward that they preferred democratic leadership (Marrow 1969, p. 126). Viewing Lewin's film today, more than fifty years later, is an exciting experience because the effects of the three leadership styles on the boys' performance in making the theatrical masks are easily detected.* Although the black-and-white film is faded and coarse-grained, the boys with a democratic leader seem to be happy and productive, those in the laissez-faire condition seem aimless, and the boys with an autocratic leader are stifled and controlled.

The second experiment did not completely overcome all of the design flaws. For example, there were only four replications of the experimental treatment, insufficient to allow for use of statistical tests of significance, and whether an order effect occurred—for example, were the results of an authoritarian leadership style affected by whether it followed a democratic or a laissez-faire leadership style in the previous six weeks?—cannot be determined. Nevertheless, the notion of manipulating group leadership styles in an experiment was ingenious and timely, given the growing threat of military dictatorships.

Margaret Mead called the leadership study a kind of "experimental anthropology," in that Lewin and the others were creating group cultures in their laboratory. The research on democratic and authoritarian groups "finally established Lewin's reputation in America" (Ash 1992). The leadership experiment was a decisive turning point in Lewin's change from individualistic psychology to social psychology. "Of course, Lippitt played a critical role in shaping Lewin's socialization, in a sense turning him to social psychology" (Cartwright 1989). As the leadership experiment brought increasing acclaim to Lewin and as he gave talks about it raptly interested audiences, the effect was to strengthen his growing interest in studying group influences on individual behavior (White 1992).

A social scientist should obviously be objective about how he or she studies an issue, although values are certainly allowed to determine what one studies. Understandably, Lewin's treatment by Germany's dictatorial government led him to study autocratic versus democratic group leadership. But did it bias how he investigated this topic? Presumably not, although there is little doubt that he wanted the democratically led groups to outperform the autocratically led groups. As Robert R. Sears, then a colleague in the Iowa Child Welfare Research Station, said, "The autocratic way he insisted on democracy was a little spectacular. There was nothing to criticize—but one could not help noticing the fire and the emphasis" (Marrow 1969, p. 127). Just how highly Lewin valued democracy is shown by his statement:

*This film is held by the Archive for the History of Psychology, University of Akron.

Democracy. . . . It is the most precious possession we have. . . . Have you noticed the peculiar mixture of desperate hope, curiosity, and skepticism with which the newly-arrived refugee from Fascist Europe looks at the United States? . . . He hates Fascism with all he has. He is more than eager to believe in this "haven for the oppressed," to see with his own eyes a people who have the Statue of Liberty standing at the gateway of a country and "equality of men" as its law. . . . Is democracy more than an empty proclamation, is it more than a phrase for politicians? Is democracy something "real"? (White and Lippitt 1980, p. viii)

Alex Bavelas, a doctoral student at Iowa, told Lewin that even people who were quite autocratic in leading a work group could be trained to acquire a democratic leadership style. Bavelas sketched out some possibilities and used them in a pathbreaking project on participative management at a manufacturing plant in Virginia.

Field Experiments in Changing Food Habits

An important series of nutritional change experiments by Kurt Lewin and his doctoral students were conducted at the Child Welfare Research Station of the University of Iowa, funded by the Food Habits Committee of the National Research Council in Washington, D.C. The committee's executive secretary, Margaret Mead, had met Lewin at a conference of the Topological Society,* held at Bryn Mawr College in Philadelphia at Christmas in 1935 (Marrow 1969, p. 113). Lewin's nutritional studies fit with World War II efforts in America to cope with food shortages, government food rationing, and needed dietary changes in order to improve public nutrition and health. A variety of food-related field experiments were carried out by the Lewinians at Iowa, including studies of eating whole wheat bread versus white bread, increasing milk consumption, and convincing mothers to give their babies cod liver oil and orange juice as well as milk. For someone with a theoretical interest in group influences on individual behavior change, the adoption of new

---

*The Topological Society was organized by Lewin as an annual series of discussions, with the first meeting in 1933. Many famous psychologists attended these sessions, along with scholars from other fields. Harold D. Lasswell presented a paper in 1936, and Fritz Heider first presented his balance theory at the 1945 meetings. The meeting expenses of the Topological Society were provided by the Laura Spelman Rockefeller Memorial, thanks to Lawrence Frank. The final meeting was held in 1965, when those present voted to disband (Marrow 1969, p. 112). In recent years the Society for the Advance of Field Theory has been organized and meets annually, usually at Rutgers University.

food habits was an intriguing applied research problem, and in the light of World War Ii, the research topic was the patriotic thing to do.

The best known of Lewin's Iowa food studies was the so-called sweetbreads study, whose objective was to increase the consumption of beef hearts, thymus (sweetbreads), liver, and kidneys—the glandular meats—which were generally considered undesirable by most Iowa housewives, who preferred to feed their families beefsteak, pork chops, and ham. These preferred meats, however, were in scarce supply and were rationed during the war, so the U.S. government encouraged consumption of the unpopular meats, which were both nutritious and a good buy.

Lewin conducted the field experiment on sweetbreads with six Red Cross volunteer groups that had previously been organized for the study of home nursing. The group members, thirteen to seventeen housewives per group living in Cedar Rapids, located near Iowa City, were already well acquainted with each other. Three of the groups received a forty-five-minute lecture that linked the problem of nutrition with the war effort. It emphasized the vitamin and mineral value of the undesirable meats, showed their economic advantages, and explained how to prepare them. Copies of recipes for cooking the glandular meats were distributed. The lectures were given by a nutritionist who was also a housewife and who described how she had prepared delicious dishes of the undesirable meats for her family. These three groups thus received the lecture condition of Lewin's field experiment.

The other three groups received a discussion-type presentation in which the same information was presented as in the lecture condition. These three discussion groups were led by Alex Bavelas, a doctoral student at Iowa who was particularly adept at group leadership. The discussion centered on obstacles that preparing the unpopular meats might encounter, such as their smell during cooking, husbands' dislike for the meats, and so forth. At the end of the meeting, the housewives were asked to indicate by a show of hands if they were willing to prepare sweetbreads within the next week.

A follow-up survey conducted several weeks after the meetings showed that "only 3 percent of the women who heard the lectures [had] served one of the meats never served before, whereas after group decision, 32 percent [had] served one of them" (Lewin 1958, p. 202). Presumably this wide difference in the effects of the two experimental treatments was due to the higher degree of involvement in the discussion condition, where the housewives played an active role, asking questions and sharing their experiences. Undoubtedly, the public commitment represented by the housewives' raising their hands at the end of the discussion group was important in achieving the 32 percent change in food behavior. But there were obvious flaws in the design of the sweetbreads field experiment: the discussion leader was not the same person as the nutritionist-lecturer, the public commitment by hand raising was not also included in the lecture condition, and only the three discussion groups were told that a later follow-up would be conducted.* These design problems made it difficult to know which factors caused the greater behavioral change in the discussion groups than in the lecture groups.

The Lewin sweetbreads experiment became a classic study of the differences between interactive interpersonal communication (represented by the discussion condition) and one-way mass communication (approximated by the lecture condition). Lewin generalized the results of the sweetbreads study, and other researches that he was conducting at Iowa, into a three-step procedure for changing behavior: unfreezing, moving, and freezing the new behavior (Lewin 1958, p. 210). Frequently, when the behavior of an individual is changed, it soon reverts to its previous state, even though a lasting change is desired.† The influence of other group members on each individual's behavior is an important factor in changing, and maintaining, such behavior. As Lewin (1943) concluded: "The group decision had a 'freezing' effect for future action."

Gatekeeping

Gatekeepers are individuals who control the flow of messages in a channel; they may withhold information, shape it, expand it, or repeat it (Shoemaker 1991, p. 1). In the sweetbreads experiment on changing food habits, Lewin found that housewives were gatekeepers of the new foods that their families ate. If a housewife decided not to serve glandular meats, her family did not eat them. The concept of gatekeeping could be applied to a wide variety of communication situations, as Lewin (1951, p. 187) stated: "This situation holds not only for food

---

*Later experiments by the Lewinians overcame many of the design shortcomings of the sweetbreads study (Pelz 1958; Radke and Klisurich 1947).

†For example, a majority of individuals who stop smoking cigarettes in smoking-cessation training classes resume their addiction within a month or two.

channels but also for the traveling of a news item through certain communication channels in a group."

In Lewin's (1947) last article before his untimely death, he theorized about the gatekeeping process in a communication system, a promising direction for further investigation. David Manning White (1950) and other communication scholars soon were studying the role of gatekeepers in a mass media institution, such as the news wire editor of a newspaper, who controls the flow of national and international news into a local newspaper. White came to the University of Iowa in 1939 to enroll in the Iowa Writer's Workshop, then directed by Wilbur Schramm. He aspired to write novels, until Schramm convinced him that this was an unattainable goal, given his writing talent (White 1991).

White earned his Ph.D. in English literature at Iowa in 1942 and left immediately for wartime work in Washington, D.C., in the Office of War Information. After the war, while a professor of journalism at Boston University, White conducted his noteworthy study of a wire editor who was responsible for selecting the news items to be published in his newspaper from the large volume of information coming in on the teletype from three news agencies. White interviewed "Mr. Gates," as he called the wire editor, for a week in February 1949, asking him why he used or did not use each of hundreds of news stories that had come in on the wire. Only about 10 percent of the news stories were used by Mr. Gates. White (1950) asked his respondent if he had any prejudices that affected his news story selection. Gates replied: "I dislike [President] Truman's economics, daylight savings time, and warm beer. . . . I am also prejudiced against a publicity-seeking minority with headquarters in Rome, and I don't help them a lot. As far as preferences are concerned, I go for human interest stories in a big way." White says that Wilbur Schramm, then at Illinois, gave him advice about the design of his wire editor study, but it was not until he was writing up his findings that he encountered Lewin's 1947 article about the Iowa housewives as gatekeepers (White 1991).

White's article on the wire editor's news story selection set off a series of similar studies of gatekeepers, as part of a research tradition on how mass media institutions function. For instance, Snider (1967) restudied the same wire editor, Mr. Gates, seventeen years later and again found that he selected news stores on the basis of what he himself liked and what he thought his readers would find interesting. Later studies in the gatekeeping tradition included a sample of news gatekeepers rather than just one. The criteria for new story selection are often quite different from those used by Mr. Gates. For example, a study of how a television station in Indianapolis processed 391 potential stories (including international, national, and local news) in a four-week period showed that gatekeeping decisions rested on which stories were easy to explain, which would attract viewers, and which could be edited with minimum effort (Berkowitz 1990). Gatekeeping was essentially a group (rather than an individual) process, as a story passed through one gate in the television station's newsroom and then on to another on its way to be broadcast.

Today Lewin's concept of gatekeeper is widely used by communication scholars, particularly in organizational communication research, and in other than just studies of news organizations. As Pamela Shoemaker (1991, p. 4) concluded from her recent review: "Gatekeeping may be a well-studied concept, and perhaps well-worn, but it is hardly worn out."

THE QUASSELSTRIPPE

Lewin often developed his theories by diagraming the relationships among his concepts on a blackboard. He thought best when he was drawing diagrams and even drew little pictures in his personal letters to other scholars. Lewin said that he could not think productively without talking to others (Lewin 1936). "The way he worked was by talking with other people. He would talk about his work, their work, it didn't matter. He talked with people individually or in groups; he was forever collaborating" (Patnoe 1988, p. 16).

This thinking-by-talking approach led Lewin to found a group called *Quasselstrippe* ("chatter line") at each of the universities where he taught. At the University of Berlin, the *Quasselstrippe* met in the Schwedisches Café, near the Psychological Institute. In Iowa City during the depression of the 1930s, the *Quasselstrippe* (dubbed the "Hot Air Club" by Lewin's Iowa students) gathered every Tuesday in the Round Window Restaurant for lunch (Marrow 1969, p. 89). The owner let Lewin's doctoral students bring their own brown-bag lunches if they would buy coffee or soft drinks to accompany their meal. The seven or eight participants, Lewin's inner group of protégés, sat around a long table (White 1992).* Typically, a student presented a research plan or discussed the interpretation of some research results. The *Quasselstrippe*

---

*In addition to the *Quasselstrippe*. Lewin also taught a doctoral-level seminar one night a week, which was open to anyone (White 1992).

discussions were open, with no criticism allowed, since they were intended to be helpful and to encourage research on field theory. Lewin was always there, of course, but he did not dominate. Anyone could talk, and everyone was encouraged to do so. Wilbur Schramm, who attended the *Quasselstrippe* in Iowa City, describes the experience as exciting and intense.* Although the weekly sessions were scheduled to last from noon to 2:00 P.M., sometimes the discussions went on for eight hours or more.

When Lewin and his group moved from Iowa City to MIT, they took the *Quasselstrippe* with them. At MIT the weekly sessions took place on Wednesday afternoons, with a blackboard, of course. After Lewin's death, when the Research Center for Group Dynamics moved to Ann Arbor, the Tuesday night seminars soon became quite large, and the faculty members did most of the talking, so the graduate students started their own weekly meetings. But without Kurt Lewin, the *Quasselstrippe* in Ann Arbor was not the same.

As Lewin's Ph.D. students completed their degrees and spread out to faculty positions at various universities, they created their own versions of the *Quasselstrippe*. Two Lewinians, John Thibaut at the University of North Carolina and Ned Jones at nearby Duke University, combined forces to organize a joint version of the *Quasselstrippe,* called the Organizational Research Group (Patnoe 1988, p. 57). Elliot Aronson, a great-grand-student of Kurt Lewin, helped establish a Tuesday night *Quasselstrippe* at the University of Minnesota and then took the idea with him when he moved to the University of Texas at Austin. Leon Festinger's version of Lewin's Quasselstrippe at the University of Minnesota and then at Stanford University was held weekly, usually on Tuesday evenings.

The role of the various *Quasselstrippes* shows that research is a very social process, one in which a free-flowing discussion of research plans and tentative results can be extremely fruitful. And they were fun too. Individuals kept coming back to the discussions each week and looked forward to the next meeting. Thinking out loud in front of one's scientific peers stimulates others to do the same. Such discussion is particularly useful in coping with the uncertainty of the research process, especially in the design stage and in interpreting the findings. The general

---

*Schramm's participation in the *Quasselstrippe* may have influenced his conception of how to teach doctoral students in the three programs in communication study that he launched in later years.

experience of the various *Quasselstrippes* was that reading completed research papers at the meetings was deadly dull and represented a poor use of the opportunity for an exciting discussion. Reporting completed research can also be threatening to the presenter, when faced with criticism. The *Quasselstrippe* gave Kurt Lewin a situation in which he could talk through his scholarly ideas, conveying his infectious enthusiasm to others. The discussions were direct, even though criticism was restricted. Morton Deutsch, who earned his Ph.D. with the Lewinian group at MIT, described the *Quasselstrippe* as "a very tough intellectual free-for-all" (Patnoe 1988, p. 93).

PARTICIPATIVE MANAGEMENT IN THE HARWOOD PAJAMA FACTORY

Lewin had long had an interest in what today is called business management, writing a book (in German), *The Socialization of the Taylor System*, in 1920. He critiqued Taylor's time-and-motion engineering as a basis for factory management, arguing instead for worker participation in humanizing the factory system (Ash 1992). Accordingly, he and his students at the University of Berlin conducted experiments on repetitive tasks, levels of aspiration, and other topics bearing on the monotony of assembly-line work.

Two decades later, after his move to the United States, in 1939, Lewin was presented with a unique opportunity to study participative management in a Harwood Manufacturing Corporation plant in Virginia. Alfred J. Marrow (1969, p. 141), a Lewin protégé, was a top officer of the company. Harwood had established a new pajama factory in Marion, Virginia, a mountainous area in which local people had little previous experience with factory work. The 600 employees were mainly women, who were paid on a daily piece-rate basis for cutting cloth and sewing pajamas. It was monotonous work, and the plant was characterized by low performance, poor morale, frequent absences and slowdowns of work, and a high rate of turnover. Overall, the new plant's production was only half that of pajama plants in the North (Marrow 1969, p. 141). Clearly, drastic action was called for. The Harwood Company invited Lewin to visit the new plant in Virginia, and after studying the problem, he recommended that management stop putting pressure on individual employees for higher production; Lewin had found that the employees thought the production goals were impossible to attain. He told the plant managers that they ought to deal with their workers as members of groups, not as individuals. Employees had been transferred frequently within the plant, essentially breaking up the existing work groups. With Lewin's encouragement, the Harwood plant brought in sixty experienced workers from another city, where a plant had closed. The new workers met management's production goals, and soon the other employees were inspired to increase their output. They realized that the production goals were attainable.

Lewin made numerous visits to the Harwood plant. The workers were initially suspicious of a psychology professor with a German accent, but Lewin won their confidence with his understanding of their problems and with his humor. He was baffled by the workers' southern drawls but soon began to pick up some of their expressions. For instance, Lewin learned to say, "That's snake oil," when an explanation was bogus (Marrow 1969, p. 143).

Lewin designed a series of experiments on participative management that were carried out from 1940 to 1947 under the direction of Lewin's doctoral students, particularly Alex Bavelas, who was appointed the full-time director of research of the factory. He was followed in this role by John R. P. French, another Lewinian. Bavelas held small-group meetings with high-producing employees in order to find out how they achieved their high performance. Out of these discussions came recommendations for action, which the plant managers agreed to implement. Employees were asked to set their own production goals, in the reinforcing context of a group setting. The workers in one part of the pajama factory decided to try for a goal of producing eighty-seven units, up from their seventy-five units, and to reach the goal in five days. They did so. This level had never been attained previously. Then the workers raised their goal to ninety units and maintained it for five months. Meanwhile, other groups in the plant, acting as a control, had not increased their production (Marrow 1969, p. 144).

The Harwood Company was losing market share and was forced to change the style of pajamas manufactured. Managers discussed this change with certain employees in groups but not with others, and the latter individuals' production dropped 35 percent after the change. But employees who had discussed the change continued at their previous level of performance. Participative management seemed to be a means of facilitating behavior change.

In yet another field experiment in the Harwood plant, supervisors were trained in democratic leadership by Bavelas. The training work-shops were highly participatory, with few lectures, instead featuring role playing and group discussions. The supervisors self-examined their leadership style and gave, and received, feedback about it. Later, similar training techniques were utilized in the National Training Laboratory in Group Dynamics at Bethel, Maine.

The series of field experiments in the Harwood manufacturing plant by Lewin and others showed that participative management led to in-creased productivity. Thus, Lewin became a well-known theorist among organizational scholars and among business management pro-fessors. He and Douglas McGregor, a business school professor at MIT, developed a friendship that explains why Kurt Lewin and his group moved to MIT from Iowa in 1945.

THE RESEARCH CENTER FOR GROUP DYNAMICS

Lewin was making frequent trips to Washington during the early 1940s in order to consult with the Office of Special Services (OSS, the prede-cessor agency to the CIA) about psychological warfare and propaganda in World War II. His colleagues in Iowa City criticized him for his fre-quent absences from the campus. At the same time Kenneth W. Spence (1907–1967), an avid promoter of Clark Hull–type behaviorism from Yale University, became chairperson of the Department of Psychology at Iowa, and led a critique of Lewin's brand of social psychology. As the University of Iowa became less hospitable to Lewin and his group, he began to look for another academic home.

Lewin and his followers were invited to MIT by Professor Douglas McGregor and President Carl Compton.* Accordingly, the Research Center for Group Dynamics located within the MIT Department of Eco-nomics and Social Sciences, and awarded Ph.D. degrees in group psy-chology. The fifteen to twenty doctoral students were taught by Lewin and four other faculty who moved with him from Iowa. Funding for the

---

*The invitation was arranged by Rensis Likert, who in August 1944 invited Lewin and McGregor to meet with him for dinner at the Cosmos Club in Washington, D.C. Then Mc-Gregor returned to MIT to convince President Compton. Meanwhile, Lewin was also negoti-ating with Professor Edward Tolman in the Psychology Department at the University of Cali-fornia at Berkeley, whose invitation was held up pending approval by the university's board of regents. Tolman's offer reached Lewin two days too late (Marrow 1969, p. 165), the first of two failed attempts by Berkeley to attract the Lewinians.

research center came mainly from the Marshall Field Fund, the Rocke-feller Foundation, and the American Jewish Congress*, plus university monies provided by MIT in return for the teaching that was done by Lewin and his staff. While Lewin was at MIT, he helped establish the Commission for Community Interrelations, an outgrowth of the Ameri-can Jewish Congress in New York, designed to conduct action programs to lessen prejudice at the community level. Lewin expected that his Re-search Center for Group Dynamics at MIT would conduct investigations on racial prejudice, and then the Commission for Community Interrela-tions would put the research findings into use.

Kurt Lewin and his intellectual followers were a tightly knit group. When Lewin moved from the University of Iowa to MIT in 1945, his key people went with him to become faculty members in the Research Center for Group Dynamics: Dorwin Cartwright, Leon Festinger, Mar-ion Raedke, and Ron Lippitt. All of the faculty were committed Lewinians, so they spoke with essentially one theoretical voice to their MIT doctoral students. For instance, the core readings in the first-year doctoral program at MIT were mainly authored or coauthored by Kurt Lewin. The cadre of Lewinian scholars trained at MIT (Harold Kelley, Stanley Shackter, Kurt Black, and John Thibaut, for example) were out-standing. All had successful careers in social psychology and carried for-ward Lewin's thinking to future generations of social psychologists.

The mass movement of Lewinians from Iowa City to Cambridge, Massachusetts, left nothing at the University of Iowa. When I became intrigued with Lewinian theory in 1955 (by taking a course in group dynamics at Iowa State University), I traveled to Iowa City in order to seek out what was left there from Lewin's nine years of influential teach-ing. It was all gone. Everything had moved to MIT and then, in 1948, on to the University of Michigan. Similarly, when Warren Bennis, now a professor of business management at the University of Southern Cali-fornia, arrived at MIT in 1951 to work on his Ph.D. degree, all of the Lewinians had moved out, except for Alex Bavelas, who had studied with Lewin at Iowa and then joined the faculty at MIT (but not in the Research Center for Group Dynamics). It is a highly unique situation in academe for an entire set of scholars and their doctoral students to move in a body from one university to another. The Lewinians did it twice.

---

*The American Jewish Congress was organized by U.S. Supreme Court Justice Louis Brandeis and other Jewish leaders who lobbied for U.S. support for Israel's independence.

The basic paradigm for Lewin-style group psychology research formed around the dependent variable of *cohesion*, the degree to which individual members fulfill group expectations. Thus, cohesion indicated the importance of the group to the individual (Cartwright and Zander 1953) and was utilized to explain the degree to which membership in a group can predict a group member's behavior change. Lewin and his followers studied what makes a group cohesive, such as how a group's activities must strengthen the individual's opportunities to achieve his or her own goals (Marrow 1969, p. 169).

Group cohesion often has beneficial effects, as Kurt Lewin generally assumed, but it can also lead to groupthink, "a deterioration of mental efficiency, reality testing, and moral judgment that results from in-group pressures" (Janis 1972, p. 11). An example of groupthink, analyzed by Janis, was the fiasco of the 1961 Bay of Pigs invasion of Castro's Cuba. The invasion was planned by bright, shrewd individuals like President John F. Kennedy and his White House advisers. In a tightly knit, cohesive group where solidarity is high, a kind of psychological contagion occurs, resulting, as in the case of the Bay of Pigs invasion, in a patchwork plan doomed to fail.

The Westgate Study

The Research Center for Group Dynamics was organized in six research programs, one of which dealt with communication and the spread of influence. During the three years that Lewin's group was at MIT, this research program conducted the Westgate housing study, an important communication investigation led by Leon Festinger. The Westgate project studied the communication network links among all of the married students living in the Westgate apartments at MIT in 1946 (Festinger, Schachter, and Bach 1950). Why did an experimental researcher like Festinger conduct this nonlaboratory study?

> I think if you just stay in the laboratory all the time, there is no way you are not going to get barren. Because the only thing you are going to learn out of a laboratory experiment is what you put into it. You are not going to see the effect of any variables that you didn't insert. You are not going to find out about any interactions that might be interesting because you have purified the thing so that you can see whether or not what you are looking for is there. I have always wanted to go back and forth between

laboratory studies and studies in the real world. Field studies, if you will. The field studies were not being done for a practical purpose. They were being done to clarify theory and get hunches and that kind of thing. The Westgate studies have no practical purpose. (Festinger, quoted in Patnoe 1988, p. 225)

Each of the households in Westgate was asked, "What three people in Westgate do you see most socially?" The resulting network data were superimposed over a map of the apartment units. Physical distance was one of the major determinants of whether a dyadic link occurred between any two households. About two-thirds of the 426 reported dyads were within the same apartment building, and no link connected individuals more than four buildings (180 feet) apart. Even among the within-building choices on the same floor, physical distance greatly affected who interacted with whom. More than half (60 percent) of the choices in Westgate were to the nearest neighbor, whose door was only twenty-two feet away. Festinger, Schachter, and Bach argued that one reason for the strong effect of space on who interacts with whom is that, with closer physical distance, any two individuals are more likely to contact each other accidentally, which may result in a friendship: "In hanging out clothes to dry, or putting out the garbage, or simply sitting on the porch, one is much more likely to meet next-door neighbors than people living four or five houses away." Children usually choose playmates who live very close by, and their parents may then become friends through the children's friendships. The chances of accidental contact between two individuals are greatly increased by spatial propinquity. The general conclusion from the Westgate study, confirmed in later network studies, is that spatial distance is one of the main determinants—and usually the main determinant—of who talks to whom (Rogers and Kincaid 1981, p. 302).

Network Research

One of the important contemporary research fronts that derives from Lewinian influences is the investigation of communication networks (or social networks, as they are also called).* In addition to the Westgate

*Another intellectual influence on contemporary network research was Jacob Moreno, who in 1934 authored an important book about sociometry, the analysis of network data that illustrates the structure of communication networks. During World War I, Moreno administered a camp of displaced persons in Europe. He observed that individuals who were allowed

study of communication networks, Alex Bavelas established a research tradition of laboratory studies of experimentally created networks like the chain, wheel, and star. Thus, one offshoot of Lewinian group dynamics evolved into mathematical research on social networks.*

Lewin had the idea that group relationships could be represented as cells with lines connecting them (he was inspired by the analogy of cell biology). Bavelas picked up Lewin's idea and developed it into a laboratory experiment on communication patterns in different network structures (Patnoe 1988, pp. 40–41). For instance, he allowed the five individuals in one network structure to exchange written notes freely with each other (the so-called wheel), while individuals in another network structure (the star) could exchange messages only with a central individual. Yet another network structure (the line) was even more restricted in who could communicate with whom. Bavelas found that networks with less restricted communication structures had higher performance in solving group problems, except that the star outperformed the wheel (which suffered from problems of information overload).

This research suggested that the communication structures of social networks can be analyzed mathematically. When the Research Center for Group Dynamics moved to the University of Michigan in 1948, Dorwin Cartwright and Leon Festinger obtained funding from the Rockefeller Foundation to employ a mathematician to collaborate with them in a quantitative conceptualization of network structure. The Michigan mathematician, Frank Harary, coauthored the resulting book on graph theory with Cartwright and Norman, who was also a mathematician (Harary, Norman, and Cartwright 1965). This volume became an important influence on the invisible college of about 700 mathematically minded network scholars today. They have their own journal, *Social Networks,* a professional association (the International Network for Social Network Analysis), and annual conferences. There is no longer much direct connection with Lewin's group dynamics followers.

---

to form their own groups in the camp were happier and better adjusted to their circumstances. Later, in the United States, Moreno promoted the use of sociometry for organizing work groups and other types of interaction.

*Bavelas remained at MIT after Lewin's death, when the other Lewin followers moved to Michigan. In 1956, Bavelas left MIT for Bell Labs and in 1960 moved on to the Stanford Business School, and in 1969 to Victoria University in Vancouver, where he spent the rest of his active career.

The Move to Ann Arbor

Lewin's last years at MIT were a crazy schedule of overwork, as his life became more and more frantic. He had always been tardy for meetings and appointments. Now he seemed distracted by his overcommitment and harried to the point of disorganization; his doctoral students at MIT seldom saw him. Lewin obtained support for his research from the American Jewish Congress in New York and eventually helped to found an applied research center in Israel,* so he commuted regularly to New York from MIT, as well as to Washington, D.C. Lewin was fundraising for several other activities, as well as for his Research Center for Group Dynamics at MIT. He worked himself into a highly stressed condition and died on February 11, 1947, at age fifty-six, of a heart attack.

After Lewin's death, Dorwin ("Doc") Cartwright directed the Research Center for Group Dynamics at MIT. The university was cutting back as federal funding for military research dried up after World War II, and continued support for the Center looked problematic. Cartwright sounded out a dozen or so universities about their interest in having the research center. Cartwright had worked for Rensis Likert in the U.S. Department of Agriculture's Program Surveys during World War II in Washington, D.C. Likert had moved his group from the USDA to the University of Michigan in Ann Arbor, where they became the Survey Research Center. Likert invited the Research Center for Group Dynamics to join his Survey Research Center. The joint unit, the Institute for Social Research, supported itself on soft money. Cartwright, his colleagues, and doctoral students moved from MIT as a unit to Ann Arbor in 1948, after three years at MIT.

"After the move to Michigan, things changed. Over the next few years the two big rooms they initially inhabited at Michigan, again ignoring status distinctions, were replaced by traditional office space. The *Quasselstrippe* became colloquia with the focus changing to the presen-

---

*Kurt Lewin became a deeply concerned Zionist while living in America (his Jewish identification was not very strong until German persecution of the Jews in Europe got underway in 1933). Lewin once was considered for a chair at Hebrew University in Jerusalem, but Sigmund Freud intervened by writing the university president, urging that the professorship be utilized to launch psychoanalysis rather than social psychology, in Israel. Lewin had a high regard for Freudian psychoanalytic theory, although he felt that it was not very scientific because an investigator could not objectively measure concepts like libido or repression. "The psychoanalytical theory has developed a system of ideas unequaled in richness and detailed elaboration in the fields of needs, dreams, and personality," said Lewin (Marrow 1969, p. 135).

tation of completed research" (Patnoe 1988, pp. 19–20). Without Kurt Lewin, the Research Center for Group Dynamics became just another excellent research organization. Some of the old magic was gone. But the research center has lived on to the present day at the University of Michigan and is still an important intellectual force in the field of social psychology. Michigan's Department of Psychology, to which the Research Center for Group Dynamics is closely linked, provides one of the best doctoral programs in the United States.

LEWIN'S STYLE

Lewin worked by talking with others; he felt that he could not think productively as an individual (Patnoe 1988, p. 16). He organized a *Quasselstrippe* at each of the universities at which he taught: Berlin, Iowa, and MIT. Lewin believed that creativity was a social process rather than an individualistic activity. He typically spent all of his workday by talking. John Thibaut, one of Lewin's doctoral students at MIT in the mid-1940s, took walks regularly with his professor along the Charles River. They discussed intellectual topics, like quasi-stationary equilibria. Thibaut's role was to take notes and then write up a record of their discussions (Patnoe 1988, p. 16). Lewin's discussions were not meandering exchanges; they were usually to an intellectual point.

Margaret Mead, the anthropologist who collaborated with Lewin in his World War II food experiments, said he was "like the fire around which other people gathered for warmth and light by which to read their own thoughts more clearly" (Marrow 1969, p. 91). Lewin had a rare ability to work with others in a way that brought out the best of their intellectual abilities. He criticized gently and enthusiastically encouraged his doctoral students. All of Lewin's famous researchers were carried out by him with his doctoral students, reported first as their dissertations and then published with Lewin as a coauthor. Kurt Lewin not only studied group communication; he used group communication with his students and colleagues as a means of planning, conducting, and interpreting research. Lewin had an unusual capacity to create scholarly environments in which very bright people felt comfortable and in which they were highly productive.

In addition to Lewin's need to be surrounded by people, he felt it necessary to visualize his theoretical ideas. The blackboard was an essential item of equipment in his doctoral seminars and in his *Quasselstrippe* discussions. Lewin invited anyone who wanted to make a point to come up to the board and diagram the idea, but he always reserved one corner of the blackboard for his own use. An individual's lifespace was diagrammed as an oval, which Lewin's students variously called "eggs," "potatoes," or "bathtubs." Inside the oval, Lewin would draw the individual's tensions, valences, and resistances. The outside of the oval represented nonpsychological factors affecting the individual's behavior of study, forces in the individual's environment.

Lewin had an almost magical touch with people. After just a brief contact, their entire life might be changed. For example, Eric Trist, a graduate student at Cambridge University in 1933 when Lewin was traveling through England on his way to teach as a visiting professor at Stanford University, was asked to show Lewin around the Cambridge campus.* After just this two hours of conversation, Trist considered himself a Lewinian, and many years later, he contacted Lewin's Research Center for Group Dynamics to set up a collaborative agreement with Trist's Tavistock Institute in London to establish a new journal, *Human Relations*. Another example of Lewin's influence on people involved Alfred Marrow, who visited Lewin at Cornell in 1934 in order to get some advice on his Ph.D. dissertation at New York University. Marrow planned to talk with Lewin for an hour or two but stayed all weekend and developed a lifelong relationship. A few years later, Marrow invited Lewin to apply his field theory to the employee relations problems at the Harwood Manufacturing Plant in Virginia, which Marrow's family owned. Thus began Lewin's research on participative management. After Lewin's death, Marrow wrote his biography. "Lewin had a special kind of personality. . . . He would meet people someplace, say at a meeting, and it changed their lives" (Cartwright 1989).

Hal Kelley, who earned his Ph.D. at the Research Center for Group Dynamics at MIT, tells this story, related to him by a friend who visited the University of Iowa in the late 1930s (Kelley 1991). His friend had noticed a cluster of individuals talking excitedly as they walked along a campus sidewalk. Some were walking backward, so that they could face the individual in the center of the group; it was Kurt Lewin.

Lewin spoke a slightly fractured English in which he sometimes used certain German words, and he pronounced some English words in a German way. For instance, he liked to disagree by saying: "Can be, but

---

*While he was leaving Cambridge, Lewin was so involved in a conversation with Trist on the railway station platform that Trist had to shove Lewin physically on board the train (M. Lewin 1992).

I sink absolute ozzer." The force of his personality overcame his linguistic deficiency in spoken conversation, but some of his books in English are difficult reading. Edward G. Boring (1929/1950, p. 725), the eminent historian of American psychology, says, in the later edition of his study: "The persuasive charm of his personality did not quicken his books." This criticism seems more accurate in describing the work of his Berlin period, which was translated into English, than such books as his *Resolving Social Conflicts* (Lewin 1948), which is quite readable.

Lewin was a vigorous missionary for his field theory approach to social psychology, but he did not use a hard-sell approach. As Boring (1929, p. 724) stated: "We shall not understand Lewin's place in American psychology in 1933–1947 except in relation to the enthusiasm which his generous, friendly, insistent zealotry created." In another passage, he spoke of "Lewin's infectious personality." Lewin's field theory had critics, especially from the enthusiasts for the S-R learning approach of Yale psychologist Clark Hull. While Lewin ably defended his field theory and disagreed with Hullian stimulus-response psychology, he always did so with a gentle smile.

Throughout his life, Kurt Lewin had a tremendous ability to interest others in his approach. Harold Kelley, now a psychology professor at UCLA, remembers him in this way: "I got this very strong sense of how enthusiastic he could become about a problem and how much he could communicate this enthusiasm to people working on it and really kind of make things seem very important and urgent and exciting. . . . It is difficult to imagine a person with all of Lewin's attributes: The charisma, the breadth of interests, the rigor and the *interest* in rigor but not a compulsion about it—and the aspirations for systematization" (Patnoe 1988, p. 64). A similar picture of Kurt Lewin emerges from a sketch provided by De Rivera (1976, pp. 8–9):

> Lewin was a person who was tremendously involved with ideas and [who] spread this excitement to those around him. He wanted to see persons in their own right, to understand them and how they saw the world. His talks with students were extremely intense and stimulating sessions which could go on for hours with complete disregard for time and place. . . . He was a person who thought most productively with others, was stimulated by the interplay of ideas, and indeed needed this sort of interchange. He was not a solitary person, who did his best thinking in isolation. . . . His only fault appears to have been that his sense of urgency often led him to try to do too much.

Morton Deutsch, who first met Kurt Lewin when deciding at which university to pursue his Ph.D. degree, described Lewin as "a *very* charismatic and exciting personality. Talking with him, he bubbled with a certain kind of enthusiasm which was very catching and involving—I was taken by him and his vision and so I decided I would go there [to the new Ph.D. program at MIT]" (Patnoe 1988, p. 91). Perhaps Joan Lasko (1991), who worked with Kurt Lewin at the University of Iowa, said it all: "He was very close to being a saint." At times, when he did not act saintly, Lasko would reprove him by saying, "*Doctor* Lewin, please!" Lewin would feel hurt because he preferred to be called "Kurt" by his students.

Leon Festinger and Cognitive Dissonance

Leon Festinger earned his Ph.D. degree at Iowa and is considered by some to be the father of experimental social psychology, rather than Lewin, his mentor.* "Among the students and associates of Kurt Lewin, [Festinger] was clearly preeminent in theoretical inventiveness and experimental ingenuity" (Smith 1983). Festinger was an important influence on all of Lewin's later students, teaching them statistical methods and experimental design. John Darley, who as a doctoral student was taught by the Lewinians, uses the metaphor of a "Lewin family." In fact, various family trees of the Lewinians have been constructed. Darley says, "If you want to look at this whole business as a social movement, Lewin is something of a Christ figure but certainly Festinger played the role of St. Paul, who made the thing happen" (Patnoe 1988, p. 209).

Festinger was born in 1919 in New York City and earned his bachelor's degree in psychology from the City College of New York. He originally came to Iowa City in 1939 in order to learn to do Lewin's Berlin-type research: individual remembering and the completion of interrupted tasks, psychological satiation, and force fields. At that time, he was not interested in social psychology (Festinger 1980). By 1939, however, the year following the autocratic-democratic leadership experiment, that is what occupied Lewin's scholarly interests. Lewin was studying group influences on individual behavior, prejudice, and

---

*Festinger argued that experimental social psychology was started by Kurt Lewin at Iowa with the idea of taking "*very complicated* social processes into the laboratory" (Patnoe 1988, p. 256). Certainly Festinger also advanced experimental social psychology in very important ways.

gatekeeping. A kind of tension existed between Lewin and Festinger (Patnoe 1988, p. 252). It was the conflict between Lewin-in-Berlin versus Lewin-in-America, between individualistic psychology and social psychology.

Festinger completed his Ph.D. at Iowa in 1942 and then taught at the University of Rochester for two years before rejoining Lewin at MIT in 1945 and later migrating with the Lewinians to the University of Michigan. But he stayed only four years before moving to Minnesota* and then to Stanford in 1955. Festinger wrote his famous book, *Cognitive Dissonance,* during his 1955–1956 year at the Center for Advanced Study in the Behavioral Sciences. The theory of cognitive dissonance immediately became hot in social psychology, communication, and in sociology. A tremendous literature developed on this topic, and Festinger is still one of the most-cited scholars in the social sciences.[†]

Festinger's cognitive dissonance theory was influenced by Fritz Heider's balance theory[‡] and by the Osgood-Tannenbaum congruity principle, as well as by Kurt Lewin's field theory and by Lewin's Gestaltist perspective from his Berlin days. The origins of the theory trace to Festinger's study of a doomsday cult, whose prophecy of the end of the world was not fulfilled (Festinger, Riecken, and Schachter 1956). The idea of an individual's attitudes versus actions being in conflict also was inspired by Festinger's reading an article about an earthquake rumor in India, which people outside the disaster area believed would reoccur. Why should people scare themselves (Evans 1980a, p. 128)? There had to be some explanation. Dissonance is the degree to which an individual faces two conflicting cognitive elements.** This concept is difficult to measure as a variable because it is so highly situational, nevertheless,

---

*While at the University of Minnesota, Festinger and Stanley Schachter, another Lewinian, trained Godfrey Hockbaum, who applied Lewinian theory to the explanation of preventive health behaviors, like getting chest X-rays. Later scholars have utilized the health belief model to investigate individual preventive health behaviors on such matters as obtaining screening exams, adopting contraceptives, and practicing AIDS prevention through safe sex (Rosenstock 1966; Becker 1974). The model has been successively revised, although it still contains such Lewinian elements as "cues-to-action."

[†]As shown by citation counts of the ISI (Institute for Scientific Information) data base.

[‡]Fritz Heider (born 1896), an Austrian psychologist and friend of Lewin who spent most of his career at the University of Kansas, described a balanced state of interpersonal relationships when a person likes, and is liked by, individuals A and B, who would then be expected to like each other.

**Festinger borrowed the term *dissonance* from the field of music, where it means the simultaneous production of two or more discordant notes, resulting in an unpleasant sound.

experimental conditions can be created to put an individual in a dissonant state, and Festinger brilliantly designed a series of such ingenious
situations.

"The appeal of the theory and of the research that supported it was
enormous. The theory was simplicity itself. . . . What students and colleagues seemed to find especially appealing was the Festinger style of
experimentation, manipulating 'social reality' through clever stage management to create conditions for which testable predictions could be
derived—in spite of the total impossibility of counting the numbers of
consonant and dissonant 'cognitive elements' or of measuring the intensity of states of dissonance directly" (Smith 1983). One effect of dissonance is for an individual to avoid exposure to conflicting messages. For
example, once an individual purchases a new car, that individual tends
to avoid advertisements for competing makes of cars. Obviously there
are communication aspects to the dissonance process. Communication
scholars were quick to begin studying Festinger's theory, and for a few
years in the late 1950s, dissonance experiments were an important type
of communication study.*

In 1968 Festinger left Stanford and social psychology for the New
School for Social Research (in New York) to work on perception, later
to study archaeology, and then to specialize in medieval history. Festinger (1980a p. 248) says: "I left the field of social psychology in 1964."
He felt that he was in a rut and needed intellectual stimulation from new
sources. Festinger died in 1991.

GROUP DYNAMICS

The idea of group dynamics, an application of Lewin's more general
field theory, began in 1946 as a training course provided by Lewin and
his staff at the MIT Research Center for Group Dynamics for the Connecticut Interracial Commission, an organization seeking to overcome
racial prejudice. The two-week training session, held at a teachers' college in New Britain, Connecticut, consisted mainly of lectures about
group psychology and prejudice, like many other training workshops
then in existence.

---

*A review of twenty years of research on cognitive dissonance led Greenwald and Ronis
(1978) to suggest that the more recent statements of the theory had evolved into defining
cognitive dissonance as "a need to preserve self-esteem, rather than a need to maintain logic-
like consistency among cognitions."

The group dynamics training movement was actually born by accident, a chance event that Lewin seized on and exploited for its training value. The 1946 Connecticut workshop staff met every evening to discuss the day's events and to plan for the next. One evening, three of the trainees asked if they could listen in on the staff's discussions. Kurt Lewin was embarrassed but said: "Yes, sure, come on in and sit down." Ron Lippitt later recalled:

> And we went right ahead as though they weren't there, and pretty soon one of them was mentioned and her behavior was described and discussed, and the trainer and the researcher had somewhat different observations, perceptions of what had happened, and she became very agitated and said that wasn't the way it happened at all, and she gave her perception. And Lewin got quite excited about this additional data and put it on the board to theorize it, and later on in the evening the same thing happened in relation to one of the other two. . . . The three at the end of the evening asked if they could come back the next night, and Lewin was quite positive that they could; we had more doubts about it. And the next night the whole 50 [participants] were there and were every night, and so it became the most significant training event of the day. (Back 1972, p. 8)

The next logical step was to cancel the training lectures that had been held during the day and to replace them with group exercises, feedback, and discussion of group and individual progress.

The next year, 1947, the group dynamics workshops were moved to the Gould Academy in Bethel, Maine, and they have met there since. Originally, the Office of Naval Research provided funds for research on group dynamics behavior that was observed during the workshops. For many years, Bethel served as the mecca for training in group dynamics, with about 100 trainees plus 50 or so training and research staff at each annual session. The workshops became less and less geared to research and more and more served as a training experience. Eventually group dynamics became a social movement, with hundreds of clones of the Bethel workshops held at various locations in the United States and abroad. All have much in common, but the group methods used at the National Training Laboratory at Bethel are usually called T-groups (for training groups). "Encounter groups" is the name used at the Esalen Institute in northern California, and "sensitivity training" is the general term utilized for Lewin-style group training (Back 1972, p. 6). The explosion of interest in group dynamic training in the 1960s affected the culture of that decade, with the Esalen Institute and EST being the best known. The group dynamics movement continues today, representing one contemporary expression of Kurt Lewin's interest in applying his field theory to real-world problems of group-influenced behavior.

CONTRIBUTIONS OF KURT LEWIN TO COMMUNICATION STUDY

Lewin succeeded in creating both a successful career for himself and a distinctive school of social psychology in America, where he "was elevated to iconic status as the founder of experimental social psychology" (Ash 1992). Kurt Lewin was a teacher-mentor for a generation of famous social psychologists: Alex Bavelas, Dorwin Cartwright, Leon Festinger, Hal Kelley, Stanley Schachter, and many others. Lewin's greatest academic influence was through the brilliant students whom he trained. After a mid-1980s series of interviews with leading social psychologists, Aron and Aron (1986, p. x) concluded: "We are now more convinced than ever that Kurt Lewin was the seminal figure for modern social psychology."

Kurt Lewin shifted from research in Berlin mainly on individual mental processes (like the Zeigarnik effect) to the effects of group communication on individual behavior (for example, the Iowa study of group leadership styles and the sweetbreads study). Lewin also moved toward more applied research, such as his wartime field experiment on changing food habits and his studies of prejudice, which were inspired by the anti-Semitism that had so strongly affected him. More generally, we see how the everyday events in Lewin's life were converted into important research ideas: for example, the waiter in the Schwedisches Café and the Zeigarnik effect, and the chance discovery of the laissez-faire leadership style.

After he left Berlin, Lewin became a more applied researcher, each of his major studies dealt with an important social problem: prejudice, nutritional improvement, and authoritarian leadership. "Certainly Lewin must be counted among those who have worked hardest to bring theory and practice together" (Sandelands 1990). Lewin's academic affiliations in America were not with departments of psychology. Instead, he was appointed in a Child Welfare Research Station (at Iowa) and a Research Center for Group Dynamics (at MIT). The nature of these university appointments implies his applied orientation. Other psychologists generally resisted applied directions. The American Psychological Association rejected Lewin's proposal to start a special division of applied psychology, so instead he founded the Society for the Study of Psychological Issues, which publishes the *Journal of Psychological Issues*. The field of psychology usually is divided organizationally at the university level into clinical psychology (that is, applied psychology) and experimental psychology, with the latter representing the higher academic prestige of the two.* Lewin was swimming against a strong current of opposition to applied work in the social sciences; nevertheless, he prevailed as a practical theorist, arguing that applications can be guided by theory and that theories can be tested by applying them to real-life social problems.

One of Lewin's students and colleagues, Ron Lippitt (1968, p. 269), commented on Kurt Lewin's orientation to social change: "Lewin had a deep sensitivity to social problems and a commitment to use his resources as a social scientist to do something about them. Thus, in the early 1940s he drew a triangle to represent the interdependence of research, training (or education), and action in producing social change." To Lewin, applied research was just another means to test a theory.

Scholarly interest in group dynamics research continued through the 1950s, a golden era for the Lewinians. But during the 1960s, the center of interest in social psychology shifted to the study of cognition, to intra-individual explanations of individual behavior. Today, small-group communication studies are relatively passé, and there is little activity in the research front that Lewin launched, so the direct intellectual influence of Kurt Lewin is diminished. References to Lewin's research and theory are seldom found in scholarly literature today, nor have they been since about 1960 (Festinger 1980, p. 241). But in several different ways, such as the group dynamics movement, the study of participative management in organizations, and in the social psychology of group influences on individual behavior, Lewinian theory lives on. Certainly Lewin's thinking continues today in the field of communication, although many of the traces (exemplified by Lewinian concepts like action research,[†] gatekeepers, and cue-to-action) are becoming increasingly difficult to recognize.

---

*In a similar style, sociology since the days of the Chicago school in the 1920s has been segregated at the university level into social work versus sociology. Political science as a discipline is often split into a school of public administration, or public affairs, or international affairs, versus a department of political science. In each case, the applied unit generally has lower academic status.

†Lewin coined the term *action research* for investigations that are intended to lead to social action by solving social problems. The action researcher is usually deeply involved with the system of study.

CHAPTER 9

CARL HOVLAND AND PERSUASION RESEARCH

Unprecedented levels of government material support during the 1940's wartime emergency went to research on social
influence via persuasive communication to change cognitions, attitudes, and behaviors. One of the most striking
yields of this 1940's national mobilization of scientific talent
was the creation of the new information/communication science discipline that grew from being unnameable in the
1930's to being a household word (at least in the chic households of the trendy elite) in the 1950's.

—William J. McGuire, "A Contextualist Theory of
Knowledge: Its Implications for Innovations
and Reform in Psychological Research"

During the 1930s and 1940s, some of the most prestigious American
social scientists were conducting communication research. Carl I. Hovland, one of the most admired experimental psychologists of his day,
also became involved in communication study. As in the case of other
forefathers of communication study, Hovland was attracted to the field
through a midlife phase change related to World War II.

Hovland launched the scholarly tradition of micro-level studies of
individual attitude change in the United States, leading to a tremendous
research literature on persuasion that continues to grow. An estimated
1,250 new publications on attitude change appear each year (McGuire
1985a, p. 258). Much as the theory and research of Paul F. Lazarsfeld
gave direction to the subdiscipline of mass communication in its early
days, the intellectual approaches of Carl Hovland in the 1940s and

I thank Sheila T. Murphy for her comments on a draft of this chapter.

Figure 9.1. Carl I. Hovland (1912–1961) at Yale University. Source: Yale University Archives, Division of Manuscripts and Archives, Yale University Library; used by permission.

1950s inspired the subdiscipline of interpersonal communication. As in the case of Lazarsfeld's surveys of media audiences, Hovland's experiments on persuasion headed communication research toward studying effects. Persuasion is "any instance in which an active attempt is made to change a person's mind" (Petty and Cacioppo 1981, p. 4). It is essentially equivalent to attitude change. It is intentional communication, a one-way attempt by a source to bring about an effect on the part of a receiver. But because persuasion is usually via interpersonal communication channels, some back-and-forth interaction usually occurs in the persuasion process.

THE LIFE AND TIMES OF CARL I. HOVLAND

Carl Hovland was born in Chicago on June 12, 1912, and attended Northwestern University for his bachelor's and his master's degrees; he earned the latter in 1934. Then he joined the Ph.D. degree program in psychology at Yale University, attracted to study with Clark L. Hull, the eminent behaviorist scholar of human learning. Psychology at Yale in the mid-1930s was particularly distinguished, for reasons that went back to an earlier, large-scale interdisciplinary program at Yale, the Institute of Human Relations.

The Institute of Human Relations

"The Yale Psychology Department was peculiarly dominant in American academic psychology in the 1930s and 1940s in a way that few other departments have been in any field for a long time" (McGuire, in press). One of the reasons was its Institute of Human Relations, a Rockefeller Foundation–funded interdisciplinary activity at Yale from 1929 to 1949. Prior to this period, psychology at Yale had had only a small faculty. The Psychology Department had been part of the Department of Philosophy until 1921 and was not particularly outstanding. But in 1924, it was granted $200,000 by the Laura Spelman Memorial Fund for a five-year improvement plan.

The Institute of Human Relations was proposed by Robert Maynard Hutchins, then the dean of the law school at Yale (later to become president of the University of Chicago), and Milton Winternitz, dean of the medical school. Both felt that a unified theory of human behavior, centered in psychology, was a fundamental basis for professional training in law and medicine. Building a strong department of psychology at Yale was seen as a priority for the university. Their proposal was enthusiastically presented to the Rockefeller Foundation by Yale president James Rowland Angell, a psychologist who had come to Yale from the University of Chicago.

Part of the initial Rockefeller Foundation funding of $2 million went to build a magnificent building for the Institute on the Yale medical campus. The building, identified as the Institute of Human Relations in foot-high letters in the concrete façade, still stands on Cedar Street and is now used as the Yale Medical School building. The building served as the meeting place for the twenty-one Yale faculty members in psychology, anthropology, sociology, psychiatry, political science, law, history, and medicine who participated in the Institute's interdisciplinary study group. In addition to the twenty-one professors already on board, the Institute's funding was used to attract additional faculty, such as the noted anthropologist Edward Sapir from Chicago and Dorothy Swaine Thomas, a sociologist (and wife of W. I. Thomas, formerly at the University of Chicago).

Initially, the Institute of Human Relations focused on interdisciplinary studies of such social problems as juvenile delinquency, automobile accidents, unemployment, mental health, residential mobility, and the administration of justice. The underlying assumption was that the better a social problem was understood, the more easily it could be solved. The interdisciplinary sweep of the Institute should produce organized knowledge from multiple perspectives, it was hoped, which could provide a more improved understanding of social problems than would just isolated facts (May 1971). Interdisciplinary study groups were set up to focus on each social problem. A study group was essentially a voluntary association of faculty members, organized under the Institute's executive committee. Publicity about the Institute's activities led the public, and some of the faculty participants, to expect solutions to the problems of unemployment, juvenile delinquency, and others, but no solutions were forthcoming from the study groups. As a midgrant evaluation by the Rockefeller Foundation, scheduled for 1934, approached, the Institute of Human Relations entered a period of questioning and self-doubt about the direction of its activities.

Clark Hull (1884–1952) stepped into this void with a proposal to form an interdisciplinary study group centered around the topic of motivation, which cut across all of the social problems being studied by the Institute's participants and across all of the academic disciplines represented in the Institute's study groups. Hull argued that the improved understanding of human motivation might provide the common ground that the Institute sought. Hull had been hired by Yale from the University of Wisconsin (where he had earned his Ph.D. degree in 1920) in 1929, mainly to teach courses in statistical methods and psychological measurement (Hilgard 1972). His research specialty was hypnosis, a topic that was not greeted with much enthusiasm by his new colleagues in psychology in New Haven, so he was looking for a new scholarly direction in 1934. He turned to experiments on conditioning and maze learning.

Hull's proposal to study motivation was built on the Russian psychologist I. P. Pavlov's theory of conditioning, joined with the functional behaviorism of John Dewey and E. L. Thorndike (May 1971). At this stage, Hull was mainly interested in animal learning, using white rats as subjects, but he and his colleagues in the Institute of Human Relations study group showed that propositions about human learning could be deduced from the same principles as applied to animal learning. The book reporting these propositions, *Mathematico-Deductive Theory of Rote Learning: A Study in Scientific Methodology,* was authored by Clark L. Hull, Carl I. Hovland, Robert T. Ross, Marshall Hall, Donald T. Perkins, and Frederick B. Fitch (1940). The authors other than Hull and Hovland were mathematicians and logicians, and the volume is highly mathematical and very difficult reading, but the book represents elegant scholarship, laying out a series of propositions about the dependent variable of learning rote material. The "mathematico-deductive" in the book's title referred to Hull's rigorous system of definitions of concepts, postulates, corallaries, theorems, and proofs, which represented his scientific methodology for advancing learning theory.

Hull's interdisciplinary seminar on motivation met every Wednesday night during the 1935–1936 academic year. At first, the seminar concerned Hull's usual approach to stimulus-response behaviorism, then, on January 22, 1936, Hull introduced certain main concepts from Freudian psychoanalysis: libido, repression, regression, fixation, and cathexis (Sears 1985, p. 214). In the mid-1930s psychoanalytic theory had not yet become academically respectable in America. Freudian theory was introduced to the Institute of Human Relations by John Dollard (born in 1900), who came to Yale in 1930 from the University of Chicago (where he had received his Ph.D. degree in sociology), and who collaborated with the anthropologist Edward Sapir (1884–1939) in work on culture and personality. Dollard had spent a year in training at the Psychoanalytic Institute in Berlin. During the 1935–1936 school year, Hull's Wednesday evening seminar explored psychoanalytic theory, stimulating considerable interest in this viewpoint, although efforts at integrating learning psychology with psychoanalysis were disappointing. A number of Yale psychologists underwent psychoanalytic training, and in 1936–1937, Hull and his group systematized psychoanalytic theory into a series of propositions, centering on the Freudian hypothesis that aggression is produced by frustration.* The main volume reporting this work is *Frustration and Aggression* by John Dollard, Neal E. Miller, Leonard W. Doob, O. H. Mowrer, and Robert R. Sears with Clellan S. Ford, Carl Iver Hovland, and Richard Sollenberger (1939). Another important book about learning, a by-product of the Hull seminar, was *Social Learning and Imitation,* by Neal E. Miller and John Dollard (1941), which showed that one rat could be taught to imitate the behavior of another rat.

These books and a series of journal articles by Hull and his associates put the Yale Department of Psychology in the front row of graduate programs in psychology. Important theories like Pavlovian conditioning and Freudian psychoanalysis were drawn upon to build a behavioristic approach to human motivation and learning, a theory that was tested in ingenious experiments. Yale became known as an exciting place at which to study, and it attracted outstanding doctoral students. Carl Hovland was one of them in 1934, and he then contributed to making Yale psychology even more distinguished.

A strengthened Department of Psychology was one of the main beneficiaries of the twenty-year Institute for Human Relations at Yale. Many of the key scholars drifted away during World War II, and in 1949, when its funding ran out, the Institute was phased out of existence.

Carl Hovland at Yale

When Hovland arrived in New Haven in 1934, Hull's Wednesday evening seminar was still a year from getting underway. Hovland participated in the seminar discussions, gaining an interdisciplinary perspective on human learning. This eclectic style in approaching a diversity of theories, rather than being wedded to a single perspective, was to characterize his later career. The bases of Hovland's learning theory, and later persuasion research, lay in an amalgamation of Clark Hull's behaviorism and psychoanalytic theory: "Behavior theory absorbed the sub-

---

*While Hull was the intellectual leader of the Wednesday night seminars, the integration of Freudian psychoanalysis and learning theory was facilitated by Mark May, who became director of the floundering institute in fall 1935. Also attending were psychologists Doob, Miller, Mowrer, Hovland, Sollenberger, Donald Marquis, and Sears; anthropologists George Peter Murdock, Ford, and John Whiting; and psychoanalysts Dollard and Earl Zinn (Sears 1985, p. 214).

ject matter, concepts, and principles from psychoanalysis but ignored the analytic method, theoretical structure, and operations that served to define the concepts" (Sears 1985, p. 215).

Hovland moved rapidly through the doctoral program, earning his Ph.D. degree in 1936, and immediately joined the Yale faculty as an assistant professor, carrying on a series of elegant learning experiments. He was Hull's protégé, but his intellect soon carried him beyond the master. Many who knew him comment on his unusual ability to conceptualize a research problem and then to design an ingenious experiment, or series of experiments, to test his theoretical hypothesis. Hovland mainly carried out learning experiments with rats in mazes, investigating the generalization of conditioned responses. His studies were so ingenious and so theoretically important that he was already well known as an experimental psychologist by age thirty. He was appointed director of doctoral studies in the Department of Psychology. His career seemed to be on a fast track to fame. But his life path was then to change in a major way. From 1942, at age thirty, when his career change occurred, until his death from cancer in 1961 at age forty-nine, Hovland mainly conducted experiments on human communication, seeking to explain the dependent variable of persuasion (attitude change). The sudden change was caused by World War II.

HOVLAND AND THE AMERICAN SOLDIER

In 1942, just after he was promoted to associate professor, Hovland took a leave of absence from Yale to direct a research program on soldiers' morale. He was convinced to change his career by meeting with Samuel Stouffer in the Pentagon. Hovland was named chief psychologist (later the title of director of experimental studies was also added) in the Research Branch of the Information and Education Division, U.S. Department of War. Stouffer wanted to hire the best experimental psychologist in the United States in order to conduct what was essentially social psychological research because he thought that most social psychologists were "too soft" methodologically (Maccoby 1987).

Sam Stouffer

Samuel A. Stouffer (1900–1960) could be very persuasive. He had been born in Sac City, a small county seat town in western Iowa, the son of a newspaper publisher. After earning his bachelor's degree at Morningside College in Sioux City, Iowa, Stouffer went on to graduate work at Harvard, where he earned a master's degree in English. Stouffer returned to Sac City from 1923 to 1926 to edit the family newspaper while his father was ill. Then he earned his Ph.D. degree in sociology at Chicago in 1930, where Robert E. Park was one of his teachers. Stouffer, however, was mainly influenced by William F. Ogburn, who was then revolutionizing Chicago sociology by introducing quantitative methods, and by L. L. Thurstone, a psychologist specializing in attitude scale construction. Stouffer's dissertation compared the attitude scores of a sample of individuals, indexing their attitudes toward prohibition (then the law of the land) with a Thurstone-type scale versus case histories of these individuals' drinking behavior during prohibition. In essence, Stouffer pitted quantitative versus qualitative measures of alcohol behavior. The two types of measures generally agreed, which helped, at least in some ways, to settle the dispute between the qualitatives and the quantitatives at Chicago.

Following his doctorate, Stouffer spent a postdoctoral fellowship year studying statistical methods at the University of London with Karl Pearson and Ronald A. Fisher, two of the most noted statisticians in the world at that time. He then taught statistics in the Department of Sociology at the University of Wisconsin from 1932 to 1934* and then returned to the faculty at Chicago, helping to turn the Department of Sociology further toward quantitative methods. Stouffer assisted the Swedish scholar Gunnar Myrdal in a Carnegie Corporation–funded analysis of Negro-white relationships in the United States, leading to Myrdal's important book, *An American Dilemma* (1944). Coordinating this huge study was an important experience for Stouffer, who in 1941 was appointed to head the army's Research Branch. He was forty-one years old and very patriotic (Hyman 1991, p. 84; Toby 1980, p. 145).

In the opinion of Paul F. Lazarsfeld, Stouffer's friend and fellow methodologist, Stouffer "never quite lost the small town attitude. And his raving success in the business world is that he was a Harvard professor with the small town behavior, which made those businessmen so secure and therefore helped them to admire him. . . . For my money, he

---

*Where he taught Ralph O. Nafziger, then a doctoral student in political science and journalism, in a statistics course. This brief contact was to influence Nafziger strongly toward quantitative methods, an orientation that he was then to transmit to early doctoral students in mass communication, especially at Minnesota and at Wisconsin, where he taught, and through his research methods textbooks, which were widely utilized (Rogers and Chaffee 1992).

was by far the most important person in the whole field [of sociol-
ogy]. . . . The main thing about Stouffer was the absolute clarity of his
thinking. . . . There was something amazingly straightforward and direct and unimpeded in his thinking and his work. Stouffer is also a very,
very good writer" (Lazarsfeld 1962b, pp. 338–348). This statement is
high praise from Lazarsfeld, who at the time was generally considered
one of the top sociologists in the United States.

Herbert Hyman (1991, p. 81) described Stouffer in this way: "Despite the sociological overlay, Stouffer never lost the look, straight talk,
and breakneck tempo of the proverbial reporter. Jacket off, shirtsleeves
rolled up, cigarette dangling from his mouth, ashes strewn all over his
vest from chain-smoking, bleary-eyed from lack of sleep and working
through the night against a deadline—such colorful eccentricities are
relevant, albeit not crucial, to explaining his influence on the [Research
Branch] staff."

Stouffer was an expert at survey research methods, and while he was
much less experienced in experimental research, he held experimentation in very high regard. "Always sophisticated and critical in his appraisal of the essentially descriptive and correlational methods of analysis of which he was master, Stouffer's admiration for the magic of
experimentation was somewhat naive" (Smith 1968, p. 279). Stouffer
was very enthusiastic about the wartime work of Hovland's experimental unit. His high expectations for experimental research were one reason why he went after Hovland, whom Stouffer thought was the best.
His choice of the Yale psychologist demonstrated Stouffer's strong belief
in methodology: Hovland was an excellent experimenter, and Stouffer
assumed that he could easily learn the subject matter (the persuasive
effects of training films) that he was to study.

The last fourteen years of his life, 1946 to 1960, Stouffer was professor of sociology and director of the Laboratory of Social Relations at
Harvard University. During this period, he helped Harvard sociology to
eminence, playing a methodological role to complement Talcott Parson,
the theoretician. He died from cancer, at age sixty.

The U.S. Army Research Branch

Social science research in the U.S. military establishment during World
War II began as a means of monitoring the troops' morale; in fact,
Stouffer's Research Branch was located within the U.S. Army's Morale
Division (later renamed the Information and Education Division). Ini-

tially, the army brass were strongly opposed to the conduct of surveys of military personnel, which they saw as a threat to the hierarchy of army discipline (Converse 1987, p. 166). In May 1941, seven months before the United States entered World War II, the U.S. secretary of war issued an official order prohibiting surveys of military personnel. Nevertheless, survey research flourished in the army from 1941 to 1945, primarily because Stouffer's unit came under General Frederick H. Osborn, "polished, aristocratic, millionaire businessman, a personal friend of the president" (Converse 1987, p. 168), who was a knowledgeable social scientist and had served on the Social Science Research Council.* Osborn helped clear away some of the military resistance to survey research, as did the obvious usefulness of the results of the early surveys that were conducted. For instance, the Research Branch found that combat infantrymen had relatively low morale and recommended that the army create a special combat badge and provide other types of motivation for infantrymen. One of the most influential products of the Research Branch was a point system for army discharge when the war was over. Policy-relevant research findings helped the Research Branch gradually sell itself to the military authorities.† Stouffer was a very effective salesman for his Research Branch. As a civilian employee of the Pentagon, he had access to the top brass and often cleared away resistance to his branch's data-gathering activities.

The Research Branch was organized in two main groups: a survey research unit, headed by Leonard S. ("Slats") Cottrell, and an experimental unit, headed by Carl Hovland. The offices of the two units adjoined in the Pentagon, and it was easy for some of the researchers to move from one unit to the other. Cottrell's survey group mainly consisted of sociologists, recruited especially from Stouffer's former doctoral students of the University of Chicago. Hovland's unit was composed predominantly of Yale psychologists and individuals who had earned their Ph.D. degrees there. About half of the staff members of the Research Branch were army personnel, and the others were civilian em-

---

*Osborn also had been president of the Carnegie Corporation, the foundation that funded the Joint Army and Navy Committee on Welfare and Recreation, established in 1941 to support welfare and recreation projects in military camps. The joint committee, chaired by Osborn, also funded a morale survey of a combat division in mid-December 1941. The survey was directed by Sam Stouffer. Shortly, Osborn was appointed as an army brigadier general in charge of the Information and Education Division (Lyons 1969, pp. 102–106).

†Although much less so in the Pacific theater, where General Douglas MacArthur was opposed to surveys of his troops.

ployees. The scholars in the Research Branch, whether officers, enlisted men, or civilians, constituted a "dense network" (Clausen 1984b), held together by the spirit of working together on a common cause.

Most of the Research Branch staff were young men and women, under thirty years of age, who were just starting their careers in social science research (Clausen 1984). Many became noted scholars in the postwar years. Stouffer's researchers included Leonard S. Cottrell, Jr., Irving Janis, Marion Harper Lumsdaine, Nathan Maccoby, Arnold Rose, Frederick D. Sheffield, M. Brewster Smith, Shirley Star, Edward A. Suchman, and Robin Williams. Consultants to Stouffer's Research Branch included Hadley Cantril, Princeton University; John Dollard, Yale University; Louis Guttman, Cornell University; Paul F. Lazarsfeld, Columbia University; Rensis Likert, Division of Program Surveys, U.S. Department of Agriculture; Quinn McNemar, Stanford University; Robert K. Merton, Columbia University; Frederick Mosteller, Harvard University; Frank Stanton, CBS; and Donald Young, Social Science Research Council (Hyman 1991). Taken together, Stouffer's staff and consultants represented the cream of American social science, with his staff consisting of up-and-comers and his consultants composed of already top figures.

Hovland's Army Experiments

The roots of persuasion theory reach out widely. For instance, Wallace Mandell, who worked with Hovland at Yale, stated: "The first persuasion study derived from our blending of Carl Rogers' observations about the importance of 'conclusion-drawing by clients' and 'credibility' of the communicator in producing attitude change, and Hovland's interest in mass communication and the use of experimental designs to study its effects" (Mandell 1992).

The core conceptual variable in Hovland's wartime studies was attitude. A tremendous amount of social science research has been devoted to measuring attitudes and to investigating factors involved in attitude change. Persuasion research has been conducted by psychologists, social psychologists, sociologists, and communication scholars. Persuasion studies represent one of the most popular single kinds of social science research, and certainly the main concept in social psychology is attitude, a positive or negative feeling toward some individual or object that serves as a predisposition to action. This definition implies that an attitude by an individual, if known, will predict the overt behavior or action by that individual at a later time.

Do attitudes really matter? Much evidence from a wide variety of studies notes that in many cases, an attitude toward a person or object does not predict or explain an individual's overt behavior regarding that person or object. Indeed, "these low correlations between attitudes and behaviors have been a scandal of the field for a half century" (McGuire 1985a, p. 251). But attitude change research is not completely worthless in explaining behavioral change. Under certain circumstances, attitudes do affect behavior.* Finding out when they do, and do not, should be one important type of persuasion research. Of course, attitude change is interesting in its own right, aside from its impact on other variables. Often we want to know what individuals' attitudes toward some object are and whether we can change such attitudes.

The study of attitudes has passed through three eras (McGuire 1985a, pp. 235–236):

1. An attitude measurement era in the 1920s and 1930s.† From 1935 to 1955 the group dynamics approach of Kurt Lewin eclipsed the study of attitude measurement.
2. A second era, in the 1950s and 1960s, focused on attitude change. This was the age of Carl Hovland. Then, during the 1965–1985 period, social perception research pushed attitude change off center stage.
3. The 1980s and 1990s represent a third-generation rekindling of interest in attitudes and in attitude systems.

Considerable methodological work was carried out to measure attitudes in the 1920s, such as by Thurstone and Chave (1929) and by Likert (1932), but then scholars did not study the process of attitude change. This kind of persuasion study did not get underway until World War II under the leadership of Carl Hovland in studies to evaluate the persuasive effects of training films on soldiers. In 1941, the U.S. government was faced with the immense task of training 15 million

---

*McGuire (1985a, p. 252) estimates that only about 10 percent of the variance in overt behavior is accounted for by attitudes.

†The concept of attitude was first used by I. W. Thomas and Florian Znaniecki (1927) in their study of Polish peasants in Poland and America.

newly drafted civilians to become fighting men. These new recruits needed to know why the United States was involved in the war, who America's enemies and allies were, how to operate complicated military equipment, and why they should fight to kill. The U.S. military services turned to the then relatively new medium of film to help accomplish these educational and motivational purposes.

In early 1942, General George C. Marshall, the U.S. army chief of staff, recruited Frank Capra, the famous Hollywood filmmaker, to produce seven fifty-minute films, the Why We Fight series. Capra, commissioned as an army lieutenant colonel, asked about one hundred of Hollywood's creative people to help him in this crash project. The Why We Fight films, which utilized a great deal of available news footage about the events leading up to U.S. involvement in the war, were propaganda messages.* Capra's two later film series, Know Your Enemy and Know Your Ally, were also intended to persuade the viewer.

In 1943, Colonel Capra of the U.S. Army's Films Division met with communication researchers of the army's Research Branch in the Pentagon in order to plan an evaluation study of the Why We Fight series. Lazarsfeld was consulting on questionnaire construction. He was at the blackboard, writing and talking with his Viennese accent, smoking a big cigar. Capra asked, "Who is he?" Hovland and his people said, "He's a professor at Columbia." Capra asked, "How much does he make?" Hovland did not know but guessed $5,000 per year, the largest figure that he could imagine. "Oh Christ," Capra said, "that's nothing. He could make ten times that much up in front of a camera [in Hollywood]" (Maccoby 1987).†

Carl Hovland was never completely converted from being an experimental psychologist running rats in learning mazes to a postwar social psychologist of persuasion. William J. McGuire, who continued in the general tradition of Hovland's research on persuasion, points out that "before the World War II work of Hovland that produced the famous *Experiments on Mass Communication* volume in *The American Soldier* series, Carl was a precocious leader in research on human learning. After the World War II work, he shifted to attitude change, but was still the Yale authority (and indeed, a world authority) on the human learning

---

*Capra was inspired to produce the U.S. propaganda films by Leni Riefenstahl's powerful pro-Hitler film *Triumph of the Will,* whose effects Capra wished to counter (Jowett 1976, pp. 320–321).

†Hyman (1991, p. 202) tells this story slightly differently but to the same effect.

topic. My dissertation was on human learning (*A Multiprocess Model for Paired Associate Learning*), and that is why he was my dissertation advisor" (McGuire 1991a). McGuire earned his Ph.D. in psychology at Yale in 1954.

The Experiments on Persuasion

The Why We Fight films were targeted at the 15 million new soldiers in the U.S. military services. To evaluate the effects of these films, Hovland and his research staff designed field experiments on one-sided versus two-sided messages, the impact of fear appeals, the effect of source credibility, and so forth. The dependent variables were the U.S. War Department's objectives for the training films, which were measured with verbal responses through pencil-and-paper techniques: knowledge of a film's contents and attitude change, such as an increased willingness to fight. Unfortunately for their scholarly purposes, the Pentagon persuasion researchers were constrained by the film messages, which were fixed: "We were greatly limited by the fact that our findings had to be derived primarily from the analysis of the effects of communications which had already been prepared by the military authorities" (Hovland 1951).

Hovland and his Pentagon colleagues were by no means the first scholars to investigate the effects of film. Earlier I mentioned the Payne Fund studies, of which the Peterson and Thurstone *Motion Pictures and the Social Attitudes of Children* (1933) investigation was best known. Children's attitudes were measured before, and after, they viewed movies about crime and war, and about such foreigners as Germans and Chinese. Rather large effects were found. Notice that the Peterson and Thurstone experiment was conducted simply to find out if movies had effects on children. Hovland and his military colleagues also measured film effects, but their experiments were designed to test theoretical hypotheses about why greater effects occurred under certain conditions.* For instance, what was the effect of a more highly credible source on individuals' attitude change? Did greater effects occur when only one side of an issue was presented, as opposed to both sides?

Hovland, Lumsdaine, and Sheffield (1949, pp. 64ff.) concluded that

---

*Actually, several attitude change experiments of this conceptual type had also been conducted prior to the wartime research program of Hovland and his associates, as Hovland (1954) was aware.

the Why We Fight films increased soldiers' knowledge of the events leading up to World War II and that attitudes were changed (although to a lesser degree than knowledge change) but that the films had no measurable effects on individuals' motivation to serve as soldiers (the ultimate objective of the orientation films). For example, in one experimental group that viewed a Why We Fight film, 41 percent of the respondents wanted to fight, while in the control group some 38 percent wanted to fight, a small difference. The finding that individuals' knowledge changes more than attitudes is a common finding in evaluations of communication interventions. And individuals' overt behavior usually changes even less than attitudes. This is the so-called hierarchy of effects.*

Each Why We Fight film was a fifty-minute documentary. Hovland and his colleagues typically carried out a before-after experimental design, with a control group of respondents. They usually gathered a one-week-later measure of the dependent variables. The persuasion scholars used equivalent forms of the questionnaire in order to avoid respondent sensitization to the measurements. In research on *The Battle of Britain,* one of the documentaries in the Why We Fight series, 4,200 military respondents provided the questionnaire data, which were gathered from the respondents in their mess halls. The soldiers on army bases were a captive audience, and thus their attention to the film was ensured. The questionnaires were anonymous, so the respondents, mainly enlisted men, did not need to fear retribution from their military superiors if they gave the "wrong" responses.

"The Army training camp provided nearly ideal circumstances for field experimentation with random assignment to experimental and control conditions" (Smith 1983). When Hovland and his associates wanted a control group in one of their field experiments, they simply marched a company of soldiers into an army mess hall, administered a questionnaire, showed them a film, administered the "after" questionnaire, and then marched them back out again. The troops did not even know they had taken part in an attitude change experiment (Smith 1992). Of course, some logistical problems arose, especially due to wartime conditions. Nathan Maccoby, one of Hovland's associates, tells of arriving at an army training base in the United States to gather data on

---

*William McGuire's notion of the hierarchy of effects is that an individual usually must pass from knowledge change to attitude change to overt behavior in a cumulative sequence of communication effects concerning some topic or issue.

the effects of the Why We Fight films and finding that the division of study had just been ordered overseas.

Hovland was famed as an experimental psychologist, and he mainly utilized experimental designs to determine the effects of the army's morale films. He did not depend solely on such highly structured and quantitative experiments, enlisting Robert K. Merton and his colleagues at Columbia University's Bureau of Applied Social Research to conduct focus interviews with small samples of soldier-respondents just after they had indicated their likes and dislikes of a training film on the Lazarsfeld-Stanton Program-Analyzer. The reason was that "the quantitative experimental design enabled one to determine the aggregate effects but provided no clues to *what it was about the film's content* that might have produced the observed effects" (Merton, with Fiske and Kendall 1956). The focus interview data helped Hovland and his staff interpret the experimental results and suggest new hypotheses for future study.

After the end of World War II, Stouffer edited The American Soldier series of four books, which included Hovland, Lumsdaine, and Sheffield's *Experiments on Mass Communication* (1949). These volumes were made possible by Sam Stouffer's derring-do. On the morning after VE Day (Victory in Europe), on May 8, 1945, before the U.S. Army could classify his accumulated data as secret, Stouffer backed a truck up to the Pentagon, loaded boxes of IBM cards onto the truck, and drove off (Maccoby 1987).* Immediately after peace was declared, Stouffer, Irving Janis, Shirley Star, M. Brewster Smith, and a few other colleagues from the Research Branch moved out of the Pentagon into rented office space at American University in Washington, D.C. There they carried out further data analysis and wrote the four-volume series of books that are collectively referred to as The American Soldier: (1) Samuel A. Stouffer, Edward A. Suchman, Leland C. DeVinney, Shirley A. Star, and Robin M. Williams, Jr. (1949), *The American Soldier: Adjustment During Army Life: Studies in Social Psychology in World War II*, Volume I, Princeton, NJ, Princeton University Press; (2) Samuel A. Stouffer,

---

*This account of how Stouffer liberated the data is corroborated by others (Schramm, in press b) but differs from that provided by Sibley (1974, pp. 41–42) and Hyman (1991, p. 84), who say that General Frederick Osborn, the officer in charge of the military research during World War II, negotiated the release of the data to the Social Science Research Council, which in turn facilitated its analysis and publication by Stouffer and his associates. In any event, the data base was extensive, with over half a million soldiers responding in 250 studies of knowledge and attitudes.

Arthur A. Lumsdaine, Marion Harper Lumsdaine, Robin M. Williams, Jr., M. Brewster Smith, Irving L. Janis, Shirley A. Star, and Leonard S. Cottrell, Jr., (1949) *The American Soldier: Combat and Its Aftermath*; (3) Carl I. Hovland, Arthur A. Lumsdaine, and Fred D. Sheffield (1949), *Experiments on Mass Communication*; and (4) Samuel A. Stouffer, Louis Guttman, Edward A. Suchman, Paul F. Lazarsfeld, Shirley A. Star, and John A. Clausen (1950), *Measurement and Prediction*. The first two volumes dealt with the survey studies of U.S. soldiers, the third volume reported Hovland and his colleagues' experimental studies of film effects, and the fourth book described the methodological advances made by the Research Branch.*

The Message-Learning Approach

Carl Hovland pioneered what is called the MLA (message-learning approach) in his wartime research on persuasion, which he continued at Yale after the war. For the nineteen years from 1942 until his untimely death in 1961, Hovland mainly pursued a series of experiments designed to explain the dependent variable of persuasion/attitude change. This paradigm, the message-learning approach (MLA), is diagrammed in Table 9.1. It consists essentially of analyzing how individuals learn from communication messages.

The independent variables are components in the Claude Shannon–type linear model of communication: SMCR (source, message, channel, receiver). Each of the Hovland-type experiments typically dealt with the effects of one dimension (or variable) of the SMCR components, for example, source credibility or fear appeals, on attitude change. Such a single component approach rules out the study of interaction effects among the components as they act together to influence attitude change. Nevertheless, Hovland pursued the understanding of persuasion in such a concerted fashion over such a long period of years and with such considerable resources that the net result of his research program was a rather thorough understanding of attitude change behavior. Hovland was ingenious in designing one study to follow up on the leads from a previous experiment, with each investigation probing further into the behavior of study. In other words, Hovland carried out a research program in which the successive series of studies added up to a

---

*Merton and Lazarsfeld also edited a book critiquing and commenting on these studies, *Continuities in Social Research* (1950), which showed how certain important concepts like reference groups emerged out of the wartime research.

TABLE 9.1
Carl Hovland's Message-Learning Approach to Attitude Change

Components in the Communication Process	Independent Variables Related to Persuasion (Attitude Change)	Illustrative Researches
Source variables	Intent to persuade Attractiveness of the source Similarity of source and receiver Power of the source Credibility of the source	Hovland and Weiss (1951); Hovland, Janis, and Kelley (1953)
Message variables	Comprehensibility Number of arguments used Rewards within the message Arousal and reduction of fear One-sided/two-sided messages Order of message presentation Message repetition Style of presentation	Hovland and others (1957)
Channel variables	Face-to-face versus mass media Channel attributes	
Receiver variables	Intelligence Self-esteem Gender differences	Janis and others (1959)

Note: A comprehensive review and synthesis of attitude change research is provided by Mc-Guire (1985a, pp. 233–346).

cumulative understanding of persuasion behavior that has never since been matched or even rivaled.

RETURN TO YALE

When Hovland returned to New Haven in 1945, he continued the tradition of persuasion research that he had begun in the Pentagon, with an almost uninterrupted continuity. Many of his wartime colleagues came with him to Yale.* In New Haven, Hovland and his co-workers

*The main participants in the persuasion research program at Yale were Irving Janis, Herbert Kelman, Harold Kelley, Arthur Gladstone, Edmund Volkhart, Arthur Lumsdaine, Muzafer Sherif, Leonard Doob, Fred Sheffield, Seymour Feshbach, Russell Clark, Elaine Bell, Bert King, Wallace Mandell, Marvin Herz, Walter Weiss, and Jepson Wulff (Hovland 1951).

followed up on leads that they had turned up in their army research, with one very important difference: the persuasion studies at Yale were more basic research, designed to formulate and test scientific propositions about the effects of communication rather than the highly applied research that was conducted to help the U.S. Army find more effective means of motivating soldiers to combat. "When Hovland came back to Yale he switched into the communication and persuasion field, but he brought an awful lot of his human learning thinking" (McGuire, in press). As Hovland (1951) stated, "We have a strong predilection for stimulus-response learning-theory formulations and . . . an attempt is made to see how far the general principles of [Hullian] behavior theory can be extended into this [persuasion] field."

Hovland's post–World War II research at Yale University from 1946 to 1961 was called "the largest single contribution . . . [to this field] any man has made" (Schramm 1985). Hovland returned to Yale University as professor and chair of the Department of Psychology, a leadership position that he did not seek but which he accepted without complaint. He also led the Yale Program in Communication and Attitude Change, which conducted more than fifty persuasion experiments. This research program was funded by a series of grants from the Rockefeller Foundation, totaling about $370,000. In 1947, Hovland was named Sterling Professor of Psychology, the most distinguished endowed professorship at Yale. He finished his brilliant but abbreviated career in a blaze of recognition.

Source Credibility and Persuasion*

Hovland, Janis, and Kelley's (1953, pp 27–31) well-known laboratory experiment on source credibility represents a core illustration of research on communication effects following a linear model. This important study isolated one communication variable, source credibility (defined as the degree to which a communication source is perceived by a receiver as trustworthy and competent), while controlling on all other variables. The design of this experiment sought to reproduce the human reception of mass media messages in a laboratory setting. In fact, although persuasion experiments are mainly considered a type of inter-

*This section is from Rogers and Kincaid (1981, pp. 36–37), and is used by permission of the Free Press.

personal communication research today, Hovland felt that he was actually studying mass communication behavior at the microlevel of individual reception of messages.* The findings from persuasion research can be utilized in either mass communication or interpersonal communication. The channel through which communication occurs is fairly irrelevant to the persuasion process.

The general procedures used in the source credibility study are a model for many subsequent communication experiments in persuasion, utilizing other independent variables. Identical communication messages were presented to two groups of randomly assigned subjects. One group was told that the message emanated from a source that they perceived as highly credible. The other group was told that the identical message came from a source perceived as low in credibility. This deception was followed for four different messages, each with a high-credibility and a low-credibility source (Table 9.2). The messages were delivered to the subjects (college students at Yale) in the form of a small booklet containing an article on each of the four topics, with the name of the source given at the end of each article. The four topics were antihistamine drugs, atomic submarines, the steel shortage, and the future of movie theaters. The high-credibility sources were the *New England Journal of Biology and Medicine,* J. Robert Oppenheimer (a famous atomic scientist), *Bulletin of the National Resources Planning Board,* and *Fortune* magazine, respectively. The low-credibility sources were a mass circulation monthly pictorial magazine; *Pravda* (the Russian newspaper); an antilabor, anti–New Deal, rightist newspaper columnist; and a movie gossip columnist. Attitude questionnaires were administered to each experimental group before, immediately after, and a month after the four articles were read by the subjects in the source credibility-persuasion experiment.

Immediately after communication took place, Hovland and his coworkers found that greater attitude change resulted from the high-credibility sources, except for the fourth topic, the future of movie theaters, where the low-credibility source led to somewhat more attitude change (Table 9.3). Four weeks after the experiments, however, the earlier differences in attitude change between the high-credibility subjects

---

*As one evidence of this point, note that the title of Hovland, Lumsdaine, and Sheffield's (1949) book summarizing their wartime persuasion research is *Experiments on Mass Communication.* Further, Hovland became interested in studying the effects of source credibility because of singer Kate Smith's radio marathon to sell U.S. war bonds (see Chapter 7).

TABLE 9.2
Design for the Experiment of Hovland and Others
on Source Credibility and Persuasion

Message Topics	High-Credibility Source for Each Topic	Low-Credibility Source for Each Topic
Antihistamine drugs: Should antihistamine drugs continue to be sold without a doctor's prescription?	*New England Journal of Biology and Medicine*	Magazine A (a mass circulation monthly pictorial magazine)
Atomic submarines: Can a practical atomic-powered submarine be built at the present time?	J. Robert Oppenheimer, the well-known nuclear scientist of the Manhattan Project	*Pravda* (a Russian newspaper)
The steel shortage: Is the steel industry to blame for the current shortage of steel?	*Bulletin of the National Resources Planning Board*	Writer A (an antilabor, anti–New Deal, rightist newspaper columnist)
The future of movie theaters: As a result of TV, will there be a decrease in the number of movie theaters in operation by 1955?	*Fortune* magazine	Writer B (a female movie gossip columnist)

Source: Hovland, Janis, and Kelly (1953, p. 28).

and the low-credibility subjects disappeared. Hovland and his colleagues concluded that the effect of source credibility is maximum at the time of communication but fades with the passage of time. This so-called sleeper effect is presumably explained by the tendency of individuals to forget the untrustworthiness of the low-credibility source over time. They remember the message but not the dubious source.*

The credibility experiment is probably the best known of the many Hovland communication experiments and formed the model research design for thousands of persuasion experiments by various scholars in

---

*A review and critique of persuasion experiments on the sleeper effect is provided by Cook and others (1979).

TABLE 9.3
Attitude Changes Resulting from High-Credibility Versus Low-Credibility Sources

Message Topic	Net Percentage of Subjects Who Changed Their Attitude in the Direction of the Communication Message	
	High-Credibility Source	Low-Credibility Source
Antihistamines	23	13
Atomic submarines	36	0
Steel shortage	23	−4
Future of movies	13	17
Means	23	7
Difference in the two means	16% (significant at the 1% level)	

Source: Hovland and others (1953, p. 30).

following years. It isolated one communication variable, a characteristic of the source, while experimentally controlling the effect of all other variables in the communication process (these effects are removed by the random assignment of individuals to the high-credibility and low-credibility conditions). Thus, the experiment followed the basic linear (source-message-channel-receiver) model of the communication process in an attempt to simulate the main elements of one-way communication and persuasion. No interpersonal communication was allowed among the subjects in each experimental group. Even in later persuasion experiments, where face-to-face, interpersonal communication was used to convey the message to the respondents (instead of the printed booklets), the most common context was the lecture, a one-way channel of communication. So even when Carl Hovland and his group studied interpersonal communication, they did not allow interaction to occur. To do so would undoubtedly have unstandardized the message that was presented to the respondents, creating an uncontrolled kind of variation in the experiment (although it would make the communication situation more natural). Thus, we see how the components approach to communication research, based on a liner model, was rather atomistic and mechanistic. The student subjects at Yale were not allowed to ask questions or to discuss the meaning of the print messages with each other. The source credibility variable was not allowed to vary in its effects through interaction with other components of the linear model like receiver characteristics (for instance, *Pravda* might have been a credible source about atomic submarines for some respondents).

The artificial situation created by this experiment aided the control of unwanted variables, contributing to the study's internal validity (defined as the degree to which an investigation controls on the effect of extraneous variables). Unfortunately, this created unreality also limits the generalization of the experiment's results to actual situations in which individuals are persuaded by credible sources. For example, people do talk to one another after they receive a message from the media. So Hovland-like persuasion experiments are relatively low on external validity, the degree to which an investigation's results are generalizable to real-world conditions. Hovland's experiments with U.S. Army privates and with Yale sophomores did not provide a strong basis for generalizability to other individuals in other circumstances.* Nevertheless, Carl Hovland's research program on persuasion represents a major intellectual contribution to communication study that has been much admired and was widely copied.

Most persuasion studies gather data about communication effects by paper-and-pencil questionnaires, a type of measurement whose validity might be questioned. For example, respondents in persuasion experiments may give socially acceptable responses. As McGuire (1991) pointed out, recent years have seen a marked advance in using physiological indicators of persuasive effects. For example, Petty and Cacioppo (1986) measured galvanic skin response and other physical effects in their persuasion studies.

Hovland and his associates at Yale University published a book about their persuasion experiments almost every year from 1953 until the time of his death in 1961: Carl I. Hovland, Irving L. Janis, and Harold H. Kelley, *Communication and Persuasion* (1953); Carl I. Hovland, Wallace Mandell, Enid H. Campbell, Timothy Brock, Abraham S. Luchins, Arthur R. Cohen, William J. McGuire, Irving L. Janis, Rosalind F. Feierabend, and Norman H. Anderson, *The Order of Presentation in Per-*

---

*As Hovland (1951) stated: "Most of us want our results to be applicable to people in general but do our experiments on a few classes in elementary psychology in our own college."

suasion (1957); Irving L. Janis, Carl I. Hovland, Peter B. Field, Harriet Linton, Elaine Graham, Arthur P. Cohen, Donald Rife, Robert P. Abelson, Gerald S. Lesser, and Bert T. King, *Personality and Persuasibility*, (1959); Milton J. Rosenberg and Carl I. Hovland, *Attitude Organization and Change* (1960); and Musafer Sherif and Carl I. Hovland, *Social Judgment: Assimilation and Contrast Effects in Communication and Attitude Change* (1961).

As William McGuire (1991) remembers, these books were usually organized by Hovland in a rather informal manner. For example, *The Order of Presentation in Persuasion* came about one day when Hovland passed McGuire on the stairs of the Yale psychology building and asked him to draft a chapter summarizing his experiments on primacy versus recency in the order of message presentation (that is, whether a message is more persuasive if the main conclusion is at the beginning or at the end of the message). Hovland then edited this paper, along with chapters by his other colleagues and by Yale doctoral students, into the book manuscript. The volume was published by Yale University Press a few months later. The entire process seemed relaxed and routine, but it was carefully orchestrated by Hovland.

Fear Appeals

One important set of persuasion experiments concerned the use of fear appeals. Is it wise to appeal to an audience with fear messages? How strong should the fear appeals be? This type of research grew out of the work of Irving Janis, one of Hovland's colleagues in the Pentagon and later at Yale: "I was interested in the dynamics of fear from my work on fear in combat" (Evans, 1980b, p. 100).

In one of the noted experiments by Janis and Feshback on preventive dental health, three levels of fear appeals were used. The third level was "all-out" fear, "showing pictures of people with cancer of the mouth and horribly deformed teeth." The intent in this study was to persuade individuals to brush their teeth regularly and to schedule dental check-ups. They found that a moderate level of fear appeal was more persuasive. "When a mass communication [message] is designed to influence an audience to adopt specific ways and means of averting a threat, the use of a strong fear appeal, as against a milder one, increases the likelihood that the audience will be left in a state of emotional tension which is not fully relieved by rehearsing the reassuring recommendations contained in the communication." "When fear is strongly aroused but is not fully relieved by the reassurances contained in a mass communication, the audience will become motivated to ignore or to minimize the importance of the threat" (Janis and Feshback 1953). The use of fear appeals can amount to playing with fire, if too strong appeals are used. But fear messages can grab an audience's attention, and, if mild fear appeals are utilized, they need not be counterproductive in bringing about attitude change.

Conclusions from Hovland's Persuasion Research

Hovland's research and theory on persuasion resulted from three influences:

1. Freudian psychoanalytic theory, a result of Hovland's participation in the Institute of Human Relations at Yale. Freudian conceptualizations influenced Hovland's persuasion research mainly through his background in Clark Hull's learning theory.
2. Hovland's methodological background as an experimental psychologist of learning, following a behaviorist approach to behavioral change, which he also learned from Clark Hull.
3. Lewin's field theory and group psychology studies, which influenced Hovland's research mainly through his collaboration with Harold Kelley, a colleague at Yale for several years who coauthored one of his most important books, *Communication and Persuasion,* with him.

Carl Hovland and his band of persuasion researchers learned a great deal during World War II and later at Yale about the process of attitude change:

1. High-credibility sources lead to more attitude change immediately following the communication act, but a sleeper effect occurs in which the source is forgotten after a period of time.
2. Mild fear appeals lead to more attitude change than strong fear appeals. Propagandists had often used fear appeals. Hovland's evidence about the effects of such appeals suggested that a source should be cautious in using fear appeals, because strong fear messages may interfere with the intended persuasion attempt.

3. One-sided messages lead to more attitude change with audiences of lower education and/or intelligence, while two-sided messages lead to more attitude change with more educated and/or intelligent audiences. Presumably more educated and intelligent individuals suspect that there are two sides to a persuasive argument, and so a one-sided presentation is accordingly less effective. Hovland and his colleagues' findings about the stronger effects of two-sided than one-sided messages contradicted the Nazi propaganda strategy of never mentioning the opposing side of an argument (Janis 1968, p. 528).

4. Stating a conclusion in a message leads to more attitude change than leaving the conclusion implicit. Here it appears that clarity about the main point of a message adds to its persuasiveness.

5. Individuals who feel socially inadequate and have low self-esteem experience more attitude change than do aggressive or socially withdrawn individuals. A strong self-concept can provide resistance to persuasive messages.

6. Active participants in the persuasion process (such as by reading a message aloud or presenting a particular point of view) have more attitude change than do more passive participants. As in the Kurt Lewin sweetbreads study, individuals who are more involved in the communication process are more likely to change their attitudes (and behavior).

7. Individuals strongly attracted to a group have less attitude change regarding an issue that is contrary to the standards of the group. This finding is similar to the generalization from group dynamics research that group cohesion encourages the individual members of a group to conform to the group's norm.

Hovland's Style

Professor Leonard Doob (1991), a close friend of Carl Hovland in the Yale Department of Psychology, remembers him as a good listener, very quite, and speaking little but with great authority. After World War II, when Hovland returned to Yale as chair of the Psychology Department, he also taught a heavy load of courses, led the large Rockefeller Foundation–funded research program on communication and attitude change, and organized another research project at Bell Labs in New Jersey. Despite these heavy demands, Hovland never complained about his work load.

Without doubt, Hovland was very, very bright. Harold Kelley (1991), a faculty colleague of Hovland at Yale after World War II, uses the word *genius* to describe him (Kelley also remembers Kurt Lewin and Leon Festinger as possessing genius qualities), as did a number of other scholars who worked closely with him. He was, without doubt, very intelligent, and this intellect was one reason for his giant stature. Wallace Mandell, who earned his Ph.D. degree with Hovland at Yale (and now is a professor at Johns Hopkins University), stated: "Carl Hovland was, in my opinion, a genius or as close to it as I have ever known. He could carry on three complex activities, edit a paper, talk on the phone, and use a slide rule, simultaneously. He was also a kind and generous man who encouraged talent and individuality in his students without the need to impose his way of thinking" (Mandell 1992).

Carl Hovland is generally described by academics who know him as a prince of a man: generous, sensitive, and mild. One individual who knew Hovland better than most others is William McGuire, the eminent social psychologist who replaced Hovland at Yale after his early death. McGuire (1991) says that although he went to Yale to study persuasion research with Hovland, who served as his doctoral adviser, his relationship with Hovland was one of friendly competition. They carried on in a joking way. When McGuire heard that Hovland was ill with cancer in 1961, he flew immediately from the University of Illinois at Urbana, where he was then teaching, to New Haven to spend a last day with Hovland. They talked about their old times together, sitting in Hovland's office until noon, when Hovland invited McGuire to lunch at a restaurant of his choice. Knowing that Hovland hated fish, McGuire suggested the most expensive seafood restaurant in New Haven. McGuire thus achieved a final advantage in his exchanges with Hovland.

Hovland was not wedded to a single theoretical perspective. Instead, he selected a particular phenomenon to investigate, say, the effects of source credibility on one-sided versus two-sided messages, and then drew on various theoretical viewpoints in designing his experimental study of the phenomena. "He [Hovland] proceeded eclectically, utilizing independent variables from a diversity of theories, bringing the insights from each convergently to bear on the phenomena of interest, using any one theory only partially but by the whole set of theories accounting as fully as possible for the observed variance in the delayed-action, primacy/recency, or whatever, phenomena" (McGuire 1985b, p. 563).

McGuire says that Hovland had "a vacuum-cleaner way of integrating things." Hovland's mind had a tremendous range, and he was interested in knowing everything. McGuire, Hovland, and several of their Yale psychology colleagues regularly drove to New Jersey for a day's consulting at Bell Labs in the 1950s. Perhaps someone would mention a new household consumer product, or a gourmet dish, or a new academic theory. Hovland would ask intelligent questions endlessly about each of these topics, until it was completely exhausted, and so was the individual who had mentioned it. On one occasion, their limousine driver mentioned that he used a new type of camera. Hovland wanted to know how it worked, what it cost, and its advantages and disadvantages. Several hours later, when they arrived at Bell Labs in New Jersey, Hovland was still asking questions about the new camera.

"I think Hovland's main talent was abstracting themes to see unifying notions behind a lot of different research, so as to see the directions that fields were moving in. He put on some performances that were really breathtaking" (McGuire, in press). Hovland was wonderful at drawing conclusions from a diversity of material and famed for pointing out intellectual connections that no one else could see. McGuire (1991) tells of his departing for an academic conference, with Hovland suggesting that he should be sure to talk to professors A, B, and C about their research, which had much in common with McGuire's then-current study. McGuire says he did not think there was any connection whatsoever, until he talked to A, B, and C. Sure enough, their work was related to his.

Carl Hovland was a quiet leader, not charismatic like Kurt Lewin or Paul F. Lazarsfeld. He was calm in nature and nonauthoritarian in leadership style. He preferred a Socratic approach, asking questions that led his discussion partner in a certain direction of thought. "Hovland's talk was economical and to the point, with few words wasted" (Schramm, in press b). But he could be persuasive.

When Hovland learned that he had cancer, he continued to work with his Yale doctoral students and conduct persuasion experiments. Finally, when he could work no more, he left his office in the Psychology Department, went to his home in New Haven, drew a bathtub full of water, and drowned himself (Schramm, in press b).

CONTRIBUTIONS OF CARL HOVLAND
TO COMMUNICATION STUDY

Like Paul F. Lazarsfeld's mass communication research, Carl Hovland's persuasion research focused on communication effects. Unlike Lazarsfeld and his students, who were finding minimal media effects in their survey research on media audiences, Hovland and his colleagues were finding that from one-third to one-half of their experimental subjects were influenced by a single exposure to a persuasive message. Hovland (1959) sought to explain this striking difference in one of his last papers to be written before his death. He noted that experimental subjects are a captive audience, and hence all are exposed to the message. Hovland's World War Ii military recruits of study were marched into an army mess hall to view one of the Why We Fight films, for example. But Lazarsfeld's survey respondents might or might not have been exposed to a particular message or medium whose effect he was studying, and even if they were exposed, the message may not have attracted their attention. Second, unfamiliar issues to the experimental subjects were studied in the typical persuasion experiment, issues with which the subjects had low ego involvement. "Substantively, work in the Yale tradition [on attitude change] skimmed the cream of exploratory research without digging definitively into the underlying processes. That is, the Yale studies typically employed trivial beliefs and attitudes that could be manipulated in the laboratory by equally trivial communicative interventions" (Smith 1983). In contrast, Lazersfeld and his group at Columbia University's Bureau of Applied Social Research often studied strongly held attitudes, like voting intentions, which were more difficult for mass communication to change. As Lazarsfeld stated: "If we visualize a learning experiment where people walk in and out as they please, where some of the most valuable effects are achieved with people who come in by mere accident, where the motivation to learn is often very low and where the possible rewards for learning are obvious neither to the experimentor nor to the subject, . . . then we can understand the frame of reference in which [mass media communication] must perform . . . [its] task" (Klapper 1960).

Carl Hovland and his group of persuasion researchers were very productive, writing almost one book per year from 1949 until the end of Hovland's life. Persuasion research continued as a popular kind of social science study in the 1950s and 1960s, when some 1,000 studies were published annually (McGuire 1985b), but the popularity of this research dropped in the 1970s and 1980s. Perhaps the energy went out of this research front because all of the original (Hovland-type) leads had been explored fully, and fresh approaches were not identified (Roloff and Miller 1980; Reardon 1981). Also, many communication scholars have begun to regard one-way communication acts as an oversimplification of the interactive, back-and-forth nature of the communication process. Nevertheless, Hovland introduced both persuasion research and the experimental method to communication study. Both his theory and method live on today.

CHAPTER 10

NORBERT WIENER AND CYBERNETICS

Genius like his rarely takes the time or trouble to grow armor to shield it from the roughness of the world, and retains the charm of childhood throughout life.

—Warren S. McCulloch, "Norbert Wiener and the Art of Theory"

The author is one of the protagonists of the proposition that science, as well as technology, will in the near and in the farther future increasingly turn from problems of intensity, substance, and energy, to problems of structures, organization, information, and control.

—John von Neumann, "Review of Norbert Wiener's Cybernetics"

Cybernetics, the theory of self-regulating systems, rests on the concept of *feedback*, defined as the control of the future conduct of a system by information about its past performance. Norbert Wiener's cybernetic theory has been applied usefully in a broad range of interdisciplinary applications: to brain functioning and neurophysiology, artificial intelligence, factory automation, prostheses, and international communication. Cybernetics also contributed directly to the rise of systems theory in the 1960s. Wiener's theory is an important influence on communication study, particularly on the Palo Alto school of interactionist communication scholars. Wiener, America's most famous mathematician, advanced communication study in important ways.

I thank Klaus Krippendorff for his comments on a draft of this chapter.

Figure 10.1. Norbert Wiener (1894–1964) at MIT.
The MIT Museum; used with permission of the MIT Historical Collection.

THE LIFE AND TIMES OF NORBERT WIENER

Norbert Wiener (1894–1964) was a boy prodigy who became the father of cybernetics. He also co-invented the idea of the entropy measure of information with Claude E. Shannon, and shares some credit with Shannon for launching information theory (and with Andrei N. Kolmogoroff, a Russian probability theorist). Yet Wiener was very insecure about his intellectual capabilities and was never certain of his academic status (Wiener 1956). "Wiener did have grave doubts all of his professional life as to whether his colleagues, especially in the United States, valued his work, and, unwarranted as these doubts were, they were very real and disturbing to him" (Levinson 1966). Perhaps his insecurity motivated him to even greater intellectual accomplishments. Certainly Wiener had an unusual personal life and was a true eccentric if America ever had one.

The dozen or so main communication theorists profiled in this book generally shared certain qualities with Norbert Wiener. They were raised by pushy parents who had high expectations for their child. Leo Wiener, Norbert's father, was a self-educated professor of Slavic languages at Harvard University, who spoke forty languages and translated Tolstoy into English (Struik 1966). He was a tough father with high expectations for his brilliant son. Leo raised Norbert to be a genius. Second, these leading communication scholars studied at the great universities of their day and associated with great minds. After Wiener graduated from Harvard with a Ph.D. in philosophy at age eighteen, he traveled to England for a postdoctoral fellowship with the philosopher and mathematician Bertrand Russell at Cambridge University. Wiener had intellectual exchanges with Max Born, John von Neumann, and other brilliant mathematicians and physicists of his day. Finally, all of these scholars taught at outstanding universities and rose rapidly to the top of their field. Wiener was a professor in the MIT Department of Mathematics for forty-five years and is regarded as America's greatest mathematician. He helped transform MIT from its earlier focus on technology to a primary concern with basic science.

One of Wiener's biographers, P. R. Masani (1990, p. 16), characterized him in the following terms: "Proverbially absent-minded, amusingly quirkish and idiosyncratic, he was fundamentally a gentle and humane soul. He was, however, given to recurrent manifestations of petulance, egoism, emotional instability, irrational insecurity, and anxiety." Wiener was an ex-prodigy, and his early formative years, firmly molded by his father, himself a genius, were not always happy. His early suffering, caused often by a breakdown of parental wisdom, left a scar on his adult personality. Wiener could be a difficult character and had warm-and-cold personal relationships with his academic colleagues throughout his career. The unique education of the young Norbert Wiener isolated him from other children his age and made him dependent on his domineering father, whose praise he craved.

The Education of a Prodigy

Norbert Wiener got his first name because his parents were introduced to each other at a club composed of admirers of the poet Robert Browning in Kansas City, where Leo Wiener was then teaching Greek, Latin, and other languages in the public schools. Norbert and his sister, Constance, were named after two of the main characters in Browning's verse play *On a Balcony* (Masani 1990, p. 30). By the time that Norbert was born, in 1894, his father, Leo, was teaching at the University of Missouri. Leo was not appointed the chair of the Department of German at Missouri in 1895, so he resigned and moved with his family to Boston, where he later joined the Department of Slavic Languages and Literature at Harvard University. Leo translated the complete works of Tolstoy into English and made other important scholarly contributions, even though he did not have a Ph.D. degree. Norbert spent the rest of his childhood in the rarefied intellectual atmosphere of the Wiener home in Cambridge, Massachusetts. Professor Walter Cannon* of the Harvard Medical School was a friend of the family. Prince Kropotkin, the Russian anarchist and geographer, visited the Wiener household (Masani 1990, p. 34), as did William James, the famous Harvard philosopher (Heims 1980).

Young Norbert displayed unusual mental abilities at an early age. When he was only eighteen months old, his nurse drew some letters in the sand while they were at the beach. Norbert watched her attentively and in two days knew the alphabet perfectly. He began reading fluently at age three and soon was reading books by Charles Darwin and other great scientists, provided to him by his father (Heims 1980, p. 6) Leo Wiener raised his son to be a vegetarian and shaped his life in other ways. In his autobiography, *Ex-Prodigy: My Childhood and Youth* (1953), Norbert Wiener recalls his painful educational experiences at the hands of his father. Leo removed his son from school at age seven and taught him a cram course in algebra and classical languages. After two years of this intensive tutoring at home, Norbert enrolled in high school, successfully competing with students seven years his senior. The elder Wiener evidently had been an effective teacher, but Leo's tutelage was a psychological torture for little Norbert. Whenever he fumbled in mathematics or grammar, his father became a tyrant, terrifying the boy and further worsening his performance, which thus enraged his father to hurl insults in German ."The lessons often ended in a family scene with a crying Norbert running into his mother's arms" (Masani 1990, p. 35). Norbert's relationship with his loving but perfectionist father put the boy in a double-bind situation from which he could not escape. Wiener's autobiography was originally entitled *The Bent Twig*.

---

*Cannon (1871–1945) earned an M.D. degree at Harvard and then was an influential professor of physiology at Harvard from 1906 to 1945. He created the concept of homeostasis to describe the general regulatory systems within the body that maintain certain consistencies, such as the body's temperature.

At age eleven, Norbert enrolled at Tufts College near Boston. He received his B.A. in mathematics cum laude in 1909, at age fifteen. When Leo enrolled him for graduate work in philosophy at Cornell University that fall, Norbert learned, through an overheard remark, that he was Jewish. His parents had withheld this fact from him, and his mother had often spoken in a derogatory way about Jews (Masani 1990, p. 41). Norbert Wiener's self-realization of his ethnic identity was a traumatic experience. While he was at Cornell, away from home for the first time, he wrote affectionate letters to his parents and sisters in Latin, German, and French, as well as English. But he was unhappy in Ithaca, and after one year, his father removed him from Cornell and enrolled him at Harvard. Norbert received his Ph.D. degree in philosophy in 1913, at age eighteen.

He also was awarded an overseas traveling fellowship by Harvard, which he spent studying mathematical philosophy with Bertrand Russell at Cambridge University. Russell had just coauthored *Principia Mathematica* with the philosopher Alfred North Whitehead, his former teacher. Norbert's doctoral dissertation at Harvard was entitled "A Comparison of the Algebra of Relatives of Schroeder and of Whitehead and Russell." In Leo Wiener's letter to Bertrand Russell, asking him to accept Norbert (dated June 15, 1913, quoted in Masani 1990, pp. 45–47), Leo stated: "Norbert graduated from College, receiving his A.B., at age of fourteen, not as the result of premature development or of unusual precocity, but chiefly as the result of careful home training, free from useless waste, which I am applying to all of my children." Bertrand Russell in a letter to Lucy Donnelly (Grattan-Guinness 1975) said, on meeting the eighteen-year-old Dr. Norbert Wiener when he arrived at Cambridge University: "The youth has been flattered, and thinks himself God Almighty—there is a perpetual contest between him and me as to which is to do the teaching."

Norbert became somewhat more emancipated from his overbearing father during his postdoctoral study in Europe. The young Wiener took two courses from Russell, becoming interested in his theory of types, paradox, and in Einstein's relativity theory. When Bertrand Russell was away from Cambridge during the spring of 1914, Wiener studied at the University of Göttingen in Germany. His postdoctoral fellowship was extended a second year, but World War I had begun in Europe and Leo decided that Norbert should return to the United States. Norbert followed Bertram Russell's advice and studied with John Dewey at Columbia University, but the experience was a disappointment for Wiener. He found Dewey's writings to be confusing, and regarded his time at Columbia as a "low point" in his career (Wiener 1953, p. 226).

After military service in World War I,* Wiener joined the Department of Mathematics at MIT in 1919 as a one-year instructor. He had found his life's niche. It was the beginning of a lengthy and happy relationship, although Wiener's faculty career at MIT started off in a dubious way, with promotions coming slowly at first. From 1919 to 1923, he studied the mathematics of the Brownian movement and "did some of the best mathematical work of this century" (Masani 1990, p. 92). In 1926, Wiener married and in a few years became a clumsy babysitter for his two daughters. He frequently traveled to conferences or to lecture in Europe, especially in Germany, where he met leading scholars in mathematics, physics, and engineering. He corresponded with Herald Bohr, Max Born, Albert Einstein, Margaret Mead, and Gregory Bateson. Eventually his career took off, and MIT began to treat him with great respect. Wiener developed intellectual interests in entropy and in the statistical nature of information. He became especially close to several electrical engineers at MIT, including Vannevar Bush (1890–1974), who was designing the differential analyzer, a kind of mechanical computing machine. Out of his collaboration with a former doctoral student from China, Y. W. Lee, Wiener in 1934 became interested in the concept of feedback, the key building block in the cybernetic theory that was to make him world famous.

The Massachusetts Institute of Technology is arguably America's most noted technical university. It is located along the banks of the Charles River in Cambridge, close to Harvard University but with quite different goals from that venerable member of the Ivy League. Harvard is old, honored, and oriented to the liberal arts. MIT is younger, functional, and oriented to science and technology. MIT students help form the public stereotype of the computer nerd, not very socially skilled but smart—very smart. Mathematics is important at MIT now, but when Wiener joined the Mathematics Department, it was mainly a service department, teaching courses for engineering majors, and MIT was mainly concerned with technology. As Wiener's stature in the field of mathematics grew, his department grew with him, rising to become an academic center for advancing the state of the art of theoretical math-

---

*One sign of Norbert Wiener's relationship with his dominating father at this time (in 1917, at age twenty-three) was that Norbert asked his father for permission to enlist in the Army.

ematics. Wiener was one of the young turks at MIT who, after about 1920, shifted its academic emphasis from technology to basic science.* MIT changed from being an engineering institute to become one of America's important research universities.

Wiener's Style

There are many anecdotes about Norbert Wiener's absent-mindedness that live on at MIT, where he was beloved and celebrated. Masani (1990, p. 349) relates the following story: One day Wiener walked from his office in the Mathematics Department to the MIT faculty club for lunch, and then, while walking back to his office, encountered a friend with whom he chatted for a few minutes. As they parted, Wiener looked bewildered and asked, "By the way, which direction was I headed when we met?" "Why, Norbert, you were headed toward your office," the friend told him "Thanks," said Wiener, "that means I have finished lunch." This incident happened in 1929.

Norbert Wiener was famed at MIT for his so-called Wiener-*wegs* (Wiener walks) on which he wandered in a random path through the Institute buildings, dropping unannounced into offices and laboratories to encounter a surprised professor or doctoral student. He often pondered deeply on these walks, with head bowed, perhaps working out a new mathematical lemma in his head. In order to avoid colliding with some object, the slay-footed, clumsy Wiener customarily trailed a forefinger along the wall of a corridor, as a means of guiding his passage down the hall. My friend Don McNeil tells of one occasion in which Norbert Wiener, trailing a finger along the wall, wheeled around a corner and into the open door of a classroom in which a large lecture class was in session. The MIT undergraduates watched with silent amazement as Professor Wiener walked around the four walls of the classroom and, still in deep contemplation and completely unaware that he had interrupted the instruction, lumbered back out the open door and on down the hall, having never looked up.

At least two MIT scholars, Dr. Robert Fano in electrical engineering and Professor Karl W. Deutsch in political science, explain their lasting academic interest in cybernetic theory to a chance encounter with the

---

*This change in focus was aided by grants from the Rockefeller Foundation's General Education Board (Heims 1980, p. 164).

great mathematician, who, on one of his Wiener-*wegs*, popped up in their office and began discussing feedback systems with them. As Deutsch (1986) recalls, his much-cited book, *The Nerves of Government: Models of Political Communication and Control* (1963), "began in 1943, when the mathematician Norbert Wiener walked into my office at MIT and recruited me at the point of a cigar into a long process of communication. It started with a discussion about my field, international politics, but soon turned to his own work on communication and control in machines, animals, and societies." Wiener was just as likely to encounter a baffled janitor or a dumbfounded undergraduate on his Wiener-*wegs*, whom he would engage in a complex discussion of Fourier analysis or Taube's problem. One can easily understand how Norbert Wiener became regarded as the most colorful character on the Institute's campus.

Deutsch (1968) has called Wiener "the most powerful and creative mind I have ever encountered." From all sides, Wiener was showered with testimony as to his brilliance. Yet as he reached middle age, in the 1930s, he began to feel uneasy about his mathematical work and worried that his academic productivity was falling off. As Norman Levinson (1966), Wiener's former doctoral student and later colleague at MIT, said: "His usual words of greeting became, 'Tell me, am I slipping?' Whether one knew what he had been doing or not, the only response anyone ever made was a strong denial. However this assurance was usually not enough and it was necessary to affirm in the strongest terms the great excellence of whatever piece of his research he himself would proceed to describe, sometimes in the most glowing terms. Altogether such an encounter was an exhausting experience." Yet Wiener's pervading insecurity about his research productivity seemed to goad him on to higher performance.

Wiener's interpersonal style was a mixture of hot and cold relationships with others. Wiener was "a moody person. At times delightful and generous, with a high good humor, he at other times reflected personal tensions in ways that made him a difficult man, hypersensitive to slights and alternating between conceit and self-deprecation . . . . He could be extremely harsh, even to old friends. He left a string of abruptly broken friendships" (Heims 1980, p. 12). In appearance and behavior, Norbert Wiener was a baroque figure, short, rotund, and myopic. . . . He was a poor listener. . . . He was a famously bad lecturer. . . . His style was often chaotic." Wiener was bigger than life in many dimensions. No one ever accused him of being sensitive in his relationships with other individuals: "All in all, it is abundantly clear that he never had the slightest idea of how he appeared in the eyes of others" (Freudenthal 1976, p. 344). Being absolutely brilliant, it seems, does not always make a happy life.

During meetings, Wiener frequently fell asleep and then awakened suddenly to fire off a comment showing that he knew exactly what had been discussed. "He would fall asleep from time to time, head on shoulder, snoring with gusto. Suddenly the snore would be interrupted; he would explode out of his sleep into full sentences which had direct and incisive relevance to the discussion that had been going on around his sleeping head. This happened so often that it could not be dismissed as a chance coincidence" (Rosenblith and Wiesner 1965b).

A colleague of Norbert Wiener, Warren S. McCulloch (1965), remembered Wiener: "Here in the halls of MIT, he was a familiar sight, standing splay foot, his cigar poised in his right hand at the level of his mouth, pouring out on student, janitor, business manager, or astounded colleague witticisms or profundities of science with equal gusto." Wiener was a nonstop talker. The public image of the befuddled, absent-minded professor is probably based more closely on Norbert Wiener than on any other individual.

THE YELLOW PERIL

Wiener became particularly interested in feedback and the design of systems as a result of his World War II research experience. It happened in 1941–1942, in MIT's Radiation Laboratory, which was established to conduct military research on improving antiaircraft fire. A special problem with antiaircraft accuracy is the relatively high speed of the airplane as a target, compared with the speed of the shell that is fired at it. In order to hit the enemy airplane, the gun must be aimed at the future position that the plane will occupy when the shell arrives on target, and by the time that the shell arrives, the plane may have taken evasive action by swerving. As a result, early in World War II most antiaircraft fire was very ineffective. The Allied antiaircraft fire against the German Luftwaffe in the 1941 Battle of Britain was particularly ineffective, with tens of thousands of shells being fired for every German plane destroyed. Improving gunfire accuracy became a high priority for the Allied military forces.

Wiener set to work with great enthusiasm on the mathematics of antiaircraft gun control. He requested a modest grant of $2,325 from the

National Defense Research Committee.* After thirteen months of day and night work, keeping himself awake by benzedrine pills, Wiener found a mathematical solution. It was a complicated solution, directed to the pure mathematician rather than to the engineer (Levinson 1966), but it could be translated into important applications for military purposes.

Wiener approached the problem of antiaircraft accuracy as a process of information transmission. Each shell that was fired was considered a message. The degree to which it approached the target was treated as information that was fed back from a radar screen to the electronic gunsight of the antiaircraft weapon, so that the next shot, fired a few seconds later, would be slightly more accurate. Gradually, the antiaircraft fire would converge on and destroy the target.

Wiener's investigation of antiaircraft fire led to his 1942 technical report, dubbed the "Yellow Peril" because of its difficult content and the yellow cover (indicating its secrecy classification). The report applied what would become cybernetic theory to the antiaircraft gunfire problem. The Yellow Peril report, dated February 1, 1942, was later declassified and published in book form in 1949 as *Extrapolation, Interpolation, and Smoothing of Stationary Time Series with Engineering Applications* (Wiener 1949). The copy of the report in the Norbert Wiener Collection at the MIT Libraries' Institute Archives and Special Collections is numbered 36 of 300 copies (each copy was numbered, for purposes of government security control). The first page or so begins as a very readable account of the problem of antiaircraft gunfire accuracy. Then the Yellow Peril report goes off into a hundred pages or so of complex mathematical formulas. MIT professor Robert Fano (1990) has called it "a real peril to read."

The report did not lead directly to improved gunsights for U.S. and British military guns, as their accuracy was being improved by other work, mainly conducted at Bell Labs (Masani 1990, pp. 182–183) and at the MIT Radiation Laboratory, where the SCR-584 radar gun control device was designed (Fagen 1978, p. 149). These improvements were particularly notable in 1944–1945 when Allied gunners shot down a very high percentage of the German V1 and V2 rockets aimed at London (Shannon 1982). But the Yellow Peril report did stimulate the

*Warren Weaver, on leave from his position at the Rockefeller Foundation for wartime duties in Washington, granted these funds to Wiener.

emergence of information theory (along with the key contributions by Claude E. Shannon) and cybernetic theory. Wiener began to think about the human operators of antiaircraft guns, who turned the cranks so as to keep a moving target in the cross-hairs of their telescope. Such consideration of man-machine problems began to take Wiener toward an interest in human neurophysiology, brain functioning, and, ultimately, intrapersonal and interpersonal communication processes.

CYBERNETICS

Feedback systems existed prior to Norbert Wiener's wartime work, of course, such as the governor that regulates the speed of a steam engine. Servomechanicisms are machines that control other machines. Examples are thermostats, the automatic pilot of an airplane, a robot on an automobile assembly line, and a heat-seeking missile. All of these servomechanisms operate through using feedback from the machine that they control (Figure 10.2). But until Norbert Wiener, there was no mathematical theory of how feedback controlled a system. Cybernetics is the theory of self-regulating systems. The term *cybernetics* was chosen by Wiener from the Greek word for "steersman" He began using the term in 1942 (Heims 1980, p. 183).

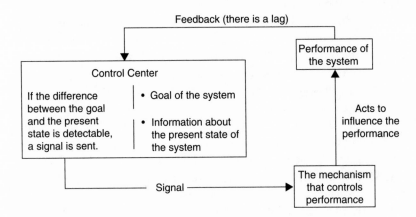

Figure 10.2. How feedback controls a system.
A cybernetic system like this one might be a thermostat controlling the temperature in a room. When the temperature of the room differs from the preset ideal temperature, the control center sends a signal to the mechanism controlling the furnace (or air conditioner), which in turn heats or cools the room. Feedback about the temperatures is then conveyed to the control center.

Feedback is the control of the future conduct of a system by information about its past performance. Thus, it is a means of controlling a system by reinserting into it the results of its past performance. In a communication system, feedback is the response by a receiver to the source's previous message, indicating its effects. Feedback allows a source gradually to self-correct the effectiveness of a series of messages, making them closer and closer to what is needed to accomplish their intent. Through its use of feedback, a system can be self-correcting. The nature of feedback inherently involves communication because the feedback process requires that information be conveyed from a receiver back to the source.

Wiener's cybernetic theory is a communication theory, concerned with how messages are exchanged between two or more units so that each influences the other. To Wiener, the units in a system might consist of a machine like an antiaircraft weapon, its human operator, and the target; or two or more humans, such as the gun operator and the officer in charge of a battery of such guns. Wiener was unique (along with Claude Shannon) among other communication theorists in including machines as possible components in a communication system.

Cybernetics deals in circular causalities in which A causes B, B causes C, and C causes A, so that A causes itself (Krippendorf 1989a, p. 443). An example of such circular causality is a speaker who modifies his or her presentation while monitoring audience reactions to it. The circular causality implied by cybernetic theory was to help lead to a major change in basic conceptions of science as the result of the systems theory movement of the 1960s.

To cyberneticians, feedback can be positive (deviation amplifying in its consequences) or negative (deviation counteracting) (Figure 10.3). To social scientists and in everyday communication, however, positive feedback usually means that the feedback message conveys a positive evaluation back to the source, as when someone in an audience tells a speaker, "You gave a good speech." For a cybernetrician, this remark would only be a partial account of the circularity involved.

Cybernetics was not just mathematical, by any means, and Wiener did not just draw upon his role as a mathematician in formulating the theory (Figure 10.4). "His role in cybernetics was not only that of an innovator but also that of a publicist, synthesizer, unifier, popularizer, prophet, and philosopher." Many nonmathematicians think of cybernetics as a mathematically demonstrated theory. It is not. "In fact, cyber-

The problem of overshooting:

1. *Positive feedback* is deviation amplifying.

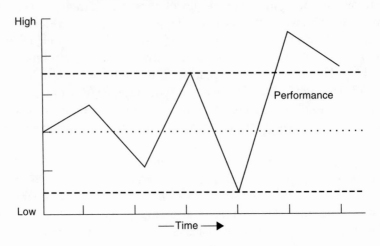

2. *Negative feedback* is deviation counteracting, bringing a system back into a stable state.

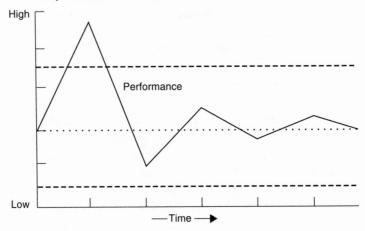

Figure 10.3.   Feedback in a cybernetic system.

We generally use the terms *positive feedback* and *negative feedback* in a different way than do cyberneticians, whose meanings for these terms are shown here.

netics is so broad that it probably cannot be viewed as a mainly mathematical theory capable of being demonstrated in the spirit of mathematics" (Levinson 1966). As Wiener (1985, pp. 323–325) stated: "The

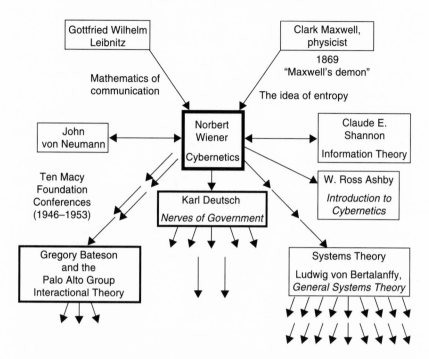

Figure 10.4. Intellectual forebears and descendants of Norbert Wiener's cybernetic theory.

whole background of my ideas on cybernetics lies in the record of my earlier work. Because I was interested in the theory of communication, I was forced to consider the theory of information and, above all, that partial information which our knowledge of one part of a system gives vs. of the rest of it. . . . Because I had some contact with the complicated mechanism of the nervous system, I knew that the world about us is accessible only through a nervous system, and that our information concerning it is confined to what limited information the nervous system can transmit. . . . These were the ideas I wished to synthesize in my book on cybernetics."

THE PHILOSOPHY OF SCIENCE CLUB

Norbert Wiener was multidisciplinary in his scholarly interests, and the disciplinary diversity of his personal networks helped him advance cybernetic theory and also assisted its wide applications. In 1933, Wiener met Dr. Arturo Rosenblueth (1890–1970), a Mexican physiologist of Hungarian descent, through his long-term family friend, Professor Walter Cannon, at the Harvard Medical School. Soon Wiener joined an interdisciplinary seminar on the scientific method led by Rosenblueth, the Philosophy of Science Club. "The role of this seminar in the genesis of cybernetics and in Wiener's life can hardly be exaggerated" (Masani 1990, p. 197). Years previously, prior to studying for his Ph.D. in philosophy, Wiener had enrolled for a doctoral degree in zoology at Harvard, but he was too clumsy for laboratory work. Perhaps his continuing interest in biological systems can be traced to his unsuccessful study of zoology.

The interdisciplinary seminar in Cambridge ended in 1944, after eleven years, when Rosenblueth was appointed head of the Department of Physiology at the National Institute of Cardiology, in Mexico City, but the Rosenblueth-Wiener collaboration continued, with the help of a $28,000 grant from the Rockefeller Foundation, through regular exchange visits in which Wiener spent one semester every other year in Mexico. The two scholars studied the human brain and the nervous system as a cybernetic system. Over the years, Wiener and Rosenblueth collaborated in this physiological research, leading to various scientific publications, most dealing with feedback systems and the nervous system. Meanwhile, Wiener was also involved with MIT colleagues, including Vannevar Bush, in computer design. Wiener explored the similarity between the functioning of the human brain and that of the computer. It was an exciting interdisciplinary area that was on the cutting edge of science.

With Warren S. McCulloch (1897–1969), a neurophysiologist at the University of Illinois Medical School in Chicago, and Walter Pitts (1923–1969), a brilliant young collaborator of McCulloch who came to study with Wiener at MIT, Wiener investigated the meaning for brain functioning of being deaf or blind or of having lost an arm or leg. McCulloch, Pitts, and Wiener concluded that an individual's pattern-recognition ability was often lost. For example, an individual whose hands had been amputated had to learn the notion of roundness through some nontactile means (Masani 1990, p. 227). This conclusion had important implications for the methodology of designing prostheses. Wiener helped inspire the "Boston Arm," which was designed by his MIT engineering colleagues on the basis of Wiener's applications of cybernetic thinking to the control of artificial limbs.

THE MACY FOUNDATION CONFERENCES

Wiener's multidisciplinary orientation, expressed in his participation in the Philosophy of Science Club and through his collaboration with Rosenblueth, McCulloch, Pitts, and others was also displayed in an important series of postwar conferences sponsored by the Josiah Macy, Jr., Foundation. (The Macy family fortune was originally made in oil and in shipping and then in the chain of Macy department stores.) Because "a member of the Macy family had been paralyzed and had been helped by a group of scientists who met at an interdisciplinary meeting," the family consequently funded a series of interdisciplinary scientific meetings —160 such conferences involving 1,350 scholars from 1940 to 1960— on such topics as aging, blood clotting, childhood liver injuries, and other medically related topics (Segal 1986, p. 159; Leeds-Hurwitz 1991). Of these many conferences, the ten meetings of the Cybernetics Group had the greatest impact.

Although the original idea of the foundation's multidisciplinary conferences was pioneered by Lawrence K. Frank, who headed the Josiah Macy, Jr., Foundation from 1936 to 1938, his replacement, Frank Fremont-Smith, was actually the guiding light for the ten conferences on cybernetics, held from 1946 to 1953. Frank was born in 1890 in Cincinnati and studied economics at Columbia University. From 1923 to 1936, he worked for the Laura Spelman Rockefeller Memorial and the Rockefeller General Education Board, a period during which he funded child welfare research institutes at Columbia University's Teachers College, the University of Iowa, the University of California at Berkeley, the University of Toronto, and the University of Minnesota. Frank has been called a raindancer for the tribe of social scientists, in that he knew how to make academic ideas grow and survive (Heims 1991, p. 62). Although Frank was no longer on the staff of the Macy Foundation at the time of the Cybernetics Conferences in 1946 (he was by then an independent consultant living in New York), he had a good deal to say about setting them up, and he participated in all ten meetings. Fremont-Smith had been Frank's assistant at the Macy Foundation and carried on the multidisciplinary activities that Frank had started.

The Participants

Warren McCulloch, neurophysiologist and a friend of Wiener, chaired the ten Macy Foundation Conferences on Cybernetics. Most were convened in the old Beekman Hotel on Park Avenue in Manhattan.* Norbert Wiener was a star of the conferences, but the list of regular participants reads like the heavy hitters of the sciences in the post–World War II period: Gregory Bateson, Lawrence K. Frank, Paul F. Lazarsfeld (who dropped out after the fifth conference), Kurt Lewin (who died in 1947), Warren S. McCulloch (chairperson), Margaret Mead, John von Neumann (who did not participate in the ninth and tenth conferences), Arturo Rosenblueth, and Norbert Wiener, the most valuable player of this scientific all-star team. Also influential was John von Neumann (1903–1957), a brilliant mathematician from Budapest, Hungary, who had migrated to America in the 1920s. While a faculty member at the Institute for Advanced Study at Princeton University, von Neumann played a key role in the design of early mainframe computers. He was a consultant to the Manhattan Project at Los Alamos, New Mexico, carrying out the complex calculations that led to the implosion detonation device for the first atomic bomb (Heims 1980). Von Neumann was also noted for his important book with Oscar Morganstern on the theory of games. He was charming and socially skilled in a way that his friend Norbert Wiener was not.

Gregory Bateson had participated in a Macy Foundation conference on central inhibition in the nervous system in 1942, at which the notion of feedback was introduced by Norbert Wiener. When Bateson went off to World War II duties in the Pacific, he found that the ideas about cybernetics that he had learned at the conference stayed with him (Segal 1986, p. 157). On his return to the United States in 1946, he contacted the Macy Foundation to ask when the next interdisciplinary conference would be held. Bateson became one of the core group for the ten Macy Conferences on Cybernetics, and he was the most influential in putting what he learned there into use as the ineractional communication viewpoint of the Palo Alto group. Bateson said, "There is certainly a piece of scientific history to be dug out of these [Macy conferences] meetings—I believe more profound and dramatic than *The Double Helix*" (Heims 1991, p 54), that is, the discovery of the structure of DNA by James Watson and Francis Crick.

Bateson's former wife, Margaret Mead, was also a core participant in the Cybernetics Group. She had earned her Ph.D. degree in anthropology at Columbia University, where Franz Boaz and Ruth Benedict were

---

*Two of the conferences were convened at Princeton, so that John von Neumann could participate more easily.

her mentors, and had carried out her dissertation fieldwork in Samoa, when she was just twenty-three years old. Mead's findings showed that the nature of male and female behavior differs tremendously among cultures. The sexual behavior expected of young men and women in Samoa would be considered abnormal in America. Mead and Bateson were a humanizing influence on the Macy conferences, focusing the discussions so that the social science applications of cybernetics did not get overlooked and also bringing the talk back down to plain English when it threatened to go off into technical jargon (von Foerster 1992).

Warren McCulloch, chair of the conferences, also played a key role in encouraging fruitful multidisciplinary exchange. He had an uncanny ability to keep the discussion moving, to halt disagreements before they became too virulent, and to know when to call on someone with a pregnant idea to speak. McCulloch was trained in medicine and psychiatry and was a neuropsychiatrist at the University of Illinois School of Medicine in Chicago.

In 1949, Heinz von Foerster, newly arrived in the United States as a refugee from Austria, was invited by McCulloch to be a guest participant in the sixth Macy conference. At this point, von Foerster had been speaking English for only four or five weeks, and his presentation at the conference in the Beekman Hotel was in appallingly inadequate language. Nevertheless, the content of his presentation about human memory was impressive, and he was nominated to edit the proceedings volumes out of the last five Macy conferences, in the hopes that this task would help him improve his English (Segal 1986, p. 159). Von Foerster's first action was to suggest that the complicated name of the conferences ("Feedback Mechanisms and Circular Causal Systems in Biology and the Social Sciences") be shortened to "Cybernetics," in light of the fact that Wiener's book *Cybernetics* was a best-seller, so the term was widely understood. Von Foerster's suggestion was greeted with applause at the sixth Macy conference, and thus the meetings came to be called by the new name. Steve Heims's book about the Macy conferences is called *The Cybernetics Group* (1991). In this case, the title refers to the Macy conference participants and to the invisible college that evolved out of their interactions in the conference.

The first Macy Foundation conference, held March 8 and 9, 1946, at the Beekman Hotel, included twenty-one scientists talking about feedback and cybernetics. Nine more of the conferences were held over the next seven years, with the same set of core participants, plus some invited guests, at each conference. These occasions provided Norbert

Wiener with a platform for his cybernetic theory and an opportunity to discuss applications of cybernetics to the social and biological sciences. At the first conference, Bateson got the inspiration from Bertrand Russell's paradox of a computer's oscillating between yes-no-yes-no, which Bateson applied to human communication problems, and (2) for report versus control functions, which he and other members of the Palo Alto school later adapted to the communication content versus communication relationship in interactional communication theory.

Interdisciplinary and Multidisciplinary

The Macy Conferences on Cybernetics were deliberately multidisciplinary in nature, bringing together a small number of scholars from widely different fields in order to explore what they could learn from each other. The focus was decidedly informal and centered on work in progress by the scholars, consisting of a core group of the dozen so individuals who participated in almost all of the ten conferences plus several scholars who were invited to a single conferences. The transaction of the last five Macy conferences (1950–1954) were edited by Heinz von Foerster and published by the Macy Foundation.

An important difference exists between *interdisciplinary* and *multidisciplinary,* although the two terms are sometimes used synonomously. *Interdisciplinary* is a type of scholarly activity falling between two disciplines, while *multidisciplinary* is a type of scholarly activity involving scholars from more than one discipline who come together to share their perspectives on a topic (Leeds-Hurwitz 1991). Wiener saw cybernetic theory as potentially unifying widely different scientific fields. He "felt that a theory of transmission of messages, although fundamental to the development of scientific thought, fell into the cracks between scientific disciplines" (Steir 1989, p. 318).

A number of multidisciplinary activities sponsored by private foundations have had an impact on communication study over the years: the Local Community Research Committee and the Social Science Research Committee at the University of Chicago from 1923 to 1932 (see Chapter 5), the Institute for Human Relations at Yale University from 1929 to 1939 (see Chapter 9), the Department of Social Relations at Harvard University after World War II, and the Center for Advanced Study in the Behavioral Sciences located at Stanford University since 1954 (see Chapter 7). The early doctoral programs in communication that were launched by Wilbur Schramm at Iowa in 1943, at Illinois in 1947, and at Stanford in 1955 were all multidisciplinary in nature, especially in their first years. The very nature of communication study demands a multidisciplinary approach, especially in the early years of this field, before it became institutionalized in universities.

The Macy Foundation conferences allowed Norbert Wiener and his theory of cybernetics to infect the social sciences, mathematics, and neurophysiology with a multidisciplinary perspective that provided a fertile ground for communication study. Perhaps the caption on *The New York Times* (March 19, 1964, p. 1) obituary for Norbert Wiener said it all: "The Father of Automation."

WIENER'S POSTWAR REBELLION

After the end of World War II, Norbert Wiener declined any federal government research grants. With the use of the atomic bomb at Hiroshima, he no longer trusted the U.S. government with his scientific work, and he broke with John von Neumann, who continued working with the federal government on technological policies. Wiener wrote a series of best-selling books—*Ex-Prodigy: My Childhood and Youth* (1953), *I Am a Mathematician: The Later Life of a Prodigy* (1956), and *God and Golem, Inc.: A Comment on Certain Points Where Cybernetics Impinges on Religion* (1964)—and became a public figure. His *Cybernetics* is a very technical book and is not easy reading. It appeared in 1948, at about the same time as the Shannon-Weaver volume, *A Mathematical Theory of Communication* (1949), which is also quite technical and mathematical. But his *Human Use of Human Beings: Cybernetics and Society* (1950) is a popular version of cybernetic theory and became a bestseller.

CONTRIBUTIONS OF CYBERNETICS TO COMMUNICATION STUDY

There is no doubt that cybernetics is a communication theory, but communication study has not been much influenced by cybernetic theory. One reason is that a certain degree of mathematical ability is necessary to understand cybernetics, or at least to conduct research cast in a cybernetic mold. Many communication scholars lack the necessary mathematical skills, although they may nevertheless be sensitized to a cybernetic viewpoint in their research. For example, feedback is certainly one of the central concepts in communication study, although only a limited amount of research has been conducted on feedback by communication scholars. Additionally, cybernetic theory competed for attention with Shannon's information theory, which appeared at approximately the same time and fit more easily with scholars' preponderant interest in studying commutation effects. Furthermore, Wiener generally opposed the extension of cybernetic theory to social science problems because he thought that human relationships are more complex than machine-machine or human-machine relationships. However, he actively participated with Arturo Rosenblueth and other biomedical scientists in applying cybernetic theory to human brain functioning and to other biological and medical problems. Finally, cybernetic theory was such a marked departure from conventional thinking in the behavioral sciences that when it was applied to many fields, its implications were strongly resisted. For example, Karl W. Deutsch, an eminent political scientist, says that when his important book on cybernetics and politics, *The Nerves of Government* (1963), appeared, "Its ideas struck many colleagues as unfamiliar, and it made its way slowly" (Deutsch 1986). However, Deutsch's book was cited 550 times in other publications over the next twenty-three years, compared to 905 citations for Norbert Wiener's *Cybernetics.*

Cybernetics as a communication theory is unique in several ways:

1. Feedback is a particular type of communication message flow, in that the information conveyed describes the system's performance at a previous point in time to itself.
2. Cybernetics implies a dynamic, processual view of behavior over time.
3. Cybernetics assumes that the control of a system lies mainly within the system itself. The results of a system's own actions provide new information by which it modifies its subsequent behavior. Thus, the system learns from itself. Information about changes in the environment affect the system only as they necessitate adjustment to feedback.

Cybernetic theory has been applied to a variety of communication situations—for example, to the relationship of television ratings to television programming, to the dynamics of public opinion polls for politicians, to human systems like organizations, and to smart weapons systems that find their own targets.

Cybernetics is gaining renewed interest today because of the newer interactive communication technologies, like computer-based electronic messaging systems, and the extensions of cybernetic thinking to language, reflexive systems, and other applications.

SYSTEMS THEORY

Systems theory is holistic; it stresses the interrelationships among the parts of a whole. Systems thinking was a reaction to the reductionist approach of classical physics, which had provided the ideal for scientific research. An example of reductionism is investigating smaller and smaller pieces or components of a phenomenon, such as the study of quarks in physics. Such reductionism removes the context of the behavior of study and also eliminates the interaction among the various parts. When the reductionist approach was taken from physics to the biological and social sciences, which study living systems, it distorted the reality of these systems. Systems theory arose in order to correct for the inappropriateness of reductionism. Systems consist of sets of components related to each other interdependently that work toward the overall objective of the whole. A system is a grouping of parts that work together in order to accomplish a set of goals (Churchman 1968).

Systems theory is actually not a theory in a strict sense but a broad paradigm, a response to the problem of reductionism, and a reaction against growing scientific specialization. C. West Churchman in his book, *The Systems Approach* (1968), criticized the approach of "sweeping in"—the tendency to look increasingly narrowly in research. Instead, we often need to look more broadly at the context and in an interdisciplinary and multidisciplinary way. Such a wide view recognizes that the solution to many social problems can best be found in the intersection of two or more disciplines rather than within a single discipline.

Systems theory thus represents "a broad shift in scientific perspective" (Buckley 1968, p. 36). It was influenced by cybernetic theory, as well as by several other theoretical movements. It arose in the 1960s and rapidly became influential in the sciences of living systems. A key figure was Ludwig von Bertalanffy, a biologist and German émigré, who taught at the University of Alberta, in Edmonton, Canada. Earlier, while at the University of Chicago, he was influenced by a lecture given by Charles Morris, the philosopher who studied with George Herbert Mead and edited Mead's potshumous book, *Mind, Self and Society* (1931). Von Bertalanffy's book, *General Systems Theory: Foundations, Development, Applications* (1968) played an important role in the subsequent spread of systems thinking.

In 1954–1955, von Bertalanffy was at the Center for Advanced Study in the Behavioral Sciences at Stanford, with Kenneth E. Boulding, an economist then at the University of Michigan; Anatol Rapoport, a biomathematician at the University of Chicago; and Ralph W. Gerard, a physiologist from the University of Illinois. They organized the Society for General Systems Research and made their first presentation of the systems approach at the Association for the Advancement of Science in 1954. Thus, the systems theory movement was launched among United States academics. Within about a decade, by the mid-1960s, systems theory had infected the social sciences in the United States: "The concept [of systems] has pervaded all fields of science and penetrated into popular thinking, jargon, and mass media. . . . Professions and jobs have appeared in recent years, which, unknown a short while ago, go under names such as systems design, systems analysis, systems engineering, and others" (von Bertalanffy 1968, p. 3).

Systems theory received an enthusiastic burst of initial enthusiasm in the 1960s because it offered an alternative to the previous scientific procedures of linear causality. "The system problem is essentially the problem of the limitations of analytical procedures in science" (von Bertalanffy 1968, p. 18). What were the shortcomings of scientific methods? The existing hypothesis-testing approaches were appropriate for understanding discrete relationships among variables, such as those encountered in physics. There scientists looked at smaller and smaller elements in order to advance knowledge. "The only goal of science appeared to be analytical, i.e., the splitting up of reality into ever smaller units and the isolation of individual causal trains" (von Bertalanffy, 1968, p. 45). But this approach was not satisfactory when studying living systems because interactions among the components of the system mean that each relationship depends on the other relationships in the system. In order to understand such complexity satisfactorily, more holistic approaches were needed. Systems theory provided such holistic thinking.

Further, living systems are open to their environment, exchanging information across their boundary. An open system is negentropic, it does not run down. In contrast, a closed system is isolated from its environment, and its energy gradually dissipates; it is entropic. Most living systems are open. In closed systems, such as in the field of physics, the final state is completely determined by initial conditions. But in open systems, a final state can be approached in a variety of ways. One of the principles of systems theory is equifinality, the idea that the same final state can be reached from different initial conditions and in different ways.

Living system typically display homeostasis, the maintenance of balance in the system. Here we see a direct connection between systems theory and cybernetics because a living system adjusts itself on the basis of feedback about its performance. An example is thermoregulation in warm-blooded mammals. When the blood becomes slightly cooler, a center in the brain is stimulated to turn on heat-producing mechanisms in the body, such as stamping our feet. The increase in body warmth is monitored by the brain center, so that the body does not become too warm (von Bertalanffy 1968, p. 43). Walter Cannon, a medical professor and physiologist at Harvard University, coined the concept of homeostasis or equilibrium in a system. Cannon's *The Wisdom of the Body*, (1932), argued that the human body acts like a self-regulating cybernetic system. For example, when the body gets too warm, it sweats, and when the perspiration evaporates, the body is cooled. When the body becomes too cold, shivering begins and the skin surface puckers up into goose bumps. Thus, the surface area exposed to cold shrinks, and the body becomes warmer.

Systems theory was applied to a wide number of scholarly fields. For example, Daniel Katz and Robert Kahn (1966) applied it to the study of organizations. James G. Miller's book, *Living Systems* (1978), established various levels of systems—from the cell, to the individual, the group, the organization, the nation, and the world. Systems at each of these levels could be analyzed using the concepts and tools of systems thinking.

Ross Ashby was an English psychiatrist who was administering a large mental hospital in London at the time that he participated in the Macy Foundation Conferences on Cybernetics, and he was known for his important book, *Design for a Brain* (1952). He made a memorable presentation to the Cybernetics Group on whether a chess-playing machine could defeat its human designer (Ashby 1952a). Then Heinz von Foerster invited Ashby to a conference at the University of Illinois at Urbana, and Ashby stayed for the next ten years, as a faculty member in von Foerster's Biological Computer Laboratory, where he conducted important research and wrote an influential book on systems theory (Ashby 1958).

Systems theory is a science of wholes that is concerned with problems of relationships and interdependence of parts of the structure. Systems thinking rejects atomistic research analyzing the communication behavior of individuals and looks instead at the networks and the relationships of an individual with others. Further, if a communication scholar accepts the systems notion of studying wholes, then the search for cause-and-effect relationships is futile. Systems thinking considers mutually interactive relationships as part of the nature of living systems.

Systems theory was the rage in the 1960s but is hardly mentioned today. This theoretical perspective was absorbed into the ongoing body of scientific scholarship. Perhaps its main point, holism, was made emphatically, and scholars do not need to be constantly reminded of it.

CHAPTER 11

CLAUDE E. SHANNON'S INFORMATION THEORY

It is hard to picture the world before Shannon as it seemed
to those who lived in it.
—John R. Pierce, "The Early Days of Information Theory"

We owe to the genius of Claude Shannon the recognition
that a large class of problems related to encoding, transmitting, and decoding information can be approached in a systematic and disciplined way: His classic paper of 1948 marks
the birth of a new chapter of Mathematics. Search should
identify implications for future work in the field of communication.
—Mark Kac, Forward to R. J. McEliece, *The Theory of
Information and Coding: A Mathematical
Framework for Communication*

Claude Shannon's information theory, first published in 1948 as two
articles in the *Bell System Technical Journal,* almost immediately had an
impact on many scientific fields.* It remains central to communication
study today; it shaped the directions taken by the field of human communication, determined many of its main concepts, and contributed toward the closer intellectual integration of this field that arose from diverse multidisiplinary roots. Shannon's theory provided the basic
paradigm for communication study; nevertheless, Shannon's concept of
information has been poorly constructed by communication scholars.
This less than full appropriation of Shannon's information theory means

*This chapter is based in part on Rogers and Valente (1992). I thank Robert Price and
Klaus Krippendorff for their comments on a draft of this chapter, and acknowledge Tom
Valente for his collaboration.

that much future work remains to be done on information theory in the field of communication.

THE HISTORICAL CONTEXT

Following the end of World War II, scientists and engineers made tremendous advances in information technology. In 1945 the first mainframe computer, ENIAC, began operation at the Moore School of Engineering at the University of Pennsylvania. MIT professor Norbert Weiner was extending his new field of cybernetics (created during World War II in order to improve the accuracy of antiaircraft gunfire) to the design of human prosthetic devices, to neurophysiology, and to communication systems. Also in 1945, Arthur C. Clarke, a British fighter pilot at the time, authored an important article in a radio journal describing the potential of communication satellites for television broadcasting. At Bell Labs in Murray Hill, New Jersey, the transistor was invented in 1949 by William Shockley, Walter Brattain, and John Bardeen, a discovery for which they received the Nobel Prize. The transistor, perhaps the most important invention of the twentieth century, is a solid state device that replaced the vacuum tube as the fundamental component of all electronics systems. In Los Alamos, New Mexico, the Princeton mathematician John von Neumann was making computer calculations in order to determine how to explode the world's first atomic bomb. The scientific success of the Manhattan Project ended the war with Japan in August 1945.

Interdisciplinary research flowered during World War II, and this intellectual cross-fertilization was important in creating the new wave of information technologies. Federal funding for these scientific projects was justified by the wartime emergency. Later, the funding continued in peacetime, as the United States squared off against the Soviet Union in the Cold War. The U.S. public believed that scientists could find the solution to almost any problem. This belief in scientific research seemed to be justified by the world events of the 1940s.

One of the most far-reaching scientific breakthroughs was Claude E. Shannon's information theory, which today underlies our fundamental understanding of communication and especially the design of new communication technologies. The concept of information, the bit, as the universal measure of information and the model of communication that grew out of Shannon's work allow us to analyze communication systems in a way that was not possible prior to Shannon. Information is the central concept in the study of communication, and Shannon's information theory became the root paradigm for communication study.

WHAT IS INFORMATION THEORY?

Claude E. Shannon proposed the concept of information in two 1948 journal articles and then in a 1949 book (with Warren Weaver), *A Mathematical Theory of Communication.* *

Information, Entropy, and the Bit

Information behaves in some unusual ways. Its value typically increases when it is selectively shared. It does not depreciate with use, although it may over time. Strangest of all, you can give information away without giving it up. Thus, it is quite different in nature from money or other forms of energy or matter. Any message is a combination of the known and the unknown, the expected and the unexpected. In a message containing only content that you already know, there is no information, so the amount of surprise in a message is an index of information.

Information is defined as a difference in matter-energy that affects uncertainty in a situation where a choice exists among a set of alternatives in a decision-making situation.[†] Information thus is decreased uncertainty. Shannon's conceptualization of information was based on an equation for entropy devised by a nineteenth-century Austrian physicist, Ludwig Boltzmann, as part of the Second Law of Thermodynamics. Entropy is the degree of uncertainty or disorganization of a system. The formula for entropy, *H,* is:

$$H = -\sum_{i=1}^{N} \log_{2Pi}^{Pi} = p \log_2 (1 / p)$$

where N is the number of possible alternatives and Pi is the probability of each alterative's being chosen. Shannon suggested by this equation

---

*The title of the 1948 two-part article, "A Mathematical Theory of Communication," was changed a year later to the book's title, "The Mathematical Theory of Communication," when it became clear that there was no competition.

[†]This definition is taken directly from Rogers (1986) but is based on Shannon's conceptualization. To inform is to give form or shape to something.

that the amount of information can be measured by the logarithm of the number of available choices, with the logarithm calculated to the base 2 rather than to the more usual base 10.* The basic unit of information is a bit, a word that is a condensation of "binary digit." Imagine an electrical switch that is either on or off, so two alternatives exist. Each should be equally probable for the choice to represent 1 bit of information. So a nonarbitrary choice among sixteen alternative messages, if the choice is completely free, equals 4 bits of information ($16 = 2^2$). Suppose there are sixteen walnut shells on a table, with a pea under one of them. If we are told that the pea is under one of the eight shells on the right, we have received 1 bit of information; the information received reduces by one-half the number of possible alternatives. Another bit might tell us whether the pea was in the front row of shells versus elsewhere. The first bit reduces the number of possible shells to eight, the second bit reduces it to four; a third could reduce it to two, and a fourth to one (this example comes from Rogers and Valente 1992). Computers are essentially composed of millions of on-off switches, which together can perform immense numbers of calculations per second. Shannon's unit for measuring information had an intuitive explanation in terms of the binary nature of switches and the holes punched or not punched in a Hollerith (IBM) card. The bit fit well with the design of computers and other information technologies based on computers.

An important advantage of Shannon's unit of measurement of information, the bit, is that it can be utilized for a wide range of types of matter-energy. The bit is a universal unit of information: ink on paper, electrical impulses passing through a copper wire, or radio waves traveling through the air, for example. In each case the amount of information can be reduced to bits.

The Shannon Model of Communication

Claude Shannon worked for Bell Labs, the elite R&D center for the U.S. telephone system, which was concerned with increasing the channel capacity of communication systems, specifically of telephone systems. "Shannon's initial goal was simple: To improve the transmission of in-

---

*The entropy measure indexes diversity or variance in a general way. When the probability of an event is lower, it is more surprising, and it contains more information, and so entropy (H) is less (Lucky 1989, p. 43).

formation over a telegraph or telephone line affected by electrical interference, or noise. The best solution, he decided, was not to improve
transmission lines but to package information more efficiently" (Horgan
1990). Shannon's two papers in 1948 proposed a set of theorems, expressed in mathematical form, dealing with the transmission of messages from one place to another. The theorems predict the dependent
variable of channel capacity, measured in bits of information. Shannon
also showed the main elements involved in communication: source,
message, transmitter, signal, noise, received signal, receiver, and destination. This composite intellectual contribution of Claude Shannon is
commonly called information theory, although Shannon (1949) referred to it as "the mathematical theory of communication."*

Communication is defined as "the process through which one mind
influences another" (Weaver 1949b, p. 3). It is thus viewed as intentional. Both Weaver and Shannon provided an identical linear model of
the components (source, message, transmitter, signal, noise, etc.) of the
communication process in their book, *The Mathematical Theory of Communication* (1949). In its simplified form, the model conveys a linear,[†]
left-to-right conception of communication (Figure 11.1). Communication scholars use it to focus on the effects of communication, especially
mass communication, though Shannon's intention was to explain the
channel capacity to carry messages, not their effects. But the linear,
source-to-receiver nature of Shannon's model led communication
scholars to add effects at the end of the chain of concepts. They looked
for explanations of the degree to which effects occurred on the basis of
such other variables as source credibility and the persuasive strategies
represented in construction of the message. In other words, they used
Shannon's conceptual variables to predict their dependent variable
rather than his. Unfortunately, use of the Shannon model by social scientists of human communication led them away from emphasizing the
subjective meanings that are created through information exchanges between individuals. The encoding and decoding of messages is a social

---

*Shannon was the first person to use the term information theory, in a 1945 classified Bell
Labs memorandum (Tropp 1984).

†Shannon's model of communication has commonly been called "linear" by communication scholars (for example, Rogers and Kincaid 1981, p. 33), meaning one-way, from left to
right. But to engineers, *linear* means noninteractive. Here we utilize the term *linear* in the
former sense.

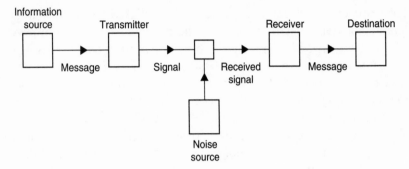

Figure 11.1. The Shannon model of communication.

"The *information source* selects a desired *message* out of a set of possible messages. . . . The *transmitter* changes the *message* into the *signal* which is actually sent over the *communication channel* from the transmitter to the *receiver*. . . . The *receiver* is a sort of inverse transmitter, changing the transmitted signal back into a message, and handing this message on to the destination. . . . In the process of being transmitted, it is unfortunately characteristic that certain things are added to the signal which were not intended by the information source. . . . All of these changes in the transmitted signal are called *noise*."

Claude E. Shannon (1949b), "The Mathematical Theory of Communication," in Claude E. Shannon and Warren Weaver (eds.), *The Mathematical Theory of Communication* (Urbana: University of Illinois), p. 34. Copyright © 1949 by the Board of Trustees of the University of Illinois; used by permission.

process, involving the human relationships among the individuals involved, as well as their individual beliefs and past experiences.

Shannon's information theory set limitations on what was considered communication: "Explicit, logical material, produced by a deliberate, formalized encoding process, and leading to successful mutual understanding." This definition of communication did not include the entire range of interactions that occur between people. For example, information theory ignored nonverbal communication (Bavelas 1990).

The Shannon model is immensely useful in explaining the essential components of a communication act (source, channel, message, receiver, noise, and feedback) to a beginning student of communication. The most influential book in translating Shannon's model into communication scholarship was David K. Berlo's *The Process of Communication* (1960). During the 1960s and early 1970s, this volume was the main textbook in university courses in communication. Generations of students were taught to understand human communication in terms of SMCR (source-message-channel-receiver), feedback, and noise. Many of these concepts have been absorbed into everyday speech by the general public. Notice that they are engineering terms. For instance, *receiver* originally meant a machine or piece of equipment to which the message-signal was sent, such as a telephone receiver, a radio receiver, or a television receiver. Communication scholars took Shannon's concept of receiver as an item of electronic equipment and converted it into a human being who receives a message. The difference, obviously, is striking. A human receiver has emotions and experiences and is a sense-making individual.

The Shannon model provided a powerful unifying force for scholars seeking to understand communication systems (McCormick 1986, pp. 34–42). The concept of information was applied in computer science, physics, molecular biology and biotechnology, psychology, and linguistics, as well as human communication. The initial enthusiasm for information theory in each of these fields gave them a common set of concepts; all shared an interest in information, although they applied it to different phenomena. The impact of information theory on the new field of communication study was especially striking. Following Shannon's publication of information theory, hundreds of schools of communication were started at U.S. universities and around the world and became tremendously attractive to students. These schools were built in part on Shannon's concepts in his mathematical theory of communication. As Klaus Krippendorff (1989b, p. 59) noted: "Within a few years of its publication [Shannon's] theory provided the scientific justification for academic programs in human communication (which sprang up largely in U.S. universities), expanded communication research to new media, created novel areas of inquiry as well as two new journals, and stimulated the development of new communication technology for handling knowledge, including in computers. The theory became a milestone in communication research and marked the transition from an industrial to an information society."

Applications of Shannon's information theory abound in everyday life. The concepts of information theory were applied to computers and to the wide range of related information technologies in which computers are a key component: telephone systems, banking, airline reservations, scientific research, weather forecasting, and hundreds of other applications of information technology. For example, we use one application of information theory every time that we listen to a compact disk or transfer text or data from a computer to a floppy disc. This application is called an error-correcting code, which is one means of overcoming noise in a message. A simple type of error-correcting code consists of determining whether there is an odd number of 1s in a string of binary numbers:

$$1 \ \ 0 \ \ 1 \ \ 1 \ \ 1 \ \ 0 \ \ 0 \ \ 0 \ \ 0 \ \ 1 \ \ 0 \ \ 1 \ \boxed{0}$$

The first twelve numbers here contain six 1s, an even number, so the string is error-coded 0. This 0, called a bit-check, is the error-correcting code. If this thirteen-number message, when received, contains five 1s, we know that an error has been made in transmission. Another type of error-correcting code consists of adding a polynomial equation at the end of a string of numbers. The decoder at the receiving end knows that any numbers diverging from the polynomial expression have been changed in transmission (Horgan 1992).

Richard Hamming (1950) conceived of the idea of error-correcting codes based on Shannon's information theory. Soon, very sophisticated error-correcting codes were created, such as those used in compact disk players. "You can run a nail file across a compact disk, and you will not hear a single hiccup on playback" (Lucky 1989, p. 69). The error-correcting code built into a compact disk will correct 8, 232 consecutive errors. Similarly, every time that a user transfers some text from a computer to a disk, the integrity of the transfer is ensured by an error-correcting code.

Shannon's theory has changed society in many profound ways. Here, we mainly analyze the considerable impacts of information theory on the field of communication study. Certain parts of Shannon's contribution, however, attracted relatively little attention by communication scholars. For instance, the set of mathematical propositions with which he specified his theory about communication channel capacity (which were investigated by electrical engineers) have seldom been investigated by communication scholars, most of whom lack the needed mathematical ability to do so. And given their predominant focus on communication effects, communication scholars were not much interested in his proposition about channel capacity.

SHANNON'S DEVELOPMENT
OF INFORMATION THEORY

Claude E. Shannon was born in 1916 in the small city of Petosky, Michigan, and was raised in nearby Gaylord, in the north-central part of Michigan's lower peninsula (Table 11.1). His father was a probate judge who supplied the young Shannon with erector sets, radio kits, and other technological toys. Claude was inclined toward science and mathematics. His childhood hero was the inventor Thomas Edison, and he was intrigued by Edgar Allen Poe's 1843 book, *The Gold Bug,* a story about solving a secret code. This early curiosity may have led to Shannon's later work in cryptography. He worked as a Western Union messenger boy in Gaylord, and his contact with telegraphy may have presaged his later work on electronic communication systems.

Shannon earned two bachelor's degrees at the University of Michigan, one in electrical engineering and one in mathematics. When he

Figure 11.2. Claude E. Shannon (born 1916) at home.
Copyright ©1983 by Stanley Rowin; used by permission.

TABLE 11.1
Major Events in the Career of Claude E. Shannon

Date	Event
1916	Born in Petosky, Michigan
1936	Earns a bachelor's degree in electrical engineering and mathematics from the University of Michigan
1940	Earns both master's and Ph.D. degrees from MIT in electrical engineering and mathematics
1940–1941	Receives a National Research Fellowship at the Institute for Advanced Study, Princeton University, to study with the mathematician Herman Weyl
1941–1956	Appointed a research mathematician at Bell Labs in New York City, where he initially conducts wartime research on cryptographic problems, while also developing information theory
1945	Publishes *A Mathematical Theory of Cryptography* as a classified memorandum at Bell Labs, which contains the essence of information theory
1948	Publishes "A Mathematical Theory of Communication," as a two-part article in the *Bell System Technical Journal*
1949	Publishes *The Mathematical Theory of Communication*
1956	Leaves Bell Labs for MIT, where in 1958 he is appointed Donner Professor of Science
1960s	Withdraws from MIT and takes early retirement

arrived for graduate work at MIT in 1936, the twenty-one-year-old Shannon became a research assistant to Vannevar Bush, operating the differential analyzer machine, a kind of mechanical computer that Bush had created. Bush, the dean of engineering at MIT and Shannon's scientific mentor, suggested to Shannon that he study the logical design of the machine for his master's thesis in electrical engineering. Shannon showed that electrical circuits could be laid out according to Boolean principles* in order to streamline the design of telephone circuits and

*Boolean mathematics had been created by George Boole a century before Shannon's work. A typical Boolean proposition states that if X or Y happens but not Z, then Q results (Horgan 1992).

computers rather than designing such circuits by conventional wisdom or by trial and error. Shannon's master's thesis, "A Symbolic Analysis of Relay and Switching Circuits," was completed in 1938 although he did not pick up the degree until two years later, and it almost immediately had profound effects on the design of telephone systems and other electronic circuits. It is considered one of the most important master's theses ever completed (Horgan 1992) and gained for Claude Shannon a reputation for brilliance.

By 1939, Shannon was beginning to think about information in a statistical sense and about how to measure it. In a four-page letter to his doctoral adviser, Vannevar Bush (then in Washington, D.C., serving as president of the Carnegie Institution), Shannon indicated just how far along his information theory had progressed (this at a point ten years before it was published): "Off and on I have been working on an analysis of some of the fundamental properties of general systems for the transmission of intelligence, including telephony, radio, television, telegraphy, etc. Practically all systems of communication may be thrown into the following general form:

$$f_1(t) \longrightarrow \boxed{T} \longrightarrow F(t) \longrightarrow \boxed{R} \longrightarrow f_2(t)$$

Where $f_1(t)$ is the intelligence to be transmitted as a function of time, T is the transmitting element, $F(t)$ represents what is actually transmitted, R is a receiving element, and $f_2(t)$ should be similar to $f_1(t)$ but in practice is distorted from $f_1(t)$ by random noise or 'static.'" Notice that Shannon in 1937 was referring to information as intelligence, but most of the other main elements in his model (see Figure 11.1) were already present. He was to polish his conceptualization and refine it over the next decade. He was in no rush to publish.

Shannon earned his Ph.D. degree in mathematics at MIT in 1940 and then, after a summer internship at Bell Labs, studied mathematics with Herman W. Weyl on a postdoctoral fellowship at the Institute for Advanced Study at Princeton University. Weyl was a noted mathematician, and the Institute for Advanced Study was a world-famous think tank that included Albert Einstein on its staff. During his 1940–1941 postdoctoral fellowship at Princeton, Shannon worked on his information theory (Pierce 1973). In fact, he had the general idea in mind while he was still at MIT back in 1939, at the time that he applied for the Na-

*This letter, dated February 16, 1939, is found in the U.S. Library of Congress, Manuscript Division, Vannevar Bush Collection, Box 102, Folder 2401.

tional Research Council postdoctoral fellowship.* The fellowship at Princeton was officially for the purpose of conducting research on the mathematics of genetic processes, the topic of his doctoral dissertation, "An Algebra for Theoretical Genetics" (1940),[†] but with the permission of Herman W. Weyl, his fellowship supervisor, he concentrated on developing information theory. In fact, for a period for several years, from 1939 to 1945, whether at MIT, Princeton, or Bell Labs, Shannon concentrated on information theory in spite of the scientific task to which he was officially assigned.

During Shannon's period at Princeton, John von Neumann supposedly told Shannon that he should use "entropy" in his emerging information theory, as no one else really understood what this concept meant (Campbell 1982; Horgan 1990). But Shannon says that he did not get the concept of entropy from von Neumann (Ellersick 1984). Shannon derived his equation for the amount of information and then realized that it was identical to the formula that physicists used to calculate the quantity known as entropy in thermodynamics (Bello 1953). This understanding helped him to realize that the communication of information is a statistical problem, an insight that was fundamental to information theory.

Prior to taking up his postdoctoral fellowship at Princeton, Shannon had had a summer job at Bell Labs, working under Thorton C. Fry in the Mathematics Department on applying the ideas from his MIT master's thesis to the design of telephone relay circuits. In September 1940, Shannon moved to Princeton, but a couple of months later, he was back at Bell Labs as a regular employee. He had dropped his fellowship because he foresaw U.S. involvement in World War II and wanted to contribute to the war effort. Thorton Fry wanted Shannon back at Bell Labs, and Warren Weaver, the Rockefeller Foundation research grants manager then on leave to direct a military research program in Washington, persuaded Shannon to study methods of improving the accuracy of antiaircraft gunfire. As Weaver wrote to Vannevar Bush,[‡]

---

*Shannon's letter of application is reproduced by Hagemeyer (1979).

[†]The problem that was central to Shannon's dissertation had grown out of his research assistantship at the biological research laboratory at Cold Spring Harbor, New York, in summer 1939. Vannevar Bush had arranged for Shannon's summer work in genetic algebra.

[‡]This letter, dated October 24, 1949, is in the U.S. Library of Congress, Manuscript Division, Vannevar Bush Collection, Box 102, Folder 2401. Weaver's letter indicates that Thorton Fry offered the Bell Labs position to Shannon in 1941 in order to help take Shannon's mind off some personal problems.

"I first got involved with Claude Shannon back in 1941. . . . At that time I persuaded him to give up a fellowship which he then had at Princeton . . . to undertake some studies in fire control design and prediction theory for old Section 7. He did some really stunning work for us." Shannon was attracted to work for Bell Labs because of two wartime research problems, cryptography and antiaircraft gunfire, both juicy problems for a mathematics whiz. And the scientific puzzles that Shannon encountered were of an ideal nature for developing information theory. The gunfire control problem was mainly posed by Norbert Wiener (see Chapter 10), but Shannon made a highly innovative exposition of its solution.

During the early 1940s while Shannon worked on cryptographic problems at Bell Labs, he lived in an apartment on Eleventh Street in Greenwich Village. His friend Barney Oliver recalls that Shannon's apartment was piled high with gadgets, equipment, and other material (Oliver 1992). Later, after Bell Labs moved from Manhattan to Morristown, New Jersey, Shannon lived in an apartment near Oliver's. He remembers Shannon as being shy and interspective. Shannon was intense and could get very involved in studying a scientific problem. Bell Labs, especially its Mathematics Department, was very permissive in allowing great freedom to its researchers to pursue whatever topic they wished. Such an organizational culture could tolerate a brilliant individualist like Shannon. He was too independent to be assigned to any task, but once he got interested in a topic, he pursued it relentlessly. So when Shannon had an opportunity to engage in improving secrecy systems during World War II, he approached it with gusto.

Shannon pushed to the limit the individual freedom for Bell Labs employees to pursue their own intellectual curiosity. While creating a chess-playing machine, for example, he played so much chess that at least one supervisor became concerned. Shannon says cheerfully, "I've always pursued my interests without much regard for financial value. I've spend lots of time on totally useless things" (Horgan 1992). Oldtimers who were at Bell Labs with Shannon in the 1940s and early 1950 remember him as a blithe spirit, riding through the corridors on a unicycle while he juggled balls. "And there were those occasional 'clop clops' as Shannon went by on his pogo stick—hardly the image of today's corporate research!" (Lucky 1989, pp. 5–6).

In 1948, in response to urging from his supervisor and his colleagues, Shannon published the two-part article in the *Bell System Technical Journal*. They represented the first publication of information theory (although Shannon had authored a classified memorandum related to this topic at Bell Labs in 1945).

John R. Pierce, a colleague of Claude Shannon at Bell Labs in 1948, described Shannon as brilliant but having to be encouraged by his supervisor, Dr. Hendrik Bode, and by his colleagues to publish his work (Pierce 1990). This view of Shannon's work habits is corroborated by Richard W. Hamming (1990) and by others who were at Bell Labs, and by Campbell (1982, p. 20), who quotes Pierce as saying that Shannon's information theory "came as a bomb, and something of a delayed action bomb." Certainly it was surprising to his colleagues at Bell Labs when Shannon published such an extraordinarily important work as his information theory, although he had been trying out components of his theory with them on a daily basis. Shannon, Pierce, and Barney Oliver often went to lunch together in the Bell Labs cafeteria in New York. As Oliver (1992) remembers it, Shannon would tell them about his thinking, perhaps by asking a series of questions. For example, Shannon would ask: "How much information is in a choice between two alternatives?" "A bit, you say, yes, well, would it matter if one alternative were more likely than the other?" "What if one alternative were very much more likely?" Shannon advanced his thinking about his information theory by discussing certain of its aspects with his work associates, but he kept the big picture of his information theory to himself. Then, in 1948, he published his information theory, a major contribution: "Rarely does it happen in mathematics that a new discipline achieves the character of a mature and developed scientific theory in the first investigation devoted to it. . . . So it was with information theory after the work of Shannon" (Khintchin 1956).

Many scholars could not completely understand information theory. They needed an interpretation and explanation that was written in nonmathematical language. It was provided by Warren Weaver, director of the Division of Natural Sciences at the Rockefeller Foundation in New York. Weaver (1894–1978) had received his doctorate in civil engineering at the University of Wisconsin in 1917, taught mathematics at Cal Tech, and then returned to Madison as professor of mathematics for a dozen years until he joined the Rockefeller Foundation in 1932, where he finished his lengthy philanthropic career as vice-president in 1959 (except for wartime service in Washington). In 1948, when Shannon's two articles on information theory appeared, Weaver was the top-ranking mathematician-scientist at the Rockefeller Foundation, and so it was natural for Chester Barnard, president of the foundation, to ask

Weaver to translate Shannon's mathematical theory of communication into less formidable language (Jorgenson 1989, p. 309). In July 1949, Weaver's article, "The Mathematics of Communication," appeared in *Scientific American* magazine. Wilbur Schramm learned of Shannon's important two-part series from Louis N. Ridenour, a physicist and dean of the graduate school at Illinois. Schramm was editor of the University of Illinois Press, and, at Ridenour's suggestion, he published a major revision of Weaver's *Scientific American* article with the two Shannon articles in a composite book *The Mathematical Theory of Communication* by Claude E. Shannon and Warren Weaver (1949).* Part II of the book is a word-for-word duplicate of Shannon's two articles except for the correction of minor errata and the addition of some references. Part I, "Recent Contributions to the Mathematical Theory of Communication," by Weaver, based on his 1949 *Scientific American* article, is primarily a discussion of how a human communication theory might be developed out of Shannon's mathematical theorems about engineering communication.[†]

The Shannon-Weaver book is one of the most widely selling academic books published by a university press. About 45,300 copies were sold from 1949 to 1990, and the rate of sales continued at more than 600 per year in the 1980s (Stockanes 1990). Further, Shannon is cited 1,472 times in the Institute for Scientific Information data base of scientific journal citations over the eighteen-year period from 1972 (when the ISI system began) through 1989. Shannon continues to be cited at about the same rate in recent as in earlier years. Shannon's total citations rank favorably with such other communication theorists as Carl Hovland, 1,327; Harold Lasswell, 1,462; Paul F. Lazarsfeld, 1,766; Robert E. Park, 1,472; Wilbur Schramm, 1,013; and Norbert Wiener, 1,267.

---

*Weaver's contribution to the book was originally part II, while Shannon's contribution was part I. However, when the book was republished prior to 1963, the order was reversed, presumably to make the work more accessible to readers who found Shannon's highly mathematical style more difficult to understand (Stockanes 1990).

[†]Because of the very fundamental differences in content between the two parts of *The Mathematical Theory of Communication,* scholars should cite either Weaver or Shannon, unless referring to the entire book. Thus, I follow the suggestion of Ritchie (1986), who argued that one source of confusion on the part of communication scholars is "the habit of citing 'Shannon and Weaver' when it is Weaver's speculations that are being quoted, under the assumption that they are somehow supported by Shannon's mathematics." When the Shannon and Weaver book is cited by communication scholars, they usually are referencing ideas from Weaver's part I rather than from Shannon's part II.

Claude Shannon's theory, first published forty-five years ago, continues to be regarded as important by contemporary scholars.

About his contribution to the Shannon-Weaver book, Weaver had this to say: "My own contribution to this book is infinitesimal as compared to Shannon's. And I am well aware of the fact that when a parade is arranged, the mouse does not march ahead of the lion. . . . I think that my section should have come first. My modest contribution . . . should entice on to the mathematical pages (making the reading of them a somewhat easier task). . . . As the thing stands, . . . it's like having a big and important party, and then introducing the guests just as they leave."*

TECHNICAL COMMUNICATION VERSUS HUMAN COMMUNICATION

Claude Shannon was careful in limiting the applicability of his information theory: "The fundamental problem of communication is that of reproducing at one point either exactly or approximately a message related at another point. Frequently the messages have meaning; that is they refer to, or are correlated according to, some system with certain physical or conceptual entities. These semiotic aspects of communication are irrelevant to the engineering problem" (Shannon 1949 p. 31). From the beginning he claimed that his model did not apply to human communication, the type of information exchange in which an individual interprets the meaning of a message. Shannon said that his model was limited to engineering or technical communication, presumably to communication through such electronic channels as the telephone, telegraph, and radio. Obviously, the process of human subjective interpretation is also involved in engineering communication, but the mathematically inclined Shannon defined the meaning aspects of human communication as beyond the scope of his conceptualization. To an engineer like Claude Shannon, human meanings and interpretations were a kind of soft data that could not be reduced to precise mathematical formulations. Warren Weaver (1949b, p. 27) provided the following example of Shannon's restricted model: "An engineering communication theory is just like a very proper and discreet girl accepting your telegram. She pays no attention to the meaning, whether it be sad, or

*Weaver to Louis Ridenour, November 17, 1949, U.S. Library of Congress, Manuscript Division, Vannevar Bush Collection, Box 102, Folder 2401.

joyous, or embarrassing." In other words, the engineering model of communication, according to Weaver, does not deal with emotions or attitudes but just with strictly cognitive content and effects in which a receiver decodes a signal in a similar way to that in which it was encoded by the source.

Weaver, in his interpretation of the Shannon model, stressed that Shannon had limited his conceptualization to engineering communication: "The word *information*, in [Shannon's] theory is used in a special sense that must not be confused with its ordinary usage. In particular, information must not be confused with meaning. In fact, two messages, one of which is heavily loaded with meaning and the other of which is pure nonsense, can be exactly equivalent, from the present viewpoint, as regards information. It is this, undoubtedly, that Shannon means when he says that 'The semiotic aspects of communication are irrelevant to the engineering aspects.' But this does not mean that the engineering aspects are necessarily irrelevant to the semiotic aspects" (Weaver 1949b, p. 8).

Weaver (1949b, p. 4), in his introductory part of the Shannon and Weaver book, identified three levels of communication problems:

Level A: How accurately can the symbols of communication be transmitted? (the technical problem).

Level B: How precisely do the transmitted symbols convey the desired meaning? (the semantic problem).

Level C: How effectively does the received meaning affect conduct in the desired way? (the effectiveness or behavioral problem).

Shannon claimed that his mathematical theory of communication dealt only with level A, which he called engineering communication or technical communication. Weaver, however, went far beyond Shannon's claim to suggest that "the mathematical theory of communication . . . particularly the more definitely engineering theory treated by Shannon, although ostensibly applicable only to Level A problems, actually is helpful and suggestive for the Level B and C problems" (Weaver 1949b, p. 24). At another point in his essay, Weaver concluded: "The analysis at Level A discloses that this level overlaps the other levels more than one could possibly naïvely suspect. Thus the theory of Level A is, at least to a significant degree, also a theory of Levels B and C" (p. 6). Weaver thus invited the wide application of Shannon's information theory to all types of intentional communication. He did not add much to Shannon's core conceptualizations of information theory, other than his optimistic broadening of its applicability, so it is appropriate to refer to *Shannon's* information theory, rather than to *Shannon and Weaver's* information theory, as is commonly done by most communication scholars.

Writing eight years after publication of his two articles on information theory, Shannon (1956) stated: "Information theory has, in the past few years, become something of a scientific bandwagon. . . . Applications are being made to biology, psychology, linguistics, fundamental physics, economics, the theory of organizations, and many other areas. In short, information is currently partaking of a somewhat heady draught of general popularity." Shannon warned that such popularity carried an element of danger: "If, for example, the human being acts in some situations like an ideal decoder, this is an experimental and not a mathematical fact, and as such must be tested under a wide variety of experimental situations." Shannon saw information theory as limited to engineering communication and warned the scientific world against applying it more broadly to all types of human communication. Nevertheless, communication scholars have not paid much attention to Shannon's warning.

INFORMATION THEORY AND CRYPTOGRAPHY

As with most other intellectual breakthroughs, Shannon's information theory grew out of previous work by other mathematicians and engineers, particularly Nyquist, Hartley, and Norbert Wiener. However, the theory was most directly related to his work on cryptography at Bell Labs during World War II. Shannon's theory of communication grew, paradoxically, out of organized attempts to *prevent* effective communication from occurring, at least to an enemy. Cryptography is the science of producing cipher systems, which allow secret communication. Cryptography makes a message private. Here again we see how seeking the solution to a practical problem can ground the development of an abstract theory.

Looking back thirty years to when he developed information theory, Shannon explained: "I started with Hartley's [1928] paper and worked at least two or three years on the problems of information and communications. . . . Then I started thinking about cryptography and secrecy systems. There is this close connection; they are very similar things, in one case trying to conceal information, and in the other case trying to transmit it" (Ellerstick 1984). Shannon's cryptography research stimulated his information theory, which he largely worked out in the five years previous to the 1945 Bell Labs classified report on his cryptographic work (Ellersick 1984). Shannon actually developed much of his information theory at home, on nights and weekends, during the 1940–1945 period. Presumably this explains the surprise of John Pierce, Shannon's colleague and supervisor at Bell Labs, when Shannon published his 1948 articles.

Cryptography transforms vocal and written messages into a coded form so that an enemy cannot understand them. During World War II, considerable cryptographic research was conducted by both the Allied and Axis powers. Bell Labs was heavily involved in the U.S. wartime activities, as might be expected, given its reputation as America's leading R&D center in electronics. During World War II, it carried out 2,000 research projects for the U.S. military, ranging from developing radar, sonar, the bazooka, bombsights, antiaircraft gun control systems, and the acoustic torpedo, to the cryptographic work on message security in radio, teletypewriter, and telephone systems (Fagan 1978, p. ix). About 2,000 of Bell Labs's 2,700 engineering staff were assigned to military projects in these years.

Cryptoanalysts in England had already had considerable success in breaking the German coding system, before Shannon and his Bell Labs co-workers began their research. The German system utilized encoding machines to scramble military messages, which the Germans transmitted by radio to their submarines, ships, and other distant forces. The encrypted messages were then decoded at the receiving end. Alan Turing, the brilliant Cambridge University mathematician working at the Government Code and Cipher School (GC&CS) at Bletchley Park (outside London), designed an Ultra machine that deciphered Enigma, the German military code. Turing's success was one of the most important turning points in World War II, aiding the British in protecting their Atlantic convoys from German submarines, helping the British know in advance about the actions of Field Marshal Erwin Rommel's Afrika Korps, and aiding greatly in the Normandy invasion.* The British suc-

---

*If the British government had known that Turing was gay, he would not have been allowed to work in cryptography research at Bletchley Park, and Britain might have lost the war (Good 1980, p. 34).

cess in cracking the German code had to be kept secret during World War II, however, or else the Germans would switch to another coding system.*

In early 1943, Alan Turing made a secret trip from Bletchley Park to the Bell Labs headquarters in New York City, where Claude Shannon was working on cryptography problems. Turing spent two months there in collaborative research on the problem of safely encoding vocal messages. Almost every day Turing and Shannon would meet to discuss their ideas about the human brain and computers. They could not, however, directly discuss the specific cryptographic projects on which they were working because such work was compartmentalized into separated partitions in order to ensure a high degree of security. Shannon told Turing about the binary digit, as a measure of information, and Turing told Shannon about his concept of the "deciban," defined as the weight of evidence that made some topic ten times as definite (Hodges 1983, pp. 249, 250). Their exchange of theoretical viewpoints was important to Shannon in building information theory in a general way, but he did not directly base it on Turing's concepts or theories. Working on cryptographic problems at Bell Labs during World War II brought Shannon in contact with some of the best minds on both sides of the Atlantic.

The seeds of information theory appeared first in a Bell Labs classified memorandum dated September 1, 1945, "A Mathematical Theory of Cryptography" (it was declassified and published in a revised form after World War II [Shannon 1949b].) Cryptographic problems fit with information theory in that the encoding of military messages into secret codes theoretically amounts to adding deceptive noise to the original messages. By using the appropriate equipment at the receiver end, the disguised message can be decoded by removing the noise (if, that is, one understands how the noise had been generated at the encoding end of the process). The classified cryptography research that Shannon conducted at Bell Labs was a specific application of Shannon's emerging information theory. Given that he was developing the theory during the same period that he worked at his Bell Labs office on cryptography, it is

---

*In order to preserve the secret that Turing had cracked the Enigma code, British Prime Minister Winston Churchill allowed the German Luftwaffe to bomb the English city of Coventry, although the British knew in advance when and where the bombing raid was scheduled. The official history of British intelligence states that both Coventry and London were known to be German targets that night, and Churchill chose to defend London.

not at all surprising that he utilized such terms as *encoding* and *noise* in the communication model (see Figure 11.1).

Shannon says: "During World War II, Bell Labs was working on secrecy systems. I'd worked on communication systems and I was appointed to some of the committees studying cryptanalytic techniques. The work on both the mathematical theory of communications and cryptology went forward concurrently from about 1941. I worked on both of them together and I had some of the ideas on one while working on the other. I wouldn't say once came before the other—they were so close together you couldn't separate them" (Kahn 1967, p. 744). The work on both the "Communication Theory of Secrecy Systems" (1949) and "A Mathematical Theory of Communication" were substantially completed by about 1944. Shannon continued to polish them, and then, in 1948, he submitted his pair of articles on information theory to the *Bell System Technical Journal.*

Shannon's important contribution in his 1949 journal article on secrecy systems was to show that redundancy provides the grounds for cryptoanalysis (Kahn 1967, p. 748). The basis of codebreaking is to assume that the most frequent letters in a secret message are cipher equivalents of *e, a, o, i, d,* and so on, and then to proceed to the least frequent letters: *p, q, x,* and *z.* The letter *e* predominates to such a degree, that *few* English sentences exist in which *e* is not the most frequent letter (Lucky 1989, p. 104). As the degree of redundancy of a coded message decreases, such as by eliminating duplication, codebreaking becomes more difficult. Alternatively, more text is needed to crack a code if a message has lower redundancy (Kahn 1967, p. 750). Redundancy is thus a kind of insurance against uncertainty and against the effect of noise in a channel. Redundancy provides, at a cost, information that reduces uncertainty and helps to overcome the effects of noise. Shannon estimated that the English language is 50 percent redundant, but later investigators revised this calculation to about 70 percent (Krippendorff 1989c, p. 317).

Shannon made important contributions to the ultrasecret "X" system of World War II, also known as SIGSALY, a telephone hot-line linking Prime Minister Winston Churchill and Presidents Franklin Delano Roosevelt and then Harry Truman. Early in the war, the Allies became convinced that the Germans had broken their code and were informed about Allied war plans, to their great strategic advantage. SIGSALY was created by British-American cryptographers as an unbreakable coding system. Shannon was asked to work out a mathematical proof that

SIGSALY was unbreakable. On the basis of his mathematical analysis using information theory, he concluded that it was impossible to crack the code, unless the Germans had the help of an Allied traitor. German intelligence was never able to break SIGSALY during the remainder of the war, although they monitored the encoded radio telephone messages daily. Shannon, in one of the first applications of the information theory that he was then evolving, greatly aided America's war effort.

It was somewhat of an accident of timing that Shannon was assigned to work on cryptographic problems when he joined Bell Labs, just as the U.S. entered World War II. It turned out to be a fortunate accident for communication theory.

INTELLECTUAL INFLUENCES ON SHANNON'S INFORMATION THEORY

Although Shannon's information theory was highly original, like other scientific advances, it built on previous contributions by other scholars. Shannon's work on cryptography problems at Bell Labs brought him into contact with two scholars, Ralph V. L. Hartley and Harry Nyquist, who were involved in the cryptography research program (Fagan 1978, p. 316). Nyquist (1924) had shown that a certain bandwidth was necessary in order to send telegraph signals at a definite rate, and Hartley (1928) had attempted to develop a theory of the transmission of information. He defined the quantity of information as the logarithm of the number of possible messages built from a pool of symbols and applied his statistical formula for entropy to the problem of signal transmission. Shannon cited both Hartley and Nyquist in his two papers on information theory, as well as Ronald A. Fisher, the English agricultural statistician who had developed a measure of information provided by the analysis of variance of an agricultural experiment.

Shannon was also aware of Norbert Wiener's work in cybernetics and cited Wiener's 1948 book in his two articles. Although Wiener's book on this topic was not published until 1949, the mathematics of his cybernetic theory was available several years earlier, during wartime, as the classified document dealing with antiaircraft gun control known as the "Yellow Peril." Wiener had recognized that the communication of information was a statistical problem. Shannon had taken a mathematics course from Norbert Wiener while he was in graduate work at MIT and had access to the Yellow Peril report while at Bell Labs from 1941

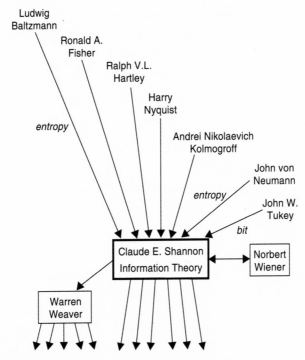

Figure 11.3. Intellectual forebears and descendants of Claude Shannon's information theory.

to 1945.* Some observers credit Wiener with being a co-discoverer of information theory.† For example, Bello (1953) says: "To MIT's eminent mathematician, Norbert Wiener, goes the major credit for discovering the new continent [of information theory] and grasping its dimensions;

*As Claude Shannon confirmed in a personal interview with Robert Price (Shannon 1982). In fact, with two Bell Labs colleagues, Shannon in 1948 authored a publication that built on the Yellow Peril report by sidestepping Wiener's formidable mathematical difficulties (Millman 1984, p. 43).

†Wiener did not seem to have fully understood Shannon's information theory, even though he wrote a review of the Shannon-Weaver book. In his autobiography, *I Am a Mathematician,* Wiener (1956, p. 263) claimed credit with Shannon for information theory: "Shannon loves the discrete and eschews the continuum. He considered discrete messages as something like a sequence of yeses and noes distributed in time, and he regarded single decisions between yes and no as the element of information. In the continuous theory of filtering, I had been led to a very similar definition of the unit of information, from what was at the beginning a considerably different point of view. In introducing the Shannon-Wiener definition of quality of information (for it belongs to the two of us equally), we made a radical departure from the existing state of the subject."

to Claude Shannon of Bell Laboratories goes the credit for mapping the new territory in detail and charting some breathtaking peaks."

Shannon was a participant in an invisible college of outstanding mathematicians and physicists that centered around John von Neumann, Norbert Wiener, John W. Tukey, and others at MIT, Bell Labs, and the Institute for Advanced Study. The intellectual climate of these scholars undoubtedly influenced Shannon's thinking in important ways (Figure 11.3).

In Shannon's 1945 Bell Labs memorandum, "A Mathematical Theory of Cryptography," he used the word *alternative* for his binary choice measure of information. In his two 1948 articles on information theory, Shannon credits John W. Tukey with suggesting the word *bit*. Tukey was a professor of mathematics and statistics at Princeton University, who also worked concurrently for Bell Labs in 1946. The story goes that several Bell Labs researchers, probably including Shannon, were meeting over lunch in the cafeteria in late 1946, bemoaning the awkwardness of the term *binary digit*. John Tukey joined the table. "With a characteristic grin, and equally characteristics down-East inflection, he asked, 'Well, isn't the word obviously *bit*?' And it was." Claude Shannon extended Tukey's use of the term *bit* to count the number of independent choices required to identify a unique entity among a certain population; Tukey had used *bit* in a more restricted sense as "the generic name of a coefficient in the expansion of a number as a sum of powers of a base" (Tropp 1984).

IMPACTS OF SHANNON'S INFORMATION THEORY

After 1948, Shannon's information theory spread rapidly and widely throughout academic communities in the physical, biological, and social sciences (Dahling 1962). Information theory was widely cited, and this influence has remained quite persistent over the years. Shannon's concept of information (measured with the entropy formula) was directly useful to communication scholars.* Perhaps that is why his the-

---

*Communication scholars who utilized an entropy-type measure in their research include Krull, Watt, and Lichty (1977), Finn (1985), Chaffee and Wilson (1977), Darnell (1970, 1972, 1976), Rogers and Kincaid (1981, pp. 281–285), Taylor (1953, 1956), Schramm (1955), and Watt and Krull (1974). The entropy measure deserves more attention from communication scientists than it has received (Finn and Roberts, 1984).

ory is usually called *information* theory rather than *communication* theory, the terminology that Shannon used for it.*

On the basis of citations to Shannon's information theory, Dahling (1962) noted that it was applied in disciplines ranging widely from biology to brain research to psychology. Horgan (1990) says that Claude Shannon wrote "the Magna Carta of the information age." Similarly enthusiastic notices about information theory come from many other sources. For example, in a review of the accomplishments of Bell Labs in the communication science field from 1925 to 1980, Millman (1984, p. 46) says: "Probably the most spectacular development in communications mathematics to take place at Bell Laboratories was the formulation in the 1940s of information theory by C.E. Shannon." It was indeed a major intellectual contribution. Robert W. Lucky, Executive Director of Research at Bell Labs, says: "I know of no greater work of genius in the annals of technological thought" (Lucky 1989, p. 37). Solomon W. Golomb, an electrical engineering professor at the University of Southern California, thinks that the importance of Shannon's information theory cannot be overstated: "It's like saying how much influence the inventor of the alphabet has had on literature" (Horgan 1992).

The universality of Shannon's conceptualization of information was applauded:[†] "By treating information in clearly defined but wholly abstract terms, Shannon was able to generalize it, establishing laws that hold good not for a few types of information, but for all kinds, everywhere" (Campbell 1982, p. 17). And Lucky (1989, p. 38) explains, "Shannon's genius lay in exposing a new way of thinking about information and communication." Information theory was a unique contribution: "The wider and more exciting implications of Shannon's work lay in the fact that he had been able to make the concept of information so logical and precise that it could be placed in a formal framework of ideas" (Campbell 1982, p. 17).

---

*In fact, Shannon never called it information theory in his two 1948 *BSTJ* articles or in his 1949 book.

[†]Shannon's information theory was generally reviewed in various publications as pioneering in nature, and treated with much acclaim. However, one review of Shannon's theory in *Mathematical Reviews* stated: "The discussion [in Shannon's two articles in the 1948 *BSTJ*] is suggestive throughout, rather than mathematical, and it is not always clear that the author's mathematical intentions are honorable" (Doob 1949). In fact, Shannon had not provided mathematical proofs for all of his work. That was to come later from others, particularly Feinstein (1958).

Looking backward at the first forty years of Shannon's theory, Verdú (1990) stated: "The revolutionary nature of Shannon's paper [the 1948 articles in the *Bell System Technical Journal*] was quickly recognized as a result of its amazing density of new ideas and its persuasive, easy-to-read style." Indeed an active band of electrical engineers and mathematicians have been advancing the research front of information theory since 1948, producing a large and growing literature of books and journal articles. Many communication scholars who only know of Shannon's 1948 articles, or more likely of the 1949 Shannon and Weaver book, would be surprised to learn how information theory has progressed in the past four decades. Shannon is not only universally acknowledged as the father of information theory on the basis of his two 1948 articles, but he also is "the most important post-1948 contributor to the subject! Nearly every one of his papers since 'A Mathematical Theory of Communication' has proved to be a priceless source of research ideas for lesser mortals" (McEliece 1977, p. 13). For example, a 1974 collection of the 49 *Key-Papers in the Development of Information Theory* (Slepian 1974) contains twelve papers by Shannon; no other author is represented more than three times.

WINDING DOWN

As sometimes occurs when a major intellectual contribution is made by a scholar relatively early in his or her career, the individual does not know what to do for a second act. In 1956, Shannon went on leave from Bell Labs as a visiting professor of electrical engineering at MIT. After a year, he resigned from Bell Labs and was appointed the Donner Professor of Science at MIT (he went on leave from MIT during the 1957–1958 academic year to be a fellow in the Center for Advanced Study in the Behavioral Sciences, one of the few to be selected from electrical engineering or mathematics). At MIT he continued to make important contributions to advancing information theory, following up on his earlier leads, but in the mid-1960s, he gradually withdrew from academic activities in the MIT departments of electrical engineering and mathematics. Shannon was a perfectionist in his teaching, believing that each of his lectures had to contain only completely original ideas (Fano 1990). He stopped answering letters, which piled up on his office desk, and eventually stopped coming to his office at MIT. Shannon took emeritus status early (at about age fifty) and also withdrew from active participation in the invisible college of electrical engineers and mathe-

maticians that had formed around the paradigm of information theory.*
He published few papers on information theory, and his former Bell
Labs colleagues suggested that he had "burned out" and had grown
tired of the theory that he had created. During the ensuing three decades, Shannon and his wife, Betty, increasingly withdrew from society,
as Shannon spent his days tinkering with various electromechanical
gadgets in his workshop in Entropy House, the Shannon's home in the
Boston suburb of Winchester.

In 1985, Shannon made a surprise visit to the International Information Theory Symposium, held at Brighton, England. "News raced
through the halls and lecture rooms that the snowy-haired man with the
shy grin who was wandering in and out of the sessions was none other
than Claude Shannon. Some of those at the conference did not even
know that he was still alive" (Horgan 1992). Robert J. McEliece, the
conference organizer, persuaded Shannon to speak to the symposium.
"He spoke for a few minutes and then—fearing that he was boring his
audience, he recalled later—he pulled three balls out of his pockets and
began juggling. The audience cheered and lined up for autographs"
(Horgan 1992). As McEliece remarked: "It was as if Newton had
showed up at a physics conference" (Horgan 1992).

Claude Shannon became fairly wealthy in middle age through his
having bought original stock in Teledyne, a high-technology electronics
company founded by Shannon's friend from his Ph.D. student days,
Henry Singleton. As Teledyne became an enormously successful company, Shannon became very well off. Then he magnified his net worth
to a level of "immense wealth" with an algorithm that he wrote to analyze his stock market portfolio (Lucky 1989).

THE IMPACT OF SHANNON'S INFORMATION THEORY
ON COMMUNICATION STUDY

Wilbur Schramm, founder of the field of communication study, popularized Shannon's work on information theory in the 1950s through
publishing the Shannon and Weaver (1949) book while he was editor
of the University of Illinois Press, authoring an article in *Journalism
Quarterly* utilizing the bit as an information measure in communication

---

*This invisible college formalized its status in 1956 as the Institute of Electrical and Elec-
tronic Engineers Information Theory Society, which holds annual conferences and publishes
the *IEEE Transaction on Information*.

research (Schramm 1955), and encouraging his students at the University of Illinois to apply information theory in communication research.*

Shannon's Model

Shannon's one-way model of the communication act (see Figure 11.1) helped set off the academic field of communication study (Rogers and Kincaid 1981, p. 33). More than any other theoretical conceptualization, it served as the paradigm for communication study, providing a single, easily understandable specification of the main components in the communication act: source, message, channel, receiver. Thus, communication investigations of the communication act could identify source variables (such as credibility), message variables (like the use of fear appeals), channel variables (such as mass media versus interpersonal channels), and receiver variables (like the persuasibility of audience individuals). Dependent variables in communication researches measured effects, such as knowledge change on the part of receivers, attitude change (persuasion), and overt behavior change like voting for a candidate or purchasing a new product.

Thus, it seemed facile to translate the Shannon (1949) model of communication into a general classificatory scheme for the variables included in communication research. The apparent simplicity of the model made it attractive to communication scholars. Notice, however, that the dependent variables are communication effects on the part of the receiver, a development that went beyond Shannon's original focus on channel capacity as the dependent variable. Two further modifications were made in Shannon's communication model by human communication scholars. First, the one-way model of a communication act was extended somewhat by adding feedback about the communication effects on the receiver. Although Shannon did not originally use the concept of feedback per se, he did present a model of source-transmitter-receiver with a "correcting device" (Shannon 1949, p. 68). Communication scholars like Berlo (1960) added, and indeed stressed, the concept of feedback in their models of human communication, influenced by Norbert Wiener's (1948) cybernetics theory. As the title of his popular textbook implied, *The Process of Communication* (1960),

*Schramm (1971, p. 7), writing twenty-three years after publication of Shannon's information theory, stated: "We felt that Shannon's information theory was a brilliant analogue which might illuminate many dark areas of our own field."

Berlo sought to conceptualize a components (SMCR) model of the communication act as a process over time. Second, the one-way conception of human communication was later modified further in communication models of convergence based on information exchange among two or more participants. Berlo's (1977) incorporation of feedback into the communication process was a step in this direction. Rogers and Kincaid (1981, pp. 37–75) depicted communication as a process in which individuals act as "transceivers," both transmitting and receiving information in order to reach common understanding. Increasingly, communication has been viewed in communication models as a process, rather than as an act, a movement away from Shannon's linear model of communication.

Shannon's Propositions about Channel Capacity

The third element of Claude Shannon's information theory, after his definition and measure of information and his model of communication, are his propositions about channel capacity. As Ritchie (1986) pointed out, Shannon's twenty-three theorems constitute "a general theory of *signal transmission*," not "a *communication* theory as students of human communication understand the term." Signal transmission is only one part of the process of human communication (Ritchie 1991, p. 8). Shannon's propositions state relationships among such concepts as channels with and without noise, the entropy of a source, channel capacity, and discrete versus continuous information (Shannon 1949).

While Shannon's conceptualization of information has been widely used by communication (and other) scholars and his model of communication has, with modifications, been given very wide attention, his propositions about channel capacity have almost been ignored by scholars of communication study. A basic reason is that human communication scholars are not much interested in channel capacity (in contrast to engineers of one-way communication systems like radio, television, and, in Shannon's conception of the communication act, one-way telephony). Shannon's main dependent variable of channel capacity did not fit well with communication scholars' primary interest in communication effects. Unlike Shannon, they do not assume that communication is constrained by limited channel capacity; instead, an assumption of abundance seems more reasonable (Ritchie 1992).

The focus on studying communication effects was encouraged by Harold D. Lasswell's famous five-questions model of communication

(*Who* says *what* to *whom* via *what channels* with *what effects?*) and by Paul
F. Lazarsfeld's close alliances with media organizations like CBS Radio
and Time-Life Corporation, sponsors of his research at Columbia
University's Bureau of Applied Social Research in the 1940s and 1950s,
who wanted to know the effects of their mass communication activities.
In recent years, this focus on effects has been questioned, and alternative models of communication (like a convergence model) have been
proposed (for example, by Rogers and Kincaid 1981).

The Concept of Information and Its Measure

One of Wilbur Schramm's Ph.D. students at the University of Illinois,
Wilson L. Taylor, developed an information-type measure of readability
called the cloze procedure (Taylor 1953, 1956), named after the Gestalt
notion of closure. Respondents are asked to fill in every fifth word in a
manuscript that has been randomly deleted.* The ability to do so correctly is an indicator of the readability of the text.

Information Theory and Communication Study

The full integrating potential of the concept of information and its measure, the bit, has not been realized in the field of communication study,
in part because the new communication paradigm was adopted by communication scholars in already-existing university departments of journalism and speech, thus dividing the emerging field of communication
study into the subdisciplines of mass communication and interpersonal
communication (Reardon and Rogers, 1989), respectively. Nor has it
been realized more broadly in the social sciences, where information
theory promised a possible means of intellectual integration (Mc-
Cormick 1986). Such integration has not occurred.

In their review of communication theories, Severin with Tankard
(1988, p. 42) stated: "The mathematical theory of communication has
been the most important single stimulus for the development of other
models and theories in communication." Shannon's information theory
provided the root paradigm for the field of communication study. The

---

*Communication scholars who have utilized Taylor's cloze procedure include Darnell
(1970), Dickens and Williams (1964), Lowry and Marr (1975), Lynch (1974), Reilly (1971),
and Taylor (1957).

first communications research institutes and the first doctoral degree–granting programs in U.S. universities began shortly after publication of Shannon's information theory. The most important institutionalizer of communication schools in U.S. universities, and the founder of the field of communication study, Wilbur Schramm, was an early enthusiast for Shannon's theory.

The timing of Shannon's information theory was important in its acceptance by communication scholars. As Berlo (1977, p. 16) noted in the late 1940s, "communication researchers were emerging from the ghetto of trade-school education and straining for the intellectual respect of their academic colleagues." Information theory looked like a route to respectability. It also looked like a means of providing a sense of universality across the different types of communication channels. It did not really matter, according to information theory, whether communication occurred by means of mass media or interpersonal channels. "Shannon implied that communication was communication, through whatever channels it occurred. The net effect of such theoretical thinking was to standardize the terminology, concepts, and model of human communication, whatever the channel" (Rogers 1986, p. 88). The concepts and model came from Claude E. Shannon.

The influence of Shannon's theory on the emerging field of communication study was tremendous. As Krippendorff (1989c, p. 314) stated: "Historically, information theory was a major stimulus to the development of communication research. It made the heretofore vague notions of information mathematically tractable, liberated it from the conflicting claims by diverse disciplines concerned with knowledge and communication technology, and legitimized research on communication and information processes."

The intellectual influence of information theory on communication study, while strong and lasting, has not been entirely positive. The influence is strong, as is indicated by the overwhelming dependence of contemporary communication scholars upon such originally engineering concepts as *source, receiver,* and *feedback* and such cryptographic terms as *noise, encoding,* and *decoding.* Shannon's model of communication, after certain changes were made by communication scholars (such as the addition of feedback), headed communication scholars toward a one-way conceptualization of communication behavior and a focus on determining communication effects. Is it fair to criticize Shannon's theory for what communication scholars did with it? "To criticize

Shannon's model as inapplicable to the complexities of human communication is to criticize a rowboat because it is not a whale" (Ritchie 1986).

Once a paradigm is accepted by scholars in an academic discipline, it provides useful guidelines for future generations of scholars, decreasing uncertainty about what topics to study, how to study them, and how to interpret research findings. However, a paradigm can be an intellectual trap, enmeshing scientists who follow it in a web of assumptions that they may not fully recognize. David K. Berlo looked back at his Ph.D. training at the University of Illinois in the 1950s: "Like many of my colleagues, I simply did not understand the underlying assumptions and theoretical consequences of what I believed, and had not grasped the limited fertility of the research tradition in which I had been trained. I did not recognize that the assumptions underlying linear causal determinism may account for the major proportion of communication events, but not account for the proportion that makes a significant difference in our lives" (Berlo 1977, p. 12). He later recognized that human communication is often unintentional and nonlinear: "An information-communication relationship may be directional as we conceive it, or it may not. If we look at the 'source' as intentional and initiatory and the 'receiver' as passive and a receptive container—e.g., if the message is stimulus and the effect is response—the relationship is directional. On the other hand, if the relationship is one in which both users approach the engagement with expectations, plans, and anticipation, the uncertainty reduction attributable to the contact may better be understood in terms of how both parties use and approach a message-event than in terms of how one person uses the contact to direct the other" (Berlo 1977, p. 20).

Today there is need for reconceptualizations of the Shannon model of communication so as to reflect the definition of communication as process, to recognize that communication often is nonlinear and unintentional, and to facilitate other important topics of study than just communication effects. Thus, gradually, communication scholars are escaping their earlier misconstruction of Claude Shannon's mathematical theory of communication, a gradual and evolutionary process that will eventually restore our faith in intellectual communities as self-correcting systems.

PART III

ESTABLISHMENT OF THE COMMUNICATION FIELD

CHAPTER 12

WILBUR SCHRAMM AND THE ESTABLISHMENT OF COMMUNICATION STUDY

Communication study has moved so fast that it has seldom
stood still for its portrait.
　　　　　　　—Wilbur Schramm, "The Nature of
　　　　　　　Communication between Humans"

All histories of academic enterprises tend to have something
patricidal about them: Embarrassing intellectual paternities
are suppressed and preferred ones put in their place. So too
with mass communication research: Its institutional birth
happened only long after its intellectual problems were established.
　　　　　　　—John Durham Peters, "Democracy and American
　　　　　　　Communication Theory: Dewey, Lippmann, Lazarsfeld"

Founding a new scientific field in U.S. universities is an extremely rare
event. Since about 1900, when the five conventional social sciences
(economics, psychology, political science, sociology, and anthropology)
had been established, very few new academic fields have developed.
Communication study is probably the most widely accepted new field
in American universities over the past ninety years. This chapter high-
lights the role of Wilbur Schramm in this unique process of founding
the new field of communication study and in gradually gaining its widespread acceptance in U.S. universities, initially in their schools of journalism.

My thinking about the role of Wilbur Schramm in founding communication study grows
out of extensive discussions with Steven H. Chaffee at Stanford University and draws at certain points on Rogers and Chaffee (1992) and Chaffee and Rogers (in press). I thank Erwin P.
Bettinghaus, James W. Dearing, Mary Schramm Coberly, Lyle M. Nelson, and John T.
McNelly for reviewing a draft of this chapter.

445

Figure 12.1. Wilbur Schramm (1907–1987) at Stanford University.
News and Information Service, Stanford University.

Wilbur Schramm (1907–1987) was the founder of the field of communication study. Without forerunners like Lasswell, Lazarsfeld, Lewin, Hovland, Wiener, and Shannon, communication study could not have achieved its present status, but it was because of Schramm, "more than anyone else, that communication could become a field of study in its own right" (Paisley 1985, p. 2). Schramm founded communication research institutes at Iowa, Illinois, and Stanford that conducted scholarly investigations, trained the new Ph.D.s in communication, and brought together the new interdisciplinary field. This institutionalization of communication study allowed an integration of theories and methods for attacking problems of human communication (Rogers 1986, p. 108). Schramm was crucial for the take-off of communication study in the years following World War II. Until Schramm, the forefounding scholars came to study communication, tarried for a few years, and then moved back to their own parent disciplines. Lazarsfeld and Hovland are examples. But Wilbur Schramm came to communication science and stayed (Rogers 1986, p. 169). He created the first university units called "communication," wrote the first textbooks for courses in communication, and awarded the first Ph.D. degrees in communication. He was the first person in the world to have the title "professor of communication" (this at the University of Illinois in 1947).

Chapter 1 describes how Wilbur Schramm came out of a creative writing program in a Department of English to launch the first academic program in communication study in the School of Journalism at the University of Iowa in 1943. Now we take up where we left off in Chapter 1, with Schramm's arrival at the University of Illinois in 1947.

APPROACHING ILLINOIS

The University of Illinois is surrounded by a flat countryside. In fact, the topography is so low that the area was too swampy to be settled in the initial westward expansion of the American frontier. Not until about 1880, when the land was drained for farming, did Champaign and Urbana, the twin cities in which the university is located, begin to grow, blessed by the crossing of two railway lines, one of them the main track linking Chicago and New Orleans. Today two interstate highways cross at Champaign-Urbana, and a variety of motels and restaurants live off the road travelers who are passing through. But the main source of livelihood is the University of Illinois, with 24,000 undergraduate students and 12,000 postgraduates. Much of this growth occurred just after World War II. The University of Illinois enrolled 17,392 students during the prewar academic year of 1940–1941 and 38,637 by the postwar years of 1947–1949. Then enrollment leveled off at about 36,000. Illinois has a large population and is rich in both agriculture and industry, so that it can support this megauniversity. Appropriately, the University of Illinois is known for its agricultural research and, especially in recent years, for its work in supercomputing.

The center of the University of Illinois campus is dominated by the Morrow Plots, a small field in which corn has been grown continuously since 1876. A metal plate at the Morrow Plots announces that they are "America's Oldest Experiment Farm." These plots helped dispel the common farmer belief that a corn crop had to be followed by hay or meadow in a crop rotation to keep up soil fertility. The Morrow Plots symbolize the importance of agriculture at this prairie university. When a new undergraduate library was constructed in 1971, two of its stories were built underground, so that the building would not shade the famous Morrow Plots.

The University of Illinois is also known historically as one of the great midwestern football powers. Red Grange, one of the most phenomenal football players of all time, starred at Illinois (this is the same Red Grange who helped convince Wilbur Schramm to leave the university after 1954, when Grange, elected to the board of trustees, voted to fire the university president, George Stoddard). Robert Zuppke, who coached Red Grange, is the namesake of Zuppke Field in the cavernous Memorial Stadium. As his final wish, Coach Zuppke was buried in a faculty cemetery across from the fifty-yard line. Zuppke is known not only for his coaching brilliance but also for refusing to offer athletic fellowships, thus destroying Illinois' football prominence for some years.

So the University of Illinois is almost a stereotype of the huge midwestern state university, flavored by a tradition of football and corn growing and computers, all in a pair of small university cities stuck out in the middle of the Midwest. It was here at Illinois, after Wilbur Schramm's arrival from Iowa City in 1947, that communication study got underway.

Getting the University Moving

When George Stoddard arrived as president just after the end of World War II, the University of Illinois had lacked strong leadership for some years, and its academic quality had been gradually deteriorating (Solberg 1991). Stoddard believed that the University of Illinois was a "sleeping giant," and he made it his personal mission to revitalize the institution.

George Stoddard (1897–1981) earned his bachelor's degree at Penn State and then studied psychology at the Sorbonne until 1923, when he went to Iowa for his Ph.D. in psychology. In 1928, he became the director of the Child Welfare Research Station, which he administered successfully for the next fourteen years as it became one of the noted child development research institutes in the United States. In the late 1920s, Stoddard conducted one of the Payne Fund studies of the effects of movies on children. Hence, he had an appreciation of mass communication research, especially studies of media effects. In 1936 he became dean of the graduate school at Iowa. In 1942, while Schramm was in Washington during World War II, Stoddard moved to Albany, to become president of the University of the State of New York.

Stoddard and Schramm had been friends and mutual admirers during their days at the University of Iowa before World War II. Both belonged to a small irreverent group called the Society for the Prevention of Cruelty to Speakers.* The SPCS whisked noted authors, who were invited to Iowa City to give public speeches, away from their audience after a few questions. Then the SPCS plied the speaker with fellowship and drinks. It was the only place in Iowa City during the Prohibition years where one could enjoy alcohol (Cartier 1988, p. 134). During this period, Dean Stoddard told his wife: "The more I look at the faculty, the more I realize the quality lacking in many of them is *imagination,* and that is what makes Will [Schramm] so interesting, so alert, so inspired" (Lerner and Nelson 1977, p. 311).

Stoddard offered the youthful Wilbur Schramm, only forty years old in 1947, the title of assistant to the president of the University of Illinois and the opportunity to join Stoddard in his get-the-university-moving-again campaign. But Schramm, although unhappy with the lack of resources at the University of Iowa, was wedded to his vision of founding communication study. In January 1947, Schramm stopped at Urbana on his way back to Iowa City from a journalism school administrators' conference in Lexington, Kentucky (Cartier 1988, p. 273). Stoddard made him an offer that he could not refuse. In essence, he invited Schramm to join his kitchen cabinet in the university administration, in exchange for creating an Institute of Communications Research for Schramm to direct. The institute was a major innovation in an American university, and in the world. It was the first degree-granting academic unit called "communication." Illinois innovated in adopting communication study because President Stoddard wanted to hire Schramm, and he paid Schramm's price for moving to Illinois: a communication research institute.

Actually, a great deal of infrastructure for communication study was already in place at Illinois, even though it was called journalism and other names rather than communication. Three years after Schramm's arrival in Urbana, in 1950, President Stoddard, who was very impressed by Schramm's leadership abilities, appointed him to be in charge of every activity at the University of Illinois that was even remotely connected with communication. Schramm was already a professor of com-

---

*In addition to Schramm and Stoddard, the sixteen members of the SPCS included Frank Luther Mott, director of Iowa's School of Journalism, and Grant Wood, the famous painter, who was then teaching an art class at the University of Iowa.

munication, of course, and director of the Institute of Communications Research and editor of the University of Illinois Press. With a stroke of Stoddard's pen, Schramm also became dean of the Division of Communication, which was established to include the existing department of advertising and the school of journalism, plus the Institute. Schramm was the first individual in America, and in the world, to hold titles like professor and dean of communication. He also was responsible for the university's broadcasting stations, veterans' affairs, a conference center, and several other activities that had some kind of communication function.* He was in essence a vice-president for special projects. Schramm was so occupied with administering this empire, in fact, that he had to strain to find time for his research projects, his doctoral students, and book writing.

Notable among the communication units at Illinois that were not assigned to Schramm was the Department of Speech. This department pursued a humanities, rather than a social scientific, approach to human communication, stressing a rhetorical perspective. The department was fairly well known in its field and was already awarding the doctorate.† Although discussions were held with the department's faculty about possibly joining Schramm's Division of Communication, the Speech Department decided to stay where it was, in the College of Literature, Arts, and Sciences. This decision by the department to go its separate way was fateful, leading to the later division of the field of communication study into the subdisciplines of mass versus interpersonal communication.

President Stoddard knew that launching communication study at Illinois was an important and risky decision in the history of U.S. higher education. In his April 21, 1947, letter to Wilbur Schramm acknowledging his acceptance of the Illinois job offer, Stoddard stated: "I have a feeling that historians of education will someday take note of this particular event."‡

---

*During his Illinois years, Schramm organized the Allerton House conference on educational television, which led the Federal Communications Commission to reserve certain channels for educational television stations. The Public Broadcasting System resulted (Nelson 1992).

†The Illinois Department of Speech did not contain work on radio and television broadcasting; if it had, it might have had more in common with Schramm's Division of Communication.

‡This letter is in the University of Illinois Archives, under the Files of the Director, Institute of Communications Research, 13/5/1, Box 4, Wilbur Schramm Personal, 1947–1949.

The Institute of Communications Research

The original idea for the research institute at Illinois did not come from Schramm or from Stoddard. A month or two prior to Stoddard's recruitment talk with Schramm in early 1947, an Illinois professor of journalism who taught courses in advertising, Dr. Charles H. Sandage, proposed establishing the Bureau of Communications Research.* He wanted to create a "Morrow Plot of Advertising" at Illinois (Sandage 1991). During his later career, Sandage became the founder of advertising teaching in America. Back in 1946, he was gathering data by mailed questionnaires from midwestern farmers about advertising effects. He was aware of the mass communication research then being conducted at the University of Iowa, by the Research Division in the University of Minnesota School of Journalism, and by Rensis Likert's Survey Research Center at the University of Michigan. Sandage cited this related work in his proposal for creating a Bureau of Communications Research at Illinois. As its name implies, he had consulted with Paul F. Lazarsfeld in the Bureau of Applied Social Research at Columbia University. Sandage asked for $10,000 per year for the proposed Illinois research institute. Sandage took his draft proposal to his boss, the director of the School of Journalism, Fred S. Siebert, who was enthusiastic about the idea and forwarded it to the university administration. There it promptly ran into trouble.

Their proposal was rejected by the university provost on December 31, 1946, who then passed it along to the president's office. President Stoddard was more positive, telling Sandage and Siebert to put their proposal on hold (this in early January 1947). The idea for creating an Institute of Communications Research at Illinois thus was in the air just prior to Schramm's recruitment by Stoddard. Here we see evidence that the important rise of communication study at Illinois was more than just Wilbur Schramm, a fact that most published accounts of this period tend to overlook.† Also involved were Sandage, Siebert, Schramm's later colleagues Ted Peterson and Jay Jensen, and the psycholinguist Charles

---

*This proposal and its accompanying correspondence, dated December 14, 1946, is found in the University Archives, University of Illinois Library, George D. Stoddard Papers, Series 2/10/1, Box 6, School of Journalism Folder.

†Late in his career, Schramm said that many aspects of his vision for communication study were constrained by the existing infrastructure at Illinois. While at Stanford, Schramm felt that he was more fully able to implement his vision (although he was somewhat constrained there too).

Osgood, whom Schramm recruited to his institute faculty. Schramm's coming to Illinois in 1947 was the catalyst. Communication study was already getting underway before he arrived, but his vision of communication study that had been born in 1942 in Washington and then worked out at Iowa from 1943 to 1947, plus his immense personal capabilities, brought communication study into actuality at Illinois in 1947.

Soon after the Institute of Communications Research was launched, in January 1948, Wilbur Schramm hosted a three-day conference at Illinois that was designed to explore future directions for communication study and, more specifically, to advise him on how to shape his new institute and the doctoral program in communication that it was to offer. This conference, funded by John Marshall of the Rockefeller Foundation with a grant of $2,000, involved many of the key figures in the early days of communication study: the forefathers Carl Hovland and Paul F. Lazarsfeld; such Bleyer children as Ralph Casey, Ralph Nafziger, and Fred Siebert; and the critical scholar Leo Lowenthal. Out of the conference papers Schramm edited *Communications in Modern Society* (1948), which was to be the first textbook for the new field.

Given his administrative responsibilities for the vast communication empire at Illinois, one might imagine that Schramm would not have time to teach, advise doctoral students, bring in research grants, conduct scholarly investigations, and write textbooks, but somehow he did. During the 1950s, he authored or edited one book in mass communication each year—for example, *Mass Communication* (1949), *Four Theories of the Press* (1956, with his Illinois colleagues Fred S. Siebert and Ted Peterson), and *Process and Effects of Communication* (1954). These books became the main texts that defined the new field of communication.*

Schramm's doctoral program in communication at Illinois had an interdisciplinary approach. The Institute of Communications Research provided a mechanism through which scholars in psychology, sociology, political science, anthropology, and electrical engineering were drawn into communication research. The Ph.D. program at Illinois was centered in the Institute, but officially it was an interdisciplinary activity under the jurisdiction of the graduate school. Importantly, the Institute was supported by "hard money" funding from the university budget,

---

*As a result of reading these books in the mid-1950s (I was then a doctoral student at Iowa State University), I felt that I understood the nature of communication study and was strongly attracted to it.

unlike Lazarsfeld's Bureau of Applied Social Research at Columbia. The Institute made more than a dozen faculty appointments and also collaborated with various departments at Illinois in several joint appointments (Maclay 1991). Funding for externally sponsored research projects was utilized for the salaries of doctoral research assistants, for travel, equipment, and other operational costs, but the faculty scholars were entirely supported by the regular university budget.* This support gave a sense of permanency to the Institute. In fact, the Institute is still there today, much as Schramm created it.

The Institute admitted about ten or twelve new doctoral students per year and has awarded five or six Ph.D. degrees annually since its first doctorate in 1951, a total of over 200 Ph.D. degrees. Originally, several years of mass media experience were a requirement for admission to the doctoral program (this prerequisite was later dropped). During the original Schramm era, from 1947 to 1955, the Institute had an annual budget from university sources of from $200,000 to $300,000. In addition, Schramm was bringing in about half a million dollars in externally funded communication research per year. Schramm at Illinois proved to be somewhat of a miracle worker in attracting big research grants: a huge U.S. Air Force contract to provide social science consultation on various military problems, funds from the National Institute of Mental Health to content analyze mass media messages about mental health, a Ford Foundation grant on how social science research findings were utilized, and a grant from the U.S. Department of State to evaluate the performance of what is today the U.S. Information Agency. This funding supported doctoral students at Illinois, so that they gained apprenticeship training in conducting communication research.

One of these doctoral students was David K. Berlo, who came to Schramm's doctoral program at Illinois in 1953 via a roundabout journey. He had been an undergraduate math major at the University of Missouri but interrupted his studies to enlist in the U.S. Air Force during the Korean War. While stationed at Chanute Air Force Base at

---

*In 1948, Schramm hired Dallas W. Smythe, an economist who had been at the Federal Communications Commission, and Harry Grace, an educational psychologist, and appointed Fred S. Siebert and Charles H. Sandage (School of Journalism) and J. W. Albig (Sociology), who were already at Illinois, to the Institute faculty. In 1949, Schramm recruited Charles Osgood, a psychologist and linguist, and Robert Hudson, a broadcaster who had worked at OWI and at CBS, to the Institute faculty. And in 1951, Schramm hired Charles Swanson, one of the first Ph.D.s in communication at Iowa, who was then teaching at Minnesota, and Joseph Bachelder, a political scientist from Washington State University.

Rantoul, Illinois, about ten miles from Urbana, he met Art Lumsdaine, who had worked with Carl Hovland during the American Soldier investigations and was then conducting Air Force research at Chanute. Berlo was finishing his bachelor's degree at the University of Illinois on a part-time basis while he was a full-time Air Force enlisted man. He asked Lumsdaine for advice about doctoral study, and Lumsdaine recommended the new Illinois doctoral program in communication. A few days later, when Berlo called on Schramm in his office on campus, he found that Lumsdaine had written a letter of recommendation about him.

Berlo was still in the Air Force during his first year in the Illinois doctoral program, and he worked full time as director of a local radio station during his second year. Five doctoral students took their qualifying examinations on the last day that Schramm was at Illinois, just before he departed for Stanford in August 1955. The celebration party was held at the home of Hideya Kumata, another one of the five, that evening in 102-degree heat. During the celebration, Gordon Sabine, then a stranger to Berlo, asked him what he would do if he were dean of a college of communication.* Never at a loss for words, Berlo went on at some length. Later someone at the party whispered to Berlo that Sabine was dean of the newly created College of Communication at Michigan State University. To Berlo's surprise, Sabine telephoned him the next morning to offer him a faculty position at MSU as soon as he completed his Ph.D. dissertation at Illinois. A year later, Berlo arrived in East Lansing to become an assistant professor. A year or two after coming to Michigan State, he was offered a position at Iowa, but Dean Sabine countered by offering Berlo the position of chair of the Department of Communication at MSU. He was twenty-nine years old. The new department was organized along lines that implemented Schramm's vision of communication study. Berlo hired faculty members out of both mass and interpersonal communication backgrounds. It probably was the first department of communication so-named in the world.[†]

A particularly key scholar in the Institute of Communications Research at Illinois was Charles Osgood (1916–1989), a psychologist and

---

*Sabine's conversation with Berlo at the celebration party was no accident. Sabine had a list of all the Illinois, Stanford, and Wisconsin doctoral students, a fairly short list, and was systematically recruiting them for the faculty in communication that he was assembling at Michigan State University (Stempel 1992).

[†]Until 1964, this department was officially called the Department of General Communication Arts.

linguist with a Ph.D. degree from Yale who had worked with Carl Hovland. Wilbur Schramm considered Osgood as his key hiree during his Illinois years. Osgood created the semantic differential, a seven-point scale on which respondents were asked to rate a series of opposite adjectives for a concept. For example, Osgood might ask respondents to rate the concept of "television" on the following adjective pairs:

Strong ____ : ____ : ____ : ____ : ____ : ____ : ____ Weak

Fast   ____ : ____ : ____ : ____ : ____ : ____ : ____ Slow

Wise   ____ : ____ : ____ : ____ : ____ : ____ : ____ Unwise

Osgood, Suci, and Tannenbaum (1957) summarized their various studies with the semantic differential in their book *The Measurement of Meaning*. They argued that the semantic differential provided one means of quantifying individuals' perceptions of a concept (which might be an object, individual, or a general noun like *television*). For some years the semantic differential was a favorite tool of communication scholars, although today it is relatively passé.

Osgood replaced Wilbur Schramm as director of the Institute of Communication Research when he left Illinois in 1955. By the Institute's fortieth anniversary, in 1988, it had produced 205 Ph.D.s in communication. Today, Illinois is regarded as having a strong doctoral program in communication, but when Schramm departed in 1955, the spotlight moved with him.

The Fall of President Stoddard

George Stoddard began to encounter problems almost from the beginning of his presidency at Illinois. He was a liberal in both politics and religion, and his liberalism generated trouble during the red scare of the McCarthy era. In one of his books, Stoddard (1943) had stated that religion is essentially superstition, a remark that made him unpopular with the Roman Catholic hierarchy of Illinois (Solberg 1991). Stoddard believed in world government and participated in various United Nations activities that took him away from the Urbana campus for extended periods of time. The university board of trustees reminded him that his primary duties were at home, but Stoddard kept on traveling. He believed in President Roosevelt's New Deal and appointed Keynesian economics professors in a department in which the older faculty hated the New Deal. As a noted University of Illinois history professor, Winston V. Solberg (1991), stated: "While a liberal, Stoddard was also dogmatic; he apparently lacked the ability to control his rages against people with whom he differed. He is reliably reported to have directed his wrath against one dean or another in front of an assemblage of deans on more than one occasion. Thus he alienated people."

Ill will was building up against President Stoddard as he zealously sought to improve the university. He moved too rapidly and was intolerant of resistance. Then came krebiozen, a mysterious chemical that was promoted as a cure for cancer by two refugee Yugoslavians, the Durouic brothers, one of whom was a medical doctor. The alleged cancer cure was said to be made from the blood serum of horses. This wonder drug was sponsored by Dr. Andrew Ivy, a well-known medical researcher who served as vice president of the University of Illinois Medical Center, located in Chicago. President Stoddard banned the use of krebiozen in the university, on scientific grounds, a policy that came in for strong criticism from cancer patients who were desperate for a cure.*

At a midnight meeting of the University of Illinois board of trustees on July 24, 1953, President Stoddard was given a vote of no confidence and forced to resign. The motion of no confidence was made by Red Grange, the former football star, who had been popularly elected to the board a few years previously. Grange had not been a very serious trustee, attending few of the board meetings and publicly criticizing the university for "buying too many pianos" (Blum 1991).

Lloyd Morey, the long-time university accountant, was appointed acting president by the board of trustees. Morey was not fond of Schramm. Documents in the University of Illinois Archives show that Acting President Morey systematically took away pieces of Schramm's communication empire. One week it was the University of Illinois Press. Shortly after, Schramm dutifully marched over to the president's office to be told that he no longer was "the Duke of Allerton Park" (the conference center). Then he was relieved of directing the university's public relations office. Later, Schramm's other nonacademic responsibilities were stripped away. But Morey could not remove Schramm's professorial duties, as he had academic tenure, and Morey did not dare to remove Schramm as director of the Institute of Communications Research

---

*Krebiozen later was proved to be nothing but mineral oil (Stoddard 1955, 1971).

or as dean of the Division of Communication. But the whole affair left a bad taste in Schramm's mouth, and his eight years of administrative experience at Illinois convinced him to avoid academic leadership positions in the future.

Schramm felt that it was time for him to move along. He was interviewed to be dean of communication at Boston University but declined. When word spread in the field that Schramm could be hired away from Illinois, several offers came his way.

THE STANFORD YEARS

Dr. Chilton R. ("Chick") Bush, chair of the Department of Communication and Journalism at Stanford University, stated in a June 29, 1970, oral history interview, that he "knew that [Wilbur Schramm] had become uncomfortable with the intellectual atmosphere at Illinois. He had three offers to leave, one being at the University of Chicago. I had several meetings with him. He came here [to Stanford] as a professor at a smaller salary than he was receiving at Illinois. . . . Bringing him to Stanford was the most important contribution I have ever made to communication research. He has had a great world impact. . . . I don't know of any field in which one man stands out so dominantly."

Chick Bush was the main recruiter of Wilbur Schramm to Stanford, but the university's administration was more than willing to go along with him. A particularly key role was played by Ernest R. ("Jack") Hilgard, a psychologist who had been impressed by Schramm during their wartime duties in the Office of War Information in Washington, D.C. In 1955, Hilgard was dean of the graduate school at Stanford University. He had a kitty of $50,000 per year, provided by the Ford Foundation, to strengthen the social sciences and readily agreed to provide Schramm's salary (Hilgard 1992). At this time, Stanford was trying to improve its academic prestige by raiding talent from other universities. Schramm arrived at Stanford with a $75,000 grant from the Ford Foundation to study the utilization of behavioral science knowledge. This grant paid half of Schramm's salary for his first four years at Stanford. Then, in 1960, Schramm brought in a four-year grant of $122,000 from the U.S. Department of Health, Education and Welfare, with Professor Robert Sears in psychology, for a study of instructional television. Schramm was continuing his legendary fund-raising record, begun at Illinois.

The Institute for Communication Research

Prior to Schramm's arrival in Palo Alto, Stanford had a Department of Speech and Drama and a separate Division of Journalism. Years previously, both had split off from the Department of English. Chick Bush made a careful analysis of the situation at Stanford and recommended that the university combine the separate pieces into a single Department of Communication and Journalism that included an Institute for Communication Research, whose purpose was to train new Ph.D.s and to conduct scholarly research on problems of interest to the mass media. Carrying out such studies would also help the academic careers of the communication faculty by expanding their records of scholarly publications. Bush, who had led the division of journalism, became chair of the new Department of Communication and Journalism in 1953 and director of the Institute for Communication Research. Two years later, Bush offered the position of institute director to Schramm, and he accepted.* Thus began the golden era at Stanford, from roughly 1955 to 1970, a period when the university dominated the field of communication study in the U.S.†

"The Institute for Communication Research [at Stanford] became the wellspring from which flowed the newest, most innovative, and most far-reaching ideas and theories in a rapidly-expanding field" (Nelson, p. 317). Stanford became the seed institution for the new field of communication study. Schramm turned out large numbers of Ph.D.s in communication during his Stanford years, and many of these new scholars rose rapidly to leadership positions in the field of communicaton: Paul J. Deutchman at Michigan State, Wayne Danielson at North Carolina and later at the University of Texas, Jack Lyle at UCLA and then at the East-West Communication Institute, and Steven H. Chaffee at the University of Wisconsin. All became deans or directors of schools of journalism. Schramm's Stanford products made important conceptual contributions as well: Max MacComb's at the University of North Carolina, in studying the agenda-setting process of the media;

---

*During his Stanford era, Schramm generally avoided administrative positions, a lesson that he had learned at Illinois. Being director of Stanford's Institute for Communication Research was a largely honorific role as the Institute was part of the Department of Communication, and the department chair carried out the administrative duties for the institute. Thus Schramm was left free to conduct research, direct the doctoral program, and teach.

†The doctoral program at Stanford had begun a couple of years prior to Schramm's arrival, and several doctoral students were already enrolled.

Godwin C. Chu at the East-West Communication Institute, in investigating international communication (somewhat later, Emile McAnany at Texas, Bob Hornik at Pennsylvania, and John Mayo at Florida State, were also to conduct pioneering studies of development communication); and Philip Tichenor at Minnesota, in examining the knowledge gap hypothesis. Several of Schramm's protégés—Ed Parker, who studied new communication technologies; Bill Paisley, who investigated knowledge utilization; and Don Roberts, who analyzed television effects on children—became faculty members at Stanford, where they produced a corps of Schramm's "grand-students."

Wayne A. Danielson (1992), a communication professor at the University of Texas at Austin, remembers the doctoral program at Stanford from 1954 to 1957, when he earned Stanford's fourth Ph.D. degree in mass communication research:

> The doctoral program was highly interdisciplinary. I took statistical methods in the Psychology Department from Quinn McNemar, and both he and Ernest Hilgard were on my doctoral committee. I also took doctoral psychology courses from Robert Sears and Leon Festinger, who distributed a draft chapter of his yet-unpublished book on *Cognitive Dissonance*. In the Sociology Department, I enrolled in courses from Paul Wallin and R.T. LaPiere. Students in communication consistently got the top grades in these doctoral courses in psychology and sociology, helping to convince us that we were competent. We were all excited to be exploring a new field, and to be enrolled in one of the very few doctoral programs [in communication] in the country.

When Danielson completed his doctorate, he was employed as an assistant professor in the School of Journalism at the University of Wisconsin for two years and then moved to the University of North Carolina at Chapel Hill, rising rapidly up the academic ranks to become dean of the School of Journalism in 1964, only seven years after receiving his Ph.D. degree.* Schramm's protégés fanned out across the U.S. during this era. As Danielson (1992) recalls, "Every university wanted to hire one of the new Stanford Ph.D.s in communication. We kept in close

---

*Danielson is also known for conducting one of the first studies of how a major news story spreads to a mass audience (Deutschmann and Danielson 1960). This classic research study set off many other news diffusion researches, which find that mass interpersonal channels are complementary in diffusing news of a presidential assassination, a major disaster, or some other big event. The media often make individuals aware of the news event, who then discuss it with friends, relatives, or work associates.

touch with each other and created a network. We formed a rump group at the Association for Education in Journalism meetings in Colorado [in 1955], in order to encourage communication research." The Stanford Ph.D.s in mass communication research infected schools of journalism at many universities with Wilbur Schramm's vision of communication study. They sought to provide the emerging field of communication study with an objective understanding of human information exchange, based on scientific research. They opposed the older generation of journalism professors, who taught their students what "should be," based on a normative perspective drawn from professional experience as a journalist.

Schramm's doctoral program at Stanford had greater influence on the field of communication study in the United States in the 1950s and 1960s than did the doctoral program that he had started previously at Illinois, perhaps because Stanford was a more prestigious university than Illinois.* The Illinois program included more of a critical perspective than did Stanford's, a difference that continues (Danielson 1992), and Stanford focuses mainly on the study of mass communication effects.

Green-Eyeshades Versus the Chi-Squares

Schramm's new doctorates in communication were called "Chi-Squares" by many of their colleagues in schools of journalism who represented a nonscientific and more vocational approach to journalism education. The term was not a compliment. A bitter conflict ensued between the "Green-Eyeshades" and the "Chi-Squares," a fundamental dispute over the epistemological basis of knowledge about human communication as it was applied in the university training of journalists. The symbol of the Green-Eyeshades is the celluloid visor once worn by newspaper copy editors to cut down on glare. The term was meant to imply that the Green-Eyeshade professors were oriented to the profession of journalism rather than to the new science of communication. The Green-Eyeshades believed that the main function of journalism education was to train students in the practical skills of reporting, writing, and editing (Lovell, 1987) and scoffed at the young communication

---

*The Illinois influence was considerable in some university communication programs, such as at Michigan State University, where David K. Berlo and Hideya Kumata, both Illinois Ph.D.s, founded an important department of communication .

scholars, whom they felt were irrelevant to the training of future journalists. The Chi-Squares, for their part, had little respect for the Green-Eyeshades. Professor Curtiss D. MacDougall of the Medill School of Journalism at Northwestern University,* who may have coined the terms, was a strong proponent of the more vocational and professional approach to journalism education.

The Green-Eyeshade versus Chi-Square battle was fought out in different ways at various universities. At Wisconsin, Daddy Bleyer, after his death in 1935, was followed as director of the journalism school by Grant Hyde, a Green-Eyeshade. In 1948, the faculty at Wisconsin revolted against Hyde, deposed him, and in 1949 brought in Ralph O. Nafziger (1896–1973), a Bleyer child who had been teaching at Minnesota for a decade or so (Durham 1992). Nafziger had earned his bachelor's degree in journalism in 1921 and then returned to Madison after a decade of newspaper experience to get his journalism master's degree in 1930 and his Ph.D. degree in political science with a minor in journalism in 1936. Nafziger enrolled in a graduate-level statistics course taught by Sam Stouffer at Wisconsin from 1932 to 1934, following Stouffer's return from a year of postdoctoral study at the University of London with Ronald A. Fisher and Karl Peason. Nafziger received some of the most expert instruction in statistical methods then available on either side of the Atlantic (Rogers and Chaffee 1992), and it had a strong influence throughout his career and, indirectly, on mass communication research. First at Minnesota and after 1949 at Wisconsin, Nafziger taught a required doctoral methodology course, Communication Media Analysis, which followed a quantitative approach. With David Manning White, Nafziger coedited two editions of a widely used methodology textbook: *Introduction to Journalism Research* (Nafziger and White 1949) and *Introduction to Mass Communication Research* (Nafziger and White 1958). Nafziger's appointment as director of the school of journalism ushered in a golden era at Wisconsin.[†] It became one of the chief training centers for producing journalism professors for other universities. They were trained in communication study, with a strong

---

*Another particularly important leader of the Green-Eyeshades was George J. Kienzle, director of the School of Journalism at Ohio State University in the 1960s.

[†]The Green-Eyeshades resisted the growing influence of Ralph Nafziger and the Chi-Squares in the Wisconsin School of Journalism, but "the new wave of research-oriented journalism and mass communication educators had the backing" of the president (McNelly 1992).

competence in using quantitative methods, and were generally oriented to investigating media effects.

The younger scholars with Ph.D. degrees in communication won the intellectual revolution in the schools of journalism bit by bit. Their scholarly approach had the approval of many university administrators, who were previously somewhat puzzled by their vocationally oriented schools of journalism, which they regarded as "something equivalent to a school of trailer park management or a school of cosmology" (Danielson 1991). The young communication professors talked the language of social science, which the university administrators generally could understand and value. They published in scientific journals, and they were promoted on the basis of their scholarly track records. The Chi-Squares represented a perspective of journalism education that fit with the norms of the U.S. research university. The Green-Eyeshade approach to journalism could not have survived in these universities.

Perley I. Reed, former director of the University of West Virginia School of Journalism, wrote to the 1965 Association for Education in Journalism (AEJ) conference: "Certain graduate-school journalism professors have . . . ceased using the universal trademark of our profession, namely journalism, and are substituting the word communication. . . . There should be only 'Schools of Journalism' and no 'Schools of Communication,' unless Western Union and Bell Telephone are the primary concepts" (Hightin 1967). The Green-Eyeshades opposed renaming "journalism" as "communication." Communication was a social science name; journalism was a vocational name.

The Green-Eyeshades also were opposed to the use of quantitative data by the Chi-Squares (as implied by the name "Chi-Square," a statistical test of significance). The new cadre of communication Ph.D.s conducted audience surveys in order to provide feedback to media institutions so that they could better fulfill the needs of audience members. For instance, say that a communication researcher found that a newspaper could increase its circulation by providing more soft news like sports, life-styles, and food tips, and less hard news. The Green-Eyeshades argued that such a recommendation might help the newspaper owners make higher profits but was in opposition to professional journalistic standards (that is, a high value on hard news).

Thus, the battle centered on whether the correct terminology was "journalism" or "communication" for university units devoted to teaching these topics, the role of the social sciences in journalism training, and the epistemological basis for understanding human communication and journalistic practice. Wilbur Schramm's vision of communication study was threatening to the Green-Eyeshades. A spokesman for the Green-Eyeshades, John Tebbel (1964), spoke of "a strong undercurrent of outrage and protect" by traditional journalism educators against the mass communication scientists.

Initially, the Green-Eyeshades had a powerful friend on their side of the conflict: the owners and publishers of newspapers, who often had considerable political clout, especially with the board of trustees of public universities. The owners and publishers doubted that the new breed of communication professors could teach anything useful to journalism students.* Gradually the industry's resistance to the Chi-Squares broke down and eventually gave way to enthusiasm, when newspapers and other media institutions became engaged in polling and market research. This type of applied communication research was of obvious value to the mass media (Danielson 1992).[†]

A key turning point in the acceptance of Schramm's vision of communication study by journalism educators was a series of rump sessions at the AEJ annual conferences. In May 1955, the American Association for Public Opinion Research (AAPOR) met in Madison, Wisconsin, and Chick Bush asked Ralph Nafziger (at Wisconsin) to invite the heads of a half-dozen departments and schools of journalism with Ph.D. programs to meet informally at Nafziger's home. At the meeting, each of the existing doctoral programs was described by a doctoral student: "This was an eye opener for a few institutions" (Troldahl 1968, p. 33). The group decided to hold a separate session on the day following the next AEJ conference in August 1955 in Colorado. Until then, the Green-Eyeshades who dominated the AEJ had managed to keep research re-

---

*In an earlier era, many newspaper editors had been opposed to hiring graduates of university schools of journalism. They believed that "the only school of journalism was a newspaper" (Schramm in press a). "The first problem of the schools of journalism was to prove themselves *practical*, which, at bottom, meant vocational" (Schramm 1947a). Once the schools of journalism were acceptable to newspaper owners, as evidenced by their hiring graduates, the schools of journalism could shape their curriculum in the direction of requiring more social sciences training and fewer skills courses in writing and editing.

[†]Dearing (1989) found that about 80 percent of the national polls about the issue of AIDS in the United States from 1983 to 1987 (each of about 1,100 respondents) were sponsored by media institutions, at an average cost of $200,000 per survey. The *Los Angeles Times* conducted an incredible thirty-five polls of voting preferences in the 1988 presidential primary in the state of Iowa. Media institutions invest so heavily in survey research because the poll results are news, which a media institution can use to sell newspapers or magazines or to earn television or radio ratings. Here is a case in which the media create news, presumably in order to earn a profit (rather than just to report the news).

ports off the conference program. Seven research papers were presented at the Colorado meetings, and the participants (they called themselves "rumpers") agreed to hold another rump session the following year, 1956, at the AEJ convention in Evanston, Illinois.

A decade later, the rump sessions evolved into the Division on Communication Theory and Methodology of AEJ, which today has several hundred members. Note that the organizers of the AEJ rump sessions were all "Bleyer children": Bush, Nafziger, and Ralph Casey.* Their actions amounted to organizing the Chi-Squares, who were then a minority in the AEJ, against the Green-Eyeshades. Bleyer children played a crucial role in preparing schools of journalism for Schramm's vision of communication study (Rogers and Chaffee 1992). Bleyer children were administrators of the journalism schools at Wisconsin, Minnesota, and Illinois, which, along with Stanford, formed a network at the top of the heap of journalism schools in the United States. These schools hired Schramm's Ph.D.s in mass communication from Stanford, who then trained a much larger body of undergraduate journalism students and mass communication doctorates, who in turn infected the rest of the schools of journalism. Thus, Schramm's vision of communication study rested on a base laid down some decades previously by Daddy Bleyer, and it was the Bleyer children who implemented Schramm's vision through schools of journalism.

Eventually, the younger generation of Chi-Squares outlived the Green-Eyeshades, which settled their dispute on an actuarial basis at most schools of journalism in the United States. But by no means is the Green-Eyeshades versus Chi-Squares debate entirely over. The battle continues in the faculties of many U.S. schools of journalism today and in print (for example, see Ron Lovell's 1987 article, "Triumph of the Chi-Squares: It's a Hollow Victory," and a set of 1988 responses such as Guido Stempel's "The Chi-Squares Strike Back").

Schramm speculated about what kind of professional school might develop out of the early schools of journalism: "In the first place, it will be a school of *communication*" (Schramm 1947a). He was wrong. Most schools of journalism, once they swung to the Chi-Square viewpoint of buying into Schramm's vision of communication study, retained "journalism" as their main title and added the words "and mass communica-

*Wilbur Schramm participated in the August 1955 Colorado rump session, stopping off en route from Urbana to his new faculty position at Stanford.

tion." As the name implies, they did not completely buy Schramm's vision, especially at the undergraduate level, where bachelors' degrees continued to be granted in "journalism."

A Bleyer-to-Schramm Palimpsest

It is quite likely that Wilbur Schramm never met Daddy Bleyer. Bleyer died in 1935 as director of the School of Journalism at Wisconsin, at a time when Schramm was an assistant professor of English literature at the University of Iowa. He would not become involved in journalism and mass communication for another eight years. His 1942 blueprint for the Iowa School of Journalism advocated an undergraduate journalism curriculum composed of one-fourth journalism skills courses and three-fourths social science and humanities courses, just the ratio that Daddy Bleyer had advocated, although Bleyer was not cited by Schramm as the source for this proportion.*

At the time of his death in 1987, Wilbur Schramm left an incomplete book manuscript in his personal computer file, *The Beginnings of Communication Study in America: A Personal Memoir*. The last chapter, for which Schramm left only the outline, was to deal with the acceptance of communication study in schools of journalism and departments of speech. One section was to be titled "Daddy Bleyer and His Children" (Rogers and Chaffee 1992). Steven Chaffee of Stanford University and I finished Schramm's (in press a) book, including the unwritten chapter. So at the time of his death, Schramm was well aware of Daddy Bleyer's important role in preparing journalism education for Schramm's vision of communication study. Most of what Schramm knew about Bleyer came through the Bleyer children, of whom Ralph Nafziger at Minnesota and then Wisconsin, Ralph Casey at Minnesota, Fred Siebert at Illinois and then at Michigan State, and Chick Bush at Stanford, were the most important links from Bleyer to Schramm.

Figure 12.2 is a palimpsest of these Bleyer-to-Schramm connections, which link across several decades to relate the two great founders (one of journalism education and the other of communication study) via four organizational settings. A palimpsest, from the Greek word for "to scrape again," comes from the reuse of ancient parchment manuscripts

---

*A few years later, however, in an article about journalism education, Schramm (1947a) approvingly cited Bleyer's ideal journalism curriculum.

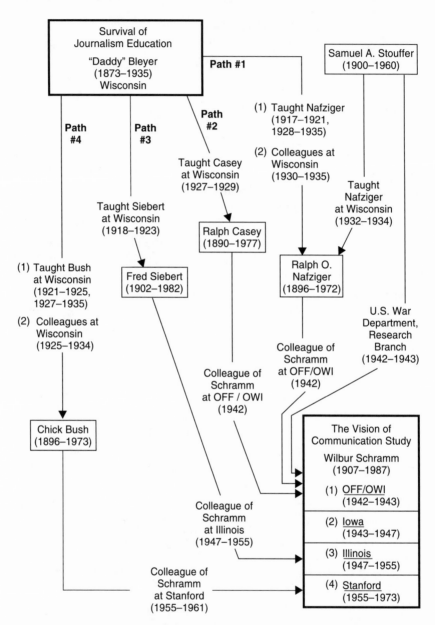

Figure 12.2. A palimpsest of the linkages from Daddy Bleyer to Wilbur Schramm. *Source:* Rogers and Chaffee (1992).

by removing previous layers of writing. To the joy of historians, the earlier layers can often be recovered by chemical or other means. Here we use palimpsest as a metaphor for the layers of history that we seek to reconstruct in understanding the Bleyer-to-Schramm academic connection.*

Now we peel back the layers of history connecting Bleyer and Schramm, starting with the most recent. First, however, we must recognize that Daddy Bleyer had a conception of journalism education that was quite different from Wilbur Schramm's vision of communication study. "Bleyer . . . created the concept of journalism as an academic field of study, while at other universities it was being treated as little more than a vocational trade" (Rogers and Chaffee 1992). Bleyer felt that schools of journalism could not survive at research universities like the University of Wisconsin unless journalism stressed its basis in the social sciences, awarded Ph.D. degrees through joint programs with the social sciences, and conducted scholarly research on journalism problems. In contrast, Schramm wanted to launch a new field. There always was a tension between these two visions, and there still is.

The most recent Bleyer-to-Schramm connection was via Chick Bush, a Bleyer child who was a colleague of Schramm's at Stanford from 1955 to 1961 (path #4 in Figure 12.1). For eight years previously (1947–1955), during Schramm's period at Illinois, he had collaborated with another former Bleyer protégé, Fred Siebert (path #3). At Iowa from 1943 to 1947, where Schramm was first implementing his vision of communication study, he did not have direct contact with a Bleyer child, but the vision was originally worked out while Schramm was at OFF/OWI in 1942–1943. Here he met regularly with Ralph Casey (path #2), a consultant to the U.S. propaganda agency, and with Ralph Nafziger (path #1) (both Bleyer children), and with Sam Stouffer, who had taught Nafziger in the graduate-level statistics course at Wisconsin and who was a consultant to OFF/OWI. Schramm's network links to the Bleyer children were important in helping him find academic homes for his research and doctoral programs in communication study, at both Illinois and Stanford, and in finding faculty jobs for his new Ph.D.s in schools of journalism.

---

*Wilbur Schramm was fond of the palimpsest as a metaphor. He insisted that *palimpsest* be included in the *International Encyclopedia of Communication,* and he wrote the entry (Schramm 1988).

International Communication

When Schramm arrived at Stanford University in 1955, he began the international phase of his career (Keever 1991). He already had completed some international work while he was an Urbana, but there his heavy administrative responsibilities meant that he could not do much traveling overseas. His first major international study was conducted during the Korean War when the U.S. Air Force sent him on a mission to Seoul, the Korean capital city that had been overrun by the North Koreans in the early months of the war and then recaptured. Schramm and John Riley, a sociologist at Rutgers University, interviewed respondents who had lived under the communist regime. Schramm was very patriotic, and his Cold Warrior orientation of that time is suggested by the title of his book reporting his findings: *The Reds Take a City* (Riley and Schramm 1951).* This research was not particularly noteworthy in an academic sense, but it led Schramm into a specialization in international communication at Stanford.

One of Schramm's pioneering studies in international communication centered on one day, November 2, 1956, when two momentous world events occurred: Soviet tanks entered Budapest to quash the Hungarian uprising, and Egypt was attacked by British, French, and Israeli armed forces in response to the Suez Canal crisis. This unique occurrence of military action by both sides in the Cold War but not against each other led to major news coverage by the world's great newspapers. Wilbur Schramm capitalized on this unusual news day by content-analyzing the way that fourteen major newspapers around the world reported the two events. His *One Day in the World's Press* (1959) showed that the ideological position of each newspaper directly affected its reporting. For example, *Pravda* splashed news of the Suez crisis across its front page but barely mentioned the Soviet military action in Hungary. The *New York Times* gave heavy coverage to both news events, but *Le Monde* concentrated particularly on Budapest. Schramm's study helped launch the field of international communication, and especially the study of international news flows, a topic that was to attract the attention of many scholars in the 1980s.†

*The results were also reported in two journal articles: Riley and Schramm (1951) and Riley, Schramm, and Williams (1951).

†In addition to Schramm's internationalizing influence on U.S. communication study, the related specialty of intercultural communication was launched by Edward Hall, whose im-

Schramm believed that the study of comparative communication systems was a sound type of scholarship. For communication study to concern only one nation, especially if it were the highly untypical United States, was unduly limiting in an intellectual sense. Schramm not only made comparative analyses himself but urged his colleagues and students to do the same. He told his colleagues in the Stanford Institute for Communication Research that he expected each of them to pursue their research specialty outside of the United States, as well as at home. Accordingly, during Schramm's years at Stanford (1955–1973), his institute became known as the most prestigious place at which to study international communication.

A further reason for Schramm's interest in international communication was his strong sense of patriotism, coupled with a belief that the main post–World War II problems for the United States lay in its Cold War conflict with the Soviet Union and in the related issue of Third World development, which U.S. foreign policy at that time defined as a struggle with the Soviet Union for the hearts and minds of people in Latin America, Africa, and Asia. Schramm wrote a very influential book, *Mass Media and National Development* (1964), summarizing the role of mass communication in development. He also conducted research on development communication, particularly on the effects of instructional television systems as a means of improving formal and informal education in nations like Colombia, El Salvador, American Samoa, and the Ivory Coast.

Finally, Schramm studied international communication because he felt it was a means to spread communication study to other nations. He formed an agreement between his Stanford Institute and the French Press Institute at the University of Paris for the exchange of faculty and students, and several books were published collaboratively. Schramm helped start communication institutes in other nations, like the Indian Institute for Mass Communication, in New Delhi. He recruited international students for his Stanford doctoral program and encouraged them to return to their home nation to launch the study of communication.

---

portant 1959 book, *The Silent Language,* was originally written as a manual for training Foreign Service employees of the U.S. Department of State (Leeds-Hurwitz 1990). Hall was an anthropologist who became interested in the effect of cultural differences on human communication through providing training to U.S. diplomatic officials, who had been particularly ineffective because they seldom spoke the language and usually knew little of the host culture. Hall coined the term *intercultural communication* in his 1959 book. This specialty has since grown to importance at the hands of communication scholars.

During its golden era from 1955 to 1970, no other doctoral training program in the United States was as international as Stanford's, and Schramm was the driving force for this international emphasis.

When Schramm retired from Stanford University in 1973 at age sixty-five, then the mandatory age of retirement, he moved to Honolulu to become director of the East-West Communication Institute, on the campus of the University of Hawaii at Manoa. The East-West Center (of which the Communication Institute was one component) had been created by the federal government to facilitate U.S.-Asian intellectual collaboration and exchange. Schramm's institute awarded study fellowships to Asian students, organized conferences of Asian and American communication scholars, conducted research, and published books and reports. So after 1973, Schramm devoted his full-time efforts to international communication. Even after he stepped down as director of the East-West Communication Institute, he continued to be active in the institute's affairs in an emeritus role. He taught briefly at the Chinese University of Hong Kong, as an endowed professor of international communication, and gradually wound down his career in Hawaii, withdrawing slowly from the center stage of communication study. He continued to write books, although they were not so frequent in appearance or as influential as previously. He no longer was involved in a doctoral training program. His vision of communication study, or at least some version of it, was already widely accepted around the world. But Schramm continued working, right up until the end. He died of a heart attack on December 27, 1987, in Honolulu. At the time he was watching television at home with his wife. After cremation, his ashes were scattered in the Pacific (Coberly 1992).

WHY WAS SCHRAMM SO INFLUENTIAL?

An important factor in Wilbur Schramm's career was his ability to write clearly, as he himself acknowledged (Schramm 1979). In fact, some admirers called him "the great summarizer." Schramm had an ability to get involved in a certain research front, quickly comprehend the main issues, identify the promising research directions, and then package this knowledge in a readable book that was free of jargon. These books of his were very influential in shaping the direction of communication research. "From 1948 to 1977, Schramm produced almost a book a year (edited or co-edited or authored) in addition to articles, book chapters, conference papers, and reports that probably number in the hundreds."

Schramm was "a phenomenally prolific writer whose work helped to shape the field during these decades [the late 1940s, through the early 1970s]" (McAnany 1988).

During his eighteen years at Stanford University, from 1955 to his retirement in 1973, Wilbur Schramm produced a flood of written work. He typed at the same rate as a professional secretary, in a rapid staccato, composing as he typed. "Some five million words and four [electric] typewriters later (he literally wore the keys off two of them), Wilbur had become unquestionably the world's leading authority in the field of communication research" (Nelson 1977, p. 317). Schramm sometimes put in a twenty-four-hour workday. His commitment to scholarly research meant that he shortchanged the time that he spent with his wife and children. He had many acquaintances and admirers but few close friends.

Schramm's books were one means through which he influenced the field of communication. In a 1979 oral history interview, he was asked which of his books he would most like to be known by. He replied, "It would be for one paragraph in *Television in the Lives of Our Children* [Schramm, Lyle, and Parker 1961]. It said: 'Perhaps the more important way to look at the effects of television on children is not what television does to children, but what children do with television.' Children are not inert. You don't shoot television at children. They fit it into what they know, what they are doing." In this interview Schramm said that his most-cited book was *Process and Effects of Communication* (1954), but his most influential book was *Television in the Lives of Our Children:* "It has led hundreds of young scholars to study the effects of television on children. And to the Surgeon General's research program on this topic, funded at $1.8 million. The original research project of 1959, on which the book is based, was funded at only $1,500." He continued: "*Mass Media and National Development* [1964] was also very influential. People come up to me all over the world and tell me how useful that book has been to them. So timing is very important. Choosing the topic of research at just the right time is crucial. I have been very lucky in choosing the topics of my research and of the books that I have written." This timing was not just luck. Schramm was so influential in his heyday that when he published a book about some new research direction, say, television effects and children, he set the agenda for communication study.

Wayne Danielson (1992), who earned his doctorate in communication at Stanford between 1954 and 1957, remembers that Schramm was an enthusiast for Shannon's information theory but not a zealot. In fact,

Schramm's job interview lecture at Stanford in early 1955 was on information theory and communication research. In Schramm's doctoral theory course at Stanford, the students read Shannon and Weaver's book, *The Mathematical Theory of Communication* (1949), and were taught to understand Shannon's model of communication and to use the bit as a measure of information. But Schramm considered Shannon's information theory as one of several models for the new field of communication study that he was launching, not the root paradigm.

Wilbur Schramm had a broad background in literature and the social sciences that ably prepared him for a new interdisciplinary field like communication study. He was intellectually curious and could become interested in a topic that was out past the edge of his field of knowledge. Shortly, he would master it. For instance, he taught himself Fortran computer programming, comprehended Shannon's information theory, and applied Freud's pleasure principle and reality principle to individuals deciding to expose themselves to entertainment versus news (Schramm 1949b). The pleasure principle motivates individuals to consume news of crime and corruption, sports, and human-interest stories for an immediate reward (that is, the pleasure principle). The reality principle (of a delayed reward) motivates individuals to consume news of public affairs, science, health, and economic matters.

Schramm was a gentleman and dealt with people in a courtly, considerate manner. He had a large ego, although it seldom showed in public. Yet he had a kind of down-home midwestern humility, which allowed him to get along with famous scholars in other fields and helped him obtain the research funding that he needed to maintain his research institutes. He possessed a powerful imagination and could see a new field of study in the pieces of mass communication and persuasion research that had accumulated in the 1930s and 1940s. Schramm's vision of communication study purposely drew on the work of famous social scientists at prestigious American universities in order to give credibility to the new field of study that he sought to create.

Schramm mixed easily with the top scholars of his day. As a master's student at Harvard, he enrolled in courses far outside his major (in American literature) with such eminent figures as Alfred North Whitehead, the philosopher. At the University of Iowa he also sought out the best minds, like Carl Seashore, George Stoddard, and Kurt Lewin, though they had little to do with Schramm's academic niche at the time. He used relationships with these authorities as intellectual bridges to other disciplines, as a means of satisfying his curiosity, and as a means of preparing to found a new field. While in Washington during World War II, Schramm had a splendid opportunity to mix with the leading social scientists of his day: Margaret Mead, Sam Stouffer, Rensis Likert, and others. At that time, Schramm was younger than these people, and it seems that he approached them in the role of an interested student-learner. He was absorbing a variety of points of view.

Schramm looked outward from the communication research institutes that he founded toward the prestigious social scientists conducting communication researches, not toward the traditional and professional units (like the schools of journalism) upon which he was building communication study. "Schramm rarely mentioned communication scholars who were already in the field, preferring to build legitimacy for Communication by asserting that esteemed figures in established social and behavioral sciences were really his colleagues. Politically, this was a shrewd strategy" (Rogers and Chaffee 1992). Thus one can understand why Schramm constructed the four founders myth: it accorded a prestigious ancestry to communication study. Schramm had relatively little to say about Daddy Bleyer and the Bleyer children and paid even less attention to rhetorical scholars in departments of speech.*

Schramm had a wide view that looked upward at great minds in high places. He identified with these noted scholars and encouraged his students to do the same. His communication doctoral programs at Iowa, Illinois, and Stanford all had strong interdisciplinary links to psychology, sociology, and political science. They were initially organized under the university's graduate school and required doctoral students to enroll in courses taught by famous psychologists and other social scientists. When Schramm's communication students earned the top grades in these tough doctoral courses, he was overjoyed. Their performance proved that the Ph.D. students in communication study were just as capable as those in the more established disciplines.

Wilbur Schramm had old-fashioned notions about the role of men and women in society. He had an Old World, respectful attitude toward women (he called his wife "Miss Betty" with a touch of magnolia in his

---

*Schramm attended only two conventions of the Association for Education in Journalism and two conventions of the International Communication Association during the last twenty-five years of his life, and on each of these occasions it was to receive a special award or to give an invited address (Rogers and Chaffee 1992).

voice), but he did not treat women students and scholars as equal to men, at least in the study of communication. For instance, in the early 1970s he referred to Dr. Aimée Dorr, an assistant professor in his Stanford Institute for Communication Research, as a "pretty little thing." His 1978 book, *Men, Messages, and Media,* appeared during the era of the feminist revolt against a male-dominated society and was criticized severely for its sexist title. After complaining petulantly about these criticisms of his book, Schramm changed the title of his second edition to the unwieldy *Men, Women, Messages, and Media* (Schramm and Porter 1982).

Schramm's gender attitudes were somewhat typical of his times. When he arrived at Stanford in 1955, Chick Bush had stated in the university catalog that women need not apply for the doctoral program in communication, presumably because they could not understand the man's world of mass media communication. Today, these attitudes of gender inequality have changed to the extent that women candidates are eagerly recruited to most doctoral programs, and women are given priority in professional hiring decisions. At most universities, more than half of the undergraduate communication students are women, and somewhat fewer than half of the graduate students in communication are female, but their professors are still more likely to be men than women, so adequate role models for the female communication students are in short supply. Although there are very few women scholars in the history recounted in this book (Margaret Mead is one of the only important figures, and she was but indirectly involved in communication study), many female communication scholars have risen to prominence in recent decades. In the past ten years, about half of the individuals elected to be president of the International Communication Association are women. Progress is being made, but gender equality is far from achieved in the field of communication.

Perhaps the considerable influence of Wilbur Schramm can be described by my observations of a day in his life at Stanford in May 1967. Schramm had invited me to give a guest lecture in his course that evening on development communication. When he telephoned with the invitation, he suggested that I arrive in Palo Alto that morning so that I could spend the day in his Institute. It was an eventful day in the field of communication study. I hung around Schramm's office in the old wooden barracks building, Cypress Hall, that housed the Institute. His door was open, and his colleagues and doctoral students dropped in and out during the day. At various times, three or four or five individuals were present at his salon.

He received numerous long-distance calls. For instance, in mid-morning he learned that one of his former Ph.D. students had not been promoted to associate professor with tenure in a West Coast university's school of journalism. Somewhat later, he talked with the U.S. Surgeon General's office in Washington about a newly funded research program on television and children. Schramm had coauthored the first major study on this topic a few years previously, reported in his book *Television in the Lives of Our Children* (Schramm, Lyle, and Parker 1961), and he recommended one of his protégés as a research manager of the surgeon general's program (several months later, it was announced that Schramm's Institute was funded by this program for a major project on the effects of television on children, as was Schramm's colleague in the Department of Psychology, Albert Bandura).

Two dozen other telephone calls interrupted my discussions that day with Schramm. Southern Illinois University wanted to hire one of his people. An old friend at the University of Oregon called to ask for advice. One of Schramm's book publishers phoned to invite him to edit a second edition of one of his classic volumes. As we got in his car to drive to Schramm's Palo Alto home for dinner, prior to meeting his 7:00 P.M.- class, he introduced me to one of the star doctoral students in his Institute, Nat Katzman (later to become my colleague at Michigan State). Following the evening class, Schramm's students invited us to join them for pizza in a campus hangout. Schramm excused himself early. I suspected that he was going home to write another book. After this day, I thought that I understood where the informal headquarters of communication study was at. It was wherever Wilbur Schramm hung his hat.

Schramm "understood that he was creating history" (Gladner 1991). No other scholar did more than Wilbur Schramm to make the vision of communication study become reality in the sense of its intellectual and institutional basis in American universities. During past decades, hundreds of university departments of communication have been launched in the United States. Most arose out of existing departments of speech, journalism, library science, and other university units emphasizing a professional or humanistic kind of communication study; others were created anew. Today communication study is a well-established academic field, tremendously diverse in the names of the schools and departments in which it is taught: communication, journalism and mass communication, speech communication, communication studies, tele-communications, and a dozen others. All trace an intellectual ancestry to Wilbur Schramm's vision of communication study.

CONTRIBUTIONS OF WILBUR SCHRAMM
TO COMMUNICATION STUDY

Wilbur Schramm was the founder of communication study. If his contribution to the field could somehow be removed, there would not be a field of communication study. It is doubtful that anyone else could have founded the field.

Any individual founding a new scientific field must have a vision for it. Schramm formed his vision in 1942 in Washington, D.C., during World War II. He returned to the University of Iowa to launch his vision of communication study in the school of journalism. The future acceptance of this perspective had been prepared by Daddy Bleyer, the pioneering journalism educator at the University of Wisconsin, and his protégés, who believed that journalism, in order to survive in research universities, needed a basis in the social sciences. Communication study would infect existing schools of journalism, at least in an initial era, rather than be implemented in newly created departments of communication. Later, more gradually and without the Green-Eyeshades versus Chi-Squares conflict that occurred in journalism, communication study also invaded departments of speech, turning them away from their humanities emphasis on rhetoric to become, in essence, departments of interpersonal communication with a strong orientation toward psychology.

In addition to his vision, Wilbur Schramm had other important qualities for founding the field of communication study. He invested long hours to implement his ideas. Schramm was a prolific and clear writer, and he authored most of the early textbooks in mass communication. He had the interpersonal charm that attracted doctoral applicants and research funding to his research institutes. His most important product was undoubtedly the new Ph.D.s in communication who fanned out across the world after studying with Schramm at Stanford, to spread the concept of communication study. Schramm gave specific direction to what was studied by the new field. He pioneered new research specialties, like international communication, development communication, and television effects on children.

Most important, Wilbur Schramm established the first academic units called "communication" at Illinois and then at Stanford. Such institutions gave visibility to the new field, providing the launching pad for its diffusion to other universities.

ACCEPTANCE OF COMMUNICATION
STUDY IN U.S. UNIVERSITIES

The highest-prestige U.S. universities tend to be private, old, and resistant to radical educational innovations, including starting a new academic field. Subjective ratings of U.S. universities generally place eight institutions at the top: Harvard, Columbia, Yale, and Princeton in the Ivy League; Stanford University; the University of Chicago; and the University of California at Berkeley and MIT. None of these prestigious universities has accepted communication study except Stanford.

The general attitude of these top-rated universities seems to be not to risk their established reputation on a new academic venture like communication study, ethnic studies, environmental studies, and feminist studies, or, in an earlier era, on the new field of sociology. The most highly regarded U.S. universities varied widely in when they accepted the discipline of sociology. "Chicago, Columbia, and Yale appointed professors of sociology in the 1890s; Harvard waited until the 1930s to create a department; Princeton and the University of California at Berkeley made their first appointments after World War II; and Johns Hopkins, the last of the Association of American Universities [the fifty-odd major research universities] to have sociology, delayed until 1959 before joining the ranks" (Lipset and Smelser 1961).

University Prestige and Adoption of Communication Study

A similar time lag to that just described for sociology occurred in the process through which American universities accepted the field of communication study. Schramm's move to Stanford University in 1955 and the founding of the doctoral program there was the key event in gaining acceptance of communication study in American universities.

Initially, communication study took over existing journalism schools, gradually shifting the teaching and study of communication in these schools from a professional perspective to a more scientific orientation. Similarly, communication study also began to invade departments of speech, changing them from the humanistic study of rhetoric toward a scientific analysis of interpersonal communication. This take-over of existing university units also divided the field of communication study into the two subdisciplines of interpersonal and mass communication.

Communication study spread first to the schools of journalism in the large midwestern universities—Wisconsin, Minnesota, and Illinois—and to Stanford. This first era of expansion occurred mainly in the 1950s. These schools of journalism were led in every case by an administrator who had been trained by Daddy Bleyer at the University of Wisconsin and had already implemented a social science basis for journalism education.

The key role of Stanford University in the diffusion of communication study centers on the fact that it is a prestigious, private, West Coast university, in contrast to the large midwestern state universities where the Bleyer children facilitated acceptance of communication study in schools of journalism. Schramm trained a new generation of Ph.D.s in communication theory and research at Stanford, who then took up faculty and administrative positions at other universities, often in schools of journalism. In every field, new Ph.D.s flow down, not up, the university prestige structure, as they take their first position as assistant professor.* It was very important for the acceptance of communication study by U.S. universities that Schramm implemented his vision at a high-prestige university like Stanford.

The forefathers of communication study were located at prestigious universities like Chicago, Yale, Columbia, and MIT. But after World War II, these universities did not adopt the innovation of communication study. The communication field has not been successful in gaining a solid foothold in Ivy League schools or at other high-prestige universities. Cornell University is an exception, but it has just begun to offer a Ph.D. degree, and Cornell's Department of Communication Arts is located in the College of Agriculture. And the University of Pennsylvania has the Annenberg School for Communication, founded in 1964, through a gift from Walter Annenberg, a wealthy media owner. Many top administrators at U.S. universities do not understand the field of communication study because they earned their doctorates at Ivy League schools where communication was not offered.

---

*This downward flow is a necessity as the highest-prestige U.S. universities produce a very high proportion of all Ph.D.s in every field.

Once many of the fifty or so U.S. research universities had adopted communication study and were producing crops of new Ph.D.s in communication,* many of these new doctorates took faculty positions at the smaller colleges and universities engaged mainly in teaching undergraduate students. By the early 1990s, an estimated 1,500 schools or departments of communication existed in the United States (Elmore 1993).[†] Thirty years previously, in 1960, there were very few.

The big spurt in the number of U.S. universities with schools or departments of communication occurred in the 1960s, with a steady growth since then. Undergraduate enrollments in communication departments skyrocketed in the 1970s and 1980s, and on many university campuses the undergraduate enrollment in communication is the largest, or one of the largest, of any university department. When the field of communication study was getting established in the 1950s and 1960s, U.S. universities were undergoing an immense expansion in both their total enrollment and their research programs. The new communication-related schools and departments benefited accordingly. Their timing was exquisite.

Today, most U.S. universities have a school or department of communication, and several universities have two or more. The field of communication study has been one of the fastest-growing academic units on U.S. university campuses for the past several decades. Data provided by the U.S. Department of Education indicate that about 50,000 bachelor's degrees in communication were awarded during 1989 (up from 11,000 in 1970), 4,000 master's degrees (up from 1,800 in 1970), and 250 doctoral degrees (up from 145 in 1970). Some 257,000 students were majoring in communication in 1993, up from

---

*Paisley (1984, p. 12) showed that twenty-one of the top forty universities (ranked by the overall quality of their graduate curriculum) in 1980 offered a Ph.D. degree in some type of communication study (communication research, journalism, speech, or information science). By 1992, I estimate that three more of these top forty universities offer a doctorate in some field of communication, for a total of twenty-four of the forty universities (60 percent).

[†]These figures are smaller than those reported by Eadie (1970), perhaps because he included university programs in mass communication, speech communication, audiology and speech correction, and drama. Using this broader definition, Eadie found that the number of communication Ph.D. degrees granted in 1976 was similar to the number in sociology and philosophy but fewer than in psychology, English, and history. The number of master's degrees in communication awarded in 1976 was greater than for any of these comparable fields. I estimate that there were about 2,000 schools and departments of communication in U.S. universities in 1993.

200,000 in 1900 (Elmore 1993). Communication study in the United States is a major growth industry.

Fitting Communication Study into Existing Structures

Compared to other social sciences like sociology, psychology, and political science, the main paradigm for communication, Schramm's vision of communication study, generally did not lead to new university departments of communication. Instead, the Schramm vision of communication study was fit into existing departments of speech and schools of journalism. These academic entities already had a long history at many universities; they had textbooks and an accumulated storehouse of knowledge and a cadre of trained professors. The new paradigm of communication study did not displace these existing academic systems of speech and journalism. Instead, it was added on, modified, and then split in two. As a result, many large universities today have a department of speech communication and also a school of mass communication (or words to a similar effect). If the university also had a library school, it evolved into a school of library and information science when the new paradigm of communication study was introduced.

The results of fitting communication study into existing, applied communication departments and schools are both positive and negative. On the negative side, the discipline of communication was bifurcated into mass communication versus interpersonal communication and perhaps into a third wing of information science (Reardon and Rogers 1988). Communication was applied to such professions as journalism, broadcasting, public relations, advertising, high school teaching, and so forth. These occupational fields stand behind the academic field of communication study, providing jobs for communication graduates. In order to prepare their students for such occupational roles, communication professors must teach their students, especially undergraduates, the practical skills of communication: effective public speaking, newswriting, film-making, how to design and pretest advertising messages.*

The academic field of communication study thus was given an ap-

---

*This applied dimension of communication study in U.S. universities is attractive to undergraduate students, in part because it leads to jobs after graduation. While the number of bachelor's degrees granted in communication went up from 17,000 in 1973 to 50,000 in 1989, the number in sociology dropped from 36,000 to 14,000 according to the U.S. Department of Education.

plied orientation, along with its theoretical dimensions. The first Ph.D. programs in communication, such as at Illinois and at Stanford, were founded along with, and as part of, an institute for applied communication research. Many university departments of communication established communication research centers, patterned, knowingly or not, after Paul Lazarsfeld's Bureau of Applied Social Research at Columbia University. Applied research can also be theory based, of course, in that a scholar can design and conduct research that answers a practical question while also testing theoretical hypotheses. But the reality of much applied communication research is that it does not contribute directly to the advancement of theory. Often an externally funded applied research results in a report to the external sponsor but not in a journal article that adds to the scholarly body of communication theory. Compared to the other social sciences, the field of communication study has a more applied perspective, along with its theoretical dimension. Such a dual orientation is a cause of certain strains, but it can also be advantageous.

Communication study is unlike the other social sciences in certain other important respects. Communication is a professional field, as well as a scientific discipline. The mass media industries (radio, television, music, print, and film) stand behind the academic field of communication, offering jobs for its graduates, helping fund its research, and providing endowments for professors and schools of communication. Visible outcroppings of this close association of the academic field with media industries are the Annenberg School for Communication (at both the University of Pennsylvania and the University of Southern California), the Newhouse School of Communication at Syracuse University, McClatchey Hall at Stanford University, the Medill School of Journalism at Northwestern University, the Pulitzer School of Journalism at Columbia University, and numerous endowed chairs like the Gallup Chair in the School of Journalism and Mass Communication at the University of Iowa. The media moguls' names are attached to schools of communication today, just as the robber barons' names show their past support for such private universities as Carnegie-Mellon, Vanderbilt, and Stanford.

The number of communication scholars in the United States is considerably smaller than the number of sociologists, at least as indicated by membership in the main professional association in each field. Compared to the 97,000 members of the American Psychological Association and the 13,000 members of the American Sociological Association (ASA), the International Communication Association (ICA) had about

2,500 members in 1993. By these measures, U.S. sociology is about five times larger than U.S. communication study, and psychology is thirty-nine times larger. One difficulty with this comparison is that the ASA is the dominant association for sociologists, while the communication field has the Speech Communication Association (with 7,000 members), the Association for Education in Journalism and Mass Communication (about 2,700 members), the American Association for Public Opinion Research (about 1,200 members), the American Society for Information Sciences (about 4,000 members), and several others, plus ICA. This lack of one main professional association shows the perceived diversity that characterizes the field of communication.

The Department of Communication at Michigan State

There is one noteworthy exception to the general tendency to fit communication study into existing university structures. It occurred at Michigan State University in East Lansing in the late 1950s, about a decade after Schramm came to Illinois in 1947 and about the time that he moved to Stanford in 1955.

Michigan State's Department of Communication at its founding (the first class of doctoral students was admitted in 1957) was the best pure expression of Wilbur Schramm's vision for communication study. Three of its four core faculty were Schramm's protégés—two from Illinois (David K. Berlo and Hideya Kumata) and one from Stanford (Paul J. Deutschmann). Unlike the doctoral programs at Iowa, Illinois, Stanford, Wisconsin, and Minnesota, the Michigan State program was headquartered in a new Department of Communication rather than in a previously existing school of journalism. This fact removed the MSU doctoral program from the inherited constraints of fitting it into a previously existing academic infrastructure. The Michigan State doctorates were in communication, rather than mass communication. The doctoral courses dealt with communication at a general level, although doctoral students could specialize in either mass communication or interpersonal communication. Wilbur Schramm presumed that departments of speech and schools of journalism would eventually change their name to "communication," as indeed many have, but only after several decades. At Michigan State, the department and its Ph.D. degree were called "communication" from the start.

The Department of Communication created at Michigan State University came about through a unique set of circumstances. Michigan in the mid-1950s was a rich state, producing 11 million automobiles per year, and Michigan State was in a rapid-growth mode, expanding rapidly from its cow-college image into a megauniversity. MSU already had a rather ho-hum school of journalism and an adequate speech department, but Michigan State's hard-driving president, John Hannah, wanted his university to become a leader in the new field of communication study. In 1955, he hired Gordon A. Sabine, dean of the School of Journalism at Oregon, who had already agreed in principle to join the Wisconsin School of Journalism, as dean of Michigan State's newly created College of Communication Arts. It included the existing units of journalism and speech.* President Hannah gave Sabine permission to go after promising young faculty members in communication and to recruit doctoral students for the Ph.D. program, set to begin in 1957. Sabine excelled as a recruiter, signing up talented individuals on his visits to Illinois, Wisconsin, and Stanford.

During the 1950s and early 1960s, three universities (Stanford, Wisconsin, and Minnesota) stood at the top of the field of communication in a network of interpersonal trust, with two other universities (Illinois and Michigan State) also interlinked closely.† These universities exchanged their most promising Ph.D.-holders as future assistant professors. For instance, Wayne Dannielson earned his Ph.D. at Stanford and became an assistant professor at Wisconsin, and Richard Carter moved in the opposite direction at the same time (this Stanford-Wisconsin exchange was called "the trade" by some observers). Percy Tannenbaum earned his Ph.D. in communication at Illinois and took his first faculty job at Wisconsin. Malcolm MacLean, Jr., received his doctorate at Wisconsin and then taught at Michigan State in the new Ph.D. program begun in 1957, joining the two Ph.D.-holders from Illinois (Berlo and Kumata) and one from Stanford (Deutschmann) as the core faculty of the doctoral program. Minnesota and Wisconsin exchanged so many bodies in both directions that their doctoral programs were twinned, although Wisconsin claimed some degree of superiority.

While most of the early doctorates from the Ph.D. communication

---

*These units refused to go along with Sabine's insistence on having a communication study backbone to the college, so Sabine created a Department of General Communication Arts in 1957, and in 1958 named David K. Berlo as chair. In 1964, the department's unwieldy name was shortened to "communication."

†The top universities in producing Ph.D.s who author journal articles, as of 1962–1971, were Wisconsin, Minnesota, Iowa, Stanford, and Illinois, with Michigan State not far behind (Cole and Bowers 1973).

programs at Illinois, Wisconsin, Minnesota, and Stanford were entering faculty positions in schools of journalism, the early Ph.D.-holders from Michigan State's Department of Communication were going to both departments of speech and schools of journalism in about equal numbers (McNelly 1992). Thus, Michigan State Ph.D.s began infecting departments of speech with Schramm's vision of communication study, gradually converting them from rhetorical analysis to becoming centrally concerned with interpersonal communication study.* The output of doctorates from Michigan State was formidable. When I taught there from 1964 to 1973, MSU was admitting thirty-five candidates each fall in communication and granting thirteen Ph.D. degrees per year, more than any other university.

THE TECHNOLOGICAL DETERMINISTS: INNIS AND McLUHAN

In recent centuries, the social impacts of various communication technologies have been studied: the printing press (Eisenstein 1968, 1969, 1979), the telegraph, the telephone (Pool, 1977, 1983a, 1983b), film (Charters 1933/1970), and television (Schramm, Lyle, and Parker 1961; Schramm, Lyle, and Pool 1963; Himmelwaite, Oppenheim, and Vince 1958). Since the 1970s, new communication technologies—the microcomputer, cable television, communication satellites, and electronic messaging systems—have diffused widely. In the face of these technological developments, the scholarly field of communication has not ignored the role of new communication technologies. It could not do so.

Two important Canadian scholars, Harold Innis and Marshall McLuhan, played a key role in calling the attention of scholars to the study of communication technologies and, more broadly, in popularizing communication study. *Technological determinism* is the belief that changes in technology cause social changes in society. Critics of technological determinism argue that a technology is usually embedded in a social structure that influences its invention, development, diffusion, and social impacts on society. Such social construction of a technology may often occur; indeed is probably always happens. But this social embeddedness of a technology does not detract from the fact that the

---

*There were, of course, other influences in the same direction, such as Carl Hovland's persuasion research and the use of experimental methods (pioneered by such speech professors as Franklin Knower).

technology may be an impetus for social change, just that it is not the sole impetus.

"Innis and McLuhan, alone among students of human society, make the history of the mass media central to the history of civilization at large. Both see the media not merely as technical appurtenances to society but as crucial determinants of the social fabric. For them, the history of the mass media is not just another avenue of historical research; rather it is another way of writing the history of Western civilization" (Carey 1967). Innis's theory of the technological determinism of communication was carried forward by Marshall McLuhan in the late 1960s and forms a background for contemporary research on the new communication technologies.

Thus the two Canadian theorists of communication technology, whose work was published in the 1950s and 1960, gained a renewed scholarly interest among communication scholars in the 1980s and 1990s.

Harold Innis

Harold Adams Innis (1894–1952) was born on an Ontario farm and grew up poor. After military service in World War I, he earned his Ph.D. degree in economics at the University of Chicago with a dissertation on the history of the Canadian Pacific Railway. He enrolled in courses at Chicago from Thorstein Veblen.* Innis studied at Chicago when Robert E. Park and George Herbert Mead were both on the faculty but did not take courses from them (Carey 1981). Nevertheless, the Chicago school was in full flower at this time (around 1920), and Innis seemed to have soaked up some of its ideas that were in the air.

Innis then accepted a faculty position in political economy at the University of Toronto, where he taught for the rest of his career. Veblen had influenced Innis to pay close attention to the intersection of technology with the geographical and institutional environment of Canada. In his first book, *The History of the Canadian Pacific Railway* (1923), Innis showed how construction of the railroad changed a society that had depended on waterborne transportation. The material determinism of Innis's "staples" thesis maintained that the historical analysis of important raw materials, like furs and wood in the case of Canada, offers a

---

*Veblen is known for such concepts as conspicuous consumption and trained incapacity and for his book, *Theory of the Leisure Class* (1926).

means of understanding a nation's political economy. Each of Innis's scholarly books was about a major Canadian industry: railroads, fur trading, and cod fishing. During the last ten years of his life, Innis turned to analyzing human communication. He began to study the wood pulp and paper industry, and this investigation led him to put communication technology in center place in his theoretical framework. Now he was no longer concerned just with the Canadian economy but rather with the historical analysis of all human civilization. His last two books, *Empire and Communications* (1950) and *The Bias of Communication* (1951), exemplify his study of communication technology in a historical context.

Innis is one of the most influential media determinists. Media determinists contend that the dominant communication technology of a civilization is central to the culture and the social structure of that society. Innis viewed communication media as the very essence of civilization. He "pursued communication in a genuinely interdisciplinary way. He . . . restored communication study to an historical foundation" (Carey 1981a). Innis became interested in the role of communication media through his early work on the influence of transportation and communication systems on Canadian frontier expansion. Later, he examined factors underlying the extension of power by the British and American empires, becoming convinced that transportation and communication were vital factors in the expansion of empires—hence, his interest in the role of communication in the historical development of civilizations. "Innis provided in communication studies, at a moment when no one else in the United States was doing so, a model of scholarly investigation that was historical, empirical, interpretive, and critical" (Carey 1981a).

In *Empire and Communication,* Innis contended that communication media are "biased" in terms of their tendency to permit control over time or space. The media used in ancient civilizations, like clay, parchment, and stone, were durable but difficult to transport. These characteristics are conducive to control over time but not over space. Hence they are time-biased. Less durable and easily transportable media such as papyrus and paper are spatially biased in being lightweight and easy to transport. Because paper permitted administration over large distances, it facilitated the geographical extension of empires and encouraged military expansion. In comparison, spoken communication, which can travel only short distances without distortion, is adequate for traditional societies, where the emphasis is on custom, continuity, community, and morality. These societies are characterized by stable and hierarchical social orders, which stifle individualism as a potential agent of change. Time-biased communication systems are found in societies with a rich oral tradition or with written technologies where access is limited to a privileged few. Moses's Ten Commandments, for example, are time-biased, because they have lasted over time.

Space-biased communication media are oriented to the present day and to the future. The emphasis is on expansion, an increase in political authority, and creation of secular institutions, with the subsequent growth of science and technical knowledge. Societies with space-biased communication media are characterized by highly efficient systems of information exchange and mass communication. Although these systems are functional, they cannot convey the richness of the oral tradition. Print, telephone, radio, and television are space-biased.*

Marshall McLuhan

While Innis was mainly interested in the effects of communication media on social organization, McLuhan focused on how communication technology changes the basic senses of hearing, seeing, touching, smelling, and tasting. Marshall McLuhan (1911–1980) was a Canadian literary critic and media determinist who became a public figure in the 1960s. He gave a tremendous popular awareness to communication study, but he also distorted this image in certain ways. Certainly he did not convey an accurate picture of the nature of communication study. With McLuhan's immense popularity came a tendency toward a simpler, monocausal explanation of social change. McLuhan claimed that when print media began to replace certain oral communication, the seeing-hearing sensory ratio was changed, leading to changes in how individuals perceive information and thus in how they think. The introduction of the phonetic alphabet, for example, led to linear thinking as individuals followed left-to-right sentences. McLuhan saw communication technology as a main cause of social change, especially at the individual level.

McLuhan was born in western Canada and grew up in a small town in Saskatchewan. His mother was a dominant intellectual figure in his life. He earned a bachelor's degree in literature from the University of Manitoba in 1932 and then traveled to England to earn a Ph.D. in En-

*Innis died in 1952, just prior to the widespread diffusion of television in North America.

glish literature at Cambridge University from 1937 to 1942. In 1947, he was appointed director of the Center for Culture and Technology at the University of Toronto. Although McLuhan acknowledged his intellectual debt to Harold Innis and both taught at the same university for several years, they had little direct contact. For instance, Innis attended the weekly McLuhan luncheons (a kind of McLuhan fan club) only a few times.

McLuhan (1969) stated, "All media, from the phonetic alphabet to the computer, are extensions of man that cause deep and lasting changes in him and transform his environment." McLuhan claimed that "the individual is perceptually modified by his own inventions" (Czitrom 1982, p. 173). Technological tools like the wheel or the alphabet extend human sense organs or body functions. Thus, a crane is an extension of the arm, and wheeled vehicles are extensions of the feet. Communication technology is an extension of the human mind, extending it to far-off parts of the world. "Both Innis and McLuhan agree that historically 'the things on which words were written down count more than the words themselves'; that is that the medium is the message" (Carey 1967). McLuhan argued that the effects of a new communication technology, like television, for instance, do not occur just on the conscious level of knowledge and opinions. The technology may also affect individuals at a subliminal level of sense ratios and patterns of perceptions. Thus McLuhan said that "the medium is the message," one of his many overstated "probes."

McLuhan became a major fad in North America in the late 1960s. His books were wildly successful best-sellers. Corporations such as General Motors and AT&T paid him huge consulting fees. At the same time academic critics skewered his ideas about how the media, especially television, were bringing about basic changes in society. McLuhan (1969) utilized the dichotomy of "hot" versus "cold" media: "Hot media are low in participation, or completion, by the audience and cool media are high in participation. A hot medium is one that extends a single human sense with high definition. High definition means a complete filling-in of data by a medium without intense audience participation. A photograph, for example, is high definition or hot, whereas a cartoon is low definition or cool, because the rough outline drawing provides very little visual data and requires viewers to fill in or complete the image [on their own]." By McLuhan's definition, television is a cool medium, inviting involvement by the viewer to give meaning to the rather vague and hazy image on the picture tube. A viewer forms the lines of dots (or pixels) that appear on the television screen into a picture. Thus the viewer becomes involved subconsciously with the television image.

Marshall McLuhan died in 1980, at age sixty-nine, of a stroke, just prior to the widespread diffusion of microcomputers and the other new interactive communication technologies based on microelectronics. His prior theorizing helped attract the attention of communication scholars to analyze these new technologies in the 1980s and 1990s.* During his lifetime McLuhan did more than any other individual to interest the general public in communication study.

COMMUNICATION STUDY IN OTHER NATIONS

Much of this book, and all of Part II, concentrated on the rise of this new field in the United States, after its early roots were planted with the European theories of Darwin, Freud, and Marx. Has there been a return migration of communication study from America to Europe? How have U.S. and European perspectives affected Latin American nations, where the study of communication is very popular, especially in Mexico and Brazil?

The main contribution of American communication to Europe has been the methodology of survey data gathering and quantitative data analysis and the U.S. focus on media effects. World War II was a major setback for university excellence. The postwar return of such Frankfurt school scholars as Max Horkheimer and Theodor Adorno helped transfer quantitative research methodologies to Europe, where they spread and are fairly widely used today. Many European communication scholars view the effects orientation of American communication study, as represented by Lasswell's five-questions model, for example, and quantitative methodologies, with a generally critical attitude. Critical scholarship is proportionately stronger in Europe than in America, and qualitative data are paid relatively more attention. Many European universities today have a department of communication, usually emphasizing mass communication, although some of the oldest and most prestigious institutions (like Oxford and Cambridge, for example) do not recognize this relatively new field. Communication study appears to be more widely institutionalized in such northern European nations as England, Germany, and the Scandinavian countries, than in the south-

*For instance, Eisenstein (1979, p. xvii) acknowledged that "Marshall McLuhan's work stimulated my historical curiosity" about the impacts of the printing press.

ern European nations with Latin cultures. Although European communication research is increasingly visible to American scholars, there is still relatively little intellectual exchange across the Atlantic, with U.S. scholars being particularly poorly informed about their continental counterparts.

Communication study is quite popular in such Latin American nations as Mexico and Brazil, where it began in the late 1960s as an outgrowth of schools of journalism. Then, during the 1970s and 1980s, the field of communication study took off. By 1992, Mexican universities had ninety-two schools of communication and enrolled about 20,000 student majors (mostly undergraduates), and Brazil had eighty schools of communication in which 3,000 professors teach an estimated 30,000 students. The typical school of communication in Latin America offers a bachelor's-level specialization in journalism, broadcasting, cinema, public relations, advertising, or organizational communication. In addition to communication skills training, each student also takes courses in communication theory and research. The main attraction of an undergraduate major in communication is the glamour of work in the mass media, and it is no accident that Mexico and Brazil have the strongest media industries in Latin America. Communication schools have proliferated in these two nations, so much so that the Brazilian government in 1987 clamped a lid on chartering additional schools of communication until a university could demonstrate that it had the trained professors and other resources necessary to provide a solid program of study.

The intellectual appeal of communication study has not been as important a factor in its popularity as has the attraction of interesting, well-paying jobs. Graduate study in Latin America has lagged, with only a few strong master's programs and very limited Ph.D. study. For instance, only eight of the eighty schools of communication in Brazil offer an M.A. degree and only three offer a doctorate. Some individuals from Latin America pursue doctoral degrees in communication at U.S. or European universities and then return to their home country as a university faculty member. Communication study in Latin America is developing as a hybrid, with certain intellectual strands drawn from North America and some from Europe, combined with certain uniquely Latin American qualities. For instance, the critical analysis and empirical study of television soap operas (*telenovelas*) is an important topic in Latin America, where this genre is popular television fare. Since the 1980s, Latin American communication scholars have turned away somewhat from their earlier interest in critical theory. Communication research is conducted not only by university scholars but also by investigators in a variety of nonuniversity research institutes. For instance, Brazil has an estimated 3,000 communication researchers, of whom about one-third are university faculty and two-thirds are in nonuniversity research institutes.

A similar explosion of student interest in communication study to that of Mexico and Brazil has occurred in Egypt and in the Republic of Korea, but in most other Asian, Middle Eastern, African, and Latin American nations, the institutionalization of the communication field has only begun. The general picture worldwide is far from that imagined by Wilbur Schramm in the late 1950s, when he began concentrating on international communication. However, Schramm's vision of communication study has spread throughout the world, occasionally to be accepted in principle and modified to suit local conditions and elsewhere to be savaged by intellectuals oriented to a different scholarly tradition. But whether criticized or accepted, Wilbur Schramm's vision of communication study has influenced everyone.

THE COMMUNICATION DISCIPLINE TODAY

Communication scholarship today is mainly empirical, quantitative, and focused on determining the effects of communication. This dominant perspective grew naturally out of the scholarly directions that Wilbur Schramm set in motion several decades ago and out of earlier communication research in sociology, social psychology, and political science. These fields, and communication study, were shaped by the social sciences' mimicking the quantification of the natural sciences, motivated by a desire for scientific respectability. Advances in measurement techniques and the widespread use of computer data analysis in the social sciences (including communication study) encouraged a quantitative style of research. "The dominant research paradigm in the social sciences is the use of statistical analysis to study human beings and their society. Basically, this paradigm involves gathering quantitative data and applying a statistical test that allows the researcher to draw conclusions" (Tankard 1984, p. 1). Most hypotheses in communication research are supported or not supported on the basis of statistical tests of significance. Probably most doctoral students in communication study today think that statistical tests are the only way to determine the fate of a hypothesis.

The previous chapters of this book traced the trend to empirical and quantitative perspectives in communication study. The great European theories came to the United States soon after the turn of the century, particularly at the hands of the Chicago school. Here, social science research became empirical in the form of observation and other qualitative research methods, with a focus on investigating the problems of social disorganization among recent European migrants to urban Chicago. Late in the golden era of the Chicago school, around 1930, the Chicago scholars began to stress quantitative and statistical methods. The shift from qualitative to quantitative methods was conflictual among the Chicago scholars.

Paul F. Lazarsfeld's Bureau of Applied Social Research utilized mainly quantitative methods in conducting communication investigations but resisted the use of the statistical tests of significance that were widely utilized after the 1940s by other social scientists. The Columbia University researchers mainly gathered data in one representative system (for example, Erie County or Decatur); they were less concerned with generalizing their findings from a random sample to a larger population (such inference is facilitated by the use of statistical methods).

The communication research by Kurt Lewin and by Carl Hovland and their followers was experimental and quantitative, and Hovland generally utilized statistical tests of significance. The first doctoral programs in communication study, created by Wilbur Schramm at Illinois and at Stanford, emphasized training in statistical methods and courses in which doctoral students read the quantitative research of Hovland, Lazarsfeld, Lewin, and Lasswell. The early dissertations at Illinois and Stanford were mainly quantitative and statistical, although use of qualitative methods were occasionally allowed when such approaches were particularly appropriate for the problem of study. Quite naturally, when Schramm's protégés left Urbana and Palo Alto to lead programs in communication study at other universities, they implemented curricula that reflected their own training. The Communication Department of Michigan State, for example, is known as a center for statistical expertise in communication research.

The early era of communication study (in the 1950s and 1960s) shaped the field in directions that were empirical, quantitative, and effects oriented. However, communication study has also exhibited alternate epistemologies that lie outside the dominant focus on quantitative approaches. For example, critical communication scholars, while relatively fewer in number, do not buy into the dominant perspective of Schramm-type communication study. The critical school pursues a different research agenda than do other communication scholars and represents one basic division in the community of communication scholars. While mainstream communication scholars look mainly at "what is," critical scholars are more interested in "what should be."

Another basic division of the field of communication study is on the basis of the research methods utilized and the theoretical perspectives that usually accompany quantitative versus qualitative methodologies. The interpretive school is an important and growing alternative to the dominant perspective of quantitative study of communication behavior. For example, since 1980, investigations of how individuals in audiences interpret media messages have begun to attract scholarly attention. How television viewers read the text of soap operas, for example, shows that each individual derives a somewhat different meaning from the same television show (Radway 1984; Livingstone 1992). This finding of differential individual interpretation of media messages should hardly be surprising, but it raises troublesome questions for most media effects studies of the past that assumed a standard message. To conventional media effects scholars, the individual differences in message interpretation are often regarded as noise—an unwelcome interference with the neat design of their studies.

In recent years another alternative perspective, cultural studies, began in England with the work of Raymond Williams (1976), who drew on Marxist theory in his investigations of working-class life, and has spread to America (Grossberg, Nelson, and Treichler 1992). Cultural studies scholars often focus on the problems of empowerment of individuals who are disadvantaged in a society by reason of their race, gender, or social class. More broadly, the cultural studies field focuses on culture, particularly as the culture of individuals affects, and is affected by, communication (Carey 1989).

A variety of theoretical and methodological perspectives are represented today in the field of communication study, and the amount of diversity may be increasing. Nevertheless, the heart of communication study is still characterized by quantitative studies of the effects of communication.

COMMUNICATION STUDY IN THE FUTURE

The doctoral programs in communication that Wilbur Schramm founded at Iowa, Illinois, and Stanford were originally oriented to mass communication, though the word *mass* did not appear in their name.

One sign of the strong tilt toward mass communication was the requirement that doctoral students have several years of experience in the mass media, ideally in newspaper journalism. An unstated reason for this requirement was so that when these students completed their Ph.D. degrees, they would be considered for employment in schools of journalism. Eventually, by the mid-1960s, the media experience requirement was changed officially in graduate school catalogs to "or equivalent," and finally it was dropped. However, most university doctoral programs are clearly either in mass communication or in interpersonal communication (the Department of Communication at Michigan State University might be one exception), as is signaled by the department's name, by the catalog description of the doctoral program, and by the makeup of the faculty. Even when the department's name is simply "communication," as at Stanford University, it is clear that a Ph.D. degree from Stanford is in mass communication.

A doctoral student who wishes to study communication, rather than mass communication or interpersonal communication, has almost no place to go, although there are an estimated 2,000 schools and departments of communication in the United States. Wilbur Schramm ended his final book manuscript, *The Beginnings of Communication Study: A Personal Memoir* (in press a), by forecasting that communication study would pass through a near-future stage of consolidation and reidentification in which university units, now called journalism, speech communication, cinema, mass communication, and information science, combine into larger units (schools and/or colleges) called simply "communication." This name change is important because it means that the past division of communication-related units on the basis of communication channel (print, film interpersonal, etc.) and the media industry that stands behind each type of communication channel will be deemphasized in favor of an intellectual unity around the core paradigm of communication study. This academic unification, Schramm expected, would happen first at the doctoral student level and more slowly, and perhaps only partially, at the undergraduate student level, where vocational specialization, rather than intellectual community, may be more appropriate in academic programs. Such future unification will put the communication-related units on the same campus together in a community of interests rather than in competition with each other, as is now the case at most large universities.

In a longer-range future era, perhaps several decades from now, Schramm expected communication study to disappear, absorbed as one important component in an eventual unification of the behavioral sciences, including, at minimum, psychology, sociology, political science, anthropology, and economics (disciplines that took their present form around 1900), centering on the study of human behavior. Schramm expected that communication study would lead this drive to unification of the behavioral sciences. Only time will tell whether the balkanization of communication study, and of the behavioral sciences, will give way to the unity that Schramm predicted.

PRINCIPAL FIGURES
IN THE HISTORY
OF COMMUNICATION STUDY

Alfred Adler (1870–1937), a Viennese follower of Sigmund Freud, who eventually broke with him to develop a distinctive brand of psychoanalysis.

Theodor Adorno (1903–1969), a member of the Frankfurt school of critical scholars. He was invited to the United States by Paul F. Lazarsfeld to work on the Radio Research Project (an unsuccessful experience) and later participated in *The Authoritarian Personality* study of prejudice.

Albert Bandura (born 1925), a Stanford University psychologist who formulated social learning theory, through which individuals mimic the behavior of others whom they observe interpersonally or in the mass media.

Gregory Bateson (1904–1980), an English anthropologist with multidisciplinary interests, who conceptualized relational communication, based on cybernetic theory. The guru of the Palo Alto group, Bateson formulated such concepts as paradox, the double bind, pragmatics of communication, and the relationship versus content dimensions of a communication act.

Bernard Berelson (1912–1979), an early social scientist of communication and a pioneer in methods of content analysis, who collaborated with Paul Lazarsfeld in the Erie County study of voting behavior.

David K. Berlo (born 1929), an early Ph.D. in communication at the University of Illinois, who founded the Department of Communication at Michigan State University, which produced a large number of communication doctorates in the 1960s and 1970s. Berlo also authored the widely used and influential textbook, *The Process of Communication* (1960).

Willard G. "Daddy" Bleyer (1873–1935), a pioneering professor of journalism at the University of Wisconsin who stressed the role of the social sciences in journalism training and who awarded Ph.D. degrees in journalism/social science to individuals ("the Bleyer children") who then became directors of schools of journalism. Bleyer's vision of journalism education in the 1930s prepared the way for the later acceptance of Wilbur Schramm's vision of communication study.

Josef Breuer (1842–1925), a well-established Viennese medical doctor from whom Freud adopted the talking cure, cofounded psychoanalysis, and with whom Freud worked out an understanding of hysteria. Freud and Breuer eventually split over the issue of childhood seduction as a cause of hysteria.

Chilton E. ("Chick") Bush (1896–1973), who earned his Ph.D. degree in journalism and political science at the University of Wisconsin under Daddy Bleyer and then led Stanford University's journalism program toward communication study. The key event in this process was hiring Wilbur Schramm in 1955.

Vannevar Bush (1908–1974), an electrical engineer at MIT and an influential science adviser in the federal government during and after World War II. Bush was Claude Shannon's mentor.

Hadley Cantril (1906–1969), a psychology professor at Princeton University who, with Frank Stanton of CBS, proposed the Radio Research Project to the Rockefeller Foundation and served as its associate director for two years. Cantril conducted an important study of powerful media effects in his investigation of how "The Invasion from Mars" radio broadcast panicked a million listeners.

August Comte (1798–1857), the father of sociology and founder of positivism, the belief that the scientific method can be applied to the study of human social behavior in order to help solve social problems.

Charles Horton Cooley (1864–1929), an early sociologist at the University of Michigan who elaborated the concepts of the primary group and the looking-glass self. Cooley was an influence on other scholars of the Chicago school.

Charles Darwin (1809–1882), founder of evolutionary theory on the basis of his interpretation of biological and geological data gathered during a five-year around-the-world trip. His theory was published in *On the Origin of the Species* (1859).

John Dewey (1859–1952), a pragmatic philosopher at the University of Chicago around the turn of the century, known for his theory of the reflex arc and for his pioneering views on progressive education.

Emile Durkheim (1858–1917), an early French sociologist who wrote *Suicide,* thus helping launch empirical and quantitative sociological analysis.

Friedrich Engels (1820–1895), collaborator with Karl Marx and coauthor with him of *The Communist Manifesto.*

Leon Festinger (1919–1991), a protégé of Kurt Lewin, noted for his theory of cognitive dissonance, defined as the unpleasant situation of an individual experiencing two conflicting cognitive elements.

Wilhelm Fleiss (1858–1928), a Berlin medical doctor with whom Freud carried on an extensive correspondence while working out the details of psychoanalytic theory.

Else Frenkel-Brunswick (1908–1958), an Austrian psychologist trained in psychoanalysis who was a co-investigator of *The Authoritarian Personality,* a study conducted at the University of California at Berkeley in the 1940s.

Sigmund Freud (1856–1939), a Viennese medical doctor who founded psychoanalytic theory as a means of treating neurotics by helping the individual understand his or her unconscious through lengthy in-depth counseling.

Erich Fromm (1900–1980), a German psychoanalyst who joined the Frankfurt school during the 1930s but later broke away while in America. He authored several important books, including *Escape from Freedom.*

George H. "Ted" Gallup (1902–1984), the polling researcher who earned his Ph.D. degree at the University of Iowa in 1928 and then taught journalism and advertising for several years. Many of his researches were sponsored by newspapers or film studios in order to learn what their audiences wanted.

Georg Wilhelm Friedrich Hegel (1770–1831), a main intellectual influence on Karl Marx when he was a university student. Marx later rejected Hegel's ideas.

Max Horkheimer (1895–1971), director of the Institute for Social Research at the University of Frankfurt in 1930; he led it in exile to New York from 1934 to 1950 and then returned to Frankfurt. Horkheimer was a key figure in forming critical theory, which draws on Marxism and psychoanalytic theory.

Carl I. Hovland (1912–1961), an experimental psychologist at Yale University who then directed a research program on persuasion in the Pentagon during World War II in order to evaluate the effects of U.S. Army training films. After 1945, Hovland led the Program in Communication and Attitude Change at Yale.

Clark Hull (1884–1952), a famed learning psychologist in Yale University's Institute of Human Relations, who drew on Freudian psychoanalytic theory to formulate his behavioral theory of learning. Hull was the academic mentor for Carl Hovland.

Robert Maynard Hutchins (1899–1977), dean of the Yale Law School when he helped launch the Institute of Human Relations, an interdisciplinary research program in which Clark Hull, Carl Hovland, and others participated. Hutchins was president of the University of Chicago in the 1930s and 1940s and chaired the Commission on Freedom and Responsibility of the Mass Media.

Harold Innis (1894–1952), a Canadian media determinist who taught political economy at the University of Toronto and influenced Marshall McLuhan.

William James (1842–1910), a pragmatic philosopher at Harvard University whose 1890 book, *The Principles of Psychology,* helped define the field.

Carl G. Jung (1875–1961), a Zurich-based follower of Sigmund Freud who made important contributions to psychoanalytic theory until he broke with Freud.

Harold D. Lasswell (1902–1978), trained as a political scientist at the University of Chicago, where he incorporated Freudian psychoanalytic theory in his research on political leaders. Lasswell pioneered the content analysis of propaganda, and created the five-questions model of communication: "*Who* says *what* to *whom* via *what channels* with *what effects?*"

Paul F. Lazarsfeld (1901–1976), a sociological methodologist who pioneered the study of mass communication effects and launched several university research institutes, the most noted of which was the Bureau of Applied Social Research at Columbia University.

Kurt Lewin (1890–1947), an important Gestalt psychologist at the University of Berlin who migrated to Cornell, Iowa, and then MIT, where he pioneered social psychological research on group dynamics and group communication.

Rensis Likert (1903–1981), director of the Division of Program Surveys, a survey research group in the U.S. Department of Agriculture from the mid-1930s until 1947, when it moved to the University of Michigan's Survey Research Center. Likert's name is known today for five-point attitude scales (with such answers as strongly agree, agree, undecided, disagree, strongly disagree).

Walter Lippmann (1889–1974), an important political columnist and adviser to a dozen U.S. presidents, who wrote the influential book *Public Opinion* (1922), which influenced communication research on public opinion and propaganda and on the agenda-setting process.

Leo Lowenthal (born 1900), a member of the Frankfurt school who migrated to the United States and worked on the Radio Research Project with Paul F. Lazarsfeld (where he made an analysis of the change from heroes of production to heroes of consumption in U.S. magazines).

Robert Lynd (1892–1970), a sociologist at Columbia University, noted for his community study (with Helen Lynd), *Middletown*. Lynd greatly aided Paul F. Lazarsfeld in helping him find academic positions when he first came to America but later was critical of Lazarsfeld's work.

Archibald MacLeish (1892–1982), a famed poet who served as the U.S. Librarian of Congress and director of the Office of Facts and Figures during World War II.

Marshall McLuhan (1911–1980), a Canadian media determinist who popularized communication in the 1950s, arguing that the communication media affected which human sense was dominant.

Herbert Marcuse (1898–1979), a Marxist-Freudian member of the Frankfurt school who wrote *One-Dimensional Man* (1965) and other important books about critical theory.

John Marshall (1903–1980), the Rockefeller Foundation official who funded the Radio Research Project directed by Paul F. Lazarsfeld and convened the Rockefeller Communication Seminar in 1939–1940, whose report helped define the field of mass communication research.

Karl Marx (1818–1883), a German intellectual exiled to Paris and then to London, where he wrote *The Communist Manifesto* and *Das Capital*, which criticized capitalism and set forth a theory of historical materialism—the notion that economic forces determine social and political structures and social change.

George Herbert Mead (1863–1931), a philosopher at the University of Chicago whose theory of symbolic interaction stressed the role of interpersonal communication in personality development. His theory was published in his posthumous *Mind, Self, and Society* (1931).

Margaret Mead (1901–1978), a well-known anthropologist who, as an official of the National Research Council during World War II, funded Kurt Lewin's sweetbreads experiment on group influences in nutritional change.

Robert K. Merton (born 1910), a sociological theorist at Columbia University who collaborated with Paul F. Lazarsfeld in mass communication research conducted by the Bureau of Applied Social Research.

C. Wright Mills (1916–1962), a colleague of Paul F. Lazarsfeld at Columbia University and a critic of his style of individual-level social analysis, especially in his 1959 book, *The Sociological Imagination*.

Charles Osgood (1916–1989), a pioneer psycholinguist at the University of Illinois who created the semantic differential for the measurement of meaning.

Osgood was director of the Institute of Communications Research, after Schramm left for Stanford in 1955.

Robert E. Park (1864–1944), the most influential member of the Chicago school from 1915 to 1935. He pioneered the study of mass communication and defined the field of sociology in America.

John Pierce (born 1910), an electrical engineer who spent most of his career at Bell Labs, where he was a colleague of Claude Shannon at the time that the latter formulated information theory.

Wilbur Schramm (1907–1987), the founder of communication study after World War II at the University of Iowa, the University of Illinois, and Stanford University. At each university, Schramm established a communication research institute, launched a doctoral program in communication study, and conducted research and authored publications that defined the field.

Carl Seashore (1866–1949), a psychologist of aural behavior and a strong intellectual influence at the University of Iowa in the 1930s and 1940s. Seashore taught Wilbur Schramm experimental methods while Schramm was a postdoctoral fellow.

Claude E. Shannon (born 1916), an electrical engineer and mathematician, trained at MIT, who formulated information theory while working on cryptographic research at Bell Labs during World War II. Shannon's information theory included a definition of the concept of information, an entropic measure of information, and propositions about communication flows.

Georg Simmel (1858–1918), an early German sociologist whose theories of the stranger, of the triad and social networks, and of urban life were important European influences on the Chicago school.

Herbert Spencer (1820–1903), a contemporary of Charles Darwin who applied evolutionary theory to explain societal progress, a view called social Darwinism. Spencer's books were popular in the United States and initially attracted Charles Horton Cooley and other early sociologists to study sociology (they later rejected Spencer's social Darwinism).

Frank Stanton (born 1908), a Ph.D. in psychology from Ohio State University who became director of research and (later) president of CBS and collaborated with Paul F. Lazarsfeld in the Radio Research Project in the late 1930s.

George Stoddard (1897–1981), an educational psychologist who directed the Child Welfare Research Station at the University of Iowa, where he hired Kurt Lewin. Stoddard later became president of the University of Illinois, where he employed Wilbur Schramm as the world's first professor of communication in 1947.

Samuel A. Stouffer (1900–1960), a small-town Iowa newspaperman who earned a Ph.D. in sociology at the University of Chicago, directed military research during World War II on soldiers' morale, and then became director of the Laboratory of Social Relations at Harvard University.

Gabriel Tarde (1843–1904), an early French sociologist whose theoretical publications influenced American scholars regarding the diffusion of innovations and social learning.

W. I. Thomas (1863–1947), author with Florian Znianecki of *The Polish Peasant in Europe and America,* the first major investigation by the Chicago school and an important early empirical study in American sociology.

Alfred Russell Wallace (1823–1913), the co-discoverer of evolutionary theory with Charles Darwin.

Paul Watzlawick (born 1921), a leading member of the Palo Alto group and coauthor of *The Pragmatics of Communication* (1962).

Warren Weaver (1894–1978), a Rockefeller Foundation official who wrote a simplification and extension of Claude Shannon's information theory, which was published with Shannon's original essay in book form (Shannon and Weaver 1949).

Max Weber (1964–1920), a particularly influential early German sociologist, noted for his concepts of bureaucracy, *verstehen,* charisma, and ideal types and for his book, *The Protestant Ethic and the Spirit of Capitalism.*

Norbert Wiener (1894–1964), an MIT mathematician who developed cybernetic theory as an outgrowth of his research on improving the accuracy of antiaircraft fire during World War II. He promulgated cybernetic theory to social scientists and to biomedical scientists in the ten multidisciplinary Macy conferences held after World War II.

Wilhelm Wundt (1832–1920), the founder of experimental psychology at the University of Leipzig about a hundred years ago.

REFERENCES

Abrams, Mark (1977). "Social Research and Market Research: The Case of Paul F. Lazarsfeld." *Journal of the Market Research Society* 19 (1):12–17.

Adorno, Theodor (1969). "Scientific Experiences of a European Scholar in America." In Donald Fleming and Bernard Bailyn (eds.), *The Intellectual Migration: Europe and America, 1930–1960,* pp. 338–370. Cambridge: Harvard University Press.

Adorno, Theodor W., Else Frenkel-Brunswik, Daniel J. Levinson, and R. Nevitt Sanford (1950/1982). *The Authoritarian Personality.* New York: Harper and Brothers; New York: Norton.

Almond, Gabriel A. (n.d.). "Harold Dwight Lasswell (1902–1978)." Unpublished paper. Harold D. Lasswell Papers, Manuscripts and Archives, Sterling Memorial Library, New Haven, Connecticut.

Anderson, Nels (1923/1961). *The Hobo: The Sociology of the Homeless Man.* Chicago: University of Chicago Press/Phoenix Books.

Anzieu, Didier (1986), *Freud's Self-Analysis.* Translated by Peter Graham. Madison, Conn.: International Universities Press.

Appignanesi, Richard, and Oscar Zarate (1979). *Freud for Beginners.* New York: Pantheon Books.

Arcenas, Elvira M. (1991). "Constructing a 'Communication' Lexicon: A Study of How 'Communication' Entered the Linguistic Mainstream of Journalism Education." Paper presented at the International Communication Association, Chicago.

Aron, Arthur, and Elaine N. Aron (1986). *The Heart of Social Psychology.* Lexington, Mass.: Lexington Books.

Ash, Mitchell G. (1992). "Cultural Contexts and Scientific Change in Psychology." *American Psychologist* 47(2):198–207.

Ashby, W. Ross (1956). *An Introduction to Cybernetics.* New York: Wiley & Sons.

Back, Kurt W. (1972). *Beyond Words: The Story of Sensitivity Training and the Encounter Movement.* New York: Russell Sage Foundation.

Bailyn, Bernard (1979). "Recollections of PFL." In Robert K. Merton, James S. Coleman, and Peter H. Rossi (eds.), *Qualitative and Quantitative Social Research: Papers in Honor of Paul Lazarsfeld,* pp. 16–18. New York: Free Press.

Bandura, Albert (1977). *Social Learning Theory.* Englewood Cliffs, N.J.: Prentice-Hall.

Barlow, Nona (1958). *The Autobiography of Charles Darwin: 1809–1892.* New York: Norton.

Barry, Robert M. (1968). "A Man and a City: George Herbert Mead in Chicago." In Michael Novak (ed.), *American Philosophy and the Future: Essays for a New Generation,* pp. 173–192. New York: Scribner's Sons.

Barton, Allen H. (1982). "Paul Lazarsfeld and the Invention of the University Institute for Applied Social Research." In Burt Holzner and Jera Nehnevajsn (eds.), *Organizing for Social Research,* pp. 17–83. Cambridge, Mass.: Schenkman.

_____ (December 18, 1991). Personal correspondence with Everett M. Rogers.

_____ (March 9, 1992). Personal correspondence with Everett M. Rogers.

Bartos, Rena (1977). "Frank Stanton: Our First CEO," *Journal of Advertising Research* 17:26–29.

Bateson, Gregory (1936/1958). *Naven: A Survey of the Problems Suggested by a Composite Picture of the Culture of a New Guinea Tribe Drawn from Three Points of View.* New York: Cambridge University Press; Stanford: Stanford University Press.

_____ (1972). *Steps to an Ecology of Mind: Collected Essays in Anthropology, Psychiatry, Evolution, and Epistemology.* New York: Ballantine.

Bateson, Gregory, and Jurgen Ruesch (1951). *Communication: The Social Matrix of Psychiatry.* New York: Norton.

Bateson, Mary Catherine (1984). *With a Daughter's Eye: A Memoir of Margaret Mead and Gregory Bateson.* New York: William Morrow.

Bavelas, Janet Beavin (1990). "Behaving and Communicating: A Reply to Motley." *Western Journal of Speech Communication* 54:593–602.

Becker, Howard S. (1953). "Becoming a Marijuana User." *American Journal of Sociology* 59:235–242.

Becker, Marshall H. (1974). "The Health Belief Model and Personal Health Behavior." *Health Education Monographs* 2:324–508.

Bello, Francis (1953). "The Information Theory." *Fortune* 48(6):136–158.

Belman, Sheldon Lary (1975). "The Idea of Communication in the Social Thought of the Chicago School." Ph.D. dissertation, University of Illinois.

Ben-David, Joseph, and Randall Collins (1966). "Social Factors in the Origins of a New Science: The Case of Psychology." *American Sociological Review* 31 (4):451–465.

Benedict, Ruth (1934). *Patterns of Culture.* Boston: Houghton Mifflin.

Beniger, James R. (1987). "Personalization of Mass Media and the Growth of Pseudo-Community." *Communication Research* 14 (3):352–371.

Benjamin, Jr., Ludy T., et al. (1992). "Wundt's American Doctoral Students." *American Psychologist* 47(2):123–131.

Benjamin, Walter (1966/1973). *Understanding Brecht.* Norfolk, England: Therford Press.

Benson, Lee (1979). "Marx's General and Middle-Range Theories of Social Conflict." In Robert K. Merton, James S. Coleman, and Peter H. Rossi (eds.), *Qualitative and Quantitative Social Research: Papers in Honor of Paul F. Lazarsfeld,* pp. 189–209. New York: Free Press.

Berelson, Bernard (1949). "What 'Missing the Newspaper Means.'" In Paul F. Lazarsfeld and Frank N. Stanton (eds.), *Communications Research, 1948–49.* New York: Harper.

———— (1959). "The State of Communication Research." *Public Opinion Quarterly* 23:1–5.

Berelson, Bernard, and Gary Steiner (1964). *Human Behavior: An Inventory of Scientific Findings.* New York: Harcourt, Brace and World.

Berkowitz, David (1990). "Refining the Gatekeeping Metaphor for Local Television News," *Journal of Broadcasting and Electronic Media,* 34:55–68.

Berlo, David K. (1960). *The Process of Communication.* New York: Holt, Rinehart and Winston.

———— (1977). "Communication as Process: Review and Commentary." In Brent D. Ruben (ed.), *Communication Yearbook 1,* pp. 11–27. New Brunswick, N.J.: Transaction Books.

———— (May 16, 1992). Personal interview with Everett M. Rogers. St. Petersburg, Florida.

Bernard, Jessie (1973). "My Four Revolutions: An Autobiographical History of the ASA." *American Journal of Sociology* 78 (4):773–791.

Bernays, Edward L. (1923). *Crystalizing Public Opinion*. New York: Horace Liveright.

———— (1928). *Propaganda*. New York: Horace Liveright.

———— (October 29, 1991). Personal correspondence with Everett M. Rogers.

Bertalanffy, Ludwig von (1968). *General System Theory: Foundations, Development, Applications*. New York: Braziller.

Bierstedt, Robert (1981). *American Sociological Theory: A Critical History*. New York: Academic Press.

Bishop, Robert L., and LaMar S. MacKay (1971). *Mysterious Silence, Lyrical Scream: Government Information in World War II*. Columbia, S.C.: Association for Education on Journalism and Mass Communication, Journalism Monographs 19.

Blau, Peter M. (1964). "The Research Process in the Study of the Dynamics of Bureaucracy." In Phillip E. Hammond (ed.), *Sociologists at Work: Essays on the Craft of Social Research*, pp. 18–57. Garden City, N.Y.: Doubleday/Anchor Books.

Bleyer, Willard G. (1910). *The Profession of Journalism*. Boston: Atlantic Monthly Press.

———— (1913). *Newspaper Writing and Editing*. Boston: Houghton Mifflin.

———— (1916). *Types of News Writing*. Boston: Houghton Mifflin.

———— (1920). *How To Write Special Feature Articles*. Boston: Houghton Mifflin.

———— (1927). *Main Currents in the History of American Journalism*. Boston: Houghton Mifflin.

———— (October 1934). "The Rise of Education for Journalism." *Quill*, pp. 12–13, 30–32.

Blum, Eleanor (October 29, 1991). Personal interview by Everett M. Rogers, Urbana, Illinois.

Blumer, Herbert (1933/1970). *The Movies and Conduct*. New York: Macmillan; New York: Arno Press.

———— (1969/1986). *Symbolic Interactionism: Perspective and Method*. Englewood Cliffs, N.J.: Prentice-Hall.

———— (May 22, 1972). Personal interview by James Carey, Department of Sociology Interviews, Box 1, Folder 2, University of Chicago Library.

Blumer, Herbert, and Philip M. Hauser (1933/1970). *Movies, Delinquency, and Crime*. New York: Arno Press.

Bogardus, E. S. (1929). "Measuring Social Distances." *Journal of Applied Sociology* 13:110–117.

――― (1933). "A Social Distance Scale." *Sociology and Social Research*. 17:265–271.

Boorstin, Daniel J. (1961). *The Image: A Guide To Psuedo-Events in America*. New York: Atheneum.

――― (1983). *The Discoverers*. New York: Vintage.

Borchers, Detlef (1988). "Paul Lazarsfeld: A Marxist on Leave." *Communication* 10:211–222.

Boring, Edwin G. (1929/1950). *A History of Experimental Psychology*. 2d ed. Englewood Cliffs, N.J.: Prentice-Hall.

Boskoff, Alvin (1969). *Theory in American Sociology: Major Sources and Applications*. New York: Thomas Crowell.

Bowles, Peter J. (1984), *Evolution: The History of an Idea*. Berkeley: University of California Press.

Bowler, Peter J. (1990). *Charles Darwin: The Man and His Influence*. Oxford: Basil Blackwell.

Bringman, Wolfgang G., William G. Balance, and Alan Krichev (1969). "Experimental Investigation of McLuhan's Ideas Concerning Effects of Hot and Cool Communications Media." *Psychological Reports* (25):447–451.

Bringmann, Wolfgang G., William D. G. Balance, and Rand B. Evans (1975). "Wilhelm Wundt 1832–1920: A Brief Biographical Sketch." *Journal of the History of Behavioral Sciences* 11:289–297.

Bronowski, Jacob (1973). *The Ascent of Man*. Boston: Little, Brown.

Brown, Steven R. (October 5, 1992). Personal correspondence with Everett M. Rogers.

Browie, Janet, and Michael Neve (eds.) (1989). Introduction to Charles Darwin, *Voyage of the Beagle*. London: Penguin.

Bryson, Lyman (1948). *The Communication of Ideas: A Series of Addresses*. New York: Harper.

Buckley, Walter (ed.) (1968). *Modern Systems Research for the Behavioral Scientist*. Chicago: Aldine.

Bulmer, Martin (1984). *The Chicago School of Sociology: Institutionalization, Diversity, and the Rise of Sociological Research*. Chicago: University of Chicago Press.

Burgess, Ernest W. (1939). "The Influence of Sigmund Freud upon Sociology in the United States." *American Journal of Sociology* 45:356–374.

Burnet, Jean (1964). "Robert E. Park and the Chicago School of Sociology: A Centennial Tribute." *Canadian Review of Sociology and Anthropology* 1:156–164.

Burrell, Gibson, and Gareth Morgan (1979). *Sociological Paradigms and Organizational Analysis*. London: Heineman.

Burston, Daniel (1991). *The Legacy of Erich Fromm*. Cambridge: Harvard University Press.

Burt, Ronald S. (1987). "Social Contagion and Innovation: Cohesion Versus Structure Equivalence." *American Journal of Sociology* 92:1287–1335.

Calder, Bobby J. (1977). "Focus Groups and the Nature of Qualitative Marketing Research." *Journal of Marketing Research* 14:353–364.

Campbell, Jeremy (1982). *Grammatical Man: Information, Entropy, Language, and Life*. New York: Simon and Schuster.

Cannon, Walter (1932). *The Wisdom of the Body*. New York: Norton.

Cantril, Hadley, and Gordon Allport (1935). *The Psychology of Radio*. New York: Harper.

Cantril, Hadley, with Hazel Gaudet and Herta Herzog (1940/1966). *The Invasion from Mars: A Study in the Psychology of Panic*. Princeton, New Jersey: Princeton University Press; New York: Harper & Row.

Capecchi, Vittorio (1978). "Paul F. Lazarsfeld: A Link Between American and European Methodology. *Quality and Quantity* 12:239–254.

Caplow, Theodore (1968). *Two Against One: Coalitions in Triads*. Englewood Cliffs, N.J.: Prentice-Hall.

Carey, James W. (1967). "Harold Adams Innis and Marshall McLuhan." *Antioch Review* 27(1):5–39.

—— (1981). "Culture, Geography, and Communications: The Work of Harold Innis in an American Context." In Liora Salter (ed.), *Culture, Communication and Dependence: The Tradition of Harold Innis*, pp. 73–91. Norwood, N.J.: Ablex.

—— (1982). "The Mass Media and Critical Theory: An American View." In

Michael Burgoon (ed.), *Communication Yearbook 6*. Newbury Park, Calif.: Sage.

———— (1989). *Communication as Culture: Essays on Media and Society*. Winchester, Mass.: Unwin Hyman.

Cartier, Jacqueline Marie (1988). "Wilbur Schramm and the Beginnings of American Communication Theory: A History of Ideas." Ph.D. dissertation, University of Iowa.

Cartwright, Dorwin (1979). "Contemporary Social Psychology in Historical Perspective." *Social Psychology Quarterly* 42(1):82–93.

———— (Mary 15, 1989). Personal interview by Everett M. Rogers, Santa Barbara, California.

Cartwright, Dorwin, and Alvin Zander (1953/1968). *Group Dynamics: Research and Theory*. New York: Harper & Row.

Caudill, Edward (1989). *Darwinism in the Press: The Evolution of an Idea*. Hillsdale, N.J.: Lawrence Erlbaum.

Chaffee, Steven H. Carlos Gomez-Palacio, and Everett M. Rogers (1990). "Mass Communication Research in Latin America: Views from Here and There." *Journalism Quarterly* 64(4):1015–1024.

Chaffee, Steven H., and John L. Hochheimer (1985). "The Beginning of Political Communication Research in the United States: Origins of the 'Limited Effects' Model." In Everett M. Rogers and Francis Balle (eds.), *The Media Revolution in America and in Western Europe*, pp. 267–296. Norwood, N.J.: Ablex.

Chaffee, Steven H., and Everett M. Rogers (eds.) (in press). In Wilbur Schramm, *The Beginnings of Communication Study in America*. Newbury Park, Calif.: Sage.

Chaffee, Steven H., and Donna G. Wilson (1977). "Media Rich, Media Poor: Two Studies of Diversity in Agenda-Holding." *Journalism Quarterly* 54:446–476.

Charters, W. W. (1933/1970). *Motion Pictures and Youth: A Summary*. New York: Macmillan; New York: Arno Press.

Christakes, George (1978). *Albion W. Small*. Boston: Twayne.

Churchman, C. West (1968). *The Systems Approach*. New York: Delacorte Press.

Clark, Jon, Cella Modgil, and Sohan Modgil (1990). *Robert K. Merton: Consensus and Controversy*. London: Falmer Press.

Clausen, John A. (1984a). "*The American Soldier* and Social Psychology: Introduction." *Social Psychology Quarterly* 47(2):184–185.

―――― (1984b). "Research on the American Soldier as a Career Contingency." *Social Psychology Quarterly* 47(2): 207–213.

Coberly, Mary Schramm (November 9, 1992). Personal correspondence with Everett M. Rogers.

Cohen, Bernard (1963). *The Press and Foreign Policy.* Princeton, N.J.: Princeton University Press.

Cohen, I. Bernard (1983). *Revolution in Science.* Cambridge: Belknap Press of Harvard University Press.

Cole, Richard, and Thomas Bowers (1973). "Research Article Productivity of U.S. Journalism Faculties." *Journalism Quarterly* 50:246–254.

Coleman, James S. (1957). *Community Conflict.* New York: Free Press.

―――― (1980a). "The Structure of Society and the Nature of Social Research." *Knowledge* 1 (3):333–350.

―――― (1980b). "Paul F. Lazarsfeld: The Substance and Style of His Work." In Robert K. Merton and Mathilda White Riley (eds.), *Sociological Traditions from Generation to Generation: Glimpses of the American Experience,* pp. 153–174. Norwood, N.J.: Ablex.

―――― (1982). Introduction to Patricia L. Kendall (ed.), *The Varied Sociology of Paul F. Lazarsfeld,* pp. 1–8. New York: Columbia University Press.

―――― (April 27, 1992). Personal interview with Everett M. Rogers, Chicago.

Coleman, James S., Elihu Katz, and Herbert Menzel (1966). *Medical Innovation: A Diffusion Study.* Indianapolis: Bobbs-Merrill.

Combs, James E., and Dan Nimmo (1993). *The New Propaganda: The Dictatorship of Palaver in Contemporary Politics.* White Plains, N.Y.: Longmans.

Converse, Jean M. (1987). *Survey Research in the United States: Roots and Emergence, 1890–1960.* Berkeley: University of California Press.

Cook, Thomas P., Charles L. Gruder, Karen M. Hennigan, and Brian R. Flay (1979). "History of the Sleeper Effect: Some Logical Pitfalls in Accepting the Null Hypothesis." *Psychological Bulletin* 86(4):662–679.

Cooley, Charles Horton (1902/1922). *Human Nature and the Social Order.* New York: Charles Scribner's Sons.

_____ (1909). *Social Organization: A Study of the Larger Mind.* New York: Charles Scribner's Sons.

_____ (1918). *Social Process.* New York: Charles Scribner's Sons.

_____ (1920). "Reflections upon the Sociology of Herbert Spencer." *American Journal of Sociology* 26:129–145.

Coser, Lewis A. (ed.) (1975). *The Idea of Social Structure: Papers in Honor of Robert K. Merton.* New York: Harcourt Brace Jovanovich.

_____ (1977). *Masters of Sociological Thought: Ideas in Historical and Social Context.* 2d ed. New York: Harcourt Brace Jovanovich.

_____ (1984). *Refugee Scholars in America: Their Impact and Their Experience.* New Haven, Connecticut: Yale University Press.

Coughlan, Neil (1975). *Young John Dewey: An Essay in American Intellectual History.* Chicago: University of Chicago Press.

Creel, George (1920), *How We Advertised America: The First Telling of the Amazing Story of the Committee on Public Information That Carried the Gospel of Americanism to Every Corner of the Globe.* New York: Harper & Brothers.

Cressey, Paul (1929/1972). *The Taxi-Dance Hall: A Sociological Study in Commercialized Recreation and City Life.* Chicago: University of Chicago Press.

Crothers, Charles (1987). *Robert K. Merton.* London: Tavistock.

Curtis, Michael (1991). "Walter Lippmann Reconsidered." Society 28(2):23–31.

Czitrom, Daniel (1982). *Media and the American Mind: From Morse to McLuhan.* Chapel Hill: University of North Carolina Press.

Dahling, Randall L. (1962). "Shannon's Information Theory: The Spread of an Idea." In Wilbur Schramm (ed.), *Studies of Innovation and of Communication to the Public,* pp. 118–139. Stanford: Stanford University, Institute for Communication Research.

Dale, Edgar (1933a/1970). *Children's Attendance at Motion Pictures.* New York: Macmillan; New York: Arno Press.

_____ (1933b/1970). *The Content of Motion Pictures.* New York: Macmillan; New York: Arno Press.

Danielian, Lucig H., and Stephen D. Reese (1989). "A Closer Look at Intermedia Influences on Agenda Setting: The Cocaine Issue of 1986." In Pamela J. Shoemaker (ed.), *Communication Campaigns about Drugs: Government, Media and the Public,* pp. 47–65. Hillsdale, N.J.: Erlbaum.

Danielson, Wayne (March 9, 1992). Personal interview by Everett M. Rogers, Austin, Texas.

Danziger, Kurt (1985). "The Origins of the Psychological Experiment as a Social Institution." *American Psychologist* 40 (2):133–140.

Darnell, Donald K. (1970). " 'Clozentropy': A Procedure for Testing English Language Proficiency of Foreign Students." *Speech Monographs* 37:36–46.

―――― (1972). "Information Theory: An Approach to Human Communication." In Richard W. Budd and Brent D. Rubin (eds.), *Approaches to Human Communication,* pp. 156–169. New York: Spartan Books.

―――― (1976). "Information Theory." In Donald K. Darnell and Wayne Brockriede (eds.), *Persons Communicating,* pp. 210–223. Englewood Cliffs, N.J.: Prentice-Hall.

Darwin, Charles (1839/1989). *Voyage of the Beagle: Charles Darwin's Journal of Researches.* New York: Penguin Books.

―――― (1958). "On Variation of Organic Things in a State of Nature; on the Natural Means of Selection; on the Comparison of Domestic Races and True Species." *Journal of the Linnaean Society of London* (*Zoology*) 3:46–50.

―――― (1859/1958). *On the Origin of Species.* New York: New American Library.

―――― (1871/1972). *The Descent of Man and Selection in Relation to Sex.* 2 vols. New York: AMS Press.

―――― (1873). *The Expression of the Emotions in Men and Animals.* London: J. Murray.

Dearborn, Mary W. (1988). *Love in the Promised Land: The Story of Anzia Yezierska and John Dewey.* New York: Free Press.

Dearing, James W. (1989). "Setting the Polling Agenda for the Issue of AIDS." *Public Opinion Quarterly* 53(3):309–329.

Delia, Jesse G. (1987). "Communication Research: A History." In Charles R. Berger and Steven H. Chaffee (eds.), *Handbook of Communication Science,* pp. 20–98. Newbury Park, Calif.: Sage.

Dennis, Everett E. (December 9, 1992). Personal correspondence with Everett M. Rogers.

de Rivera, Joseph (1976). *Field Theory as Human Science: Contributions of Lewin's Berlin Group.* New York: Gardner Press.

Deutsch, Karl W. (1963). *The Nerves of Government: Models of Political Communication and Control.* New York: Free Press.

———— (1986). "This Week's Citation Classic." *Current Contents* 18(19):18.

Deutschmann, Paul J., and Wayne Danielson (1960). "Diffusion of the Major News Story." *Journalism Quarterly* 37:345–355.

Dewey, John (1896). "The Reflex Arc Concept in Psychology." *Psychological Review* 3:357–370.

———— (1927). *The Public and Its Problems.* Chicago: Swallow Press.

Dickens, Milton, and Frederick Williams (1964). "An Experimental Application of 'Cloze' Procedure and Attitude Measures to Listening Comprehension." *Speech Monographs* 31:103–108.

Dimmick, John, and Eric W. Rothenbuhler (1987). "Competitive Displacement in the Communication Industries: New Media in Old Environments." In Ronald E. Rice (ed.), *The New Media: Communication Research, and Technology,* pp. 287–308. Newbury Park, Calif.: Sage.

Diner, Steven J. (1975). "Department and Discipline: The Department of Sociology at the University of Chicago, 1892–1920." *Minerva* 12(4):514–533.

———— (1980). *A City and Its Universities: Public Policy in Chicago, 1892–1919.* Chapel Hill: University of North Carolina Press.

Dobson, Velma, and Darryl Bruce (1972). "The German University and the Development of Experimental Psychology." *Journal of the History of Behavioral Science* 8:204–207.

Dobyns, Henry F, Paul L. Doughty, and Harold D. Lasswell (eds.) (1964). *Peasants, Power, and Applied Social Change.* Newbury Park, Calif.: Sage.

Dollard, John, Neal E. Miller, Leonard W. Doob, O. H. Mowrer, and Robert R. Sears, with Clellan S. Ford, Carl Iver Hovland, and Richard T. Sollenberger (1939). *Frustration and Aggression.* New Haven: Yale University Press.

Doob, J.L. (1949). "Review of Shannon's *A Mathematical Theory of Communication.*" *Mathematical Reviews* 29:133.

Doob, Leonard (October 10, 1991). Personal interview by Everett M. Rogers, New Haven, Connecticut.

Dorfman, Ariel, and Armand Mattelart (1971/1975). *How to Read Donald Duck: Imperialist Ideology in the Disney Comic.* New York: International General.

Durham, Frank (1992). "Cultural History of a Curriculum: The Search for Salience." *Journalism Educator,* 47(4):14–21.

Dysinger, W. S., and Christian A. Ruckmick (1933/1970). *The Emotional Responses of Children to the Motion Picture Situation.* New York: Macmillan; New York: Arno Press.

Eadie, William F. (1979). "Earned Degree Trends in Communication Studies, 1960–1976." *Communication Education* 28:294–300.

Eastman, Max (December 1941). "John Dewey," *Atlantic Monthly* 168:671–685.

Eisenberg, Eric M. (1984). "Ambiguity as Strategy in Organizational Communication." *Communication Monographs* 51:227–242.

Eisenstein, Elizabeth (1968). "Some Conjectures about the Impact of Printing on Western Society and Thought: A Preliminary Report." *Journal of Modern History* 40 (1):3.

———— (1969). "The Advent of Printing and the Problem of the Renaissance." *Past and Present* 45:19–89.

———— (1979). *The Printing Press as an Agent of Change: Communications and Cultural Transformation in Early-Modern Europe,* vol. 1. Cambridge: Cambridge University Press.

Elmore, Garland C. (1993). *The Communication Disciplines in Higher Education: A Guide to Academic Programs in the United States and Canada.* Second edition. MacLean, VA: Speech Communication of America.

Ekman, Paul (1973). *Darwin and Facial Expression: A Century of Research in Review.* New York: Academic Press.

Ellenberger, Henri F. (1970). *The Discovery of the Unconscious: The History and Evolution of Dynamic Psychiatry.* New York: Basic Books.

Ellersick, F.W. (1984). "A Conversation with Claude E. Shannon." *IEEE Communications Magazine* 22 (5):123–126.

Emery, Edwin, and Joseph P. McKerns (1987), *AEJMC: 75 Years in the Making.* Columbia, S.C.: Association for Education in Journalism and Mass Communication, Journalism Monographs 104.

Ennis, James G. (1992). "The Social Organization of Sociological Knowledge: Structural Models of the Intersections of Specialties." *American Sociological Review* 57:259–265.

Eulau, Heinz (1962). "The Maddening Methods of Harold D. Lasswell: Some Philosophical Underpinnings." *Journal of Politics* 30:3–24.

_____ (1968). "The Behavioral Movement in Political Science: A Personal Document." *Social Research* 35:1–29.

_____ (1977). "The Hoover Elite Studies Revisited." *Social Science History* 1(3):392–400.

Evans, Richard I. (1980a). "Leon Festinger," In *The Making of Social Psychology: Discussions with Creative Contributors*, pp. 125–135. New York: Gardner Press.

_____ (1980b). "Irving Janis." In *The Making of Social Psychology: Discussions with Creative Contributors*, pp. 97–111. New York: Gardner Press.

Fagen, M. D. (ed.) (1978). *A History of Engineering and Science in the Bell System: National Service in War and Peace (1929–1975)*. Murray Hill, N.J.: Bell Telephone Laboratories.

Fano, Robert (November 29, 1990). Personal interview by Everett M. Rogers, Cambridge, Massachusetts.

Faris, Ellsworth (1944). "Robert E. Park: 1864–1944." *American Sociological Review* 9:322–325.

Faris, Robert E. L. (1970). *Chicago Sociology, 1920–1932*. Chicago: University of Chicago Press.

_____ (May 24, 1972). Personal interview by James Carey, Department of Sociology Interviews, Box 1, Folder 1, University of Chicago Library.

_____ (November 1, 1990). Personal interview by Everett M. Rogers, Coronado, California.

Farr, Robert M. (1983). "Wilhelm Wundt (1832–1920) and the Origins of Psychology as an Experimental and Social Science." *British Journal of Social Psychology* 22:289–301

Feinstein, Amiel (1958). *Foundations of Information Theory*. New York: McGraw-Hill.

Fern, Edward F. (1982). "The Use of Focus Groups for Idea Generation: The Effects of Group Size, Acquaintanceship, and Moderator on Response Quantity and Quality." *Journal of Marketing Research* 19:1–13.

Festinger, Leon (1957). *A Theory of Cognitive Dissonance*. Stanford: Stanford University Press.

_____ (1980). "Looking Backward." In Leon Festinger (ed.), *Retrospections on Social Psychology*, pp. 236–254. New York: Oxford University Press.

Festinger, Leon, Henry W. Riecken, and Stanley Schachter (1956). *When Prophecy Fails.* Minneapolis: University of Minnesota Press.

Festinger, Leon, Stanley Schachter, and Kurt Bach (eds.) (1950). *Social Pressures in Informal Groups: A Study of Human Factors in Housing.* Stanford: Stanford University Press.

Finn, Seth (1985). "Information Theoretic Measures of Reader Enjoyment." *Written Communication* 2 (4):358–376.

Finn, Seth, and Donald F. Roberts (1984). "Source, Destination, and Entropy: Reassessing the Role of Information Theory in Communication Research." *Communication Research* 11:453–476.

Fisher, Seymour, and Roger P. Greenberg (1977). *The Scientific Credibility of Freud's Theories and Therapy.* New York: Basic Books.

Foerster, Heinz von (June 11, 1992). Personal interview with Everett M. Rogers, Pescadero, California.

Forman, Henry James (1933). *Our Movie-Made Children.* New York: Macmillan.

Fox, Richard Wightman (1983). "Epitaph for Middletown: Robert S. Lynd and the Analysis of Consumer Culture." In Richard Wightman Fox and T. J. Jackson (eds.), *The Culture of Consumption: Critical Essays in American History,* pp. 103–141. New York: Pantheon Books.

Frazier, P. Jean, and Cecilie Gaziano (1979). *Robert E. Park's Theory of News, Public Opinion, and Social Control.* Lexington, KY: Association for Education and Mass Communication, Journalism Monographs 64.

Freeman, John, and Michael T. Hannan (1989). "Setting the Record Straight on Organizational Ecology: Rebuttal to Young." *American Journal of Sociology* 95 (2):425–439.

Freeman, Lucy (1972). *The Story of Anna O.* New York: Walker.

Freud, Sigmund (1900/1913). *The Interpretation of Dreams.* London: G. Allen.

_____ (1901/1989). *The Psychotherapy of Everyday Life.* New York: New American Library.

_____ (1905a/1960). *Jokes and Their Relation to the Unconscious.* New York: Norton.

_____ (1905b/1949). *Three Essays on the Theory of Sexuality.* London: Image Publishing.

Freudenthal, Hans (1976). "Norbert Wiener." In David L. Sills (ed.), *Dictionary of Scientific Biography,* 14:344–347. New York: Charles Scribners.

Freund, Michael (1978). "Sociography: The Marienthal Story." *Austria Today* 3:55.

—— (January 24, 1991). Personal correspondence with Everett M. Rogers.

Frisby, David (1984). *George Simmel.* London: Tavistock Publications.

Fromm, Erich (1941). *Escape from Freedom.* New York: Rinehart.

—— (1955). *The Sane Society.* Greenwich, Conn: Fawcett Premier.

—— (1956). *The Art of Loving.* New York: Bantam.

—— (1962). *Beyond the Chains of Illusion: My Encounter with Marx and Freud.* New York: Simon & Schuster/Touchstone.

——, with D.T. Suzuki and R. DeMartino (1960). *Zen Buddhism and Psychoanalysis.* New York: Harper & Row.

Garfield, Eugene (1980). "Citation Measures of the Influence of Robert K. Merton." *Transactions of the New York Academy of Sciences,* ser. II, 29:61–74.

Geertz, Clifford (1973). *The Interpretation of Cultures: Selected Essays.* New York: Basic Books.

Gillette, J.M. (1928). "Urban Influence and Selection." In *Papers and Proceedings at the American Sociological Society,* pp. 1–14. Chicago: University of Chicago Press.

Gitlin, Todd (1978). "Media Sociology: The Dominant Paradigm." *Theory and Society* 6:205–253.

Gladner, Timothy Richard (1990). "Education and the Mass Media: The Origins of Mass Communications Research in the United States, 1939–1955." Ph.D. dissertation, University of Illinois.

—— (November 22, 1991). Personal correspondence with Everett M. Rogers.

Glock, Charles Y. (1979). "Organizing Innovation for Social Science Research and Training." In Robert F. Merton, James S. Coleman, and Peter H. Rossi (eds.), *Qualitative and Quantitative Social Research: Papers in Honor of Paul F. Lazarsfeld.* New York: Free Press.

Goffman, Erving (1959). *The Presentation of Self in Everyday Life.* Garden City, N.Y.: Doubleday.

—— (1961). *Asylums: Essays on the Social Situation of Mental Patients and Other Inmates.* Garden City, N.Y.: Anchor Books.

────── (1963). *Stigma*. Englewood Cliffs, N.J.: Prentice-Hall.

────── (1979). *Gender Advertisements*. New York: Harper & Row.

Goist, Park Dixon (1971). "City and 'Community': The Urban Theory of Robert Park." *American Quarterly* 23:46–59.

Goldman, Nancy (1973). "Biographical Sketch." In Leonard S. Cottrell, Jr., Albert Hunter, and James F. Short, Jr. (eds.), *Ernest W. Burgess on Community, Family, Delinquency*. Chicago: University of Chicago Press.

Goldsen, Joseph M. (September 19, 1991). Personal interview by Everett M. Rogers, San Francisco.

Goleman, Daniel (August 1978). "Bateson: Journey of a Generalist." *Psychology Today,* pp. 44–45.

Good, I. J. (1980). "Pioneering Work on Computers at Bletchley." In N. Metropolis, J. Howlett, and Gian-Carlo Rota (eds.), *A History of Computing in the Twentieth Century,* pp. 31–45. New York: Academic Press.

Goodspeed, Thomas Wakefield (1916/1972). *A History of the University of Chicago: The First Quarter Century*. Chicago: University of Chicago Press.

Gould, Stephen Jay (1980). *The Panda's Thumb: More Reflections in Natural History*. New York: Norton.

Grant, Peter R. (1991). "Natural Selection and Darwin's Finches." *Scientific American* 265(4):82–87.

Grattan-Guinness, I. (1975). "Wiener on the Logics of Russell and Schroder: An Account of His Doctoral Thesis, and of His Discussion of It with Russell." *Annals of Science* 32:103–132.

Greenberg, George S. (1977). "The Family Interactional Perspective: A Study and Examination of the Work of Dan D. Jackson." *Family Process* 16(4):385–412.

Greenwald, Anthony G., and David L. Ronis (1978). "Twenty Years of Cognitive Dissonance: Case Study of the Evolution of a Theory." *Psychological Review* 85(1):53–57.

Greenwood, M. (1949). "Pearson, Karl." In L. G. Wichham Legg (ed.), *The Dictionary of Natural Biography, 1931–40,* pp. 681–684. London: Oxford University Press.

Grossberg, Lawrence, Cary Nelson, and Paula Treichler (1992). *Cultural Studies*. London: Routledge.

Hagemeyer,   Frederich   Wilhelm   (1979).   "Die   Entstehung   von

Informationskonzepten in der Nachrichtentechnik: Eine Fallstudie zur Theoriebildung in der Technik in Industrie—und Kriegsforschung" (The Emergence of Concepts of Information in Information Technology: A Case Study of Theory Formation in Technology within Industrial and Military Research Programs. Doctoral thesis, Free University of Berlin.

Haley, Jay (1971). "A Review of the Family Therapy Field." In Jay Haley (ed.), *Changing Families: A Family Therapy Reader,* pp. 1–12. New York: Grune & Stratton.

—— (1976). "Development of a Theory: A History of a Research Project." In Carlos E. Sluzki and D. C. Ransom (eds.), *Double Bind,* pp. 59–110. New York: Grune & Stratton.

Hall, Calvin S., and Gardner Lindzey (1957). *Theories of Personality.* New York: Wiley.

Hall, Edward (1959). *The Silent Language.* Garden City, N.Y.: Doubleday.

Hamming, Richard W. (1950). "Error Detecting and Error Correcting Codes." *Bell System Technical Journal,* 26(2):147–160.

Hamming, Richard W. (September 4, 1990). Personal correspondence with Everett M. Rogers.

Hannan, Michael T., and John Freeman (1977). "The Population Ecology of Organizations." *American Journal of Sociology* 82:929–964.

—— (1989). *Organizational Ecology.* Cambridge: Harvard University Press.

Harary, Frank, Robert Z. Norman, and Dorwin Cartwright (1965). *Structural Models: An Introduction to the Theory of Directed Graphs.* New York: Wiley.

Hartley, H. V. L. (1928). "Transmission of Information." *Bell System Technical Journal* 7:535–563.

Harvey, Lee (1987). *Myths of the Chicago School of Sociology.* Aldershot, England: Avebury.

Hawkins, Hugh (1972). *Between Harvard and America: The Educational Leadership of Charles W. Eliot.* New York: Oxford University Press.

Haworth, Lawrence, (1960). "The Experimental Society: Dewey and Jordan." *Ethics* 71:27–40.

Heider, Fritz (1946). "Attitudes and Cognitive Organization." *Journal of Psychology* 21:107–112.

Heilbut, Anthony (1983). *Exiled in Paradise: German Refugee Artists and Intellectuals in America from the 1930's to the Present.* Boston: Beacon Press.

Heims, Steve J. (1980). *John von Neumann and Norbert Wiener: From Mathematics to the Technologies of Life and Death.* Cambridge: MIT Press.

———— (1991). *The Cybernetics Group.* Cambridge: MIT Press.

Held, David (1980). *Introduction to Critical Theory: Horkheimer to Habermas.* Los Angeles: University of California Press.

Hilbert, Richard A. (1980). "Covert Participant Observation: On Its Nature and Practice." *Urban Life* 9:51–77.

Hilgard, Ernest R. (1987). *Psychology in America: A Historical Survey.* New York: Harcourt Brace Jovanovich.

———— (March 11, 1992a). Personal interview by Everett M. Rogers, Stanford, California.

———— (November 11, 1992b). Personal correspondence with Everett M. Rogers.

Himmelwaite, Hilde, A. N. Oppenheim, and Pamela Vince (1958). *Television and the Child.* New York: Oxford University Press.

Hinkle, Roscoe C. (1980). *Founding Theory of American Sociology 1881–1915.* Boston: Routledge and Kegan.

Hodges, Andrew (1983). *Alan Turing: The Enigma.* New York: Simon and Schuster.

Hofstadter, Richard (1944/1955). *Social Darwinism in American Thought.* Boston: Beacon Press.

Holaday, P. W., and George D. Stoddard (1933/1970). *Getting Ideas from the Movies.* New York: Macmillan; New York: Arno Press.

Hollonquist, Tore, and Edward A. Suchman (1944/1979). "Listening to the Listener: Experiences with the Lazarsfeld-Stanton Program Analyzer." In Paul F. Lazarsfeld and Frank N. Stanton (eds.), *Radio Research, 1942–43,* pp. 265–334. New York: Duell, Sloan, and Pearce; New York: Arno Press.

Hook, Sidney (1939). *John Dewey: An Intellectual Portrait.* New York: John Day.

Horgan, John (June 1990). "Claude E. Shannon: Unicyclist, Juggler, and Father of Information Theory." *IEEE Information Theory Society Newsletter.*

———— (April 1992). "Claude E. Shannon." *IEEE Spectrum,* pp. 72–75.

Horkheimer, Max (1937). "Traditionelle und Kritische Theorie." *Zeitschrift für Sozialforschung* 6 (2):245–295. "Traditional and Critical Theory." Translated by Matthew J. O'Connell. In Max Horkheimer (ed.), *Critical Theory: Selected Essays,* pp. 188–243. New York: Herder and Herder.

Horkheimer, Max, et al. (1936). *Studien über Autorität und Familie.* Paris: Felix Alcan.

Hornstein, Gail A. (1992). "The Return of the Repressed: Psychology's Problematic Relations with Psychoanalysis, 1909–1960." *American Psychologist* 47(2):254–263.

Horowitz, Louis Irving (1983). *C. Wright Mills: An American Utopian.* New York: Free Press.

Horton, Donald, and R. R. Wohl (1956). "Mass Communication and Para-Social Interaction: Observations on Intimacy at a Distance." *Psychiatry* 19(3):215–229.

Hovland, Carl I. (1951). "Changes in Attitude Through Communication." *Journal of Abnormal and Social Psychology* 46:424–437.

———— (1954). "Effects of the Mass Media of Communication." In Gardner Lindzey (ed.), *Handbook of Social Psychology.* vol. 2: *Special Fields and Applications,* pp. 1062–1103. Cambridge, Mass.: Addison-Wesley.

———— (1959). "Reconciling Conflicting Results from Experimental and Survey Studies of Attitude Change." *American Psychologist* 14:8–17.

Hovland, Carl, Irving Janis, and Harold Kelley (eds.) (1953). *Communication and Persuasion: Psychological Studies of Opinion Change.* New Haven: Yale University Press.

Hovland, Carl I., Arthur A. Lumsdaine, and Fred D. Sheffield (1949). *Experiments on Mass Communication: Studies in Social Psychology in World War II,* vol. 3. New Haven: Yale University Press.

Hovland, Carl I., and Walter Weiss (1951). "The Influence of Source Credibility on Communication Effectiveness." *Public Opinion Quarterly* 15:635–650.

Hovland, Carl I., Wallace Mandell, Enid H. Campbell, Timothy Brock, Abraham S. Luchins, Arthur R. Cohen, William J. McGuire, Irving L. Janis, Rosalind F. Feierabend, and Norman H. Anderson (1957). *The Order of Presentation in Persuasion.* New Haven: Yale University Press.

Hoyt, Palmer (1943). "OWI in 1943: Coordinator and Service Agency." *Journalism Quarterly* 20(4):320–325.

Hudson, Robert B. (1977), "The Illinois Years." In Daniel Lerner and Lyle M. Nelson (eds.), *Communication Research: A Half-Century Appraisal,* pp. 311–316. Honolulu: University Press of Hawaii.

Hughes, Everett C. (1964). "Robert E. Park." *Sociological Eye* 2:543–549.

Hughes, Helen MacGill (1968). "Robert E. Park." In David Sills (ed.), *International Encyclopedia of the Social Sciences,* pp. 416–419. New York: Macmillan.

Hull, Clark L, Carl I. Hovland, Robert T. Ross, Marshall Hall, Donald T. Perkins, and Frederick B. Fitch (1940). *Mathematico-Deductive Theory of Rote Learning.* New Haven: Yale University Press.

Hunt, Morton (January 28, 1961). "A Profile: Robert K. Merton." *New Yorker.*

Hurwitz, Donald (1988). "Market Research and the Study of the United States Radio Audience." *Communication* 10(2):223–241.

Hutchins, Robert Maynard (March 29, 1937). Letter to Harold D. Lasswell, Folder 7, President's Papers, Department of Political Science (Appointments and Budgets, 1925–1939), University of Chicago Regensdorf Library, Department of Special Collections.

Hyman, Herbert H. (1979). "The Effects of Unemployment: A Neglected Problem in Modern Social Research." In Robert K. Merton, James S. Coleman, and Peter H. Rossi (eds.), *Qualitative and Quantitative Social Research: Papers in Honor of Paul F. Lazarsfeld,* pp. 282–298. New York: Free Press.

–––––– (1991). *Taking Society's Measure: A Personal History of Survey Research.* New York: Russell Sage Foundation.

Ikenberry, Stanley O., and Renee C. Friedman (1972). *Beyond Academic Departments.* San Francisco: Jossey-Bass.

Innis, Harold A. (1923/1971). *The History of the Canadian Pacific Railway.* Toronto: University of Toronto Press.

–––––– (1950/1971). *Empire and Communication.* Toronto: University of Toronto Press.

–––––– (1951). *The Bias of Communication.* Toronto: University of Toronto Press.

Iyengar, Shanto, and Donald R. Kinder (1987). *News That Matters: Agenda-Setting and Priming in a Television Age.* Chicago: University of Chicago Press.

Jahoda, Marie (1979). "PFL: Hedgehog or Fox?" In Robert K. Merton, James S. Coleman, and Peter H. Rossi (eds.), *Qualitative and Quantitative Social Research: Papers in Honor of Paul F. Lazarsfeld,* pp. 3–9. New York: Free Press.

–––––– (1983). "The Emergence of Social Psychology in Vienna: An Exercise in Long-Term Memory." *British Journal of Social Psychology* 22:343–349.

Jahoda, Marie, Paul F. Lazarsfeld, and Hans Ziesel (1933/1971). *Marienthal: The Sociography of an Unemployed Community*. Chicago: Aldine-Atherton. First published in 1933 as *Die Arbeitslosen von Marienthal: Ein Soziographischer*. Leipzig: Hirzl.

James, William (1920). *Letters to William James II*. Boston: Atlantic Monthly Press.

Janis, Irving L. (1972). *Victims of Groupthink: A Psychological Study of Foreign-Policy, Decisions, and Fiascoes*. Boston: Houghton Mifflin.

Janis, Irving L., and Seymour Feshback (1953). "Effects of Fear-Arousing Communications." *Journal of Abnormal and Social Psychology* 48 (1):78–92.

Janis, Irving L., Carl I. Hovland, Peter B. Field, Harriet Linton, Elaine Graham, Arthur R. Cohen, Donald Rife, Robert P. Abelson, Gerald S. Lesser, and Bert T. King (1959). *Personality and Persuasibility*. New Haven: Yale University Press.

Jay, Martin (1973). *The Dialectical Imagination: A History of the Frankfurt School and the Institute of Social Research, 1923–1950*. Boston: Little, Brown.

———— (1988). "Urban Flights: The Institute of Social Research between Frankfurt and New York." In Thomas Bender (ed.), *The University and the City: From Medieval Origins to the Present*, pp. 232–248. New York: Oxford University Press.

Jones, Ernest (1953). *The Life and Work of Sigmund Freud*. Vol. 1: *The Formative Years and the Great Discoveries 1856–1900*. New York: Basic Books.

———— (1955). *The Life and Work of Sigmund Freud*. Vol. 2: *Years of Maturity, 1901–1919*. New York: Basic Books.

———— (1957). *The Life and Work of Sigmund Freud*. Vol. 3: *The Last Phase, 1919–1939*. New York: Basic Books.

Jorgenson, Jane (1989). "Weaver, Warren (1894–1978)." In Eric Barnouw (ed.), *International Encyclopedia of Communication*, p. 309. New York: Oxford University Press.

Jowett, Garth S. (1976). *Film: The Democratic Art*. Boston: Little, Brown.

———— (1987). "Propaganda and Communication: The Re-Emergence of a Research Tradition." *Journal of Communication* 37(1):97–114.

———— (1992). "Social Science as a Weapon: The Origins of the Payne Fund Studies, 1926–1929." *Communication* 13:211–225.

————, and Victoria O'Donnell (1986). *Propaganda and Persuasion*. Newbury Park, Calif.: Sage.

Kac, Mark (1977). Foreword, to R. J. McEliece, *The Theory of Information and Coding: A Mathematical Framework for Communication.* Reading, Mass.: Addison-Wesley.

Kadushin, Charles (May 13, 1991). Discussion with Everett M. Rogers, Los Angeles.

Kahn, David (1967). *The Codebreakers: The Story of Secret Writing.* New York: Macmillan.

Kaplan, Jeremiah (November 27, 1991). Personal interview by Everett M. Rogers, New York.

Katz, Daniel, and Robert Kahn (1966). *The Social Psychology of Organizations.* New York: Wiley.

Katz, Elihu (1987), "Communication Research Since Lazarsfeld." *Public Opinion Quarterly* 51:525–526.

―――― and Paul F. Lazarsfeld (1955). *Personal Influence: The Part Played by People in the Flow of Mass Communication.* New York: Free Press.

Keever, Beverly Ann (1991). "Wilbur Schramm: On Windwagons and Sky Busters: Final Regrets of a Mass Communication Pioneer." *Mass Communication Review* 1:3–26.

Kelley, Harold H. (July 30, 1991). Personal interview by Everett M. Rogers, Los Angeles.

Kendall, Patricia (1970). "Note on Significance Tests." In Robert K. Merton, George G. Reader, and Patricia L. Kendall (eds.), *The Student-Physician: Introductory Studies in the Sociology of Medical Education,* pp. 301–305. Cambridge: Harvard University Press.

Khintchin, A. I. (1956). "On the Fundamental Theorems of Information Theory." *Uspekhi Matematicheskikh Nauk* 9:54–63.

Klapper, Joseph T. (1960). *The Effects of Mass Communication.* New York: Free Press.

Knight, Isabel F. (1984). "Freud's 'Project': A Theory for *Studies on Hysteria.*" *Journal of the History of the Behavioral Sciences* 20:340–358.

Komarovsky, Mirra (1940). *The Unemployed Man and His Family: The Effect of Unemployment upon the Status of the Man in Fifty-Nine Families.* New York: Dryden Press.

Krippendorff, Klaus (1989a). "Cybernetics." In Erik Barnouw (ed.), *International Encyclopedia of Communication,* pp. 443–446. New York: Oxford University Press.

_____ (1989b). "Shannon, Claude (1916–)." In Erik Barnouw (ed.), *International Encyclopedia of Communication*, pp. 59–61. New York: Oxford University Press.

_____ (1989c). "Information Theory." In Erik Barnouw (ed.), *International Encyclopedia of Communication*, pp. 314–320. New York: Oxford University Press.

Krull, Robert, James H. Watt, Jr., and Lawrence W. Lichty (1977). "Entropy and Structure: Two Measures of Complexity in Television Programs." *Communication Research* 4 (1):61–86.

Kuhn, Manfred H., and Thomas S. McPartland (1954). "An Empirical Investigation of Self-Attitudes." *American Sociological Review* 19(1):68–76.

Kuhn, Thomas S. (1962/1970). *The Structure of Scientific Revolutions*. 2d ed. Chicago: University of Chicago Press.

Kunkel, John H. (1986). "The Vicos Project: A Cross-Cultural Test of Psychological Propositions." *Psychological Record* 36:451–466.

Küppers, Bernd-Olaf (1990). *Information and the Origin of Life*. Cambridge: MIT Press.

Kurtz, Lester R. (1984), *Evaluating Chicago Sociology: A Guide to the Literature, with an Annotated Bibliography*. Chicago: University of Chicago Press.

Kurzweil, Edith (1989). *The Freudians: A Comparative Perspective*. New Haven: Yale University Press.

Lagemann, Ellen Condliffe (1989). "The Plural Worlds of Educational Research." *History of Education Quarterly* 29(2):185–214.

Lasko, Joan (August 23, 1991). Personal interview by Everett M. Rogers, Los Angeles.

Lasswell, Harold (1923). "Chicago's Old First Ward." *National Municipal Review* 12:127–131.

_____ (1925). "Prussian Schoolbooks and International Amity." *Journal of Social Focus* 3:718–722.

_____ (1927/1938/1971). *Propaganda Technique in the World War*. New York: Knopf; New York: Peter Smith; and Cambridge: MIT Press.

_____ (1930/1960). *Psychopathology and Politics*. New York: Viking Press; Chicago: University of Chicago Press.

_____ (1941). "The Garrison State and the Specialists on Violence." *American Journal of Sociology* 46:455–468.

—— (1948). "The Structure and Function of Communication in Society." In Lyman Bryson (ed.), *The Communication of Ideas: A Series of Addresses,* pp. 37–51. New York: Harper. Reprinted in Wilbur Schramm and Donald F. Roberts (eds.) (1971). *The Process and Effects of Mass Communication,* pp. 84–99. Rev. Ed. Urbana: University of Illinois Press.

—— (1951a). *The World Revolution in Our Time.* Stanford: Stanford University Press.

—— (October 15, 1951b). "HDL Summary of Activities." Unpublished paper.

—— (1971). Introduction to Harold D. Lasswell, *Propaganda Technique in World War I,* pp. ix–xvii. Cambridge: MIT Press.

—— (1972). "Communication Research and Public Policy." *Public Opinion Quarterly* 36:301–310.

Lasswell, Harold D., Ralph D. Casey, and Bruce L. Smith (1935). *Propaganda and Promotional Activities: An Annotated Bibliography.* Minneapolis: University of Minnesota Press.

Lasswell, Harold D., and Nathan Leites (eds.) (1949). *Language of Politics: Studies in Quantitative Semantics.* New York: George Stewart.

Latour, Bruno, and Steven Woolgar (1979). *Laboratory Life: The Social Construction of Scientific Facts.* Newbury Park, Calif.: Sage.

Lazarsfeld, Paul F. (1925). "Über die Perihlbewegung des Merkuz aus der Einsteinschen Gravitationstheorie." Ph.D. thesis, University of Vienna.

—— (1932). "An Unemployed Village." *Character and Personality,* 147–151.

—— (1940). *Radio and the Printed Page: An Introduction to the Study of Radio and Its Role in the Communication of Ideas.* New York: Duell, Pearce and Sloan.

—— (1941). "Remarks on Administrative and Critical Communications Research." *Studies in Philosophy and Social Science* 9 (1):2–16.

—— (1947). Introduction to Hans Zeisel, *Say It with Figures,* pp. xv–xviii. New York: Harper & Row.

—— (1954). *Mathematical Thinking in the Social Sciences.* New York: Free Press.

—— (November 29, 1961a). Tape-recorded oral history interview by Joan Gordon, Columbia University, Butler Library, Oral History Research Office.

—— (December 8, 1961b). Tape-recorded oral history interview by Joan Gordon, Columbia University, Butler Library, Oral History Research Office.

—— (January 8, 1962a). Tape-recorded oral history interview by Joan Gordon, Columbia University, Butler Library, Oral History Research Office.

—— (August 16, 1962c). Tape-recorded oral history interview by Joan Gordon, Columbia University, Butler Library, Oral History Research Office.

—— (1962d). "The Sociology of Empirical Social Research." *American Sociological Review* 27 (6):757–767.

—— (1962e). "Some Problems of Organized Social Research." In Paul F. Lazarsfeld, Lawrence R. Klein, and Ralph W. Tyler (eds.), *The Behavioral Sciences: Problems and Prospects.* Boulder, Colo.: Institute of Behavioral Science.

—— (1969a). "An Episode in the History of Social Research: A Memoir." In Donald Fleming and Bernard Bailyn (eds.), *The Intellectual Migration: Europe and America, 1930–1960,* pp. 270–337. Cambridge: Belknap Press of Harvard University Press.

—— (1969b). "From Vienna to Columbia." *Columbia Forum*, pp. 31–36.

—— (1972). *Qualitative Analysis: Historical and Critical Essays.* Boston: Allyn and Bacon.

—— (August 6, 1973). Letter to Ed McLuskie, Columbia University, Butler Library, Oral History Research Office.

—— (February 21, 1975a). Tape-recorded oral history interview by Ann Pasanella, Columbia University, Butler Library, Oral History Research Office.

—— (March 12, 1975b). Tape-recorded oral history interview by Ann Pasanella, Columbia University, Butler Library, Oral History Research Office.

—— (April 12, 1975c). Tape-recorded oral history interview by Ann Pasanella, Columbia University, Butler Library, Oral History Research Office.

—— (April 19, 1975d). Tape-recorded oral history interview by Ann Pasanella, Columbia University, Butler Library, Oral History Research Office.

—— (1975e). "Working with Merton." In Lewis A. Coser (ed.), *The Idea of Social Structure: Papers in Honor of Robert K. Merton,* pp. 35–60. New York: Harcourt Brace Jovanovich.

—— (June 8, 1976). Videotaped interview, Columbia University, Butler Library, Rare Book and Manuscript Collection, Box 11, Series 3.

_____ (1982). "An Episode in the History of Social Research: A Memoir." in Patricia L. Kendall (ed.), pp. 11–73. *The Varied Sociology of Paul F. Lazarsfeld.* New York: Columbia University Press.

_____ Lazarsfeld, Paul F., Bernard Berelson, and Hazel Gaudet (1944/1948/1968). *The People's Choice: How the Voter Makes Up His Mind in a Presidential Campaign.* New York: Duell, Sloan and Pearce; New York: Columbia University Press.

Lazarsfeld, Paul F., Hadley Cantril, and Frank Stanton (1939). "Current Radio Research in Universities." *Journal of Applied Psychology* 23:201–204.

Lazarsfeld, Paul F., and Anthony R. Oberschall (1965). "Max Weber and Empirical Social Research." *American Sociological Review* 30:185–199.

Lazarsfeld, Paul F., and Morris Rosenberg (eds.) (1955). *The Language of Social Research: A Reader in the Methodology of Social Research.* New York: Free Press.

Lazarsfeld, Paul R., William H. Sewell, and Harold L. Wilensky (eds.) (1967). *The Uses of Sociology.* New York: Basic Books.

Lazarsfeld, Paul F., and Frank N. Stanton (eds.) (1942). *Radio Research, 1941.* New York: Duell, Sloan, and Pearce.

_____ (eds.) (1944/1979). *Radio Research, 1942–43.* New York: Duell, Sloan, and Pearce; New York: Arno Press.

_____ (eds.) (1949). *Communications Research, 1948–1949.* New York: Duell, Sloan and Pearce; New York: Harper.

Lazarsfeld, Paul F., and Wagner Thielens (1953). *The Academic Mind: Social Scientists in a Time of Crisis.* New York: Free Press.

Lazarsfeld, Sofie (1932/1934). *Wie die Frau den Mann erlebt.* Vienna, Verlag für Sexual Wissenschaft Schneider. Translated and published in English as *Rhythm of Life: A Guide to Sexual Harmony for Women.* London: Routledge and Son.

Leeds-Hurwitz, Wendy (1990). "Notes in the History of Intercultural Communication: The Foreign Service Institute and the Mandate for Intercultural Training." *Quarterly Journal of Speech* 76:262–281.

_____ (1991). "Crossing Disciplinary Boundaries: The Macy Conferences on Cybernetics as a Case Study in Multidisciplinary Communication." Paper presented at the American Society for Cybernetics, Amherst, Massachusetts.

Lengermann, Patricia M. (1979). "The Founding of the ASR: The Anatomy of a Rebellion." *American Sociological Review* 44:185–198.

Lerg, Winfried B. (1977). "Paul Felix Lazarsfeld und die Kommunikation Forschung: Ein Biobibliographisches Epitaph." *Publizistik* 1:72–87.

Lerner, Daniel (1958). *The Passing of Traditional Society: Modernizing the Middle East*. New York: Free Press.

Lerner, Daniel and Lyle M. Nelson (eds.) (1977). *Communication Research: A Half-Century Appraisal*. Honolulu: University Press of Hawaii.

Levine, Donald N. (1989). "Simmel as a Resource for Sociological Metatheory." *Sociological Theory* 7 (2):161–173.

Levine, Donald N., Elwood B. Carter, and Eleanor Miller Gorman (1976). "Simmel's Influence on American Sociology." *American Journal of Sociology* 84(4):813–845, and 84(5):1112–1132.

Levinson, Daniel (1990). "The Authoritarian Personality Revisited: Forty Years Later." Paper presented at the International Society of Political Psychology, Washington, D.C.

Levinson, Norman (1966). "Wiener's Life," *American Mathematical Society Bulletin*. 72:1–32.

Levy, Mark R. (1982). "The Lazarsfeld-Stanton Program Analyzer: An Historical Note." *Journal of Communication* 28:30–38.

Lewin, Kurt (1920). *Die Sozialisierung des Taylorsystems: Eine grundsätzliche Untersuchung zur Arbeits- und Berufs-Psychologie (The Socialization of the Taylor System: A Fundamental Investigation in Industrial and Occupational Psychology)*. Berlin-Fichtenau: Verlag Gesellschaft und Erziehung.

_____ (1936). "Some Social-Psychological Differences Between the United States and Germany." *Character and Personality* 4:265–293.

_____ (1941). "Self-Hatred Among Jews." *Contemporary Jewish Record* 4:219–232.

_____ (1947a). "Frontiers in Group Dynamics: I, Concept, Method, and Reality in Social Science, Social Equilibria, and Social Change." *Human Relations* 1 (1):5–42.

_____ (1947b). "Frontiers in Group Dynamics: II, Channels of Group Life, Social Planning and Action Research." *Human Relations* 1(2):179–193.

_____ (1948). *Resolving Social Conflicts: Selected Papers on Group Dynamics*. New York: Harper and Brothers.

_____ (1951). *Field Theory in Social Science: Selected Theoretical Papers*. New York: Harper and Brothers.

———— (1958). "Group Decision and Social Change." In Eleanor E. Maccoby, Theodore M. Newcomb, and Eugene L. Hartley (eds.), *Readings in Social Psychology,* pp. 197–211. 3d ed. New York: Holt, Rinehart and Winston.

Lewin, Kurt, and Ronald Lippitt (1938). "An Experimental Approach to the Study of Autocracy and Democracy: A Preliminary Note." *Sociometry* 1:292–300.

Lewin, Kurt, Ronald Lippitt, and R. K. White (1939). "Patterns of Aggressive Behavior in Experimentally Created Social Climates." *Journal of Social Psychology* 10:271–299.

Lewin, Miriam A. (1976). "Psychological Aspects of Minority Group Membership: The Concepts of Kurt Lewin." In Thomas Blass (ed.), *Contemporary Social Psychology: Representative Readings,* pp. 128–137. Itasca, Ill.: Peacock.

———— (June 8, 1992). Personal interview with Everett M. Rogers, Cos Cob, Connecticut.

Lewis, David L., and Richard Smith (1980). *American Sociology and Pragmatism: Mead, Chicago Sociology and Symbolic Interaction.* Chicago: University of Chicago Press.

Liebes, Tamar and Elihu Katz (1990). *The Export of Meaning: Cross-Cultural Reading of Dallas.* New York: Oxford University Press.

Likert, Rensis (1932). "A Technique for the Measurement of Attitudes." *Archives of Psychology* 22(140):5–55.

Lincourt, John M., and Peter H. Hare (1973). "Neglected American Philosophers in the History of Symbolic Interactionism." *Journal of the History of the Behavioral Sciences* 9(4):333–338.

Lindstrom, Fred B., and Ronald A. Hardert (1988). "Kimball Young on Founders of the Chicago School." *Sociological Perspectives* 31 (3):269–297.

Lippitt, Ronald (1968). "Kurt Lewin" In David L. Sills (ed.), *International Encyclopedia of Social Sciences.* New York: Macmillan.

Lippmann, Walter (1922/1965). *Public Opinion.* New York: Harcourt Brace; New York: Free Press.

———— (1925). *The Phantom Public.* New York: Harcourt, Brace.

Lippmann, Walter, and Charles Merz (August 4, 1920). "A Test of the News." *New Republic,* pp. 3–42.

Lipset, David (1980). *Gregory Bateson: The Legacy of a Scientist.* Boston: Beacon Press.

Lipset, Seymour Martin (1955). "The Department of Sociology." In R. Gordon Hoxie, Sally Falk Moore, Joseph Dorfman, Richard Hofstadter, Theodore W. Anderson, Jr., John D. Millett, and Seymour Martin Lipset (eds.), *A History of the Faculty of Political Science, Columbia University,* pp. 284–303. New York: Columbia University.

Lipset, Seymour Martin, and Neil Smelser (1961). "Change and Controversy in Recent American Sociology." *British Journal of Sociology* 12:41–51.

Lipset, Seymour Martin, Martin A. Trow, and James S. Coleman (1956). *Union Democracy: The Internal Politics of the International Typographical Union.* New York: Free Press.

Livingstone, Sonia M. (1992). "The Resourceful Reader: Interpreting Television Characters and Narratives." In Stanley A. Deetz (ed.), *Communication Yearbook 15,* pp. 58–90. Newbury Park, Calif.: Sage.

Lovell, Ron (October 1987). "Triumph of the Chi-Squares: It's a Hollow Victory." *Quill,* pp. 22–25.

Lowenberg, Bert James (1933). "The Reaction of American Scientists to Darwinism." *American Historical Review* 38:687–701.

Lowenthal, Leo (1944/1979). "Biographers in Popular Magazines." In Paul F. Lazarsfeld and Frank N. Stanton (eds.), *Radio Research: 1942–1943,* pp. 507–548. New York: Duell, Sloan and Pearce; New York: Arno Press.

Lowery, Shearon A., and Melvin L. DeFleur (1988). *Milestones in Mass Communication Research: Media Effects.* 2d ed. New York: Longman.

Lowry, Dennis T., and Theodore J. Marr (1975). "Clozentropy as a Measure of International Communication Comprehension." *Public Opinion Quarterly* 39:301–312.

Lubasz, Heinz, (1975). "Review of Martin Jay's *The Dialectical Imagination.*" *History and Theory* 27:200–212.

Lucky, Robert W. (1989). *Silicon Dreams: Information, Man, and Machine.* New York: St. Martin's Press.

Lynch, F. D. (1974). "Clozentropy: A New Technique for Analyzing Audience Response to Film." *Speech Monographs* 41:245–252.

Lynd, Robert S. (1939). *Knowledge for What? The Place of Social Science in American Culture.* Princeton, N.J.: Princeton University Press.

Lynd, Robert S., and Helen Merrell Lynd (1929). *Middletown: A Study in American Culture.* New York: Harcourt, Brace.

―――― (1937). *Middletown in Transition.* New York: Harcourt, Brace.

Lyons, Gene M. (1969). *The Uneasy Partnership: Social Science and the Federal Government in the Twentieth Century.* New York: Russell Sage Foundation.

McAnany, Emile G. (1988). "Wilbur Schramm, 1907–1987: Roots of the Past, Seeds of the Present." *Journal of Communication* 38(4):109–122.

McCaul, Robert L. (1959). "Dewey's Chicago." *School Review* 67:258–280.

―――― (March 25, 1961). Dewey and the University of Chicago: Part I, July 1894–March 1902." *School and Society* 85:152–157.

―――― (April 8, 1961). "Dewey and the University of Chicago: Part II, April 1902–May 1903." *School and Society,* 85:179–183.

―――― (April 22, 1961). "Dewey and the University of Chicago: Part III, September 1903–June 1904. *School and Society,* 85:202–206.

Maccoby, Nathan (October 21, 1987). Personal interview by Everett M. Rogers, Stanford, California.

McCombs, Maxwell E. (1981). "The Agenda-Setting Approach." In Dan D. Nimoro and Keith R. Sanders (eds.), *Handbook of Political Communication,* pp. 121–140. Newbury Park, Calif.: Sage.

―――― and Donald L. Shaw (1972). "The Agenda-Setting Function of Mass Media." *Public Opinion Quarterly* 36:176–187.

McCormick, Thelma (1986). "Reflections on the Lost Vision of Communication Theory." In Sandra J. Ball-Rokeach and Muriel G. Cantor (eds.), *Media, Audience, and Social Structure,* pp. 34–42. Newbury Park, Calif.: Sage.

McCulloch, Warren S. (1965). "Norbert Wiener and the Art of Theory." *Journal of Nervous and Mental Disease* 140 (1):16.

McDougal, Myres S. (July 11, 1991a). Personal correspondence with Everett M. Rogers.

―――― (October 10, 1991b). Personal interview by Everett M. Rogers, New Haven, Connecticut.

McEliece, R. J. (1977). *The Theory of Information and Coding: A Mathematical Framework for Communication.* Reading, Mass.: Addison-Wesley.

McElwain, Max (1991). *Profiles in Communication: The Hall of Fame of the University of Iowa School of Journalism and Mass Communication.* Iowa City: Iowa Center for Communication Study.

McGuire, William J. (1983). "A Contextualist Theory of Knowledge: Its

Implications for Innovation and Reform in Psychological Research." *Advances in Experimental Social Psychology* 16:1–47.

———— (1985a). "Attitudes and Attitude Change." In Gardner Lindzey and Elliot Aronson (eds.), *Handbook of Social Psychology*. Vol. 2: *Special Fields and Applications*, pp. 233–346. 3d ed. New York: Random House.

———— (1985b). "Toward Social Psychology's Second Century." In Sigmund Koch and David E. Leary (eds.), *A Century of Psychology as Science*, pp. 558–590. New York: McGraw-Hill.

———— (1986). "The Vicissitudes of Attitudes and Similar Representational Constructs in Twentieth Century Psychology." *European Journal of Social Psychology* 16:89–130.

———— (January 7, 1991a). Personal correspondence with Everett M. Rogers.

———— (October 11, 1991b), Personal interview by Everett M. Rogers, New Haven, Connecticut.

———— (in press). "Persuasion and Communications at Yale." in Everette E. Dennis and Ellen Wartella (eds.), *American Communication Research: The Remembered History*. New York: Freedom Forum Media Studies Center.

MacIver, R.M. (1968). *As a Tale That Is Told: The Autobiography of R. M. MacIver*. Chicago: University of Chicago Press.

McLuhan, Marshall (1964). *Understanding Media: The Extensions of Man*. New York: McGraw-Hill.

———— (1969). "Playboy Interview: Marshall McLuhan." *Playboy*, pp. 53–74, 158.

McLuskie, Clarence Edward, Jr. (1975). "A Critical Epistemology of Paul Lazarsfeld's Administrative Communication Inquiry." Ph.D. dissertation, University of Iowa.

McMurray, Robert N. (January 4, 1933). "When Men Eat Dogs." *Nation*, pp. 15–18.

McNelly, John T. (January 3, 1992a). Personal correspondence with Everett M. Rogers.

———— (August 11, 1992b). Personal interview by Everett M. Rogers, Madison, Wisconsin.

McQuail, Dennis, and Sven Windhal (1981). *Communication Models for the Study of Mass Communication*. New York: Longman.

McSween, Charles (1987). "Code Blue: The Demise of Symbolic Interactionism in Communication Theory." Unpublished paper. Los Angeles: University of Southern California, Annenberg School for Communication.

Malthus, Thomas (1797/1914). *Essays on the Principles of Population*. London: Everyman.

Mandell, Wallace (January 3, 1992). Personal correspondence with Everett M. Rogers.

Mann, Thomas (1961). *The Genesis of a Novel*. London: Secker and Warburg.

Marcuse, Herbert (1955). *Eros and Civilization*. Boston: Beacon Press.

—— (1964). *One-Dimensional Man*. Boston: Beacon Press.

Marrow, Alfred J. (1969). *The Practical Theorist: The Life and Work of Kurt Lewin*. New York: Basic Books.

Marshall, John (January 24, 1973). Tape-recorded oral history interview by Pauline Medow, Columbia University, Butler Library, Oral History Research Office.

—— (September 26, 1977). Interview by Ann Pasanella, Columbia University, Butler Library, Oral History Research Office.

Marvick, Dwaine (ed.) (1977). *Harold D. Lasswell on Political Sociology*. Chicago: University of Chicago Press.

—— (1980). "The Work of Harold D. Lasswell: His Approach, Concerns, and Influence." *Political Behavior* 2(3):219–229.

Marx, Karl (1867/1967). *Das Kapital*. New York: L.W. Schmidt.

—— (1973). *On Society and Social Change*. Chicago: University of Chicago Press.

Marx, Karl, and Friedrick Engels (1848/1978). "The Communist Manifesto." In Robert Tucker (ed.), *The Marx-Engels Reader,* pp. 469–500. New York: Morton.

Masani, P. R. (1990). *Norbert Wiener, 1894–1964*. Basel: Birkheuser Verlag.

Matthews, Fred H. (1977). *Quest for an American Sociology: Robert E. Park and the Chicago School*. Montreal: McGill-Queen's University Press.

May, Mark A. (1971). "A Retrospective View of the Institute of Human Relations at Yale." *Behavior Science Notes* 3:141–172.

Mayer, Martin, (1972). *About Television*. New York: Harper & Row.

Mead, George Herbert (1934). *Mind, Self and Society*. Chicago: University of Chicago Press.

Mead, Margaret (1928). *Coming of Age in Samoa.* New York: Blue Ribbon Books.

Meltzer, Bernard N., and John W. Petras (1970). "The Chicago and Iowa Schools of Symbolic Interactionism." In Tamatsu Shibutani (ed.), *Human Nature and Collective Behavior Papers in Honor of Herbert Blumer.* Englewood Cliffs, N.J.: Prentice Hall, pp. 3–17.

Merelman, Richard M. (1981). "Review Article: Harold D. Lasswell's Political World: Weak Tea for Hard Times." *British Journal of Political Science* 11:471–499.

Merriam, Charles E. (1919). "American Publicity in Italy." *American Political Science Review* 13(4):541–555.

Merton, Robert K. (1938). "Social Structure and Anomie." *American Sociological Review* 3:672–682.

———— (1949/1957/1968). *Social Theory and Social Structure.* New York: Free Press.

———— (1979). "Remembering Paul Lazarsfeld." In Robert K. Merton, James S. Coleman, and Peter H. Rossi (eds.), *Qualitative and Quantitative Social Research: Papers in Honor of Paul F. Lazarsfeld,* pp. 19–22. New York: Free Press.

———— (1987). "The Focussed Interview and Focus Groups: Continuities and Discontinuities." *Public Opinion Quarterly* 51:550–566.

———— (October 9, 1991). Personal interview by Everett M. Rogers, New York.

———— (February 29, 1992). Personal correspondence with Everett M. Rogers.

———— (in press). "On Paul Lazarsfeld: The Master Surveyor." In Everette E. Dennis and Ellen Wartella (eds.), *American Communication Research: The Remembered History.* New York: Freedom Forum Media Studies Center.

Merton, Robert K., with Marjorie Fiske and Alberta Curtis (1946/1958/1971). *Mass Persuasion: The Social Psychology of a War Bond Drive.* New York: Harper and Brothers.

Merton, Robert K., Marjorie Fiske, and Patricia L. Kendall (1956/1990). *The Focused Interview: A Manual of Problems and Procedures.* 2d ed. New York: Free Press.

Merton, Robert K., and Patricia L. Kendall (1946). "The Focused Interview." *American Journal of Sociology* 51:541–557.

Merton, Robert K., and Paul F. Lazarsfeld (eds.) (1950). *Continuities in Social Research: Studies on the Scope and Methods of "The American Soldier."* New York: Free Press.

Metz, Robert (1975). *CBS: Reflections in a Bloodshot Eye.* Chicago: Playboy Press.

Meyer, Alan S., Lucy N. Friedman, and Paul F. Lazarsfeld (1973). "Motivational Conflicts Engendered by the On-Going Dicusssion of Cigarette Smoking." In William L. Dunn, Jr. (ed.), *Smoking Behavior: Motives and Incentives.* pp. 243–254. Washington, D.C.: V. H. Winston & Sons.

Mielke, Keith W., and Milton Chen (1983). "Formative Research for 3-2-1 Contact: Methods and Insights." In M. Howe (ed.), *Learning from Television,* pp. 31–55. London: Academic Press.

Miles, Matthew (1979). "Qualitative Data as an Attractive Nuisance: The Problem of Analysis." *Administrative Science Quarterly* 24:590–601.

Miller, James Grier (1978). *Living Systems.* New York: McGraw-Hill.

Miller, Jonathan, and Borin Van Loon (1982). *Darwin for Beginners.* New York: Pantheon Books.

Miller, Neal E., and John Dollard (1941). *Social Learning and Imitation.* New Haven: Yale University Press.

Millman, S. (ed.) (1984). *A History of Engineering and Science in the Bell System: Communications Sciences (1925–1980).* Murray Hill, N.J.: AT&T Bell Laboratories.

Mills, C. Wright (1951). *White Collar: The American Middle Classes.* New York: Oxford University Press.

——— (1956). *The Power Elite.* New York: Oxford University Press.

——— (1959). *The Sociological Imagination.* New York: Grove Press.

Moeller, Leslie G. (November 16, 1970). Oral history interview by W. J. Zima and Gary Wade, State Historical Society of Wisconsin, Madison.

Morawski, J. G. (1986). "Organizing Knowledge and Behavior at Yale's Institute of Human Relations." *Isis* 77:219–242.

Moreno, Jacob L. (1934/1953). *Who Shall Survive? Foundations of Sociometry, Group Psychotherapy and Sociodrama.* Washington, D.C.: U.S. Government Printing Office, Nervous and Mental Disease Monograph 58; Washington, D.C.: Beacon House.

Morgan, David L. (1988). *Focus Groups as Qualitative Research.* Qualitative Research Methods Volume 16. Newbury Park, Calif.: Sage.

Morgan, David L., and Margaret T. Spanish (1984). "Focus Groups: A New Tool for Qualitative Research." *Qualitative Sociology* 7:253–270.

Morrison, David (1976a). Paul Lazarsfeld: The Biography of an Institutional Innovator." Ph.D. dissertation, Leicester University.

―――― (1976b). "Paul Lazarsfeld 1901–1976: A Tribute." *Osterreichische Zeitschrift für Soziologie* 213:7–9.

―――― (1978). "Kultur and Culture: The Case of Theodor W. Adorno and Paul F. Lazarsfeld." *Social Research* 45 (2):331–355.

―――― (1988). "The Transference of Experience and the Impact of Ideas: Paul Lazarsfeld and Mass Communication Research." *Communication* 10:185–209.

Morrison, Denton E., and Ramon E. Henkel (eds.) (1970). *The Significance Controversy: A Reader.* Chicago: Aldine.

Motley, Michael T. (1990). "On Whether One Can(not) Not Communicate: An Examination via Traditional Communication Postulates." *Western Journal of Speech Communication* 54:1–20.

Mott, Frank Luther (1991/1950). *American Journalism: A History of Newspapers in the United States Through 260 years: 1690 to 1950.* New York: Macmillan.

Mullins, Nicholas C. (1973). *Theories and Theory Groups in Contemporary American Sociology.* New York: Harper & Row.

Muth, Rodney (1990). "Harold Dwight Lasswell: A Biographical Profile." In Rodney Muth, Mary M. Finley, and Marcia F. Muth (eds.), *Harold D. Lasswell: An Annotated Biography,* pp. 1–48. New Haven: New Haven Press.

Muth, Rodney, Mary M. Finley, and Marcia F. Muth (eds.) (1990). *Harold D. Lasswell: An Annotated Biography.* New Haven: New Haven Press; also Dordrecht (Netherlands): Kluwen Academic Publishers.

Mutz, Diana E. (1987). "Political Alienation and Knowledge Acquisition." In Margaret McLaughlin (ed.), *Communication Yearbook 10,* pp. 470–498. Newbury Park, Calif.: Sage.

Mydral, Gunnar (1944). *An American Dilemma* New York: Harper and Brothers.

Nafziger, Ralph O. (July 8, 1970). Oral history interview by David Clark, State Historical Society of Wisconsin, Madison.

Nafziger, Ralph O., and David Manning White (eds.) (1949). *Introduction to Journalism Research.* Baton Rouge: Louisiana State University Press.

―――― (eds.) (1958). *Introduction to Mass Communication Research.* Baton Rouge: Louisiana State University Press.

Nelson, Harold L. (1987). "Founding Father: Willard Grosvener Bleyer, 1873–1935." *Journalism Monographs* 104:5–6.

Nelson, Lyle M. (1977). "The Stanford Years." In Daniel Lerner and Lyle M. Nelson (eds.), *Communication Research: A Half-Century Appraisal,* pp. 317–324. Honolulu: University Press of Hawaii.

—— (November 19, 1992). Personal correspondence with Everett M. Rogers.

Neurath, Paul (1983). "Paul F. Lazarsfeld and the Institutionalization of Empirical Social Research." In Robert B. Smith (ed.), *A Handbook of Social Research Methods,* pp. 365–382. Cambridge, Mass.: Ballinger.

Nyquist, H. (1924). "Certain Factors Affecting Telegraph Speed." *Bell System Technical Journal* 3:324–346.

Odum, Howard W. (1951). *American Sociology: The Story of Sociology in the United States through 1950.* New York: Longmans, Green.

Oliver, Bernard M. (June 2, 1992). Personal interview by Everett M. Rogers, Palo Alto, California.

Osgood, Charles E., George J. Suci, and Percy H. Tannenbaum (1957/1975). *The Measurement of Meaning.* Urbana: University of Illinois Press.

Osgood, Charles E., and Percy H. Tannenbaum (1955). "The Principle of Congruity in the Prediction of Attitude Change." *Psychological Review* 62:42–55.

Oukrop, Carol Christensen (1965). "A History of the University of Iowa School of Journalism, from Its Founding in 1924 under C.H. Weller, Through the Tenure of Wilbur Schramm as Director, June, 1947." Master's thesis, University of Iowa.

Pacanowsky, Michael (1988). "Communication in the Empowering Organization." In James A. Anderson (ed.), *Communication Yearbook 11,* pp. 356–404. Newbury Park, Calif.: Sage.

Paisley, William (1984). "Communication in the Communications Sciences," in Brenda Dervin and Melvin J. Voigt (eds.), *Progress in the Communication Sciences.* Norwood, N.J.: Ablex, pp. 1–43.

Park, Robert E. (1922). *The Immigrant Press and Its Control.* New York: Harper.

—— (1923). "The Natural History of the Newspaper." *American Journal of Sociology* 28:273–289.

—— (1929a). "Life History." Unpublished paper. University of Chicago Library, Department of Special Collections, Ernest W. Burgess Papers, Box 1F, Folder 1.

———— (1929b). "The City as a Social Laboratory." In T.V. Smith and Leonard D. White (eds.), *Chicago: An Experiment in Social Science Research.* Chicago: University of Chicago Press.

———— (1922b/1982). "Notes on the Origins of the Society for Social Research." *Journal of the History of the Behavioral Sciences* 18(4):337–338.

———— (1950/1974). *Race and Culture.* New York: Free Press (edited by Everett Cherrington Hughes, Charles S. Johnson, Jitsuichi Masuoke, Robert Redfield, and Lewis Wirth, *The Collected Papers of Robert Ezra Park, Volume 1,* New York: Arno Press).

Park, Robert E., and Ernest W. Burgess (1924). *Introduction to the Science of Sociology.* Chicago: University of Chicago Press.

Parsons, Talcott (1949). *The Structure of Social Action.* New York: Free Press.

Pasanella, Ann (1990). "The Mind Traveler: Searching for the History of the Columbia School of Communication Research Through the Paul Lazarsfeld Papers at Columbia University." New York: Columbia University, Gannett Center for Media Studies.

———— (October 31, 1992). Personal correspondence with Everett M. Rogers.

Patnoe, Shelley (1988). *A Narrative History of Experimental Social Psychology: The Lewin Tradition.* New York: Springer-Verlag.

Peel, J. D. Y. (1971). *Herbert Spencer: The Evolution of a Sociologist.* New York: Basic Books.

Pelz, Edith Bennett (1958). "Some Factors in Group Decision." In Eleanor E. Maccoby, Theodore M. Newcomb, and Eugene L. Hartley (eds.), *Readings in Social Psychology,* pp. 212–219. 3d ed. New York: Holt, Rinehart and Winston.

Perry, Helen Swick (1982). *Psychiatrist of America: The Life of Harry Stack Sullivan,* Cambridge: Belknap Press of Harvard University Press.

Persons, Stow (1990). *The University of Iowa in the Twentieth Century: An Institutional History.* Iowa City: University of Iowa Press.

Peters, Charles C. (1933/1970). *Motion Pictures and Standards of Morality.* New York: Macmillan; New York: Arno Press.

Peters, John Durham (1989). "Democracy and American Communication Theory: Dewey, Lippmann, Lazarsfeld." *Communication* 11:199–220.

Peterson, Ruth C., and L. L. Thurstone (1933/1970). *Motion Pictures and the Social Attitudes of Children.* New York: Macmillan; New York: Arno Press.

Petty, Richard E., and John T. Cacioppo (1981). *Attitudes and Persuasion: Classic and Contemporary Approaches.* Dubuque, Iowa: William C. Brown.

_____ (1986). "The Elaboration Likelihood Model of Persuasion." *Advances in Experimental Social Psychology* 19:123–205.

Philipsen, Gerry (1975). "Speaking 'Like Men' in Teamsterville: Cultural Patterns of Role Enactment in an Urban Neighborhood." *Quarterly Journal of Speech* 61:13–22.

_____ (1976). "Places for Speaking in Teamsterville." *Quarterly Journal of Speech* 62:15–25.

Pierce, J. R. (1973). "The Early Days of Information Theory." *IEEE Transactions on Information Theory* IT-19:3–8.

_____ (August 17, 1990). Personal interview by Everett M. Rogers, Stanford, California.

Pool, Ithiel de Sola (1969). "Content Analysis and the Intelligence Function." In Arnold A. Rogow (ed.), *Politics, Personality, and Social Science in the Twentieth Century: Essays in Honor of Harold D. Lasswell,* pp. 198–223. Chicago: University of Chicago Press.

_____ (ed.) (1977). *The Social Impact of the Telephone.* Cambridge: MIT Press.

_____ (1983a). *Technologies of Freedom.* Cambridge: Belknap Press of Harvard University Press.

_____ (1983b). *Forecasting the Telephone: A Retrospective Technology Assessment.* Norwood, N.J.:Ablex.

Ithiel de Sola Pool with others (1952/1970). *The Prestige Press: A Comparative Study of Political Symbols.* Cambridge: MIT Press.

Prewitt, Kenneth (1991). "Social Sciences and Private Philanthropy: The Quest for Social Relevance." Paper presented at the Conference on Foundations, the Research University, and the Creation of Knowledge, Centennial of the University of Chicago.

Pulitzer, Joseph (May, 1904). "The College of Journalism." *North American Review* 178:641–680.

Punch, Maurice (1986). *The Politics and Ethics of Fieldwork.* Newbury Park, Calif.: Sage.

Putnam, Linda L., and Michael E. Pacanowsky (eds.) (1983). *Communication and Organizations: An Interpretive Approach.* Newbury Park, Calif.: Sage.

Qualter, T.H. (1962). *Propaganda and Psychological Warfare.* New York: Random House.

―――― (1985). *Opinion Control in the Democracies.* New York: St. Martin's Press.

Quandt, Jean B. (1970). *From the Small Town to the Great Community: The Social Thought of Progressive Intellectuals.* New Brunswick, N.J.: Rutgers University Press.

Quinton, Anthony (1974). "Critical Theory: On the Frankfurt School." *Encounter* 43–53.

Radke, Marian, and Dana Klisurich (1947). "Experiments in Changing Food Habits." *Journal of the American Dietetic Association* 24:403–409.

Radway, Janice A. (1984). *Reading the Romance: Women, Patriarchy, and Popular Literature.* Chapel Hill: University of North Carolina Press.

Raushenbush, Winifred (1979). *Robert E. Park: Biography of a Sociologist.* Durham, N.C.: Duke University Press.

Reardon, Kathleen K. (1981). *Persuasion: Theory and Context.* Newbury Park, Calif.: Sage.

Reardon, Kathleen K., and Everett M. Rogers (1988). "Interpersonal Versus Mass Communication: A False Dichotomy?" *Human Communication Research* 15 (2):284–303.

Reilly, Richard R. (1971). "A Note on 'Clozentrophy': A Procedure for Testing English Language Proficiency of Foreign Students." *Speech Monographs* 38:350–353.

Rieber, Robert W. (1989). "In Search of the Impertinent Question: An Overview of Bateson's Theory of Communication." In Robert W. Rieber (ed.), *The Individual, Communication, and Society: Essays in Memory of Gregory Bateson,* pp. 1–28. New York: Cambridge University Press.

Riley, John W., and Wilbur Schramm (1951a). *The Reds Take a City: The Communist Occupation of Seoul.* New Brunswick, N.J.: Rutgers University Press.

―――― (1951b). "Communication in the Sovietized State, as Demonstrated in Korea." *American Sociological Review* 16:757–766.

Riley, John W., Wilbur Schramm, and Fred W. Williams (1951). "Flight from Communism: A Report on Korean Refugees." *Public Opinion Quarterly* 15:274–284.

Riley, Mathilda White (1960). "Membership of the American Sociological Association 1950–1959." *American Sociological Review* 25:914–926.

Ritchie, David (1986). "Shannon and Weaver: Unraveling the Paradox of Information." *Communication Research* 13:278–298.

Ritchie, David (1991). *Information.* Newbury Park, Calif.: Sage.

_____ (1992). "Conceptualizing Information in Human Communication: Is the 'Scarce Resources' Assumption Useful?" Unpublished paper. Portland State University, Department of Communication.

Robinson, Gertrude J. (1988). "Here Be Dragons: Problems in Charting the United States' History of Communication Studies." *Communication* 10 (2):97–119.

Rockefeller Communication Seminar (October 17, 1940a), *Needed Research in Communication.* New York, Rockefeller Foundation Report. U.S. Library of Congress, Papers of Lyman Bryson, Box 18.

_____ (November 1, 1940b). *Public Opinion and the Emergency.* New York, Rockefeller Foundation Report. U.S. Library of Congress, Papers of Lyman Bryson, Box 18.

Rockefeller Foundation (January 18, 1941). *Memorandum on Communications Conference.* New York, Rockefeller Foundation Report. U.S. Library of Congress, Papers of Lyman Bryson, Box 18.

Rogers, Everett M. (1983). *Diffusion of Innovations.* New York: Free Press.

_____ (1985). "The Empirical and Critical School of Communication." In Everett M. Rogers and Francis Balle (eds.), *The Media Revolution in America and in Western Europe.* pp. 219–235. Norwood, N.J.: Ablex.

_____ (1986). *Communication Technology: The New Media in Society.* New York: Free Press.

_____ (1992). "On Early Mass Communication Research." *Journal of Broadcasting and Electronic Media* 36(4):467–471.

_____ (1993). "Looking Back, Looking Forward: A Century of Communication Study." In Philip Gaunt (ed.), *Beyond Agendas: New Directions in Communication Research.* pp. 19–39. Westport, Conn.: Greenwood.

Rogers, Everett M., and Steven H. Chaffee (1992). "Communication and Journalism from Daddy Bleyer to Wilbur Schramm: A Palimpsest." Paper presented at the Association for Journalism and Mass Communication, Montreal.

Rogers, Everett M., and James W. Dearing (1988). "Agenda-Setting Research: Where Has It Been, Where Is It Going?" In James A. Anderson (ed.), *Communication Yearbook,* pp. 555–594. Newbury Park, Calif.: Sage.

Rogers, Everett M., James W. Dearing, and Dorine Bregman (1993). "The Anatomy of Agenda-Setting Research." *Journal of Communication,* 43(2):68–84.

Rogers, Everett M., James W. Dearing, and Soonbum Chang (1991). *AIDS in the 1990s: The Agenda-Setting Process for a Public Issue.* Columbia, SC: Association for Education in Journalism and Mass Communication, Journalism Monographs 126.

Rogers, Everett M., and D. Lawrence Kincaid (1981). *Communication Networks: Toward a New Paradigm for Research.* New York: Free Press.

Rogers, Everett M., and Thomas Valente (1992). "A History of Information Theory in Communication Research." In Jorge Reina Schement and Brent Reuben (eds.), *Information and Behavior* 4:35–56.

Rogers, L. Edna (September 6, 1992). Personal correspondence with Everett M. Rogers.

Rogers, L. Edna, and Richard V. Farace (1975). "Analysis of Relational Communication in Dyads: New Measurement Procedures." *Human Communication Research* 1:222–239.

Rogow, Arnold A. (ed.) (1969). *Politics, Personality and Social Science in the Twentieth Century: Essays in Honor of Harold D. Lasswell.* Chicago: University of Chicago Press.

Rokeach, Milton (1960). *The Open and Closed Mind.* New York: Basic Books.

Roloff, N. E., and Gerald R. Miller (eds.) (1980). *Persuasion: New Directions in Theory and Research.* Newbury Park, Calif.: Sage.

Rosenberg, Milton J., and Carl I. Hovland (1960). *Attitude Organization and Change.* New Haven: Yale University Press.

Rosenberg, Milton J., et al. (1960). *Attitude Organization and Change: An Analysis of Consistency among Attitude Components.* New Haven: Yale University Press.

Rosenblith, Walter A., and Jerome B. Wiesner (1965). "Norbert Wiener: 1894–1964." *Journal of Nervous and Mental Disease* 140 (1):3–8.

Rosengren, Karl Erik (1983). "Communication Research: One Paradigm or Four?" *Journal of Communication* 33 (3):185–207.

Rosenstock, Irwin M. (1966). "Why People Use Health Services." *Millbank Memorial Fund Quarterly* 44:94–127.

Ross, Donald K. (1957). "Willard G. Bleyer and Journalism Education." *Journalism Quarterly* 34 (3):466–474.

Ross, Dorothy (1991). *The Origins of American Social Science.* New York: Cambridge University Press.

Rosten, Leo (1937). *The Washington Correspondents.* New York: Harcourt, Brace.

_____ (1941). *Hollywood: The Movie Colony, the Movie Makers.* New York: Harcourt, Brace.

_____ (1969). "Harold Lasswell: A Memoir." In Arnold A. Rogow (ed.), *Politics, Personality, and Social Science in the Twentieth Century: Essays in Honor of Harold D. Lasswell,* pp. 1–13. Chicago: University of Chicago Press.

Rowland, Willard D. Jr. (1983). *The Politics of TV Violence: Policy Uses of Communication Research.* Newbury Park, Calif.: Sage.

Rubenstein, Robert, and Harold D. Lasswell (1966). *Sharing the Power in a Psychiatric Hospital.* New Haven: Yale University Press.

Rucker, Darnell (1969). *The Chicago Pragmatists.* Minneapolis: University of Minnesota Press.

Ruiz [no given name] (1979). *Marx for Beginners.* New York: Pantheon Books.

Ryan, Bryce, and Neal C. Gross (1943). "The Diffusion of Hybrid Seed Corn in Two Iowa Communities." *Rural Sociology* 8:15–24.

Sahakian, William S. (1974). *Systematic Social Psychology.* New York: Chandler.

Samelson, Franz (1986). "Authoritarianism from Berlin to Berkeley: On Social Psychology and History." *Journal of Social Issues* 42 (1):191–208.

Sandage, Charles H. (October 29, 1991). Personal interview by Everett M. Rogers, Urbana, Illinois.

Sandelands, Lloyd E. (1990). "What Is So Practical About Theory? Lewin Revisited." *Journal for the Theory of Social Behavior* 20 (3):235–262.

Sanford, R. Nevitt (September 10, 1984). "This Week's Citation Classic: Adorno and Others' *The Authoritarian Personality.*" *ISI Current Contents,* p. 16.

_____ (1986). "A Personal Account of the Study of Authoritarianism: Comment on Samelson." *Journal of Social Issues* 42 (1):209–214.

Schmidt, John C. (1986). *Johns Hopkins: Portrait of a University.* Baltimore: Johns Hopkins University Press.

Schramm, Wilbur Lang (1935). *Approaches to a Science of English Verse.* Iowa City: University of Iowa.

—— (1942–1943). "A Confidential and Shameless Biography of Wilbur Schramm." Folder L3, Schramm Papers, Iowa City, University of Iowa Libraries, Special Collections Department.

—— (1947a). "Education for Journalism: Vocational, General, or Professional?" *Journal of General Education* 1 (2):90–98.

—— (1947b). *Windwagon Smith and Other Yarns.* New York: Harcourt, Brace.

—— (ed.) (1948). *Communications in Modern Society.* Urbana: University of Illinois Press.

—— (ed.) (1954). *The Process and Effects of Mass Communication.* Urbana: University of Illinois Press.

—— (1955). "Information Theory and Mass Communication." *Journalism Quarterly* 32:131–146.

—— (1959a). "Comments on Berelson." *Public Opinion Quarterly* 23(1):6–9.

—— (1959b). *One Day in the World's Press.* Stanford: Stanford University Press.

—— (1964). *Mass Media and National Development.* Stanford: Stanford University Press.

—— (1971). "The Nature of Communication between Humans." In Wilbur Schramm and Donald F. Roberts (eds.), *Process and Effects of Mass Communication,* pp. 3–53. Rev. ed. Urbana: University of Illinois Press.

—— (1978). *Men, Messages, and Media: A Look at Human Communication.* New York: Harper & Row.

—— (March 30, 1979). Personal interview by John Stevens, conducted at the University of Michigan, Ann Arbor, and held in the Wisconsin Historical Society, Madison.

—— (1980). "The Beginnings of Communication Research in the United States." In Dan Nimmo (ed.), *Communication Yearbook 4,* pp. 73–82. New Brunswick, N.J.: Transaction Books.

—— (April 14, 1981). "There Were Giants in the Earth in These Days." Les Moeller lecture, Iowa City, University of Iowa, School of Journalism and Mass Communication.

―――― (1985). "The Beginnings of Communication Study in the United States." In Everett M. Rogers and Francis Balle (eds.), *The Media Revolution in America and Western Europe.* pp. 200–211. Norwood, N.J.: Ablex.

―――― (1988). "Palimpsest." In Erik Barnouw (ed.), *International Encyclopedia of Communication.* New York: Oxford University Press.

―――― (in press a). "The Master Teachers." In Everette E. Dennis and Ellen Wartella (eds.), *American Communication Research: The Remembered History.* New York: Freedom Forum Media Studies Center.

―――― (in press b). *The Beginnings of Communication Study in America: A Personal Memoir.* Newbury Park, Calif.: Sage.

Schramm, Wilbur, Jack Lyle and Edwin B. Parker (1961). *Television in the Lives of Our Children.* Stanford: Stanford University Press.

Schramm, Wilbur, Jack Lyle, and Ithiel de Sola Pool (1963). *The People Look at Educational Television.* Stanford: Stanford University Press.

Schramm, Wilbur, and William E. Porter (1982). *Men, Women, Messages, and Media: Understanding Human Communication.* 2d ed. New York: Harper and Row.

Schramm, Wilbur, and John Riley (1951). *The Reds Take a City: The Communist Occupation of Seoul with Eye-Witness Accounts.* New Brunswick, N.J.: Rutgers University Press.

Schramm, Wilbur, and Donald Roberts (eds.) (1971). *The Process and Effects of Mass Communication.* Rev. ed. Urbana: University of Illinois Press.

Schultz, Duane (1975). *A History of Modern Psychology.* 2d ed. New York: Academic Press.

Seaman, Melvin (1959). "Alienation." *American Sociological Review* 24:783–791.

Sears, Robert R. (1985). "Psychoanalysis and Behavior Theory, 1907–1965." In Sigmund Koch and David E. Leary (eds.), *A Century of Psychology as Science,* pp. 208–220. New York: McGraw-Hill.

Segal, Lynn (1986). *The Dream of Reality: Heinz von Foerster's Constructionism.* New York: Norton.

Selvin, Hanan C. (1957). "A Critique of Tests of Significance in Survey Research." *American Sociological Review* 23:519–527.

―――― (1976). "Durkheim, Booth and Yule: The Non-Diffusion of an Intellectual Innovation." *Archives of European Sociology* 17:39–51.

Serevin, Werner J., with James W. Tankard, Jr. (1988). *Communication Theories: Origins, Methods, Uses.* 2d ed. New York: Longman.

Shannon, Claude E. (1940). "An Algebra for Theoretical Genetics." Ph.D. dissertation, MIT.

—— (1945). "A Mathematical Theory of Cryptography." Memorandum. New York: Bell Telephone Laboratories.

—— (1948). "A Mathematical Theory of Communication." *Bell System Technical Journal* 27:379–423, 623–656.

—— (1949a). "Communication in the Presence of Noise." *Proceedings of the I.R.E.* 37:10–21.

—— (1949b). "Communication Theory of Secrecy Systems." *Bell System Technical Journal* 28:656–715.

—— (1949c). "The Mathematical Theory of Communication." In Claude E. Shannon and Warren Weaver (eds.), *The Mathematical Theory of Communication,* pp. 29–125. Urbana: University of Illinois Press.

—— (1956). "The Bandwagon." *IEE Transactions on Information Theory* 2 (3):3.

—— (July 28, 1982). Personal interview with Robert Price, Boston.

Shannon, Claude E., and Warren Weaver (1949). *The Mathematical Theory of Communication.* Urbana: University of Illinois Press.

Sheingold, Carl A. (1973). "Social Networks and Voting: The Resurrection of a Research Agenda." *American Sociological Review* 38:712–720.

Sheriden, Phyllis Barker (1979). "The Research Bureau in a University Context: A Case History of a Marginal Institution." D.Ed. thesis, Columbia University.

Sherif, Muzafer, and Carl I. Hovland (1961). *Social Judgement: Assimilation and Contrast Effects in Communication and Attitude Change.* New Haven: Yale University Press.

Shibutani, Tamotsu (November 3, 1990). Personal interview with Everett M. Rogers, Santa Barbara, California.

Shils, Edward (1970). "Tradition, Ecology, and Institution in the History of Sociology." *Daedulus* 49 (4):760–825.

—— (1981). "Some Academics, Mainly in Chicago." *American Scholar* 50:179–196.

────── (ed.) (1991). *Remembering the University of Chicago: Teachers, Scientists, and Scholars.* Chicago: University of Chicago Press.

Shoemaker, Pamela (1991). *Gatekeeping.* Newbury Park, Calif.: Sage.

Shonle, Ruth (1926). "Suicide: A Study of Personal Disorganization." Ph.D. dissertation, University of Chicago.

Shuttleworth, Frank K., and Mark A. May (1933/1970). *The Social Conduct and Attitudes of Movie Fans.* New York: Macmillan; New York: Arno Press.

Sibley, Elbridge (1974). *Social Science Research Council: The First Fifty Years.* New York: Social Science Research Council.

Sieber, Sam D. (1972). *Reforming the University: The Role of the Social Research Center.* New York: Praeger.

Siebert, Frederick S. (April 21, 1970). Oral history interview by Robert V. Hudson, Historical Society of Wisconsin, Madison.

Siebert, Fred S., Theodore Peterson, and Wilbur Schramm (1956). *Four Theories of the Press.* Urbana: University of Illinois Press.

Sills, David L. (1957). *The Volunteers: Means and Ends in a National Organization.* New York: Free Press.

────── (1981). "Surrogates, Institutes, and the Search for Convergences: The Research Style of Paul F. Lazarsfeld." *Contemporary Sociology* 10:351–361.

────── (1987). "Paul F. Lazarsfeld: 1901–1976." In National Academy of Sciences (ed.), *Bibliographical Memoirs,* 56:251–282. Washington, D.C.: National Academy Press.

Simmel, Georg (1922/1955). *The Web of Group-Affiliations.* Translated by Kurt F. Wolf and Reinhard Bendix. New York: Free Press.

Sinclair, Upton (1906/1981). *The Jungle.* New York: Bantam Books.

Singhal, Arvind, and Everett M. Rogers (1989a). "Pro-Social Television for Development in India." In Ronald E. Rice and Charles Atkin (eds.), *Public Communication Campaigns,* pp. 331–350. Newbury Park, Calif.: Sage.

────── (1989b). *India's Information Revolution.* Newbury Park, Calif.: Sage.

Slepian, David (1974). *Key Papers in the Development of Information Theory.* New York: IEEE Press.

Sloan, William David (ed.) (1990). *Makers of the Media Mind: Journalism Educators and Their Ideas.* Hillsdale, N.J.: Lawrence Erlbaum.

Smith, Adam (1776/1986). *The Wealth of Nations.* New York: Penguin Books.

Smith, Bruce Lannes (1969). "The Mystifying Intellectual History of Harold D. Laswell." In Arnold A. Rogow (ed.), *Politics, Personality, and Social Science in the Twentieth Century: Essays in Honor of Harold D. Lasswell,* pp. 41–105 Chicago: University of Chicago Press.

Smith, Bruce Lannes, Harold Lasswell, and Ralph D. Casey (1946). *Propanganda, Communication, and Public Opinion.* Princeton, N.J.: Princeton University Press.

Smith, David, and Phil Evans (1982). *Marx's Kapital for Beginners.* New York: Pantheon Books.

Smith, Dennis (1988). *The Chicago School: A Liberal Critique of Capitalism.* New York: St. Martin's Press.

Smith, James Allen (1991). *The Idea Brokers: Think Tanks and the Rise of the New Policy Elite.* New York: Free Press.

Smith, M. Brewster (1950). "Review of *The Authoritarian Personality.*" *Journal of Abnormal and Social Psychology* 45:775–779.

—— (1968). "Samuel A. Stouffer." In David L. Sills (ed.), *International Encyclopedia of the Social Sciences,* 15:277–280. New York: Macmillan.

—— (1983). "The Shaping of American Social Psychology: A Personal Perspective from the Periphery." *Personality and Social Psychology Bulletin* 9 (2):165–180.

—— (1990). "Else Frenkel-Brunswik: 1908–1958." In A. N. O'Connell and N. F. Russo (eds.), *Women in Psychology,* pp. 88–95. Westport, Conn.: Greenwood Press.

—— (March 12, 1992). Personal interview by Everett M. Rogers, Santa Cruz, California.

Smith, Sally Bedell (1990). *In All His Glory: The Life of William S. Paley.* New York: Simon and Schuster/Touchstone.

Smith, T.V., and Leonard D. White (1929). *Chicago: An Experiment in Social Science Research.* Chicago: University of Chicago Press.

Snider, Paul B. (1967). "Mr. Gates Revisited: A 1966 Version of the 1949 Case Study." *Journalism Quarterly* 44:419–427.

Solberg, Winston U. (November 15, 1991). Personal correspondence with Everett M. Rogers.

Spencer, Herbert (1891). *The Study of Sociology*. New York: Appleton.

Sproule, J. Michael (1987). "Propaganda Studies in American Social Science: The Rise and Fall of the Critical Paradigm." *Quarterly Journal of Speech* 73:60–78.

————— (1989). "Social Responses to Twentieth-Century Propaganda." In Ted J. Smith III (ed.), *Propaganda: A Pluralistic Perspective,* pp. 5–22. New York: Praeger.

————— (1991). "Propaganda and American Ideological Critique." In James A. Anderson (ed.), *Communication Yearbook 14,* pp. 211–239. Newbury Park, Calif.: Sage.

Spykman, Nicholas J. (1966). *The Social Theory of Georg Simmel*. New York: Atherton Press.

Stanton, Frank (November 29, 1991). Personal correspondence with Everett M. Rogers.

————— (November 30, 1992). Personal correspondence with Everett M. Rogers.

Starck, Kenneth (December 27, 1991). Personal correspondence with Everett M. Rogers.

Steel, Ronald (1981). *Walter Lippmann and the American Century*. New York: Vintage Books.

Stehr, Nico (1982). "A Conversation with Paul F. Lazarsfeld." *American Sociologist* 17:150–155.

Steiner, Linda (1992). *Construction of Gender in Newsreporting Textbooks*. Columbia, S.C.: Association for Education in Journalism and Mass Communication, Journalism Monographs 135.

Steir, Frederick (1989). "Wiener, Norbert (1894–1964)." In Eric Barnow (ed.), *International Encyclopedia of Communication,* pp. 318–319. New York: Oxford University Press.

Stempel, Guido H. III (January 1988). "The Chi-Squares Strike Back: Academic Research Presents an Opportunity, Not a Threat." *Quill,* pp. 30–31.

————— (November 5, 1992). Personal correspondence with Everett M. Rogers.

Stivens, Eugene, and Susan Wheelan (eds.) (1986). *The Lewin Legacy: Field Theory in Current Practice*. Berlin: Springer-Verlag.

Stockanes, Harriet (December 11, 1990). Personal correspondence with Everett M. Rogers.

Stocking, George (1979). *Anthropology at Chicago: Tradition, Discipline, Department*. Chicago: University of Chicago Press.

Stoddard, George D. (1943). *The Meaning of Intelligence*. New York: Macmillan.

–––––– (1950). "Carl Emil Seashore: 1866–1949." *American Journal of Psychology* 63:456–462.

–––––– (1955). *Krebiozen: The Great Cancer Mystery*. Boston: Beacon Press.

–––––– (1971). "An Autobiography." In Robert J. Havighurst (ed.), *Leaders in American Education*. pp. 321–354. Chicago: University of Chicago Press.

Stonequist, Everett V. (1937). *The Marginal Man*. New York: Charles Scribner's Sons.

Stouffer, Samuel A. (February 17, 1941). Letter to Frederick C. Mills, Columbia University, Butler Library, Rare Books and Manuscript Library.

Stouffer, Samuel A., Arthur A. Lumsdaine, Marion H. Lumsdaine, Robin M. Williams, Jr., M. Brewster Smith, Irving L. Janis, Shirley A. Star, and Leonard S. Cottrell, Jr. (1949a). *The American Soldier: Combat and Its Aftermath: Studies in Social Psychology in World War II*. Princeton, N.J.: Princeton University Press.

Stouffer, Samuel A., Edward A. Suchman, Leland C. DeVinney, Shirley A. Star, and Robin M. Williams, Jr. (1949b). *The American Soldier: Adjustment During Army Life: Studies in Social Psychology in World War II*. Princeton, N.J.: Princeton University Press.

Stouffer, Samuel A., Louis Guttman, Edward A. Suchman, Paul F. Lazarsfeld, Shirley A. Star, and John A. Clausen (1950). *Measurement and Prediction: Studies in Social Psychology in World War II*. Princeton, N.J.: Princeton University Press.

Struik, Dirk J. (1966). "Norbert Wiener: Colleague and Friend." *American Dialog*, 34–37.

Sullivan, Harry Stack (1953). *The Interpersonal Theory of Psychiatry*. New York: Norton.

Sulloway, Frank J. (1979). *Freud, Biologist of the Mind: Beyond the Psychoanalytic Legend*. New York: Basic Books.

–––––– (1991). "Reassessing Freud's Case Histories: The Social Construction of Psychoanalysis." *Isis* 82:245–275.

Szasz, Thomas (1978). *The Myth of Psychotherapy: Mental Healing as Religion, Rhetoric, and Repression*. Garden City, N.Y.: Anchor Press/Doubleday.

Sztompka, Piotr (1986). *Robert K. Merton: An Intellectual Profile.* New York: St. Martin's Press.

Tankard, James W., Jr. (1984). *The Statistical Pioneers.* Cambridge, Mass.: Schenckman.

_____ (1990). "Maxwell McCombs, Donald Shaw and Agenda-Setting." In William D. Sloan (ed.), *Makers of the Media Mind: Journalism Educators and Their Ideas,* pp. 278–285. Hillsdale, N.J.: Lawrence Erlbaum.

Tarde, Gabriel (1903). *The Laws of Imitation.* Translated by Elsie Clews Parsons. New York: Holt.

Taylor, Wilson L. (1953). "'Cloze Procedure': A New Tool For Measuring Readability." *Journalism Quarterly* 30:415–453.

_____ (1956). "Recent Development in the Use of Cloze Procedure." *Journalism Quarterly* 33:42–48.

_____ (1957). "'Cloze' Readability Scores as Indices of Individual Differences in Comprehension and Aptitude." *Journal of Applied Psychology* 41:19–26.

Tebbel, John (October 10, 1964). "What's Happening to Journalism Education?" *Saturday Review,* pp. 103–104, 109.

Thomas, William I., and Florian Znaniecki (1927/1984). *The Polish Peasant in Europe and America.* New York: Knopf; Urbana: University of Illinois Press.

Thorne, Barrie (1990). "Science with a Conscience: A Review of Ellen Fitzpatrick's *Endless Crusade: Women Social Scientists and Progressive Reform. Women's Review of Books* 7(9):22.

Thrasher, Frederic M. (1927/1963). *The Gang: A Study of 1,313 Gangs in Chicago.* Chicago: University of Chicago Press.

Thurstone, L. L., and E. J. Chave (1929). *The Measurement of Attitude: A Psychophysical Method and Some Experiments with a Scale for Measuring Attitude Toward the Church.* Chicago: University of Chicago Press.

Tichener, E. B. (1921). "Wilhem Wundt." *American Journal of Psychology* 32(2):161–178.

Toby, Jackson (1980). "Samuel A. Stouffer: Social Research as a Calling." In Robert K. Merton and Mathilda White Riley (eds.), *Sociological Traditions from Generation to Generation: Glimpses of the American Experience,* pp. 131–151. Norwood, N.J.: Ablex.

Torgerson, Douglas (1990). "Origins of the Policy Orientation: The Aesthetic Dimension in Lasswell's Political Vision." *History of Political Thought,* 40(2):339–351.

_____ (July 16, 1991). Personal correspondence with Everett M. Rogers.

Towers, Wayne M. (1977). "Lazarsfeld and Adorno in the United States: A Case Study in Theoretical Orientations." In Brent D. Ruben (ed.), *Communication Yearbook 1,* pp. 133–145. New Brunswick, N.J.: Transaction Books.

Trahair, Richard C. S. (1981–1982). "Elton Mayo and the Early Political Psychology of Harold D. Lasswell." *Political Psychology* 3:170–198.

Troldahl, Verling C. (1968). "Perspectives in Studying Communication." Unpublished manuscript. East Lansing, Michigan State University, Department of Communication.

Tropp, Henry S. (1984). "Origin of the Term Bit." *Annals of the History of Computing* 6 (8):152–155.

Trujillo, Nick, and George Dionisopoulos (1987). "Cop Talk, Police Stories, and the Social Construction of Organizational Drama." *Central States Speech Journal* 33:196–209.

Turner, Ralph H. (1967). Introduction to *Robert E. Park on Social Control and Collective Behavior,* pp. ix–xivi. Chicago: University of Chicago Press.

Turner, Stephen Park, and Jonathan H. Turner (1990). *The Impossible Science: An Institutional Analysis of American Sociology.* Newbury Park, Calif.: Sage.

Valente, Thomas (1991). "Thresholds and the Critical Mass in the Diffusion of Innovations." Ph.D. dissertation, University of Southern California.

Van Maanen, John (1988). *Tales of the Field: On Writing Ethnography.* Chicago: University of Chicago Press.

Veblen, Thorstein (1926). *Theory of the Leisure Class.* New York: Vanguard Press.

Verdú, Sergio (September 1990). "The First Forty Years of the Shannon Theory." *IEEE Information Theory Society Newsletter,* pp. 1, 4–10.

von Bertalanffy, Ludwig (1968). *General Systems Theory: Foundations, Development, Applications.* New York: Braziller.

von Neumann, John (May 1949). "Review of Norbert Wiener's *Cybernetics.*" *Physics Today,* pp. 33–34.

Wallace, Alfred Russell (1858). "On the Tendency of Varieties to Depart Indefinitely from the Original Type." *Journal of the Proceedings of the Linnaean Society of London (Zoology)* 3:53–62.

Waring, Ethel B. (March 14, 1964). Oral history interview, conducted by

Dolores Greenberg, Cornell University Library, Department of Manuscripts and University Archives.

Wartella, Ellen, and Byron Reeves (1985). "Historical Trends in Research on Children and the Media: 1900–1960." *Journal of Communication* 35:118–133.

Washington, Booker T., with the collaboration of Robert E. Park (1912). *The Man Farthest Down: A Record of Observation and Study in Europe.* Garden City, N.Y.: Doubleday, Page.

Watt, James H., Jr. and Robert Krull (1974). "An Information Theory Measure for Television Programming." *Communication Research* 1 (1):44–89.

Watzlawick, Paul (1981). "Hermetic Pragmaesthetics or Unkempt Thoughts about an Issue of *Family Process.*" *Family Process* 20:401–403.

Watzlawick, Paul, Janet Helmick Beavin, and Don D. Jackson (1967). *Pragmatics of Human Communication: A Study of Interaction Patterns, Pathologies, and Paradoxes.* New York: Norton.

Weakland, John H. (May 14, 1992). Personal interview with Everett M. Rogers, Palo Alto, California.

Weaver, Warren (July 1949a). "The Mathematics of Communication." *Scientific American* 181:11–15.

――― (1949b). "Recent Contributions to the Mathematical Theory of Communication." In Claude E. Shannon and Warren Weaver (eds.), *The Mathematical Theory of Communication,* pp. 1–28. Urbana: University of Illinois Press.

Weber, Marianne (1926/1975). *Max Weber: Ein Lebensbild.* Tübingen, Germany: J. C. B. Mohr.

Weber, Max (1930). *The Protestant Ethic and the Spirit of Capitalism.* Translated by Talcott Parsons. London: Allen and Unwin.

――― (1946). *From Max Weber: Essays in Sociology.* Translated by Hans Gerth and C. Wright Mills. New York: Oxford University Press.

Westbrook, Robert B. (1991). *John Dewey and American Democracy.* Ithaca, N.Y.: Cornell University Press.

Westley, Bruce H., and Malcolm S. MacLean, Jr. (1955). "A Conceptual Model for Communications Research." *Audio-Visual Communication Review* 3 (4):3–12.

Westrum, Ron (1991). *Technologies and Society: The Shaping of People and Things.* Belmont, Calif.: Wadsworth.

White, David Manning (1950). "'The Gate Keeper': A Case Study in the Selection of News." *Journalism Quarterly* 27:283–390.

———— (December 9, 1991). Personal correspondence with Everett M. Rogers.

White, Norton, and Lucia White (1962). *The Intellectual Versus the City: From Thomas Jefferson to Frank Lloyd Wright.* Cambridge: MIT Press.

White, Ralph K. (1943). "The Case for the Tolman-Lewin Interpretation of Learning." *Psychological Review,* 5 (3):157–186.

White, Ralph K. (June 5, 1992). Personal interview with Everett M. Rogers, Cockeysville, Maryland.

White, Ralph K., and Ronald Lippitt (1980). *Autocracy and Democracy: An Experimental Inquiry.* New York: Harper and Brothers.

Wiebe, Gerhard (May 18, 1981). Personal correspondence with Mark R. Levy.

Wiener, Norbert (February 1, 1942). *The Extrapolation, Interpolation, and Smoothing of Stationary Time Series with Engineering Applications.* Report to the National Defense Research Council. Cambridge, Mass.: MIT.

———— (1948). *Cybernetics: Or Control and Communication in the Animal and the Machine.* Cambridge: MIT Press.

———— (1949). "The Mathematical Theory of Communication: Review." Manuscript, MIT Libraries, Institute Archives and Special Collections.

———— (1950). *The Human Use of Human Beings: Cybernetics and Society.* Boston: Houghton Mifflin.

———— (1953). *Ex-Prodigy: My Childhood and Youth.* Cambridge: MIT Press.

———— (1956). "What Is Information Theory?" *IRE Transactions on Information Theory* IT-2:48.

———— (1964). *God and Golem, Inc.: A Comment on Certain Points Where Cybernetics Infringes on Religion.* Cambridge: MIT Press.

———— (1985). *Collected Works with Commentaries.* Cambridge: MIT Press.

Wilbers, Steven (1980). *The Iowa Writers' Workshop: Origins, Emergence, and Growth.* Iowa City: University of Iowa Press.

Wilder, Carol (1978). "From the Interactional View: A Conversation with Paul Watzlavick." *Journal of Communication* 28:35–45.

_____ (1979). "The Palo Alto Group: Difficulties and Directions of the Interactional View for Human Communication Research." *Human Communication Research* 5:171–186.

_____ (May 21, 1987). Personal interview by Everett M. Rogers, New Orleans.

Williams, Frederick, Ronald E. Rice, and Everett M. Rogers (1988). *Research Methods and New Media.* New York: Free Press.

Williams, Raymond (1976). *Keywords.* London: Fontana.

Williams, Robin M. Jr. (1984). "Field Observations and Surveys in Combat Zones," *Social Psychology Quarterly* 47(2):186–192.

Winett, Richard A. (1986). *Information and Behavior: Systems of Influence.* Hillsdale, N.J.: Lawrence Erlbaum.

Winkin, Yves (1992). "Baltasound as the Symbolic Capital of Social Interaction." Paper presented at the International Communication Association, Miami.

_____ (July 27, 1992). Personal correspondence with Everett M. Rogers.

Winkler, Allan M. (1978). *The Politics of Propaganda: The Office of War Information 1942–1945.* New Haven: Yale University Press.

Wirth, Louis (1926/1929). "The Ghetto: A Study in Isolation." Ph.D. dissertation, University of Chicago (published as *The Ghetto* in 1929 by the University of Chicago Press).

Wishbow, Nina (1987). "Applying the Concept of the Double Bind to Communication in Organizations." In Sari Thomas (ed.), *Studies in Communication,* pp. 114–121. Norwood, N.J.: Ablex.

Wolf, William B. (1973). "The Impact of Kurt Lewin on Management Thought." *Academy of Management Proceedings,* 322–325.

Young, Ruth C. (1988). "Is Population Ecology a Useful Paradigm for the Study of Organizations?" *American Journal of Sociology* 94(1):1–24.

_____ (1989). "Reply to Freeman and Hannan and Britlain and Wholey." *American Journal of Sociology* 95 (2):445–446.

Zajonc, R. B. (1992). "Cognition and Communication in Social Psychological Perspective." Paper presented at the Katz-Newcomb Lecture, Ann Arbor, University of Michigan.

Zeigarnik, Bluma (1927). "Über Behalten von erledigten und unerledigten Handlungen." *Psychologische Forschung* 9:1–85.

Zeisel, Hans (1947/1985). *Say It with Figures.* New York: Harper & Row.

_____ (1976–1977). "In Memoriam: Paul Felix Lazarsfeld, 1901–1976." *Public Opinion Quarterly* 40 (4):556–557.

_____ (1986). "Forensic Sociologist." *Journal of Advertising Research* 26:39–42.

Zorbaugh, Harvey Warren (1929). *The Gold Coast and the Slum: A Sociological Study of Chicago's Near North Side.* Chicago: University of Chicago Press.

INDEX OF NAMES

INDEX OF SUBJECTS